Frommer's®

W9-BCC-077

Madrid

2nd Edition

by Peter Stone

Here's what the critics say about Frommer's:

"Amazingly easy to use. Very portable, very complete."

—*Booklist*

"Detailed, accurate, and easy-to-read information for all price ranges."
—*Glamour Magazine*

"Hotel information is close to encyclopedic."

—*Des Moines Sunday Register*

"Frommer's Guides have a way of giving you a real feel for a place."
—*Knight Ridder Newspapers*

1807
WILEY
2007

Wiley Publishing, Inc.

Published by:

Wiley Publishing, Inc.

111 River St.
Hoboken, NJ 07030-5774

ISBN: 978-0-470-04728-6

Editor: Alexis Lipsitz Flippin
Production Editor: Michael Brumitt
Cartographer: Anton Crane
Photo Editor: Richard Fox
Anniversary Logo Design: Richard Pacifico
Production by Wiley Indianapolis Composition Services

Front cover photo: Museo Nacional Centro de Arte Reina Sofia: People looking at
Picasso's painting *Guernica.*
Back cover photo: Plaza Mayor, with statue of Felipe III and the Panaderia, its facade
painted with allegorical figures.

For information on our other products and services or to obtain technical support, please
contact our Customer Care Department within the U.S. at 800/762-2974, outside the
U.S. at 317/572-3993 or fax 317/572-4002.

Wiley also publishes its books in a variety of electronic formats. Some content that
appears in print may not be available in electronic formats.

Manufactured in the United States of America

5   4   3   2   1

Contents

8   Strolling Around Madrid   198

9   Shopping in Madrid   211

10   Madrid After Dark   224

11   Side Trips from Madrid   243

Appendix A: Madrid in Depth   279

List of Maps

An Invitation to the Reader

In researching this book, we discovered many wonderful places—hotels, restaurants, shops, and more. We're sure you'll find others. Please tell us about them, so we can share the information with your fellow travelers in upcoming editions. If you were disappointed with a recommendation, we'd love to know that, too. Please write to:

Frommer's Madrid, 2nd Edition
Wiley Publishing, Inc. • 111 River St. • Hoboken, NJ 07030-5774

An Additional Note

Please be advised that travel information is subject to change at any time—and this is especially true of prices. We therefore suggest that you write or call ahead for confirmation when making your travel plans. The authors, editors, and publisher cannot be held responsible for the experiences of readers while traveling. Your safety is important to us, however, so we encourage you to stay alert and be aware of your surroundings. Keep a close eye on cameras, purses, and wallets, all favorite targets of thieves and pickpockets.

About the Author

Born in London, England, **Peter Stone** started his working life in the Foreign Office in Downing Street before moving on to translating and journalism. He has resided over 27 years in different areas of Spain including Málaga, Barcelona, Alicante, Palma de Mallorca, and Las Palmas de Gran Canaria, and also lived in Greece and North Africa. A lifelong lover of Hispanic culture, history, and language, he made Madrid his home in 1998, and his publications on the Spanish capital include *Madrid Escapes.* He has contributed to a wide variety of international magazines and guidebooks, including *Time Out, Insight,* and *Intelliguide,* and is the author of *Frommer's Barcelona,* 2nd Edition.

Other Great Guides for Your Trip:

Frommer's Spain
Frommer's Europe
Spain For Dummies
MTV Spain

Frommer's Star Ratings, Icons & Abbreviations

Every hotel, restaurant, and attraction listing in this guide has been ranked for quality, value, service, amenities, and special features using a **star-rating system.** In country, state, and regional guides, we also rate towns and regions to help you narrow down your choices and budget your time accordingly. Hotels and restaurants are rated on a scale of zero (recommended) to three stars (exceptional). Attractions, shopping, nightlife, towns, and regions are rated according to the following scale: zero stars (recommended), one star (highly recommended), two stars (very highly recommended), and three stars (must-see).

In addition to the star-rating system, we also use **seven feature icons** that point you to the great deals, in-the-know advice, and unique experiences that separate travelers from tourists. Throughout the book, look for:

Finds	Special finds—those places only insiders know about
Fun Fact	Fun facts—details that make travelers more informed and their trips more fun
Kids	Best bets for kids and advice for the whole family
Moments	Special moments—those experiences that memories are made of
Overrated	Places or experiences not worth your time or money
Tips	Insider tips—great ways to save time and money
Value	Great values—where to get the best deals

The following **abbreviations** are used for credit cards:

AE American Express	DISC Discover	V Visa
DC Diners Club	MC MasterCard	

Frommers.com

Now that you have this guidebook to help you plan a great trip, visit our website at **www. frommers.com** for additional travel information on more than 3,500 destinations. We update features regularly to give you instant access to the most current trip-planning information available. At Frommers.com, you'll find scoops on the best airfares, lodging rates, and car rental bargains. You can even book your travel online through our reliable travel booking partners. Other popular features include:

- Online updates of our most popular guidebooks
- Vacation sweepstakes and contest giveaways
- Newsletters highlighting the hottest travel trends
- Online travel message boards with featured travel discussions

What's New in Madrid

Madrid is undergoing dynamic transitions. Here is a sampling of the latest happenings.

THE CITYSCAPE The **"Greening of Madrid"** plan by mayor Ruiz-Gallardón has involved the planting of hundreds of thousands of trees, shrubs, and flowers both in and around the city. The most ambitious project (and still in progress) is covering the whole Príncipe Pío section of the Manzanares River—which together with the M-30 bypass road is being diverted underground—and turning the surface into a pedestrianized zone of pathways and gardens that will link up with the Casa del Campo to make one huge green area. An out-of-town walkway and cycle path designed to eventually encompass the whole city is also nearing completion, and both projects are scheduled to be finished by early 2007.

High rises (high, that is, for Spain though still modest by Chicago or Singapore standards) are sprouting just beyond Plaza Castilla where urban Madrid continues its inexorable expansion north. Four office and apartment towers—each more than 200m (656 ft.) tall—are due for completion by early 2007. At the same time, newly created **suburbs** like Sanchinarro—huge shopping centers at their core—struggle to find a personality among the cranes and concrete.

TO SMOKE OR NOT TO SMOKE Though the campaign wasn't quite as successful as the antismoking lobby would have liked, the January 2006 law aimed at cutting down the ubiquitous Spanish tendency to smoke in every possible *rincón* has had some effect. It's effectively banned smoking in all official workplaces and throughout the entire Metro system (which makes a welcome change from the days when at 7am on a bitter winter's morn you'd find yourself on a chilly platform inhaling the Winston or Ducado fumes of waiting commuters). In bars, however, the decision was left to the owner's discretion—and in 99% of cases smoking was still allowed (except in locales larger than 100m/328 ft., where a small smoke-free zone had to be observed). For nonsmokers, Madrid has some totally fume-free oases such as Dosa Grill and the increasingly ubiquitous Starbucks cafes. Madrid is still a long way from California, but there is talk of stricter laws being imposed in 2007. For more, see p. 118.

GETTING THERE Barajas airport had its capacity and area considerably expanded when its new terminals 4 and 4S were opened in February 2006. Initial glitches—delays, poor flight information—were gradually ironed out, and today the new zone is a model of 21st-century style and efficiency. All four terminals are linked by a new bus service that runs direct from Avenida America station and replaces the former one that operated from Plaza Colon. Terminal 2 is also linked by direct Metro line with the center. New airlines are entering the market on a regular basis, one of the latest being **easyJet**—the booming U.K. cut-rate flight company—which opened offices at the airport in September 2006.

For more information, see chapter 2.

GETTING AROUND   Large stretches of the Metro—lines 3 and 7 in particular—were closed throughout summer 2006 to undergo major upgrades that involved the widening of platforms and provision of newly designed trains with increased space for passengers and improved air-conditioning/heating. In the expanding north of the city, the innovative circular **Metronorte** Metro and brand-new *tren ligero* (a sort of streamlined tram service) linking satellite towns such as Pozuelo and San Sebastian de los Reyes with the city center, are due to be in operation by the beginning of 2007. Meanwhile, **Chamartín**, one of the city's two major railway stations, will see completion of a renovated and expanded Metro and train junction as well as a brand-new under-ground bus terminal.

There was good news for all night hedonists in May 2006, when a new half-hourly *buhometro* (literally, "owl metro") bus service came into operation at week-ends in the center, following Metro routes and filling the gap between the last Metro train at 2am and the first the next day at 6am.

For more on getting around, see chapter 4.

ACCOMMODATIONS   The face of Madrid's hotel scene is changing at all levels, from deluxe lodgings to budget choices. The **High Tech** chain of hotels is one of several imaginative chains that have launched appealing new lodgings in the last couple of years. **Vincci** (www.vinccihoteles.com) is a case in point. Its **Vincci Centrum,** Cedaceros 4 (© 91-360-47-20), and **Vincci Soho,** Prado 18 (© 91-141-41-00), are stylishly cool and close to the action. The **Petit Palace** and **Hoteles Catalonia** groups in turn specialize in tastefully renovated older buildings offering updated accommodation plus state-of-the-art Internet facilities. Of the 20 **Petit Palace** hotels that have recently sprung up in Madrid, we've picked the **Ducal,** Calle Hortaleza 3 (© 91-521-10-43), between Chueca and the Gran Vía, for its location and charm. Our **Hoteles Catalonia** choice is **Catalonia Centro,** Goya 49 (© 91-781-49-49), in the stylish Salamanca district.

Newest boy on the block is the **Room-Mate Hotel** group (www.room-mate-hoteles.com), which opened no less than three hostelries in Madrid in 2006. Their trendily minimalistic **Hotel Alicia,** Calle del Prado 2 (© 91-389-60-95), is in the sought-after Huertas zone.

Young travelers are well catered to at a duo of brand-new basic but switched-on hostels: **Cat's Hostel,** Calle Cañizares 6 (© 91-369-28-07), in Huertas and **Mad-hostel,** Calle de la Cabeza 24 (© 91-506-48-40), in Lavapiés. Both opened in 2006 and offer bargain-price no-frills accommodation (four to 14 sharing rooms or dormitories) with access to fast Internet facilities.

For details, see chapter 5.

DINING   One of the hottest new dining sensations in the Spanish capital is actually an Arab restaurant—**Mosaiq,** Calle Caracas 21 (© 91-308-44-46), with its Moroccan-style decor and cuisine of North African delights, including chicken *tagine.*

Two other "in" spots are the cool, somewhat misleadingly named **Kikuyu,** Barbara de Braganza 4 (© 91-319-66-11), which charms its clientele with delicious vegetarian and Levante rice dishes; and ultra-chic **Bazaar,** Calle Libertad 21 (© 91-523-39-05), whose inventive dishes and people-watching appeal makes it a veritable mecca for Madrileño youth.

If you're in a hurry but want quality fast food, the choices are growing, including the above-mentioned smoke-free **Dosa Grill.** At press time, the unimaginatively named, brightly decorated **Fast Good,** Calle Padre Damián (© **91-343-06-55**), had just opened, with exquisite light salads and tasty fresh dishes actually inspired by superchef Ferran Adrià.

For details, see chapter 6.

ATTRACTIONS On the cultural front, there's been a massive, multimillion-dollar expansion in all three of the major museums in the "Golden Triangle" of art. At a cost of nearly $100 million, **Museo del Prado ("El Prado"),** Paseo del Prado (© **91-330-28-00**), is aiming to double its floor space. Much of its expansion is underground. The long-delayed extensions planned next to the **Church of the Jerónimos Reales** and in the nearby renovated **Casón del Buen Retiro** (to house some of the **El Prado** paintings) are now expected to be completed by 2007.

Not to be outdone, **Museo Nacional Centro de Arte Reina Sofía,** Santa Isabel 52 (© **91-467-50-62**), has allocated $95 million to open new galleries and a 450-seat auditorium. Its ultimate goal is to turn itself into the Madrid version of Paris's Centre Pompidou.

The **Thyssen-Bornemisza,** Paseo del Prado 8 (© **91-369-01-51**), expanded into two adjoining buildings with 16 new galleries in 2005. This greatly increased the space needed for its permanent collection and provided new galleries for temporary exhibitions.

For details, see chapter 7.

SHOPPING Though Madrid is hardly short of large U.S.–style commercial centers these days, they can't seem to stop building more. The latest addition, launched in May 2006 and claiming to be the biggest hypermarket in the country, is **Plenilunio,** with more than 200 locales, situated on the Eisenhower junction of the Barcelona highway between the easterly suburb of Canillejas and Barajas airport.

Opened in 2005, **Hartley's Good Bookshop** at Calle Padilla 74 (© **91-401-90-77**), in the Salamanca district, is the newest of Madrid's English-language bookshops. The shop sells copies of both old and new books as well as original English videos. Presentations of new books are sometimes held, and there are reading evenings for children.

For details, see chapter 9.

1

The Best of Madrid

Madrid is on a roll. Never a city to let the grass grow under its feet, the Spanish capital is experiencing unprecedented change thanks to the efforts of the visionary mayor Alberto Ruiz-Gallardón—a man compared by some, however tongue in cheek, to a pharaoh. In 2005 the mayor launched a new 7-year city program aimed at transforming the capital into a world-class cosmopolitan center, with improved Metro and rail transport and the expansion of new *barrios*, or districts, especially in the north of the city where a *tren ligero* (a smaller, streamlined Talgo-shaped tram similar to those successfully operating in Bilbao) is scheduled to be in operation by spring 2007. Though the completion of all this work was originally timed to coincide with Madrid's expected nomination as venue for the 2012 Olympics, the city's disbelief at being beaten for the honor by London was quickly forgotten (maudlin introspection is not part of the feisty Madrileño temperament). In fact, many completion schedules have been brought forward to coincide with the municipal elections of May 2007.

Two new terminals at Barajas airport were inaugurated in February 2006, more than doubling the city's international traffic and making the airport the third busiest in Europe, while Chamartín railway station is being totally rebuilt to merge with a renovated Metro station and a new underground regional and long-distance bus terminal. Each of the four skyscrapers currently under construction (Torres Repsol, Espacio, Sacyr, and Cristal) will outstrip Torre Picasso in the AZCA Business Center as the highest building in town; at the same time, pedestrian and subway underpasses are being tunneled and countless streets and avenues widened, all aimed at improving road access. The roadwork may prove a bone of contention for frustrated and quietly—or not so quietly—seething Madrileño drivers who see their priority of getting to work on time thwarted by cranes, bulldozers, excavations, and scaffoldings until the job gets done. On the other hand, public transportation is being upgraded almost by the month, particularly on the much-used and excellent-value Metro (p. 70).

The cultural mix of the 5-million-plus population is also changing radically, with an influx of immigrants from South American and Eastern European countries taking over many of the service and blue-collar jobs. Many are Ecuadorians, who are busy opening cafes, shops—especially bakeries—and *locutorios* (long-distance phone-call centers). Meanwhile the Russians, Romanians, Poles, and Czechs who work on many of the building sites and in practical fields such as plumbing and carpentry have shown great versatility both in their work and in picking up Spanish. It's all a great change from the homogeneous Madrid of a few years back when foreign residents totaled barely 1%.

Ecological changes abound, too. Madrid is now officially one of the "greenest" cities in Europe, with verdant areas springing up every year thanks to an ecologically aware town hall. The Retiro, with its flowers, fountains, and boat-filled lake, and the huge Casa del Campo moorland, with its copses and bird life, are the city's twin lungs, aided by the regular flow of pure mountain air from the Guadarramas 97km (60 miles) away. Alberto Ruiz-Gallardón's improvement plans also cover the planting of hundreds of thousands of trees in newly created green zones—intersected by walking and cycling lanes—both in and around the city. His Manzanares River development is particularly ambitious, with both river and M-30 highway running underground while the surface becomes a pedestrianized parkland that connects with the Casa del Campo. (In summer 2006 the crusading mayor also launched a battle against "light pollution" by announcing a future ban on practically all neon lights in the city center, so that Madrileños would be able to see the stars on cloudless nights.)

In a sense, the Spanish capital hasn't changed at all: It has always been an awesome blend of tradition and dynamism. At its heart is the vintage Madrid of Los Austrias, the Plaza Mayor, and the Palacio Real, still exuding centuries-old atmosphere and ringed in turn by regenerated *castizo* (traditional) districts like Chueca, Malasaña, and Lavapiés (the latter's population epitomizing the new ethnically varied Madrid). The San Isidro and Virgen de la Almudena fiestas are celebrated with their customary color and vigor. Shopping, dining, and cultural options are plentiful and remarkably varied. And the spontaneous nonstop lifestyle continues to thrive, with bars (more than 18,000 of them) opening from 5:30am onwards for coffee and *churros* and closing late (or never shutting at all if you include the after-hours bars), and weekend dawn traffic jams of cars and night buses blocking the city thoroughfares as revelers weave their way to, from, or between their favorite spots.

1 The Most Unforgettable Madrid Experiences

- **Sitting in *Sol* or *Sombra* at the Bullfights:** A bullfight can be one of the most evocative and memorable events in Spain, and the best place by far to see one is at the country's biggest *plaza de toros* (bullring) at **Ventas** (on the eastern border of Madrid's Salamanca district close to the M-30 highway). Tickets are either *sol* (sunny side) or *sombra* (in the shade); you'll pay more to get out of the sun. Peak time for attending bullfights is during the capital's San Isidro fiestas in May, when 4 consecutive weeks of daily *corridas* feature some of the biggest names in the bullfighting world. See p. 186.

- **Seeing the Masterpieces at El Prado:** One of the world's premier art museums, on a par with the Louvre, El Prado is home to some 4,000 masterpieces, many of them acquired by Spanish kings. The wealth of Spanish art is staggering—everything from Goya's *Naked Maja* to the celebrated *Las Meninas (The Maids of Honor)* by Velázquez (my favorite) and the dark vision of Goya's *Disasters of War* etchings. El Prado also boasts a number of Botticellis, Titians, and French Impressionists, but don't try to take it all in in 1 day: The museum's overall collection is simply too vast to absorb in a single visit. See p. 168.

- **Feasting on Tapas in the *Tascas*:** Tapas, those delicious bite-size portions washed down with wine, beer, or sherry, are reason enough to go to Madrid! Original favorites were cured ham or *chorizo* (spicy sausage). Today you might sample *gambas* (deep-fried shrimp), *boquerones* (anchovies marinated in vinegar), *albóndigas* (meatballs), *tortillas* (tiny omelets), or *calamares* (squid). Among the best areas for a *tapeo* (tapa "crawl") are bustling Plaza de Santa Ana and the labyrinthine Cava Baja. See chapter 6.

- **Lounging in an Outdoor Cafe:** In summer Madrileños live it up on café

Rising from the Ashes

As with that fateful September 2001 attack in New York City and the July 2005 bombings in London's underground, the resilient spirit of the city's inhabitants survived Madrid's own terrorist-inflicted tragedy on March 11, 2004, when Al Qaeda bombed suburban-line trains in and close to Atocha station, killing nearly 200 people. "We were all on that train" became a popular slogan. Madrid bounced back, albeit in a politically changed environment. Three days after the outrage, the PSOE Socialist Party, led by José Rodríguez Zapatero, unexpectedly won the elections and ended the 8-year government of the PP Conservative Party under Jose Maria Aznar. The PSOE introduced a radical new agenda, taking action to withdraw Spanish troops from Iraq, introduce more female politicians into Parliament, pass a law allowing homosexual marriages, and approve a controversial Estatut-(statute) giving the province of Catalonia more autonomy—all of which was strenuously opposed by the opposition PP.

terrazas till the early hours. Prized spots are the wide tree-lined Paseo del Pintor Rosales on the western edge of the Argüelles district, overlooking the Casa del Campo, and the elegant cosmopolitan swathe of the Paseo de la Castellana, Paseo del Prado, and Paseo de Recoletos. In Lavapiés, the colorful Calle Argumosa also offers a fashionable spill of alfresco bars. See chapter 6.

- **Relaxing in a Genuine Literary Cafe:** Once upon a time the city had several distinguished old-world cafes where intellectuals, artists, and lesser mortals would gather to enjoy a leisurely chat or stimulating *tertulia* (social gathering). Today the sole survivors of these legendary 19th-century watering holes are the ornate **Gran Café de Gijón** (✆ **91-521-54-25**) and the more austere **Café Comercial** (✆ **91-521-56-55**), both graced with traditional columns and high windows with views of the ever-changing scenes outside. Lingering unhurriedly over a coffee in either is a real treat. See pages 142 and 208.
- **Shopping the Rastro:** Madrid's teeming flea market represents a tradition that's 500 years old. The place really gets going from around 9am on, with shoulder-to-shoulder stalls stretching down Calle Ribera de Curtidores. Real or fake antiques, secondhand clothing, porn films, Franco-era furniture, paintings (endless copies of Velázquez), old books, religious relics, and plenty of just plain junk are for sale. These streets also contain some of the finest permanent antiques shops in Madrid. *Warning:* Keep an eagle eye on your wallet or purse; this is a pickpocket's paradise. See p. 219.
- **Sunday Strolling in the Retiro:** Spread across 140 leafy hectares (350 acres) the statue- and tree-filled Parque de Retiro was originally designed as the gardens of Buen Retiro palace, occupied by Philip IV in the 1630s. In 1767 Charles III opened part of the gardens to the general public. On Sunday mornings before lunch vendors hawk their wares, magicians perform their acts, fortunetellers read tarot cards, and large Disney-style moving models of Tweety Bird and Bugs Bunny delight the kids. In the central lake (presided over by a 1902 monument to Alfonso XII) you can rent a boat and laze away the hours

on the glittering waters. See chapter 6.

- **Picnicking in the Casa del Campo:** On a hot summer's day enjoy an alfresco repast in the shade of a fragrant pine in the heart of Madrid's largest park and look back at the shimmering city skyline. Afterward go boating on the lake or take the kids to the zoo or Parque de Atracciones. You can get here by *teleférico* chair lift or by Metro to **Lago.** See p. 187.

- **Nursing a Drink at Chicote** (© 91-532-67-37): The 1930s interior at Madrid's most famous bar looks the same as it did during the Spanish Civil War. Shells might have been flying along the Gran Vía, but the international press corps covering the war drank on. Postwar regulars included writers, artists, and film stars like Frank Sinatra and Ava Gardner. Today it's one of the smart, sophisticated spots to rendezvous in Madrid. See p. 238.

- **Experiencing the** *Movida:* Very roughly translated as the "shift," or the "movement," *movida* characterizes post-Franco life in the capital after Madrileños threw off the yoke of dictatorship and repression, giddily drinking, dancing, and generally having a ball à la Almodóvar. To get the feel of this still inexhaustible phenomena, head for the highly liberated nocturnal (and after-hours) fun zones of Chueca, Huertas, and Malasaña, and sample the big clubs around Calle Arenal like **Palacio Gaviria** (© 91-256-60-69). See p. 235.

- **Wandering around the Monasterio de las Descalzas Reales:** A haven of unexpected peace in the bustling heart of Madrid, barely a stone's throw from the Gran Vía, this charming former medieval palace was converted into a monastery in the 16th century by Philip II's sister Juana. Ornate frescoes, Flemish tapestries, and paintings by the likes of Titian and Zurbarán fill its chapel-lined interior. Only 20 visitors are allowed in at a time, so be prepared to wait. See p. 181.

- **Exploring the Real Monasterio de San Lorenzo de El Escorial** (49 km/30 miles from Madrid): Philip II, who commissioned this monastery in the 1530s, envisioned it as a spiritual fortress against the distractions of the secular world. Today it remains the best living example of religious devotion in Renaissance Spain. Within its huge granite walls—more awesome than beautiful—are the tombs of Spanish kings and a priceless repository of ancient books, tapestries, and masterpieces by Goya, Velázquez, and other artistic giants. See p. 256.

2 The Best Splurge Hotels

- **Hesperia Madrid** (© 91-210-88-00): It's a member of "The Leading Hotels of the World"—and you'll see why as soon as you check in to this Catalan-owned gem with its ultra-smart fittings, sophisticated amenities, and hint-of-Far-East decor. Add to this the hotel's Michelin-rated Santceloni restaurant (see "The Most Unforgettable Dining Experiences," below), and you have one of the most highly regarded lodgings in Madrid. See p. 104.

- **Park Hyatt Villa Magna** (© 800/223-1234 from the USA or Canada or © 91-587-12-34 from Spain): A recognized "in" place favored by movie stars and high-ranking politicians, the Villa Magna enjoys a prestigious reputation almost unique in the city. It's also got a full-service business center stocked with access to translators, word processors, even a well-informed technology concierge. Behind its elegant garden setting is a classically styled hotel boasting top facilities and the highest standards of service. See p. 104.

- **The Ritz** (© **800/225-5843** from the USA or Canada or 91-701-67-67 from Spain): In spite of an increasing number of impressive rivals, the Belle Epoque Ritz remains a world apart.

Now approaching its 100th anniversary, this granddaddy of Madrid's luxury hotels has seen monarchs and dictators come and go. Backed by gardens in the loveliest part of the Paseo del Prado, the hotel has an incomparable setting and superb decor matched only by the inimitable service and attention to detail. Ah, but be prepared to pay accordingly. See p. 104.

3 The Best Moderately Priced Hotels

- Built in 1966 and still going strong, the reasonably priced **Fiesta Gran Hotel Colón** (© **91-573-59-00**) lies west of Retiro Park in a relatively safe area of Madrid that's easily connected to the center by subway. It's nicely maintained and kept up-to-date, offering well-designed bedrooms with comfortably traditional furnishings. See p. 107.
- Ideally located in a popular tiny square close to the Plaza Mayor, the

19th-century **Hostal Persal** (© **91-369-46-43**) offers good-value family-size rooms as well as fine meals. See p. 92.
- If the prospect of bedding down in a peaceful setting within easy reach of the center tickles your fancy, then the **Residencia El Viso** (© **91-564-03-70**) is for you. It has comfortable rooms, a friendly atmosphere, and a leafy patio where you can enjoy home-cooked meals. See p. 113.

4 The Most Unforgettable Dining Experiences

- The **Sobrino de Botín** (© **91-366-30-26**) may be touristy these days, but the setting and atmosphere of the city's oldest restaurant (some say the oldest eatery in the world) more than compensate. Rafters, beams, and nooks abound, and the effective service is accompanied by some first-rate Castilian specialties, such as *lechón* (suckling pig). See p. 127.
- **Zalacaín** (© **91-561-48-40**): This is definitely money-is-no-object time, but with unsurpassable Basque and French cuisine like this, you can let yourself go for once. Still one of the very best gourmet rendezvous in Madrid, it's holding out well against the fashionable tsunami of Catalan nouvelle cuisine. See p. 152.

- **La Broche** (© **91-399-34-37**): For those who favor tradition-shattering Catalan delights, the dining room of the Hotel Occidental Miguel Angel (p. 110) provides some of the most imaginative offerings in the city, with chef Sergi Arola emulating the culinary style of his much-vaunted mentor Ferran Adrià. See p. 158.
- **Santceloni** (© **91-210-88-40**): A stylish repository of fine Mediterranean cuisine located in the immaculate Hesperia Madrid hotel (p. 104), this elite locale is for many the tops in town. Chef Santi Santamaría conjures up inspired Catalan dishes such as fennel-based John Dory. See p. 152.

5 The Best Things to Do For Free

- **Enjoy the Weekend Cultural Treats:** Saturday afternoons and Sunday mornings are free at the Museos Naval, de America, Arqueológico Nacional, and Nacional Centro de Arte Reina Sofia. The tiny Casa Museo de Lope de Vega is free on Saturdays, and Sunday morning–only treats include the famed El Prado and Museos Sorolla, Casa de la Moneda, and Nacional de Artes Decorativas. See chapter 7.
- **Don't Forget Weekday Freebies:** Some of the private museums (such as Lazaro Galdiano and Cerralbo) are free on Wednesdays (Cerralbo is also free on Sun), while the Museo San Isidro in Plaza San Andrés gives you a gratis daily rundown on the city's history. Attractions that are permanently free include the Bolsa (Stock Exchange), Museo Municipal, Casa de America, private Fundación art exhibitions such as La Caixa and Juan March, and the Conde Duque cultural center. See chapter 7.
- **Take an Ecclesiastical Trip Back in Time:** We're particularly fond of Madrid's two oldest churches, hidden in the heart of the Austrias district. They're both tiny, giving you an idea of what Madrid must have been like with a population of just around 10,000. **San Nicolás de los Servitas** (full title: San Nicolás de Bari de los Servitas) was named after an Italian saint, and its 12th-century Arabic *torre* rises above a narrow lane just behind the Calle Mayor. Nearby **San Pedro el Leal** (also known as San Pedro el Viejo) has the best-preserved 14th-century Mudéjar brick tower in the capital. No charge for either, of course—though you may care to leave something in the collection box to help toward the preservation of these two gems. See chapter 7.
- **Stroll in the Parks:** Madrid's best central *parques* are particularly rewarding to explore, especially the **Retiro,** with its rose garden, fountains, statues (including the **Angel Caído,** or Fallen Angel, depicting Lucifer), central lake, **Casa de Vacas,** and 19th-century **Palacios de Cristal** and **Velazquez** cultural showrooms. Below the Palacio Real, the **Campo del Moro** has a verdant neatness more associated with northern Europe, while on the edge of Argüelles the **Parque del Oeste**'s marked nature trails wend their way down past an international selection of trees and plants to the River Manzanares (where you can view the **Ermita de San Antonio de la Florida**'s Goyan frescoes). See chapter 7.
- **See Madrid's "Little Egypt":** On the ridge overlooking the Casa de Campo, you can visit the **Templo de Debod,** a unique slice of Egypt in Spain. It's the real McCoy, shipped stone by stone from the banks of the Nile. See chapter 7.
- **Be a Politician for a Day (or Morning, Anyway):** Visit the **Congreso de los Diputados** on Saturday mornings and imagine yourself changing the direction of the Spanish nation. No need to book: Just turn up at 10am (except during the summer recess). See chapter 8.

6 The Best Stuff to Bring Home

- **Leather:** Leather has long been one of Spain's most highly valued products, and best buys range from stylish belts and handbags to handmade shoes and fine jackets. Check out top shops like Loewe in the Gran Vía and

Farrutx in Calle Serrano. Or rummage through Sunday's Rastro flea market for a secondhand bargain. See chapter 9.

- **Ceramics:** Though this is not a Madrid specialty, you'll find a wide selection of ceramic vases, dishes, and jugs from nearby towns such as Toledo and Talavera de la Reina, some of whose wares have the style and finesse of fine art. You'll also find plenty of choices from areas farther afield such as Seville, Granada, and Manises in Valencia province. Visit the Antigua Casa Talavera (p. 217) for some of the best choices. See chapters 9 and 11.

- **Porcelain:** Porcelain ornaments similar in style to the Italian Capodimonte are made by the Valencian company Lladró, and, though considered rather twee by some, are extremely popular with most visitors. Check out Lasarte in the Gran Vía. See chapter 9.

- **Capes:** If your taste runs to the slightly eccentric, now's your chance to buy a genuine Spanish cape *(capa)* and surprise your friends as you arrive at the theater in style! The place to find them is Capas Seseña (p. 216). See chapter 9.

7 The Best Unique Inns

- **La Taberna de Antonio Sánchez** (℡ **91-539-78-26**): You can't get more traditional than this much-copied 200-year-old original, a vintage example of Old Madrid complete with zinc counter, carved wooden bar top, barrels, honest wines, and a genial bartender. Formerly patronized by painters and playwrights, this small cavelike locale has also had long associations with the bullfight world. (The bull's head on the wall is not there just for decoration.) See p. 165.

- **Casa Pedro** (℡ **91-734-02-01**): Perhaps because of its location up in the northern suburbs, few people realize this atmospheric eating spot—the second oldest in all Madrid—even exists. Yet it's barely half an hour away by Metro, and the unique experience of dining on fine Castilian fare in a rambling 19th-century house guarantees that any trip here is well worth it. See p. 167.

- **Casa Alberto** (℡ **91-429-93-56**): Another genuine oldie, this charismatic tavern has been around since 1827. The dark maroon exterior and tunnel-like interior with its zinc bar top, bullfight pictures, and engravings on the walls create the ideal ambience to enjoy a tasty tapa or three. The restaurant at the rear provides more substantial versions of the traditional seafood and Castilian meat dishes available. See p. 136.

8 The Best Museums

- **El Prado:** The spectacular Prado is no mere museum, but a fully formed travel experience. It's worth a journey to Spain just to see it. See p. 168.

- **Museo Lázaro Galdiano:** This rare collection demonstrates the evolution of enamel and ivory crafts from the Byzantine era to 19th-century Limoges. Of almost equal importance are displays of superb medieval gold and silver work along with Italian Renaissance jewelry. Reopened in 2003 after 18 months of renovations, the museum also contains galleries with rare paintings, everything from Flemish primitives to works by Spanish masters of the golden age, including El Greco, Murillo, and Zurbarán. The museum also has paintings from Goya's "Black Period" and works by the English and Italian masters Constable and Tiepolo. See p. 183.

- **Thyssen-Bornemisza Museum:** Madrid's acquisition of this treasure trove of art in the 1980s was one of the greatest coups in European art history. Amassed by a Central European collector beginning around 1920, and formerly displayed in Lugano, Switzerland, the 700 canvasses, with works by artists ranging from El Greco to Picasso, are arranged in chronological order. The collection rivals the legendary holdings of the queen of England herself. See p. 169.

- **Museo Cerralbo:** This 19th-century mansion evokes the genuine aura of a sumptuous restoration residence. Formerly owned by the 17th marquis of Argüelles, it houses one of the most personal collections in Madrid. Works by Zurbarán and El Greco, especially the latter's *Ecstasy of St. Francis of Assisi,* are among its highlights, and the upper floor contains a unique collection of Western and Oriental armor and weapons. See p. 182.

- **Museo Sorolla:** Visit the great Valencian artist's own house in the residential heart of the Spanish capital. Built in 1910 and bequeathed as a museum by his wife after his death, its trademark works are luminous Levante coast beach scenes, with women in white dresses backed by an azure Mediterranean sea. The museum was reopened in 2002 after a spell of tasteful refurbishment. See the artist's eccentrically furnished studio complete with a Turkish sofa on which he took his siesta. See p. 184.

- **Reina Sofia:** Spain's number-one modern art exhibition. Regulars on show include Dalí, Tàpies, and Klein, and an ever-interesting series of temporary exhibits ranges from the anarchic to mainstream. The outside glass-walled elevator is popular with kids. See p. 172.

2

Planning Your Trip to Madrid

This chapter is devoted to the where, when, and how of your trip: the advance planning required to get it together and take it on the road.

1 Visitor Information

TOURIST OFFICES You can begin your info search with Spain's tourist offices located in the following places:

In Madrid The **Patronato Municipal de Turismo (Municipal Tourist Board),** Plaza Mayor 3 (Metro: Sol; © **91-588-16-36;** www.munimadrid.es/turismo), can provide up-to-date information on what to do and where to go in the Spanish capital; it's open Monday to Friday 10am to 8pm and Saturday 10am to 3pm. Other tourist offices are located at Duque de Medinaceli 2, the Barajas Airport (Terminal 1), Puerta de Toledo, and the Chamartín rail station (open hours vary).

In the United States For information before you go, contact the **Tourist Office of Spain,** 666 Fifth Ave., Fifth Floor, New York, NY 10103 (© **212/265-8822**). It can provide sightseeing information, events calendars, train and ferry schedules, and more. Elsewhere in the United States, branches of the Tourist Office of Spain are located at: 8383 Wilshire Blvd., Suite 956, Beverly Hills, CA 90211 (© **323/658-7188**); 845 N. Michigan Ave., Suite 915E, Chicago, IL 60611 (© **312/642-1992**); and 1221 Brickell Ave., Suite 1850, Miami, FL 33131 (© **305/358-1992**).

In Canada Contact the **Tourist Office of Spain,** 102 Bloor St. W., Suite 3402, Toronto, Ontario M5S 1M9, Canada (© **416/961-3131**).

In Great Britain Write to the **Spanish National Tourist Office,** 22–23 Manchester Sq., London W1M 5AP (© **020/ 7486-8077**).

WEBSITES You can find lots of great information at the following sites. (See **"Online Traveler's Toolbox"** later in this chapter for more websites.)

Spain in General TURESPAÑA (Tourism in Spain official website; www. spain.info), **Tourist Office of Spain** (www.okspain.org), **All About Spain** (www.red2000.com), **Cybersp@in** (www. cyberspain.com).

Madrid **Madrid by All About Spain** (www.red2000.com), **Time Out: Madrid** (www.timeout.com), **Soft Guide Madrid** (www.softguides.com), **Web Madrid** (www.webmadrid.com), **Chamber of Commerce of Madrid** (www.descubre madrid.com/en/index.asp).

2 Entry Requirements & Customs

ENTRY REQUIREMENTS

A valid **passport** is all that an American, British, Canadian, or New Zealand citizen needs to enter Spain. (Australians, however, need a visa—see below.)

Spain

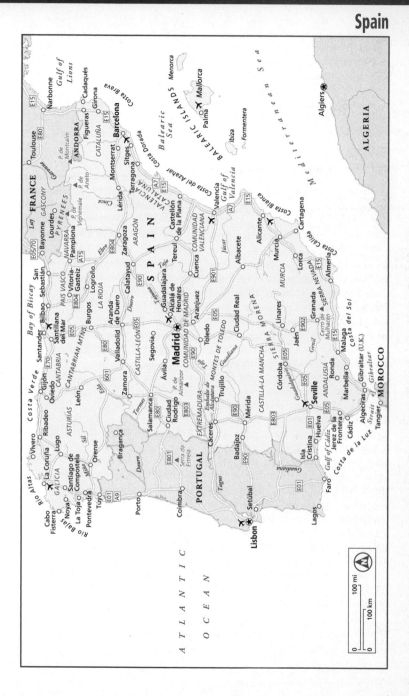

The websites listed below provide downloadable passport applications as well as the current fees for processing passport applications. For an up-to-date, country-by-country listing of passport requirements around the world, go to the "Foreign Entry Requirement" Web page of the U.S. State Department at **http:// travel.state.gov**.

PASSPORTS

In the United States You can apply for passports in person at one of 13 regional offices or by mail. To apply, you'll need a passport application form, available at U.S. post offices and federal court offices, and proof of citizenship, such as a birth certificate or naturalization papers; an expired passport is also accepted. First-time applicants for passports pay $60 ($40 if under 18). Persons 18 or older who have an expired passport that's not more than 12 years old can reapply by mail. The old passport must be submitted along with new photographs and a pink renewal form (DSP-82). If your expired passport is more than 12 years old, or if it was granted to you before your 16th birthday, you must apply in person. The fee is $40. Call © **202/647-0518** at any time for information. You can also write to Passport Service, Office of Correspondence, Department of State, 1111 19th St. NW, Suite 510, Washington, DC 20522-1075. To find your regional passport office, either check the U.S. State Department website (http://travel.state. gov) or call the National Passport Information Center (NPIC) number (© **877/ 487-2778**) for automated information. The cost is 35¢ per minute for 24-hour automated service, or $1.05 per minute 9am to 3pm for live operator service.

In Canada Citizens may go to one of 28 regional offices located in major cities. Alternatively, you can mail your application to the Passport Office, External Affairs and International Trade Canada,

Ottawa, ON K1A 0G3. Post offices have application forms. Passports cost C$60, and proof of Canadian citizenship is required, along with two signed identical passport-size photographs. Passports are valid for 5 years. For more information, call © **800/567-6868** or go to www. dfait-maeci.gc.ca/passport/menu.asp.

In Great Britain British subjects may visit or apply to one of the regional offices in Liverpool, Newport, Glasgow, Peterborough, Belfast, or London for a standard 10-year passport (5-yr. passport for children under 16). The fee is £28, You can also apply in person at a main post office or travel agency. Two photos must accompany the application. For more information regarding fees, documentation requirements, and to ask for an emergency passport, contact the London Passport office at © **0870/521-0410** or go to www.ukpa.gov.uk.

In Australia Citizens may apply at the nearest post office. Provincial capitals and other major cities have passport offices. Application fees are subject to review every 3 months. Call © **02/13-12-32** or visit www.passports.gov.au for the latest information. Australians must pay for a departure tax stamp costing A$20 at a post office or airport; children 11 and under are exempt. Australian citizens will also need a visa to enter Spain. Apply at a Spanish consulate well before departure time. Spanish consulates are located at 31 Market St., Sydney, NSW 2000 (© **02/ 9261-2433**), and at 766 Elizabeth St., Melbourne, VIC 3000 (© **03/9347-1966**).

In New Zealand Citizens may go to their nearest consulate or passport office to obtain an application, which may be filed in person or by mail. To obtain a 10-year passport, proof of citizenship is required, plus a fee of NZ$80. Passports are processed at the New Zealand Passport Office, Documents of National Identity

Division, Department of Internal Affairs, 47 Boulcott House St., Wellington (© **0800/22-50-50;** www.passports. govt.nz).

In Ireland Residents can apply for a 10-year passport at the **Passport Office,** Setanta Centre, Molesworth St., Dublin 2 (© **01/671-1633;** www.irlgov.ie/iveagh or www.oasis.gov.ie). The charge is 58€. Those under age 18 and over 65 must apply for a 12€ 3-year passport. Applications are sent by mail. You can also apply at 1A South Mall, Cork (© **021/272-525)** or at most main post offices. Irish citizens living in North America can contact the Irish Embassy, 2234 Massachusetts Ave., NW, Washington, DC 20008 (© **202/462-3939;** www.irelandemb. org). The embassy can issue a new passport or direct you to one of three North American consulates that have jurisdiction over a particular region; the charge is $80. Allow plenty of time before your trip to apply for a passport; processing normally takes 3 weeks but can take longer during busy periods (especially spring). And keep in mind that if you need a passport in a hurry, you'll pay a higher processing fee. For security reasons passport applications cannot be downloaded online.

VISAS

No visas are required for U.S. visitors to Spain providing your stay does not exceed 90 days. Australian visitors, however, need a visa (see "Passports," above).

MEDICAL REQUIREMENTS

For information on medical requirements and recommendations, see "Health & Safety," p. 25.

CUSTOMS
WHAT YOU CAN BRING INTO SPAIN

You can bring most personal effects and the following items duty-free: two still cameras and 10 rolls of film per camera, tobacco for personal use, 1 liter each of liquor and wine, a portable radio, a tape recorder, a typewriter, a bicycle, sports equipment, fishing gear, and two hunting weapons with 100 cartridges each.

WHAT YOU CAN TAKE HOME FROM SPAIN
U.S. Citizens

Returning **U.S. citizens** who have been away for 48 hours or more are allowed to bring back, once every 30 days, $400 worth of merchandise duty-free. You'll be charged a flat rate of 10% duty on the next $1,000 worth of purchases. Be sure to have your receipts handy. On gifts, the duty-free limit is $100.

For more specifics on what you can bring back and the corresponding fees, download the invaluable free pamphlet *Know Before You Go* online at **www.cbp. gov.** (Click on "Travel," and then click on "Know Before You Go! Online Brochure.") Or contact **U.S. Customs & Border Protection (CBP),** 1300 Pennsylvania Ave., NW, Washington, DC 20229 (© **877/287-8667)** and request the pamphlet.

Canadian Citizens

Canada allows its citizens a C$750 exemption, and you are allowed to bring back duty-free 200 cigarettes, 2.2 pounds of tobacco, 40 imperial ounces (1.2 qt.) of liquor, and 50 cigars. In addition, you are allowed to mail gifts to Canada from abroad at the rate of C$60 a day, provided they are unsolicited and aren't alcohol or tobacco (write on the package: "Unsolicited gift, under $60 value"). All valuables should be declared on the Y-38 Form before departure from Canada, including serial numbers of, for example, expensive foreign cameras that you already own. *Note:* The C$750 exemption can be used only once a year and only after an absence of at least 7 days.

For a full summary of Canadian rules, write for the booklet *I Declare,* issued by the **Canada Border Services Agency** (© **800/461-9999** in Canada, or 204/983-3500; www.cbsa-asfc.gc.ca).

U.K. Citizens

If you're a citizen of the **United Kingdom,** you can buy wine, spirits, or cigarettes in an ordinary shop in any other European Union country and bring home *almost* as much as you like. (U.K. Customs and Excise does set theoretical limits.) But if you buy your goods in a duty-free shop, then the old rules still apply—you're allowed to bring home 200 cigarettes and 2 liters of table wine, plus 1 liter of spirits or 2 liters of fortified wine. If you're returning home from a non-E.U. country, the same allowances apply, and you must declare any goods in excess of these allowances. British customs tends to be strict and complicated in its requirements.

For further details, get in touch with **HM Customs and Excise Office,** Passenger Enquiry Point, Wayfarer House, Great South West Road, Feltham, Middlesex, TW14 8NP (© **0845/010-9000;** from outside the U.K., 020/8929-0152), or consult its website at www.hmce.gov.uk.

Australian Citizens

The duty-free allowance in **Australia** is A$400 or, for those under 18, A$200. Australian citizens are allowed to mail gifts to Australia from abroad duty-free to a limit of A$200 per parcel. There are no other restrictions on unsolicited gifts; however, you could be subject to a customs investigation if you send multiple parcels of the same gift to the same address. Upon returning to Australia, citizens can bring in 250 cigarettes or 250

grams of loose tobacco, and 1.125 liters of alcohol. If you're returning with valuable goods you already own, such as foreign-made cameras, you should file form B263. A helpful brochure, available from Australian consulates or customs offices, is *Know Before You Go.* For more information, contact **Australian Customs Services,** GPO Box 8, Sydney NSW 2001 (© **02/9213-2000** or 1300/363-263; www.customs.gov.au).

New Zealand Citizens

The duty-free allowance for **New Zealand** is NZ$700. New Zealanders are allowed to mail gifts to New Zealand from abroad duty-free to a limit of NZ$70 per parcel. Beware of sending multiple parcels of the same gift to the same address; a customs investigation could await your return home. Citizens over 17 years of age can bring in 200 cigarettes, or 50 cigars, or 250 grams of tobacco (or a mixture of all three if their combined weight doesn't exceed 250g); plus 4.5 liters of wine and beer, or 1.125 liters of liquor. New Zealand currency does not carry import or export restrictions. Fill out a certificate of export, listing the valuables you are taking out of the country; that way, you can bring them back without paying duty. Most questions are answered in a free pamphlet available at New Zealand consulates and Customs offices: *New Zealand Customs Guide for Travellers, Notice no. 4.* For more information, contact **New Zealand Customs,** The Customhouse, 17–21 Whitmore St., Box 2218, Wellington (© **04/473-6099** or 0800/428-786; www.customs.govt.nz).

3 Money

If there is one thing old Spaniards wax nostalgically over, it's certainly not the police state they experienced under the dictatorship of Franco, but the prices paid back then. How they miss the days

when you could go into a restaurant and order a meal with wine for 50 pesetas.

Regrettably, Spain is no longer a budget destination. In Madrid, you can

The Euro, the U.S. Dollar & the British Pound

Euro €	U.S. $	U.K. £	Euro €	U.S. $	U.K. £
1.00	1.25	0.69	75.00	63.75	51.75
2.00	2.50	1.38	100.00	125.00	69.00
3.00	3.75	2.07	125.00	156.25	86.25
4.00	5.00	2.76	150.00	187.50	103.50
5.00	6.25	3.45	175.00	218.75	120.75
6.00	7.50	4.14	200.00	250.00	138.00
7.00	8.75	4.83	225.00	281.25	155.25
8.00	10.00	5.52	250.00	312.50	172.50
9.00	11.25	6.21	275.00	343.75	189.75
10.00	12.50	6.90	300.00	375.00	207.00
15.00	18.75	10.35	350.00	437.50	241.50
20.00	25.00	13.80	400.00	500.00	276.00
25.00	31.25	17.25	500.00	625.00	345.00
50.00	62.50	34.50	1,000.00	1,250.00	690.00

often find hotels charging the same prices as in London or Paris.

Taken as a whole, though, Madrid remains slightly below the cost-of-living index of other major European capitals. Unless the current monetary situation is drastically altered, there is a very favorable exchange rate in Spain when you pay in U.S. dollars.

Prices in Madrid are generally high, but you get good value for your money. Hotels are usually clean and comfortable, and restaurants generally offer good cuisine and ample portions made with quality ingredients. Trains are fast and on time, and most service personnel treat you with respect.

In Madrid, many prices for children—generally defined as ages 6 to 17—are lower than for adults. Fees for children under 6 are generally waived.

CURRENCY: THE EURO

In January 2002, the largest money-changing operation in history led to the deliberate obsolescence of many of Europe's individual national currencies, including the Spanish peseta. In its place was substituted the euro (abbreviation EUR), a currency that, at this writing, was based on the fiscal participation of a dozen nations of Europe. Exchange rates of participating countries are locked into a common currency fluctuating against the dollar. For more details on the euro, check out **www.europa.eu.int/euro**.

For American Readers At the euro's inception, the U.S. dollar and the euro traded on par (that is, $1 approximately equals 1€). But in recent years the euro has gained strength against the dollar and in converting prices to U.S. dollars, we used the current conversion rate of 1€ = $1.25. For up-to-the minute exchange rates between the euro and the dollar, check the currency converter website **www.xe.com/ucc**.

For British Readers At this writing, £1 equals approximately US$1.82, and trades at 1.45€. These were the rates of exchange used to calculate the values in the table below.

(For up-to-date rates at any time, check the Universal Currency Converter website: www.xe.com/ucc.)

Exchange rates are more favorable at the point of arrival. Nevertheless, it's often helpful to exchange at least some money before going abroad. Currency and traveler's checks (for which you'll receive a better rate than cash) can be changed at all principal airports, though standing in line at the *cambio* (exchange bureau) in Madrid's Barajas airport could make you miss the next bus leaving for downtown. Before leaving home, therefore, order a few euros in advance from the following: **American Express** (© **800/221-7282;** www.americanexpress.com), **Thomas Cook** (© **800/223-7373;** www.thomascook.com), or **Capital for Foreign Exchange** (© **888/842-0880**).

Upon arrival in Madrid, it's best to exchange currency or traveler's checks at a bank, not a *cambio,* hotel, or shop. Note the rates and ask about commission fees; it can sometimes pay to shop around and ask the right questions.

Many Madrid hotels don't accept dollar- or pound-denominated checks; those that do will almost certainly charge for the conversion. In some cases, they'll accept countersigned traveler's checks or a credit card, but if you're prepaying a deposit on hotel reservations, it's cheaper and easier to pay with a check drawn on a Spanish bank.

This can be arranged by a large commercial bank or by a specialist such as **Ruesch International,** 700 11th St. NW, 4th Floor, Washington, DC 20001-4507 (© **800/424-2923;** www.ruesch.com), which performs a wide variety of conversion-related tasks, usually for only $5 to $15 per transaction.

If you need a check payable in euros, call Ruesch's toll-free number, describe what you need, and note the transaction number given to you. Mail your dollar-denominated personal check (payable to Ruesch International) to the address above. Upon receiving this, the company will mail a check denominated in euros for the financial equivalent, minus the $2 charge. The company can also help you with many different kinds of wire transfers and conversions of VAT (value-added tax, known as IVA in Spain), refund checks, and also will mail brochures and information packets on request. Brits can contact **Ruesch International Ltd.,** Marble Arch Tower, 14 Floor, 55 Bryanston St., London W14 7AA, England (© **0207/563-3300**).

ATMs

The easiest and best way to get cash away from home is from an ATM (automated teller machine), sometimes referred to as a "cash machine," or a "cashpoint." *Note:* In Spain only four-digit numbers are valid, so be sure to change any five- or six-digit

---

(Tips Emergency Cash—The Fastest Way

If you need emergency cash over the weekend when all banks and American Express offices are closed, you can have money wired to you from **Western Union** (© **800/325-6000;** www.westernunion.com). You must present valid ID to pick up the cash at the Western Union office. However, in most countries, you can pick up a money transfer even if you don't have valid identification, as long as you can answer a test question provided by the sender. Be sure to let the sender know in advance that you don't have ID. If you need to use a test question instead of ID, the sender must take cash to his or her local Western Union office, rather than transferring the money over the phone or online.

PIN number to a four-digit number before you go.

The **Cirrus** (© **800/424-7787;** www.mastercard.com) and **PLUS** (© **800/843-7587;** www.visa.com) networks span the globe; look at the back of your bank card to see which network you're on, and then call or check online for ATM locations at your destination. Be sure you know your PIN and daily withdrawal limit before you depart. *Note:* Remember that many banks impose a fee every time you use a card at another bank's ATM, and that fee can be higher for international transactions (up to $5 or more) than for domestic ones (where they're rarely more than $2). In addition, the bank from which you withdraw cash may charge its own fee. For international withdrawal fees, ask your bank.

CREDIT CARDS

Credit cards are another safe way to carry money. They also provide a convenient record of all your expenses, and they generally offer relatively good exchange rates. You can withdraw cash advances from your credit cards at banks or ATMs, provided you know your PIN. Keep in mind that you'll pay interest from the moment of your withdrawal, even if you pay your monthly bills on time. Also, note that many banks now assess a 1% to 3% "transaction fee" on **all** charges you incur abroad (whether you're using the local currency or your native currency).

American Express, Visa, MasterCard, and Diners Club credit cards are all widely accepted in Spain.

TRAVELER'S CHECKS

Traveler's checks are accepted in Spain at banks, travel agencies, hotels, and some shops, and you can buy them at most banks before you leave. They are offered in denominations of $20, $50, $100, $500, and sometimes $1000. Generally, you'll pay a service charge ranging from 1% to 4%. The most popular traveler's checks are offered by **American Express** (© **800/807-6233** or © 800/221-7282 for card holders—this number accepts collect calls, offers service in several foreign languages, and exempts Amex gold and platinum cardholders from the 1% fee.); **Visa** (© **800/732-1322**)—AAA members can obtain Visa checks for a $9.95 fee (for checks up to $1,500) at most AAA offices or by calling © **866/339-3378;** and **MasterCard** (© **800/223-9920**).

American Express, Thomas Cook, Visa, and **MasterCard** offer **foreign currency traveler's checks,** which are useful if you're traveling to one country, or to the euro zone; they're accepted at locations where dollar checks may not be.

If you carry traveler's checks, keep a record of their serial numbers separate from your checks in the event that they are stolen or lost. You'll get a refund faster if you know the numbers.

4 When to Go

CLIMATE

Spring and fall are ideal times to visit Madrid. May and October are the best months, in terms of both weather and crowds. In my view, however, the balmy month of May (with an average temperature of 61°F/16°C) is the most glorious time for making your own discovery of the Spanish capital.

In summer, it's hot, hot, and hotter still, with Madrid at times feeling like the inside of an oven. The Spanish capital has dry heat; the temperature can reach 95°F (35°C) or more in July, 75°F (24°C) in September.

August is the month when Madrid is at its most peaceful—that's when many of its inhabitants have escaped to the mountains or are sunning themselves on the Atlantic or Mediterranean coasts. About 75% of the city's restaurants and shops also decide that it's time for a vacation, but visitors usually find enough for their needs. The only problem is the heat, which can sometimes reach afternoon maximums of 104°F (40°C), though the abundance of air-conditioned locales and soothing lack of crowds produces a unique daylong siesta atmosphere.

Weather Chart for Madrid

	Jan	Feb	Mar	Apr	May	June	July	Aug	Sept	Oct	Nov	Dec
Temp (°F)	42	45	49	53	60	69	76	75	69	58	48	43
Temp (°C)	6	7	9	12	16	21	24	24	21	14	9	6
Rainfall (in.)	1.60	1.80	1.20	1.80	1.50	1.00	.30	.40	1.10	1.50	2.30	1.70

HOLIDAYS

Holidays include January 1 (New Year's Day), January 6 (Feast of the Epiphany), March 19 (Feast of St. Joseph), Good Friday, Easter Monday, May 1 (May Day), June 10 (Corpus Christi), June 29 (Feast of St. Peter and St. Paul), July 25 (Feast of St. James), August 15 (Feast of the Assumption), October 12 (Spain's National Day), November 1 (All Saints' Day), December 8 (Immaculate Conception), and December 25 (Christmas).

No matter how large or small, every city or town in Spain also celebrates its local saint's day. (In Madrid, it's **May 15 [St. Isidro].**) You'll rarely know what the local holidays are in your next destination in Spain. Always try to keep money on hand, because you may arrive in town only to find banks and stores closed. In some cases, intercity bus services are suspended on holidays.

CALENDAR OF EVENTS

The Madrileño calendar is a colorful kaleidoscope of saint's days, fiestas, and bullfights. Art exhibitions are perennial features and during the hot summers you can enjoy concerts in the Retiro Park as well as other open areas. Check with the **Municipal Tourist Board** for details (© **91-588-16-36;** www.munimadrid.es/turismo).

The dates given below may not be precise. Sometimes the exact days may not be announced until 6 weeks before the actual festival. Go to **www.spain.info**, the official website for **TURESPAÑA** (Tourism in Spain), if you're planning to attend a specific event.

THE BIG THREE FIESTAS

Fiesta de San Isidro: Madrileños run wild during this 10-day celebration honoring their city's patron saint. Food fairs, Castilian folkloric events, street parades, parties, music, dances, bullfights, and other festivities mark the occasion. Local couples known as *chulos* and *chulapas* parade in *castizo* (traditional 19th-century) dress and enjoy feasts, *romerías* (festivals), and music acts in key spots like the Plaza Mayor. The largest number of consecutive daily bullfights are held during this fiesta. Make hotel reservations early. Expect crowds and traffic (and beware of pickpockets). Second week in May.

Virgen de la Paloma: This lively festival belies the midsummer image of Madrid as a temporarily lethargic ghost city with practically everyone out of town basking on the Levante and Cantabrian coasts. On August 15, the Latina quarter becomes a crowded riot of street bunting, drinking stalls, live music, and kids' events. The highlight is the procession. Early to mid-August.

The Autumn Festival: The **Festival de Otoño** is the best music festival in Spain, with a lineup that attracts the cream of the European and South American musical communities. The usual roster of chamber music, symphonic pieces, and orchestral works is supplemented by a program of *zarzuelas* (operettas or musical reviews), as well as Arabic and Sephardic pieces composed during the Middle Ages. Make hotel reservations early, and for tickets write to **Festival de Otoño,** Plaza de España 8, 28008 Madrid (© **91-580-25-75**). October and November (dates vary year to year).

THE YEAR AT A GLANCE
January

Three Kings Day (Día de los Reyes). Parades are staged throughout the main arteries of the city in anticipation of the Feast of the Epiphany (Jan 6). Parades usually take place on January 5 or 6.

February

ARCO (Madrid's International Contemporary Art Fair). One of the biggest draws on Spain's cultural calendar, this exhibit showcases the best in contemporary art from Europe and America. At the Crystal Pavilion of the Casa de Campo, the exhibition draws galleries from throughout Europe, the Americas, Australia, and Asia, who bring with them the works of regional and internationally known artists. To buy tickets, you can contact El Corte Ingles at © **91-418-88-00,** or Madrid Rock at © **91-547-24-23.** The cost is between 19€ and 23€ ($24–$29). You can get schedules from the tourist office closer to the event. Dates vary, but usually mid-February.

Madrid Carnaval. The carnival kicks off with a big parade along the Paseo de la Castellana, culminating in a masked ball at the Círculo de Bellas Artes on the following night. Fancy-dress competitions last until February 28, when the festivities end with a tear-jerking "burial of a sardine" at the Fuente de los Pajaritos in the Casa de Campo. This is followed that evening by a concert in the Plaza Mayor. Call © **91-429-31-77** for more information. Dates vary.

March

Semana Santa (Holy Week). Although many of the country's smaller towns stage similar celebrations (notably in Zamora, Valladolid, and Seville), the festivities in Madrid are among the most elaborate. From Palm Sunday until Easter Sunday a series of processions with hooded penitents moves to the piercing wail of the *saeta*, a love song to the Virgin or Christ. *Pasos* (heavy floats) bear images of the Virgin or Christ. Again, make hotel reservations way in advance. Call Madrid's Municipal Tourist Board for details (© **91-588-16-36**). Usually last week of March.

April

Bullfights. Holy week traditionally kicks off the season in Madrid. This national pastime affords the visitor an unparalleled insight into the Spanish temperament.

Tips On Time in Spain

In Spain, a time change occurs the first weekend of spring. Many unsuspecting visitors have arrived at the airport late and missed their planes. If you're visiting the country in early spring, always ask when the time change occurs.

May

Dos de Mayo. May 2 sees the commemoration of the valiant but unsuccessful uprising against occupying French forces during the Peninsula War in 1808, which was brutally repressed and stirringly immortalized in Goya's famous *Los Fusilamientos del 3 de Mayo* painting of firing-squad victims. Rock concerts and flamenco shows take place in the Dos de Mayo square in Malasaña, where the rebellion began, as well as in other parts of the city.

Fiesta de San Isidro. This 10-day celebration honors the city's patron saint. See "The Big Three Fiestas," above.

Feria del Libro. This annual book fair is located in the Retiro Park. Leading international novelists and historians come to promote their latest works, and the number of stands increases annually. The *feria* covers 2 weeks from late May to early June.

June

Corpus Christi. A major holiday on the Spanish calendar, this event is marked by big processions in Madrid, as well as in nearby cathedral cities like Toledo. Around early June.

July

Veranos de la Villa. Called "the summer binge" of Madrid, this program presents folkloric dancing, pop music, classical music, *zarzuelas* (operettas or musical reviews), and flamenco at various venues throughout the city.

Open-air cinema is a feature in the Parque del Retiro. Ask at the various tourist offices for complete details (the program changes every summer). Sometimes admission is charged, but often these events are free. Mid-July until the end of August.

August

Fiestas of Lavapiés and Virgen de La Paloma, Madrid. These two fiestas begin with the Lavapiés on August 1 and continue through the hectic La Paloma celebration on August 15, the day of the Virgen de la Paloma. Thousands of people race through the narrow streets. Apartment dwellers hurl buckets of cold water onto the crowds below to cool them off. Children's games, floats, music, flamenco, and *zarzuelas,* along with street fairs, mark the occasion. For more information, call 🕾 **91-429-31-77.** August 1 to 15. For more on La Paloma, see "The Big Three Fiestas," above.

October

Autumn Festival, Madrid. This cultural program features a series of operatic, ballet, dance, music, and theatrical performances. See "The Big Three Fiestas," above.

December

Día de los Santos Inocentes. On this countrywide holiday, the Spanish play many practical jokes and in general do *loco* things to one another—it's the Spanish equivalent of April Fools' Day. December 28.

5 Travel Insurance

TRAVEL INSURANCE AT A GLANCE

The cost of travel insurance varies widely, depending on the cost and length of your trip, your age and health, and the type of trip you're taking, but expect to pay between 5% and 8% of the vacation itself. You can get estimates from various providers through **InsureMyTrip.com.** Enter your trip cost and dates, your age, and other information, for prices from more than a dozen companies.

Since Spain for most of us is far from home, and a number of things could go wrong—lost luggage, trip cancellation, a medical emergency—consider the following types of insurance.

Check your existing insurance policies before you buy travel insurance to cover trip cancellation, lost luggage, medical expenses, or car rental insurance. You're likely to have partial or complete coverage. But if you need some, ask your travel agent about a comprehensive package. The cost of travel insurance varies widely, depending on the cost and length of your trip, your age and overall health, and the type of trip you're taking. Insurance for extreme sports or adventure travel, for example, will cost more than coverage for a European cruise. Some insurers provide packages for specialty vacations, such as skiing or backpacking. More dangerous activities may be excluded from basic policies.

- **Access America** (② 800/284-8300; www.accessamerica.com)
- **Travel Assistance International** (② **800/821-2828;** www.travel assistance.com)
- **Travel Guard International** (② 800/ 826-1300; www.travelguard.com)
- **Travel Insured International** (② **800/243-3174;** www.travel insured.com)

- **Travelex Insurance Services** (② **800/228-9792;** www.travelex-insurance.com)

TRIP-CANCELLATION INSURANCE (TCI)

There are three major types of trip-cancellation insurance—one, in the event that you prepay a European tour that gets cancelled, and you can't get your money back; a second when you or someone in your family gets sick or dies, and you can't travel (but beware that you may not be covered for a preexisting condition); and a third, when bad weather makes travel impossible. Some insurers provide coverage for events like jury duty; natural disasters close to home, like floods or fire; even the loss of a job. A few have added provisions for cancellations because of terror activities. Always check the fine print before signing on, and don't buy trip-cancellation insurance from the tour operator that may be responsible for the cancellation; buy it only from a reputable travel insurance agency. Don't overbuy. You won't be reimbursed for more than the cost of your trip.

Trip-cancellation insurance will help retrieve your money if you have to back out of a trip or depart early, or if your travel supplier goes bankrupt. Permissible reasons for trip cancellation can range from sickness to natural disasters to the State Department declaring a destination unsafe for travel.

For more information, contact one of the following recommended insurers: **Access America** (② 866/807-3982; www.accessamerica.com); **Travel Guard International** (② 800/826-4919; www.travel guard.com); **Travel Insured International** (② 800/243-3174; www.travel insured.com); and **Travelex Insurance Services** (② 888/457-4602; www.travelex-insurance.com).

MEDICAL INSURANCE

Most health insurance policies cover you if you get sick away from home—but check, particularly if you're insured by an HMO. With the exception of certain HMOs and Medicare/Medicaid, your medical insurance should cover medical treatment—even hospital care—overseas. However, most out-of-country hospitals make you pay your bills *up front* and send you a refund after you've returned home and filed the necessary paperwork. Members of **Blue Cross/Blue Shield** can now use their cards at select hospitals in most major cities worldwide (contact © **800/ 810-BLUE** or www.bluecares.com for a list of hospitals).

Some credit cards (American Express and certain gold and platinum Visas and MasterCards, for example) offer automatic flight insurance against death or dismemberment in case of an airplane crash if you charged the cost of your ticket to the card.

If you require additional medical insurance, try **MEDEX International,** 9515 Deereco Rd., Timonium, MD 21093- 5375 (© **888/MEDEX-00** or 410/453- 6300; fax 410/453-6301; www.medex assist.com) or **Travel Assistance International** (© **800/821-2828;** www.travel assistance.com), 9200 Keystone Crossing, Suite 300, Indianapolis, IN 46240 (for general information on services, call the company's Worldwide Assistance Services, Inc., at © **800/777-8710**).

The cost of travel medical insurance varies widely. Check your existing policies before you buy additional coverage. Also, check to see if your medical insurance covers you for emergency medical evacuation. If you have to buy a one-way same-day ticket home and forfeit your nonrefundable round-trip ticket, you may be out big money.

LOST-LUGGAGE INSURANCE

On flights within the U.S., checked baggage is covered up to $2,500 per ticketed passenger. On international flights (including U.S. portions of international trips), baggage coverage is limited to approximately $9.07 per pound, up to approximately $635 per checked bag. If you plan to check items more valuable than what's covered by the standard liability you may purchase "excess valuation" coverage from the airline, up to $5,000. See if your homeowner's policy covers your valuables, get baggage insurance as part of your comprehensive travel-insurance package, or buy Travel Guard's "BagTrak" product.

Before you leave home, compile an inventory of all packed items and a rough estimate of the total value to ensure you're properly compensated if your luggage is lost. You will only be reimbursed for what you lost, no more. Be sure to take any valuables or irreplaceable items with you in your carry-on luggage. If your main luggage is lost, immediately file a lost-luggage claim at the airport, giving full details of all contents, as most airlines enforce a 21-day deadline. Most airlines require that you report delayed, damaged, or lost baggage within 4 hours of arrival.

Once you've filed a complaint, persist in securing your reimbursement; there are no laws governing the length of time it takes for a carrier to reimburse you.

If you arrive at a destination without your bags, ask the airline to forward them to your hotel; they are required to deliver luggage, once found, directly to your house or destination free of charge and will usually comply. The airline may reimburse you for reasonable expenses, such as a toothbrush or a set of clothes, but the airline is under no legal obligation to do so.

Lost luggage may also be covered by your homeowner's or renter's policy. Many platinum and gold credit cards cover you as well. If you choose to purchase additional lost-luggage insurance, be sure not to buy more than you need.

Buy in advance from the insurer or a trusted agent (prices will be much higher at the airport).

CAR-RENTAL INSURANCE (LOSS/DAMAGE WAIVER OR COLLISION DAMAGE WAIVER)

If you hold a private auto insurance policy, you are probably not covered in Spain for loss or damage to the car, or liability in case a passenger is injured. The credit card you used to rent the car may provide some coverage.

Check your own auto insurance policy, the rental company policy, and your credit card coverage for the extent of coverage. Is your destination covered? Are other drivers covered? How much liability is covered if a passenger is injured? (If you rely on your credit card for coverage, you may want to bring a second credit card with you, as damages may be charged to your card, and you may find yourself stranded with no money.)

6 Health & Safety

STAYING HEALTHY

Spain should pose no major health hazards. Yes, the rich cuisine—garlic, olive oil, and wine—may give some travelers mild diarrhea, so take along some anti-diarrhea medicine, moderate your eating habits, and even though the water is generally safe, drink mineral water only. Fish and shellfish from the polluted Mediterranean should only be eaten cooked, though in Madrid most seafood comes from the cleaner Atlantic-washed northern provinces and you might risk the odd raw *percebe* (goose barnacle) if you can afford it.

If you're traveling around Spain (particularly southern Spain) over the summer, limit your exposure to the sun, especially during the first few days of your trip and, thereafter, from 11am to 2pm. Use a sunscreen with a high protection factor and apply it liberally. Remember that children need more protection than adults do.

The water is safe to drink throughout Spain; however, do not drink the water in mountain streams, regardless of how clear and pure it looks.

GENERAL AVAILABILITY OF HEALTH CARE

No shots of any sort are required before traveling to Spain. Once there, medicines for a wide variety of common ailments from colds to diarrhea can be obtained over the counter at local chemists or *farmacias*. Generic equivalents of common prescription drugs are also usually available in Spain. (However, it does no harm to bring OTC medicines with you to be on the safe side.)

Contact the **International Association for Medical Assistance to Travelers (IAMAT; (C) 716/754-4883** or, in Canada, 416/652-0137; **www.iamat.org**) for specific tips on travel and health concerns in Spain and for lists of local, English-speaking doctors. The United States **Centers for Disease Control and Prevention** ((C) **800/311-3435;** www.cdc.gov) provides up-to-date information on health hazards by region or country and offers tips on food safety. The website **www.trip prep.com**, sponsored by a consortium of travel medicine practitioners, may also offer helpful advice on traveling abroad. You can find listings of reliable clinics overseas at the **International Society of Travel Medicine** (www.istm.org).

COMMON AILMENTS

CHANGE OF DIET You'll have no need to go on a tempting cholesterol binge if you really don't want to. Vegetarians can follow their usual diet pattern in Madrid, as an increasing number of vegetarian eating spots is available (see also "Vegetarian Visitors," later and "Going Green in Madrid," p. 125) as well as a

Avoiding "Economy-Class Syndrome"

Deep vein thrombosis, or as it's know in the world of flying, "economy-class syndrome," is a blood clot that develops in a deep vein. It's a potentially deadly condition that can be caused by sitting in cramped conditions—such as an airplane cabin—for too long. During a flight (especially a long-haul flight), get up, walk around, and stretch your legs every 60 to 90 minutes to keep your blood flowing. Other preventative measures include frequent flexing of the legs while sitting, drinking lots of water, and avoiding alcohol and sleeping pills. If you have a history of deep vein thrombosis, heart disease, or another condition that puts you at high risk, some experts recommend wearing compression stockings or taking anticoagulants when you fly; always ask your physician about the best course for you. Symptoms of deep vein thrombosis include leg pain or swelling, or even shortness of breath.

multitude of *herbolarios,* or health food shops.

HIGH-ALTITUDE HAZARDS   Madrid is nearly 2,000 feet above sea level, but this does not usually trigger respiratory problems. Care should be taken, however, if you decide to climb up to the top of the 7,500-foot-high Guadarrama mountains—a feat performed by a surprising number of people on the steep but relatively easy path access from Cotos.

SUN EXPOSURE   Madrid has a dry, sunny climate (more than 300 cloudless days a year), and it's best to take protective measures against sunburn and heatstroke. This is particularly valid in May and June when the days are long and the sun's rays are deceptively intense. The temperatures at those times are not as oppressive as those of July and August, when you feel more inclined to stay in the shade or seek solace in an air-conditioned locale.

Visitors with eyesight problems should also take care to avoid the sun's strong glare, using prescribed sunglasses.

WHAT TO DO IF YOU GET SICK AWAY FROM HOME

Spanish medical facilities are among the best in the world. If a medical emergency arises, your hotel staff can usually put you in touch with a reliable doctor. If not, contact the American embassy or a consulate; each one maintains a list of English-speaking doctors. Medical and hospital services aren't free, so be sure that you have appropriate insurance coverage before you travel.

Pack prescription medications in your carry-on luggage. Carry written prescriptions in generic, not brand-name form, and dispense all prescription medications from their original vials. Also bring along copies of your prescriptions in case you lose your pills or run out.

We list Madrid **hospitals** and **emergency numbers** under "Fast Facts," p. 74.

If you suffer from a chronic illness, consult your doctor before your departure. Pack **prescription medications** in your carry-on luggage, and carry them in their original containers, with pharmacy labels—otherwise they won't make it through airport security. Carry the generic name of prescription medicines, in case a local pharmacist is unfamiliar with the brand name.

For travel abroad, you may have to pay all medical costs upfront and be reimbursed later. See "Medical Insurance," under "Travel Insurance," above.

STAYING SAFE
TERRORISM

Since the Al Qaeda bomb attacks on three suburban trains in and around Atocha station on March 11, 2004, resulting in the deaths of 200 people, both political and public attention in Spain has been strongly focused on the global nature of terrorism now threatening Western society.

A direct or indirect consequence of the massacre was that after a massive protest demonstration of two million people in the streets of the city, voters unexpectedly returned the Socialist party to power in the March 14 general elections. (The policy of the new president Rodríguez Zapatero had always been to oppose the war in Iraq, and one of his first acts was to authorize the full withdrawal of Spanish troops from that country just over 3 months later.)

Life in Madrid continued more or less unchanged after this event, even though the memory of it remains indelible. To date there is nothing to suggest that Islamic terrorism constitutes a more serious threat in Madrid than in any other major world city. U.S. tourists traveling to Spain should, however, exercise caution and refer to the guidance offered in the Worldwide Caution Public Announcements issued in the wake of the September 11, 2001, terrorist attacks, now also bearing in mind the 2004 tragedy in Madrid.

The homegrown terrorist problem of ETA, the Basque separatist movement, has meanwhile taken a more hopeful turn. After 4 decades of deadly bomb attacks on police and public (even including tourists), the ETA announced a "permanent" ceasefire in 2006. Subsequent negotiations between the PSOE government helmed by the pragmatic Rodríguez Zapatero and the outlawed Herri Batasuna party, the front for ETA, have led to cautious optimism for a peaceful settlement of the problem. The opposition PP party under Mariano Rajoy is, however, adamant in their refusal to support any form of discussion with what they regard as simply a terrorist group and have successfully stage-managed several mass demonstrations of protest to this effect. Therefore, the outcome at press time remains largely in doubt.

A smaller Marxist group, GRAPO, which also mounted several attacks since 1999 and killed three people, has in recent years been inactive.

"CONVENTIONAL" CRIME

While most of Spain has a moderate rate of "conventional" crime, and most of the estimated one million American tourists enjoy trouble-free visits to Spain each year, the principal tourist areas have been experiencing an increase in violent crime. Madrid has reported growing incidents of muggings and violent attacks, and older tourists and Asian-Americans seem to be particularly at risk. Criminals frequent tourist areas and major attractions such as museums, monuments, restaurants, hotels, beach resorts, trains, train stations, airports, subways, and ATMs.

Reported incidents have occurred in key tourist areas, including the zones around the Prado Museum and Atocha train station, and parts of Old Madrid like Sol, El Rastro flea market, and Plaza Mayor. Travelers should exercise caution, carry limited cash and credit cards, and leave extra cash, credit cards, passports, and personal documents in a safe location. Crimes have occurred at all times of day and night, though visitors—and residents—are more vulnerable in the early hours of the morning.

Thieves often work in teams or pairs. In most cases, one person distracts a victim while the accomplice performs the robbery. For example, a stranger might wave a map in your face and ask for directions or "inadvertently" spill something on you. While your attention is diverted, an accomplice makes off with the valuables.

Attacks can also be initiated from behind, with the victim being grabbed around the neck and choked by one assailant while others rifle through the belongings. A group of assailants may surround the victim, maybe in a crowded popular tourist area or on public transportation, and only after the group has departed does the person discover he/she has been robbed. Some attacks have been so violent that victims have needed to seek medical attention afterward.

Theft from parked cars is also common. Small items like luggage, cameras, or briefcases are often stolen from parked cars. Travelers are advised not to leave valuables in parked cars and to keep doors locked, windows rolled up, and valuables out of sight when driving. "Good Samaritan" scams are unfortunately common. A passing car will attempt to divert the driver's attention by indicating there is a mechanical problem. If the driver stops to check the vehicle, accomplices steal from the car while the driver is looking elsewhere. Drivers should be cautious about accepting help from anyone other than a uniformed Spanish police officer or Civil Guard.

The loss or theft abroad of a U.S. passport should be reported immediately to the local police and the nearest U.S. embassy or consulate. U.S. citizens may refer to the Department of State's pamphlet, "A Safe Trip Abroad," for ways to promote a trouble-free journey. The pamphlet is available by mail from the Superintendent of Documents, U.S. Government Printing Office, Washington, DC 20402, via the Internet at www.gpoaccess.gov/index.html, or via the Bureau of Consular Affairs home page at http://travel.state.gov.

DEALING WITH DISCRIMINATION

As Madrid's population slowly becomes more international, overt racial prejudice—never a dominant issue here anyway—appears to be diminishing, though as the sidebar "A Note on Discrimination," below, points out, there will always be a hardcore group of people, such as the fascist fringe supporters of certain Spanish football clubs, whose attitude is affected simply by the color of a person's skin.

Still, since the March 11 bombings of 2004, there has been a slight hardening of attitudes towards Arabic nationalities by certain members of the community. Some residents' attitudes towards Latin Americans have been soured by the appearance (in relatively small numbers) of young L.A.–style South American criminal gangs such as the Latin Kings and Dominicans Don't Play in the outer areas of the city.

On the sexual front, the city is as liberal as any regarding gay lifestyles, including homosexual marriages, which are widely accepted (see "Gay & Lesbian Travelers," below).

Solo female travelers and residents can also live a reasonably hassle-free existence (see "Women Travelers" in "Specialized Travel Resources," below).

7 Specialized Travel Resources

TRAVELERS WITH DISABILITIES

Most disabilities shouldn't stop anyone from traveling. There are more options and resources out there than ever before.

Because of Madrid center's narrow roads and endless flights of stairs, visitors with disabilities may have difficulty getting around the city. But conditions are slowly improving: Newer hotels are more sensitive to the needs of persons with disabilities, and the more expensive restaurants are generally wheelchair-accessible. In general, however, most places have very limited, if any, facilities for people with

A Note on Discrimination

A fierce sense of national pride might lead many Spaniards to bristle at the suggestion that racism is a problem in their country, but recent events and a new report by Amnesty International have brought to the fore concerns over racism and racial profiling in Spain. In January 2002, Rodney Mack, an African American and the principal trumpet player with the Barcelona Symphony Orchestra, was attacked and beaten in Madrid by four police officers who later said they mistook the musician for a car thief. The thief had been described as a black man of roughly Mr. Mack's height, and a police official later admitted that Mack was singled out because of "the color of his skin and his height." In April 2002, Amnesty International cited the Mack case in an exhaustive report accusing Spain of "frequent and widespread" mistreatment of foreigners and ethnic minorities. The report investigated more than 320 cases of abuse from 1995 to 2002, including deaths and rapes while in police custody, as well as beatings, verbal abuse, and the use of racial profiling by police. The report claims that an increase in racist attacks in Spain has coincided with a dramatic growth in the country's immigrant population over the last 20 years. Spanish officials, however, rejected the report, and Congressman Ignacio Gil-Lázaro of Spain's ruling Popular Party said, "The police and Civil Guard confront immigration in a deeply humanitarian way."

While Amnesty's report may rightfully dispel the notion that Spain is exempt from the problems of racism, it does not suggest that the country is Europe's only offender. In recent years, Amnesty has pointed at race-based abuses in numerous European nations, including Austria, Greece, and Italy, as well as in the United States. Travelers of color may have a perfectly enjoyable trip in Spain, but visitors to the area should travel with the knowledge that racism and xenophobia is a growing concern. If you encounter discrimination or mistreatment while traveling in Spain, please report it to your embassy immediately.

—John Vorwald

disabilities, so travelers should consider taking an organized tour specifically designed to accommodate their needs.

Many travel agencies offer customized tours and itineraries for travelers with disabilities. One of the best organizations serving the needs of persons with disabilities (wheelchairs and walkers) is **Flying Wheels Travel,** 143 W. Bridge, P.O. Box 382, Owatonna, MN 55060 (© **800/ 535-6790** or 507/451-5005; www.flying wheelstravel.com), which offers various escorted tours and cruises internationally.

Others include **Access-Able Travel Source** (© **303/232-2979;** www.access-able. com); and **Accessible Journeys** (© **800/ 846-4537** or 610/521-0339; www. disabilitytravel.com).

You can also obtain a free copy of *Air Transportation of Handicapped Persons,* published by the U.S. Department of Transportation. Write for Free Advisory Circular No. AC12032, Distribution Unit, U.S. Department of Transportation, Publications Division, M-4332, Washington, DC 20590.

If you're flying around Spain, the airline and ground staff will help you on and off planes and reserve seats for you with sufficient legroom, but it is essential to arrange for this assistance *in advance* by contacting your airline.

For the blind or visually impaired, the best source is the **American Foundation for the Blind (AFB;** ✆ **800/232-5463;** www.afb.org) 15 W. 16th St., New York, NY 10011 (✆ **800/232-5463** to order information kits and supplies, or 212/502-7600). It offers information on travel and various requirements for the transport and border formalities for Seeing Eye dogs. It also issues identification cards to those who are legally blind.

Other organizations that offer assistance to travelers with disabilities include **MossRehab** (www.mossresourcenet.org) and **SATH (Society for Accessible Travel & Hospitality;** ✆ **212/447-7284;** www. sath.org). **AirAmbulanceCard.com** is now partnered with SATH and allows you to preselect top-notch hospitals in case of an emergency.

The community website **iCan** (www. icanonline.net/channels/travel) has destination guides and several regular columns on accessible travel. Also check out the quarterly magazine *Emerging Horizons* (www.emerginghorizons.com), and *Open World* magazine, published by SATH.

For British Travelers with Disabilities The annual vacation guide *Holidays and Travel Abroad* costs £5 from **Royal Association for Disability and Rehabilitation (RADAR),** Unit 12, City Forum, 250 City Rd., London EC1V 8AF (✆ **020/7250-3222;** www.radar.org.uk). RADAR also provides a number of information packets on such subjects as sports and outdoor vacations, insurance, financial arrangements for persons with disabilities, and accommodations in nursing care units for groups or for the elderly. Each of these fact sheets is available for £2. Both the fact sheets and the holiday guides can be mailed outside the United Kingdom for a nominal postage fee.

GAY & LESBIAN TRAVELERS

In 1978, Spain legalized homosexuality among consenting adults. In April 1995, the parliament of Spain banned discrimination based on sexual orientation.

Madrid is one of the country's major gay centers. The action is mainly located in the *castizo* quarter of **Chueca** between the Gran Vía and Calle Genova (p. 69). Clubs here range from the relatively sedate to the downright outrageous, and there are also a couple of gay-theme bookshops. The tiny Plaza de Chueca bustles with outdoor cafe life in summer and is a good spot for impromptu encounters.

To learn about gay and lesbian travel in Spain, you can secure publications or join data-dispensing organizations before you go. *Frommer's Gay & Lesbian Europe* has chapters on Madrid (as well as on Barcelona, Sitges, and Ibiza, other key gay rendezvous places).

On the magazine front, *Our World,* 1104 N. Nova Rd., Suite 251, Daytona Beach, FL 32117 (✆ **904/441-5367;** www.ourworldmag.com), is devoted to options and bargains for gay and lesbian travel worldwide. It costs $35 for 10 issues. And *Out and About,* 995 Market St., 14th Floor, San Francisco, CA (✆ **800/929-2268;** www.outandabout. com), is noted for its "straight" reporting on the best gay or gay-friendly hotels, gyms, clubs, and other places, with coverage of destinations throughout the world. Aimed for the most upscale gay male traveler, it costs $49 a year for 10 information-packed issues and has been praised by everybody from *Travel + Leisure* to the *New York Times.*

Gay.com Travel (✆ **800/929-2268** or 415/644-8044; www.gay.com/travel or www.outandabout.com), is an excellent online successor to the *Out & About* magazine. It provides regularly updated information about gay-owned, gay-oriented, and gay-friendly lodging, dining, sight-seeing, nightlife, and shopping establishments in every important destination worldwide.

The **International Gay & Lesbian Travel Association (IGLTA),** 4331 N. Federal, Suite 304, Ft. Lauderdale, FL 33308 (© **800/448-8550** or 954/776-2626; www.iglta.com), encourages gay and lesbian travel worldwide. With around 1,200 member agencies, it specializes in networking travelers with the appropriate gay-friendly service organization or tour specialist. It offers a quarterly newsletter, marketing mailings, and a membership directory that is updated four times a year. For an online directory of gay- and lesbian-friendly travel businesses, go to their website and click on "Members."

Travel agents who are IGTA members will be tied into this organization's vast information resources.

SENIOR TRAVEL

Many discounts are available for seniors traveling to Madrid, but often you need to be a member of an association to obtain them.

For information before you go, write for the free booklet, *101 Tips for the Mature Traveler,* available from **Grand Circle Travel,** 347 Congress St., Suite 3A, Boston, MA 02210 (© **800/221-2610** or 617/350-7500; www.gct.com).

One of the most dynamic travel organizations for seniors is **Elderhostel,** 75 Federal St., Boston, MA (© **877/426-8056;** www.elderhostel.org). Established in 1975, it operates an array of programs throughout Europe, including Spain. Most courses last around 3 weeks and are a good value, since they include airfare, accommodations in student dormitories or modest inns, all meals, and tuition. Courses involve no homework, are not graded, and are often liberal arts oriented. These are not luxury vacations, but they are fun and fulfilling. Participants must be at least 55 years old. A companion

must be at least 50 years old; spouses may participate regardless of age. **ElderTreks** (© **800/741-7956;** www.eldertreks.com) offers small-group tours to off-the-beaten-path or adventure-travel locations, restricted again to travelers 50 and older.

SAGA Holidays, 222 Berkeley St., Boston, MA 02116 (© **800/343-0273;** www.sagaholidays.com), runs tours for seniors 50 and older. Many tours are all-inclusive; all cover air transfers and accommodations. Insurance, both baggage and medical, is also included in the net price of the tours.

In the United States, the best organization to join is the **AARP,** 601 E St. NW, Washington, DC 20049 (© **800/424-3410** or 202/434-AARP; www.aarp.org). Members get discounts on hotels, airfares, and car rentals. AARP offers members a wide range of benefits, including *AARP: The Magazine* and a monthly newsletter. Anyone over 50 can join.

FAMILY TRAVEL

Madrid may suffer the stresses and strains of a bustling metropolis, but it is in fact a very good destination for families with **children.** In the Casa del Campo parkland beside the city there's the zoo and Parque de Atracciones, while nearby amenities include the Faunia ecocenter and Warner's Movie World. For more on children's attractions in the city, see the "Especially For Kids" section, p. 189.

To locate accommodations, restaurants, and attractions that are particularly kid-friendly, refer to the "Kids" icon throughout this guide. Suites are sometimes available, which saves considerably on having to pay for two doubles rooms.

For some general tips on family travel, check our very own *Frommer's 500 Places to Take Your Kids Before They Grow Up,* which can be purchased via Frommers.com or www.amazon.com.

Note that children traveling to Spain with companions other than their own parents should have a notarized letter from their parents to this effect. For full entry requirements to Spain, check the **www. travel.state.gov** website.

WOMEN TRAVELERS

In the capital women are as emancipated as in any other major European city. If a degree of machismo still exists, it is minimal today, and women are increasingly reaching high positions in all walks of life. For women exploring the city on their own, the degree of hassle experienced is scarcely different from that found in Paris or London.

For general advice to female travelers, check out the award-winning website **Journeywoman** (www.journeywoman. com), a "real life" women's travel-information network where you can sign up for a free e-mail newsletter and get advice on everything from etiquette and dress to safety; or the travel guide *Safety and Security for Women Who Travel* by Sheila Swan and Peter Laufer (Travelers' Tales, Inc.), offering commonsense tips on safe travel.

MULTICULTURAL TRAVELERS

As Madrid becomes increasingly multicultural, especially in areas such as Lavapiés (p. 69), visitors and residents of all nationalities are naturally accepted by what is in effect a fairly open-minded society. A person of a different race or skin color rarely draws more than a second glance, unlike a few decades back, when a dark face was a rarity in a 99% *castizo* city.

That said, instances of racial conflict are not unknown, though these tend to involve African, Arabic, and Latin American locals rather than multinational visitors.

For general views on travel for African-Americans, check out the following: **Black Travel Online** (www.blacktravel online.com) posts news on upcoming events and includes links to articles and travel-booking sites. Agencies and organizations that provide resources for black

travelers include **Rodgers Travel** (© 800/ 825-1775; www.rodgerstravel.com); the **African American Association of Innkeepers International** (© 877/422-5777; www.africanamericaninns.com); and **Henderson Travel & Tours** (© 800/ 327-2309 or 301/650-5700; www. hendersontravel.com), which has specialized in trips to Africa since 1957. For more information, check out the following collections and guides: *Go Girl: The Black Woman's Guide to Travel & Adventure* (Eighth Mountain Press), a compilation of travel essays by writers including Jill Nelson and Audre Lorde; *The African American Travel Guide* by Wayne Robinson (Hunter Publishing; www.hunterpublishing.com); *Steppin' Out* by Carla Labat (Avalon); *Travel and Enjoy Magazine* (© 866/266-6211; www.travelandenjoy.com); and *Pathfinders Magazine* (© 877/977-PATH; www. pathfinderstravel.com), which includes articles on everything from Rio de Janeiro to Ghana as well as information on upcoming ski, diving, golf, and tennis trips.

STUDENT TRAVEL

If you're traveling internationally, you'd be wise to arm yourself with an **International Student Identity Card (ISIC)**, which offers substantial savings on rail passes, plane tickets, and entrance fees. It also provides you with basic health and life insurance and a 24-hour help line. The card is available from **STA Travel** (© 800/781-4040 in North America; www.sta.com or www.statravel.com; or www.statravel.co.uk in the U.K.), the biggest student travel agency in the world. If you're no longer a student but are still under 26, you can get an **International Youth Travel Card (IYTC)** from the same people and it entitles you to some discounts (but not on museum admissions).

Travel CUTS (© 800/667-2887 or 416/614-2887; www.travelcuts.com) offers similar services for both Canadians and U.S. residents. Irish students may prefer to turn to **USIT** (© **01/602-1600;** www.usitnow.ie), an Ireland-based specialist in student, youth, and independent travel.

Student travelers should check out the **Madhostel** and **Cat's Hostel** in chapter 5 for two of the best-value young-at-heart accommodations in the city.

SINGLE TRAVELERS

On package vacations, single travelers are often hit with a "single supplement" cost added to the base price. To avoid it, you can agree to room with other single travelers or find a compatible roommate before you go from one of the many roommate-locator agencies.

Uniworld, 16000 Ventura Blvd., Encino, CA 91436 (© **800/733-7820** or 818/382-7820), specializes in single tours for the mature person. It arranges for you to share an accommodation with another single person or gets you a low-priced single supplement. Uniworld specializes in travel to certain districts of England, France, Spain, Italy, and Scandinavia.

For more general information, check out Eleanor Berman's latest edition of *Traveling Solo: Advice and Ideas for More Than 250 Great Vacations* (Globe Pequot), a guide with advice on traveling alone, either solo or as part of a group tour.

8 Planning Your Trip Online

Researching and booking your trip online can save time and money. Then again, it may not. It is simply not true that you always get the best deal online. Most booking engines do not include schedules and prices for budget airlines, and from time to time you'll get a better last-minute price by calling the airline directly, so it's best to call the airline to see if you can do better before booking online.

Some sites, such as Expedia.com, will send you **e-mail notification** when a cheap fare becomes available to your favorite destination. Some will also tell you when fares to a particular destination are lowest.

TRAVEL PLANNING & BOOKING SITES

Keep in mind that because several airlines are no longer willing to pay commissions on tickets sold by online travel agencies, these agencies may either add a $10 surcharge to your bill if you book on that carrier—or neglect to offer those carriers' schedules.

The list of sites below is selective, not comprehensive. Some sites will have evolved or disappeared by the time you read this.

- **Travelocity** (www.travelocity.com or www.frommers.travelocity.com) and **Expedia** (www.expedia.com) are among the most popular sites, each offering an excellent range of options. Travelers search by destination, dates, and cost.

- **Orbitz** (www.orbitz.com) is a popular site launched by United, Delta, Northwest, American, and Continental airlines. (Stay tuned: At press time, travel-agency associations were waging an antitrust battle against this site.)

- **Qixo** (www.qixo.com) is another powerful search engine that allows you to search for flights and accommodations from some 20 airline and travel-planning sites (such as Travelocity) at once. Qixo sorts results by price.

- **Priceline** (www.priceline.com) lets you "name your price" for airline tickets, hotel rooms, and rental cars. For airline tickets, you can't say what time you want to fly—you have to accept any flight between 6am and

Frommers.com: The Complete Travel Resource

For an excellent travel-planning resource, we highly recommend **Frommers. com** (www.frommers.com), voted Best Travel Site by *PC Magazine.* We're a little biased, of course, but we guarantee that you'll find the travel tips, reviews, monthly vacation giveaways, bookstore, and online-booking capabilities to be thoroughly indispensable. Special features include our popular **Destinations** section, where you can access expert travel tips, hotel and dining recommendations, and advice on the sights to see in more than 3,500 destinations around the globe; the **Frommers.com Newsletter,** with the latest deals, travel trends, and money-saving secrets; and our **Travel Talk** area featuring **Message Boards,** where Frommer's readers post queries and share advice, and where our authors sometimes show up to answer questions. Once you finish your research, the **Book a Trip** area can lead you to Frommer's preferred online partners' websites, where you can book your vacation at affordable prices.

10pm on the dates you've selected, and you may have to make one or more stopovers. Tickets are nonrefundable, and no frequent-flier miles are awarded.

SURFING FOR AIRFARES

Most airlines now offer online-only fares that even their phone agents know nothing about. For the websites of airlines that fly to and from your destination, go to "Getting There," p. 38.

Other helpful websites for booking airline tickets online include:

- www.biddingfortravel.com
- www.cheapflights.com
- www.hotwire.com
- www.kayak.com
- www.lastminutetravel.com
- www.opodo.co.uk
- www.sidestep.com
- www.site59.com
- www.smartertravel.com

SURFING FOR HOTELS

In addition to **Travelocity, Expedia, Orbitz, Priceline,** and **Hotwire** (see "Travel Planning & Booking Sites,"

above), the following websites will help you with booking hotel rooms online:

- www.hotels.com
- www.quickbook.com
- www.travelaxe.net
- www.travelweb.com
- www.tripadvisor.com

It's a good idea to **get a confirmation number** and **make a printout** of any online booking transaction.

SURFING FOR RENTAL CARS

For booking rental cars online, the best deals are usually found at rental-car company websites, although all the major online travel agencies also offer rental-car reservations services. Priceline and Hotwire work well for rental cars, too; the only "mystery" is which major rental company you get, and for most travelers the difference between Hertz, Avis, and Budget is negligible.

TRAVEL BLOGS AND TRAVELOGUES

To read a few blogs about Madrid, try **www.travelblog.org/Europe/Spain/Madrid.**

Other blogs include:
- www.gridskipper.com
- www.salon.com/wanderlust
- www.travelblog.com
- www.worldhum.com
- www.writtenroad.com

9 The 21st-Century Traveler

INTERNET ACCESS AWAY FROM HOME

Travelers have any number of ways to check their e-mail and access the Internet on the road. Of course, using your own laptop—or even a PDA (personal digital assistant) or electronic organizer with a modem—gives you the most flexibility. But even if you don't have a computer, you can still access your e-mail and even your office computer from cybercafes.

WITHOUT YOUR OWN COMPUTER

There is now a wide choice of cybernet cafes in central Madrid, most of them quite reasonably priced. Here are two useful addresses:

- **BBiGG,** Alcalá 21 (© **91-521-92-07;** www.bbigg.com; Metro: Sol), is open 24 hours and has 300 flat-screen PCs.
- **easyEverything,** Montera 10 (© **91-523-55-63;** Metro: Sol), is open 24 hours and has a cafe, music, and friendly staff members.

To find more cybercafes in your destination, check **www.cybercaptive.com** and **www.cybercafe.com**.

Aside from these formal cybercafes, most **youth hostels** nowadays have at least one computer you can get to the Internet on. And most **public libraries** across the world offer Internet access free or for a small charge. Avoid **hotel business centers** unless you're willing to pay exorbitant rates.

Most major airports now have **Internet kiosks** scattered throughout their gates. These kiosks, which you'll also see in shopping malls, hotel lobbies, and tourist information offices around the world, give you basic Web access for a per-minute fee that's usually higher than cybercafe prices. The kiosks' clunkiness and high price mean they should be avoided whenever possible.

To retrieve your e-mail, ask your **Internet service provider (ISP)** if it has a Web-based interface tied to your existing e-mail account. If your ISP doesn't have such an interface, you can use the free **mail2web** service (www.mail2web.com) to view and reply to your home e-mail. For more flexibility, you may want to open a free, Web-based e-mail account with **Yahoo! Mail** (http://mail.yahoo.com). (Microsoft's Hotmail is another popular option, but Hotmail has severe spam problems.) Your home ISP may be able to forward your e-mail to the Web-based account automatically.

If you need to access files on your office computer, look into a service called **GoToMyPC** (www.gotomypc.com). The service provides a Web-based interface for you to access and manipulate a distant PC from anywhere—even a cybercafe—provided your "target" PC is on and has an always-on connection to the Internet (such as with Road Runner cable). The service offers top-quality security, but if you're worried about hackers, use your own laptop rather than a cybercafe computer to access the GoToMyPC system.

Note: Tailor-made for visitors who haven't brought a computer with them, the innovative high-tech **Petit Palace** hotels provide free state-of-the-art Wi-Fi connections. Two Petit Palace hotels are included in chapter 5, and altogether no less than 18 others are scattered around the city—not bad for a company that's only been operating 2 years.

WITH YOUR OWN COMPUTER

Wi-Fi (wireless fidelity) is the buzzword in computer access, and more and more hotels, cafes, and retailers are signing on as wireless "hotspots" from where you can get high-speed connection without cable wires, networking hardware, or a phone line (see below).

T-Mobile Hotspot (www.t-mobile. com/hotspot) serves up wireless connections at more than 1,000 Starbucks coffee shops nationwide. **Boingo** (www.boingo. com) and **Wayport** (www.wayport.com) have set up networks in airports and high-class hotel lobbies. iPass providers (see below) also give you access to a few hundred wireless hotel lobby setups. To locate other hotspots that provide **free wireless networks** in cities around the world, go to **www.personaltelco.net/ index.cgi/WirelessCommunities**.

You can get Wi-Fi connection one of several ways. Many laptops sold in the last year have built-in Wi-Fi capability (an 802.11b wireless Ethernet connection). Mac owners have their own networking technology, Apple AirPort.

For those with older computers, an 802.11b/**Wi-Fi card** (around $50) can be plugged into your laptop. You sign up for wireless access service much as you do cellphone service, through a plan offered by one of several commercial companies that have made wireless service available in airports, hotel lobbies, and coffee shops, primarily in the U.S. (followed by the U.K. and Japan). Best of all, you don't need to be staying at the Four Seasons to use the hotel's network; just set yourself up on a nice couch in the lobby. The companies' pricing policies can be byzantine, with a variety of monthly, per-connection, and per-minute plans, but in general you pay around $30 a month for limited access—and as more and more companies jump on the wireless bandwagon, prices are likely to get even more competitive.

For dial-up access, most business-class hotels throughout the world offer dataports for laptop modems, and a few thousand hotels in the U.S. and Europe now offer free high-speed Internet access. In addition, major ISPs have **local access numbers** around the world, allowing you to go online by placing a local call. The **iPass** network also has dial-up numbers around the world. You'll have to sign up with an iPass provider, who will then tell you how to set up your computer for your destination(s). For a list of iPass providers, go to www.ipass.com and click on "Individuals Buy Now." One solid provider is **i2roam** (www.i2roam.com; (2) **866/811-6209** or 920/235-0475).

If Wi-Fi is not available at your destination, most business-class hotels throughout the world offer dataports for laptop modems, and a few thousand hotels in the U.S. and Europe now offer free high-speed Internet access using an Ethernet network cable. You can bring your own cables, but most hotels rent them for around $10. **Call your hotel in advance** to see what your options are.

In addition, major ISPs have **local access numbers** around the world, allowing you to go online by simply placing a local call. Check your ISP's website or call its toll-free number and ask how you can use your current account away from home, and how much it will cost.

If you're traveling outside the reach of your ISP, the **iPass** network has dial-up numbers in most of the world's countries. You'll have to sign up with an iPass provider, who will then tell you how to set up your computer for your destination(s). For a list of iPass providers, go to www.ipass.com and click on "Individual Purchase." One solid provider is **i2roam** ((2) **866/811-6209** or 920/235-0475; www.i2roam.com).

Wherever you go, bring a **connection kit** of the right power and phone adapters, a spare phone cord, and a spare Ethernet

Online Traveler's Toolbox

Veteran travelers usually carry some essential items to make their trips easier. Following is a selection of handy online tools to bookmark and use.

General:

- **Airplane Food** (www.airlinemeals.net)
- **Airplane Seating** (www.seatguru.com and www.airlinequality.com)
- **Foreign Languages for Travelers** (www.travlang.com)
- **Maps** (www.mapquest.com)
- **Subway Navigator** (www.subwaynavigator.com)
- **Time and Date** (www.timeanddate.com)
- **Travel Warnings** (http://travel.state.gov, www.fco.gov.uk/travel, www. voyage.gc.ca, or www.dfat.gov.au/consular/advice)
- **Universal Currency Converter** (www.xe.com/ucc)
- **Visa ATM Locator** (www.visa.com), **MasterCard ATM Locator** (www. mastercard.com)
- **Weather** (www.intellicast.com and www.weather.com)

On Madrid:

- **Local Scene:** The www.madridman.com website run by American resident Scott Martin gives you chatty background information on where to stay and what to do once you're in Madrid.
- **Restaurants:** The site www.spain.info has a good section on Madrid attractions, especially eating spots.
- **Weekly Events:** Check the **Metrópoli** section of *El Mundo* newspaper on Fridays (www.elmundo.es) for the most comprehensive summary of everything going on in the capital (in Spanish only).
- **Mad About Madrid:** The www.madaboutmadrid.com website gives you a further rundown on city events in English.

network cable—or find out whether your hotel supplies them to guests.

ELECTRICITY

In Spain the electricity connection is 220 volts though it may occasionally be 125 volts. A two-prong plug is needed to connect appliances into the mains. (For further details, see the "Electricity" section of "Fast Facts: Madrid" in chapter 4.)

CELLPHONE USE

The three letters that define much of the world's wireless capabilities are GSM (Global System for Mobiles), a big, seamless network that makes for easy cross-border cellphone use throughout Europe and dozens of other countries worldwide. In the U.S., T-Mobile, AT&T Wireless, and Cingular use this quasi-universal system; in Canada, Microcell and some Rogers customers are GSM, and all Europeans and most Australians use GSM. If your cellphone is on a GSM system, and you have a world-capable multiband phone such as many Sony Ericsson, Motorola, or Samsung models, you can make and receive calls across civilized areas around much of the globe. Just call your wireless operator and ask for "international roaming" to be activated on your account. Unfortunately, per-minute charges can be high—usually $1 to $1.50

in Western Europe and up to $5 in places like Russia and Indonesia.

RENTING A PHONE

For many, **renting** a phone is a good idea. (Even worldphone owners will have to rent new phones if they're traveling to non-GSM regions, such as Japan or Korea.) While you can rent a phone from any number of overseas sites, including kiosks at airports and at car-rental agencies, we suggest renting the phone before you leave home. North Americans can rent one before leaving home from **InTouch USA** (© **800/872-7626;** www.intouch-global.com) or **RoadPost** (© **888/290-1606** or 905/272-5665; www.roadpost.com). InTouch will also, for free, advise you on whether your existing phone will work overseas; simply call © **703/222-7161** between 9am and 4pm EST, or go to **http://intouchglobal.com/travel.htm**.

Cellphone rental from **OnSpanish-Time.com** will deliver the phone to your hotel. Call © **91-523-21-59** (toll-free in the U.S. or Canada: 800/240-6993) or go to www.onspanishtime.com.

Another useful website for phone rentals is **www.gomadrid.com**.

BUYING A PHONE

Buying a phone can be economically attractive, as many nations have cheap prepaid phone systems. Once you arrive at your destination, stop by a local cell-phone shop and get the cheapest package; you'll probably pay less than $100 for a phone and a starter calling card. Or go to **OnSpanishTime.com** (www.onspanishtime.com) for information on buying a phone. Note that local calls may be as low as 10¢ per minute, and in many countries incoming calls are free.

Wilderness adventurers, or those heading to less-developed countries, might consider renting a **satellite phone ("satphone")**. It's different from a cellphone in that it connects to satellites and works where there's no cellular signal or ground-based tower. You can rent satellite phones from RoadPost (see above). InTouch USA (see above) offers a wider range of sat-phones but at higher rates. Per-minute call charges can be even cheaper than roaming charges with a regular cellphone, but the phone itself is much more expensive.

10 Getting There

BY PLANE

Any information about fares or even flights in the highly volatile airline industry is not written in stone; even travel agencies with banks of computers have a hard time keeping abreast of last-minute discounts and schedule changes.

Below is a list of major airlines that fly to Madrid. For up-to-the-minute information, check with a travel agent or the individual airlines.

THE MAJOR AIRLINES

FROM NORTH AMERICA Flights to Madrid from the U.S. East Coast take 6 to 7 hours, depending on the season and prevailing winds.

The national carrier of Spain, **Iberia Airlines** (© **800/772-4642;** www.iberia.com), offers more routes to and within Spain than any other airline, with non-stop service to Madrid from both New York and Miami. From Miami, Iberia takes off for at least eight destinations in Mexico and Central America, and in cooperation with its air partner, Ladeco (an airline based in Chile), to dozens of destinations throughout South America as well. Iberia also flies from Los Angeles to Madrid, with a brief stop in Miami; and offers services to Madrid through Montreal two and three times a week, depending on the season. Also available

> **Tips Europass: A Cost-Cutting Technique**
>
> A noteworthy cost-cutting option is Iberia's **Europass**. Available only to passengers who simultaneously arrange for transatlantic passage on Iberia and a minimum of two additional flights, it allows passage on any flight within Iberia's European or Mediterranean dominion for $250 for the first two flights and $133 for each additional flight. This is especially attractive for passengers wishing to combine trips to Spain with, for example, visits to such far-flung destinations as Cairo, Tel Aviv, Istanbul, Moscow, or Munich. For details, contact Iberia (© **800/772-4642;** www.iberia.com). Iberia's main Spain-based competitor is **Air Europa** (© **888/238-7672;** www.air-europa.es), which offers nonstop service from New York's JFK Airport to Madrid, with continuing service to major cities within Spain; fares are competitive.

are attractive rates on fly/drive programs within Iberia and Europe.

Iberia's fares are lowest if you reserve an APEX (advance-purchase excursion) ticket at least 21 days in advance, schedule your return 7 to 30 days after your departure, and leave and return between Monday and Thursday. Fares, which are subject to change, are lower during off-season. Most transatlantic flights are on carefully maintained 747s and DC-10s, and in-flight services reflect Spanish traditions, values, and cuisine.

American Airlines (© 800/433-7300; www.aa.com) offers daily nonstop service to Madrid from its massive hub in Miami, with excellent connections from there to the rest of the airline's impressive North and South American network.

Delta (© 800/241-4141; www.delta.com) maintains daily nonstop service from Atlanta (centerpiece of its worldwide network) to Madrid. Delta's Dream Vacation department maintains access to fly/drive programs, land packages, and escorted bus tours through the Iberian Peninsula.

Since 1991, United Airlines (© 800/241-6522; www.ual.com) has flown passengers nonstop every day to Madrid from Washington, D.C. United also offers fly/drive programs and escorted motor coach tours.

Continental Airlines (© 800/231-0856; www.continental.com) offers between six and seven nonstop flights per week, depending on the season, to Madrid from Newark, New Jersey, an airport many New York residents prefer.

US Airways (© 800/428-4322; www.usairways.com) offers daily nonstop service between Philadelphia and Madrid. US Airways offers connections to Philadelphia from more than 50 cities throughout the United States, Canada, and The Bahamas.

Most U.S.-based carriers offer service solely to Madrid; once in Madrid, Spain's airline, Iberia, offers low fares to cities throughout the country.

FROM GREAT BRITAIN The two major carriers that fly between the United Kingdom and Spain are **British Airways** (© **0845/773-3377,** or 020/8759-5511 in London; www.british-airways.com) and **Iberia** (© **020/7830-0011** in London). In spite of the frequency of their routes, however, I suspect most vacationing Brits fly charter (discussed later).

More than a dozen daily flights, on either BA or Iberia, depart from both London's Heathrow and Gatwick airports. The Midlands is served by flights from Manchester and Birmingham, two major airports that can also be used by Scots flying to Spain. Approximately seven flights a day go between London and Madrid (trip time: 2–2½ hr.). The best air deals on scheduled flights from the U.K. are those requiring a Saturday-night stopover.

Low-cost flights are now provided from a variety of British cities to Madrid by **easyJet.** No tickets are issued and no specific seats allocated (though families with children do have priority). All bookings are made by e-mail. Check www. easyjet.com.

Ryanair is also operating bargain-priced flights from London Stansted to Valladolid (currently 2½ hours by bus or train from Madrid but soon to be accessible by an hour-long high-speed train). Check www. ryanair.com for full flight details.

NEW AIR TRAVEL SECURITY MEASURES

In the wake of the terrorist attacks of September 11, 2001, in New York—and subsequently March 11, 2004, in Madrid—the airline industry began implementing sweeping security measures in airports. Expect a lengthy check-in process and extensive delays. Although regulations vary from airline to airline, you can expedite the process by taking the following steps:

- **Arrive early.** Arrive at the airport at least 2 hours before your scheduled flight.

- **Try not to drive your car to the airport.** Parking and curbside access to the terminal may be limited. Call ahead and check.

- **Don't count on curbside check-in.** Some airlines and airports have stopped curbside check-in altogether, whereas others offer it on a limited basis. For up-to-date information on specific regulations and implementations, check with the individual airline.

- **Be sure to carry plenty of documentation.** A government-issued photo ID (federal, state, or local) is now required. You may need to show this at various checkpoints. With an e-ticket, you may be required to have with you printed confirmation of purchase, and perhaps even the credit card with which you bought your ticket. This varies from airline to airline, so call ahead to make sure you have the proper documentation. And be sure that your ID is **up-to-date;** an expired driver's license, for example, may keep you from boarding the plane altogether.

- **Know what you can carry on—and what you can't.** Travelers in the United States are now limited to one carry-on bag, plus one personal bag (such as a purse or a briefcase). The FAA has also issued a list of newly

---

Tips What You Can Carry On—and What You Can't

The Transportation Security Administration (TSA), the government agency that now handles all aspects of airport security, has devised new restrictions for carry-on baggage, not only to expedite the screening process but to prevent potential weapons from passing through airport security. Passengers are now limited to bringing just one carry-on bag and one personal item onto the aircraft (previous regulations allowed two carry-on bags and one personal item, like a briefcase or a purse). In summer 2006, in response to the foiled terrorist plot in England (which involved liquid explosives), the agency released an updated list of items passengers are not allowed to carry onto an aircraft. For the latest information, go to the TSA's website **www.tsa.gov.**

Tips Getting Through the Airport

- Arrive at the airport 1 hour before a domestic flight and 2 hours before an international flight; if you show up late, tell an airline employee and he or she will probably whisk you to the front of the line.
- Beat the ticket-counter lines by using airport electronic kiosks or even online check-in from your home computers, from where you can print out boarding passes in advance. Curbside check-in is also a good way to avoid lines.
- Bring a current, government-issued photo ID such as a driver's license or passport. Children under 18 do not need government-issued photo IDs for flights within the U.S., but they do for international flights to most countries.
- Speed up security by removing your jacket and shoes before you're screened. In addition, remove metal objects such as big belt buckles. If you've got metallic body parts, a note from your doctor can prevent a long chat with the security screeners.
- Use a TSA-approved lock for your checked luggage. Look for Travel Sentry certified locks at luggage or travel shops and Brookstone stores (or online at www.brookstone.com).

restricted carry-on items; see the box "What You Can Carry On—and What You Can't."

- **Prepare to be searched.** Expect spot-checks. Electronic items, such as a laptop or cellphone, should be readied for additional screening. Limit the metal items you wear on your person.
- **It's no joke.** When a check-in agent asks if someone other than you packed your bag, don't decide that this is the time to be funny. The agents will not hesitate to call an alarm.
- **No ticket, no gate access.** Only ticketed passengers will be allowed beyond the screener checkpoints, except for those people with specific medical or parental needs.

GETTING INTO TOWN FROM THE AIRPORT

There are good links from **Madrid's Barajas Airport** (terminals 1, 2, and 3 at present) by Metro to the city center

(1€/$1.25) and by special direct bus (3€/$3.75) to the Plaza de Colón. A new public bus service (no. 200; 1€/$1.25) also runs from the airport to the centrally located Avenida de America bus and Metro terminus.

Inside the airport free shuttle buses operate between new long-haul Terminals 4 and 4S (the Satellite building) and the other terminals. (There is also an automated passenger transport system [APM] between 4 and 4S.)

If you've rented a car and are driving into the city yourself, check www.asirt.org/roadwatch.htm and www.onemotoring.com for a rundown on international road signs. (Some of the links here can be a bit hit or miss, though.)

FLYING FOR LESS: TIPS FOR GETTING THE BEST AIRFARE

Passengers within the same airplane cabin are rarely paying the same fare. Business travelers who need to purchase tickets at the last minute, change their itinerary at a moment's notice, or get home for the weekend pay the premium rate. But passengers who can book their ticket either **long in advance or at the last minute** may pay a fraction of the full fare.

Here are a few other easy ways to save.

- If your schedule is flexible, ask if you can secure a cheaper fare by **staying an extra day** or by **flying midweek** at less busy hours (such as after 7pm). (Many airlines won't volunteer this information.)
- **Take advantage of APEX fares.** Advance-purchase booking, or APEX, fares are often the key to getting the lowest fare. You generally must be willing to make your plans and buy your tickets as far ahead as possible: The **21-day APEX** is seconded only by the **14-day APEX,** with a stay of 7 to 30 days. Because the number of seats allocated to APEX fares is sometimes less than 25% of plane capacity, the early bird gets the low-cost seat. There's often a surcharge for flying on a weekend, and cancellation and refund policies can be strict.
- **Watch for sales.** You'll almost never see sales during July and August or the Thanksgiving or Christmas seasons, but at other times you can get great deals. Note, however, that the lowest-priced fares are often nonrefundable, require advance purchase of 1 to 3 weeks and a certain length of stay, and carry penalties for changing dates of travel.
- Join a **travel club** such as **Moment's Notice** (② **718/234-6295;** www. moments-notice.com) or **Sears Discount Travel Club** (② **800/433-9383** or 800/255-1487 to join; www. travelersadvantage.com), which supply unsold tickets at discounted prices. You pay an annual membership fee to get the club's hot line number. Of course, you're limited to

what's available, so you have to be flexible.

- **Join frequent-flier clubs.** It doesn't cost a cent, but it does entitle you to better seats, faster response to phone inquiries, and prompter service if your luggage is stolen or your flight is canceled or delayed, or if you want to change your seat. And you don't have to fly to earn points; frequent-flier credit cards can earn you thousands of miles for doing your everyday shopping. With more than 70 mileage awards programs on the market, consumers have never had more options. To play the frequent-flier game to your best advantage, consult Randy Petersen's **Inside Flyer** (www. insideflyer.com). Petersen and friends review all the programs and post regular updates on changes in policies and trends.
- Search the **Internet** for cheap fares (see "Planning Your Trip Online" earlier).
- Keep an eye on **local newspapers** for promotional specials or fare wars, when airlines lower prices on their most popular routes.
- Try to **book a ticket in its country of origin.** If you're planning a one-way flight from Johannesburg to Bombay, a South Africa–based travel agent will probably have the lowest fares. For multi-leg trips, book in the country of the first leg; for example, book New York–London–Amsterdam–Rome–New York in the U.S.
- **Consolidators,** also known as bucket shops, are great sources for international tickets. Basically, they're just big travel agents who get discounts for buying in bulk and pass some of the savings on to you. Start by looking in Sunday newspaper travel sections; U.S. travelers should focus on the *New York Times, Los Angeles Times,* and *Miami Herald.* U.K. travelers

should search in the *Independent, The Guardian,* or *The Observer. Beware:* Bucket shop tickets are usually nonrefundable or rigged with stiff cancellation penalties, often as high as 50% to 75% of the ticket price, and some put you on charter airlines, which may leave at inconvenient times and experience delays. I've gotten great deals on many occasions from **Cheap Tickets** (℘ 800/377-1000; www.cheaptickets.com) and **STA Travel** (℘ 800/781-4040; www.statravel.com) who've been the world's lead consolidator for students since purchasing Council Travel, and whose fares are competitive for travelers of all ages. **ELTExpress** (Flights.com; ℘ 800/TRAV-800; www.eltexpress.com) has excellent fares worldwide, particularly to Europe. It also has "local" websites in 12 countries. **FlyCheap** (℘ 800/FLY-CHEAP; www.1800flycheap.com), owned by package-holiday megalith MyTravel, has especially good fares to sunny destinations.

- Look for **packages offered by local airlines or travel agencies.** From Madrid, **Air Europa** (www.air-europa.es) and the national airline Iberia often provide special flight offers to regional destinations. Check with local travel agents like **Viajes Iberia** (www.viajesiberia.com; not to be confused with Iberia Airlines) and **Viajes Marsans** (www.marsans.es), both of which have various branches throughout the city and can arrange inclusive hotel and flight deals with inland and coastal places of interest. Other local agencies that provide inclusive flight or train and hotel packages to various parts of Spain include **Solplan** (www.solplan.es) and **JuliaTours** (www.juliatours.es).

TIPS FOR BRITISH TRAVELERS

A regular fare from the United Kingdom to Spain is extremely high, so savvy Brits usually call a travel agent for a deal—either a charter flight or some special air-travel promotion. These so-called deals are almost always available, because of the great interest in Spain as a tourist destination. Another way to keep costs down is by purchasing an **APEX (advance-purchase excursion) ticket.** Alternatively, a **PEX (public excursion fare) ticket** offers a discount without the strict booking restrictions. You might also ask the airlines about a **Eurobudget ticket,** which has restrictions or length-of-stay requirements.

British periodicals are always full of classified advertisements touting "slashed" fares to Spain. Good sources include the London-based magazine *Time Out,* the daily travel section of London's *Evening Standard,* and the Sunday edition of almost any newspaper.

Most vacationing Brits looking for air-flight bargains go charter. Delays can be frequent (some last 2 whole days and nights), and departures are often at inconvenient hours. Booking conditions can also be severe, and one must read the fine print carefully and deal with only a reputable travel agent. Stays rarely last a month, and booking must sometimes be made at least a month in advance, although a 2-week period is sometimes possible.

Charter flights leave from some British regional airports for Madrid airports. Figure on saving approximately 10% to 15% off regularly scheduled flight tickets. Recommended companies include **Trailfinders** (℘ 020/7937-5400 in London; www.trailfinders.com) and **Avro Tours** (℘ 020/8715-0000 in London).

In London, many bucket shops (airline consolidators; see "Flying for Less: Tips for Getting the Best Airfare," above) situated around Victoria Station and Earls Court offer low fares. Make sure the company you deal with is a member of the IATA, ABTA, or ATOL. These umbrella organizations will help you out if anything goes wrong.

CEEFAX, a British television information service included on many home and hotel TVs, runs details of package holidays and flights to Europe and beyond. Just switch to your CEEFAX channel to find a menu of listings that includes travel information.

Also check out the **easyJet** and **Ryanair** flights mentioned earlier in "The Major Airlines."

GETTING THERE BY CAR

If you're touring the rest of Europe in a rented car, you might, for an added cost, be allowed to drop off your vehicle in a Madrid.

Highway approaches to Spain are across France on expressways. The most popular border crossing is near Biarritz, but there are 17 other border stations between Spain and France. If you plan to visit the north or west of Spain (Galicia), the Hendaye-Irún border is the most convenient frontier crossing. If you're going to Barcelona or Catalonia and along the Levante coast (Valencia), take the expressway in France to Toulouse, then the A-61 to Narbonne, and then the A-9 toward the border crossing at La Junquera. You can also take the RN-20, with a border station at Puigcerdà.

If you're driving from Britain, make sure you have a cross-Channel reservation, as traffic tends to be very heavy, especially in summer.

The major ferry crossings connect Dover and Folkestone with Dunkirk. Newhaven is connected with Dieppe, and the British city of Portsmouth with Roscoff. Taking a car on the ferry from Dover to Calais on **P & O Ferries** (© 800/677-8585 in North America or 08705/20-20-20; www.poferries.com) costs £99 ($188) and takes 1¼ hours. This cost includes the car and two passengers.

One of the fastest crossings is by hovercraft from Dover to Calais. It costs

more than the ferry, but it takes only about half an hour. For reservations and information, call **Hoverspeed** (© 800/677-8585 for reservations in North America, or 0870/240-8070 in England; www.hoverspeed.com). The hovercraft takes 35 minutes and costs £138 to £215 ($262–$409) for the car and two passengers. The drive from Calais to the border would take about 15 hours.

You can take the Chunnel, the underwater Channel Tunnel linking Britain (Folkestone) and France (Calais) by road and rail. **Eurostar** tickets, for train service between London and Paris or Brussels, are available through Rail Europe (© 800/EUROSTAR; www.eurostar.com for information). In London, make reservations for Eurostar at © 0870/530-00-03. The tunnel also accommodates passenger cars, charter buses, taxis, and motorcycles, transporting them under the English Channel from Folkestone, England, to Calais, France. It operates 24 hours a day, 365 days a year, running every 15 minutes during peak travel times, and at least once an hour at night. Tickets may be purchased at the tollbooth at the tunnel's entrance. With "Le Shuttle," gone are the days of weather-related delays, seasickness, and advance reservations.

Once you land, you'll have about a 15-hour drive to Spain.

If you plan to transport a rental car between England and France, check in advance with the rental company about license and insurance requirements and additional drop-off charges. And be aware that many car-rental companies, for insurance reasons, forbid transport of one of their vehicles over the water between England and France.

CAR RENTALS Many of North America's biggest car-rental companies, including Avis, Budget, and Hertz, maintain offices throughout Spain. Although several Spanish car-rental companies exist, we've received lots of letters from readers of previous editions telling us they've had hard times resolving billing irregularities and insurance claims, so you might want to stick with the U.S.-based rental firms.

Note that tax on car rentals is a whopping 15%, so don't forget to factor that into your travel budget. Usually, prepaid rates do not include taxes, which will be collected at the rental kiosk itself. Be sure to ask explicitly what's included when you're quoted a rate.

Avis (© **800/331-1212;** www.avis. com) maintains about 100 branches throughout Spain, including about a dozen in Madrid. If you reserve and pay for your rental by telephone at least 2 weeks before your departure from North America, you'll qualify for the company's best rate, with unlimited kilometers included.

You can usually get competitive rates from **Hertz** (© **800/654-3131;** www. hertz.com) and **Budget** (© **800/472-3325;** www.budget.com); it always pays to comparison shop. Budget doesn't have a drop-off charge if you pick up a car in one Spanish city and return it to another. All three companies require that drivers be at least 21 years of age and, in some cases, not older than 72. To be able to rent a car, you must have a passport and a valid driver's license; you must also have a valid credit card or a prepaid voucher. An international driver's license is not essential, but you might want to present it if you have one; it's available from any North American office of the American Automobile Association (AAA).

Two other agencies of note include **Kemwel Holiday Auto** (© **877/820-0668;** www.kemwel.com) and **Auto Europe** (© **800/223-5555;** www.auto europe.com).

Many packages include airfare, accommodations, and a rental car with unlimited mileage. Compare these prices with the cost of booking airline tickets and renting a car separately, in order to see if these offers are good deals. Internet resources can make comparison shopping easier. **Expedia** (www.expedia.com) and **Travelocity** (www.travelocity.com) help you compare prices and locate car-rental bargains from various companies nationwide. They will even make your reservation for you once you've found the best deal. See "Planning Your Trip Online," earlier in this chapter, for tips.

Most cars rented in Spain are stick shift, not automatic. Most have air-conditioned, and nearly all use unleaded gas.

DRIVING RULES   Spaniards drive on the right side of the road. Drivers should pass on the left; local drivers sound their horns when passing another car and flash their lights at you if you're driving slowly (slowly for high-speed Spain) in the left lane. Autos coming from the right have the right-of-way.

Spain's express highways are known as *autopistas,* which charge a toll, and *autovías,* which don't. To exit in Spain, follow the SALIDA (exit) sign, except in Catalonia, where the exit sign says SORTIDA. On most express highways, the speed limit is 120kmph (75 mph). On other roads, speed limits range from 90kmph (56 mph) to 100kmph (62 mph). You will see many drivers far exceeding these limits.

The greatest number of accidents in Spain is recorded along the notorious Costa del Sol highway, Carretera de Cádiz.

If you must drive through Madrid—or any other Spanish city—try to avoid morning and evening rush hours. Never park your car facing oncoming traffic, as that is against the law. If you are fined by the highway patrol *(Guardia Civil de Tráfico),* you must pay on the spot. Penalties for drinking and driving are very stiff (N.B. **breathalyzers** are far more strictly used than in the past).

MAPS   For one of the best overviews of the Iberian Peninsula (Spain and Portugal), get Michelin map no. 990 (folded version) or map no. 460 (spiral-bound version). For more detailed looks at Spain, Michelin has a series of six maps (nos. 441–446) showing specific regions, complete with many minor roads.

For extensive touring, purchase *Mapas de Carreteras—España y Portugal*, published by Almax Editores and available at most leading bookstores in Spain. This cartographic compendium of Spain provides an overview of the country and includes road and street maps of some of its major cities.

The American Automobile Association (www.aaa.com) publishes a regional map of Spain that's available free to members at most AAA offices in the United States. Incidentally, the AAA is associated with the **Real Automóvil Club de España (RACE; ☎ 90-240-45-45;** www.race.es). This organization can supply helpful information about road conditions in Spain, including tourist and travel advice.

It will also provide limited road service, in an emergency, if your car breaks down.

BREAKDOWNS   These can be a serious problem. If you're driving a Spanish-made vehicle that needs parts, you'll probably be able to find them. But if you are driving a foreign-made vehicle, you may be stranded. Have the car checked before setting out on a long trek through Spain. On a major motorway you'll find strategically placed emergency phone boxes. On secondary roads, call for help by asking the operator to locate the nearest Guardia Civil, which will put you in touch with a garage that can tow you to a repair shop.

As noted above, the Spanish affiliate of AAA can provide limited assistance in the event of a breakdown.

All highways within Spain radiate outward from Madrid, connecting on both inward and outward journeys with the M-30 and M-40 highways that encircle the city. The following are the major highways into Madrid, with information on driving distances to the city:

Highways to Madrid

Route	From	Distance to Madrid
N-I	Irún	507km (315 miles)
N-II	Barcelona	626km (389 miles)
N-III	Valencia	349km (217 miles)
N-IV	Cádiz	625km (388 miles)
N-V	Badajoz	409km (254 miles)
N-VI	Galicia	602km (374 miles)

GETTING THERE BY BUS

Bus travel to Spain is possible but not popular—it's quite slow. But coach services do operate regularly from major capitals of Western Europe to Madrid, from which bus connections can be made to Seville. The busiest routes are from London and are run by **Eurolines Limited,** 52 Grosvenor Gardens, London SW1W 0AU (☎ **0990/143-219** or 020/7730-8235). The journey from London's

Victoria Station to Madrid is provided by two services: Service 180 is an express from Victoria Station to Madrid, departing London daily at 9pm, arriving in Madrid the following day at 9:30pm; and Service 181 leaves London at 9pm on the first day, arriving in Madrid at 12:30am on the third day.

If you're touring the rest of Europe in a rented car, you might, for an added cost, be allowed to drop off your vehicle in Madrid.

GETTING THERE BY TRAIN

If you're already in Europe, you may want to get to Spain by train, especially if you have a Eurailpass. Even if you don't, the cost is moderate. Rail passengers who visit from Britain or France should make *couchette* (bunk beds in a sleeper car) and sleeper reservations as far in advance as possible, especially during the peak summer season.

Since Spain's rail tracks are of a wider gauge than those used for French trains (except for the Talgo and Trans-Europe-Express trains), you'll probably have to change trains at the border unless you're on an express train (see below). For long journeys on Spanish rails, seat and sleeper reservations are mandatory.

The most comfortable and fastest trains in Spain are the AVE, Altaria, TER, Talgo, and Electrotren. You will have to pay a supplement to ride on these fast trains, however. Both first- and second-class fares are sold on Spanish trains. Tickets can be purchased in either the United States or Canada at the nearest office of French Rail or from any reputable travel agent. Confirmation of your reservation will take about a week.

If you want your car carried, you must travel Auto-Expreso in Spain. This type of auto transport can be booked only through travel agents or rail offices once you arrive in Europe.

To go from London to Spain by rail, you'll need to change not only the train but also the rail terminus in Paris. In Paris it's worth the extra bucks to purchase a Talgo express or a "Puerta del Sol" express—that way, you can avoid having to change trains once again at the Spanish border. Trip time from London to Paris is about 6 hours; from Paris to Madrid, about 15 hours or so, which includes 2 hours spent in Paris changing trains and stations. Many rail passes are available in the United Kingdom for travel in Europe.

The main train station for arrivals from the north is **Chamartín** (the other main station is **Atocha,** which serves the south and east). From here there are direct Metro routes to all parts of Madrid. (For details of these train stations, see page 47.) The Barcelona-to-Madrid Talgo currently takes 5½ hours, but this will be cut by 2 hours by 2008. Other high-speed times to and from Madrid are: Seville (AVE), 2½ hours; Valencia (Altaria). 3½ hours; and Málaga (Talgo), 4¼ hours.

11 Packages for the Independent Traveler

Package tours are simply a way to buy the airfare, accommodations, and other elements of your trip (such as car rentals, airport transfers, and sometimes even activities) at the same time and often at discounted prices.

Before you start your search for the lowest airfare, you may want to consider booking your flight as part of a travel package such as an escorted tour (see below for details) or a package tour. What you lose in adventure, you'll gain in time and money saved when you book accommodations,

and maybe even food and entertainment, along with your flight.

Package tours are not the same thing as escorted tours. With a package tour, you travel independently but pay a group rate. Packages usually include airfare, a choice of hotels, and car rentals, and packagers often offers several options at different prices. In many cases, a package that includes airfare, hotel, and transportation to and from the airport will cost you less than just the hotel alone would have, had you booked it yourself.

> **Tips   Ask Before You Go**
>
> Before you invest in a package deal or an escorted tour:
> - Always ask about the **cancellation policy.** Can you get your money back? Is there a deposit required?
> - Ask about the **accommodations choices and prices** for each. Then look up the hotels' reviews in a Frommer's guide and check their rates online for your specific dates of travel. Also find out what types of rooms are offered.
> - Request a complete **schedule.** (Escorted tours only)
> - Ask about the **size** and demographics of the group. (Escorted tours only)
> - Discuss what is included in the **price** (transportation, meals, tips, airport transfers, etc.). (Escorted tours only)
> - Finally, look for **hidden expenses.** Ask whether airport departure fees and taxes, for example, are included in the total cost—they rarely are.

That's because packages are sold in bulk to tour operators—who resell them to the public at a cost that often drastically undercuts standard rates.

RECOMMENDED PACKAGE TOUR OPERATORS

One good source of package deals is the airlines themselves. Most major airlines offer air/land packages. See "By Plane," earlier in this chapter; most airlines offer packages that may include car rentals and accommodations in addition to your airfare.

The best place to start your search is the travel section of your local Sunday newspaper. Also check the ads in the back of national travel magazines like *Travel + Leisure, National Geographic Traveler,* and *Condé Nast Traveler.* One of the biggest packages in the Northeast, **Liberty Travel** (© 888/271-1584; www.libertytravel. com), usually boasts a full-page ad in Sunday papers. **American Express Travel** (© 800/941-2639; www.travel impressions.com) is another option.

Among the airline packagers, **Iberia Airlines** (© 800/772-4642 or 902/400/ 500 in Spain; www.iberia.com) leads the way. **Discover Spain Vacations** (© 800/ 227-5858; www.farandwide.com), the

marketing arm of Iberia, is the most reliable tour operator and the agency used for air and land packages to Madrid. Naturally, round-trip airfares on Iberia are included in the deal. Several fly/drive packages are also offered.

Other packages for travel in Spain are offered by **United Airlines** (© 800/241-6522; www.ual.com), **American Airlines Vacations** (© 800/321-2121; www.aa vacations.com), and **Delta Vacations** (© 800/872-7786; www.deltavacations. com). Also worth a look are **Continental Airlines Vacations** (© 800/301-3800; www.covacations.com) and **United Vacations** (© 888/854-3899; www.united vacations.com). Several big **online travel agencies**—Expedia, Travelocity, Orbitz, Site59, and Lastminute.com—also do a brisk business in packages.

Solar Tours (© 800/388-7652; www. solartours.com) is a wholesaler that offers a number of package tours to Madrid.

Spanish Heritage Tours (© 800/456-5050; www.shtours.com) is known for searching for low-cost airfare deals to Spain—round-trips from the U.S. to Madrid for $429 or to Málaga for $529. The tour agent also features both air and land packages to Madrid.

12 Escorted General-Interest Tours

Escorted tours are structured group tours, with a group leader. The price usually includes everything from airfare to hotels, meals, tours, admission costs, and local transportation.

Despite the fact that escorted tours require big deposits and predetermine hotels, restaurants, and itineraries, many people derive security and peace of mind from the structure they offer. Escorted tours—whether they're navigated by bus, motor coach, train, or boat—let travelers sit back and enjoy the trip without having to drive or worry about details. They often take you to the maximum number of sights in the minimum amount of time with the least amount of hassle. They're particularly convenient for people with limited mobility and can be a great way to make new friends.

On the downside, you'll have little opportunity for serendipitous interactions with locals. The tours can be jam-packed with activities, leaving little room for individual sightseeing, whim, or adventure—plus they often focus on the heavily touristed sites, so you miss out on many a lesser-known gem.

RECOMMENDED ESCORTED TOUR OPERATORS

There are many escorted tour companies to choose from, each offering transportation to and within Spain, prearranged hotel space, and such extras as bilingual tour guides and lectures. Many of these tours to Spain include excursions to Morocco or Portugal.

Some of the most expensive and luxurious tours are run by **Abercrombie & Kent International** (℗ 800/323-7308 or 630/954-2944; www.abercrombiekent. com), including deluxe 13- or 19-day tours of the Iberian Peninsula by train. Guests stay in fine hotels, ranging from a medieval palace to the exquisite modern Hesperia Madrid hotel on Avenida Castellana.

Trafalgar Tours (℗ 800/854-0103 or 212/689-8977; www.trafalgartours.com) offers a number of tours of Spain. One of the most popular offerings is an 18-day trip called "The Best of Spain" (this land-only package is $1,735; with land and air, it's $2,155–$2,565).

Insight Vacations' "Highlights of Spain" is an 11-day tour that begins in Madrid, sweeps along the southern and eastern coasts, and concludes in Madrid. The company offers the tour for $1,370 to $1,785 including airfare, accommodations, and some meals. For information, contact your travel agent or Insight International (℗ **800/582-8380;** www.insight vacations.com).

Petrabax Tours (℗ **800/634-1188;** www.petrabax.com) attracts those who prefer to see Spain by bus, although fly/drive packages are also offered, featuring stays in *paradores* (high-standard, state-run hotels—some modern, some in historic buildings). A number of city packages are also available, plus a 10-day trip that tries to capture Spain in a nutshell, with stops in places ranging from Madrid to Granada.

Recently, more and more special-interest tours to Madrid and Castile are being offered, including tours by **Archetours, Inc.** (℗ **800/770-3051;** www.archetours. com), which features tours devoted to Spanish architecture.

13 Getting Around Madrid

BY CAR

Exploring the city center by car is certainly not a good idea unless you want to get stuck in one of the semi-permanent traffic jams. Parking in town is another big problem. Best to forget it.

On the other hand, a car can be very useful for touring Madrid province, particularly if you want to really get off the beaten track—although bus and train transport to all the main places of interest (such as Chinchón, Alcalá de Henares, Aranjuez, El Escorial) is extremely efficient and economical (see chapter 11 for more details).

If you do decide to rent a car (see "Getting There" section, earlier), driving is on the right, and the speed limit on minor road varies between 40km and 70km per hour and on motorways is 110km (68 miles) per hour. Toll roads exist between major cities, and charges vary according to the distance covered.

Most cars run on unleaded gas, and there's no shortage of gas stations. Automatic transmission cars are rare—most have the manual four-gear system–though air-conditioning is now a standard on most cars. Breathalyzers are now being used with more frequency. The limit amounts to two standard glasses of beer or wine, so take care when washing down those tapas and hitting the road.

BY TRAIN

Cercanías (suburban line trains) provide excellent low-cost transport to major towns in Madrid province such as Alcalá de Henares, Aranjuez, and San Lorenzo de El Escorial (p. 72).

If you want to go farther afield, high-speed trains operate to a variety of major cities such as Seville, Valencia, and Barcelona from **Atocha.** Northern cities such as Bilbao are reached from **Chamartín.** (For more details, see "Getting There by Train," above.)

BY BUS

Buses run from several bus stations to towns of interest in Madrid province such as Chinchón and Torrelaguna (see chapter 11 for more details).

Outside of the Community of Madrid, two main bus stations, Méndez Alvaro and Avenida de America, operate economical but rapid coach services to most Spanish cities.

14 Tips on Accommodations

LANDING THE BEST ROOM

Somebody has to get the best room in the house. It might as well be you. You can start by joining the hotel's frequent-guest program, which may make you eligible for upgrades. A hotel-branded credit card usually gives its owner "silver" or "gold" status in frequent-guest programs for free. Always ask about a corner room. They're often larger and quieter, with more windows and light, and they often cost the same as standard rooms. When you make your reservation, ask if the hotel is renovating; if it is, request a room away from the construction. Ask about nonsmoking rooms, rooms with views, rooms with twin, queen- or king-size beds. If you're a light sleeper, request a quiet room away from vending machines, elevators, restaurants, bars, and discos. Ask for a room that has been most recently renovated or redecorated.

If you aren't happy with your room when you arrive, ask for another one. Most lodgings will be willing to accommodate you.

See chapter 5 for detailed information on all types of accommodations.

RENTING & HOUSE-SWAPPING

Interested in living like the Madrileños live? A rental agency called **The Right Vacation Rental Company** (www.the rightvacationrental.com) rents properties right in the heart of the old Austrias district. You can also rent a weekend Casa Rural (country cottage or flat) up in the mountains or down in the wooded valleys of the richly varied Comunidad de Madrid, barely an hour away from the city center. This provides a relaxing break from the pressures and stimulations of the big city and gives you an idea of what life is like in Madrid province. For more rental properties, check out **www.turismo sierraoeste.com** or **www.alorustico.com**.

House-swapping is becoming a more popular and viable means of travel; you stay in their place, they stay in yours, and you both get an authentic and personal feel for a place, the opposite of the escapist retreat that many hotels offer. Try **Home-Link International** (www.homelink.org), the largest and oldest home-swapping organization, founded in 1952, with more than 11,000 listings worldwide ($75 for a yearly membership). It has a number of apartments available for exchange in Madrid.

15 Recommended Books, Films & Music

BOOKS
ART & ARCHITECTURE
The Moors contributed much to Spanish culture, leaving Spain with a distinct legacy that is documented in Titus Burckhardt's **Moorish Culture in Spain** (McGraw-Hill).

Spain's most famous artist was Pablo Picasso. The most controversial book about the late painter is **Picasso, Creator and Destroyer** by Arianna Stassinopoulos Huffington (Simon & Schuster).

Spain's other headline-grabbing artist was Salvador Dalí. In **Salvador Dalí: A Biography** (Dutton), author Meryle Secrest asks: Was he a mad genius or a cunning manipulator?

FICTION
The most famous Spanish novel is **Don Quixote**, by Miguel de Cervantes. Readily available everywhere, it deals with the conflict between the ideal and the real in human nature. Although the work of Cervantes has attained an almost mystical significance in the minds of many Spaniards, in the words of Somerset Maugham, "It would be hard to find a work so great that has so many defects." Nicholas Wollaston's **Tilting at Don Quixote** (André Deutsch Publishers) punctures any illusions that the story of the half-crazed Don is only a matter of good and rollicking fun.

Ernest Hemingway completed many works on Spain, none more notable than his novels of 1926 and 1940, respectively: **The Sun Also Rises** (Macmillan) and **For Whom the Bell Tolls** (Macmillan), the latter based on his experiences in the Spanish Civil War.

Don Ernesto (the name Hemingway was known by in Spain) also wrote the English-language classic on bullfighting, **Death in the Afternoon** (various editions).

BIOGRAPHY
Despite the unparalleled fame of Miguel de Cervantes in Spanish literature, very little is known about his life. One of the most searching biographies of the literary master is Jean Canavaggio's **Cervantes,** translated from the Spanish by J. R. Jones (Norton).

The latest biography on one of the 20th century's most durable dictators is **Franco: A Concise Biography** (Thomas Dunne Books), which was released in the spring of 2002. Gabrielle Ashford Hodges documents with great flair the Orwellian repression and widespread corruption that marked the notorious regime of this "deeply flawed" politician.

Andrés Segovia: An Autobiography of the Years 1893–1920 (Macmillan), with a translation by W. F. O'Brien, is worth seeking out.

TRAVELOGUE/HISTORY
Denounced by some as superficial, James A. Michener's **Iberia** (Random House) remains the classic travelogue on Spain.

The *Houston Post* claimed that this book "will make you fall in love with Spain."

For a very different, but dated, view of Spain, read W. Somerset Maugham's ***Don Fernando*** (Ayer), with the famed English author's comments on everything from the Spanish diet to *Don Quixote.*

For an interesting selection of anecdotes and pieces written over the years on the capital, read ***Madrid: A Travellers Companion*** (Constable) by Hugh Thomas, author of the classic in-depth Spanish Civil War.

A more personal view of the city is provided in Elizabeth Nash's highly individual ***Madrid: A Cultural and Literary Companion*** in Signal Books' "Cities of the Imagination" series.

If you want the full lowdown on the monuments and historical background of Castile, check out Hispanophile Alistair Boyd's ***Companion Guide to Madrid and Central Spain*** (Collins).

Finally, a succinct and offbeat introduction to the capital's surrounding towns and villages is provided in Peter Stone's ***Madrid Escapes*** (Santana Books).

FILMS SET IN MADRID

One of the city's most enthusiastic chroniclers on celluloid has been **Pedro Almodóvar** (Oscar winner in 1999 for the best foreign language movie ***All About My Mother***). Though his unique comic vision has not been altogether appreciated by many Madrileños—many of whom regard his stylish films as perverse kitsch sagas of marginals and neurotics—atmospheric sub-classics such as ***Women on the Edge of a Nervous Breakdown*** and ***What Have I Done to Deserve This?*** create their own hilarious Madrileño sub-world in which the female plays a surprisingly dominant role.

More soberingly straight and dramatic are the social-commentary works of **Carlos Saura,** ranging from his early ***Los Golfos*** and ***De Prisa, De Prisa*** (both about young Madrileño criminals in the Franco era) to the '90s ***Taxi*** (on urban racism in the city). His trilogy of realistic musicals, ***Carmen, Tango,*** and ***Flamenco,*** shows another facet of this leading director's talents.

The highly unprolific Victor Erice (three films in 30 years) created an indelible image of an artist's struggle in ***The Quince Tree Sun,*** shot entirely on location in the garden of real-life artist Antonio Lopez' own rambling Chamartín house. Strictly for cineastes, this one.

MUSIC

Three major composers of Spanish classical music stand out: **Isaac Albeñiz,** a child prodigy who played in piano concerts at the age of 4, for his *Iberia* suite; **Manuel de Falla,** an ascetic Andaluz from Cádiz, for his *Three Cornered Hat* ballet; and **Enrique Granados** with his lively *Goyescas.*

The most talented musician of modern times was cellist **Pablo (Pau) Casals,** while today's leading opera singer is **Placido Domingo.**

3

Suggested Madrid Itineraries

You can cover quite a few of central Madrid's monuments and architectural highlights in just a day. But the more time you have available, the more justice you can do to the wealth of sights in and near the city. Here are some recommendations on how best to spend your time.

1 The Best of Madrid in 1 Day

This is going to be a very busy day if you want to do the city's key sights full justice. Start with the not-to-be-missed **Prado** museum, for many the highlight of a Madrid visit. Then, after sauntering briefly though the neighboring **Botanical Garden,** take in the sights around the **Puerta del Sol** and **Plaza Mayor.** After lunch, explore the historic **Austrias** district, the heart of old regal Madrid. Round off your day with a coffee or aperitif in the adjoining **Plaza de Oriente** and enjoy the view of the **Royal Palace.** *Note:* Varying seasonal hours of some attractions may require modification of the itinerary below; check the individual listings of these sights in chapter 7 for year-round opening and closing times.

❶: Prado Museum ❀❀❀
Your minutes are precious here, so pick out a few choice masterpieces (such as Velázquez's *Las Meninas*) and concentrate on your favorites. It will be difficult not to be sidetracked with such a wealth of beauty around you, but try to confine your time to a mere hour instead of the half-day you really need to do this place justice. If you're making this visit on a Sunday morning, admission is free, so expect to see longer-than-usual lines of eagerly waiting tourists.

❷: Botanical Gardens ❀❀❀
Adjoining the museum, this delightfully compact backwater of calm and greenery was founded by Charles III. It had over 650 plant species when it opened in 1755; now you can count the wide variety of flowers, shrubs, and ancient trees in thousands. As you wander its sylvan pathways,

it's hard to believe you're in the heart of a big city.

❸: Paseo del Prado ❀❀
Also the work of Charles III, this tree-lined gem, where you can walk shaded by a huge mellow archway of green, is for our money the most beautiful *paseo* in Madrid, if not all Spain. Incomprehensible 2006 plans to chop down most of these ancient trees and "open up" the whole avenue to make it more "touristically attractive" have so far been scotched thanks to strong opposition by Thyssen Museum owner "Tita" Cervera, widow of Baron Thyssen, and a host of other prominent Madrileños. At press time, however, it's still not clear what will happen.

❹: Congreso de Diputados ❀
Reach here after turning left at the **Neptuno** fountain. At the Plaza del Congreso

Madrid Itineraries

The Best in 1 Day

1 Prado Museum
2 Botanical Gardens
3 Paseo del Prado
4 Congreso de Diputados
5 Ateneo de Madrid
6 Casa Museo de Lope de Vega
7 La Mallorquina Pastelería
8 Puerta del Sol
9 Plaza Mayor
10 Cava Baja's Casa Lucio
11 Austrias District
12 Plaza Oriente
13 Café Oriente

The Best in 2 Days

1 Retiro Park
2 Thyssen-Bornemisza Museum
3 Cibeles
4 Circulo de Bellas Artes
5 The Círculo de Bellas Artes Cafe
6 Real Academia de Bellas Artes de San Fernando
7 Convento de las Descalzas Reales
8 Casa Ciriaco
9 Palacio Real
10 Almudena Catedral
11 Parque de las Vistillas
12 Campo del Moro
13 Ermita de San Antonio de la Florida
14 Casa Mingo

The Best in 3 Days

1 Reina Sofia
2 Plaza del Cascorro/Rastro
3 Plaza de Lavapies Café Barbieri
5 Anton Martín Market
6 Filmoteca Cine Doré
7 Plaza Tirso de Molina
9 La Corrala Casa Lastra Sidrería
10 Templo de Debod
11 Teleférico de Madrid
12 Casa de Campo
13 Lago

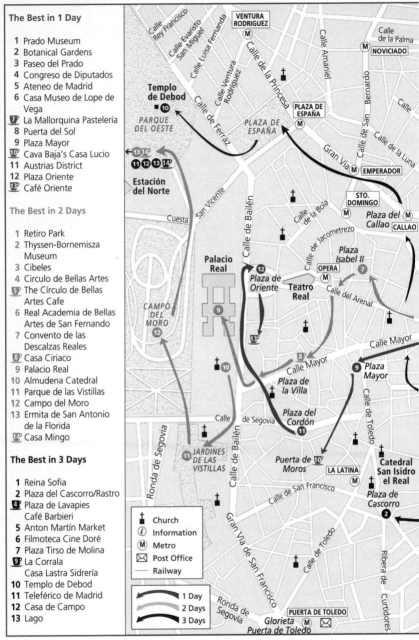

Church
Information
Metro
Post Office
Railway

1 Day
2 Days
3 Days

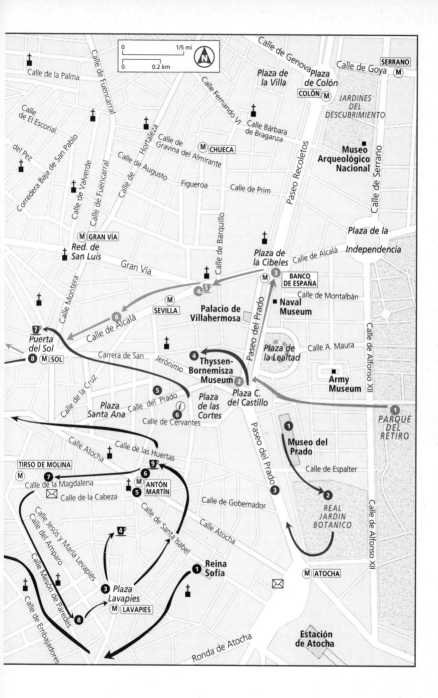

admire the neoclassical facade, granite pillars, and bronze statues of lions outside this mid-19th-century parliamentary building designed by Pascual y Colomer. Here the fate of the state is discussed—often heatedly—and a botched coup was attempted in 1981 (bullet holes in the ceiling of the Sessions Chamber date from that inauspicious occasion). Bring your passport if you want to pay a Saturday morning visit.

❺: Ateneo de Madrid ✦

This 19th-century bastion of culture exudes a time-warp atmosphere. Wander in, ask politely to see the well-worn lounges with their wooden walls and high chandeliers, and imagine yourself back in the time of Unamuno, Ortega y Gasset, and other literary giants of the "Generation of '98" (that's 1898). Though the impressive upstairs library (members only, but you can peer through the glass door) now boasts Internet facilities, the mellow historic surroundings remain incongruously as they were more than a century ago.

❻: Casa Museo de Lope de Vega ✦

Probably the smallest museum in town, this well-preserved medieval house was the home of Spain's most famed and prolific 16th-century playwright and has a secret hidden gem of a garden at the rear. Ironically, it's located on a street named for the dramatist's rival, novelist Cervantes. Best to book ahead; it has severe limitations on the size of visiting groups.

> 🕖 Rest your weary legs in **La Mallorquina Pastelería**'s rather secretive upstairs cafe, where the laid-back atmosphere contrasts pleasantly with the frenzy of the congested bar-cum-shop below. Great coffee plus a variety of cholesterol-filled pastries including a favorite of the Balearic island, *ensaimada,* which may tempt you into spoiling your lunch. Puerta del Sol 8. ✆ **91-521-12-01.**

❽: Puerta del Sol ✦✦✦

Named after the sun-emblazoned gate of a medieval fort that once stood here, this compact and ever-crowded urban hub, Madrid's answer to Times Square, is the only plaza in the city that still bears the name *puerta* (gate). Highlights are its 18th-century clock, whose chimes have marked the jubilant beginning of many a New Year, and emblematic little statue of *El Oso y el Madroño* (The Bear and the Strawberry Tree). It's said to be the geographical center of the country—although the nearby town of Parla also claims this privilege.

❾: Plaza Mayor ✦✦✦

Fly back to **San José** in time to connect with your departing flight home. If you have extra time, feel free to head back into Manuel Antonio National Park, do some souvenir shopping, or simply laze around your hotel pool. You've earned it.

> 🕙 Lunch in **Cava Baja**'s **Casa Lucio** restaurant, a favorite of King Juan Carlos and visiting stars, dignitaries, and heads of state including George W. Prize dish is the outwardly simple *huevos estrellados,* (a fry of eggs and wafer-thin potatoes), here raised to a fine art. On a grander scale, the oven-baked beefsteaks are out of this world. Try to get a first-floor table for the best atmosphere. See p. 126.

⓫: Austrias District ✦✦✦

The narrow streets of Cuchilleros and Cavas Baja and Alta and the charming plazas de la Cebada and de la Paja are at the heart of 16th-century Madrid, dating from the period when the Habsburgs ruled Spain. Here you'll find the city's oldest—and smallest—churches, **San Nicolas de las Servitas** and **San Pedro el Viejo,** twin reminders of a time when Madrid was a modest town of some 10,000 inhabitants. The tiny Morería section on its western fringe was once the Jewish quarter.

⑫: Plaza Oriente ★★

Built over the remains of the old wooden Habsburg palace that burned down in the 17th century, this attractive French-style semicircular plaza has statues of the kings of Spain clustered around a central equestrian statue of Philip IV. A favorite with photographers of all nationalities, it's one of our favorite spots for relaxing over a drink.

⑬ The great attraction of the **Café de Oriente** ★★ is not so much its plush mock Baroque interior as the outside terrace area, which overlooks the square and magnificent facade of the Palacio Real (which you'll visit on your second day). Here you can sip your Campari and soda in an atmosphere of historic splendor. Plaza de Oriente. ℂ **91-541-39-74.** See p. 132.

2 The Best of Madrid in 2 Days

On your first day, follow the 1-day tour, above. On your second day start early with a stroll in the Retiro Park, then pay a quick visit to the famed Thyssen Gallery in the leafy Paseo del Prado (you'll only have time to pick out a few favorites—the Dutch masterpieces, for example). Then go up Alcalá street from nearby Cibeles fountain, taking in the Circulo de Bellas Artes, passing San Jerónimo and—after the Puerta del Sol—the Convento de las Descalzas Reales. In the afternoon take in the cathedral and the Royal Palace. Afterward descend to the Campo del Moro park and wander along the lesser-known River Manzanares area to the tiny chapel of San Antonio de la Florida where Goya is buried.

❶: Retiro Park ★★★

Start with an early breakfast and a stroll among the joggers and tai chi exercisers as far as the *Estanque* (lake) in the **Retiro Park.** Once the sole playground of royals, this rectangular oasis of greenery has been a popular rendezvous for residents ever since it was opened up to the public in 1868.

❷: Thyssen-Bornemisza Museum ★★★

More exquisite art if you're game. This superb multifaceted gallery, founded by the late Baron Hans Heinrich and his wife Carmen "Tita" Rivera, reopened in 2004 with a new extension for temporary exhibitions. To get a rough idea of the museum's vast range, we suggest you take a peep first at the Dutch masters and then at masterpieces by modernists Klee, Braque, and Picasso.

❸: Cibeles

Madrid's most famous fountain lies at the meeting point of Alcalá and the Paseo del Prado opposite the Banco España and main Post Office (Palacio de Comunicaciones). Soccer team Real Madrid's successes are celebrated by fans jumping in the water. An over-excessive spree a year or so back caused one of the goddess's hands to go missing. It was replaced at great cost, and the hapless students responsible received a sobering fine.

❹: Círculo de Bellas Artes

An Art Deco gem with exhibitions in various salons as well as a neighboring cinema cafe (see box below). You can also pop up to the top floor and look at the library, even if you're not a member.

5 The **Círculo de Bellas Artes'** spacious and well-worn cafe evokes a turn-of-the-20th-century aura, with its ceiling chandeliers, recumbent statue of a naked lady, and high, wide windows overlooking the junction of Alcalá and the Gran Vía. Morning TV interviews with both established and up-and-coming politicians are often held against this backdrop, so you might get a glimpse of some future Spanish president. Calle Marqués de Casa Riera 2. © 91-360-54-00. See p. 143.

6: Real Academia de Bellas Artes de San Fernando 🗺🗺

Time for a quick peep at another unmissable temple of art, located just up Alcalá on the way to Sol. This one's the oldest in Madrid and remarkable for its wealth of Spanish and Dutch masters. If nothing else, see the roomful of Goyas.

7: Convento de las Descalzas Reales

An oasis of calm set down in the midst of urban mayhem, this 16th-century convent feels hundreds of kilometers from Madrid instead of just a stone's throw from the Gran Vía, though admittedly you'll experience a slight sense of rush as you "do" the array of corridors and paintings in around 20 minutes. Some of these guided visits have commentary in Spanish only, so take a guidebook with you to be on the safe side.

8 After this surfeit of culture, tuck into a satisfying lunch at one of Madrid's genuine remaining traditional eating spots, **Casa Ciriaco**, in central Calle Mayor. Photos of eminent figures from the past hang on the inner restaurant's walls; here is where pre-'30s radical thinkers used to meet to put the world right. Anti-royalists once threw a bomb at Alfonso XIII from one of the balconies. (He was unharmed, though many others were less fortunate.) These days the mood is neither anarchic nor intellectual, but the hearty Castilian food is great. Calle Mayor 84. © 91-559-50-66. See p 132.

9: Palacio Real 🗺🗺

A Bourbon monument of granite and white stone, this vast Italian-designed 18th-century palace is one of Madrid's greatest architectural assets. Though it's not used much by today's royal family, official ceremonies are often held here—be sure to check that it is open before your visit. Fifty of its nearly 3,000 sumptuous salons are accessible to the public. If you come at midday on the first Wednesday of the month (July and Aug excepted), you'll catch the colorful changing of the guard.

10: Almudena Catedral

Built over an unbelievably protracted period of 110 years—during which time its originally projected Gothic style eventually gave way to neoclassicism—this bright but rather vacuous 20th-century creation pales in comparison with the 11th-century mosque that long preceded it. Worth a look for its 16th-century image of the Virgin of the Almudena in the crypt, polychrome funeral casket of San Isidro, and controversial abstract stained-glass windows, which provide some welcome color.

11: Parque de las Vistillas

Located at the southern end of the Puente de Segovia viaduct close to the secretive Capilla del Cristo de los Dolores, this tiny area of parkland offers some of the best views in the city. Below you lies the green expanse of the Casa del Campo, while over to the northeast you can see the distant purple-gray Guadarrama mountains, snow-capped in winter. During the San Isidro and Virgen de la Paloma fiestas, lively verbenas (fairs) held here fill the night air with music.

12: Campo del Moro 🗺

Though the name has 11th-century Moorish connotations (when the city was under siege), the charming Campo del Moro is in fact laid out like a rather lush English park. Designed in 1844 and first opened in 1931, it was closed during the Franco era and finally reopened to the public in 1983. Today you can stroll at leisure among the flower beds, lawns, and fountains and enjoy the marvelous view of the Palacio Real towering above.

⑬: Ermita de San Antonio de la Florida (Panteón de Goya) 🏵🏵

Halfway along the Paseo de la Florida which runs parallel to the River Manzanares, you'll find this delightful domed hermitage—the right-hand one of an identical couple. Some of Goya's most evocative frescoes (beautifully restored in 1996) depict the Miracles of Saint Anthony on the interior of the cupola.

The artist himself is buried in front of the altar.

> **14º Casa Mingo** 🏵🏵 Great place for sampling cider—still or fizzy—and stuff cooked in it, like delicious calories-loaded *chorizo*. A mere stone's throw from the Ermita de San Antonio de la Florida, it used to be a popular student's hangout. Although it's not so cheap these days and sees many more tourists than students, it's still great fun, either inside under the rafters and beside the barrels or outside on the roof on hot summer evenings. Paseo de la Florida 34. ℂ **91-547-79-18.** See p. 164.

3 The Best of Madrid in 3 Days

One of the best and most surprising things about Madrid is how quickly one can move from the narrow, alleyed medieval urban core to green wooded parkland. For the first 2 days, follow the itineraries above. Then, if you have room for another unforgettable artistic experience, pop into the **Reina Sofía** museum for a tantalizing glimpse at Spain's premier modern collection (highlighted by Picasso's *Guernica*). Alternatively, if it's a Sunday you can visit Madrid's famed open-air **Rastro** market. Then take a stroll around the old southern district of **Lavapiés**—one of Madrid's most atmospheric *castizo* areas—with its *corralas, tabernas,* and village-style multi-ethnic shops. In the afternoon travel by Metro to parkside Argüelles and from there take a **funicular** ride over the Manzanares River into the huge **Casa del Campo.** Walk down through the parklands to **Lago** for a sunset aperitif in one of the many lakeside cafes.

❶: Reina Sofia 🏵🏵🏵

Completing Madrid's trio of top art museums is this veritable mecca of modernity. You may not go for the hyper-functional exterior—an uncompromising blend of concrete, glass, and steel—but there's no doubt the Dalís and Tàpies inside are worth anyone's time. If you see only one thing, though, it has to be Picasso's ground-breaking *Guernica,* once considered so inflammatory a work it needed half a dozen guards close by to ensure no one tried to vandalize it. Now there's one guard around at the most.

❷: Plaza del Cascorro/Rastro

If your visit is on a Sunday, you might want to switch your stop at the Reina Sofia for a bargain-hunting visit here. This small square is at the top of Ribera de Curtidores where the Sunday **Rastro** flea market is held. The small but stirring monument at its center is in honor of a young soldier, Eloy Gonzalo, who died on a suicide mission to Cuba while defending Spain's last Latin American possession in 1898. Saying *hola* to Eloy as you enter the square is said to bring good luck.

❸: Plaza de Lavapiés 🗝🗝

Steep, narrow lanes, many of them pedestrianized, converge on this dusty triangular plaza, once the heart of a medieval Jewish stronghold. In just the past decade its traditional *castizo* atmosphere has been replaced by a bohemian multi-ethnic scene, populated by Senegalese, Chinese, Moroccans, Turks, and Indians. Explore the district's eclectic array of shops, cafes, and eating spots and check out the new Valle-Inclán theater. Borderline seedy, the square positively bustles with life.

> 📷 The intriguingly rundown high-ceilinged **Café Barbieri** on Calle Ave María just off the square has a vaguely bohemian ambience that goes with the territory. A cavernous, moodily lit spot where you can enjoy a reflective coffee or something stronger in the stimulating midst of the Lavapiés melting pot, it also offers a nice range of teas. Calle Ave María 45.© 91-527-36-58.

❺: Antón Martín Market

A short puff uphill from Calle Ave María brings you to Plaza Antón Martín, where you can browse one of Madrid's most typical old two-story markets. Stalls here sell a colorful selection of food from all over Spain as well as from tropical regions. Throbbing with life and color, it's the antithesis of the bland supermarket. You'll also find a good herbs and olive oil section and a friendly alcove cafe where you can hear youngsters banging out their steps on the floor of the flamenco dance school overhead.

❻: Filmoteca Cine Doré

Situated next to the market, Madrid's most enchanting cinema has an Art Deco exterior and a traditional theater interior. The place itself looks a scene from an Almodóvar flick and shows the most eclectic range of films in town. It also has a cafe and a small bookshop and in summer runs open-air shows on the roof. All films are in their original language, and the entrance fee is a bargain.

❼: Plaza Tirso de Molina

Built on the site of a former convent and originally known as the Plaza del Progreso, this square at the northern end of Lavapiés was renamed after the great Golden Age playwright in 1941. In 2005 it was converted from an attractive if slightly seedy 19th-century plaza into an extended but characterless semi-pedestrianized zone with children's play areas and flowerbeds set amid the original trees. Although Tirso (or Fray—Friar—Gabriel Téllez, his real name) might not be too pleased to see some of the apparently homeless denizens hanging around his statue today, they're harmless enough and even manage to add an aura of Zola-esque earthiness to an area now dominated by concrete.

❽: La Corrala 🗝🗝

During the 19th century, many of Madrid's working-class population lived in tenements like these. With their characteristic patios and open balconies, these tenements symbolized a basic communal lifestyle that made few concessions to individual privacy. In today's (comparatively) less sociable world, most of these buildings have disappeared; the few that remain have subsequently achieved near-museum status. This one in Calle Meson de Paredes is the best-preserved, though you can only view it from outside.

> 🍴 **Casa Lastra Sidrería.** Good Asturian fare in a homey tavern setting. It can be expensive, so the fixed-menu lunch is the best value, especially if it includes *merluza* (hake). Go easy on the heady house cider if you want to do the rest of the day justice. Calle Olivar 3. © **91-369-08-37.** See p. 140.

⑩: Templo de Debod

Take the Metro to Argüelles to see this and the following sights. Of all Madrid's fascinating attractions, none is more incongruous than the Egyptian Temple of Debod, poised high on the edge of the Parque del Oeste on the site of the former Montaña barracks and enjoying great views. The temple and two of its original three gateways were transported from their Nile-side habitat in 1968 in thanks for Spain's help with the Aswan Dam. Inside the temple are depictions of a Theban god with a ram's head symbolizing fertility. This is one of the city's major freebie attractions.

⑪: Teleférico de Madrid

For the best aerial view of the southern side of Madrid, take this 2.5km (1½ mile) cable-car ride across the River Manzanares and Parque del Oeste into the Casa de Campo. An upbeat, rather dated, commentary in Spanish extols the beauties of the Palacio Real and Ermita de San Antonio de la Florida (or Panteón de Goya) as they float below. Departure point is in the middle of the splendid Paseo de Pintor Rosales, whose fortunate apartment owners not only enjoy unrivaled vistas but also on warm days can relax in the best array of terrace cafes you'll find in the city.

⑫: Casa de Campo

Thanks to this immense area of pines and shrubs (nearly 4,500 acres in all), Madrid claims to have a bigger total of green zones than any other European capital. In olden days kings hunted wild boar here. Today predators in the form of prostitutes parade on the westerly fringe roads. The green expanse's central trails and footpaths are quite free from such salacious influences, however, and ideal for family picnics and strolls.

⑬: Lago

Surprisingly little known, this circular lake with its high, gushing central fountain in the southeast corner of the Casa del Campo is the ideal spot for a relaxing rowboat outing. Around the edge of the lake, an enticing choice of alfresco eating spots beckons like *tabernas* on some Greek island. Here you can enjoy superb views of the city skyline, dominated by the classic outline of the Palacio Real.

> 🍵 Enjoy an evening drink in one of the open-air spots beside the lake. In winter, return to Austrias.

4

Getting to Know Madrid

The center of the Spanish capital is a huddle of medieval alleyways and squares whose most elegant reminder of old Habsburg Madrid is the zone between the Royal Palace and Plaza Mayor. Dissecting it is the Manhattan-style Gran Vía, while across the wide, modern Castellana avenue leading north to the Plaza Castilla are the spacious charms of Retiro Park, which embraces 19th-century residential areas. Fanning out around Madrid, expanding suburbs and fashionable American-style satellite towns are gradually absorbing much of the capital's booming five-million-plus population.

At its heart the city remains as vibrant, sociable, and exciting as ever. This chapter provides a brief orientation of its various multifaceted *barrios,* or districts, as well as detailed advice on how to get around by public transport (very good value) or even on foot (even better value). Additionally, the "Fast Facts" section helps you to find everything you need from babysitters to late-night pharmacies.

1 Orientation

ARRIVING

BY PLANE   Madrid's international airport, **Barajas,** lies 15km (9 miles) east of the center. The airport has four terminals—three for international traffic (terminals 2, 3, and 4), and one (terminal 1) for domestic. Terminals 1 to 3, all easily reached from the city center by bus or Metro, are connected by a moving sidewalk. The vast and impressively modernistic Terminals 4 and 4S, which opened in February 2006, have greatly increased the amount of international traffic handled by the airport and are currently reached by bus either from the Colon underground terminal in the center of Madrid, from Barajas town (which adjoins the airport), or from Terminal 2. (By 2007, a Metro link is scheduled to operate from the city center directly to Terminals 4 and 4S.) All terminals have a wide selection of shops and eating spots. For flight information, call © **90-235-35-70.** *Note:* It's usually best to allow half an hour to get from the center to the airport.

The most frequent and economical route into the city center from Barajas airport is by **bus:** Take number 200 bus from Terminals 1 and 2 or 204 bus from Terminal 4. Both these red-colored municipal buses take you to the Avenida de America **Metro (subway)** and coach station. A one-way ticket costs 1€ ($1.25), and lines operate daily from 6am to 11:30pm. Travel time runs from 20 and 30 minutes, depending on the traffic. Please note that only euros are accepted on this service. (For more information, contact the **municipal bus service** at © **90-250-78-50;** Spanish only spoken). From the Avenida de America Metro, lines 4, 6, 7, and 10 link up with the rest of central Madrid.

Madrid

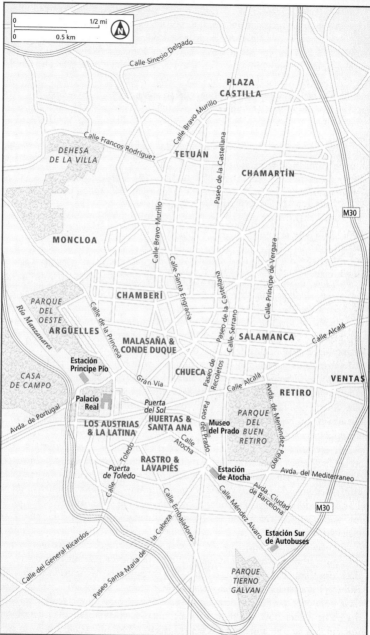

0 1/2 mi
0 0.5 km

Calle Sinesio Delgado

PLAZA CASTILLA

Calle Bravo Murillo

Calle Francos Rodriguez

DEHESA DE LA VILLA

TETUÁN

CHAMARTÍN

Paseo de la Castellana

M30

MONCLOA

Calle Bravo Murillo

Calle Santa Engracia

Parque del Oeste

CHAMBERÍ

Calle Principe de Vergara

Río Manzanares

ARGÜELLES

Calle de la Princesa

MALASAÑA & CONDE DUQUE

Paseo de la Castellana

Calle Serrano

SALAMANCA

Calle Alcalá

CASA DE CAMPO

Estación Principe Pío

Gran Vía

CHUECA

Paseo de Recoletos

Calle Alcalá

VENTAS

RETIRO

Palacio Real

Puerta del Sol

HUERTAS & SANTA ANA

Museo del Prado

Paseo del Prado

PARQUE DEL BUEN RETIRO

Avda. de Menéndez Pelayo

Avda. de Portugal

LOS AUSTRIAS & LA LATINA

Calle Atocha

Calle Toledo

RASTRO & LAVAPIÉS

Puerta de Toledo

Calle

Estación de Atocha

Avda. del Mediterraneo

Avda. Ciudad de Barcelona

M30

Calle del General Ricardos

Calle Embajadores

Calle Santa Maria de la Cabeza

Calle Méndez Alvaro

Estación Sur de Autobuses

Paseo Santa Maria de la Cabeza

PARQUE TIERNO GALVAN

Another convenient way to reach the center is via **Metro line 8** (marked pink on the metro map), which departs from Terminal 2. Fitted with luggage racks, trains make the trip in only 12 minutes with three stops along the way. A one-way ticket costs 1€ ($1.25), and the line operates daily from 6am to 1:30am. Trains from Barajas arrive at the Nuevos Ministerios section of Madrid, north of the center. From here you'll have access to two other Metro lines, 10 bus routes, and a number of commuter train lines. The facility at Nuevos Ministerios also has 34 check-in counters for departing flights such as those on Iberia. It's possible to check your luggage and receive boarding passes up to 24 hours in advance, except for the popular Madrid/Barcelona air shuttle.

Terminals 1, 2, and 4 are all linked by a **free airport bus shuttle** called **Bustránsit,** which runs every few minutes.

If you go by **taxi,** expect to pay 25€ to 30€ ($31–$38) and up, plus surcharges, for the trip to the airport and for baggage handling. If you take an unmetered limousine, make sure to negotiate the price in advance.

For more airport information, call the Barajas Airport Authority company **Aena** at ℰ **90-240-47-04** (English spoken) or contact its website **www.aena.es.**

BY TRAIN   Madrid has two major railway stations: **Atocha** (Av. Ciudad de Barcelona next to the Glorieta del Emperador Carlos V; Metro: Atocha RENFE) and **Chamartín** (just above Plaza Castilla at Agustín de Foxá; Metro: Chamartín) and one smaller station, **Estación Príncipe Pío** (also known as Norte; Paseo del Rey 30; Metro: Príncipe Pío).

Originally designed by the late-19th-century architect Alberto del Palacio in a classic Industrial Revolution amalgam of iron and glass, the impressive, ever-expanding **Atocha** now boasts a comprehensive range of shops, restaurants, and cafes, as well as an indoor tropical garden/conservatory complete with frond-covered ponds inhabited by turtles (don't feed them!). Trains to and from the station connect mainly with southern and eastern Spanish destinations. The high-speed AVE trains to Cordoba (2 hr.) and Seville (2 hr., 40 min.; total refund if it's more than 10 min. late!) depart from Atocha, as do Altaria trains to Valencia (3 hr., 30 min.) and Barcelona (5 hr., 30 min.). You check in at an imposing airport-departure-style lounge.

Chamartín, currently in the throes of a drastic renovation, is scheduled for expansion by 2007 into a combined Metro, train, and bus *intercambiador,* or junction. The new bus station will eventually replace the current antiquated and congested Plaza Castilla terminus. The Metro station reopened in May 2006 after months of renovation work and by spring 2007 should accommodate four lines instead of the present three. Chamartín currently also has *cercanías* (suburban train line) connections with Atocha and Nuevos Ministerios. Long-distance trains from here connect with northern cities such as Santander, Burgos, Bilbao, San Sebastian, and Barcelona (a slower service than from Atocha, however) and to many European capitals.

Príncipe Pío, nestled below the Palacio Real close to the Manzanares River, is also known as the Estación Norte. (In Franco's time when it served as the main exit and arrival point for northern European destinations, it was often referred to as the Estación de Francia.) Although the station contains a vast commercial center of shops and eating spots, plus a multiscreen cinema, its sphere of operations has nevertheless become more local, in large part providing a commuter connection with El Escorial, Alcalá de Henares, and nearby "dormitory" towns as well as with neighboring provincial capitals such as Avila.

The Fast and the Furious

The Spanish railway system is getting faster and more efficient by the year, while still managing to be a highly affordable means of transport. The quickest way to get to Toledo (30 min.) is now by train. Outstripping that are plans for new high speed AVE by 2007 between Madrid and Valladolid which will do the 200 kilometer trip in 55 minutes (stopping en route after a mere 22 min. at Segovia), and an Altaria connection with Valencia which will take an amazing hour and a half—cutting nearly 2 hours off the present schedule. Barcelona's connection will be similarly reduced from its present 5½-hour duration to 3¼ hours, more than halving its 7½ hour slog of a mere 3 years back.

For information on connections from any of these stations, call **RENFE (Spanish Railways)** at © **90-224-02-02,** daily 7am to 11pm. (For a Eurailpass to travel from Madrid to other European countries including neighboring Portugal, visit www.rail europe.com.)

For tickets, go to the principal office of **RENFE,** Alcalá 44 (© **91-506-63-29;** Metro: Banco de España). The office is open Monday through Friday 9:30am to 8pm.

BY BUS   Madrid has two major bus terminals *(Estaciones de Autobuses)* and two smaller terminals providing long and shorter distance bus services to and from Madrid. Though their journeys take longer than those of the faster trains, they are comfortable and economical and use excellent highway systems.

The biggest bus terminal, covering mainly southern and southeastern destinations such as Granada, Sevilla, Málaga, and Valencia with the operator Auto Res (visit www.auto-res.net for timetables and routes), is **Estación Sur,** Calle Méndez Alvaro (© **91-468-42-00;** Metro: Méndez Alvaro). It's also the focal point for a wide variety of international destinations ranging from Morocco to Romania.

At the underground **Avenida de America** station nearer the center, Continental Auto provides services to northern and northeastern cities including Oviedo, Santander, Bilbao, San Sebastian, Pamplona, and Barcelona.

Conde Casal, close to the northeastern corner of the Retiro Park, operates services to surrounding Castilian destinations such as Zamora, Salamanca, and Cuenca as well as to Alicante and the Costa Blanca.

From the smaller **Príncipe Pío** terminus opposite the railway station of the same name (see above), La Sepulvedana runs buses to Segovia and other destinations near Madrid.

BY CAR   Driving in congested Madrid is a nightmare and even potentially dangerous. It always feels like rush hour, although "official" rush hours are Monday through Saturday from 8 to 10am, 1 to 2pm, and 4 to 6pm. Parking is next to impossible except in expensive garages. About the only time you can drive around Madrid with a minimum of hassle is in August, when thousands of Madrileños have taken their cars and headed for Spain's vacation oases. Save your car rentals for excursions *from* the capital. If you drive into Madrid from another city, ask at your hotel for the nearest garage or parking possibility and leave your vehicle there until you're ready to leave.

For more information on renting a car before you leave home (and the savings you may get by doing that) or getting a car en route in a neighboring country and driving there, see chapter 2.

4–5° izda.: A Miniguide to Deciphering the Mystery of Madrid Addresses

The numbers and abbreviations in Spanish addresses can seem complicated when the hotel, pension, gallery, or private residence is located *above* the ground floor. (*Remember:* In Europe, the ground floor is the ground floor, and is the equivalent to the first floor in the U.S. The first floor in Europe is the one above the ground floor, which is equivalent to the second floor in the U.S.) Once you understand what all the symbols and abbreviations mean, however, you'll find that addresses in Spain are actually quite detailed and specific, explaining where the establishment is located with the utmost precision. Also note that in Spain, as in many other European countries, the building number comes after the street name. Here is a brief explanation of how addresses work:

The first number represents the number of the address on a particular **street** (for example, Hotel Adler is at Calle Velázquez 33). Sometimes the address may cover two street numbers, separated by a dash or the word *y,* which means "and" (for example, Hotel Occidental is at Miguel Angel 29–31 while Hotel Tryp Ambassador is at Cuesta Santo Domingo 5 y 7).

The second number, or the number after the street number(s), is followed by a ° (degree symbol). This represents the *piso* **(floor)** that the establishment is on. For instance, Hotel Riesco is at Calle Correo 2–3°, which means the hotel is on the third floor at number 2 on Calle Correo; Hotel Astoria is at Carrera de San Jerónimo 30–32–5°, which means the hotel is on the fifth floor at nos. 30–32 on Carrera de San Jerónimo.

After a number with a degree symbol, you may see a third item. This will really only apply to a private residence or a small gallery. If there are only

VISITOR INFORMATION

The most convenient **tourist office** is near the American Express office, on Duque de Medinaceli 2, Banco de España (② **91-429-31-77;** Metro: Plaza de España); it's open Monday through Friday 9am to 7pm and Saturday 9:30am to 1pm. Ask for a street map of the next town on your itinerary, especially if you're driving. The staff here can give you a list of hotels and *hostales* (hostels) but cannot recommend any particular lodging.

CITY LAYOUT

All roads lead to Madrid, which has outgrown its previous boundaries and is branching out in all directions.

MAIN ARTERIES & SQUARES   Every new arrival must find the **Gran Vía,** which cuts a bow-shaped east-west swath across the city between the neoclassical **Metrópolis** building near the Banco de España and the **Plaza de España,** where you'll find one of Europe's tallest skyscrapers, the Edificio España. As you walk along it noting the changing styles of buildings on either side, you're actually time-traveling through the 4 decades it took to construct the avenue between the early and mid-1900s. Home to two units on a particular floor, you might see **izda.** or **dcha.** These abbreviations for the *izquierda* (left) or *derecha* (right), respectively, signal the location of the establishment within the building. For example, the Guillermo de Osma Art Gallery is at Claudio Coello 4–1° izda., which means the gallery is on the left side of the first floor of no. 4 on Claudio Coello. Alternatively, if the establishment is on a floor containing more than two apartments or galleries (generally, there may be up to six), you might see something with a superscript *a* or *o,* representing the unit number, such as 1° or 1ª *(primero/a)* for the first unit, 3° or 3ª *(tercero/a)* for the third unit, and so on. For example, Calle de Ferraz 32–34–2°–5° designates the fifth unit on the second floor at nos. 32–34 on Calle de Ferraz, and Calle del Amparo 21–3°–6ª is the sixth unit on the third floor of no. 21 on Calle del Amparo.

And just to complicate matters even more, finding an address within Madrid's grand boulevards and cramped meandering streets can sometimes be a problem, primarily because of the way buildings are numbered. On most streets, the numbering begins on one side and runs consecutively until the end, resuming on the other side and going in the opposite direction. Thus, no. 50 could be opposite no. 250. But there are many exceptions to this system. That's why it's important to know the cross street as well as the number of the address you're looking for. In fact, some addresses don't have a number at all. What they have is the designation *s/n,* which means *sin número* (without number). For example, the address of the Panteón de Goya (Goya's Tomb) is Glorieta de San Antonio de la Florida s/n.

the largest concentration of department stores, hotels, restaurants, and movie houses in the city, it's superseded only by **Calle Serrano** for chic quality shopping.

South of the Gran Vía lies the **Puerta del Sol,** the starting point for all road distances within Spain. Dominated by the 18th-century Casa de Correos (seat of the regional government), whose New Year clock chimes are traditionally witnessed by exhilarated crowds, all eating their 12 grapes in time with the chimes, the crescent-shaped square is perennially lively. Its symbolic statue, *Oso y el Madroño (Bear and the Strawberry Tree),* is a favorite rendezvous spot. It's also a prime hunting ground for pickpockets and purse-snatchers, so take care. **Calle de Alcalá** begins here at Sol and runs for 4km (2½ miles).

The **Plaza Mayor** lies at the heart of Old Madrid and is an attraction in itself, with its mix of Habsburg, French, and Georgian architecture. Pedestrians pass under the arches of the huge square onto the narrow streets of the old town, where you can find some of the capital's most intriguing restaurants and *tascas,* serving tasty tapas and drinks. The colonnaded ground level of the plaza is filled with shops, many selling souvenir hats of turn-of-the-20th-century Spanish sailors or army officers. On the weekend, stamps and rare coins are sold at stalls. Concerts, shows, and exhibitions are often held here, and at *Navidad* it's a child's delight with a proliferation of Christmas trees and stalls selling gifts. The lavish *Reyes* (or Three Kings) processions start from here on January 6 amid much excitement.

Warning: Be on the lookout for thieves here, especially late at night.

The area south of the Plaza Mayor—known as *barrios bajos* and including the zones of Lavapiés and Embajadores—is made up of narrow cobblestone streets lined with 16th- and 17th-century architecture. To the west is the elegant historic barrio of the Austrias, most of whose buildings sprang up during the Habsburg rule. From the northwest corner of Plaza, follow the **Arco de Cuchilleros,** a street packed with markets, restaurants, flamenco clubs, and taverns, to explore this zone. In a narrow atmospheric street called the **Cava Baja,** just before you reach the Plaza de la Cebada, you'll find the largest concentration of trendy wine bars, homely *tabernas,* and *posada* (inn) style restaurants in all Madrid (see also "Neighborhoods in Brief," below). The nearby **Plaza de la Paja,** close to the city's two oldest churches, was actually the heart of the city and its main marketplace during the medieval period.

On the western edge of this area is the diminutive Muslim Madrid zone, which is centered on Las Vistillas, just below the Almudena cathedral and Royal Palace—the zone enjoys views towards the distant Guadarramas. Below it to the west is the Campo del Moro park, the Manzanares River with its bordering walkways, and the great green expanse of the Casa del Campo.

Close to the beginnings of the Gran Vía and just below its junction with Calle Alcalá, you'll find the grand **Plaza de la Cibeles,** with its fountain to Cybele, "the mother of the gods," main post office (known as "the cathedral of post offices"), and 19th-century French- and Viennese-styled Banco de España. From Cibeles, the wide **Paseo de Recoletos** begins a short run north to Plaza de Colón. From this latter square rolls the serpentine central artery of Madrid: **Paseo de la Castellana,** flanked by expensive shops, apartment buildings, luxury hotels, and foreign embassies.

Heading south from Cibeles is **Paseo del Prado,** where you'll find one of Madrid's major attractions, the **Museo del Prado,** as well as the **Jardín Botánico** (Botanical Garden). The *paseo* leads to the Atocha Railway Station. To the east of the garden lies **Parque del Retiro,** a magnificent park once reserved for royalty, with rose gardens, wide walkways, terrace cafes, fountains, statues (including the only one in the world dedicated to the devil), musicians and entertainers, a rowing lake (the Estanque), and Madrid's finest homage to the Industrial Revolution era: the iron-, tile-, and glass-built **Casa de Cristal (Crystal Palace)** inspired by its 19th-century London namesake.

STREET MAPS Arm yourself with a good map before setting out. Falk publishes the best, and it's available at most newsstands and kiosks in Madrid. The free maps given away by tourist offices and hotels aren't really adequate for more than general orientation, as they don't list the maze of little streets that is Old Madrid.

NEIGHBORHOODS IN BRIEF

Madrid can be divided into three principal districts: The old traditional **Center,** with the Puerta del Sol and Gran Vía at its heart and surrounding 17th-century Austrias and *castizo* Argüelles, Chueca, Malasaña, Chamberí, and Lavapiés districts all offering the most tourist interest; the newer **Ensanche** area, which includes the classy Salamanca barrio and cosmopolitan Castellana avenue and features some of the best shops and hotels; and the **Periphery,** which contains modern suburbs ranging from easterly Ciudad Lineal to the burgeoning northern area of Sanchinarro, and is of little interest to visitors.

The Center

The Austrias & Plaza Mayor With its alleys and tiny plazas, the **Austrias** quarter was named after the 17th-century monarchs of Spain and contains the city's most evocative churches. In 1617 the **Plaza Mayor** became its hub, and today is one of the key nighttime centers of tourist activity. Filled with taverns and bars, it is bounded by Calle Mayor, Cava de San Miguel, and Calle de la Cruz. Westwards from the Plaza the above-mentioned Arco de Cuchilleros is filled with Castilian restaurants and taverns; while cavelike touristy locales called *mesones*—hewn into the base of Cava de San Miguel's old five-story buildings at the northern end of the plaza—provide wine, tapas, and musical entertainment.

Puerta del Sol Just east of the Plaza Mayor, the semicircular "Gateway to the Sun" is no less thronged with visitors at night, though its attractions are more peripheral, ranging from the shops and department stores of northerly traffic-free Preciados to the countless array of bars and nightspots lining the narrow alleys of the southerly Huertas district.

Gran Vía/Plaza de España Gran Vía is the city's main street, limned with cinemas, department stores, and the headquarters of banks and corporations. It ends at the Plaza de España, where bronze figures of Don Quixote and his faithful squire, Sancho Panza, are set in a park beside a fountain overlooked by the stark 1950s Torre España and Edificio Europa buildings.

Argüelles/Moncloa Just to the northeast of Plaza España is **Argüelles,** a compact barrio of narrow, crisscrossing lanes sandwiched between promenade-like Pintor Rosales (which runs along the edge of the Parque del Oeste) and the shop-filled Calle Princesa, which leads up to **Moncloa.** The latter is home to the kitsch '50s Ministerio del Aire building and a huge university campus area bounded by the green recreational zones of Puerta de Hierro to the north and Cea Bermúdez and Bravo Murillo avenues to the east. Students haunt its cafes, *tascas,* and more recently, its wine bars.

Chueca This old, atmospheric area north of the Gran Vía includes the narrow streets of Hortaleza, Infantas, Barquillo, and San Lucas. It's the center of Madrid's gay scene, with dozens of clubs and restaurants of all price ranges and nationalities. At night the whole area is very lively, especially in the tiny main square.

Malasaña Centered around the famed (but innocuous) Plaza Dos de Mayo, this traditional barrio is named for a teenage seamstress, Manuela Malasaña, who became an unwitting martyr for the Spanish cause during the Peninsula War, when the scissors she was carrying for her work were interpreted as a lethal weapon by the occupying French forces and she was summarily tried and executed. Its grid system of narrow, crisscrossed, lanes is bordered by traditional (and now largely renovated) 19th-century buildings. Its many music bars are patronized at night by hard rock and grunge fans.

Chamberí Though actually built in the late 19th century outside the old city walls, this formerly working-class zone is neither grungy nor gay like its southern neighbors but more low-keyed and upmarket. The focal point is the circular Plaza Olavide. This barrio offers an attractive selection of restaurants, bookshops, art galleries, and museums, such as the charming Museo Sorolla.

Lavapiés In decay until a few decades back, this former medieval working-class quarter south of the Plaza Mayor (earlier mentioned as the *barrios bajos*) has seen many of its lanes turned into pedestrian zones, houses tastefully converted into studio flats, and a polyglot ambience born out of the recent influx of immigrants from North Africa and the Middle East. The neighborhood, a blend of the international and earthy bohemian, has become one of the most evocative and stimulating in Madrid.

The Ensanche

Salamanca Quarter Ever since Madrid's city walls came tumbling down in the 1860s, the district of Salamanca to the east has been one of the most fashionable places to live in Madrid. Calle Serrano marks the western border of this neighborhood and is lined with international shops, stores, and boutiques. The U.S. Embassy is located halfway up the avenue, close to the Lázaro Galdiano Museum.

Castellana/Recoletos/Paseo del Prado Not a real city district, this long continuous avenue is Madrid's north-south axis, its name changing along the way. In summer its large medians serve as home to open-air terraces filled with animated crowds. Many restaurants and hotels are located both on it and along its side streets. The **Castellana** is the longest and most modern section, descending from Plaza Castilla to Colon Square and including the skyscraper AZCA business center, the huge Santiago Bernabeu soccer stadium, and a choice of top hotels en route. Shorter and more intimate is **Recoletos,** linking Colon with Cibeles. Its central median is often reserved for antique book fairs, and its most famous buildings include the National Library and the Gran Café de Gijón. Leading from Cibeles down to Atocha, the **Paseo del Prado** is the elegant final stretch. Tree-shaded and maturely beautiful, it's home to such incomparable city gems as the Neptune statue, the Bolsa (Stock Exchange), the Ritz hotel, the Museo del Prado, and the Botanical Gardens.

The Periphery

Ciudad Lineal This was originally envisioned as the progressive face of Madrid, and its elegant, tree-lined outer avenue is named after its idealistic 19th-century planner Arturo Soria. Today the rest of the district's "attractions"—more crassly commercial than classy—are centered on the large Alcalanorte commercial complex. Unfortunately, there's little here to make the visitor stop en route to two of the city's best parks, **El Capricho** and **Juan Carlos 1.**

Sanchinarro This neighborhood is the still-unfinished face of 21st-century Madrid. Its ultra-modern apartments are grouped around a giant Corte Inglés center, and new rail services including the *tren ligero* (see "Getting Around," below) are scheduled to link it with the center and further outlying new areas such as Las Tablas by spring 2007.

2 Getting Around

Though Madrid is growing all the time, with new suburbs springing up out of nowhere, finding your way around the city is rendered easy by the well-planned public system of Metro, bus, and train transport. The Metro in particular has undergone a huge expansion and modernization program since 2000, first extending as far as Barajas airport and as far south as Arganda del Rey (29km/18 miles from the center) and today mushrooming even further. Out of a total of 12 lines, all easily identified by their different colors on the underground map, no less than seven (1 to 5, 7, and 11) are being extended; work is due for completion by 2007. Also in that year a new

Making Conversation with a Madrileño

In Madrid it's tactful to avoid discussing Gibraltar, the late General Franco's regime, and politics in general until you're totally sure of your ground. Also avoid criticizing national activities—controversial elsewhere but not in Madrid—such as bullfights. (In more radical areas like the Basque Country and Cataluña, where Madrid tends to be regarded as the unacceptable face of authority, you may have more leeway in discussing these topics.) Sports such as soccer football and attractions of different regions of the country are good topics to discuss—many Madrid inhabitants originally came from another part of Spain and still retain a strong link with their home province, so if you know something about it they will be appreciative.

Metronorte line (complementing the 3-year-old *Metrosur* line linking the southern satellite towns of Mostoles, Fuenlabrada, and Leganes) is scheduled to reach as far as Alcobendas and San Sebastian de los Reyes on the northeasterly outskirts; and a ***tren ligero*** (literally, "light train" or jet-age tram similar to the service currently operating in Bilbao and eastern Barcelona) will be running on separate lines to the affluent westerly residential towns of Pozuelo de Alarcón and Boadilla del Monte and new northern suburbs of Sanchinarro and Las Tablas.

Note: See the inside front cover for a comprehensive map of the Madrid Metro, or go to www.metromadrid.es, and look at the top right corner to change to the English page. Other outlying new towns are easily reached by the excellent *cercanías* (suburban line) train service. Buses currently operate a full-time day service and reduced night service with 20 routes operating between midnight and 5am. Taxis are widely available and still remain a good value by international standards. Private transport (car or bike) is best avoided in the city center for reasons given below.

BY SUBWAY (METRO)

The Metro system is perfectly straightforward to learn and use and by far the quickest, simplest, and cheapest way to travel about the city. The central converging point is Sol station and trains run every 3 to 5 minutes during the day and every 10 to 15 minutes at night. Services begin at 6am (7am on Sundays) and finish around 1:30 am. It's advisable to avoid rush hours 8 to 10 am, 1 to 2 pm, and 4 to 6 pm. The fare is 1.00€ ($1.25) for a one-way trip on zone A stops (central) and 1.50€ ($1.85) for zone A and B stops (includes trips to Outer Madrid stations such as Arganda del Rey on line 9 and Mostoles on Metrosur). You can save money on public transportation by purchasing a combined ten-in-one *metrobus* ticket costing 6.15€ ($7.70) from any Metro ticket office counter or vending machine as well as at most *estancos* (shops selling tobacco and stamps) and in many newspaper kiosks. It covers zone A stops plus trips on red metropolitan buses. For information, call © **91-429-31-77.** In the past couple of years the *Metro* facilities have been radically improved. Shiny comfortable modern trains are gradually replacing the older—barely post Civil War—stock and stations have been modernized, redecorated in brighter colors, and more warmly lit. Formerly lax no smoking rules are now rigidly enforced and traveling underground is now an altogether more agreeable experience (except, inevitably, during the above-mentioned rush hours).

BY BUS

A 150-line network of red-colored buses also services the city and suburbs, with routes clearly shown at each stop on a schematic diagram. The buses, which have the first and last stop on their routes clearly marked, are fast and efficient because they travel along special lanes. Schedules operate generally between 6am and 11:30pm, and the time between buses varies from 5 to 20 minutes depending on the service. The efficient and long-established night service operating half-hourly from midnight to 3am and hourly from 3 to 6am with departure points at Cibeles and Sol was considerably bolstered in May 2006 with the introduction of a quarter-hourly *buhometro* (literally "night owl" Metro) weekend and fiesta-day bus service, which follows all the routes usually covered by the Metro when it closes down between 1:30am and 6 or 7am. As with the Metro, these bus services charge 1€ ($1.25) per zone A (central) ride and 6.15€ ($7.70) for a 10-trip *metrobus* ticket. In addition to being available at the above-mentioned Metro counters, vending machines, *estancos* (tobacconists), and newspaper kiosks, tickets are also sold at **Empresa Municipal de Transportes,** Alcántara 24 (© **91-406-88-00**), where you can buy a guide to the bus routes. The office is open daily from 8am to 2pm.

BY CERCANÍAS TRAIN

This excellent provincial train service has 10 lines (C-1 to C-10) operating economically and punctually to a variety of key towns radiating outwards from the capital, from Aranjuez to San Lorenzo de El Escorial. The tiniest and most dramatic is the elderly narrow-gauge C-9 train that climbs from Cercedilla—reached by C-8b from Madrid center—through towering pine forests to Cotos 5,000 feet up in the Guadarrama mountains. **Atocha** station (Glorieta del Emperador Carlos V; Metro: Atocha RENFE) is the best departure point for southerly destinations and **Chamartín** station (Calle Agustín de Foxá; Metro: Chamartín) for northerly ones, though trains run between the two stations and either can, in practice, be used for all destinations. Tickets (one-way or round-trip) can be bought at station ticket offices or from machines on which the destinations are clearly marked.

BY TAXI

Cab fares are pretty reasonable, and Madrid city cabs are easy to identify. They're white with a red band and a small insignia of a bear and madroño tree, symbols of Madrid, on the side. You can either hail them in the street or pick them up at taxi stands, located all over the city. If they're free *(libre),* a green light on the roof indicates this. When you flag down a taxi, the meter should register 1.35€ ($1.70); for every kilometer thereafter, the fare increases by .65€ (81¢).

A supplement is charged for trips to the railway station or the bullring, as well as for rides on Sunday and holidays. The ride to and from Barajas Airport carries a 4€ ($5) surcharge, and there is a 2€ ($2.50) supplement from railway stations. A 1.35€ ($1.70) supplement is charged on Sunday and holidays; and a .80€ ($1) supplement is tacked on at night (after 11pm). You may also be charged a fee for each suitcase handled by the driver. It's customary to tip at least 10% of the fare.

Instead of a regular taxi, you can take an **AeroCITY** shuttle service (© **91-571-50-47**), transporting you in an air-conditioned minivan to your doorstep in Madrid. This service is sometimes less expensive than a regular taxi, depending on the number of people traveling in the vehicle at one time. Service is 24 hours daily.

Warning: Make sure the meter is turned on when you get into a taxi. Otherwise, a driver will have to assess the cost of the ride off the top of his head, and his assessment, you can be sure, will involve higher mathematics.

You may also encounter unmetered taxis that hire out for the day or the afternoon. These are legitimate, but some drivers operate as gypsy cabs. Since they're not metered, they often charge high rates. These unmetered cabs are easy to avoid—always take either a black taxi with horizontal red bands or a white one with diagonal red bands.

Note: If you take a taxi outside the city limits, the driver is entitled to charge you twice the rate shown on the meter.

To call a taxi, dial ℭ **91-447-51-80.**

BY CAR

You may have indeed gotten to Madrid by car, but you won't need a car once you get there; driving in Madrid is a nightmare (see "Arriving: By Car," earlier in this chapter). If you drive into Madrid from another city, ask at your hotel for the nearest garage or parking possibility and leave your vehicle there until you're ready to leave.

For details on driving to Madrid, see "Getting There by Car," in chapter 2.

If you decide you want to rent a car while in Madrid to explore its environs or even to move on, you have several choices. In addition to its office at Barajas Airport (ℭ **91-393-72-22**), **Avis** has a main office in the city center at Gran Vía 60 (ℭ **91-547-20-48**). **Hertz,** too, has an office at Barajas Airport (ℭ **91-393-72-28**) and another in the heart of Madrid in the Edificio España, Gran Vía 88 (ℭ **91-542-58-03**). **Budget Rent-a-Car** (known in Spain as Interrent) maintains its headquarters at Barajas Airport (ℭ **91-393-72-16**).

BY BICYCLE

The twin dangers of inhaling polluted air and getting knocked off your vehicle by hordes of impatient car drivers make riding a bike in the city center a dicey proposition. But some parts of the capital are ideal for enjoying a spin on two wheels, such as the wooded parklands of the Casa del Campo and Dehesa de la Villa, both of which are full of easily navigable trails. In addition, some city streets (Calle Fuencarral, for example, between the Bilbao and Quevedo roundabouts) are closed to traffic on Sunday from 11am to 2pm, giving you a brief hassle-free opportunity to explore urban areas on two wheels.

You can rent a bike from the following two companies at reasonable prices. **KaracoSpor** (Calle Tortosa 8; ℭ **91-539-96-33;** www.karacol.com; open daily 10:30am–3pm and 5–8pm; Metro: Atocha) rents bicycles for 15€ ($19) per day. A cash deposit of 50€ ($63) and photocopy of your passport are required. Its offices are conveniently located near the Atocha railway station, making it easy to put the bike on the train and journey in relaxed style to such amenable places as Aranjuez, where the terrain is flat and you can explore parks and riverside trails.

At **Bicimanía** (Calle Palencia 20; ℭ **91-533-11-89;** www.bicimania.com; open Mon–Sat 10:30am–2pm and 5–8:30pm; Metro: Alvarado), located in the western Tetuan district, you can rent bike for both all-day or weeklong excursions. It costs you 15€ ($19) for a single weekday, 24€ ($30) for a whole weekend or 80€ ($100) for the week, and a cash deposit of 150€ ($188) is required (500€/$625 for bikes with back suspension). You'll also need to bring a copy of your passport.

FAST FACTS: Madrid

American Express For your mail or banking needs, you can go to the American Express office at the corner of Marqués de Cubas and Plaza de las Cortes 2, across the street from the Palace Hotel (© **91-322-55-00** or 91-322-54-45; Metro: Gran Vía). Open Monday through Friday from 9am to 7:30pm and Saturday from 9am to 2pm.

ATM Networks/Cashpoints PLUS, Cirrus, and other networks connecting automated-teller machines operate in Spain, and ATMs are plentiful in Madrid. See "Money" section in chapter 2.

Babysitters Most major hotels can arrange for babysitters, called *canguros* (literally, kangaroos) or *niñeras.* Usually the concierge keeps a list of reliable nursemaids and will contact them for you, provided you give adequate notice. Rates vary considerably but are usually reasonable. Although many babysitters in Madrid speak English, don't count on it.

Business Hours While many **shops**—especially the smaller ones—retain the traditional opening and closing times of 9 or 10am to 2pm and 5 to 8 or 9pm, many are now switching to a more flexible and extended *horario,* often staying open through lunchtime. Large stores such as the Corte Inglés and the Casa del Libro bookshop follow the latter schedule, for example, as do hypermarkets like Al Campo and Carrefour. **Banks** are open Monday to Friday from 8:30am to 1:30pm; some banks extend their hours to 5pm on Thursdays or open on Saturday mornings.

Car Rentals Should you want to rent a car while in Madrid, you have several choices. In addition to its office at Barajas Airport (© 91-393-72-22), **Avis** has a main office in the city center at Gran Vía 60 (© 91-547-20-48). **Hertz,** too, has an office at Barajas Airport (© 91-393-72-28), and another in the heart of Madrid in the Edificio España, Gran Vía 88 (© 91-542-58-05). **Budget** maintains its offices at Barajas Airport (© 91-393-72-16). It's known in Spain as Interrent.

Currency The euro replaced the Spanish peseta as the country's national currency in 2002. See "Money" section in chapter 2.

Currency Exchange The currency exchange at Chamartín railway station (Metro: Chamartín) is open 24 hours and gives the best rates in the capital. If you exchange money at a bank, ask about the minimum commission charged.

Many banks in Spain still charge a 1% to 3% commission with a minimum charge of 3€ ($3.75). However, branches of **Banco Central Hispano** charge no commission. Branches of **El Corte Inglés,** the department store chain, offer currency exchange facilities at various rates. You get the worst rates at street kiosks such as Chequepoint, Exact Change, and Cambios-Uno. Although they're handy and charge no commission, their rates are very low. Naturally, **American Express** offices offer the best rates on their own checks. ATMs are plentiful in Madrid.

Dentist For an English-speaking dentist, contact the **U.S. Embassy,** Serrano 75 (© **91-587-22-00**); it maintains a list of dentists who have offered their services to Americans abroad. For dental services, also consult **Unidad Médica Anglo-Americana,** Conde de Arandá 1 (© **91-435-18-23**). Office hours are Monday through Friday 9am to 8pm and Saturday 10am to 1pm, and there is a 24-hour answering service.

Doctor For an English-speaking doctor, contact the **U.S. Embassy,** Serrano 75 (© **91-587-22-00**).

Driving Rules See "Getting Around," p. 70.

Drugstores For a late-night pharmacy, look in the daily newspaper under *Farmacias de Guardia* to learn which drugstores are open after 8pm. Or go to any pharmacy, which, even if closed, always posts a list of nearby pharmacies that are open late that day. Madrid has hundreds of pharmacies, but one of the most central is **Farmacia Gayoso,** Arenal 2 (© **91-521-28-60**; Metro: Puerta del Sol). It is open Monday through Saturday 9:30am to 9:30pm.

Electricity As in the rest of Europe, the electricity connection is 220 volts, though on rare occasions it's 125 volts. Many hotels have 110-volt North American-style outlets for electric razors. For other appliances, you'll need a transformer, unless there is a voltage switch. You'll need a two-prong plug to connect into the mains.

Embassies/Consulates If you lose your passport, fall seriously ill, get into legal trouble, or have some other serious problem, your embassy or consulate can help. These are the Madrid addresses and hours: The **United States Embassy,** Calle Serrano 75 (© **91-587-22-00**; Metro: Núñez de Balboa), is open Monday through Friday 9am to 6pm. The **Canadian Embassy,** Núñez de Balboa 35 (© **91-423-32-50**; Metro: Velázquez), is open Monday through Friday 8:30am to 5:30pm. The **United Kingdom Embassy,** Calle Fernando el Santo 16 (© **91-319-02-00**; Metro: Colón), is open Monday through Friday 9am to 1:30pm and 3 to 6pm. The **Republic of Ireland** has an embassy at Claudio Coello 73 (© **91-576-35-00**; Metro: Serrano); it's open Monday through Friday 9am to 2pm. The **Australian Embassy,** Plaza Diego de Ordas 3, Edificio Santa Engracia 120 (© **91-441-93-00**; Metro: Ríos Rosas), is open Monday though Thursday 8:30am to 5pm and Friday 8:30am to 2:15pm. Citizens of **New Zealand** have an embassy at Plaza de la Lealtad 2 (© **91-523-02-26**; Metro: Banco de España); it's open Monday through Friday 9am to 1:30pm and 2:30 to 5:30pm.

Emergencies A centralized number for fire, police, or ambulance is © **112.**

Holidays For full information on holidays and fiestas, see the "Calendar of Events," in chapter 2.

Hospitals/Clinics **Unidad Médica Anglo-Americana,** Conde de Arandá 1 (© **91-435-18-23**; Metro: Retiro), is not a hospital but a private outpatient clinic offering the services of various specialists. This is not an emergency clinic, although someone on the staff is always available. The daily hours are from 9am to 8pm. For a real medical emergency, call © **112** for an ambulance.

Hotlines For up-to-date information on events and attractions in Madrid, call the **town hall** © **010** (this number is valid all over Spain). Also see "Emergencies," above.

Internet Access If you just have to check your e-mail, head for **Net Café,** San Bernardo 81 (© **91-594-09-99**; http://netcafe.cl), open daily 11am to 2am,

(5€/$6.25 per hour). For details of other locales and contacts, see "Online Traveler's Toolbox" and "The 21st-Century Traveler," in chapter 2.

Language English is still not as widely spoken or understood as in the popular Mediterranean coastal zones such as the Costa del Sol, Costa Brava, and Mallorca. Best to take a concise phrasebook to help you along. Frommer's very own **"Spanish Phrasebook & Culture Guide"** (Wiley; 2006) fits the bill nicely here, covering a variety of subjects from socializing and shopping to health and safety, with relevant advice sections on all these points. See Appendix B at the back of this book for a glossary of vocabulary words.

Laundromats, Laundries & Dry Cleaning Try a self-service facility, Lavandería Donoso Cortés, Donoso Cortés 17 (© **91-446-96-90**; Metro: Quevedo); it's open Monday to Friday 9am to 2pm and 3:30 to 8pm, Saturday 9am to 2pm. A good dry-cleaning service is provided by the El Corte Inglés department store at Raimundo Fernández Villaverde 79 (© **91-418-88-00**; Metro: Gregorio Marañón), where the staff speaks English.

Legal Aid Should you happen to break the law and get arrested, you will be assigned an *abogado de oficio,* or duty solicitor, free of charge. You'll also be allowed to phone your consul, who will put you in touch with an English-speaking lawyer.

Liquor Laws The legal age for drinking beer, wine, and spirits is 18. Few countries have such a widely available source of alcoholic drinks and more generous hours in which they are available. Opening hours of bars and establishments selling liquors vary widely. They can open at 6am or even slightly earlier and usually close at 2am at the latest. Nightclubs, late night bars, and after-hours establishments fill the remaining hours up to and after dawn. Supermarkets sell alcoholic drinks from 9 or 10 am till closing time around 9 or 10 pm.

Lost & Found Be sure to tell all of your credit card companies the minute you discover your wallet has been lost or stolen and file a report at the nearest police precinct. (Your credit card company or insurer may require a police report number or record of the loss.) Most credit card companies have an emergency toll-free number to call if your card is lost or stolen; they may be able to wire you a cash advance immediately or deliver an emergency credit card in a day or two. The toll-free numbers for lost credit cards are as follows: **Visa** (© **900/99-11-24**); **MasterCard** (© **900/97-1231**); and **American Express** (© **1/715-343-7977**) (global hotline).

If you need emergency cash over the weekend when all banks and American Express offices are closed, you can have money wired to you via **Western Union** (© **800/325-6000**; www.westernunion.com).

Luggage Storage & Lockers These can be found at both the Atocha and Chamartín railway terminals, as well as the major bus station at the Estación Sur de Autobuses, Calle Méndez Alvaro (© **91-468-42-00**; Metro: Méndez Alvaro). Storage is also provided at the air terminal beneath the Plaza de Colón.

Mail The local postage system is both reliable and efficient, though services such as FedEx are available if you prefer to use them. Postage rates, in euros, for postcards and letters to the States from Spain are as follows:

	Standard	Urgent	Registered
Up to 20 grams	0.78	2.75	2.98
20–50 grams	1.66	3.75	3.86
50–100 grams	2.38	4.65	4.58
100–200 grams	4.85	7.10	7.05
200–350 grams	8.90	11.00	11.10
350–100 grams	18.00	20.25	20.20

Post your letters in the post office itself or in yellow post boxes called *buzones*. Buy stamps in an *oficina de correos* (post office) or—if you don't fancy queuing—in an *estanco* (a government-licensed tobacconist easily recognized by its brown and yellow logo). For information on the central post office in Madrid, see "Post Office," below. For general information, check the Spanish Post Office website: www.correos.es.

Newspapers & Magazines The Paris-based *International Herald Tribune,* which sometimes includes an English-language version of *El País* (see below), is sold at most newsstands in the tourist districts, as is *USA Today,* the *Financial Times,* the *Wall Street Journal,* and European editions of *Time* and *Newsweek.* Top Spanish newspapers are *El País, El Mundo, ABC,* and *La Razón.* The *Guía del Ocio,* a small magazine sold in newsstands, contains entertainment listings and addresses in Spanish, as does the *Metrópoli,* which comes with *El Mundo* free on Fridays. *InMadrid* is an English-language freebie available at tourist offices, as well as some bookshops, bars, and cinemas. *TBS the Broadsheet,* with general subjects on Spain in English, is sold at various kiosks, bookshops, and bars frequented by English-speaking visitors (such as Irish pubs) (TBS, Plaza de Canalejas 6; © **91-523-74-80;** www.tbs.com.es).

Police In an emergency, dial © **112.**

Post Office If you don't want to receive your mail at your hotel or the American Express office, direct it to *Lista de Correos* at the central post office in Madrid. To pick up mail, go to the window marked *Lista,* where you'll be asked to show your passport. Madrid's central office is in Palacio de Comunicaciones at Plaza de la Cibeles (© **91-396-20-00).**

Postal Codes Postal codes for the Madrid area are five-digit numbers beginning with 28. For example, the Retiro area is 28001 and the Gran Vía 28013. Codes vary from one side of a street to the other, however, and you may find addresses even in a specific area with differing numbers. Therefore, it's best to simply check each address (a hotel, say, or a restaurant) individually.

Radio & TV On short-wave radio you can hear the Voice of America and the BBC daily. There is also an English-language radio program in Madrid called "Buenos Días" (Good Morning), which airs many useful hints for visitors; it's broadcast Monday to Friday from 6 to 8am on 657 megahertz. Radio 80 broadcasts news in English Monday to Saturday from 7 to 8am on 89 FM. Some TV programs are broadcast in English in the summer months. Many hotels—but regrettably not most of the budget ones I recommend—also bring in satellite-TV programs in English.

Restrooms Some public restrooms are available, including those in the Parque del Retiro and on Plaza de Oriente across from the Palacio Real. Otherwise, you can always go into a bar or *tasca,* but you should order something. The major department stores, such as Galerías Preciados and El Corte Inglés, have good, clean restrooms. For some amusing anecdotes on bathroom experiences in Madrid, among many other world-wide spots, check out www.thebathroom diaries.com.

Safety Because of an increasing crime rate in Madrid, the U.S. Embassy has warned visitors to leave valuables in a hotel safe or other secure place when going out. Your passport may be needed, however, as the police often stop foreigners for identification checks. The embassy advises against carrying purses and suggests that you keep valuables in front pockets and carry only enough cash for the day's needs. Be aware of those around you and keep a separate record of your passport number, traveler's check numbers, and credit card numbers.

Purse snatching is common, and criminals often work in pairs, grabbing purses from pedestrians, cyclists, and even from cars. A popular scam involves one miscreant's smearing the back of the victim's clothing, perhaps with mustard, ice cream, or something worse. An accomplice then pretends to help clean up the mess, all the while picking the victim's pockets.

Every car can be a target, parked or just stopped at a light, so don't leave anything in sight in your vehicle. If a car is standing still, a thief may open the door or break a window in order to snatch a purse or package, even from under the seat. Place valuables in the trunk when you park and always assume that someone is watching to see whether you're putting something away for safekeeping. Keep the car locked while driving.

Smoking New smoking rules came into effect on January 1, 2006, regarding bars, cafes, and workplaces. (For full details see the "Up in Smoke" box in chapter 6, p. 118).

Taxes There are no special city taxes for tourists, except for the VAT (value-added tax; known as IVA in Spain), levied nationwide on all goods and services, ranging from 7% to 33%. In Madrid the only city taxes are for home and car owners, which need not concern the casual visitor. For information on how to recover VAT, see chapter 9.

Telephones If you don't speak Spanish, you'll find it easier to telephone from your hotel, but remember that this can be very expensive—most hotels impose a surcharge on every operator-assisted call. In some cases it can be as high as 40% or more. On the street, phone booths (known as *cabinas*) have dialing instructions in English; you can make local calls by inserting a .25€ coin for 3 minutes. For example, if you wanted to call the British Embassy in Washington, D.C., you would dial 00-1-202-588-7800.

To call Madrid: If you're calling Madrid from the United States:

1. Dial the international access code: **011.**
2. Dial the country code for Spain: **34.**
3. Dial **1** for Madrid and then the number. So the whole number you'd dial would be 011-34-1-000-0000. (**Note:** If you are dialing a Madrid number from within Spain the prefix code is **91.**)

To make international calls from Madrid:

1. Dial 00 and then the country code (U.S. or Canada 1, U.K. 44, Ireland 353, Australia 61, New Zealand 64).
2. Dial the area code and number. For example, if you wanted to call the British Embassy in Washington, D.C., you would dial 00-1-202-588-7800.

For directory assistance: Dial © 11818 if you're looking for a number inside Spain, and dial © 11825 for numbers to all other countries.

For operator assistance: If you need operator assistance in making an international call, dial © 1008 (for Europe, Morocco, Tunisia, Libya, and Turkey) or 1005 (for the USA and all other countries), and © 1009 if you want to call a number in Spain.

Rechargeable online phonecard system: Planet Phone Cards (www.planetphone cards.com) offer a wide range of phone cards online.

Toll-free numbers: Numbers beginning with **900** in Spain are toll-free, but calling a 1-800 number in the States from Spain is not toll-free. In fact, it costs the same as an overseas call.

In Madrid some smaller establishments, especially bars, discos, and a few informal restaurants, don't have phones. Further, many summer-only bars and discos secure a phone for the season only and then get a new number the next season. Many attractions, such as small churches or even minor museums, have no staff to receive inquiries from the public.

In 1998, all telephone numbers in Spain changed to a nine-digit system instead of the six- or seven-digit method used previously. Each number is now preceded by its provincial code for local, national, and international calls. For example, when calling to Madrid from Madrid or another province within Spain, telephone customers must dial 91-123-4567. Similarly, when calling Valladolid from within or outside the province, dial 979-123-4567.

When in Spain, the access number for an **AT&T** calling card is © **800/CALL-ATT**. The access number for **Sprint** is © **800/888-0013**.

More information is also available on the **Telefónica** website at www. telefonica.es.

Time Spain is 6 hours ahead of Eastern Standard Time in the United States. Daylight saving time is in effect from the last Sunday in March to the last Sunday in September.

Tipping Don't overtip. The government requires restaurants and hotels to *include* their service charges—usually 15% of the bill. However, that doesn't mean you should skip out of a place without dispensing an extra euro or two. The following are some guidelines:

Your hotel porter should get 0.90€ ($1.10) per bag. Maids should be given 1€ ($1.25) per day, more if you're generous. Tip doormen .90€ ($1.10) for assisting with baggage and .75€ (94¢) for calling a cab. In top-ranking hotels, the concierge will often submit a separate bill, showing charges for newspapers and other services; if he or she has been particularly helpful, tip extra. For cab drivers, add about 10% to the fare as shown on the meter. At airports, such as Barajas in Madrid and major terminals, the porter who handles your luggage will present you with a fixed-charge bill.

In both restaurants and nightclubs, a 15% service charge is added to the bill. To that, add another 3% to 5% tip, depending on the quality of the service. Waiters in deluxe restaurants and nightclubs are accustomed to the extra 5%, which means you'll end up tipping 20%. If that seems excessive, you must remember that the initial service charge reflected in the fixed price is distributed among all the help.

Barbers and hairdressers expect a 10% to 15% tip. Tour guides expect 2€ ($2.50), although a tip is not mandatory. Theater and bullfight ushers get from .30€ to .45€ (38¢–56¢).

Useful Phone Numbers

U.S. Dept. of State Travel Advisory: ℂ **202/647-5225** (manned 24 hr.)

U.S. Passport Agency: ℂ **202/647-0518**

U.S. Centers for Disease Control International Traveler's Hotline: ℂ **404/332-4559**

Water Over the past 2 years the rain in Spain has been even less than usual, with reservoir supplies at just over 50% capacity. At press time, this has not incurred any restrictions on use or deterioration in the quality of the water. In general it is perfectly okay to drink the tap water in Madrid, though a wide selection of bottled mineral water is available in shops, bars, and restaurants if you'd rather play safe.

5

Where to Stay

Madrid's hotels may be expensive, but the city's wide range of accommodations is among the finest in the world. Just a century ago, no hotel in Madrid could match the top hotels of London or Paris, but 1906 marked a turning point. Alfonso XIII—nearing the date of his royal wedding to Victoria of Battenberg—was shamed by the lack of high-quality hotels. With the opening of the Ritz 2 years later, a renaissance of the capital's top hostelries began, and a gradual revision and expansion of the capital's lesser lodgings followed.

Today more than 65,000 hotel rooms blanket the city—from *grand luxe* bedchambers fit for a prince to bunker-style beds in the hundreds of neighborhood *hostales* and *pensiones* (low-cost boardinghouses).

In recent years, overall lodging quality has improved, thanks to stricter laws and renovations. Most of the older Madrid hostelries in Madrid that previously failed to meet the new standards have finally been brought up to snuff.

Three-quarters of my recommendations are modern—at least inside—with an increased emphasis on innovative and creative character rather than the bland mass corporate style of many of the late-20th-century creations.

A prime example is the superb Catalan-owned **Hesperia Madrid** in the Castellana (p. 104). Another eye-catcher is the five-star flagship of the prestigious Silken chain, **Puerta de America,** each of whose 12 floors has been designed by a different architect and whose controversially flamboyant red, orange, and yellow exterior can be seen from miles away.

Particularly impressive is the boom of the High Tech chain of **Petit Palace** hotels (in just 3 years nearly 20 have appeared in Madrid!). Like those of the burgeoning **Hoteles Catalonia** group, these hotels are mainly located in tastefully renovated 19th-century buildings. They offer chic accommodation as well as state-of-the-art Internet facilities and are well suited to business and leisure travelers alike. Our favorite is one of the most central, the **Petit Palace Ducal,** just off the Gran Vía.

Equally imaginative in combining a clinical jet-age style with traditional locations are the excellent-value **Room-Mate Hotels** (www.room-matehoteles.com), three of which opened in Madrid in 2006 (see **Hotel Alicia,** p. 91).

Meanwhile, young budget travelers should take a look at the new switched-on face of Madrid youth hostels in the bohemian corners of Huertas (**Cat's Hostel;** p. 92) and Lavapiés (**Madhostel;** p. 93).

SAVING ON YOUR HOTEL ROOM

A hotel's "rack rate" is the official published rate—I use these prices to help you make an apples-to-apples comparison. The truth is, *hardly anybody pays rack rates* and, with the exception of smaller B&Bs, you can usually pay quite a bit less than the rates shown below. If you decide to come to Madrid during the very hot months of July and August (in reality the capital's "low season"), you'll usually pick up some bargains in the higher-priced hotels at lower rates than those we officially quote below. Check directly with your hotel of choice by Internet, or run through the database of the regularly updated website **www.venere.com**, which, by cutting out booking agents, is able to offer some of the most competitive rates available. High seasons are Easter and Christmas, so avoid those periods if you can.

Here's how I've organized the price categories:

- **Very Expensive,** $300 and up
- **Expensive,** $200 to $290
- **Moderate,** $130 to $199
- **Inexpensive,** under $130

These are all high-season prices, with no discounts applied. But *always* peruse the category above your target price—you might just find the perfect match, especially if you follow the advice below. *Note to single travelers:* Single rates may be available in some of the accommodations listed in this chapter—call the hotel directly for specific rates.

- **Ask about special rates or other discounts.** Ask whether a less expensive room than the first one quoted is available, or whether any special rates apply to you. You may qualify for corporate, student, military, senior, or other discounts. Mention membership in AAA, AARP, frequent-flier programs, or trade unions, which may entitle you to special deals as well. Find out the hotel policy on children—do kids stay free in the room or is there a special rate?
- **Dial direct.** When booking a room in a chain hotel, you'll often get a better deal by calling the individual hotel's reservation desk than at the chain's main number.
- **Book online.** Many hotels offer Internet-only discounts, available through the hotel's website or through Expedia or Travelocity. Priceline and Hotwire allow you to "bid" for a room, though you will have to pay with a credit card up-front without knowing the exact hotel. *Note:* If you book online, you may not be able to ask for certain preferences, such as a quiet room.
- **Remember the law of supply and demand.** Resort hotels are most crowded and therefore most expensive on weekends, so discounts are more common for midweek stays. Business hotels in downtown locations are busiest during the week, so you can expect deals over the weekend. Many hotels have high-season and low-season prices, and booking the day after high season ends (like in Sept for beachfront beds) can mean savings.
- **Look into group or long-stay discounts.** If you come as part of a large group, you should be able to negotiate a bargain rate, since the hotel can then guarantee occupancy in a number of rooms. Likewise, if you're planning a long stay (at least 5 days), you might qualify for a discount. As a general rule, expect 1 night free after a 7-night stay.
- **Avoid excess charges and hidden costs.** When you book a room, confirm whether the hotel charges for parking. Use your own cellphone, pay phones, or prepaid phone cards instead of hotel phones, which have exorbitant rates. Don't be tempted by the room's minibar offerings: Most hotels charge through the nose for water, soda, and snacks. Ask about local taxes and service charges, which can be 15% or more.

- **Book an efficiency or look into *apartotels*.** A room with a kitchenette allows you to shop for groceries and cook your own meals. This can be a big money saver, especially for families on long stays. For details on *apartotels,* hotel/apartment hybrids, see "Self-Catering Lodgings," below.
- **Consider enrolling in hotel "frequent-stay" programs,** which are upping the ante lately to win the loyalty of repeat customers. Frequent guests can now accumulate points or credits to earn free hotel nights, airline miles, in-room amenities, merchandise, tickets to concerts and events, discounts on sporting facilities—and even credit toward stock in the participating hotel, in the case of the Jameson Inn hotel group. Perks are awarded not only by many chain hotels and motels (Hilton HHonors, Marriott Rewards, Wyndham ByRequest, to name a few), but individual inns and B&Bs. Many chain hotels partner with other hotel chains, car-rental firms, airlines, and credit-card companies to give consumers additional incentive to do repeat business
- **Investigate reservations services.** These outfits usually work as consolidators, buying up or reserving rooms in bulk, and then dealing them out to customers at a profit. They do garner deals that range from 10% to 50% off, but remember, the discounts apply to rack rates—inflated prices that people rarely end up paying. You're probably better off dealing directly with a hotel, but if you don't like bargaining, this is certainly a viable option. Most of them offer online reservation services as well. Here are a few of the more reputable providers: **Hotel Locators** (© 800/423-7846; www.hotellocators.com); **Accommodations Express** (© 800/950-4685; www.accommodationsexpress.com); **Hotel Discounts** (© 800/715-7666; www.hoteldiscount.com); and **Quikbook** (© 800/789-9887, includes fax-on-demand service; www.quikbook.com).

Note: Rates given in this chapter do not include the government IVA room tax, which is an additional 7%.

WHERE THE HOTELS ARE LOCATED

In Madrid, hotel locations vary in character, atmosphere, and distance from the center. Here's a run down on the neighborhoods covered and the type of accommodation available in each of them. (To help you decide on which is most suitable for you, check "Which Neighborhood Should I Stay In?" below.)

The largest concentration of hotels can be found around **Atocha** Railway Station and the **Gran Vía,** and though bargain seekers will find great pickings there, I've downplayed these two popular, but noisy, districts in my search for the most outstanding places to stay. The central areas near **Sol** and **Plaza Mayor,** which provide a further comprehensive cross-section of accommodation, also tend to be on the boisterous side, as you would expect in such busy central locations.

The smart **Plaza de las Cortes,** just above the **Paseo del Prado,** offers select and slightly quieter hotels as does the **Argüelles** area just west of the **Plaza España.** A number of newer hotels sit away from the center, especially on the streets just off the **Paseo de la Castellana**—a particularly popular choice for business travelers thanks to the proximity of the AZCA center's international offices and easy Metro access to Barajas airport (15 min.) from expanded and modernized **Nuevos Ministerios** station.

Cosmopolitan **Chamberí** and **Salamanca** districts, above the Malasaña district and Retiro Park respectively, offer some of the most exclusive hotels in the city; while the residential zone of **Chamartín,** home of Madrid's other main railway station and great hub of Plaza Castilla, features a variety of leisure- and business-oriented hotels.

SELF-CATERING LODGINGS

Madrid also has a small number of *apartotels.* These combine the best of hotel and apartment facilities, and are designed for more self-sufficient visitors looking for the freedom to cook. Units come equipped with basic kitchen facilities and a hotel restaurant. Maid service is usually provided and the minimum stay is a week, though if time is no object, monthly or even longer stays are available. **Sol, Chamberí,** and **Argüelles** (in **Plaza España**) all offer apartotel accommodations.

TRAVELERS WITH DISABILITIES

In recent years newer hotels have incorporated ramps, wider elevators, and even adapted rooms (mainly in higher-category hotels) to better accommodate travelers with disabilities. But you should always check with the hotel in advance about specific needs and facilities available. **The FAMMA Association,** Calle Galileo 69 (© **91-593-35-50;** www.servicon.es/famma) provides a useful guide to access for those with disabilities in Madrid.

AGENCIES

Check out **Madrid & Beyond** (© **91-758-00-63;** www.madridandbeyond.com), an Anglo-American travel company based in Madrid. Staffed by an enthusiastic, English-speaking team of U.K. and U.S. expats, they provide an in-depth knowledge of Spain, and recommend and reserve quality hotels both in Madrid and throughout the country (useful if you're thinking of doing some wider traveling). Their aim is to match each customer's taste and budget with a particular property, and arrange a variety of activities, including walking and cycling tours.

Travel agency **Viajes Aira** (© **91-305-42-24;** fax 91-305-84-19; open 7am–midnight) takes hotel bookings at its Terminal 1 and 2 desks at Barajas airport's arrival

---

Tips **Which Neighborhood Should I Stay In?**

If you like to be in the heart of the action, don't mind a bit of noise, and appreciate real value for money, then look at the varied selection of hotels around the **Gran Vía, Puerta del Sol,** and **Plaza Mayor.** You can't get more central and you won't find a wider variety of day and night amenities right on your doorstep. Also not far to stumble home to after raiding the department stores or painting the town red!

If your taste matches something more stylish and less frenetic yet within easy walking distance of the center, **Argüelles** and **Chamberí** are more likely to fit the bill. The hotels I recommend here are pleasantly located and ideal for shopping and eating out. These barrios are both chic and traditional.

If you'd rather be a bit farther away from the central bustle, then take a look at the modern, elegant hotels in and around the **Paseo de la Castellana** and the residential **Salamanca** and **Chamartín** districts, all of which offer laid-back comforts and quality accommodation within a 15-minute Metro ride of the **Puerta del Sol.**

Tips **If You Have an Early Flight**

Unless absolutely necessary, it's worth making the journey into Madrid rather than staying at bleak Barajas, where the airport is located. If you find that you have to stay here, one of the best options is **Tryp Barajas**, Av. de Logroño 35, 28042 (© **91-747-77-00;** fax 91-747-87-17), a government-rated four-star hotel amid spacious grounds. With a classic modern decor, it is comfortable and inviting, offering midsize to spacious units costing 135€ ($169) for a double or 336€ ($420) for a suite. The 270-unit, three-floor hotel also has a restaurant, bar, and room service, plus babysitting and a pool. Each air-conditioned room comes with TV, minibar, hair dryer, and safe.

Another member of the Tryp chain, the 80-unit **Tryp Alameda**, Av. de Logroño 100, 28042 (© **91-747-48-00;** fax 91-747-89-28), is a case of two peas in a pod. When one hotel overflows, the other fills in the gap. Rooms are fairly bland but comfortable. The only difference is that this hotel has a small gym. A restaurant and bar are on-site, and amenities include room service, laundry, babysitting, sauna, and pool. In the room are air-conditioning, TV, minibar, hair dryer, and safe. Rates range from 155€ to 205€ ($194–$256) for a double, to 326€ ($407) for a suite. Both chain members have free 24-hour shuttle service to the airport.

A final possibility is the **Hotel Villa de Barajas,** Av. de Logroño 331, 28042 (© **91-329-28-18;** fax 91-329-28-04), a government-rated three-star member of the Best Western chain. Simpler than the two Tryp choices above, it charges only 93€ ($116) for a double room. Each midsize unit comes with a TV and phone as well as air-conditioning, and on-site are a restaurant and bar. It too offers free shuttle service to the airport.

These hotels accept all major credit cards.

area. The agency doesn't charge a booking fee and focuses mainly on hotels in the moderate- or midrange category (around 100€–150€/$125–$188 for a double).

The privately run **Brújula** agency has booking desks at each of Madrid's two main railway stations (Atocha: © **91-539-11-73;** Chamartín: © **91-315-78-94;** open 7:15am–9:30pm). The agency charges a booking fee of 2.50€ ($3) and covers every category of hotel, from inexpensive to five-star.

AMENITIES & EXTRAS

Note that in the hotel amenity details, mention of private bathrooms is made *only* if all the rooms in the hotel in question do *not* come with a bathroom. In some hotel bathrooms in Madrid, you may encounter a European phenomenon known as a **hip bath.** This bathtub is about half the length of a standard tub, large enough to sit in but not long enough lie in. Think of it as a half-size or sit-down tub. In the reviews that follow, I have noted those hotels containing bathrooms with hip baths. Also, breakfast is not included in the quoted rates unless otherwise specified. And don't forget that a 7% government room tax is added to all rates.

RESERVATIONS   Most hotels require at least a day's deposit before they will reserve a room for you. Preferably, this can be accomplished with an international money order or, if agreed to in advance, a personal check or credit card number. You can usually cancel a room reservation 1 week ahead of time and get a full refund. A few hoteliers will return your money up to 3 days before the reservation date, but some will take your deposit and never return it, even if you cancel far in advance. Many budget hotel owners operate on such a narrow margin of profit that they find just buying stamps for airmail replies too expensive by their standards. Therefore, it's important that you enclose a prepaid International Reply Coupon with your payment, especially if you're writing to a budget hotel. Better yet, call and speak directly to the hotel of your choice or send a fax.

If you're booking into a chain hotel, such as a Hyatt or a Forte, you can call toll-free in North America and easily make reservations over the phone. Whenever such a service is available, toll-free numbers are indicated in the individual hotel descriptions.

If you arrive without a reservation, begin your search for a room as early in the day as possible. If you arrive late at night, you have to take what you can get, often for a much higher price than you'd like to pay.

Upon checking in, you'll be asked for your ID (identity card or passport) and to sign a registry form.

RATINGS Spain officially rates its hotels by star designation, from one to five stars. Five stars is the highest rating in Spain, signaling a deluxe establishment complete with all the amenities and the high tariffs associated with such accommodations. Top of the range are the **Gran Lujo** hotels such as the **Ritz** and **Hesperia Madrid,** while standard five-star residences are beaten by the likes of **Westin Palace** and **Orfila.** Most of the establishments recommended in this guide tend to be three- and four-star hotels, as epitomized by solid midrange recommendations like the **Claridge.** Hotels granted one and two stars—like the **Santander** and **Persal**—are generally less comfortable, with limited plumbing and other physical facilities, but are often perfectly clean and decent places. Similarly endowed *pensiones* (guesthouses), like the homely **Armesto** and **Riesco,** land at the bottom of the range aimed at dedicated budget travelers. In inexpensive hotels, by the way, be warned that you'll have to carry your bags to and from your room. Don't expect bellboys or doormen to be around to it for you.

FROMMER'S STAR-RATING SYSTEM These ratings reflect my personal evaluation of a hotel, based on a variety of overall factors ranging from atmosphere and character to facilities and standard of service. Those in the Very Expensive and Expensive categories are on a scale of one (highly recommended) to three stars (exceptional). Those in the Moderate and Inexpensive categories rate from zero (recommended) to two stars (very highly recommended). If, after a stay in one of the hotels listed in this guide, you have any views on the level of recommendation—or lack of it—please let me know.

PARKING This is a serious problem. Few hotels have garages for the simple reason that many buildings turned into hotels were constructed before the invention of the automobile. Street parking is rarely available, and even if it is, you run the risk of having your car broken into. If you're driving into Madrid, most hotels (and most police) will allow you to park in front of the hotel long enough to unload your luggage. Someone on the staff can usually pinpoint the location of the nearest garage in the neighborhood, often giving you a map showing the way—be prepared to walk 2 or 3 blocks to your car. Parking charges given in most hotel listings are the prices these neighborhood garages charge for an average-size vehicle.

- **Best Historic Hotel:** Inaugurated by Alfonso XIII in 1910, **The Ritz** (✆ **800/ 225-5843** in the U.S., or ✆ 91-701-67-67), the gathering place of Madrid society, is still the capital's leading luxury choice. This Edwardian hotel is mellower than ever before, the old haughtiness of former management gone with the wind—it long ago rescinded its policy of not allowing movie stars as guests. *Note:* In summer a tie is no longer obligatory and dress tends to be more informal (though the hotel still draws the line at shorts). The rich and famous continue to parade through its portals; today in the lobby you're likely to encounter nearly anyone, from the secretary-general of NATO to Paloma Picasso. See p. 104.

- **Best for Business Travelers:** The concierge at the **Park Hyatt Villa Magna** (✆ **800/223-1234** in the U.S., or ✆ 91-587-12-34) is one of the most skillful in Madrid, well versed in procuring virtually anything a traveler could conceivably need during a trip to the Spanish capital. One floor below lobby level, this five-star hotel's business center is well stocked with access to translators, word processors, scanners, fax machines, photocopiers, and even a well-informed technology concierge. There's a branch of Hertz car rental on the premises, and enough stylish conference rooms (staffed with butlers and stocked with caviar if the nature of your business meeting calls for it) to provide a place for any sales or executive meeting. See p. 104.

- **Best for a Romantic Getaway:** The **Santo Mauro Hotel** (✆ **91-319-69-00**) opened in 1991 in a villa designed by a French architect and built in 1894 for the duke of Santo Mauro. As a sign of the times, more recent visitors have included Julia Roberts and Richard Gere. The lavish property has an ageless grace, although it has been updated to state-of-the-art condition. In good weather guests retreat to a beautiful garden pavilion and enjoy many facilities such as a gym and indoor pool. Even though it's situated in Madrid, it's resortlike in nature. If you can afford it, go for one of the suites with a fireplace. See p. 110.

- **Best Fashionable Hotel:** A former rundown apartment house, the **Hotel Villa Real** (✆ **91-420-37-67**) has blossomed into a fashionable address, opposite the Cortes and next to the Palace Hotel. A member of the famed Catalan-owned Derby chain, this is a 19th-century building of classic French architecture. The marble bathrooms are extremely stylish, and Roman mosaics are a special feature in many rooms—fine views have earned it the name "Balcony of the Retiro." Some of the town's most important movers and shakers can be found in the cocktail bar. A chic rendezvous patronized by the cognoscenti of Spain, this is where you'd invite the duchess of Alba for tea. See p. 90.

- **Best Hotel Lobby for Pretending You're Rich:** The **Westin Palace Hotel** (✆ **800/325-3535** in the U.S., ✆ 800/325-3589 in Canada, or ✆ 91-360-80-00), between the Prado and the Cortes, is a Victorian wedding cake of a place. To sit and people-watch in this lobby—the grandest Belle Epoque lobby in Madrid—is to be at the epicenter of Spanish political life. Head for the dazzling stained-glass cupola of the main rotunda lounge, and take in the fanciful ceiling frescoes and the custom-made carpets along the way. See p. 91.

- **Best-Designed New Hotel:** The **Silken Puerta de America** (✆ **91-744- 54-00**) is the bright star of the famed Silken group. This startlingly innovative hotel has been created by no less than 12 key designers and architects, one for each of its dozen floors. See p. 113.

Where to Stay in Central Madrid

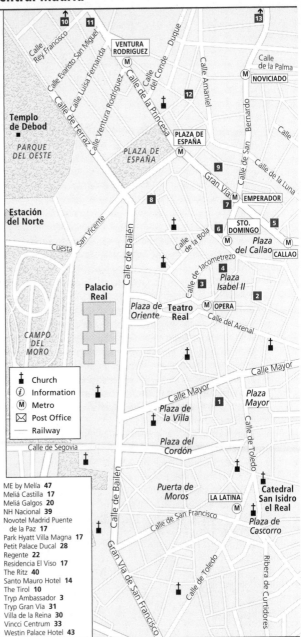

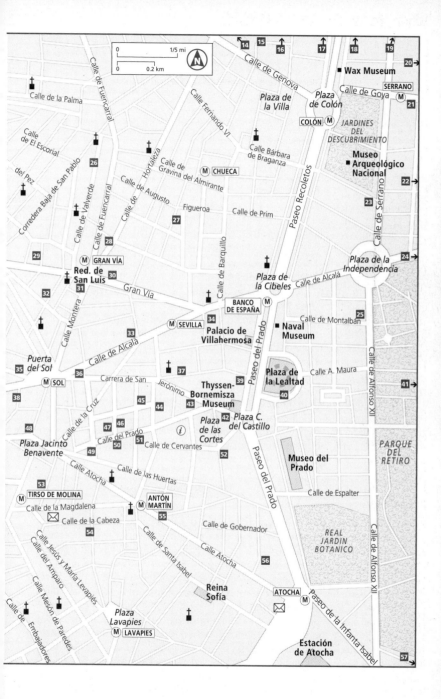

- **Best Hotel Service:** There are grander hotels in Madrid, but it's hard to find a staff as highly motivated, professional, and efficient as the one at the **Castellana InterContinental Hotel** (© **800/327-0200** in the U.S., or © 91-310-02-00). Room service is offered around the clock, and the staff is adept at solving your Madrid-related problems. Nothing seems to make them lose their cool, even when there's a long line at the desk. See p. 109.

- **Best Location: ME By Meliá** (© **97-701-60-00**) is for those who want to be in the heart of Old Madrid, within easy walking distance of all those midtown Hemingway haunts. Dozens of the finest tapas bars are literally at your doorstep, and you can stroll among the flower vendors, cigarette peddlers, and lottery-ticket hawkers, enjoying an atmosphere that's missing from the newer and more modern section of Madrid. See p. 99.

- **Best Hotel Health Club: The Ritz** (© **800/225-5843** in the U.S., or © 91-701-67-67) is not only the most historic hotel in Madrid, but it's also got a state-of-the-art fitness center on its top floor. The 533-sq.-m (1,727-sq.-ft.) gym overlooks the Prado Museum, Los Jerónimos Church, and the tree-lined Paseo del Prado. All Ritz guests have complimentary use of most of the center's services and facilities, which include English-speaking professional trainers, the latest exercise equipment, saunas, UVA rays, dressing rooms, showers, lockers, and an outside jogging trail that's open March to October. See p. 104.

- **Best for Families:** The family-friendly, chain-run **Novotel Madrid** (© **800/221-4542** in the U.S., or © 91-724-76-00) on the outskirts of town is a good place for the whole clan. Rates are reasonable, and the bedrooms can easily be arranged to sleep children. There's also a pool, and the breakfast buffet is one of the most generous in Madrid. Children 15 and under stay free in their parents' room. See p. 108.

- **Best Budget Hotel:** In the very heart of Old Madrid, off the Plaza Mayor, **Hostal la Macarena** (© **91-365-92-21**) has been housing readers comfortably and well—all for an affordable price—for decades. Surrounded by ancient buildings, the little inn is modest itself, but its welcome is warm, its staff accommodating, and its price is right. See p. 100.

1 Near the Plaza de las Cortes

VERY EXPENSIVE

Hotel Villa Real 🌟🌟🌟   It's not on the same level as the Ritz, but it is the first major hotel nearby to give the Westin Palace serious competition. Until 1989, the Villa Real was little more than a rundown 19th-century apartment house across a three-sided park from the Spanish parliament *(Congreso de los Diputados)* between Puerta del Sol and Paseo del Prado. Since then, developers have poured lots of *dinero* into renovations to produce this stylish hotel patronized by the cognoscenti of Spain, and today it's a member of the prestigious Derby chain. The facade combines an odd mix of neoclassical and Aztec motifs and is guarded by footmen and doormen. Rooms at the Villa Real are more consistent in quality than those offered by its neighbor, the Palace (see below), but lack the latter's mellow charm and patina. The interior contains a scattering of modern paintings amid neoclassical detailing. Highlights are its proliferation of Roman mosaics—among the largest private collections in Spain.

Each of the accommodations offers soundproofing, a sunken salon with leather-upholstered furniture, and built-in furniture accented with burl-wood inlays.

Although rooms aren't imaginative, they're mostly large, with separate sitting areas and big, bright, well-equipped bathrooms.

Plaza de las Cortes 10, 28014. (✆) **91-420-37-67.** Fax 91-420-25-47. www.derbyhotels.es. 115 units. 190–350€ ($237–$437) double; 300€–450€ ($375–$562) suite. AE, DC, MC, V. Parking 20€ ($25). Metro: Sevilla or Banco de España. **Amenities:** Restaurant; bar; health club; room service; babysitting; laundry service; dry cleaning. *In room:* A/C, TV, minibar, hair dryer, safe.

Westin Palace Hotel ✿✿✿   The Palace is an ornate Victorian wedding cake known as the *gran dueña* of Spanish hotels. It had an auspicious beginning, inaugurated personally by King Alfonso XIII in 1912, and covers an entire city block in the historical and artistic area. The property was a military hospital during the civil war, and when it reverted back to hotel status, politicians, artists, and celebrities formed a strong part of its clientele. It faces the Prado and Neptune Fountain and lies within walking distance of the main shopping center and the best antiques shops. Some of the city's most intriguing *tascas* and restaurants are a short stroll away.

Architecturally, the Palace captures the grand pre–World War I style, with an emphasis on space and comfort; a stunning atrium dominates the ground floor public areas. Although it doesn't achieve the snob appeal of its nearby siblings, the Ritz and the Villa Real, it's one of the largest hotels in Madrid and offers first-class service. The air-conditioned hotel has conservative, traditional rooms, boasting plenty of space, large, immaculate bathrooms, and lots of extras. Accommodations vary widely, with the best rooms found on the fourth, fifth, and sixth floors. Rooms on the side are noisy and lack views. Many rooms appear not to have been renovated for some time.

Plaza de las Cortes 7, 28014. (✆) **800/325-3535** in the U.S., (✆) 800/325-3589 in Canada, or (✆) 91-360-80-00. Fax 91-360-81-00. www.palacemadrid.com. 465 units. 400€ ($500) double; from 500€ ($625) suite. AE, DC, MC, V. Parking 20€ ($25). Metro: Banco de España. **Amenities:** 2 restaurants; bar; lounge; gym; sauna; room service; babysitting; laundry. *In room:* A/C, TV, minibar, hair dryer, safe.

2 Huertas

MODERATE

Hotel Alicia ✿   Even newer than the Catalonia Las Cortes, this pristine member of the Room Mate chain first opened its doors in April 2006. Other members of the group include **Mario,** near Opera, and **Laura,** an *apartotel* near the Descalzas Reales Convent; a fourth hotel, **Oscar,** is due for completion in December 2006. All share the same imaginative modernistic style. The compact and friendly Alicia is the fruit of prestigious interior designer López Otero, who has converted the original early-20th-century industrial building with taste and flair. It's beautifully positioned overlooking Santa Ana Square, and the rooms' large windows capitalize on the view and provide generous amounts of light. Accommodation ranges from doubles and suites to duplexes with their own small private pool. The hotel closes in August.

Calle del Prado 2, 28014. (✆) **91-389-60-95.** Fax: 91-369-47-95. www.room-matehoteles.com. 34 units. From 110€ ($137) double; 155€ ($194) suite; 210€ ($262) duplex. AE, DC, MC, V. Metro: Sol or Tirso de Molina. **Amenities:** Reception; lounge. *In room:* A/C, flat-screen TV, Wi-Fi Internet.

Hotel Catalonia Las Cortes ✿   This is one of the newest hotels in the charming Hoteles Catalonia chain to appear in Madrid. Opened in January 2006, it occupies a renovated 18th-century house halfway between the Cortes square and lively Plaza Santa Ana. All rooms have been furnished in a tastefully classical style but feature every modern amenity. The staff is particularly friendly and helpful. The small restaurant provides ample buffet breakfasts.

Calle de Prado 6, 28014. ⊘ **91-389-60-51.** Fax: 91-389-60-52. www.hoteles-catalonia.com. 65 units. 100€ ($125) double. AE, DC, MC, V. Metro: Sol or Tirso de Molina. **Amenities:** Restaurant (breakfast only). *In room:* AC, satellite TV.

Hostal Persal ⚐ Totally refurbished at the beginning of the millennium, this upmarket 1870s *hostal* was originally built as a town house. It's situated in an attractive square close to the lively Plaza Santa Ana and Plaza Mayor, and is just a short stroll from the Prado museum. The *hostal* is an ideal family choice—it boasts large bargain-priced rooms that can accommodate up to four. The sunny restaurant area is noted for its generous portions at breakfast time, and the hotel staff is commendably industrious and friendly.

Plaza del Angel 12, 28012. ⊘ **91-369-46-43.** Fax 91-369-19-52. www.hostalpersal.com. 80 units. 75€ ($94) double; 105€ ($131) triple; 120€ ($150) quad. AE, DC, MC, V. Metro: Sol or Tirso de Molina. **Amenities:** Cafe; laundry; concierge. *In room:* A/C, satellite TV.

INEXPENSIVE

Cat's Hostel *Finds* This lively youth hostel, set in a converted 18th-century mansion, is extremely spacious, and the rich-colored tiles and attractive archways of the ground floor lounge and adjoining patio—complete with gushing fountain—are evocatively Moorish in style. Most of the predominantly young visitors here, however, are generally less interested in the decor than in taking advantage of the endless 'round-the-clock bars and nightspots within a stone's throw of the place, not to mention the impromptu celebrations regularly held in the lounge. (These include the famous Casa Patas flamenco hall, which is on the same street; see p. 231.) True to the hostel's feline associations, the reception is always open. (Cats don't sleep at night, so neither does the staff.) Rooms range from functional private doubles to basic but adequate dormitories accommodating up to 14. The cozy basement cave-bar prides itself, somewhat riskily, on serving the "cheapest beers in Madrid."

Calle Cañizares 6, 28012. ⊘ **91-369-28-07.** Fax: 91-429-94-79. www.catshostel.com. Double 20€ ($25) per person; dormitories for up to 14 persons 16€ ($20) per person, all with shared bathrooms. Breakfast included. **Amenities:** Cave-bar; 24-hr. reception; special surprise fiestas; free left-luggage facilities; laundry; visiting DJs; satellite TV; free internet; kitchen for guest use. *In room:* Safe.

3 Lavapiés

INEXPENSIVE

Hostal Astoria ⚐ *Value* This excellent-value *hostal* is famed for its welcoming atmosphere and friendly staff. Located conveniently close to the Puerta del Sol and the bars and nightlife of the Huertas district, it provides a good base for exploring the city center. Rooms are comfortable, with adjoining bathrooms (with half baths). Ask for a room at the back where you can enjoy peace and quiet away from busy Carrera San Jerónimo.

Carrera de San Jerónimo 30–32–5°, 28014. ⊘ **91-429-11-88.** Fax 91-429-20-23. www.hostal-astoria.com. 26 units. 63€ ($79) double. MC, V. Metro: Sevilla. *In room:* TV, radio, hair dryer, safe.

Hostal Cervantes *Value* One of Madrid's most pleasant family-run hotels, the Cervantes is much appreciated by Frommer's readers and has been for years. You'll take a tiny birdcage-style elevator to the immaculately maintained second floor of this stone-and-brick building. Each room contains a comfortable bed, spartan furniture, and a tiny bathroom with a tub/shower combination. No breakfast is served, but the owners, the Alfonsos, will direct you to a nearby cafe. The establishment is convenient to the Prado, Retiro Park, and the older sections of Madrid.

(Finds) Life in a Former Bordello

Time was, Spanish dons didn't go to the present **Hotel Mónaco**, Barbieri 5, 28004 Madrid (ℂ **91-522-46-30**; fax 91-521-16-01), just to sleep—at least not alone. Once a closely guarded "secret" address, the Mónaco wasn't exactly what the French called a *maison de tolerance.* In other words, the prostitutes didn't work on the premises. The Spanish don arrived for his night out with his lady already selected from somewhere else in Madrid. He was then rented a room with his mistress. Even King Alfonso XIII, noted for his eccentricity (including the then-revolutionary wearing of pink shirts) came here with his favorite of the moment. He preferred room 20, if you're interested in nostalgia. Today the bedrooms have been restored and are furnished much in their old style, including riotous neo-rococo moldings, lavish bathtubs for that cozy two-in-a-tub session, and ceiling mirrors to better observe the action in bed. The location is on one of Madrid's inner city streets with almost more bars and restaurants than any other. A total of 34 units are rented, costing 72€ ($90) for a double, with parking costing 12€ to 15€ ($15–$19) extra. On-site is a bar, and each accommodation is air-conditioned with TV, hair dryer, and safe; American Express, Discover, MasterCard, and Visa are accepted. Metro: Gran Vía.

Cervantes 34, 28014. ℂ **91-429-83-65.** Fax 91-429-27-45. 14 units. 45€ ($56) double. MC, V. Metro: Antón Martín. **Amenities:** Lounge. *In room:* TV, safe.

Hostal Oporto ✦ (Value) Tucked away in a narrow road behind the Thyssen Museum, this clean, immaculately kept *hostal* is a real find for the frugal traveler. You get not only a decent, comfortable bedroom with private bathroom with shower, but a friendly welcome and an accommodating staff as well. In summer the small to mid-size bedrooms get rather hot, but a ceiling fan keeps the air stirred up. The decor is a bit tacky, but you're not paying for style. Some of the larger accommodations are suitable for three or more persons.

Calle Zorrilla 9, 28014 ℂ/fax **91-429-78-56.** www.hostaloporto.com. 12 units. 42€ ($53) double; 58€ ($73) triple. MC, V. Metro: Sevilla. **Amenities:** Laundry service. *In room:* TV.

Madhostel (Finds) The "mad" here really does mean "like crazy" and is not just an abbreviation of Madrid. This jet-age version of the old youth-hostel format is an ideal choice for younger travelers looking for a fun stay in the city, with a permanent party atmosphere. Located in a spacious 19th-century *corrala* building in the heart of Lavapiés, with a high terrace offering unexpected Mary Poppins–style rooftop views of old Madrid, it provides basic but sociable rooms accommodating up to six persons with or without private bath and of mixed or single genders. The chummy insomniac staff make sure you feel at home whatever the hour.

Calle de la Cabeza 24, 28012. ℂ **91-506-48-40.** Fax: 91-506-48-41. www.madhostel.com. Rooms for 4 to 6, with private bathroom 20€ ($25) per person; with shared bathroom 18€ ($23) per person. Breakfast is included. **Amenities:** Communal lounge and kitchen; bar; flamenco stage for Spanish or pop shows; laundry; 24-hr. reception; free Internet and Wi-Fi. *In room:* A/C, safe, private or shared bathrooms.

4 Near the Plaza España

EXPENSIVE

Hotel Husa Princess ✪   This prestigious 10-story hotel is well located on leafy Calle Princesa, and runs north of Plaza España—an ideal spot to enjoy true comfort in a relaxed setting a short stroll from the very heart of Madrid. The hotel is especially popular with airline staff, so the top two floors offer special "steward services" including coffee in the mornings and tapas in the afternoon; rooms have classic reproductions by the likes of Goya and Zurbarán. Mediterranean-style cuisine is the specialty of the hotel's attractive **Malvasia** dining room. If you're a fitness enthusiast, the hotel's very own gym and sports facilities are another bonus.

Calle Princesa 40, 28008. ✆ 91-542-21-00. Fax 91-542-73-28. www.hotelhusaprincesa.com. 275 units. 330€ ($413) double; 485€–780€ ($606–$975) suite. AE, DC, MC, V. Parking 25€ ($31). Metro: Ventura Rodríguez. **Amenities:** Restaurant; bar; indoor pool; health club; sauna; 24-hr. room service; laundry service. *In room:* A/C.

MODERATE

Apartotel Rosales ✪   The modern, well-appointed Rosales offers generously-sized hotel and studio apartment accommodations. Although the studios have no kitchens, excellent-value meals are available in the hotel's cafe and restaurant. Attractively situated in the Argüelles district just to the west of the Plaza España, it's just a short walk from the terrace cafes of the Pintor Rosales promenade and the *teleférico* chair lift operating on weekends to the Casa del Campo. There's no shortage of neighborhood shops, ranging from small *colmados* to Cortes Inglés stores, and if you feel like a stroll among the greenery, the charming Parque del Oeste is close by.

Calle Marqués de Urquijo 23, 28008. ✆ 91-542-03-51. Fax 91-559-78-70. 40 units. 130€ ($163) double; 152€–175€ ($190–$219) apt. AE, DC, V. Parking 14€ ($18). Metro: Argüelles. **Amenities:** Restaurant; health club; business center; room service; laundry service; nonsmoking rooms. *In room:* A/C, TV, safe.

Casón del Tormes   This attractive hotel is around the corner from the Royal Palace and Plaza de España. Behind a four-story red-brick facade with stone-trimmed windows, it overlooks a quiet one-way street. A long, narrow lobby contains a marble floor opening into a separate room. Guest rooms are generally roomy and comfortable with color-coordinated fabrics and dark wood, including mahogany headboards. Bathrooms are very small but with adequate shelf space. Motorists appreciate the public parking lot near the hotel.

Calle del Río 7, 28013. ✆ 91-541-97-46. Fax 91-541-18-52. www.bestwestern.com/es/hotelcasondeltormes. 63 units. 99€ ($124) double; 123€ ($154) triple. AE, DC, MC, V. Parking nearby 16€ ($20). Metro: Plaza de España. **Amenities:** Restaurant; bar; room service; babysitting; laundry service; dry cleaning. *In room:* A/C, TV, hair dryer, safe.

5 On or Near the Gran Vía

EXPENSIVE

Hotel A. Gaudí ✪   In a turn-of-the-20th-century building in the heart of Madrid, this hotel is located in a beautifully restored landmark modernist building that has retained its early-20th-century neo-Plateresque facade. It was constructed in 1898 by Emilio Salas y Cortés, one of the teachers of the great Barcelona architect Gaudí, and was overhauled in 1998. Some of the most important attractions of Madrid are within an easy walk, including the Prado, the Thyssen Museum, and the Plaza Mayor with its rustic taverns. The bedrooms come in a number of sizes, but each is comfortably furnished and beautifully maintained. Lovers of Catalan cuisine will enjoy dining in the Gaudí's stylish **Pedrera** restaurant.

Gran Vía 9, 28013. Ⓒ **91-531-22-22.** Fax 91-531-54-69. www.hoteles-catalonia.es. 184 units. 172€–186€ ($215–$233) double; 300€ ($375) suite. AE, DC, MC, V. Metro: Gran Vía. **Amenities:** Restaurant; bar; Jacuzzi; sauna; room service; laundry service. *In room:* A/C, TV, minibar, hair dryer, safe.

Hotel Arosa 🏵 ⓥ*alue*   A favorite with both international and business visitors, this first-rate modern hotel is situated between the Gran Vía and Sol, close to all the main shopping and a wide variety of bars, cafes, and eating spots. Recent sweeping renovations have left the rooms fully soundproofed and spotlessly equipped with comfortable wooden furnishing and pristine marble shower and bathrooms. Some pricier units have balconies overlooking the main drag where you can sip a sherry as you watch the traffic and crowds. The public-area decor may appeal to aficionados of post-*movida* kitsch (the movement, a renaissance of the arts after years of dictatorial creative repression) and admirers of movies by Pedro Almodóvar.

Calle Salud 21, 28013. Ⓒ **91-532-16-00.** Fax 91-531-31-27. www.bestwestern.es/arosa.html. 139 units. 173€ ($216) double. AE, DC, MC, V. Metro: Gran Vía. Pets are allowed. **Amenities:** Restaurant; bar; concierge; room service (7am–11pm); laundry service. *In room:* A/C, TV w/satellite programs and pay movies, dataport, radio, minibar, hair dryer, safe.

Hotel Best Western Premier Santo Domingo 🏵   This stylish, carefully decorated hotel rises from a position adjacent to the Gran Vía, a 2-minute walk from the Plaza de España. It was inaugurated in 1994, after an older building—containing the main law courts of the Spanish Inquisition—was gutted and reconfigured into the comfortable and atmospheric structure you'll see today. The marble-lined entrance opens into an elegant art-filled interior filled with 18th-century ceramics, copies of Golden Age paintings, and romantic prints. Rooms are decorated individually, each in a style a wee bit different from that of its neighbor, in pastel-derived shades. Some contain gold damask wall coverings, faux tortoiseshell desks, and striped satin bedspreads. Bathrooms are generally spacious and outfitted with ceramics and marble slabs. The best units are the fifth-floor doubles, especially those with furnished balconies and views over the tile roofs of Old Madrid. Each is soundproofed to guard against noise from the street and from its neighbors. The hotel restaurant is heavy with vegetarian dishes.

Plaza Santo Domingo 13, 28013. Ⓒ **91-547-98-00.** Fax 91-547-59-95. www.hotelsantodomingo.com. 120 units. Mon–Thurs 179€–203€ ($224–$254) double; Fri–Sun 149€–179€ ($186–$224) double. Breakfast free Sat–Mon mornings; otherwise, 11€ ($14) extra. AE, DC, MC, V. Parking nearby 17€ ($21). Metro: Santo Domingo. **Amenities:** Restaurant; bar; room service; babysitting; laundry service; dry cleaning. *In room:* A/C, TV, minibar, hair dryer, safe.

Hotel Emperador 🏵🏵   This well-run hotel is located in central Madrid right on the Gran Vía. Though officially for members only, its **Club Emperador** has long been a favorite hangout for residents and visitors alike. Even more popular is that rarity among Madrid hotels, a rooftop pool, open here in summer from 11am to 9pm to the delight of guests seeking a cool, refreshing dip. The city views are stunning, too. The spacious, traditionally furnished rooms enjoy a tranquil atmosphere in spite of the noisy neighboring thoroughfare, and service is discreetly attentive. This is one of the capital's most popular hotels, so early booking here is strongly advised.

Gran Vía 54, 28013. Ⓒ **91-547-28-00.** Fax 91-547-28-17. www.emperadorhotel.com. 241 units. 203€ ($254) double; 490€ ($613) suite. AE, DC, MC, V. Metro: Gran Vía. **Amenities:** Bar; outdoor pool; health club; concierge; business center; salon; room service (7am–midnight); babysitting; laundry service; rooms for those w/limited mobility. *In room:* A/C, TV, minibar, hair dryer, safe.

Tryp Gran Vía 🐾   A member of the famed international Tryp chain, this centrally located hotel is ideally located right on the bustling Gran Vía surrounded by bars, cafes, and eating spots, and is in easy reach of the main shops and museums. Service is efficient and attentive and public areas are comfortably and tastefully furnished. All rooms are neat, airy, and well equipped. Some have special provisions for travelers with disabilities.

Gran Vía 25, 28013. ℂ **91-522-11-21.** Fax 91-521-24-24. www.solmelia.com. 175 units. 105€ ($131) double. AE, DC, MC, V. Parking nearby 20€ ($25). Metro: Gran Vía. **Amenities:** Restaurant; bar/cafeteria; buffet breakfast lounge; rooms for those w/limited mobility. *In room:* A/C, TV, radio, minibar, hair dryer, safe.

MODERATE

Hotel Atlántico   Refurbished in stages between the late 1980s and 1994, this hotel occupies five floors of a grand turn-of-the-20th-century building on one of Madrid's most impressive avenues. Established in 1989 as a Best Western affiliate, it offers security boxes in relatively unadorned but well-maintained guest rooms, which have been insulated against noise. Accommodations are rather small. The hotel contains an English-inspired bar serving drinks and snacks that's open 24 hours a day.

Gran Vía 38, 28013. ℂ **800/528-1234** in the U.S. and Canada, or ℂ 91-522-64-80. Fax 91-531-02-10. www.hotel-atlantico.com. 80 units. 160€ ($200) double. Rates include breakfast. AE, DC, MC, V. Parking nearby 17€ ($21). Metro: Gran Vía. **Amenities:** Restaurant; bar; laundry service; dry cleaning. *In room:* A/C, TV, minibar, hair dryer, safe.

Hotel Liabeny   The Liabeny, behind an austere stone facade, is in a prime location midway between the Gran Vía and Puerta del Sol. It has seven floors of comfortable, contemporary rooms, which are newly redecorated but a bit pristine. They are of a good size and functionally furnished with comfortable beds and neatly organized bathrooms, mainly with shower stalls.

Calle Salud 3, 28013. ℂ **91-531-90-00.** Fax 91-532-74-21. www.liabeny.es. 222 units. 150€ ($188) double; 165€ ($206) triple. AE, MC, V. Parking 12€ ($15). Metro: Puerta del Sol or Gran Vía. **Amenities:** Restaurant; 2 bars; room service; babysitting; laundry service; dry cleaning. *In room:* A/C, TV, minibar, hair dryer, safe.

Petit Palace Ducal   Opened in 2003, this chic member of the High Tech chain of hotels is located on the southern fringe of Chueca close to the Gran Vía. Singles, couples, and families alike are well catered to, and the young staff is most welcoming. The overall mood is stylishly innovative with red-black decor and free high-speed Internet access on flat-screen PCs in all rooms. Top rooms have a tiny terrace. It's not cheap, but it's good value for what you get.

Calle Hortaleza 3, 28004. ℂ **91-521-10-43.** fax 91-521-50-64. www.hthoteles.com. 58 units. Single 102€ ($128); double 140€ ($175). AE, DC, MC, V. Metro: Gran Vía. **Amenities:** Bar; business center; Internet access. *In room:* A/C, TV, minibar, hair dryer, safe, high-speed Internet.

INEXPENSIVE

Anaco   Modest yet modern, the Anaco is just off the Gran Vía but opens onto a tree-shaded plaza. It's for those who want a clean resting place for a good price, and don't expect much more. The rooms are compact and contemporary, with built-in headboards, reading lamps, and lounge chairs. Each has a compact tiled bathroom. Ask for one of the five terraced rooms on the top floor, which rent at no extra charge. English is spoken here. A municipally operated garage is nearby.

Tres Cruces 3, 28013. ℂ **91-522-46-04.** Fax 91-531-64-84. www.anacohotel.com. 40 units 65€–86€ ($81–$108) double; 110€–115€ ($138–$144) triple. AE, DC, MC, V. Parking nearby 14€ ($18). Metro: Gran Vía, Callao, or Puerta del Sol. **Amenities:** Restaurant; bar; room service; babysitting; laundry service; dry cleaning. *In room:* A/C, TV, hair dryer, safe.

Green Hotel El Prado   You might get the feeling that this hotel is both overbooked and understaffed. But it has comfortable rooms, relatively reasonable rates, and a well-scrubbed interior less than a decade old. You'll register in a somewhat claustrophobic lobby and then head upstairs to a room that's cozy and sleekly outfitted with contemporary-looking, full-grained walls and partitions. Each unit comes with a small tiled bathroom with shower. Other than breakfast, no meals are served.

Calle Prado 11, 28014 Madrid. ✆ **91-369-02-34.** Fax 91-429-28-29. www.green-hoteles.com. 50 units. 120€–150€ ($150–$188) double. AE, MC, V. Metro: Antón Martín. **Amenities:** Restaurant; bar, cafe; room service; babysitting; laundry service; dry cleaning *In room:* A/C, TV, minibar, hair dryer.

Hostal Alcázar Regis   Conveniently located in the midst of Madrid's best shops is this post–World War II building, complete with a circular Greek-style temple as its crown. On the building's fifth floor, you'll find long and pleasant public rooms, wood paneling, lead glass windows, parquet floors, crystal chandeliers, and high-ceilinged guest rooms.

Gran Vía 61, 28013. ✆ **91-547-93-17.** 10 units. 44€ ($55) double. No credit cards. Metro: Plaza de España or Santo Domingo. **Amenities:** Lounge; laundry service; dry cleaning. *In room:* A/C, TV, safe.

High Tech Avenida   This immaculately converted three-floor hotel—formerly the modest Hostal Nuevo Gaos—has been renovated and expanded into an ultra-smart, high-tech residence with free ADSL Wi-Fi connections in all rooms and a public business center. The decor is neat, smart, and stylishly minimalistic, and the ensuite bathrooms all have shower and tub. Facilities for visitors with disabilities are provided and there are rooms for both smokers and nonsmokers. Pets are also allowed. The hotel is centrally located between the Gran Vía and Puerta del Sol, and shops, stores, and cafes are all virtually on your doorstep. If you feel like a night on the town without going too far, the popular Torre Bermejas flamenco club is just across the street.

Calle de Mesonero Romanos 14, 28013. ✆ **91-532-71-07.** Fax 91-532-71-06. www.hthoteles.com. 68 air-conditioned units. 90€–150€ ($112.50-$187.50) double. AE, DC, MC, V. Parking 11€ ($13). Metro: Callao or Gran Vía. **Amenities:** Restaurant serving buffet breakfasts; lounge; business center, laundry service; dry cleaning. *In room:* (High-tech) PC, exercise bike, and sauna; (Family) king-size bed, bunks, and free cots.

Regente *(Value)*   This traditional budget hostelry is on the same street as Hostal Nuevo Gaos, close to a variety of eating spots, bars, and shopping highlights such as FNAC and the Corte Inglés; also, it is located just a few steps way from Madrid's great central artery, the Gran Vía. Some of its facilities are updated, but the simple decor and furnishings are from another era, with an austere atmosphere, spartan rather than homely. Excellent value, though, and with something for both the young and young at heart to enjoy. Be warned: It can get noisy at times.

Calle de Mesonero Romanos 9, 28013. ✆ **91-521-29-41.** Fax 91-532-30-14. 154 units. 100€ ($125) double. AE, DC, MC, V. Parking. Metro: Callao or Gran Vía. **Amenities:** Restaurant; bar/cafeteria; car-rental desk; laundry service; dry cleaning; nonsmoking rooms. *In room:* A/C, TV, radio, hair dryer, safe, Wi-Fi.

Villa de la Reina *(🔆)*   The owners of this hotel took an early-20th-century neoclassical building and restored it. The architecture of the past has been respected, although the hotel is fully up-to-date with all the modern amenities. Living here was never this good—take the bathrooms, for instance. Each contains such extras as scales, bathrobes, magnifying mirror, and vast selection of toilet articles. The rooms are well furnished in a classical style and handsomely decorated, enhanced by high ceilings and large windows flooding the space with light. The breakfast buffet is about the finest along the Gran Vía—we counted 60 home-baked products on one morning alone. A special feature is the 24-hour **Club H10,** which offers affordable meals plus free non-alcoholic drinks.

Gran Vía 22, 28013 Madrid. © **91-523-91-01.** Fax 91-521-75-22. www.hotelvilladelareina.com. 74 units. 140€–200€ ($175–$250) double; 215€–335€ ($269–$419) suite. AE, DC, MC, V. Parking 15€ ($19). Metro: Gran Vía. **Amenities:** Restaurant; bar; 24-hr. room service; laundry service; dry cleaning; nonsmoking rooms. *In room:* A/C, TV, dataport, minibar, hair dryer, safe.

6 Near the Puerta del Sol

EXPENSIVE

Hotel Palacio San Martín ♠   You can enjoy the best of both worlds at this multifaceted hotel that offers totally up-to-date facilities in a tastefully converted 15th-century mansion, whose courtyard served as a resting place for coaches on their journeys across Spain. In fact, it's two buildings merged into one, and from 1800 until 1951 it was the atmospheric site of the U.S. Embassy in Spain. (The ambassador was so at home here at the end of the embassy's tenure that he at first refused to move to the new modern building on Calle Serrano.) After reverting to its original status as a private residence, it opened as a hotel in 2002. As an ultimate concession to modern needs, some floors are nonsmoking. Outstanding period features include the original facade and inner courtyard as well as wood paneling and stucco ceilings in the rooms. Both the splendid rooftop restaurant and the highly coveted presidential suite (complete with its own Jacuzzi) provide fine views of the historic and picturesque Austrias area. Many rooms overlook the Plaza de las Descalzas. Best bets are those on the fifth floor with balconies. Parking is in a nearby garage with a separate exit straight to the hotel.

Plaza de San Martín 5, 28013. © **91-701-50-00.** Fax 91-701-50-10 www.intur.com. 93 units. 160€ ($200) double; 210€ ($263) suite. AE, DC, MC, V. Parking nearby 17€ ($21). Metro: Sol. **Amenities:** Restaurant (rooftop); health club; business center; 24-hr. room service; laundry service; nonsmoking rooms. *In room:* A/C, TV w/pay movies, dataport, radio, minibar, safe.

Hotel Preciados ♠ *Kids*   One of Madrid's newest hotels has been created from a historic 1861 structure. The original facade, entryway, grand staircase, and other architectural details have been retained, but everything else has been reconstructed from scratch for modern comfort. The five-floor hotel, which opened in 2001, is close to such landmarks as the royal palace, the opera house, and the Puerta del Sol (the very center of Madrid). Children are especially welcome here, and there are special facilities for them such as extra beds that can be added to the standard rooms and even a special kiddies menu in the restaurant. Bedrooms are midsize to spacious, and the bathrooms have all new plumbing. The on-site restaurant, serving a savory Mediterranean cuisine, used to be the famous Café Varela, a favorite of Madrid's literati.

Preciados 37, 28013. © **91-454-44-00.** Fax 91-454-44-01. www.preciadoshotel.com. 73 units. 125€–260€ ($156–$325). MC, V. Parking 18€ ($23). Metro: Puerta del Sol or Santo Domingo/Callao. **Amenities:** Restaurant; bar; room service; babysitting; laundry service; dry cleaning; dance club. *In room:* A/C, TV, minibar, hair dryer, safe.

ME By Meliá ♠   Basking behind an ornate government-protected stone façade that dates back to 1923, this famed hotel has changed character dramatically over the passing decades. In the beginning, it was the rather staid Palacio de los Condes de Teba, occasionally enlivened by legendary regulars like bullfighter Manolete who would give lavish parties and attract mobs in the square below. Next, after being refurbished and upgraded by the prestigious Tryp Hotel Group, it became the Reina Victoria, more elegant but generally patronized by less colorful figures. In October 2006, under the guiding hand of Sol Meliá, which owns Tryp, it metamorphosed into today's gleaming state-of-the-art, high-tech hotel, which aims at satisfying the sophisticated demands of today's global travelers. All the latest communications facilities, from high-speed Internet to video conferences, are available. The furnishing and decor are luxuriously modern and the impressive range of accommodations covers deluxe and supreme standard double rooms, self-contained studios, and top-quality suites. Some units are soundproofed and some have adjoining facilities. All bathrooms have hydromassage showers. The famous neighboring Plaza Santa Ana has also seen sweeping renovations in recent years, resulting in more space for an increasingly lively array of terrace cafes. The action here begins about 8:30am and goes on until well past midnight, so be warned: Though atmospheric, it's not the place for the "noise-sensitive."

Plaza Santa Ana 14, 28012. ⓒ **91-701-60-00.** Fax 91-522-03-07. **www.mebymelia.com.** 191 units. 200€–260€ ($250–$325) double; 350 € ($437.50) studio; 450–700€ ($562.50–$875) suite. AE, DC, MC, V. Metro: Tirso de Molina or Sol. **Amenities:** Restaurant; bar; health club; business center; 24-hr. room service; babysitting; laundry service; dry cleaning. *In room:* A/C, TV/DVD, free Wi-Fi, iPod connection, hair dryer, safe, CD player.

Tryp Ambassador 🅐   In the 19th century the dukes of Granada made their town house home in Madrid, but from the early 1990s on it's been the property of the Tryp hotel chain. Many of the original features—such as the romantic *invernadero* (greenhouse)—have been retained and the result is a lavishly restored, four-story historic hotel with grand public areas that's interconnected via a sunny lobby to a six-story annex containing about 60% of the establishment's rooms. All rooms are conservatively modern and outfitted in white and salmon accented with mahogany. Most are large and soundproofed and come with twin beds. Bathrooms contain marble tub/shower combos, robes, and deluxe toiletries.

Cuesta Santo Domingo 5 y 7, 28013. ⓒ **91-541-67-00.** Fax 91-559-10-40. www.solmelia.es. 183 units. 245€ ($306) double; from 330€ ($413) suite. AE, DC, MC, V. Metro: Opera or Santo Domingo. **Amenities:** Restaurant; bar; room service; babysitting; laundry service; dry cleaning. *In room:* A/C, TV, minibar, hair dryer, safe.

MODERATE

Hostal Madrid *Value*   Although its attractive facade dates from the 18th century, this small, well-run hotel boasts modern, state-of-the-art facilities. Conveniently located in the lively central zone between Sol and the Plaza Mayor, it offers both conventional rooms for singles and couples and small fully equipped apartments for families or groups of friends. Run by a youthful and welcoming staff that offers discount passes for city clubs and entertainment locales, it has a special appeal for younger visitors. The atmosphere is free and easy and you can come and go as you please with your own key (no need to check in at reception).

Calle Esparteros 6–2°, 28012. ⓒ **91-522-00-60.** Fax 91-532-35-10. www.hostal-madrid.com. 15 units. 75€ ($94) double; 90€ ($113) triple; 120€ ($150) quad. MC, V. Metro: Sol. **Amenities:** Hotel safe. *In room:* TV.

Hotel Carlos V   Ideally positioned in a pedestrian-only street just off the Puerta del Sol, this modest family-run hotel is close to all central amenities. The second-floor restaurant and lounge areas are comfortable and attractive, and accommodations obligingly cater to a variety of party sizes offering connecting rooms, top-floor rooms with sun terraces, and group or family units.

Calle Maestro Victoria 5, 28013. ✆ **91-531-41-00.** Fax 91-531-37-61. www.hotelcarlosv.com. 67 units. 125€ ($156) double. Rates include continental breakfast. AE, DC, MC, V. Parking nearby 14€ ($18). Metro: Sol. **Amenities:** Restaurant; bar; concierge; room service (8am–11pm); laundry service; airport transfer. *In room:* A/C, TV, dataport, minibar, hair dryer, safe.

Hotel Opera 🌟🌟 *Finds*   Don't judge this little discovery by its dreary facade or its narrow windows; it livens up considerably once you enter. Set close to the royal palace and the opera house, this hotel isn't regal but features wood paneling and a tinted-glass-decorated interior. It also offers first-rate comfort and a warm welcome from its English-speaking staff. Guest rooms range from medium to surprisingly spacious, each with first-rate furnishings. Rooms on high floors enjoy views of Plaza Isabel II and the Teatro Real. Bathrooms are excellent, clad in marble with dual basins. The Opera remains one of Madrid's relatively undiscovered boutique hotels.

Cuesta de Santo Domingo 2, 28013 ✆ **91-541-28-00.** Fax 91-541-69-23. www.hotelopera.com. 79 units. 115€ ($144) double. AE, DC, MC, V. Parking nearby 12€ ($15). Metro: Opera. **Amenities:** Restaurant; bar; laundry service; dry cleaning. *In room:* A/C, TV, minibar, hair dryer, safe.

Vincci Centrum 🌟   In one of Madrid's most central locations, this hotel is convenient to the Gran Vía (Madrid's main street), Paseo del Prado, and Puerta del Sol (the city's exact center). It's part of the wave of minimalist hotel designs sweeping the Spanish capital. During the week, most of the clients are commercial travelers; on weekends, vacationers fill the rooms. A sleek modern design prevails in the midsize guest rooms, which come with bathrooms with immaculately tiled walls. The atmosphere is stylishly comfortable and most inviting. (A sister hotel, the **Vincci Soho,** with similar facilities, opened in early 2006 at Calle Prado 18 in the Huertas district; see www.vinccihoteles.com.)

Calle Cedaceros 4, 28014 Madrid. ✆ **91-360-47-20.** Fax 91-522-45-15. www.vinccihoteles.com. 85 units. 220€ ($275) double. AE, DC, MC, V. Metro: Sevilla. **Amenities:** Restaurant-cafe; bar; limited room service; laundry service; dry cleaning; nonsmoking rooms. *In room:* A/C, TV, dataport, minibar, hair dryer, safe.

INEXPENSIVE

Hostal la Macarena 🌟 *Value*   Known for its reasonable prices and praised by readers for its warm hospitality, this unpretentious *hostal* is run by the Ricardo González family. A 19th-century facade with Belle Epoque patterns stands in ornate contrast to the chiseled simplicity of the ancient buildings facing it. The location is one of the *hostal's* assets: It's on a street (a noisy one) immediately behind Plaza Mayor near one of the best clusters of *tascas* in Madrid. Rooms range from small to medium and are all well kept, with modest furnishings and comfortable beds. Windows facing the street have double panes. Bathrooms are tiny and contain stall showers.

Cava de San Miguel 8, 28005 ✆ **91-365-92-21.** Fax 91-364-27-57. 25 units. 65€ ($81) double; 90€ ($113) triple; 110€ ($138) quad. MC, V. Metro: Sol, Opera, or La Latina. **Amenities:** Bar; lounge. *In room:* TV, hair dryer.

Hostal la Perla Asturiana   Ideal for those who want to stay in the heart of old Madrid (1 block off Plaza Mayor and 2 blocks from Puerta del Sol), this small, family-run place welcomes you with a courteous staff at the desk 24 hours a day for security and convenience. You can socialize in the small, comfortable lobby adjacent to the reception area but stay here for the cheap prices and location, not grand comfort. Each of the small rooms comes with a comfortable bed plus a simple and adequate bathroom with a shower unit. Many inexpensive restaurants and tapas bars are nearby. No breakfast is served.

Plaza Santa Cruz 3, 28012. ✆ **91-366-46-00**. Fax 91-366-46-08. www.perlaasturiana.com. 33 units. 45€–50€ ($56–$63) double; 60€ ($75) triple. MC, V. Metro: Sol. **Amenities:** Lounge; laundry service; dry cleaning. *In room:* TV.

Hostal Residencia Americano

Americano, on the third floor of a five-floor building, is suitable for those who want to be in the thick of Puerta del Sol. Most of the guest rooms are outside chambers with balconies facing the street and all have been refurbished. The rooms are small, especially when three or four guests are crowded in. Bathrooms are bleak, clean cubicles with showers. No breakfast is served.

Puerta del Sol 11, 28013 ✆ **91-522-28-22**. Fax 91-522-11-92. 44 units. 45€ ($56) double; 60€ ($75) triple; 70€ ($88) quad. AE, MC, V. Metro: Sol. **Amenities:** Lounge. *In room:* TV.

Hostal Residencia Lisboa

My only complaint about the Lisboa, on Madrid's most famous restaurant street, is that it can be a bit noisy. The hotel is a neat, modernized town house with compact rooms and a staff that speaks five languages. Most of the rooms, on four floors of this old building, are small, but a few are comfortably larger. Most come equipped with a double bed, some with twins. Bathrooms are small, mainly with shower stalls. The Lisboa does not serve breakfast, but budget dining rooms, cafes, and *tascas* surround the neighborhood.

Ventura de la Vega 17, 28014. ✆ **91-429-98-94**. Fax 91-429-46-76. hostallisboa@inves.es. 26 units. 55€ ($69) double. AE, DC, MC, V. Parking nearby 13€ ($16). Metro: Puerta del Sol. **Amenities:** Lounge; babysitting; laundry service; dry cleaning. *In room:* A/C, TV, hair dryer, safe.

Hostal Riesco *Value*

Run by the same family for over a quarter of a century, this third-floor hotel nestles in the very heart of the city on the corner of a street overlooking the Puerta del Sol. The gently rising, polished-wooden entry stairs and slow-moving traditional elevator—which only goes to even-numbered floors—belong to another era, and the genial decor includes stucco ceilings and bright gold fittings. Some of the rooms have small terraces with colorful flowers and plants. This is one of the best budget-value hotels in central Madrid.

Calle Correo 2–3°, 28012. ✆ **91-522-26-92**. Fax 91-532-90-88 28 units. 50€ ($63) double; 70€ ($88) triple. No credit cards. Metro: Sol. **Amenities:** Lounge.

Hotel Francisco 1

Regular visitors who used to patronize the now-disbanded Hotel París on the other side of the Puerta del Sol can now stay at this sister establishment in the newly pedestrianized Calle Arenal, just a short stroll away from Opera square, the Plaza Mayor, and other attractions of the historic Austrias district. It's a genial homely place that's been around for some time, and its laidback atmosphere is a welcome reminder of the less frenetic Madrid of yesteryear. The decor is neat but unostentatious, and the clean and comfortable rooms are rated standard or superior (the latter being worth that little extra in summer as they alone have air-conditioning). If you prefer relative peace and quiet to the nonstop cacophony of city life, ask for an interior room. The Francisco has been run by the same family for many years and the staff is very friendly and obliging.

Arenal 15, Calle 28013. ✆ **91-521-64-96** or **91-548-02-04**. Fax 91-542-28-99. www.hotelfrancisco.com. 121 units. 80€–110€ ($100–$137.50) standard or superior double. Rates include breakfast. AE, DC, MC, V. Metro: Sol. **Amenities:** Breakfast restaurant; bar; TV room; game room; laundry service; dry cleaning. *In room:* (Standard) TV, safe, no phone; (Superior) A/C, TV, safe.

Hotel Inglés ✦

You'll find this little hotel (where Virginia Woolf used to stay) on a central street lined with *tascas*. Behind the red-brick facade is a modern, impersonal hotel with contemporary, well-maintained rooms. The lobby is air-conditioned, but guest rooms are not; guests who open their windows at night are likely to hear noise from the enclosed courtyard, so light sleepers beware. Rooms come in a variety of shapes, most of them small, and some in the back are quite dark. Tiled bathrooms are cramped but tidily maintained, with shower stalls.

Calle Echegaray 8, 28014. ℭ **91-429-65-51.** Fax 91-420-24-23. 58 units. 90€ ($113) double; 115€ ($144) suite. AE, DC, MC, V. Parking 12€ ($15). Metro: Sevilla. **Amenities:** Cafeteria; bar; health club; conference facilities; room service; babysitting; laundry service; dry cleaning. *In room:* TV, hair dryer, safe.

Hotel Santander ☆ *Value*   First opened in the 1920s, the cozy and character-filled Santander is a modest but stalwart highlight of Huertas district. Located on a long, narrow street renowned for its variety of polyglot attractions—from Japanese restaurants to vintage tiled *tabernas*—it is a stone's throw from a wealth of other lively hedonistic amenities in Plaza Santa Ana and Plaza del Angel. Rooms are clean, neat, and feature high-ceilings; a separate small alcove in some suite-sized units has enough space for you to take breakfast in. It's a genuine low-cost bargain, and the plain ambience is enhanced by warm and friendly service.

Calle Echegaray 1, 28014. ℭ **91-429-95-51.** Fax 91-369-10-78. 35 units. 70€ ($88) double. MC, V. Metro: Sevilla. **Amenities:** Laundry; safe. *In room:* TV.

SELF-CATERING

Apartamentos Turísticos Príncipe 11   Located just off Plaza Santa Ana and a short stroll from the Plaza Mayor, these modern self-contained 40-sq.-m (431-sq.-ft.) units are ideally placed for all central Madrid's shops, bars, and nightspots. Accommodations mainly comprise studios and apartments, but also include a small number of suites and large family flats. There are also *buhardillas* (attics or penthouses) with spacious terraces. All flats have fully equipped kitchenettes and bathrooms with washing machines.

Calle Príncipe 11, 28012. ℭ **902-113-311.** Fax 91-429-42-49. www.atprincipe11.com. 36 units. 75€ ($94) 2-person studio; 100€ ($125) 4-person studio; 120€ ($150) 2-person suite; 150€ ($188) 6-person apt. AE, DC, MC, V. Metro: Sol. *In apt:* A/C, laundry, dataport, TV, kitchenette, maid service, safe.

7 Near Cibeles

MODERATE

Hotel Suecia ☆   As part of a plan to establish closer ties between Sweden and Spain, the Suecia was launched in the mid-1950s by Swedish Prince Bertil. Set in a quiet street next to the Circulo de Bellas Artes and a short stroll from Alcalá and the Cibeles roundabout, it's a pleasant place to stay, in easy reach of all central sights. Rooms are bright and comfortable, and the spacious lobby opens into a bar area where an international breakfast buffet includes a variety of hot and cold dishes to get your day off to a good start. The top floor offers a small balcony where you can relax after lunch. (A plaque at the entrance claims that this was also yet another spot frequented by Hemingway during his legendary sojourns in Madrid.)

   Note: At press time, the Suecia was closed indefinitely. Please call to see if the hotel plans to reopen by the time you visit.

Calle Marqués de Casa Riera 4, 28014. ℭ **91-531-69-00.** Fax 91-521-71-41. www.hotelsuecia.com. 128 units. 180€ ($225) double. AE, DC, MC, V. Parking nearby 20€ ($25). Metro: Banco de España. **Amenities:** Restaurant; bar; cafe; concierge; 24-hr. room service; babysitting; laundry service; nonsmoking floor. *In room:* A/C, TV, minibar, hair dryer, safe.

8 Near Atocha Station

EXPENSIVE

NH Nacional ⓕ   This stately hotel was built around 1900 to house the hundreds of passengers flooding into Madrid through the nearby Atocha railway station. In 1997, a well-respected nationwide chain, NH Hotels, ripped out much of the building's dowdy interior, reconstructing the public areas and bedrooms into a smooth, seamless decor that takes maximum advantage of the building's tall ceilings and large spaces. The entrance area impressively boasts a marble hall with Gothic columns and an overhead glass copula. In the bedrooms the Belle Epoque trappings of another day have been replaced with modern designer decor, even avant-garde art, giving the units a welcoming ambience, and those facing the exterior enjoy good views of the Botanical Gardens. Rooms also come equipped with immaculately kept bathrooms. Today the Nacional is a destination for dozens of corporate conventions.

Paseo del Prado 48, 28014. ⓒ 91-429-66-29. Fax 91-369-15-64. www.nh-hoteles.es. 214 units. 200€–220€ double ($250–$275); 450€ ($563) suite. AE, DC, MC, V. Metro: Atocha. **Amenities:** Restaurant; bar; room service; babysitting; laundry service; dry cleaning. *In room:* A/C, TV, minibar, hair dryer, safe.

MODERATE

Hotel TRH Cortezo   Just off Calle de Atocha, which leads to the railroad station of the same name, the Cortezo is a short walk from Plaza Mayor and Puerta del Sol. The accommodations are comfortable but simply furnished, with contemporary bathrooms. Beds are springy and the furniture is pleasantly modern; many rooms have sitting areas with a desk and armchair. The public rooms match the guest rooms in freshness. The hotel was built in 1959 and last renovated in 1997.

Dr. Cortezo 3, 28012. ⓒ 91-369-01-01. Fax 91-369-37-74. 88 units. 80€–125€ ($100–$156) double; 160€ ($200) suite. AE, DC, MC, V. Parking 20€ ($25). Metro: Tirso de Molina. **Amenities:** Restaurant; bar; room service; babysitting; laundry service; dry cleaning. *In room:* A/C, TV, minibar, hair dryer, safe.

Husa Paseo del Arte   It's a mere trot across the road to the modern Centro de Arte Reina Sofía, and an easy 5- to 10-minute stroll up the tree-shaded Paseo del Prado to the nearby art meccas of the Prado and Thyssen-Bornemisza. Opened on the site of the former Hotel Mercátor in 2006, the Paseo del Arte is noted for its naturally lit modular lounge and comfortable air-conditioned guest rooms and suites, 16 of which are equipped for guests with disabilities. Business visitors have access to a conference room and state-of-the-art Internet facilities, and fitness-minded guests can enjoy the gymnasium. The **Trazos** restaurant offers buffet breakfasts and traditional a la carte dinners as well as a fixed daily lunch menu. There's a separate section for nonsmokers. The hotel has a garage with 80 parking spaces and is very close to the main Atocha railway station.

Calle Atocha 123, 28012. ⓒ 91-298-48-00. www.husa.es/en. 260 units. 120€–240€ ($150–$300) double; 200€–350€ ($187.50–$437.50) junior suite. AE, DC, MC, V. Parking 12€ ($15). Metro: Atocha. **Amenities:** Restaurant; cafeteria; bar; 2 lounges; 24-hr. reception; conference room; Internet connection; limited room service; terrace; solarium; gym; babysitting; laundry service; dry cleaning. *In room:* A/C, TV, minibar, hair dryer.

INEXPENSIVE

Hotel Mediodía ⓥ*alue*   Located in a renovated 18th-century building at the end of the Paseo del Prado, this excellent-value hotel is just across the road from the Botanical Gardens and famed open-air bookstalls of the gently rising Calle Claudio Moyano. The comfortable converted period rooms still retain the original wooden floors, and some have uninterrupted views of Atocha station. Homey and comfortable, the Mediodía is noted for its friendly and attentive service.

Plaza de Emperador Carlos V 8, 28012. (ℰ **91-527-30-60**. Fax 91-527-30-66. 165 units. 75€ ($94) double. AE, MC, V. Metro: Atocha. **Amenities:** Lounge. *In room:* TV.

9 Near Retiro/Salamanca

VERY EXPENSIVE

Hesperia Madrid 🎔🎔🎔   Luxury without frills is the keynote of this ultramodern Catalan-owned hotel ideally located in a fashionable part of the Castellana Avenue and an accredited member of the Leading Hotels of the World. Cool minimalism with Asian overtones dominates, underscored by the lobby's exquisite lime trees and stylish atrium. Rooms are immaculately compact, with top-quality fixtures and fittings, fashionable bathroom toiletries, and added luxuries such as a choice of pillows from a special pillow menu. Tiny Japanese gardens and chic individual designs dot the building; among its most prized rooms is the deluxe presidential suite, which enjoys marvelous city views from the split-level terrace. Also highly impressive is the **Santceloni** dining room, which has already earned itself a Michelin rating. The staff is efficient, friendly, and exceptionally attractive (another part of the hotel's charismatic appeal). Suites have their own butler.

Paseo de la Castellana 57, 28046. (ℰ **91-210-88-00**. Fax 91-210-88-99. www.hesperia.com. 171 units. 420€ ($525) double; 750€–3,950€ ($938–$4,938) suite. AE, DC, MC, V. Parking 23€ ($29). Metro: Rubén Darío. **Amenities:** Restaurant; bar; access to health club; sauna; business center; concierge; salon; 24-hr. room service; babysitting; laundry service; nonsmoking rooms and floor; limousine service. *In room:* A/C, TV, minibar, safe, Wi-Fi.

Park Hyatt Villa Magna 🎔🎔🎔   One of the finest hotels in Europe, the Park Hyatt is nine stories of rose-colored granite set behind a bank of pines and laurels on the city's most fashionable boulevard. It's an even finer choice than the Palace or Villa Real and is matched in luxury, ambience, and service only by the Ritz, whose age gives it a richer patina.

Separated from the busy boulevard by a parklike garden with beautiful cedar trees, the hotel has contemporary lines. In contrast, its interior recaptures the style of Carlos IV, with paneled walls, marble floors, and bouquets of fresh flowers. Almost every film star shooting on location in Spain stays here, and heads of state and senior politicians also feature high among the regulars. As if to emphasize this diversity of clientele, both the fitness and business facilities are excellent. Rooms in this luxury palace are plush but dignified and decorated in Louis XVI, English Regency, or Italian Provincial style.

Paseo de la Castellana 22, 28046. (ℰ **800/223-1234** in the U.S. and Canada, or (ℰ 91-587-12-34. Fax 91-431-22-86. www.madrid.hyatt.com. 182 units. 525€ ($656) double; from 775€ ($969) suite. AE, DC, MC, V. Parking 19€ ($24). Metro: Gregorio Marañón. **Amenities:** 2 restaurants; 2 bars; health club; car-rental desk; business services; salon; room service; babysitting; laundry service; dry cleaning. *In room:* A/C, TV, minibar, hair dryer, safe.

The Ritz 🎔🎔🎔   The Ritz is the most legendary hotel in Spain. With soaring ceilings and graceful columns, it offers all the luxury and pampering you'd expect of a grand hotel. Although the building has been thoroughly modernized, great effort was expended to retain its Belle Epoque character and architectural details.

No other Madrid hotel, except the Palace, has a more varied history. One of *Les Grands Hôtels Européens,* the Ritz was built in 1908 by King Alfonso XIII with the aid of César Ritz. It looks out onto the circular Plaza de la Lealtad in the center of town, near 120-hectare (300-acre) Retiro Park, facing the Prado, the Palacio de Villaher-mosa, and the Stock Exchange. The Ritz was constructed when costs were relatively low and when spaciousness and luxury were the standard. Its facade has even been des-ignated a historic monument. The glory days of 1910 live on in the rooms with their spacious closets, antique furnishings, and hand-woven carpets. Bathrooms are spa-cious, with robes, dual basins, and deluxe toiletries. The hotel requests that male guests wear a jacket and tie after 11am in the public areas. Nonetheless, casual wear, even blue jeans, is seen at the hotel, but such guests are conspicuous by their lack of what the Spanish call *gracia*. A special treat to enjoy here for guests or visitors alike is the famed brunch in the *Goya* restaurant or on the beautiful summer garden terrace. (*Warning:* It's not cheap!)

Plaza de la Lealtad 5, 28014. ℭ **800/225-5843** in the U.S. and Canada, or ℭ 91-701-67-67. Fax 91-701-67-76. www.ritz.es. 167 units. 675€–725€ ($844–$906) double; from 1,250€ ($1,563) suite. AE, DC, MC, V. Parking 25€ ($31). Metro: Banco de España. **Amenities:** Restaurant; bar; health club; sauna; car-rental desk; room service; laun-dry service; dry cleaning. *In room:* A/C, TV, minibar, hair dryer, safe.

EXPENSIVE

Catalonia Centro ⋔   Inaugurated in June 2005, this superbly refurbished 19th-century building is now one of the Hoteles Catalonia group's most prestigious new Madrid hotels. Combining period character with fully modern amenities, it stands six stories high, like most of the surrounding buildings in the Salamanca district. Bay windows and decorative grilles are key features on the hotel's traditional brick facade, and the well-equipped rooms have parquet floors and warm wood furnishings.

Goya 49, 28001. ℭ **91-781-49-49.** Fax: 91-781-49-48. www.hoteles-catalonia.com. 88 units. 143€–232€ ($179–$290) double. AE, DC, MC, V. Metro: Goya. **Amenities:** Restaurant; laundry; Wi-Fi Internet access. *In room:* A/C, TV, hair dryer, safe.

Hesperia Emperatriz ⋔   This hotel lies just off the wide Paseo de la Castellana. Built in the 1970s, it has been recently renovated in a combination of Laura Ashley and Spanish contemporary styles by Madrid's trendiest firm, Casa & Jardín. Rooms are comfortable and classically styled in cheery yellows and salmons and come with neatly kept bathrooms. Ask for a room on the seventh floor, where you get a private terrace at no extra charge. Best of all—and understandably in great demand—is the eighth-floor Emperatriz suite with its spacious balcony.

López de Hoyos 4, 28006. ℭ **91-563-80-88.** Fax 91-563-98-04. www.hesperia-emperatriz.com. 158 units. 250€ double ($313); 450€ ($563) suite. AE, DC, MC, V. Metro: Gregorio Marañón. **Amenities:** Restaurant; bar; salon; room service; babysitting; laundry service; dry cleaning. *In room:* A/C, TV, minibar, hair dryer, safe.

Hotel AC Palacio del Retiro ⋔⋔   This finely renovated luxury hotel enjoys an unrivalled location just across the road from El Retiro park (ask for a room at the front if you want to enjoy the exceptional views). It's also only a short stroll from here to Madrid's "golden triangle" of great art museums and Calle Serrano's sophisticated shops. A nationally registered early-20th-century building, the hotel combines mag-nificent traditional architecture with ultra-elegant modern decor that's notable for its inventive use of glass and marble. Public areas and rooms alike are coolly spacious and furnished with immaculate taste. Modern facilities include a business area with Inter-net access and staff support, as well as a well-equipped fitness center. There are special rooms for clients with disabilities and nonsmokers, and some rooms have intercon-necting facilities. All have ensuite bathrooms equipped with hydromassage Jacuzzis. To facilitate your arrival, a shuttle service is available to and from the airport.

Alfonso XII, 14. 28014. (C) **91-523-74-60**. Fax 91-523-74-61. www.ac-hotels.com. 51 units. 350 € ($437.50) double. AE, DC, MC, V. Parking 20 € ($25). Metro: Retiro. **Amenities:** Restaurant; bar; 24-hr. front desk; meeting room; room service; TV room; health club with Turkish bath, sauna, and massages; babysitting; laundry service. *In room:* AC, TV, Wi-Fi, minibar, hair dryer, safe.

Hotel Adler 🌟🌟   The Adler stands at the intersection of Velázquez and Goya streets in a location nicknamed "the golden triangle of art" (near El Prado, Reina Sofía, and the Thyssen-Bornemisza collection). One of the newest and most elegant places to stay in Madrid, it offers grand comfort in a converted 18th-century *palacete* complete with neoclassical decor and an interior designed by Pascual Ortega, and featuring works by modernist artists such as Tàpies and Chillida. The Serrano district's exclusive shops are also near at hand. The classic building has been carefully restored and offers gracious comfort in a setting that retains the feel of the 1880s but with decidedly modern touches. Bedrooms are user friendly—you live and sleep in ultimate comfort with luxe furnishings and totally modernized bathrooms—and charming *áticos* (penthouse rooms) provide the much-sought-after fifth-floor accommodations. The on-site restaurant is one of the better hotel dining rooms in this upmarket section of town.

Calle Velázquez 33, 28001. (C) **91-426-32-20**. Fax 91-426-32-21. www.travel-in-madrid.com/hotel/adler/english. htm. 45 units. 330€–380€ ($413–$475) double; 450€ ($563) suite. AE, DC, MC, V. Metro: Velázquez. **Amenities:** Restaurant; bar; room service; babysitting; laundry service; dry cleaning. *In room:* A/C, TV, minibar, hair dryer, safe.

Hotel Alcalá 🌟   This enduring hotel has a justifiably high reputation. Its long-established staff is renowned for its friendly and highly attentive service, while the warm period atmosphere is enhanced by original wooden floors and traditional fittings. All rooms have been individually designed and refurbished, and central units overlook a charming garden patio. Each level has a particularly individual room with decor planned by one of Spain's top modern designers, Agatha Ruix de la Prada, who runs a boutique in the city. Retiro Park is just across the road whenever you feel like a stroll among the greenery. For night owls, the hotel serves a *madrugada* (dawn) breakfast highlighted by the inevitable high-calorie *chocolate con churros*.

Calle Alcalá 66, 28009. (C) **91-435-10-60**. Fax 91-435-11-05. www.nh-hotelews.com. 146 units. 215€–235€ ($269–$294) double. AE, DC, MC, V. Parking 18€ ($23). Metro: Príncipe de Vergara. **Amenities:** Restaurant; bar; concierge; room service (7am–11pm); laundry service; nonsmoking rooms. *In room:* A/C, TV w/pay movies, video games, radio, minibar, hair dryer.

Hotel Wellington 🌟   Located in one of Salamanca district's most fashionable avenues, the Wellington is one of those grand old Madrid hotels that's seen slightly better days. Built at the beginning of the 1950s, it still impresses with its French-style entrance and warmly intimate lobby, and its rooms are comfortable and stylish. Rates are comparatively low, and added bonuses include an adjoining gourmet restaurant **(Goizeko Wellington)** and a garden area with an outdoor summer pool. It's a popular meeting place for the bullfight fraternity, especially during the May fiesta period of Madrid's patron saint, San Isidro, when the cream of *torero* (bullfighting) society puts in an appearance.

Calle Velázquez 8. 28001. (C) **91-575-44-00**. Fax 91-576-41-64. www.hotel-welllington.com. 276 units. 295€ ($369) double; 395€ ($494) suite. AE, DC, MC, V. Parking 20€ ($25). Metro: Retiro. **Amenities:** Restaurant; bar; outdoor pool (June 15–Sept 15); business center; limousine service; salon; babysitting; laundry service; nonsmoking rooms. *In room:* A/C, TV, dataport, radio, minibar, hair dryer, safe.

Kids Family-Friendly Hotels

Meliá Castilla Children can spend hours and all their extra energy in the hotel's swimming pool and gymnasium. On the grounds is a showroom exhibiting the latest European automobiles. Hotel services include babysitting, providing fun for kids and parents too. © **91-567-50-00.**

The Tirol This centrally located government-rated three-star hotel is a favorite of families seeking good comfort at moderate price. It has a cafeteria. © **91-548-19-00.**

Jardín de Recoletos ☆ (Value)   Built in 1999, this hotel welcomes its guests to the chic Salamanca district of Madrid. It is close to both the financial district and the best shops. A contemporary apartment hotel, it stands on a street of little noise but close to the Plaza Colón, one of the major traffic arteries of Madrid. The inviting lobby has sleek marble floors and a stained-glass ceiling; adjacent is a combined cafe and restaurant. Most of the rooms are rather spacious and attractively decorated in a traditional style, with small sitting and dining areas, wood trim, creamy white walls, and comfortable furniture in yellow and champagne. Unusual for Madrid, the accommodations come with well-equipped kitchenettes. If you want to pay extra, you can book either a unit rated "superior" or else a suite that offers a hydromassage bathroom and a big terrace.

Gil de Santivañes 6, 28001 © **91-781-16-40.** Fax 91-781-16-41. www.jardinerecoletos.com. 43 units. 190€ ($238) double; 245€–260€ ($306–$325) suite. Rates include buffet breakfast. AE, DC, MC, V. Parking 9€ ($11). Metro: Serrano. **Amenities:** Restaurant; cafe; limited room service; laundry service; dry cleaning. *In room:* A/C, TV, dataport, kitchenette, minibar, hair dryer, iron, safe, beverage maker.

Meliá Galgos   A prominent member of the large Sol Meliá hotel group, the lush, spacious Galgos is located close to the Castellana avenue on a trendy Salamanca district street noted for its art galleries. Popular with leisure seekers, it's also particularly well equipped for business travelers, boasting no less than 11 conference rooms. The comfortable rooms—which don't skimp on space—come with a generous selection of amenities, and the first-rate restaurant serves prodigious anti-diet breakfasts.

Calle Claudio Coello 139, 28006. © **91-562-66-00.** fax 91-562-76-62. www.solmelia.com. 200€ ($250) double. AE, DC, MC, V. Parking 24€ ($30) per day. Metro: Rubén Darío. **Amenities:** Restaurant; bar; 11 conference rooms; Internet access; gym with sauna. *In room:* A/C, TV, pay movies.

MODERATE

Fiesta Gran Hotel Colón ☆   East of Retiro Park, Gran Hotel Colón is just a few minutes from the city center by subway. Built in 1966, it offers comfortable yet reasonably priced accommodations in a modern setting. More than half of the accommodations have private balconies, and all contain traditional furniture, much of it built-in. Rooms vary in size but most offer roomy comfort, dark wood beds, and adequate closet space. Bathrooms are small, with stall showers, but with suitable shelf space. Other perks include two dining rooms, a covered garage, and bingo games. One of the Colón's founders was an interior designer, which accounts for the unusual stained-glass windows and murals in the public rooms and the paintings by Spanish artists in the lounge.

Pez Volador 1–11, 28007. ℂ **91-573-59-00.** Fax 91-573-08-09. www.fiesta-hotels.com. 359 units. 120€–155€ ($150–$194) double. AE, DC, MC, V. Parking 15€ ($19). Metro: Sainz de Baranda. **Amenities:** Restaurant; bar; health club; sauna; salon; room service; babysitting; laundry service; dry cleaning. *In room:* A/C, TV, minibar, hair dryer, safe.

Gran Hotel Velázquez ✦

This is one of the most attractive medium-size hotels in Madrid, with plenty of comfort and convenience. Opened in 1947 on an affluent residential street near the center of town, it has a 1930s-style Art Deco facade and a 1940s interior filled with well-upholstered furniture and richly grained paneling. Several public rooms lead off a central oval area. As in many hotels of its era, the rooms vary. Some are large enough for entertaining, with a small separate sitting area. All contain piped-in music and walk-in closets. Bathrooms are decorated in marble or tiles, with either stall showers or tubs.

Calle Velázquez 62, 28001. ℂ **91-575-28-00.** Fax 91-575-28-09. www.chh.es. 146 units. 245€ double ($306); from 350€ ($438) suite. AE, DC, MC, V. Parking nearby 20€ ($25). Metro: Velázquez. **Amenities:** 2 restaurants; bar; salon; room service; babysitting; laundry service; dry cleaning. *In room:* A/C, TV, minibar, hair dryer, safe.

Hotel Mora

This modest but comfortable five-story hotel, located right beside the tree-lined Paseo de Prado and directly opposite the Botanical Gardens, is just a short stroll from both the Atocha railway station and Reina Sofia and Prado museums. Refurbished throughout, the traditional hotel has a bright comfortable lounge with stylish cream pillars and an adjoining bar-cafeteria with a variety of breakfasts, from continental to American. Staff is very friendly and the rooms neat and well appointed.

Paseo del Prado 32, 28014. ℂ **91-420-15-69.** Fax 91-420-05-64. 62 units. 80€ ($100) double. AE, DC, MC, V. Metro: Atocha. **Amenities:** Lounge; bar/cafeteria. *In room:* A/C, TV, safe.

Novotel Madrid Puente de la Paz

Novotel was originally intended to serve the hotel needs of a cluster of multinational corporations with headquarters 2.4km (1½ miles) east of the center of Madrid, but its guest rooms are so comfortable and its prices so reasonable that tourists have begun using it as well. Opened in 1986, it is located on the highway, away from the maze of sometimes confusing inner-city streets, which makes it attractive to motorists.

Bedrooms are laid out in a standardized format whose popularity in Europe has made it one of the hotel industry's most notable success stories. Each contains a well-designed bathroom, in-house movies, and soundproofing. The sofas, once their bolster pillows are removed, can be transformed into comfortable beds for children. The English-speaking staff is well versed in both sightseeing attractions and solutions to most business-related problems.

Calle Albacete 1 (at Av. Badajos), 28027. ℂ **800/221-4542** in the U.S. and Canada, or ℂ 91-724-76-00. Fax 91-724-76-10. www.novotel.com. 240 units. 175€ ($219) double. Children 15 and under stay free in parent's room. AE, DC, MC, V. Parking 17€ ($21). Metro: Barrio de la Concepción. If you're arriving by car, exit from M-30 at Barrio de la Concepción/Parque de las Avenidas, just before reaching the city limits of central Madrid, and then look for the chain's trademark electric-blue signs. **Amenities:** Restaurant; bar; pool; health club; sauna; room service; babysitting; laundry service; dry cleaning. *In room:* A/C, TV, minibar, hair dryer, safe.

INEXPENSIVE

Hostal Armesto *Value*

Tucked away on a side road a short walk from the Paseo del Prado, this unpretentious little *hostal* is run by a friendly and helpful couple. The excellent-value rooms are neat and clean, and each has its own private shower. Ask for a rear-view room with views over the charming and secluded private garden of the adjoining San Agustín palace.

Calle San Agustín 6–1°, 28014. C 91-429-90-31. 6 units. 50€ ($63) double. MC, V. Metro: Antón Martín. **Amenities:** Room service. *In room:* TV, fan.

Hotel Claridge
This contemporary building, last renovated in 1994, is southeast of the Retiro Park, close to the Conde Casal bus station (which offers services to Cuenca among other places) and about 5 minutes from the Prado by taxi or subway. Soft carpets and triple glazing ensure that the entrance and public areas are soothingly quiet. Rooms are well organized and pleasantly styled, though small and compact. They include small, well-organized bathrooms. You can take your meals in the hotel's cafeteria and relax in the modern lounge.

Plaza Conde de Casal 6, 28007 C 91-551-94-00. Fax 91-501-03-85. 150 units. Mon–Thurs 90€–115€ ($113–$144) double; Fri–Sun 75€–80€ ($94–$100) double; 160€ ($200) suite. AE, DC, MC, V. Metro: Conde de Casal. **Amenities:** Restaurant; bar; laundry service; dry cleaning. *In room:* A/C, TV, hair dryer, safe.

10 Chamberí

VERY EXPENSIVE

Castellana InterContinental Hotel 🕊🕊
Solid, spacious, and conservatively modern, this is one of Madrid's most reliable hotels. Originally built in 1963, the Castellana InterContinental lies behind a barrier of trees in a neighborhood of apartment houses and luxury hotels. Its high-ceilinged public rooms are gorgeous, with terrazzo floors and giant abstract murals pieced together from multicolored stones and tiles. Former infamous celebrities like Oliver Reed, who (not always welcomingly) livened the place up in the '70s, have given way today to a more staid business-oriented clientele. Most of the accommodations have private balconies and traditional furniture, and most rooms provide generous living space with safes and very large beds, often king size. Bathrooms are tiled and well equipped.

Paseo de la Castellana 49, 28046 C 800/327-0200 in the U.S., or C 91-310-02-00. Fax 91-319-58-53. 310 units. 375€–450€ ($469–$563) double; from 950€ ($1,188) suite. AE, DC, MC, V. Parking 20€ ($25). Metro: Gregorio Marañón. **Amenities:** 3 restaurants; bar; health club; sauna; solarium; salon; room service; babysitting; laundry service. *In room:* A/C, TV, minibar, hair dryer, bathrobes, safe.

Hotel Orfila 🕊🕊 *Finds*
Though not as spectacular as Santo Mauro, this small 19th-century palace in a residential area is a gem and a classic example of elegant, tasteful decoration. Many visitors are deserting such old favorites as Villa Magna or the Westin Palace to stay here for its peaceful and laid-back atmosphere. In 1886 it was a family home but in the 1990s was converted to a luxury hotel that still pays homage to its Belle Epoque past with such features as its imposing central stairway. Back in the 1920s this distinguished Relais & Châteaux member boasted its own theater and literary salon. Public lounges in turn evoke its former aristocratic associations, and the lobby is installed in what used to be the courtyard of the town house, where horse-drawn carriages pulled in. The midsize to spacious bedrooms are decorated in a rich 19th-century style that would make one of the old *grandes señores* feel at home. The hotel also offers an Art Nouveau restaurant, **El Jardín de Orfila,** serving an international cuisine. Diners usually savor an aperitif first in the palace garden.

Orfila 6, 28010. C 91-702-77-70. Fax 91-702-77-72. www.hotelorfila.com. 32 units. 290€–375€ ($363–$469) double; from 565€ ($706) suite. AE, DC, MC, V. Metro: Alonso Martínez. **Amenities:** Restaurant; bar; room service; babysitting; laundry service; dry cleaning. *In room:* A/C, TV, minibar, hair dryer, safe.

Santo Mauro Hotel 🏵🏵🏵   This hotel offers even more style and elegance than the InterContinental (see above). It opened in 1991 in what was once a neoclassical villa built in 1894 for the duke of Santo Mauro. Set within a garden and done in a French style, it's decorated with rich fabrics and Art Deco accents and furnishings. The former library is now a gourmet restaurant (p. 158), and the ballroom has been transformed into a very stylish conference room. Another plus is the indoor swimming pool with a vaulted ceiling. Staff members outnumber rooms by two to one. Each of the rooms contains an audio system with a wide choice of tapes and CDs as well as many lovely details, like raw silk curtains, Persian carpets, antique prints, and parquet floors. Accommodations are spacious throughout and come in combinations ranging from studios to duplex suites. Celebrity guests have included stars Madonna and Julia Roberts, as well as British soccer player David Beckham and his wife, Victoria (formerly "Posh Spice" of the Spice Girls).

Calle Zurbano 36, 28010. 📞 **91-319-69-00.** Fax 91-308-54-77. www.ac-hoteles.com/ac_stomauro.htm. 54 units. 300€–375€ ($375–$469) double; from 420€ ($525) suite. AE, DC, MC, V. Parking 15€ ($19). Metro: Rubén Darío or Alonso Martínez. **Amenities:** Restaurant; bar; indoor heated pool; health club; sauna; room service; massage; babysitting; laundry service; dry cleaning. *In room:* A/C, TV, minibar, hair dryer.

EXPENSIVE

Gran Hotel Conde Duque 🏵   Attractively located in a quieter corner of central Madrid, this relaxing hotel nestled beside a tree-lined plaza is just a short stroll from Plaza España. Run with homey efficiency by a Basque family, it has an ambience and clientele that are predominantly Spanish. Its rooms combine modern and traditional furnishings, with large, well-equipped bathrooms and polished wooden floors. Museums and central attractions are within easy reach, and visitors can make use of neighboring health spa facilities, including a sauna.

Plaza Conde del Valle Suchil 5, 28015. 📞 **91-447-70-00.** Fax 91-448-35-69. www.hotelcondeduque.es. 143 units. 220€–265€ ($275–$331) double. AE, DC, MC, V. Parking 20€ ($25). Metro: San Bernardo. **Amenities:** Restaurant; bar; health club; airport transfer; limousine service; car-rental desk; business center; 24-hr. room service; babysitting; laundry service. *In room:* A/C, TV, dataport, radio, minibar, hair dryer, safe.

Hotel Occidental Miguel Angel 🏵   Just off Paseo de la Castellana, this hotel is sleek and modern. It opened its doors in 1975 and has been renovated periodically ever since. It has a lot going for it: ideal location, contemporary styling, good furnishings, an efficient staff, and plenty of comfort. There's an expansive sun terrace on several levels, with clusters of garden furniture surrounded by paintings of semitropical scenes. The soundproof rooms are done in color-coordinated fabrics and carpets, and in many cases reproductions of classic Iberian furniture; each has a superbly comfortable bed.

Miguel Angel 29–31, 28010. 📞 **91-442-00-22.** Fax 91-442-53-20. 263 units. 250€–310€ ($313–$388) double. AE, DC, MC, V. Parking 18€ ($23). Metro: Gregorio Marañón. **Amenities:** 2 restaurants; bar; pool; health club; sauna; salon; room service; babysitting; laundry service; dry cleaning. *In room:* A/C, TV, minibar, hair dryer, safe.

Hotel Zurbano   Located at the modern confluence of Nuevos Ministerios and Castellana Avenue, near the Corte Inglés store and AZCA business center, the Zurbano is just 15 minutes by direct Metro service from both the heart of Madrid and Barajas airport. A member of the renowned NH hotel group, it combines comfortable soundproofed rooms—which certainly don't skimp on space—with a stylish modern decor that includes modern Hispanic art reproductions. Popular with both business visitors and foreign language students attending local schools, it has a lively polyglot atmosphere.

Calle Zurbano 79–81, 28003. ☎ **91-441-45-00.** Fax 91-441-32-24. www.nh-hoteles.com. 260 units. 195€ ($244) double; 295€ ($369) suite. AE, DC, MC, V. Metro: Gregorio Marañón. **Amenities:** Restaurant; bar; cafe; concierge; businesses center; room service (7am–midnight); laundry service; nonsmoking floors; rooms for those w/limited mobility. *In room:* A/C, TV, dataport, radio, minibar, hair dryer.

MODERATE

Hotel Orense ☞   At first glance, you might mistake this silver-and-glass tower for one of many upscale condominium complexes surrounding it on all sides. Stylish and streamlined, with a design inaugurated in the late 1980s and renovated in 1996, it offers reproduction Oriental carpets and conservatively contemporary furniture that's comfortable, tasteful, and upscale. Accommodations are equipped along the lines of a private apartment, which makes them appropriate for a stay of up to several weeks. (In fact, management rents some of them to international corporations for long-term lodging and office space.) All rooms contain private bathrooms with tubs.

Pedro Teixeira 5, 28020 ☎ **91-597-15-68.** Fax 91-597-12-95. www.hotelorense.com. 140 units. Mon–Thurs 150€–225€ ($188–$281) double; Fri–Sun 95€ ($119) double. AE, DC, MC, V. Metro: Santiago Bernabeu. **Amenities:** Restaurant; bar; room service; laundry service; dry cleaning. *In room:* A/C, TV, minibar, hair dryer, safe.

INEXPENSIVE

Hostal Residencia Don Diego ☞   On the fifth floor of an elevator building on a peaceful tree-lined avenue, Don Diego is in a combination residential/commercial neighborhood that's relatively convenient to many of the city monuments. The vestibule contains an elegant winding staircase with iron griffin heads supporting its balustrade. The hotel is warm and inviting, filled with leather couches and comfortably angular but attractive furniture. Rooms are a bit small but comfortable for the price. Bathrooms are cramped but adequate, with shower stalls. The English-speaking staff is both friendly and service oriented, and keeps the place humming along efficiently.

Calle de Velázquez 45, 28001. ☎ **91-435-07-60.** Fax 91-431-42-63. 58 units. 80€ ($100) double; 115€ ($144) triple. MC, V. Metro: Velázquez. **Amenities:** Cafeteria; laundry service; dry cleaning. *In room:* A/C, TV, safe.

SELF-CATERING

Apartotel NH Prisma ☞   No skimping of space here in these 50-sq.-m (538-sq.-ft.) suites, which have been designed for both work and play and enjoy combined apartment and hotel amenities in the same building. In addition to the lounge, kitchenette, and bathroom, there's an office if you're here on business. If you don't feel like self-catering, you can eat in the hotel restaurant. Located in Chamberí district, it's close to the Castellana and AZCA business center with its banking and insurance offices. The Puerta del Sol and Plaza Mayor are just a few minutes away by Metro, and if you enjoy swimming, one of Madrid's best outdoor pools, Isabel II (open June–Sept only), is a short walk away next to Calle Bravo Murillo.

Calle Santa Engracia 120, 28003. ☎ **91-441-93-77.** Fax 91-442-58-51. 103 units. 80€–150€ ($100–$188) double. AE, MC, V. Metro: Ríos Rosas. **Amenities:** A/C, restaurant, cafe, bar, laundry, dry cleaning. *In apt:* Satellite TV w/pay movies, dataport, video games, kitchen, maid service, room service.

Apartotel Tribunal   These well-appointed apartments are situated in the heart of Madrid between Chamberí and the Gran Vía, just a few steps from the Tribunal Metro. Fully equipped for do-it-yourself living, they also enjoy hotel-style facilities such as maid service and a 24-hour reception desk. Ask for an exterior apartment for views of the Municipal museum, with its baroque facade opposite.

Calle San Vicente Ferrer 1, 28004. ℂ **91-522-14-55.** Fax 91-523-42-40. 106 units. www.apartotel-tribunal.com. 80€ ($100) double. AE, DC, MC, V. Metro: Tribunal. **Amenities:** 24-hr. reception desk; laundry service; maid service. *In room:* A/C, TV, hair dryer.

11 Chamartín

EXPENSIVE

The Cuzco ✦ Popular with businesspeople and tour groups, the Cuzco lies in a commercial neighborhood of big buildings, government ministries, and the main Congress Hall. The Chamartín railway station is only a 10-minute walk north, so this is a popular and convenient place to stay. The 15-floor structure, set back from Madrid's longest boulevard, has been redecorated and modernized many times since it was completed in 1967. The rooms are spacious, with separate sitting areas, video movies, and modern furnishings. Bathrooms come equipped with tub/shower combos.

Paseo de la Castellana 133, 28046. ℂ **91-556-06-00.** Fax 91-556-03-72. 330 units. 190€ ($238) double; from 225€ ($281) suite. AE, DC, MC, V. Parking 20€ ($25). Metro: Cuzco. **Amenities:** Restaurant; bar; health club; sauna; salon; room service; massage; babysitting; laundry service; dry cleaning. *In room:* A/C, TV, minibar, hair dryer, safe.

Don Pío This top-value hotel lies directly opposite the Chamartín station and close to the busy Plaza Castilla. Luxury standards combined with attentive service make this a firm favorite with both business and holiday clientele. Traditional furnishings and dark wooden paneling welcome you in the entrance lobby, and the large, stylish rooms all have marble-finished bathrooms complete with hydromassage bathtubs. The hotel's attractive restaurant nestles under a sunny atrium filled with plants and encased by a glass-domed roof. All central amenities are just a quarter of an hour away by Metro, and if you enjoy swimming, a superb outdoor public pool lies just up the road.

Av. Pío XII, 25, 28016. ℂ **91-353-07-80.** Fax 91-353-07-81. 41 units. www.hoteldonpio.com. 165€ ($206) double. AE, DC, MC, V. Parking 12€ ($15). Metro: Pío XII. **Amenities:** Restaurant; cafe; concierge; business center; room service (7am–12:30am); laundry service. *In room:* A/C, TV, dataport, minibar, hair dryer.

Eurobuilding ✦ Even while the Eurobuilding was on the drawing boards, the rumor was that this government-rated five-star sensation of white marble would provide "a new concept in deluxe hotels." It's actually two hotels linked by a courtyard, away from the city center, but right in the midst of apartment houses, boutiques, nightclubs, first-class restaurants, and the modern Madrid business world. Also close by are the Palacio de Congresos and Santiago Bernabeu football (soccer) stadium. The more glamorous of the twin buildings is the main one, named Las Estancias de Eurobuilding. It contains only suites, all recently renovated in pastel shades. Ornately carved gold-and-white beds, large terraces for breakfast and cocktail entertaining—all are tastefully coordinated. Across the courtyard the neighbor Eurobuilding contains less impressive but still very comfortable double rooms, many with views from private balconies of the formal garden below. Added attractions for guests are two swimming pools, one outdoor and one indoor, and a **Spa Elyseum,** with thermal cure programs, opened in 2004.

Calle Padre Damián 23, 28036. ℂ **91-353-73-00.** Fax 91-345-45-76. 490 units. 245€–265€ ($306–$331) double; from 490€ ($613) suite. AE, DC, MC, V. Parking 22€ ($28). Metro: Cuzco. **Amenities:** Restaurant; bar; indoor pool; health club; sauna; room service; babysitting; laundry service; dry cleaning. *In room:* A/C, TV, minibar, hair dryer, safe.

Hotel Nuevo Madrid ✦ Open since February 2005, this member of Spain's famed HUSA chain of hotels is just across the M-30 east of Chamartín station in northeast

Madrid close to the Ifema fairgrounds. It's an ideal choice for both business and leisure visitors looking for relaxed accommodation away from the center yet in easy reach of the hotspots when necessary. The comfortably furnished rooms, some nonsmoking, have state-of-the-art amenities including Internet access.

Calle Bausá 27, 28033. ☎ **91-298-26-02.** Fax 91-298-26-01. 226 units. 90€ ($113) double. AE, DC, MV, V. Metro: Pío XII or Duque de Pastrana. **Amenities:** Restaurant; bar; lounge. *In room:* A/C, digital TV, Internet access, work desk, minibar, hair dryer, safe.

MODERATE

Hotel Aristos ⊕ (Value)   Renovated in 2000, this relaxing hotel is in Chamartín's residential corner of Pío XII not far from the Eurobuilding (see above) and a mere 15 minutes from Barajas airport. One of its main attractions is the garden where you can lounge and take a drink. Each of the medium-size rooms has a small terrace and modern furniture. All units contain bathrooms with tub/shower combos.

Av. Pío XII 34, 28016. ☎ **91-345-04-50.** Fax 91-345-10-23. 23 units. 180€ ($225) double. AE, DC, MC, V. Parking 12€ ($15). Metro: Pío XII. **Amenities:** Restaurant; lounge; room service; laundry service; dry cleaning. *In room:* A/C, TV, minibar, hair dryer, safe.

Hotel Chamartín   This brick-sided hotel soars nine stories above the northern periphery of Madrid. It's part of the massive modern shopping complex attached to the Chamartín railway station, although once you're inside your soundproofed room, the noise of the railway station will seem far away. The owner of the building is RENFE, Spain's government railway system, but the nationwide chain that administers it is HUSA Hotels. The hotel lies 15 minutes by taxi from both the airport and the historic core of Madrid and sits atop one of the capital's busiest Metro stops. The well-appointed rooms are good size, with cushiony furnishings. Especially oriented to the business traveler, the hotel offers a video screen that posts the arrival and departure of all of Chamartín station's trains.

Agustín de Foxá, 28036. ☎ **91-334-49-00.** Fax 91-733-02-14. www.husa.es. 378 units. 165€ ($206) double; from 265€ ($331) suite. AE, DC, MC, V. Metro: Chamartín. Bus: 5. **Amenities:** Restaurant; lounge; car-rental desk; room service; laundry service; dry cleaning. *In room:* A/C, TV, minibar, hair dryer, safe.

Residencia El Viso ⊕ (Finds)   If your dream of Madrid is a peaceful and relaxing backwater in easy striking distance of the city center, then look no further than El Viso. Set in a converted 1930s Art Deco villa on a tree-lined residential barrio 15 minutes from bustling Sol, it seems to be in another world. Its uniquely personal atmosphere is as charming as the setting. A spiral staircase rises from the lounge, and the intimately comfortable rooms all have en suite bathrooms. Though essentially renowned as a top-notch bed-and-breakfast locale, it also provides delicious lunches that are cooked by its owner, María, and when the weather is warm, served on the shaded garden patio.

Calle Nervión 8, 28002. ☎ **91-564-03-70.** Fax 91-564-19-65. elviso@estanciases.es. 12 units. 140€ ($175) double. AE, DC, MC, V. Parking nearby 20€ ($25). Metro: República Argentina. **Amenities:** Restaurant; health club; business center; 24-hr. room service; laundry service. *In room:* A/C, TV w/pay movies, radio, minibar, safe.

12 Avenida America

Hotel Silken Puerta de America ⊕   The multicolored facade of this striking new hotel, part of the prestigious Silken hotel group, brightens up the predominantly gray cityscape around the Avenida de America bus and Metro terminal. More remarkable still is its artistic pedigree: Each of its 12 floors has been designed by a top international architect, from Norman Foster to Arata Isosaki. The individual rooms and suites stimulate with their comfortable furnishings and imaginative decor, while the spacious public areas reflect a liberating ambience of clean, pure images, such as the minimalist **Marmo** cocktail lounge with its gleaming Carrara marble bartop. The elegant **Lágrimas Negras** dining room is noted for its Spanish-oriented cuisine. You can work off any hedonistic indulgences in the hotel's wide-ranging fitness facilities.

Avenida de America 41, 28002. ✆ **91-744-54-00.** fax 91-744-54-01. www.hoteles-silken.com/HPAM. 342 units. 200€–300€ ($250–$375) double. AE, DC, MC, V. Metro: Avenida de America. **Amenities:** Restaurant; bar/cafe; lounge; covered swimming pool; sauna; gym; garden; babysitting; room service; laundry; dry cleaning; Wi-Fi; garden; facilities for travelers with disabilities. *In room:* A/C, TV, minibar, hair dryer, safe.

6

Where to Dine

Madrid boasts the most varied cuisine and the widest choice of dining opportunities in Spain. At the fancy tourist restaurants, prices are comparable to those in New York, London, or Paris, but there are many low-cost taverns and family restaurants as well.

Breakfasts are served in cafes or in your hotel between 7:30 and 10am, although if you want to make a very early start of it, you'll find the occasional bar open around 5:30 or 6am.

It's the custom in Madrid to consume the big meal of the day from 2 to 4pm. After a recuperative siesta, Madrileños then enjoy tapas. Indeed, no culinary experience would be complete without a tour of the city's many tapas bars (see "An Early Evening *Tapeo*" on p. 144 and "The Best of the *Tascas*" on p. 165).

All this nibbling is followed by a light supper in a restaurant, usually from 9:30pm to as late as midnight. Many restaurants, however, start serving dinner at 8pm to accommodate visitors from other countries who don't like to dine so late.

Many of Spain's greatest chefs have opened restaurants in Madrid, energizing the city's culinary scene. Gone are the days when mainly Madrileño food was featured, which meant Castilian specialties such as *cocido* (a chickpea-and-sausage stew) or roasts of suckling pig or lamb. Now, you can take a culinary tour of the country without ever leaving Madrid—from Andalusia with its *gazpacho* and *rabo de toro* (braised bull's tail) to Asturias with its *fabada* (a rich pork stew)

and *sidra* (cider) to the Basque country, which has the most sophisticated cuisine in Spain. The city also has a host of Galician and Mediterranean restaurants. Amazingly, although Madrid is a landlocked city surrounded by a vast arid plain, you can order some of the freshest seafood in the country here.

International restaurants also abound. You can take your pick from a variety of European, Latin American, North African, and Asian eating spots.

Meals include service and tax (7%–12%, depending on the restaurant) but not drinks, which can add to the tab considerably.

In most cases service can seem perfunctory by U.S. standards. Waiters are matter-of-fact and do not fawn over you, nor do they return to the table to ask how things are. This can seem off-putting at first, but if you observe closely you'll see that Spanish waiters typically handle more tables than American waiters and that they generally work quickly and more efficiently. Top restaurants such as Zalacaín (p. 152) have a formal dress policy (jacket and tie for men).

Follow the local custom and don't overtip. Theoretically, service is included in the price of the meal, but it's customary to leave an additional 10%.

The recommended restaurants in this chapter are categorized by the average cost of one entree, an appetizer, and glass of wine. **Very Expensive** means a meal averages $50 per person and up; **Expensive,** $30 to $50; **Moderate,** $20 to $30; and **Inexpensive,** under $20.

Where to Dine in Central Madrid

Alfredo's Barbacoa **28**
Alkalde **32**
Al Mounia **27**
Al Natural **60**
El Amparo **32**
Annapurna **24**
Arce **35**
Artemisa **52**
Asador Frontón **62**
La Atalaya **28**
Automático **66**
Bajamar **14**
Balear **22**
Bali **18**
La Bardemcilla **35**
La Barraca **41**
Las Batuecas **15**
Bazaar **39**
Belagua **23**
El Bocaíto **40**
El Bodegón **30**
Biotika **54**
El Bierzo **38**
La Bola **11**
El Borbollón **27**
La Botillería de Maxi **3**
La Broche **24**
El Buey **33**
Cabo Mayor **16**
Café del Círculo de Bellas
  Artes **45**
Café de Oriente **6**
El Caldero **55**
Caripén **12**
Carmencita **38**
Casa Alberto **49**
Casa Benigna **28**
Casa Ciriaco **7**
Casa Labra **47**
Casa Lastra Sidería **54**
Casa Lucio **1**
Casa Mingo **13**
Casa Mundi **64**
Casa Paco **4**
Casa Pedro **28**
Casa Vallejo **19**
La Cava Real **20**
El Cenador del Prado **51**
Ceres **15**
Cervecería Alemania **49**
Cervecería
  Santa Bárbara **21**
El Chaflán **28**
Champagnería Gala **48**
La Chata **1**
Ciao Madrid
  (2 branches) **20 and 26**
Comme-Bio **5**
Cornucopia **9**
El Cosaco **2**
Las Cuatro Estaciones **16**
La Dame Noire **37**
Delfos **11**
Do Salmon **51**
Donzoko **48**
Dosa Grill Café **39**
Económico Soidemersol **66**
Edelweiss **57**
Elqui **63**
El Estragón **2**
Errota-Zar **60**
El Espejo **34**
La Esquina del Real **7**
Extremadura **42**
La Falsa Modestia **54**

Finca de Susana **52**
Foster's Hollywood **30**
La Fuencisla **17**
Los Galayos **5**
La Galette **33**
La Gamella **63**
Ginza Sushi Restaurant **53**
Goizeko Kabi **28**
El Granero de Lavapiés **66**
Gran Café de Gijón **27**
Gula Gula **43**
Horcher **63**
Iroco **33**
Isla del Tesoro **16**
Julian de Tolosa **3**
Jockey **25**
Kikuyu **26**
Lhardy **52**
Malacatín **42**
Masaniello **2**
El Mentidero de la Villa **36**
Mesón las Descalzas **10**
El Molino de los Porches **13**
Mosaiq **26**
Museo del Jamón **50**
Nabucco **22**
Nicomedes **30**
Nodo **32**
O'Pazo **16**
El Olivo **28**
Paellería Valenciana **42**
La Paloma **30**
Pedro Larumbe **31**
El Pescador **30**
Platerías Comedor **49**
La Posada de la Villa **3**
Príncipe de Viana **28**
Príncipe y Serrano **28**
Ribeiro do Miño **19**
Salvador **42**
San Mamés **15**
Santceloni **24**
El Schotis **1**
Siam **6**
Bar Salamanca **1**
Sobrino de Botín **5**
Suntory **28**
La Taberna de Antonio
  Sánchez **56**
Taberna del Alabardero **8**
Taberna de la Daniela **33**
Taberna Toscana **48**
Taj **57**
Teatriz **29**
La Terraza del Casino **44**
Thai Gardens **32**
Tienda de Vinos **35**
Tocororo **49**
La Trainera **30**
La Trucha **46**
La Vaca Argentina **7**
La Vaca Verónica **33**
El Viajero **2**
26 de Libertad **42**
Urban Cowboy **58**
Viridiana **61**
Viuda de Vacas **1**
WokCafe **42**
Zalacaín **26**
Zara **42**

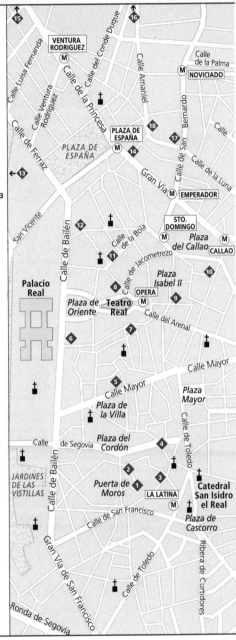

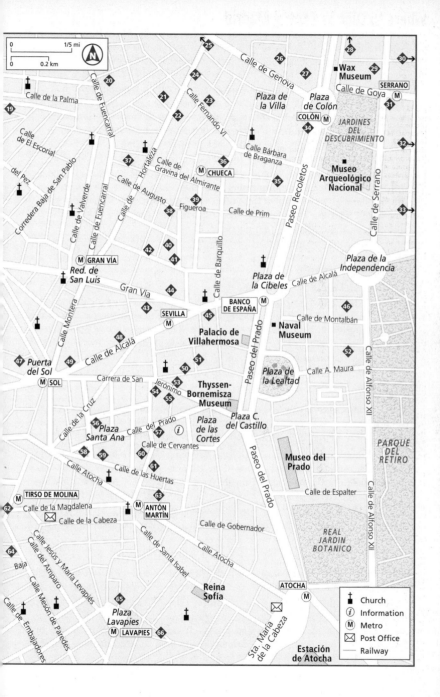

117

Up in Smoke

At the beginning of 2006 Spain instituted a smoking ban in office buildings, malls, and cultural centers and on public transportation. Cafes, bars, and restaurants were allowed to decide whether smoking on the premises should be permitted or not. Unwilling to lose customers, the vast majority of these businesses opted for the former, much to the dismay of Spain's anti-smoking lobby. Although premises over 100 square meters in area are now required to have a small nonsmoking zone, totally smoke-free locales remain almost as rare in Madrid as a pub in Saudi Arabia. Nicotine haters can nevertheless find solace in clear-aired oases such as the inimitable **Starbucks** and vegetarian **Elqui** (p. 141). Two more 100% nonsmoking newcomers to watch for are the light-filled "gourmet" fast-food joint **Dosa Grill Café,** Calle Libertad 17 (Chueca; ℂ **91-360-47-50**), and the intimate new-style organic food and wine spot, **Urban Cowboy,** Calle de Cañizares 14 (Huertas) ℂ **61-921-99-70**).

FIXED-PRICE MENUS

Order the *menú del día* (**menu of the day**) or *cubierto* (**fixed price**)—both fixed-price menus based on what is fresh at the market that day. These are the dining bargains in Madrid, although often lacking the quality of more expensive a la carte dining. Each generally includes a first course, such as fish soup or hors d'oeuvres, followed by a main dish, plus bread, dessert, and the wine of the house. You won't have a large choice. The *menú turístico* is a similar fixed-price menu, but for many it's too large, especially at lunch. Only those with big appetites will find it the best bargain.

DRINKS

BEER   Madrid's favorite *cerveza* is the home-brewed **Mahou,** which comes in light and dark versions and is served draught or by the bottle. Also popular and widely available locally are **Aguila** from Valencia and **Cruzcampo** from Seville.

WINE   **Rioja** from the province of La Rioja adjoining Navarra is by far the best and most popular quality *vino tinto,* followed by **Ribera del Duero** from nearby Valladolid. **Rueda** (Valladolid again), **Penedès** (Cataluña), and the expensive **Albariño** (Galicia) are the favorite whites. Though the capital has its own regional **Vinos de Madrid**—modest wines but admirable for quaffing—these are still sadly undervalued and struggling to find a niche. You may find them in the cave bars behind the Plaza Mayor.

CIDER   Still or fizzy **sidra** is the favorite drink in Asturian eating spots such as Casa Mingo (p. 164) and Casa Lastra (p. 140). *Warning:* The still version is stronger than you'd think.

SPIRITS   Adventurous imbibers can try **orujo,** a fiery liquor or *aguardiente* (made from the stalks and skins of grapes) that tastes like a rough grappa and is sometimes offered free after a meal. **Magno** and **Carlos 1,** mellow **coñacs** from Cádiz, or **Pacharán,** a rose-purple anise-flavored **sloe gin** spirit from Navarra, are more conventional after-dinner tipples.

CAVA   Spain's answer to champagne is best from Cataluña (though recent political differences between the capital and Barcelona led to a not-too-successful boycott of the stuff). Look for **Codorniu** and **Freixenet.** Up-and-coming rivals from Extremadura and Toledo aren't bad either.

CAFETERIAS

These are generally not self-service establishments but restaurants serving light, often American, cuisine. Go for breakfast instead of dining at your hotel, unless it's included in the room price. Some cafeterias offer no hot meals, but many feature combined plates of fried eggs, French fries, veal, and lettuce-and-tomato salad, which make adequate fare, or snacks like hot dogs and hamburgers.

1 Restaurants by Cuisine

AMERICAN
Alfredo's Barbacoa (Chamartín, $, p. 162)
Foster's Hollywood (Near Plaza República Argentina, $, p. 165)

ARGENTINE
La Vaca Argentina (Near Plaza España, $$, p. 146)
La Vaca Verónica (Plaza de las Cortes & Huertas, $, p. 139)

ASTURIAN
Casa Lastra Sidrería (Lavapiés, $$$, p. 140)

ASTURIAN/SPANISH
Casa Mingo (Near Plaza República Argentina, $, p. 164)

BASQUE
Alkalde ✿ (Retiro/Salamanca, $$$, p. 153)
Arce ✿ (On or near the Gran Vía, $$$, p. 135)
Asador Frontón ✿ (Plaza Mayor & Austrias, $$$, p. 126)
Belagua (Chamberí, $$$, p. 158)
El Amparo ✿✿ (Retiro/Salamanca, $$$, p. 153)
Errota-Zar (Plaza de las Cortes & Huertas, $$, p. 138)
Goizeko Kabi ✿ (Chamartín, $$, p. 162)
Príncipe de Viana ✿ (Chamartín, $$$, p. 162)

BASQUE/FRENCH
El Borbollón (Paseo de Recoletos, $$$, p. 142)
La Paloma ✿ (Retiro/Salamanca, $$$, p. 154)
Pedro Larumbe ✿ (Retiro/Salamanca, $$$, p. 155)

BASQUE/SPANISH/ MADRILEÑO
San Mamés ✿ (Cuatro Caminos, $$$, p. 166)
Taberna del Alabardero (Puerta del Sol, $$, p. 133)

CALIFORNIAN/CASTILIAN
La Gamella ✿✿ (Retiro/Salamanca, $$$, p. 154)

CANTABRIAN
La Atalaya (Near Plaza República Argentina, $, p. 165)

CASTILIAN
Bar Salamanca (Plaza Mayor & Austrias, $, p. 128)
Café del Círculo de Bellas Artes ✿ (Near Plaza de la Cibeles, $, p. 143)
Casa Alberto (Plaza de las Cortes & Huertas, $$, p. 136)
Casa Ciriaco (Puerta del Sol, $$, p. 132)
Casa Lucio ✿ (Plaza Mayor & Austrias, $$, p. 126)
Casa Pedro (Fuencarral, $$$, p. 167)
El Bierzo (Chueca, $, p. 150)

El Molino de los Porches ✿ (Near Plaza España, $$$$, p. 145)

Julian de Tolosa (Plaza Mayor & Austrias, $$$, p. 126)

Príncipe y Serrano ✿ (Near Plaza República Argentina, $$, p. 164)

Viuda de Vacas ✿ (Plaza Mayor & Austria, $, p. 130)

CATALAN

La Broche ✿✿ (Chamberí, $$$, p. 158)

CUBAN

Tocororo (Plaza de las Cortes & Huertas, $$, p. 139)

Zara (Chueca, $$, p. 150)

EURO-AMERICAN

Cornucopia (Puerta del Sol, $$, p. 132)

EXTREMADURAN

Extremadura (Chueca, $$, p. 148)

Nicómedes ✿ (Arturo Soria District, $$, p. 163)

FRENCH

Caripén ✿ (Puerta del Sol, $$$, p. 131)

La Dame Noire (Chueca, $$, p. 149)

La Esquina del Real (Puerta del Sol, $$$, p. 131)

FRENCH/BASQUE

La Cava Real ✿✿ (Chamberí, $$, p. 160)

FRENCH/SPANISH

Café de Oriente (Puerta del Sol, $$, p. 132)

GALICIAN

Do Salmon (Plaza de las Cortes & Huertas, $$, p. 137)

O'Pazo ✿ (Cuatro Caminos, $$$, p. 166)

Ribeiro do Miño (Chueca, $, p. 150)

GERMAN

Edelweiss (Near Plaza de la Cibeles, $$, p. 143)

GERMAN/INTERNATIONAL

Horcher ✿ (Retiro/Salamanca, $$$, p. 154)

GREEK

Delfos (Puerto del Sol, $, p. 134)

INDIAN

Annapurna (Chamberí, $$, p. 159)

Taj (Near Plaza de la Cibeles, $, p. 144)

INDONESIAN

Bali ✿ (Near Plaza España $$, p. 145)

INTERNATIONAL

El Espejo (Paseo de Recoletos, $$, p. 142)

El Viajero (Plaza Mayor & Austrias, $, p. 129)

Gula Gula (On or near the Gran Vía, $, p. 135)

Iroco (Retiro/Salamanca, $, p. 157)

Jockey ✿✿✿ (Chamberí, $$$$, p. 158)

26 de Libertad (Chueca, $, p. 151)

Viridiana ✿✿ (Retiro/Salamanca, $$$, p. 156)

Zalacaín ✿✿✿ (Retiro/Salamanca, $$$$, p. 152)

INTERNATIONAL/BASQUE/ SPANISH

El Bodegón (Retiro/Salamanca, $$$, p. 153)

INTERNATIONAL/ NO SMOKING

Dosa Grill (Chueca, $, p. 118)

Urban Cowboy (Huertas, $, p. 118)

ITALIAN

Ciao Madrid (Chueca and Chamberí $$, p. 148 and 159)

La Falsa Molestia (Lavapiés, $, p. 141)

Masaniello (Plaza Mayor & Austrias, $, p. 130)

Nabucco (Chueca, $, p. 150)

Teatriz ✿ (Retiro/Salamanca, $$, p. 157)

THE TRAVELOCITY GUARANTEE

...THAT SAYS EVERYTHING YOU BOOK WILL BE RIGHT, OR WE'LL WORK WITH OUR TRAVEL PARTNERS TO MAKE IT RIGHT, RIGHT AWAY.

To drive home the point,
we're going to use the word "right" in every single sentence.

Let's get right to it. Right to the meat! Only Travelocity guarantees everything about your booking will be right, or we'll work with our travel partners to make it right, right away. Right on!

Here's a picture taken smack dab right in the middle of Antigua, where the Guarantee also covers you.

The Guarantee covers all but one of the items pictured to the right.

Now, you may be thinking, "Yeah, right, I'm so sure." That's OK; you have the right to remain skeptical. That is until we mention help is always right around the corner. Call us right off the bat, knowing our customer service reps are there for you 24/7. Righting wrongs. Left and right.

For example, what if the ocean view you booked actually looks out at a downright ugly parking lot? You'd be right to call – we're there for you. And no one in their right mind would be pleased to learn the rental car place has closed and left them stranded. Call Travelocity and we'll help get you back on the right track.

Now if you're guessing there are some things we can't control, like the weather, well you're right. But we can help you with most things – to get all the details in righting,* visit travelocity.com/guarantee.

*Sorry, spelling things right is one of the few things not covered under the Guarantee.

I'd give my right arm for a guarantee like this, although I'm glad I don't have to.

travelocity
You'll never roam alone.

JAPANESE

Donzoko (Puerta del Sol, $$, p. 133)
Ginza Sushi Bar (Plaza de las Cortes & Huertes, $$, p. 138)
Nodo (Near Plaza República Argentina, $$$, p. 163)
Suntory ⚅ (Retiro/Salamanca, $$$, p. 155)
WokCafe (Chueca, $, p. 152)

MADRILEÑO

Casa Mundi (Chamberí, $$, p. 159)
La Bola (Near Plaza España, $$, p. 145)
La Botillería de Maxi (Plaza Mayor & Austrias, $, p. 129)
Malacatín (Plaza Mayor & Austrias, $, p. 129)
Taberna de la Daniela ⚅ (Retiro/Salamanca, $$, p. 157)

MEDITERRANEAN

Champagnería Gala (Plaza de las Cortes & Huertas, $$, p. 137)
El Cenador del Prado ⚅ (Plaza de las Cortes & Huertas, $$, p. 137)
El Mentidero de la Villa ⚅ (Chueca, $$$, p. 147)
El Olivo ⚅⚅ (Chamartín, $$$, p. 161)
Kikuyu (Chamberí, $$, p. 160)
Las Cuatro Estaciones ⚅⚅⚅ (Chamberí, $$$, p. 159)
Santceloni ⚅⚅⚅ (Retiro/Salamanca, $$$$, p. 152)

MEDITERRANEAN/ASIAN

Bazaar (Chueca, $$, p. 147)

MEDITERRANEAN/ SCANDINAVIAN

Casa Benigna (Near Plaza República Argentina, $$, p. 163)

MOROCCAN

Al Mounia ⚅ (Paseo de Recoletos, $$$, p. 141)
Mosaiq ⚅ (Chamberí, $$, p. 160)

MURCIAN

El Caldero ⚅ (Plaza de las Cortes & Huertas, $$, p. 137)

PAELLA/SEAFOOD

Balear (Chamberí, $$, p. 159)

RUSSIAN

El Cosaco (Plaza Mayor & Austrias, $, p. 128)

SEAFOOD

Bajamar (Near the Plaza España, $$$, p. 145)
Cabo Mayor ⚅⚅ (Chamartín, $$$, p. 161)
El Pescador ⚅ (Retiro/Salamanca, $$$, p. 154)
La Trainera ⚅ (Retiro/Salamanca, $$$, p. 155)

SPANISH

Casa Vallejo (Chueca, $$, p. 148)
Económico Soidemersol (Lavapiés, $, p. 141)
El Buey (Retiro/Salamanca, $$, p. 156)
El Chaflán ⚅ (Chamartín, $$$$, p. 160)
El Schotis ⚅ (Plaza Mayor & Austrias, $$, p. 127)
Gran Café de Gijón ⚅ (Paseo de Recoletos, $$, p. 142)
La Chata (Plaza Mayor & Austrias, $, p. 129)
La Fuencisla ⚅ (Chueca, $$$, p. 147)
Las Batuecas (Cuatro Caminos, $, p. 166)
La Trucha (Plaza de las Cortes & Huertas, $$, p. 139)
Los Galayos ⚅⚅ (Plaza Mayor & Austrias, $$, p. 127)
Mesón las Descalzas (On or near the Gran Vía, $, p. 136)
Platerías Comedor (Puerta del Sol, $$, p. 133)
Sobrino de Botín ⚅⚅ (Plaza Mayor & Austrias, $$, p. 127)
Tienda de Vinos ("El Comunista"; Chueca, $, p. 151)

SPANISH/BASQUE
Carmencita (Chueca, $, p. 150)
Salvador (Chueca, $$, p. 149)

SPANISH/INTERNATIONAL
Finca de Susana (Puerta del Sol, $, p. 134)
La Terraza del Casino ✵✵✵ (Puerta del Sol, $$$$, p. 130)
Lhardy ✵✵ (Puerta del Sol, $$$$, p. 131)

SPANISH/GRILLED MEAT
La Posada de la Villa (Plaza Mayor & Austrias, $$, p. 127)

SPANISH/ASIAN
Nodo (Retiro/Salamanca, $$, p. 163)

SPANISH/TAPAS
El Bocaíto ✵ (Chueca, $$, p. 148)
Casa Labra (Puerto del Sol, $, p. 133)
La Bardemcilla ✵ (Chueca, $$, p. 149)
Museo del Jamón (Puerta del Sol, $, p. 134)

STEAK
Casa Paco ✵✵ (Puerta del Sol, $$, p. 136)

TAPAS
Automático ✵ (Lavapiés, $, p. 140)
Cervecería Alemania (Near Plaza República Argentina, $, p. 164)
Cervecería Santa Bárbara (Near Plaza República Argentina, $, p. 164)

La Taberna de Antonio Sánchez ✵ (Lavapiés, $, p. 165)
Taberna Toscana (Plaza de las Cortes & Huertas, $, p. 140)

THAI
Siam (Near Plaza España, $$, p. 146)
Thai Gardens ✵✵ (Retiro and Salamanca, $$$, p. 156)

VALENCIAN
La Barraca (On or near the Gran Vía, $$$, p. 135)
Paellería Valenciana (On or near the Gran Vía, $, p. 136)

VEGETARIAN
Al Natural (Near Plaza de la Cibeles, $, p. 143)
Artemisa (Plaza de las Cortes & Huertas, $, p. 139)
Ceres (Cuatro Caminos, $, p. 166)
Comme-Bio (Puerta del Sol, $, p. 134)
El Estragón (Plaza Mayor & Austrias, $, p. 128)
El Granero de Lavapiés (Lavapiés, $, p. 141)
Elqui (Lavapiés, $, p. 141)
Isla del Tesoro (Malasaña, $, p. 146)
La Biotika (Plaza de las Cortes & Huertas, $$, p. 138)

VEGETARIAN/INTERNATIONAL
La Galette (Retiro/Salamanca, $$, p. 156)

- **Best for a Romantic Dinner: El Amparo** (✆ **91-431-64-56**) sits in one of Madrid's most elegant enclaves, with cascading vines on its facade. You can dine grandly on nouveau Basque cuisine, enjoying not only the romantic ambience but also some of the finest food in the city. A sloping skylight bathes the interior with sunlight during the day, and at night lanterns cast soft, flattering glows, making you and your date look luscious. See p. 153.
- **Best for a Business Lunch:** For decades the influential leaders of Madrid have come to **Jockey** (✆ **91-319-24-35**) to combine power lunches with one of the true gastronomic experiences in Madrid. In spite of increased competition, Jockey is still among the favorite rendezvous sites for heads of state, international celebrities, and diplomats. It's the perfect place to close that business deal with your Spanish partner—he or she will be impressed with your selection. See p. 158.

- **Best for a Celebration:** At night the whole area around Plaza Mayor becomes one giant Spanish fiesta, with singers, guitar players, and bands of roving students serenading for their sangria and tapas money. Since 1884 it has always been party night at **Los Galayos** (℃ **91-366-30-28**) too, with tables and chairs set out on the sidewalk for people-watching. The food's good as well—everything from suckling pig to roast lamb. What else would you expect from the best eating spot in the Plaza Mayor? See p. 127.

- **Best View:** The cafe tables on the terrace of the **Café de Oriente** (℃ **91-541-39-74**) afford one of the most panoramic views of classical buildings and monuments in Madrid—a view that takes in everything from the Palacio Real (Royal Palace) to the Teatro Real. Diplomats, even royalty, have patronized this place, known for its good food and attractive Belle Epoque decor, which includes banquettes and regal paneling. See p. 132.

- **Best Decor: Las Cuatro Estaciones** (℃ **91-553-63-05**) has the most spectacular floral displays in Madrid. These flowers, naturally, change with the seasons, so you never know what you'll see when you arrive to dine. The entrance might be filled with hydrangeas, chrysanthemums, or poinsettias. The food is equally superb, a magnificent blend of classical and modern, but it's the stunningly modern and inviting decor that makes Las Cuatro Estaciones the perfect place for a lavish dinner on the town. See p. 159.

- **Best for Kids: Foster's Hollywood** (℃ **91-564-63-08**) wins almost hands-down. Since 1971 it has lured kids with Tex-Mex selections, one of the juiciest hamburgers in town, and what a *New York Times* reporter found to be "probably the best onion rings in the world." The atmosphere is fun too, evoking a movie studio with props. See p. 165.

- **Best Basque Cuisine:** Some food critics regard **Zalacaín** (℃ **91-561-48-40**) as the best restaurant in Madrid. Its name comes from Pío Baroja's 1909 novel, *Zalacaín El Aventurero,* but its cuisine comes straight from heaven. When the maitre d' suggests a main dish of cheeks of hake, you might turn away in horror—until you try it. Whatever is served here is sure to be among the finest food you'll taste in Spain—all the foie gras and truffles you desire, but many innovative dishes to tempt the palate as well. See p. 152.

- **Best American Cuisine:** Not everything on the menu at **La Gamella** (℃ **91-532-45-09**) is American, but what there is here is choice, inspired by California. Owner Dick Stephens, a former choreographer, now runs this prestigious restaurant in the house where the Spanish philosopher Ortega y Gasset was born. Even the king and queen of Spain have tasted the savory fare, which includes everything from an all-American cheesecake to a Caesar salad with strips of marinated anchovies. It's also known for serving what one food critic called, "the only edible hamburger in Madrid," and that palate had tasted the hamburger at Foster's Hollywood (see above). Its wine list is comprehensive, covering a wide range of national and world vintages. See p. 154.

- **Best Continental Cuisine:** Although the chef at the small but enchanting **El Mentidero de la Villa** (℃ **91-308-12-85**) roams the world for culinary inspirations, much of the cookery is firmly rooted in French cuisine. Continental favorites are updated here and given new twists and flavors, sometimes betraying a Japanese influence. From France come the most perfect noisettes of veal (flavored with fresh tarragon) that you're likely to be served in Spain. Even the Spanish dishes have been updated and are lighter and subtler in flavor. See p. 147.

- **Best Seafood:** On the northern edges of Madrid, **Cabo Mayor** (© **91-350-87-76**) consistently serves the finest and freshest seafood in the country. Members of the royal family are likely to come here for their favorite seafood treats, which might be a savory kettle of fish soup from Cantabria (a province between the Basque country and Asturias), or stewed *besugo,* or sea bream (also known as porgy) flavored with thyme. Even the atmosphere is nautically inspired. See p. 161.

- **Best Steakhouse:** Spanish steaks at their finest are offered at **Casa Paco** (© **91-366-31-66**). Señor Paco was the first in Madrid to sear steaks in boiling oil before serving, so that the almost-raw meat continues to cook on the plate, preserving the natural juices. This Old Town favorite also has plenty of atmosphere, and has long been a celebrity favorite as well. See p. 136.

- **Best Roast Suckling Pig:** Even hard-to-please Hemingway agreed: The roast suckling pig served at **Sobrino de Botín** (© **91-366-30-26**) since 1725 is the best and most aromatic dish in the Old Town. You'd have to travel to Segovia (home of the specialty) for better fare than this. Under time-aged beams, you can wash down your meal with Valdepeñas or Aragón wine. See p. 127.

- **Best Cocido:** Malacatín (© **91-365-52-41**). *Cocido madrileño* is the capital's favorite dish, a hearty combo of chickpeas, cabbage, salt pork, beef, and chicken designed to combat the winter cold. If you like it, come here: Having raised it to the peak of perfection, they've decided to serve nothing else. The restaurant is small, atmospheric, and an excellent value—the fixed price also includes wine and dessert. Prior booking of both dish and table are essential. See p. 129.

- **Best Wine List:** Although it may no longer be considered the finest restaurant in Madrid, as it once was, **Horcher** (© **91-532-35-96**) does have one of the city's most laudable wine lists. The cuisine is also just as good as it ever was, but there's so much competition these days that other shining stars have toppled Horcher, now in its third generation of ownership, from its throne. Nevertheless, its wine cellars have won praise from kings and gourmands throughout Europe. It offers not only Spain's best vintages but also those from the rest of the continent. Trust the sommelier: He's one of the best in the business, and his advice is virtually always spot-on. See p. 154.

- **Best Value Lunch:** For quality, good service, and simple but imaginative dishes (like chargrilled vegetables and fresh pan-fried rice) at a highly competitive price, the bright, modern **Finca de Susana** (© **91-369-35-57**) beats most of its rivals hands down. You need to arrive earlier than usual in Spain for the bargain three-course lunch (say 1:30pm) in order to avoid the lines (no reservations). See p. 134.

- **Best Vegetarian Fare: Al Natural** (© **91-369-47-09**). Obviously, politicians' gourmet tastes are changing—this totally "green" eating spot situated right behind the *Congreso de Diputados* enjoys the patronage of many a parliamentary member. Rice, vegetables, and veggie pizzas feature strongly, though some *platos* have chicken or fish included. Its 60 places are packed by midday, so try to get here early for lunch. See p. 143.

- **Best Place for Sherry: La Venencia** (© **91-429-62-61**). This cavernous bar sells sherry and nothing else, from ultra-dry *manzanillas* to hearty *olorosos,* in an uncompromisingly preserved, rundown, untampered setting. This means flaking tobacco-brown walls with tattered sherry posters, old barrels, and a basic wooden bar top where the barman chalks up your tab as you go along. Olives, Manchego

Tips   Going Green in Madrid

Being a "veggie" no longer means being an outsider in the Spanish capital. A recent naturalism and biology festival held in the Retiro's Casa de Cristal signposted the capital's changing attitude to food. In the past decade the traditional dominance of carnivore-oriented establishments has been challenged by a small but growing number of vegetarian restaurants. In this chapter you'll find 10 of the best (see "Restaurants by Cuisine," earlier).

You don't have to confine yourself to 100% green establishments to get the goods, though, as many standard Spanish eating spots offer a large choice of noncarnivorous *platos.*

Apart from the ubiquitous tortilla (made, *naturalmente,* with eggs Spanish-style and not from cornmeal Mexican-style), check out the menus for dishes like *pimientos fritos* (fried peppers), *berengenas al horno* (eggplant baked in the oven), *calabaza guisada* (stewed pumpkin), *setas al jerez* (mushrooms cooked in sherry), and *pisto* (Spain's answer to ratatouille, with tomatoes, peppers, eggplant, zucchini, and onions all cooked in oil and garlic: Avoid the Manchego version, though—this has bits of ham in it). *Jamón* (Mountain or cooked, Serrano or York) is scarcely regarded as "real" meat in Spain and can even appear in apparently innocuous dishes such as *caldo* (broth), so confirm with the waiter before you order.

Arabic, Indian, and Italian restaurants may also provide what you're looking for, with their inventive range of couscous, rice, and pasta-based dishes, and if fish is an acceptable option, there are, of course, plenty of seafood restaurants to choose from, though these tend to be expensive. (Check the restaurant listings below for top-value spots such as Ribeiro do Miño.)

Potato power: Anyone wanting a *ración,* or single dish, of something cheap and meat-free should try *patatas bravas* (potatoes sautéed brown and served in a picante sauce). Between Sol and Tirso de Molina there's a trio of eating spots all called Las Bravas and all specializing in this simple but filling dish, though it's also widely available in tapas bars.

cheese, and mountain ham are on the concise no-nonsense tapas list. Check out the sitting area with tables and chairs at the back. See p. 239 in chapter 10.

- **Best Wine Bar: Aloque** (© **91-528-36-62**). No less than 200 *vinos* are on offer at this understated modern bodega-taberna hidden away along a narrow lane in medieval multiethnic Lavapiés. In addition to the inevitable Riojas and Penedès, you'll find some exciting new wines from hitherto undervalued areas like Yecla and Toro. Sit at the bar or at tables in a small alcove. Good incentive: a la carte *raciones* if you get peckish. See p. 237 in chapter 10.
- **Best Tapas: El Bocaíto** (© **91-532-12-19**). Cited as a favorite snack 'n' wine locale by Oscar-winning cineaste Pedro Almodóvar, the stylish little Bocaíto, set in the heart of bohemian Chueca, will usually serve a free miniportion of *cecina* (smoked beef) or something similar with your vino before offering a wealth of marine delights that ranges from *salmonetes* (red mullet) to *pescaítos* (small fried fish). See p. 148.

- **Best "Celebrity" Bar: La Bardemcilla** (© **91-521-42-56**). The "Bardem" bit comes from the name of Spain's number-one movie family, the equivalent of the Fondas to the States and the Redgraves to the U.K. Actress mother Pilar's son Javier—Oscar nominated for his performance as a homosexual Cuban writer in *Before Night Falls* in 2001—is co-owner with his sister Mónica; and tapas and *raciones* are accordingly named after other movies he's made: croquetas "Jamón, Jamón" and tortilla "Perdita Durango," for example. It's a warm, stylish bar with an ever-so-slightly pretentious ambience. Comfortable restaurant at the back. See p. 149.

2 Plaza Mayor & Austrias

EXPENSIVE

Asador Frontón ⊕ BASQUE   Brainchild of former top pelota star Miguel Ansorena, this Basque bastion of hearty fare opened in 1980, on the first floor of a building overlooking Tirso de Molina square. As befits Spain's most macho province, the Asador specializes in grilled man-size meat dishes of the highest quality and its *chuletones de buey* (huge beef steak chops) are second to none. No need to be daunted by their size—when served they are cut into strips for two to share. A popular starter is *pimientos del piquillo* (spicy peppers), and fish also features impressively in the form of *rape a la brasa* (grilled angler fish, also shared by two). Finish your meal with the house's own *cuajada* (junket) or *panchineta* (cream-filled puff pastry). Such has been the Frontón's success that it's expanded to two other branches in the northern part of the city, notably in Calle Pedro Mugaruza, near Cuzco, where the menu is even broader.

Plaza Tirso de Molina 7 (entrance via Calle Jesús y María 1). © **91-369-16-17**. Main courses 20€–25€ ($25–$31.25). AE, DC, MC, V. Oct–Apr daily; June–July and Sept Mon–Sat 1–3:30pm, 9–11pm. Closed Aug. Metro: Tirso de Molina.

Julian de Tolosa CASTILIAN   Set in a 19th-century building in the center of Cava Baja, this popular eating spot is renowned for its generous-sized quality steaks. The charming two-level dining area, with its red-brick walls, wooden beamed ceiling, and subtle halogen lighting, occupies the ground floor and basement areas. Maitre d' Angela Halty will guide you through the contents of the succinct menu and its accompanying wine list of full-bodied reds. Supreme highlight is the legendary *chuletón de buey* (huge ox steak—rated as one of the best in Madrid), supported by tasty basics such *alubias rojas de Tolosa* (red Tolosa beans) and *pimientos del piquillo* (baked spicy peppers). Fresh *espárragos* (asparagus) and *cogollos* (lettuce hearts) are summer favorites. Also first rate are the *merluza* (hake) and salty Idiazábal cheese. It's all good but not cheap. Don't forget to check the prices before you order!

Cava Baja 18. © **91-365-82-10**. Main courses 18€–25€ ($22.50–$31.25). AE, DC, MC, V. Mon–Sat 1:30–4pm and 9pm–midnight; Sun 1:30–4pm. Metro: La Latina.

MODERATE

Casa Lucio ⊕ CASTILIAN   Set on a historic street whose edges once marked the perimeter of Old Madrid, this is a venerable *tasca* with all the requisite antique accessories. Dozens of cured hams hang from hand-hewn beams above the well-oiled bar. Among the clientele is a stable of sometimes surprisingly well-known public figures—perhaps even the king of Spain. Here's where Laura Bush lunched with then-president Aznar's wife and Queen Sofía during a state visit to Spain by George W. a couple of years back. The two dining rooms, each on a different floor, have whitewashed walls, tile floors, and exposed brick. A well-trained staff offers classic Castilian food, which might include Jabugo ham with broad beans, shrimp in garlic sauce, hake with green sauce, several types of roasted lamb, and a thick steak served sizzling hot on a heated platter, called *churrasco de la casa*. The gourmet showpiece, however, is a modest *campo* dish called *huevos estrellados*, literally "broken eggs" mixed with potatoes and here raised to a fine art.

Cava Baja 35. ✆ **91-365-32-52**. Reservations recommended. Main courses 15€–22€ ($18.75–27.50). AE, DC, MC, V. Sun–Fri 1–4pm; daily 9pm–midnight. Closed Aug. Metro: La Latina.

El Schotis ✦ SPANISH   El Schotis was established in 1962 on one of Madrid's oldest and most historic streets. A series of large and pleasingly old-fashioned dining rooms is the setting for an animated crowd of Madrileños and foreign visitors, who receive ample portions of conservative, well-prepared vegetables, salads, soups, fish, and above all, meat. Specialties of the house include roast baby lamb, grilled steaks and veal chops, shrimp with garlic, fried hake in green sauce, and traditional desserts. Although one reader found everything but the gazpacho ho-hum, this local favorite pleases thousands of diners annually. There's a bar near the entrance for tapas and before- or after-dinner drinks.

Cava Baja 11. ✆ **91-365-32-30**. Reservations recommended. Main courses 12€–20€ ($15–$25); fixed-price menu 21€ ($26.50). AE, DC, MC, V. Mon–Sat 1–4pm and 8:30pm–midnight; Sun 1–4pm. Metro: Puerta del Sol or La Latina.

La Posada de la Villa SPANISH/GRILLED MEAT   This historic inn founded in 1642 offers a modern, more sanitized version of the earthy, grilled cuisine that fed the stonemasons who built the building's thick walls. Within a trio of dining rooms whose textured plaster and old stonework absolutely reeks of Old Castile, you'll find a hardworking staff and a menu that focuses on a time-honored specialty—roasted baby lamb—that's ordered more often than anything else on the menu. Other excellent choices include different versions of hake, Madrid-style tripe, and the rich, savory stew (*cocido madrileño*) that many local residents remember fondly from the days of their childhood. Notice that many of the chairs have brass plaques bearing the names of famous patrons—I saw one labeled "Janet Jackson" last time!

Cava Baja 9. ✆ **91-366-18-60**. Reservations recommended. Main courses 12€–20€ ($15–$25). DC, MC, V. Daily 1–4pm; Mon–Sat 8pm–midnight. Closed Aug. Metro: La Latina.

Los Galayos ✦✦ SPANISH   Its location is among the most desirable in the city, on a narrow side street about three steps from the arcades of Plaza Mayor. Within two separate houses, the restaurant has flourished on this site since 1894. In summer, cascades of vines accent a series of tables and chairs on the cobblestones outside, perfect for tapas sampling and people-watching. Some visitors consider an evening here among the highlights of their trip to Spain.

The ambience inside evokes Old Castile, with vaulted or beamed ceilings in several dining rooms. The Grande family, your multilingual hosts, prepares traditional versions of fish, shellfish, pork, veal, and beef in time-tested ways. Suckling pig, baby goat, and roasted lamb are almost always featured.

Calle Botoneras 5. ✆ **91-366-30-28**. Reservations recommended. Main courses 10€–25€ ($12.50–$31.25). AE, DC, MC, V. Daily 8:30am–1am. Metro: Puerta del Sol or Tirso de Molina.

Sobrino de Botín ✦✦ SPANISH   Ernest Hemingway made this restaurant famous. In the final two pages of his novel *The Sun Also Rises,* Jake invites Brett to Botín for the Segovian specialty of roast suckling pig, washed down with Rioja Alta.

As you enter, you step back to 1725, the year the restaurant was founded. You'll see an open kitchen with a charcoal hearth, hanging copper pots, an 18th-century tile oven for roasting the suckling pig, and a big pot of soup whose aroma wafts across the tables. Painter Francisco Goya was once a dishwasher here. Your host, Antonio, never loses his cool—even when he has 18 guests standing in line waiting for tables.

The two house specialties are roast suckling pig and roast Segovian lamb. From the a la carte menu, you might try the fish-based "quarter-of-an-hour" soup. Good main dishes include baked Cantabrian hake and filet mignon with potatoes. The dessert list features strawberries (in season) with whipped cream. You can accompany your meal with Valdepeñas or Aragón wine, although most guests order sangria.

Calle de Cuchilleros 17. (©) **91-366-30-26** or 91-366-42-17. Reservations required. Main courses 16€–50€ ($20–$62.50); fixed-price menu 30€ ($37.50). AE, DC, MC, V. Daily 1–4pm and 8pm–midnight. Metro: La Latina or Opera.

INEXPENSIVE

Bar Salamanca *(Finds* CASTILIAN   It's well worth squeezing in to sample the hearty bargain fare at this a small and friendly watering (and eating) hole in the generally pricey Cava Baja. As in any Castilian locale worth its salt, the specialties here range from a full-bodied *cocido* to a variety of roasts, especially lamb. Other prime *raciones* to enjoy include *croquetas* (croquettes), *albóndigas* (meatballs), and *champiñones al cabrales* (mushrooms cooked with strong blue Asturian cheese). The comprehensive wine list covers Riojas, Ribera del Dueros, and Albariños by the glass or bottle.

Cava Baja 31. (©) **91-366-31-10.** Main courses 5€–10€ ($6.25–$12); set lunches 7€–9€ ($8.75–$11.25). No credit cards. Tues–Thurs 1–4pm and 8:30pm–midnight; Fri–Sat 1–4pm and 8:30–1am; Sun 1–4:30pm. Metro: La Latina.

El Cosaco RUSSIAN   One of the few Russian restaurants in Madrid sits adjacent to one of the most charming and evocative squares in town. Inside, you'll find a trio of dining rooms outfitted with paintings and artifacts from the former Soviet Union. Menu items seem to taste best when preceded with something from a long list of vodkas, many of them from small-scale distilleries you might not immediately recognize. Items include rich and savory cold-weather dishes that seem a bit incongruous in the sweltering heat of Madrid, but which you might find as satisfying alternatives to the all-Spanish restaurants in the same neighborhood. Examples include beef Stroganoff; quenelles of pike-perch with fresh dill; and thin-sliced smoked salmon or smoked sturgeon that's artfully arranged with capers, chopped onions, and chopped hard-boiled eggs. Red or white versions of borscht make a worthy starter, and blinis, stuffed with caviar or paprika-laced beef, are always excellent.

Plaza de la Paja 2. (©) **91-365-35-48.** Reservations recommended. Main courses 8€–18€ ($10–$22.50). AE, DC, MC, V. Daily 9pm–midnight; Sat–Sun 1:30–3:30pm. Metro: La Latina.

El Estragón VEGETARIAN   Set beside the Austrias' historic Plaza de la Paja (literally, Square of the Straw), this delightful New Age veggie outpost offers a homely ambience with 20-odd tables set on three levels amid a decor of checkered tablecloths, russet terra-cotta tiles, and plaid curtains. The menu offers an eclectic choice of vegetarian dishes, from a vegetable-filled risotto verde to soy *albóndigas* (meatballs)—even a *cordon bleu* steak that contains no meat (only vegetables). Popular appetizers are almond soup or pepper tart, and few can resist finishing with the delicious homemade chocolate tart with truffles. Unlike most green eating spots, it does in fact also have *pinchos* (kabobs) at the bar. The weekday fixed-lunch menu is good value, but be warned: On weekends it doubles in price. An added bonus for website fanatics is the free Internet access.

Plaza de la Paja or Costanilla de San Andrés 10. © **91-365-89-92.** Main courses 10€–15€ ($12.50–$18.75). Set lunch 12€ ($15). Set dinner 20€ ($25). AE, DC, MC, V. Daily 1:30–5pm; 8:30pm–midnight. Metro: La Latina.

El Viajero INTERNATIONAL   This bustling three-story restaurant is located right on Plaza de la Cebada close to the Rastro market and the labyrinthine lanes of Lavapiés. Grilling is the big thing here with an emphasis on Uruguayan *chorizo* (a sausage of red peppers and pork), *salchichas* (sausages), and beef, but the wide-ranging choice also covers salads, *pinchitos* (shish kabobs), and couscous. Prices are very reasonable, and there's a first-rate prix-fixe menu. Lunch times tend to be packed, and market visitors make it particularly busy on Sundays. On sunny summer days you can eat on the terrace and enjoy the view.

Plaza de la Cebada 11. © **91-366-90-64.** Main courses 5€–18€ ($6.75–$22.50). Prix-fixe lunch 11.50€ ($14.40). AE, DC, MC, V. Tues–Sat 2–4:30pm and 9pm–12:30am; Sun 2–4:30pm. Closed last 2 weeks of Aug. Metro: La Latina.

La Botillería de Maxi MADRILEÑO   A source of endless bad puns from "offally good" to the "offal truth," this genial old-style spit-and-sawdust establishment, located in the quieter lane parallel to Cava Baja, specializes in just that. Offal, or—to be more precise—dishes like *callos* (tripe in a rich sauce) or *entresijos* and *gallinejas* (the latter two are deep-fried lamb's gizzards, *gallinejas* generally being of a slightly higher quality). Acquired tastes or not, there are many who find these essentially *madrileño* dishes delicious from the word go, especially at Maxi's, where you can be sure they're as good as it gets. If the thought of munching internal organs makes you squeamish—however well cooked and presented they may be—then there are the old standby *raciones* of aromatic *jamón Serrano* or pungent *cabrales* cheese to fall back on. And whatever you have you must accompany it with the hearty house red wine.

Cava Alta 21. © **91-365-12-49.** Main courses 7€–14€ ($8.75–$17.50); set lunch Sat–Mon 10€ ($12.50), Tues–Fri 10€ ($12.50). No credit cards. Tues–Sat 1–4pm and 8:30pm–midnight; Sun 12:30–6pm. Metro: La Latina.

La Chata SPANISH   The cuisine here is Castilian, Galician, and northern Spanish. Set behind a heavily ornamented tile facade, the place has a stand-up tapas bar at the entrance and a formal restaurant in a side room. Many locals linger in the darkly paneled bar, which is framed by hanging Serrano hams, cloves of garlic, and photographs of bullfighters. Full meals might include roast suckling pig, roast lamb, *calamares en su tinta* (squid in its own ink), grilled filet of steak with peppercorns, or omelets flavored with strips of eel.

Cava Baja 24. © **91-366-14-58.** Reservations recommended. Main dishes 12€–18€ ($15–$22.50). AE, MC, V. Thurs–Mon 12:30–5pm; daily 8pm–1am. Metro: La Latina.

Malacatín *(finds)* MADRILEÑO   Tucked away in a narrow street off the Plaza Cascorro, a stone's throw from the Rastro market, is this tiny century-old slice of old *castizo* Madrid. It's a tiny taberna where you sit on benches at basic wooden trestle tables and enjoy the place's one and only main dish: *cocido*. A very reasonably priced set menu includes wine (usually Valdepeñas) and dessert. If you feel like a tapa beforehand you can sample *morcillas de León* (blood sausage from León) or *bacalao frito* (fried cod) at the bar—or a *caldo* (consommé) in cold weather—but don't forget to leave room for the prodigious main meal. As there are only two sittings—both at lunchtime—you'll need to be prepared for a siesta afterward anyway. Reservations at least 1 day beforehand are essential.

Calle de la Rueda 5. ℭ **91-365-52-41.** Set lunch 20€ ($25). Mon–Sat 1:30–4:30pm (seatings at 2:30 and 3:30pm). No credit cards. Closed July–Aug. Metro: La Latina.

Masaniello ITALIAN   This warmly hospitable rustic-style *trattoria* (named after a Naples revolutionary) is a lone unexpected outpost of Italian color in the midst of Cava Baja's proliferation of tabernas, wine bars, and former coaching houses transformed into atmospheric *castizo* restaurants. Here *pasta* instead of *cocido* rules the day and you can enjoy real pizzas cooked in a genuine pizza oven by an Italian chef. The honest, down-to-earth Napoletana is a solid favorite, but under owner Luigi Fabriccini's guiding hand other more innovative specialties also fill the menu—among them, *parmesana de berengena* (eggplant cooked in Parmesan cheese), *calzone, pappardelle,* or *spaghetti mare e monte.* Accompany your meal with a fine Chianti and end with the marvelous homemade *tiramisu,* if you have room (not forgetting a fiery *grappa* or *zambuca* with your espresso if you want the full treatment).

Cava Baja 28. ℭ **91-364-54-86.** Main courses 8€–16€ ($10–$20). DC, MC, V. Sept–June Tues 9pm–1am, Wed–Sun 2–4pm, and 9pm–1am; July Tues–Sun 9pm–1am. Closed Aug. Metro: La Latina.

Viuda de Vacas ⚜ *Finds* CASTILIAN   Cross the threshold of this beloved Madrileño taberna, tucked away in a tranquil corner of the Austrias district, and you're back in another age. The central zinc bar top, tiny coal-fueled fireplace, and creaky spiral stairway to the first floor tell you this is one central eating spot that trendy "renovators" have not managed to get their hands on. The building dates from the late 18th-century and owes its mood of uncompromising period charm to the friendly Casanova family, now in their third generation of ownership. The place is especially popular with chic 30-somethings (be prepared for a lively atmosphere as the evening progresses). Service is informal, and ultratiled walls and basic wooden tables complete the unspoiled *castizo* setting. Inventive dishes, accompanied by an excellent-value *Jumilla* house wine, are the order of the day. After a starter of *calabacines gratinados* (baked zucchini cooked in garlic, onions, and parsley and covered with grated cheese), *berengenas a la crema* (eggplant in a wine-based creamy sauce), or *pimientos del padrón* (hot chunky green peppers), you might follow up with a hearty *rabo de toro* (braised bull's tail cooked in thyme and garlic), *dorada al horno* (sea bream baked in oil, white wine, parsley, and bread crumbs), *gallina en pepitoria* (cockerel in almond-butter sauce), or *codornices rellenos de foie gras y setas* (quail stuffed with foie gras and mushrooms). Round off the meal with delicious homemade *natillas* or egg custard.

Cava Alta 23. ℭ **91-366-58-47.** Reservations recommended. Main courses 10€–17.50€ ($12.50–$21.90). MC, V. Mon–Wed, Fri–Sat 1:30–4:30pm and 9:30pm–midnight; Sun 1:30–4:30pm. Closed last 2 weeks of Sept. Metro: La Latina.

3 Puerta del Sol

VERY EXPENSIVE

La Terraza del Casino ⚜⚜⚜ SPANISH/INTERNATIONAL   The city's most imaginative chef, Ferran Adrià, isn't in Madrid. He's still tending those pots and pans in the little town of Roses near Girona in Catalonia. But the innovative master of cuisine created all the dishes on the menu here and flies in regularly to see that his cooks are following his orders. His luxe restaurant in Madrid lies on the top floor of the Casino in Madrid, a historical building and a former gentlemen's club with a history going back to 1910. Even the grand dons of those days surely didn't dine as well as you can today.

Adrià's dishes are exquisite, and food critics (and I concur) are always writing about taste "explosions" in your mouth. His Catalan restaurant is El Bulli, meaning "innovative" in Spanish. The same name could apply to this Madrid dining hot spot that provides a panoramic view of the heart of Madrid and can be reached by an elevator or up a sweeping 19th-century staircase designed to impress. The decor is classically restrained with high ceilings and crystal chandeliers. The exquisite food uses fresh seasonal ingredients and reinterprets Spanish dishes. An example is *raya* (skate) in oil and saffron with parsley purée and nuts on a bed of finely diced fries. More traditional dishes include the succulent *merluza a la gallega* (Galician hake), *crema de la fabada asturiana* (creamed Asturian bean soup), and the steeply priced *jamón Jabugo* (cured ham from acorn-fed pigs) served with a *menestra* (mixed vegetables) al dente. Only French champagne and Spanish wines are listed, and one of the best is the rounded woody red, the Ribera del Duero from the province of Valladolid.

Alcalá 15. ☏ **91-521-87-00.** www.casinodemadrid.es. Main courses 25€–35€ ($31.25–$43.75); fixed-price menu 70€ ($87.50). AE, DC, MC, V. Mon–Fri 1–3:30pm and 9–11:30pm; Sat 9–11:30pm. Closed Aug. Metro: Sevilla.

Lhardy ☏☏ SPANISH/INTERNATIONAL   This is Madrid's longest-running culinary act. Lhardy has been a Madrileño legend since opening in 1839 as a gathering place for the city's literati and political leaders. At street level is what may be the most elegant snack bar in Spain. Within a dignified antique setting of marble and hardwood, cups of steaming consommé are dispensed from silver samovars into delicate porcelain cups, and rows of croquettes, tapas, and sandwiches are served to stand-up clients who pay for their food at a cashier's kiosk near the entrance. The ground-floor deli and takeout service is open daily from 9am to 3pm and 5 to 9:30pm.

The real culinary skill of the place, however, is on Lhardy's second floor, where you'll find a formal restaurant decorated in the ornate Belle Epoque style of Isabel Segunda. Specialties of the house include fish, pork, veal, tripe in a garlicky tomato and onion wine sauce, and *cocido,* the celebrated chickpea stew of Madrid. *Soufflé sorpresa* (baked Alaska) is the dessert specialty.

Carrera de San Jerónimo 8. ☏ **91-521-33-85.** Reservations recommended in the upstairs dining room. Main courses 14€–25€ ($17.50–$31.25). AE, DC, MC, V. Mon–Sat 1–3:30pm and 8:30–11pm. Closed Aug. Metro: Puerta del Sol.

EXPENSIVE

Caripén ☏ FRENCH   This restaurant stands in a historic district near the Royal Opera House and the Spanish Senate. It was once El Tablao, the flamenco club of Lola Flores, one of the most famous of all Spanish dancers. Its Art Deco decor has been restored, and instead of flamenco, you get the inspired French bistro cookery of Daniel Boute. The restaurant is especially popular with the Madrid locals, or *gatos* (cats), because it serves until 3am when most other quality establishments are shuttered. (Local residents are called *gatos* because they like to roam about at night.) Go for the *mejillones de roca* (mussels in white wine and cream sauce), a perfectly prepared steak tartare, *foie* with *setas* (duck liver and mushrooms), or skate in black butter. You can finish off with such desserts as tiramisu, freshly made fruit tarts, or crepes.

Plaza de la Marina Española 4. ☏ **91-541-11-77.** Reservations recommended on weekends. Main courses 15€–22.50€ ($18.75–$28). MC, V. Mon–Sat 9pm–3am. Closed Aug. Metro: Opera/Santo Domingo.

La Esquina del Real FRENCH   Next to the Teatro Real you'll find this restaurant in an impressive 17th-century building with an ancient stone facade, thick granite walls, and the original wooden beams supporting old ceilings. This place has a sophisticated atmosphere, yet prices are very reasonable. One Madrid food critic recently called this spot one of the city's "best kept" culinary secrets. The hospitable owner and chef, Marcel Magossian, extends a hearty welcome to patrons and feeds them well. Fresh ingredients are transformed into tasty concoctions, like large prawns with a delicate flavoring of raspberry vinaigrette or roast oxtail with mashed potatoes and fresh mushrooms. A rather common dish, veal fricassee in mushroom sauce, is transformed into something sublime here. To end your repast, you might opt for a combination platter of warm cheese, tarte tatin, or ice cream with a crunchy caramel sauce flambéed at your table.

Calle de la Unión 8. ℂ 91-559-43-09. Reservations recommended on weekends. Main courses 25€–34€ ($31.25–$42.50). AE, MC, V. Mon–Fri 2–4pm and 9pm–midnight; Sat 9pm–midnight. Closed last 2 weeks of Aug. Metro: Opera.

MODERATE

Café de Oriente FRENCH/SPANISH   The Oriente is a cafe-and-restaurant complex, the cafe being one of the most popular in Madrid. From the cafe tables on its terrace, there's a spectacular view of the Palacio Real (Royal Palace) and the Teatro Real. The dining rooms—Castilian upstairs, French Basque downstairs—are frequented by royalty and diplomats. Typical of the refined cuisine are vichyssoise, fresh vegetable flan, and many savory meat and fresh-fish offerings. Service is excellent. Most visitors, however, patronize the cafe, trying if possible to get an outdoor table. The cafe is decorated in turn-of-the-20th-century style, with banquettes and regal paneling, as befits its location. Pizza, tapas, and drinks (including Irish, Viennese, Russian, and Jamaican coffees) are served.

Plaza de Oriente 2. ℂ 91-541-39-74. Reservations recommended in restaurant only. Restaurant main courses 15€–24€ ($18.75–$30); cafe tapas 3.60€–7.25€ ($4.50–$9.05), coffee 4€ ($5). AE, DC, MC, V. Daily 1–4pm and 9pm–midnight. Metro: Opera.

Casa Ciriaco CASTILIAN   In business for more than 90 years, this longtime favorite taberna-cum-restaurant is still run by the same family. Lying only 2 blocks from the Palacio Real, it has on occasion served dinners to members of the royal family and other impressive guests, among them bullfighters, artists, and scholars. These distinguished diners are drawn to the unpretentious family atmosphere and the time-tested recipes. Nouvelle cuisine here means anything served in 1900, including the classic Madrid tripe, an acquired taste for many diners. One of the most enticing offerings is *perdiz* (partridge) served with fava beans. Hare is another good choice, served here with white beans. A good appetizer is a plate of the grilled prawns, or start with one of the hearty soups of the day, including a specialty of Castile: *sopa castellana* (seafood soup). A few fish dishes appear, including mountain trout, and *conchinillo asado* (roast suckling pig) is a specialty. Wash everything down with a glass of Toledo wine.

Calle Mayor 84. ℂ 91-559-50-66. Reservations recommended. Main courses 12€–24€ ($15–$30). MC, V. Thurs–Tues 1–4:30pm and 8pm–12:30am. Closed Aug. Metro: Sol.

Cornucopia EURO-AMERICAN   Set on a narrow side street adjacent to the medieval Plaza de Descalzas Reales, this restaurant occupies the mezzanine level of what was originally a 19th-century private palace. Its glamour and allure derive from its ownership by four partners, two of whom (Jennifer Cole and her cohort, Kimberly Manning) are American; the others are French-born François and Spanish-born Fernando. Set inside a pair of elegant and airy dining rooms whose gleaming parquet floors remain from the original decor, the restaurant displays frequently changing paintings, all available for sale. Menu items include mussels with fennel and a roasted red pepper sauce over black fettuccine, grilled baby hen with mushrooms and sherry sauce, and grilled pork tenderloin stuffed with brie and bacon and served with a pome-granate-apple compote and a red wine reduction sauce. Desserts are sumptuous and might include a dollop of such original homemade ice creams as *mojito*. Named after the classic Cuban cocktail, it's flavored with mint, lemon, and rum. The food is well pre-pared, the ingredients are fresh, and the staff is among the most welcoming in Madrid.

Calle Flora 1. ℃ **91-547-64-65.** Reservations recommended. Main courses 9€–18€ ($11.25–$22.50); fixed-price lunch (Tues–Sat only) 10€ ($12.50). AE, DC, MC, V. Tues–Sat 1:30-4pm; Tues–Sun 9pm–1:30am Closed 1 week in Aug. Metro: Opera or Callao.

Donzoko JAPANESE   Now in its third decade, the Donzoko is one of Madrid's longest established Japanese eating spots. Its location on lively Echegaray street makes it particularly popular with party-going groups of young clientele, as does the monu-mental menu, which covers every everything from sushi to sukiyaki (veal strips with wok-cooked vegetables for two; often viewed by Madrileños as a Nipponese version of their *cocido*). Sashimi and prawn tempura also grace the list, and of course *sake* (rice wine) is the appropriate drink for the occasion. Decor is functional to weird—you're greeted by a metal water fountain on the small entrance patio—and the service is attentively cool.

Calle Echegaray 3. ℃ **91-429-57-20.** Main courses 10€–25€ ($12.50–$31.25). AE, DC, MC, V. Mon–Sat 1:30–3:30pm and 8:30–11:30pm. Metro: Sevilla.

Platerías Comedor SPANISH   One of the most charming dining rooms in Madrid, Platerías Comedor has richly brocaded walls evocative of 19th-century Spain. Busy socializing may take place on the plaza outside, but this serene oasis makes few concessions to the new generation in its food, decor, or formally attired waiters. Spe-cialties include beans with clams, stuffed partridge with cabbage and sausage, duck liver with white grapes, tripe a la Madrid, veal stew with snails and mushrooms, and guinea hen with figs and plums. Follow up any of these with the passion-fruit sorbet. Many restaurants have sprouted up in recent years that serve better food, but Platerías Comedor continues to thrive as a culinary tradition—its old-fashioned atmosphere is hard to come by.

Plaza de Santa Ana 11. ℃ **91-429-70-48.** Reservations recommended. Main courses 12€–18€ ($15–$22.50). AE, DC, MC, V. Tues-Sat 1:30–4pm and 8:30pm–midnight; Sat 9pm–midnight. Metro: Sol.

Taberna del Alabardero BASQUE/SPANISH   In close proximity to the Royal Palace, this little Spanish classic is known for its selection of tasty tapas, ranging from squid cooked in wine to fried potatoes dipped in hot sauce. Photographs of famous former patrons, including Nelson Rockefeller and the race-car driver Jackie Stewart, line the walls. The restaurant in the rear is said to be one of the city's best-kept secrets. Decorated in typical tavern style, it serves a savory Spanish and Basque cuisine with market-fresh ingredients.

Felipe V 6. ℃ **91-547-25-77.** Reservations required for restaurant only. Bar: tapas 2.90€–9€ ($3.60–$15); glass of house wine 1.80€ ($2.25). Restaurant: main courses 14€–20€ ($18–$25). AE, DC, MC, V. Daily 8am–1am. Metro: Opera.

INEXPENSIVE

Casa Labra SPANISH/TAPAS   Founded in 1860 and run by the Molina family for the past 6 decades, the mellow brown-walled Casa Labra is located a mere stone's throw from the Puerta del Sol. Said to have started as a favorite meeting spot of the 19th-century socialist party, it's one of the center's oldest and most popular tapa bars, invariably crowded and full of atmosphere. Of the many tidbits on offer, the delicious deep-fried cod croquettes (croquetas de bacalao) are a must, accompanied by the house's modestly priced Valdepeñas wine. The adjoining restaurant provides a more relaxed and secluded eating experience and is priced accordingly.

Tetuan 12 (✆) **91-532-14-05.** Tapas 2€–3€ ($2.50–$3.75). Main courses 12€–20€ ($15–$25). Daily 9:30am–3:30pm, 6–11pm. Metro: Sol.

Comme-Bio VEGETARIAN

This restaurant opened in 2001 with two branches, one in the central Calle Mayor and the other in Chamberí district. Each serves soups, seitanes, risottos, and pastries (as well as some tempting nonvegetarian "biological" meat dishes)—complete with an additional special kiddie menu—in a bright open buffet dining area with large windows, a terrace, and a special air-conditioned section for smokers. The adjoining shop dispenses a comprehensive range of organic products—right down to ecologically approved pet food!

Mayor 30. (✆) **91-354-63-22.** Main courses 8€–20€ ($10–$25); buffet lunch 12€ ($15). DC, MC, V. Daily 1:30–4pm and 8:30pm–midnight. Metro: Sol.

Delfos GREEK

Located right in the heart of town, this is one of Madrid's smartest Greek eating spots, offering the full gamut of Hellenic fare and then some. The atmosphere is friendly and the taberna-style decor gets you in the right mood to enjoy the food. Pikalia megali is the ideal full-bodied appetizer, combining many familiar Greek tidbits on a single platter including taramasalata, tzatziki, black olives, feta cheese, and dolmades (stuffed grape leaves). The Hellenes' favorite meat, lamb, scores highly here: Try the delicious Delfos version cooked with nuts and honey. Anise-flavored ouzo is the ideal aperitif to kick off with and for those who've acquired the taste, the tangy resinated white wine, retsina, accompanies the meal to perfection. Though it is deceptively quaffable, beware: In sufficient quantities it packs quite a kick.

Cuesta de Santo Domingo 14. (✆) **91-548-37-64.** Main courses 8€–16€ ($10–$20); set lunch 10€ ($13). AE, DC, MC, V. Tues–Sun 1:30–4:30pm and 8pm–2:30am. Metro: Santo Domingo.

Finca de Susana (Finds) SPANISH/INTERNATIONAL

Set on a quiet street close to Alcalá and a short walk from the Puerta del Sol, this airy, open-plan restaurant with bright, modern decor offers a winning combination of inventive quality cuisine and highly affordable prices. Vegetables in tempura batter and an exceptional choice of rice and fish dishes head the individual specialties, and the desserts are simple and delicious. Service is smart and efficient, and best value is its set weekday lunch. Understandably, it's a popular place, so you should plan to dine here earlier than the usual Spanish hours—there's no booking ahead and queues soon gather, especially at lunchtime.

Calle Arlaban 4. (✆) **91-369-35-57.** Main courses 6€–12€ ($7.50–$15); set lunch 8€ ($10). AE, DC, MC, V. Daily 1–3:45pm and 8:30–11:45pm. Metro: Sevilla.

Museo del Jamón SPANISH/TAPAS

The displays on the walls of this unique establishment explain the bewildering name: "The Museum of Ham." As in an art exhibition, large amounts of different kinds of hams—cured by a variety of methods—hang from the ceilings. The popular chorizos are hooked in rows reminiscent of one of those scenes in Golden Age paintings. This is indeed a real museum of the most celebrated fast food in Spain. On certain nights, the tavern offers live entertainment in the dining area upstairs, often a guitarist. The paella for two is reasonably priced. The aged *jamón Serrano* is a great delicacy, now highly prized at tapas bars throughout Spain, Europe, and North America. You might try it in small sandwiches known as *bocattas* or as an always-available tapa. The daily menu is varied and served in generous portions. Service is efficient, though not too friendly, but customers don't seem to mind.

Carrera de San Jerónimo 6 (1 block east of Puerta del Sol). © **91-521-03-46.** *Menú del día* 8€–12€ ($10–$15); *platos combinados* 3€–5€ ($3.75–$6.25). MC, V. Daily 9am–12:30am. Metro: Sol.

4 On or near the Gran Vía

EXPENSIVE

Arce *✦* BASQUE   Arce has brought some of the best modern interpretations of Basque cuisine to Madrid, thanks to the enthusiasm of owner/chef Iñaki Camba and his wife, Theresa. Within a comfortably decorated dining room, you can enjoy dishes made of the finest ingredients using flavors designed to dominate your taste buds. Examples include a salad of fresh scallops and an oven-baked casserole of fresh boletus mushrooms, seasoned lightly so that the woodsy vegetable taste comes through. Look for unusual preparations of hake and seasonal variations of such game dishes as pheasant and woodcock.

Augusto Figueroa 32. © **91-522-59-13.** Reservations recommended. Main courses 18€–38€ ($23–$48). AE, DC, MC, V. Mon–Fri 1:30–4pm; Mon–Sat 9pm–midnight. Closed the week before Easter and Aug 15–31. Metro: Chueca.

La Barraca VALENCIAN   La Barraca is like a country inn right off the Gran Vía, and it's a longtime local favorite. The food, frankly, used to be better, but perhaps my tastes have changed since my student days. This Valencian-style restaurant is a well-managed establishment recommended for its tasty Levante cooking. There are four different dining rooms, three of which lie one flight above street level; they're colorfully cluttered with ceramics, paintings, photographs, Spanish lanterns, flowers, and local artifacts. The house specialty, paella a la Barraca, is made with pork and chicken. Specialties in the appetizer category include *desgarrat* (a salad of cod and red peppers), mussels in a white-wine sauce, and shrimp sautéed with garlic. In addition to the recommended paella, you can select at least 16 rice dishes, including black rice and queen paella. Main-dish specialties include brochette of angler and prawns and rabbit with *fines herbes*. Lemon-and-vodka sorbet brings the meal to a fitting finish.

Reina 29–31. © **91-532-71-54.** Reservations recommended. Main courses 12€–25€ ($15–$31). AE, DC, MC, V. Daily 1–4pm and 8:30pm–midnight. Metro: Gran Vía or Sevilla. Bus: 1, 2, or 74.

INEXPENSIVE

Gula Gula INTERNATIONAL   Don't go here if you want a quiet meal for two. Situated on a first floor in a prominent Gran Vía locale and enjoying unexpectedly good views, this place is brash and noisy: ideal for party animals and out-on-the-town revelers. Stag or hen parties may be at the neighboring table, and the background music is either unrestrained disco or a singing act performed by resident drag queens. Leather-clad waiters keep the mood going, and the no-limits-on-how-much-you-eat buffet, including one hot dish and a plentiful salad, is very reasonable. Or you can opt for a salad only or a special dish such as *rocambola de gambas* (shrimp extravaganza).

Gran Vía 1. © **91-522-87-64.** Lunch buffet 11.50€ ($14); dinner buffet 17.50€ ($22). AE, DC, MC, V. Sun–Wed 1–4:30pm and 9:30–11:30pm; Thurs–Sat 1–4:30pm and 9:30pm–2:30am. Metro: Sevilla.

Mesón las Descalzas SPANISH   Las Descalzas, a recommended tavern-style restaurant, has a massive tapas bar that's often crowded at night. Behind a glass-and-wood screen is the restaurant section, its specialties including kidneys with sherry, *sopa castellana* (seafood soup), Basque-style hake, crayfish, shrimp, oysters, clams, and paella with shellfish. There is folk music for entertainment.

Postigo San Martín 3. ⓒ **91-522-72-17.** Reservations recommended. Main courses 12€–18€ ($15–$23); fixed-price menu 10€ ($13). AE, DC, MC, V. Daily 1–4pm and 8pm–midnight. Metro: Callao.

Paellería Valenciana VALENCIAN   This lunch-only restaurant ranks as one of the best values in the city. The specialty is paella, which you must order by phone in advance. Once you arrive, you might begin with a homemade soup or the house salad, and then follow with the rib-sticking paella, served in an iron skillet for two or more only. Among the desserts, the chef's special pride is razor-thin orange slices flavored with rum, coconut, sugar, honey, and raspberry sauce. A carafe of house wine comes with the set menu, and after lunch the owner comes around dispensing free cognac.

Caballero de Gracia 12. ⓒ **91-531-17-85.** Reservations recommended. Main courses 9.50€–20€ ($12–$25). AE, MC, V. Mon–Sat 1:30–4:30pm. Metro: Gran Vía.

5 Plaza de las Cortes & Huertas

MODERATE

Casa Alberto CASTILIAN   One of the oldest *tascas* in the neighborhood, Casa Alberto dates from 1827 and has thrived ever since. On the street level of a house where Miguel de Cervantes lived briefly in 1614, it contains an appealing mixture of bullfighting memorabilia, engravings, and reproductions of Old Masters paintings. Many visitors opt only for the tapas, continually replenished from platters on the bar, but a sit-down dining area offers more substantial meals. Specialties include fried squid, shellfish in vinaigrette sauce, chorizo in cider sauce, and several versions of baked or roasted lamb.

Huertas 18. ⓒ **91-429-93-56.** Reservations recommended. Main courses 12€–21€ ($15–$26). AE, DC, MC, V. Tues–Sat 1–4pm; Tues–Sun 8:30pm–midnight. Metro: Antón Martín.

Casa Paco ⓐⓐ STEAK   Madrileños defiantly name Casa Paco, just beside the Plaza Mayor, when someone dares to denigrate Spanish steaks. They know that here you can get the thickest, juiciest, tastiest steaks in Spain, priced according to weight. Señor Paco sears his steaks in boiling oil before serving them on plates so hot that the almost-raw meat continues to cook, preserving the natural juices. Located in the Old Town, this two-story restaurant has three dining rooms, but reservations are imperative. If you face a long wait, sample the tapas at the bar in front. Around the walls are autographed photographs of notables.

Casa Paco isn't just a steakhouse; you can start with fish soup and proceed to grilled sole or baby lamb, or try *Casa Paco cocido,* the house version of Madrid's famous chickpea and pork soup. As tempting as the fresh shellfish looks, it is sold at no set price but "at market rates," which change from day to day. The bill for your appetizers might equal the national budget for Nepal. You might top it off with one of the luscious desserts, but Paco no longer serves coffee. It made customers linger, keeping tables occupied while potential patrons had to be turned away.

Plaza Puerta Cerrada 11. ⓒ **91-366-31-66.** Reservations required. Main courses 12€–20€ ($15–$25); fixed-price menu 27€ ($34). DC, MC, V. Mon–Sat 1–4pm and 8:30pm–midnight. Closed Aug. Metro: Sol, Opera, or La Latina. Bus: 3, 21, or 65.

Champagnería Gala MEDITERRANEAN   This restaurant makes its reputation on its Catalan paellas but also on *fideuàs,* which is similar to the more famous rice dish except noodles are used instead. The waiters will offer you a choice of more than a dozen *fideuàs* or paellas ranging from *negra* (cooked in squid's ink) to *vasca* (with traditional *bacalao,* or cod, with clams and leeks). Run by a group of women, the restaurant has an airy, inviting setting that is partially grass covered and includes a plant-filled patio. It's found on a little back street near the Reina Sofía and Calle Atocha. Regional bean stews and other items round out the menu. But most visitors come here just to sample the paellas or *fideuàs,* which can be meat, half-meat, half-fish, or else with just beef, seafood, or chicken—your choice. In-the-know diners consume their meals with *cava,* the sparkling wine of Catalonia. At the end of the meal, you'll be expected to drink dessert wine from a *porrón,* a traditional "drinking bottle" rather than a glass.

Moratín 22, Santa Ana. ✆ **91-429-25-62.** Reservations required. Main courses 10€–15€ ($13–$19). No credit cards. Daily 1–4:30pm and 9:30–11pm. Metro: Antón Martín.

Do Salmon (*Value*) GALICIAN   As the name implies, this is a predominantly seafood restaurant offering good solid *gallego* specialties such as *pulpo a la feira* (octopus cooked in olive oil and with paprika sauce) as well as national favorites like *lenguado en salsa tartare* (grilled sole in rich tartar sauce). Hearty meat dishes also feature on the menu, and for carnivores I recommend the traditional *codillo con grelos* (ham knuckle with turnip tops). The service is quietly impersonal and the decor unspectacular— verging on mid-1950s drab—but the quality of the food is what counts. Portions are generous (no measly nouvelle cuisine rationing here) and prices extremely reasonable, which is why the place has a staunch band of loyal regulars.

Calle León 4. ✆ **91-429-39-52.** Main courses 8€–18€ ($10–$23); set lunch (Tues–Fri only) 11.50€ ($14). AE, MC, V. Tues–Sun 1–4pm and 9pm–midnight. Closed mid-Aug to mid-Sept. Metro: Antón Martín.

El Caldero (*Finds*) MURCIAN   Set on the narrow pedestrianized Huertas street, this is probably the only restaurant in Madrid specializing in dishes from the little-known Levante province of Murcia. It was founded 30 years ago by Antonio Valero and is now run by his son Alfredo, who provides the same high standard of marine cuisine. As with its more famous neighbor Valencia, Murcia's regional specialty is rice, served here in a variety of dishes headed by *paella* and *arroz al caldero* (rice cooked in seafood and shellfish stock). The fish in general is excellent, especially the *dorada a la sal* (gilthead bream cooked in salt), and fresh Levantine vegetables also feature prominently on the menu in dishes such as *verduras a la piedra.* Its prize *postre* (dessert), *tocino del cielo* (a light pudding made with egg yolk and syrup), is mouthwateringly delicious. The favorite beverage to swig down with these culinary delights is *sangría de cava* (champagne sangria).

Calle Huertas 15. ✆ **91-429-50-44.** Main courses 12€–25€ ($15–$31). AE, DC, MC, V. Daily 1:30–4pm; Tues–Sat 9pm–midnight. Closed mid-Aug to mid-Sept. Metro: Antón Martín.

El Cenador del Prado (*Finds*) MEDITERRANEAN   Founded by brothers Ramón and Tomás Herranz 2 decades back, this eccentrically beautiful eating spot is like no other in Madrid. In the anteroom, an attendant will check your coat into an elaborately carved armoire before the maitre d' ushers you into one of a trio of rooms. Two of the rooms have cove moldings, English furniture, and floor-to-ceiling gilded mirrors. A third room is ringed with lattices and flooded with sun from a skylight. Bright maroon and orange walls and glittering chandeliers create a modernist-cum-baroque mood.

The main dining area basks in a glass-domed conservatory setting, while the small private adjoining salon has the air of an 18th-century *palacete*. Cuisine is a blend of Hispanic and Middle East Mediterranean with exquisite entrees like hummus with peppers and superb main fish courses such as *rodaballo con leche merengada* (turbot cooked in cinnamon-flavored milk). You might also enjoy such specialties as crepes with salmon and Iranian caviar, a salad of red peppers and salted anchovies, a casserole of snails and oysters with mushrooms, a ceviche of salmon and shellfish, potato-leek soup studded with tidbits of hake and clams, sea bass with candied lemons, veal scaloppine stuffed with asparagus and garlic sprouts, or medallions of venison served with pepper-and-fig chutney. The fixed *menú de degustación* is very good value.

Calle del Prado 4. ℱ 91-429-15-61. Reservations recommended. Main courses 13€–25€ ($16–$31); fixed-price menu 25€ ($31); vegetarian menu 20€ ($25). AE, DC, MC, V. Mon–Fri 1:45–4pm; Mon–Sat 9pm–midnight. Closed Aug 12–19. Metro: Sevilla or Antón Martín.

Errota-Zar BASQUE   Next to the House of Deputies and the Zarzuela Theater, Errota-Zar means "old mill," a nostalgic reference to the Basque country, home of the Olano family, owners of the restaurant.

A small bar at the entrance displays a collection of fine cigars and wines, and the blue-painted walls are adorned with paintings of Basque landscapes. The restaurant has only about two dozen tables, which can easily fill up. The Basque country is long known as the gastronomic capital of Spain, and Errota-Zar provides a fine showcase for its cuisine.

Try such appetizers as the rare tolosa kidney bean or fried anchovies. Many Basques begin their meal with a *tortilla de bacalao* (salt cod omelet). For main dishes, sample the delights of *chuletón de buey* (oxtail), along with grilled vegetables, or *kokotxas de merluza en aceite* (the cheeks of the hake fish cooked in virgin olive oil). Hake cheeks may not sound appetizing, but Spaniards and many foreigners praise this dish. You might opt instead for *foie al Pedro Jiménez* (duck liver grilled and served with a sweet wine sauce). The best homemade desserts are *cuajada de la casa*, a thick yogurt made from sheep's milk, or *tarta de limón*, a lemon cake. You might also try rice ice cream in prune sauce.

Jovellanos 3, 1st floor. ℱ 91-531-25-64. Reservations recommended. Main courses 18€–22€ ($23–$28); *menú completo* 30€ ($38). AE, DC, MC, V. Mon–Sat 1–4pm and 9pm–midnight. Closed last half of Aug. Metro: Banco España or Sevilla.

Ginza Sushi Restaurant JAPANESE   This favorite Oriental eating spot is located just opposite the Palaca Hotel and around the corner from the Thyssen museum. You can choose between a self-service bar if you're in a hurry and a sit-down restaurant if you want to take your time and relax. The specialty in both is sushi, of course, and the fish is first rate. Vegetable dishes such as tempura are also highly recommended

Plaza de las Cortes 3. ℱ 91-429-76-19. Main courses 10€–25€ ($13–$31). AE, DC, MC, V. Tues–Sun lunch and dinner. Metro: Banco de Espana.

La Biotika *(Finds* VEGETARIAN   Vegetarian cuisine doesn't get a lot of attention in most Madrid restaurants, but this discovery is a rare exception. Opening east of the landmark Plaza Santa Ana, it is intimate and charming. It serves the capital's best macrobiotic vegetarian cuisine, and does so exceedingly well. I always begin with one of the homemade soups, which are made fresh daily, and then have one of the large, fresh salads. The bread is also made fresh daily. One specialty is a "meatball without meat" (made with vegetables but shaped like a meatball). Tofu with zucchini and many other offerings appear daily.

Amor de Dios 3. ✆ 91-429-07-80. Main courses 6€–10€ ($7.50–$13). *Menú del día* 8€–9.50€ ($10-12). No credit cards. Daily 1–4pm and 8–11pm. Metro: Antón Martín.

La Trucha SPANISH   With its Andalusian tavern ambience, La Trucha boasts a street-level bar and small dining room with arched ceiling and whitewashed walls. The decor is made festive with hanging braids of garlic, dried peppers, and onions. On the lower level the walls of a second bustling area are covered with eye-catching antiques, bullfight notices, and other bric-a-brac. There's a complete a la carte menu including *trucha* (trout), *verbenas de ahumados* (a selection of smoked delicacies), a glorious stew called *fabada* (made with beans, Galician ham, black sausage, and smoked bacon), and a *comida casera rabo de toro* (home-style oxtail). No one should miss nibbling on the *tapas variadas* in the bar.

If this branch turns out to be too crowded, there's another **Trucha** at Núñez de Arce 6 (✆ **91-532-08-82**).

Manuel Fernández González 3. ✆ **91-429-58-33.** Reservations recommended. Main courses 15€–30€ ($19–$38). AE, MC, V. Daily 12:30–4pm and 7:30pm–midnight. Metro: Antón Martín or Sevilla.

Tocororo CUBAN   This is Madrid's finest Cuban restaurant. The nostalgia is evident in the pictures of old Havana and in the paintings of famous artists such as Lam y Mattos adorning the walls. The wait staff is as lively as the pop Cuban music playing on the stereo. The dishes are typical Caribbean dishes, such as *ceviche* (marinated fish), *ropa vieja* (shredded meat served with black beans and rice), or lobster enchilada. If you prefer a simpler repast, try a selection of *empanadas y tamales* (fried potato pastries and plantain dough filled with onions and ground meat). Special cocktails of the house include *mojito* (rum, mint, and a hint of sugar) and daiquiris. In winter there is live Cuban music. With a discreet but pleasant ambience, this restaurant is located in the zone of *La Marcha* (most of the bars and discos are in this area).

Calle del Prado 3 (at the corner of Echegaray). ✆ **91-369-40-00.** Reservations required Thurs–Sat. Main courses 13€–18€ ($16–$23); fixed-price menu 10€ ($13). AE, DC, MC, V. Tues–Wed 1:30–4pm and 8:30pm–midnight; Thurs–Sun 1:30–4pm and 8:30pm–1:30am. Closed last 2 weeks Feb and last week Sept. Metro: Sevilla.

INEXPENSIVE

Artemisa VEGETARIAN   There are two branches of this very popular and established vegetarian establishment. The most popular is probably this modern and simply decorated eating spot in the heart of bohemian Huertas parallel to Calle Echegaray. For starters try the inventive *crema de ortiga* (nettle cream), *sopa de menta y calabacín* (mint and pumpkin soup), or *quiche de puerros* (leek quiche). Main courses include an excellent vegetarian paella, and you can sip an "ecological" wine with your meal. Choose from over 20 different versions of herbals teas to accompany your dessert (give the *pastel persa*, Persian pastry, a try). A second branch is located at Tres Cruces 4 (✆ **91-521-87-21;** Metro: Callao).

Ventura de la Vega 4. ✆ **91-429-50-93.** Main courses 9€–12€ ($11–$15); set menu 10.50€ ($13). AE, DC, MC, V. Daily 1:30–4pm and 9pm–midnight. Metro: Sevilla.

La Vaca Verónica ARGENTINE   "Veronica the Cow" is the charmingly eccentric name for this culinary haven located in the heart of Huertas district. Healthy pasta and salad dishes predominate, and *carabineros* (large grilled shrimp) and generous-sized *filetes* are among its eclectic seafood and meat choices. The set menus are exceptionally good value, and if you have a sweet tooth—and aren't counting the calories—the *tarta de chocolate* is a must. The colorful decor reflects the restaurant's Argentine origins.

Calle Moratín 38. ✆ **91-429-78-27.** Main courses 8€–16€ ($10–$20). Set menu 13.50€ ($17). AE, DC, MC, V. Sun–Fri 2–4pm and 9pm–midnight; Sat 9pm–midnight. Metro Antón Martín.

Taberna Toscana TAPAS   Many Madrileños begin their nightly *tasca* crawl here. The ambience is that of a village inn that's far removed from 20th-century Madrid. You sit on crude country stools, under sausages, peppers, and sheaves of golden wheat that hang from the age-darkened beams. The long, tiled bar is loaded with tasty tidbits, including the house specialties: *lacón y cecina* (boiled ham), *habas* (broad beans) with Spanish ham, and chorizo—almost meals in themselves. Especially delectable are the kidneys in sherry sauce and the snails in hot sauce.

Manuel Fernández y Gonzales 10. ✆ **91-429-60-31.** Beer (caña) 1.20€ ($1.50), glass of wine from 1€ ($1.25) tapas 3€–11€ ($3.75–$14). MC, V. Tues–Sat noon–4pm and 8pm–midnight. Metro: Sol or Sevilla.

6 Lavapiés

EXPENSIVE

Casa Lastra Sidrería ASTURIAN   Some visitors come here because they've heard this establishment serves "Austrian cuisine." Actually, the food is inspired by the cuisine of Asturias, a province of Spain in the northwest. Since 1926, this tavern has attracted a devoted following, particularly among homesick Asturians. The decoration is in a regional style, with cowbells, dried sausages, "pigtails" of garlic, and wood clogs. This restaurant and cider house—the national drink of the province—is known for serving very big portions, which means you might skip the starters. However, if you do indulge, I'd recommend *fabes con almejas* (white beans with clams) or *chorizo a la sidra* (spicy Spanish sausage cooked in cider). As a main course, *merluza* (hake) is also cooked in cider. If you're here in winter, order a fabulous *fabada,* the meat, sausage, and bean casserole of the province. Milk-fed lamb is roasted to perfection, and goat meat is yet another specialty, as is a cheese made from a blend of milk from goats, sheep, and cows. For dessert, locals order *carbayón,* which is made from sweetened egg yolks and almonds, although this may be too sweet for most tastes. Everything is washed down with cider, which might be more potent than you think.

Calle Olivar 3. ✆ **91-369-08-37.** Reservations not required. Main courses 15€–25€ ($19–$31). Fixed-price menu (Mon–Thurs) 13.50€ ($17). AE, DC, MC, V. Thurs–Tues 1–5pm; Thurs–Sat and Mon–Tues 8pm–midnight. Closed July. Metro: Antón Martín.

INEXPENSIVE

Automático ✦ *Finds* TAPAS   This classic tapas hangout is among the most popular in Lavapiés, and in summer its terrace—one of many in lively Argumosa street—draws animated crowds of habitués and visitors. On Sundays, when the nearby Rastro market is in full swing, it's packed to the gills. Atmosphere aside, the inventive and bargain-priced range of tidbits you get with your *caña* of beer or *chato* of wine is something else. *Bacalao* (salt cod), *mojama* (salted tuna), *cecina* (jerked beef), *migas* (fried bread crumbs), *morcilla patatera* (traditional blood sausage), and homemade pâtés line its comprehensive repertoire. On winter evenings recorded blues and jazz classics enliven the indoor lounge/bar.

Argumosa 17. ✆ **91-530-99-21.** Tapas/*raciones* 1.75€–9.50€ ($2.20–$12). MC, V. Tues–Sun 7pm–12:30am; Fri–Sat 12:30pm–12:30am. Metro: Lavapiés.

Económico Soidemersol SPANISH   As the name implies, this is a place where you can dine without straining the budget. Formerly known simply as the Económico, it's a legendary eating spot that has preserved its traditional food and friendly neighborhood atmosphere while undergoing renovations and opening a sunny outside terrace. Go for standards like *gazpacho, lentejas* (lentils), *tortilla,* and *callos* (tripe). If you're feeling ultra-adventurous, try the chewy *oreja* (pig's ears). (Incidentally, its name—if you forget the *sol* part—is *remedios* spelled backward, and *remedios* means cures or remedies. Enough said.)

Argumosa 9. ☏ **91-539-73-71.** Main courses 6€–10€ ($7.50–$13); set lunch 10.50€ ($13). MC, V. Daily 1–5pm and 8pm–midnight. Closed mid-Aug to mid-Sept. Metro: Lavapiés.

El Granero de Lavapiés VEGETARIAN   Another Lavapiés pioneer, the Granero (Granary, no less) shot onto the green scene just before the Elqui. Its low-priced ever-changing menu is based on seasonably fresh vegetables. Choose according to the time of year you visit from dishes like *lombarda con puré de patatas* (red cabbage with potato purée), *croquetas de champiñón* (mushroom croquettes), and *berengenas con tofú* (eggplant with tofu). Among the more conventional dishes is the ever-dependable gazpacho. Positively nonsmoking.

Argumosa 10. ☏ **91-467-76-11.** Main courses 6€–12€ ($7.50–$15). Set lunch 9.50€ ($12). No credit cards. Daily 1–4pm and 8:30–11pm. Metro: Lavapiés.

Elqui (Finds VEGETARIAN   The city's number-one self-service vegetarian eating spot sprang up just over 7 years ago in the burgeoning international melting pot of Lavapiés. Its inventive combinations of cereals cooked with fresh vegetables soon earned it a large following, and today its bargain all-you-can-eat lunchtime buffet of *ensaladas,* main hot dishes, and *postres* is a sellout—so best get there early. Mediterranean dishes such as hummus, couscous, and nut and ricotta crepes feature strongly on its very reasonable a la carte evening menu, and the *plato de baile* of brown rice, mushrooms, asparagus, and tofu is a must. There's a short list of organic wines and a wider range of herbal teas. Caffeine and nicotine are definitely out. The Elqui also arranges 8-hour-long vegetarian cooking courses.

Buenavista 18. ☏ **91-468-04-62.** Main courses 6€–10€ ($7.50–$13). Set buffet lunch 10.50€ ($13). No credit cards. Tues–Thurs, Sun 1:45–4pm; Fri–Sat 1:45–4pm and 9–11:30pm. Closed last 3 weeks Aug. Metro: Antón Martín or Lavapiés.

La Falsa Molestia ITALIAN   This archly named trattoria-style dinner club is a one of the liveliest Italian eating spots in town. Single-dish specialties range from *bruschetta* to *scamorze* (a melted cheese specialty), and there's a mind-bending choice of salads. Freshly made raviolis, lasagnas, and spaghettis fill the a la carte selection, and the choice of mineral waters is as wide as you're likely to find anywhere. The dinner club serves no lunches but stays open late and provides its own musical entertainment if you feel peckish after a disco session or flamenco show.

Magdalena 32. ☏ **91-420-32-38.** Main courses 9€–16€ ($11–$20); set menu 9€ ($11). No credit cards. Wed–Sun 5pm–3am. Metro: Antón Martín.

7 Paseo de Recoletos

EXPENSIVE

Al Mounia ✦ MOROCCAN   Widely acknowledged as the top Moroccan eating spot in Madrid, the Al Mounia first opened in 1968 under the auspices of owner-host

Sahri and his daughter, stunning a then more traditional and provincial scene with its exotic cumin- and pistachio-flavored cuisine, atmospheric mosaics, embossed tiled decor, and high standards of service. Today it's particularly popular with couples or party groups. The imaginative *maghrebi* menu extends far beyond the conventional couscous, and gourmet standouts are its delicious *pastilla* (pigeon pie) and *metaui* (Berber roast lamb). After the meal sample from the outrageously delicious Oriental pastries and dried fruits from the dessert trolley, accompanied ideally by fresh mint tea. The restaurant's cellar includes a selection of excellent Moroccan wines.

Calle de Recoletos 5. ℂ 91-435-08-28. Main courses 18€–30€ ($23–$38). AE, MC, V. Tues–Sat 1:30–3:30pm and 9pm–midnight. Closed Semana Santa and Aug. Metro: Banco de España.

El Borbollón BASQUE/FRENCH   The welcoming Castro family presides over this little charmer lying between Calle Serrano and Paseo de Recoletos, near both Plaza Cibeles and Plaza Colón. For 2 decades they have welcomed some of the more discerning palates in Madrid. Eduardo Castro, the chef, is a local personality and a whiz in the kitchen. He is known for such dishes as a perfectly grilled *rape* (monkfish). Steak is cooked with savory green peppers, and a chateaubriand appears enticingly drenched in whiskey. Fresh turbot and hake appear regularly on the menu, and rich game dishes such as partridge are featured in the autumn. Choice cutlets of Segovian lamb are awakened with garlic cloves. Fresh flowers and bucolic art make for a soothing decor.

Paseo de Recoletos 7. ℂ 91-431-41-34. Main courses 15€–22€ ($19–$28). AE, DC, MC, V. Daily Mon–Sat 1–4pm and 9pm–midnight. Metro: Retiro or Plaza Colón.

MODERATE

El Espejo ⊛ INTERNATIONAL   Here you'll find good food and one of the most perfectly crafted Art Nouveau decors in Madrid. If the weather is good, you can sit at one of the outdoor tables and be served by uniformed waiters who carry food across the busy street to a green area flanked with trees. I prefer a table inside, within view of the tile maidens with vines and flowers entwined in their hair. Upon entering, you'll find yourself in a charming cafe/bar, where many visitors linger before heading toward the spacious dining room. Dishes include grouper ragout with clams, steak tartare, guinea fowl with Armagnac, and duck with pineapple. Try profiteroles with cream and chocolate sauce for dessert.

Paseo de Recoletos 31. ℂ 91-308-23-47. Reservations required. *Menú del día* 22.50€ ($29). AE, MC, V. Daily 1–4pm and 9pm–midnight. Metro: Colón. Bus: 27 or 45.

Gran Café de Gijón ⊛ SPANISH   If you want food and atmosphere like it was in Franco's heyday, drop in here. Each of the old European capitals has a coffeehouse that traditionally attracts the literati—in Madrid it's the Gijón, which opened in 1888 in the heyday of the Belle Epoque. Artists and writers still patronize this venerated old cafe, many of them spending hours over one cup of coffee. Open windows look out onto the wide *paseo,* and a large terrace is perfect for sun worshippers and bird-watchers. Along one side of the cafe is a stand-up bar; on the lower level is a restaurant. In summer, sit in the garden to enjoy a *blanco y negro* (black coffee with ice cream) or a mixed drink.

Paseo de Recoletos 21. ℂ 91-521-54-25. Reservations required for restaurant. Main courses 15€–24€ ($19–$30); fixed-price menu 11.50€–24€ ($14–$30). AE, DC, MC, V. Sun–Fri 7am–1:30am; Sat 7am–2am. Metro: Banco de España or Colón.

8 Near Plaza de la Cibeles

MODERATE

Edelweiss GERMAN   This soberly styled German standby has provided good-quality food and service at moderate prices since World War II. Here you will be served hearty portions of food, mugs of draft beer, and fluffy pastries; that's why there's always a wait.

Start with Bismarck herring, and then dive into goulash with spaetzle or *Eisbein* (pigs' knuckles or *codillo de cerdo*) with sauerkraut and mashed potatoes (minimum two persons), the most popular dish at the restaurant. Finish with the homemade apple tart or Black Forest gâteau. The decor is vaguely German, with travel posters and wood-paneled walls. Edelweiss is air-conditioned in summer.

Jovellanos 7. ℰ **91-521-03-26.** Reservations recommended. Main courses 12€–24€ ($15–$30); fixed-price lunch 17.50€ ($22). AE, DC, MC, V. Daily 1–4pm and Mon–Sat 8pm–midnight. Metro: Cibeles. Bus: 5.

INEXPENSIVE

Al Natural VEGETARIAN   The charming Al Natural, situated on a quiet road just behind the Congreso building, is as exotic a vegetarian mecca as you could wish to find and a soothing escape for both the weary city explorer and occasional stressed political celebrity. Its atmospheric decor and healthily inventive dishes make a winning combination. The painted backdrop of fruit and greenery is subtly illuminated by amber lighting, luxuriant plants hang from the ceiling, and the background music is sensual and relaxing. The dining area is surrounded by warm wood paneling. Among the many veggie treats on offer, I recommend the *pita napolitana* (Neapolitan-style pita bread), *escalope de seitán y roquefort* (escalope of seitan and Roquefort cheese), and *champiñones Stroganoff* (mushrooms Stroganoff). Round off the meal with a healthy *yogur biológico* and *tila* (chamomile) tea.

Zorilla 11. ℰ **91-369-47-09.** Main courses 12€–22€ ($15–$28); set menu 13.50€ ($17). AE, DC, MC, V. Daily 1–4pm and 8pm–midnight. Metro: Banco de España.

Café del Círculo de Bellas Artes ℱ *Finds* CASTILIAN   This former members-only club is now open to the general public, and if you dine out here, you may still get the feeling you're crashing a private party (a time-honored tradition in Madrid, incidentally). With its 1920s-style ceilings, chandeliers, artistic statues, and soaring pillars, the cafe lies in an arts center. It's the best place to take a refueling stop when you're so tired you confused van Gogh with the Goyas at the Thyssen or the Real Academia de Bellas Artes.

Locals don't even know the place by its formal name, having nicknamed it *la pecera,* or aquarium. The food and drink are served in a palatial hall. At lunchtime join politicians and bankers from the nearby parliament or the Banco de España to enjoy a variety of pork, beef, fresh fish, and chicken dishes—the menu is rotated daily. Hopefully, you'll be here on the day the chef decides to prepare his robust *cocido,* the "granddaddy of Spanish stews." It will put hair on your chest, even if you're a woman. At night a more artsy crowd flocks to the place, devouring the succulent tapas such as shrimp and fresh anchovies and the rum cocktails that make you think you're back in Barbados. Only tapas are served at night, but if you order three or four they become meals unto themselves.

Calle Alcalá 42. ℰ **91-521-69-42.** Lunch main courses 12€ ($15) each. Evening tapas 2.90€–6.50€ ($3.60–$8.10). MC, V. Sun–Thurs 9:30am–1am; Fri–Sat 9:30am–3am. Metro: Banco de España.

Moments An Early Evening *Tapeo*

What's more fun than a pub-crawl in London or Dublin? In Madrid, it's a *tapeo,* and you can drink just as much or more than in those far-northern climes. One of the unique pleasures of Madrid, a *tapeo* is the act of strolling from one bar to another to keep yourself amused and fed before the fashionable Madrileño dining hour of 10pm.

Most of the world knows that tapas are Spain's delectable appetizers, and restaurants around the world now serve them. In Madrid they're served almost everywhere, in *tabernas, tascas,* bars, and cafes.

Although Madrid took to tapas with a passion, they may have originated in Andalusia, especially around Jerez de la Frontera, where they were traditionally served to accompany the sherry produced there. The first tapa (which means a cover or lid) was probably *chorizo* (a spicy sausage) or a slice of cured ham perched over the mouth of a glass to keep the flies out. Later, the government mandated that bars serve a "little something" in the way of food with each drink to dissipate the effects of the alcohol. This was important when drinking a fortified wine like sherry; its alcohol content generally ranges from 15% to 18%, higher than that of normal table wines. Bottom line: Eating a selection of tapas as you drink will help preserve your sobriety.

Tapas can be relatively simple: toasted almonds; slices of ham, cheese, or sausage; potato omelets; or the ubiquitous olives. They can be more elaborate too: a succulent veal roll; herb-flavored snails; *gambas* (shrimp); a saucer of peppery *pulpo* (octopus); stuffed peppers; *anguila* (eel); *cangrejo* (crabmeat salad); *merluza* (hake) salad; and even bull testicles.

Each bar in Madrid gains a reputation for its rendition of certain favorite foods. One bar, for example, specializes in very garlicky grilled mushrooms, usually accompanied by pitchers of sangria. Another will specialize in *gambas.* Most chefs are men in Madrid, but at tapas bars or *tascas,* the cooks are most often women—often the owner's wife.

For a selection of my favorite bars, see "The Best of the *Tascas*" on p. 165. There are literally hundreds of others, many of which you'll discover on your own during your strolls around Madrid.

Taj INDIAN   If curry is your thing, then don't be put off by the sounds and appearance of this somewhat unchic eating spot—complete with artificial flowers and banal background Muzak. Attractively situated on a peaceful lane between the Cortes and Cibeles, it offers the real McCoy: genuinely hot lamb and tandoori chicken curries as well as a comprehensive *degustación* choice of entrees such as samosas, pakora, naan bread, and Bombay duck. The friendly and attentive staff makes the visit all the more enjoyable.

Calle Marqués de Cubas 6. ② 91-531-50-59. Main courses 8€–18€ ($10–$23); set lunch 12€ ($15). AE, DC, MC, V. Mon–Thurs 1–4pm and 8:30–11:30pm; Fri–Sun 1–4pm and 8:30pm–midnight. Metro: Banco de España.

9 Near the Plaza España

EXPENSIVE

Bajamar SEAFOOD   Bajamar, one of the best fish houses in Spain, is right in the heart of the city. Both fish and shellfish are flown in fresh daily, the prices depending on what the market charges. Lobster, king crab, prawns, and soft-shell crabs are all priced according to weight. There is a large array of reasonably priced dishes as well. The service is smooth and professional, and the menu is in English. For an appetizer order the half-dozen giant oysters or rover crayfish. The special seafood soup is a most satisfying meal in itself; the lobster bisque is also worth trying. Some of the noteworthy main courses include turbot Gallego style, seafood paella, and baby squid cooked in its ink. The simple desserts include the chef's custard.

Gran Vía 78. ℰ **91-559-59-03.** Reservations recommended. Main courses 22€–65€ ($28–$81). AE, DC, MC, V. Daily 1–4pm and 8pm–midnight. Metro: Plaza de España.

El Molino de los Porches CASTILIAN   This authentic Castilian *asador* serves tasty grilled meats and fish. The *cordero* (lamb) and *cochinillo* (baby pig) are both good choices, as is the wild beef raised on the grassland plains of Andalusia. This spot is a popular hangout for bullfighters and their entourages. It's also a popular place for weddings and receptions (with musical groups performing), so book in advance and don't be surprised if things get a bit noisy. The big attraction here, as in many restaurants on this attractive Argüelles avenue bordering the parklands of the Parque del Oeste, is the outdoor terrace area, where you can relax in summer (if it's not too hot).

Paseo del Pintor Rosales 1. ℰ **91-548-13-36.** Daily 1:45–4:30pm and 8:45pm–midnight. Set menu 30€ ($38). AE, DC, MC, V. Free car park. Metro: Ventura Rodriguez.

MODERATE

Bali INDONESIAN   The one and only Indonesian restaurant in town, Bali has long been a refuge for hedonists seeking an exotic alternative to the hearty Castilian fare. Go for the *rijsttafel*, a delicious selection of Oriental tapas served up on a candle-heated grill. Or sample the excellent set menu. Individual recommended main dishes include *pollo satay* (grilled chicken skewers) with peanut sauce.

San Bernardino 6. ℰ **91-541-91-22.** Mon–Sat lunch and dinner, Sun lunch only; call for hours. Set menu 30€ ($38) AE, DC, MC, V. Metro: Plaza de Espana.

La Bola MADRILEÑO   This is *the taberna* in which to savor the 19th century. Just north of the Teatro Real, it's one of the few restaurants (if not the only one) left in Madrid with a blood-red facade; at one time, nearly all fashionable restaurants were so coated. Time stands still inside the restaurant, with its traditional atmosphere, gently polite waiters, Venetian crystal, and aging velvet. Ava Gardner and her entourage of bullfighters dined here. Grilled sole, filet of veal, and roast veal are regularly featured. Basque-style hake and grilled salmon are well recommended. The highlight: traditional Madrileño *cocido* cooked in earthenware pots by wood fire (although connoisseurs feel that it's become rather lightweight in its efforts to cater to an increasingly international clientele). Refreshing dishes to begin your meal include grilled shrimp, red-pepper salad, and lobster cocktail.

Calle de la Bola 5. ℰ **91-547-69-30.** Reservations required. Main courses 14€–24€ ($18–$30). No credit cards. Mon–Sat 1–4pm; daily 8:30–11pm. Metro: Opera. Bus: 1 or 2.

Vineyards & Wineries

Spanish wines are some of the best in the world, and the country's famed *Riojas* and *Penedeses* are widely available and remarkably affordable. Better value still—and barely known even in the rest of Spain—are the honest traditional wines emerging from Madrid province's own underrated vineyards.

Three of the top wine-producing regions in the Madrid province are **Colmenar de Oreja, San Martín de Valdeiglesias,** and **Chinchón. Colmenar de Oreja's** prize-winning red and white Jesús Díaz wines are made from the Malvar and Airén grapes, while **San Martín de Valdeiglesias'** strong (13%–13.5% alcohol) Señoría de Valderrábano reds are made from the Garnacha variety. **Chinchón** (of anise fame) also produces a hearty and palatable red called Viña Galinda. Look for these and other Comunidad de Madrid wines from Arganda del Rey and Villarejo del Salvanés in the supermarkets and restaurants. They're worth a try.

For wider information on Spanish wines in general, contact **Wines from Spain,** c/o the Commercial Office of Spain, 405 Lexington Ave., 44th Floor, New York, NY 10174-0331 (② **212/661-4959;** www.winesfromspain.com).

La Vaca Argentina ARGENTINE   Located close to the Opera House and Isabel II square, this is one of several branches of the popular Argentine chain that caters wholeheartedly to serious carnivores. Decor, as in the other restaurants, is modern and functional, though the genuine cowhide-lined walls are a nod to its land of origin. Service tends to be distracted, even coolly distant (perhaps the waiters yearn for the far-off pampas). Steaks are suitably huge but well matched by the delicious salads and imaginative pasta dishes. Among the tasty Argentine starters is *empanada* (small meat pie) in chile sauce.

Calle Cañas del Peral 2. ② 91-541-33-18. www.lavacaargentina.net. Main courses 12€–30€ ($15–$38). Daily 1–4:30pm and 9pm–12:30am. Metro: Opera.

Siam THAI   A near-Buddhist sense of calm and peace fills this intimate eating spot, located in a quiet zone close to other polyglot restaurants just a short stroll from the Plaza España. Specializing in delicacies from Thailand, where multilingual Texan owner David Haynes lived many years before moving to Madrid to create this genuine labor of love, it's one of the best Asian eating spots in town. Authentic imported ingredients are used in creating gourmet treats such as hot prawn soup, spicy green curry, and rehashed veal cooked with cashews and limes. Among the simple but delicious desserts are oranges in rosewater, and you can choose from a wide range of special teas. The fixed-price lunch menu is a very good value.

Calle San Bernardino 6. ② 91-559-83-15. Main courses 10€–18€ ($15–$23); set lunch 11.50€ ($14). Daily 1–4pm and 8pm–midnight. Metro: Plaza España or Noviciado.

10 Malasaña

INEXPENSIVE

Isla del Tesoro VEGETARIAN   A vegan's delight on Madrid's modestly expanding green scene, "Treasure Island" has been a mainstay of bohemian Malasaña for quite a while. Universal vegetarian dishes are imaginatively prepared, and the restaurant, surprisingly, does not frown on the increasingly ostracized smoker client. The adventurous menu of the day regularly changes its choice from country to country, and the Japanese tray of specialties is particularly inventive. Try the *buen rollito,* which consists of pasta stuffed with fruit, cheese, fresh spinach, and nuts or the ever-popular main salad buffet.

Calle Manuela Malasaña 3. ☏ **91-593-14-40.** Main courses 9€–14€ ($11–$18); set lunch 10.50€ ($13). Mon–Sat 1:30–4pm and 9pm–12:30am; Sun 9am–12:30am. Metro: Bilbao.

11 Chueca

EXPENSIVE

El Mentidero de la Villa ✿ MEDITERRANEAN   The Mentidero ("Gossip Shop" in English) is a truly multicultural experience. The owner describes the cuisine as "modern Spanish with Japanese influence and a French cooking technique." That may sound confusing, but the result is an achievement; each ingredient manages to retain its distinct flavor. The kitchen plays with such adventuresome combinations as veal liver in sage sauce; a spring roll filled with fresh shrimp and leeks; noisettes of veal with tarragon; filet steak with a sauce of mustard and brown sugar; and medallions of venison with purée of chestnut and celery. One notable dessert is the sherry trifle. The postmodern decor includes trompe l'oeil ceilings, exposed wine racks, ornate columns with unusual lighting, and a handful of antique carved merry-go-round horses.

Santo Tomé 6. ☏ **91-308-12-85.** Reservations required. Main courses 25€–35€ ($31–$44). AE, DC, MC, V. Mon–Fri 1:30–4:30pm; Mon–Sat 9pm–midnight. Closed Aug. Metro: Alonso Martínez or Colón. Bus: 37.

La Fuencisla ✿ SPANISH   Near El Museo Romántico is this small but comfortable restaurant that for nearly half a century has been serving meals in the traditional Spanish style. A family business, La Fuencisla (named as an offering to the Virgin of Segovia) is run by Señor and Señora de Frutos. Señor de Frutos greets the visitors in the front while the Señora creates tasty homemade meals in the kitchen. The dishes are typical of the Segovian kitchen, and ingredients are prepared according to time-tested recipes. No dish is more typical than the grilled chops of milk-fed lamb, praised by gastronomes. Begin with fresh asparagus in country butter and aromatic garlic or savory mussels in a marinara sauce. Filet of tuna freshly baked in the oven is another pleaser. For desserts, the cooks always prepare homemade tarts, which are especially good when the fresh fruit comes in. Otherwise, you might opt for the rice pudding or *flan de coco* (coconut pudding).

San Mateo 4. ☏ **91-521-61-86.** Reservations recommended. Main courses 15€–22€ ($19–$28); *menú completo* 36€ ($45). AE, DC, MC, V. Mon–Sat 2–4pm and 9pm–1am. Closed Aug. Metro: Tribunal.

MODERATE

Bazaar MEDITERRANEAN/ASIAN   Enjoying tremendous vogue in Madrid is this popular restaurant, frequented largely by an attractive set of Madrileño youth. On a recent visit we spotted three dead ringers for Paris Hilton. The decor is light, stylish, and airy; the talk hip and sophisticated. The chef's repertoire of dishes is creative, vigorous, and vibrant. Typical of the zest is a starter of fresh tomato soup made with basil ice cream. More old-fashioned, typical fare is also served, including a tasty chicken curry, a savory kettle of stew beef, and tantalizingly flavored chicken brochettes. For dessert, we recommend the locally fabled *chocolatísimo,* a medley of chocolate delights.

Calle Libertad 21. ✆ **91-523-39-05.** Reservations not required. Main courses 7.50€–15€ **($9.40–$19).** AE, MC, V. Mon–Sat 1:15–4pm and 8:30–11:45pm. Metro: Chueca.

Casa Vallejo SPANISH   This hardworking bistro with a not terribly subtle staff offers less exposure to international clients than some of its competitors. Despite that, you'll find a sense of culinary integrity that's based on a devotion to fresh ingredients and a rigid allegiance to time-tested Spanish recipes. Occupying a turn-of-the-20th-century building, it contains room for only 42 diners at a time. Menu items include garlic soup; tartlets layered with tomatoes, zucchini, and cheese; a ragout of clams and artichokes; croquettes of chicken; breast of chicken garnished with a fricassee of fresh wild mushrooms; pork filet; duck breast in orange or prune sauce; and creamy desserts. Budget gourmands in Madrid praise the hearty flavors here, the robust cookery, and the prices.

Calle San Lorenzo 9. ✆ **91-308-61-58.** Reservations recommended. Main courses 7.50€–18€ **($9.40–$23);** fixed-price menu (Mon–Fri) 12€–18.50€ **($15–$23).** MC, V. Mon–Sat 2–4pm; Tues–Sat 9:30pm–midnight. Metro: Tribunal or Alonso Martínez.

Ciao Madrid ITALIAN   These two highly successful Italian restaurants are run by members of the extended Laguna family. The older of the two is the branch on Calle Apodaca, established about a dozen years ago; its cohort entered the scene in the early 1990s. Both maintain the same hours, prices, menu, and a decor inspired by the tenets of minimalist Milanese decor, with good-tasting food items that include risottos and pastas, such as ravioli or tagliatelle with wild mushrooms. No one will mind if you order pasta as a main course (lots of clients here do, accompanying it with a green salad). If you're in the mood for a more substantial main course, consider osso buco, veal scaloppine, chicken or veal parmigiana, and any of several kinds of fish. (See also the Chamberí branch, p. 159.)

Calle Apodaca 20. ✆ **91-447-00-36.** Reservations recommended. Pastas 8€–12€ **($10–$15);** main courses 12€–20€ **($15–$25).** AE, DC, MC, V. Mon–Fri 1:30–3:45pm; Mon–Sat 9:30pm–midnight. Closed Sept. Metro: Tribunal. There's another location at Calle Argensola 7 (✆ **91-308-25-19;** closed Aug; Metro: Alonso Martínez).

El Bocaíto ✦ SPANISH/TAPAS   Inside this 150-year-old house, four original columns of wood encircle the high ceiling, and bullfighting posters adorn the white-tile walls. Behind a bar shaped into two horseshoes, the staff cooks and prepares some of the most appreciated tapas in Madrid. The selection ranges from simple delights such as *ajos tiernos en aceite* (tender garlic in olive oil), cured Serrano ham, *gambas fritas* (fried shrimp), and green asparagus in scrambled eggs to some very sophisticated delicacies, such as *bacalao con caviar* (salt cod pâté with caviar). The famous *mejimecha* (marinated mussels with ham and onions in béchamel sauce) is sublime, as are the anchovies of the house and tasty croquettes. The prices for the tapas range from 5.40€ to 7.20€ **($6.75–$9).** Don Miguel Benavente, the chef and owner for more than 3 decades, recommends the *plato combinado* (a combination platter of all tapas), which, together with a glass of the very palatable Rioja house wine, is available at a cost of 10€ **($12).** A selection of the culinary treats on offer includes lentils with *chorizo* (Spanish sausage), *merluza* (hake), *osso buco al horno* (braised veal shank), and typical Andalusian and Castilian dishes.

Calle Libertad 4–6 ✆ **91-532-12-19.** Reservations recommended. Main courses 12€–20€ **($15–$25).** MC, V. Mon–Fri 1–4pm and 8:30pm–midnight; Sat 8:30pm–midnight. Closed last 2 weeks Aug. Metro: Chueca.

Extremadura EXTREMADURAN   In case you're wondering, Extremadura is the most westerly province in central Spain, famed until recently mainly for the fact that

Spain's two great New World explorers, Cortés and Pizarro, came from here. During the past decade its cuisine has also started making waves, and this homely restaurant serves up hearty traditional regional dishes with a few stylish and eccentric touches of its own. The heartiness comes with the entrees, more than generous portions of cheeses, pâtés, and salads, while the main-course fish and meat dishes are accompanied by such specialty fare as *ortigas* (cooked nettles), *borrajas* (borage), and *criadillas de tierra* (truffles). Venison ragout, roast kid, fresh trout, and *migas* (fried bread crumbs with meat, tomatoes, and grapes) are among the top regional highlights, and the *menú de degustación* is just the job if you've a big appetite. Excellent-value Extremadura wines dominate the cellar, and fiery homemade *orujos* (*eau de vies* complete with soused snakes or lizards in the bottle) are the ideal after-dinner *digestif.*

Calle Libertad 13. ✆ **91-531-89-58**. Main courses 10€–18€ ($13–$23). *Menú de degustación* 25€ ($31). DC, MC, V. Tues–Sat 1–4pm, 8pm–midnight. Metro: Chueca.

La Bardemcilla ★ (Finds SPANISH/TAPAS

Formerly known as the Café Latino, this warm Chueca locale was renovated a few years back and is now run by the cinematic Bardem family (Javier, sister Mónica, brother Carlos, and mother Pilar). Family photos and scenes from movies bedeck the walls, and tapas and *raciones* bear names from Bardem films (mostly Javier's). Mingle with the largely cool clientele at the comfortable bar near the entrance and sample a *caña* and *croquetas*, or enjoy a more leisurely dinner in the noisy and comfortable restaurant at the back. *Solomillo a la luna* (sirloin steak) and *chuletas de cordero* (lamb chops) are recommended main dishes on the carnivore-oriented menu, and there's an interestingly varied wine list.

Augusto Figueroa 47. ✆ **91-521-42-56**. Tapas 2.75€–7.50€ ($3.40–$9.40). Main courses 12€–22€ ($15–$28). AE, MC, V. Mon–Fri noon–4:30pm and 8pm–2:30am; Sat 8pm–2am. Metro: Chueca.

La Dame Noire FRENCH

This is one for lovers of the pseudo baroque, a tongue-in-cheek locale where maroon-orange walls with artificial protruding legs and leopard skins, overhead fans, candles, and gilt prevail. The leather-clad waiters look like epicene extras in a minor Almodóvar movie, and the food is all but eclipsed by the kitsch atmosphere. But not quite. The set-price Gallic-style dinner incorporates a variety of tasty dishes, from *mejillones a la crema* (creamed mussels), goat's cheese salad, and Burgundian snails to pepper or tartare steak. Desserts include rich chocolate pastel and tarte tatin. Choose a reasonably priced Navarra wine to accompany the meal.

Calle Pérez Galdós 3. ✆ **91-531-04-76**. Set dinner (wine not included) 19.50€ ($24). AE, DC, MC, V. Sun–Thurs 9pm–midnight; Fri–Sat 9pm–2am. Metro: Gran Vía or Tribunal.

Salvador SPANISH/BASQUE

This is a robust, macho enclave of Madrid. The owner of this bustling restaurant, José Blasquez García, configured it as a mini-museum to his hobby and passion, the Spanish art of bullfighting. Inside, near a bar that stocks an impressive collection of sherries and whiskies, you'll find the memorabilia of years of bull-watching, including photographs of great matadors beginning in the 1920s, and agrarian artifacts used in the raising and development of fighting bulls. The menu is as robust and two-fisted as the decor, featuring macho-size platters of oxtail in red-wine sauce; different preparations of hake, one of which is baked delectably in a salt crust; stuffed peppers, fried calamari, and shrimp; and for dessert, the local version of *arroz con leche* (rice pudding).

Calle Barbieri 12. ✆ **91-521-45-24**. Reservations recommended. Main courses 12€–25€ ($15–$31). AE, MC, V. Mon–Sat 1:30–4pm and 9–11:30pm. Closed Aug. Metro: Chueca.

Zara CUBAN   Small, cozy, and lively. That's Zara, the joint creation of Pepe Martínez and Inés Llanos, who forsook their native Caribbean island 4 decades ago to set up this landmark of Cuban cuisine in central Madrid. Prices are reasonable, the service is first-rate, and it's well worth waiting in a queue to sit at one of the check-clothed tables if the place is busy (which is most of the time). Recommended are the *arroz con frijoles y cerdo* (rice with pork and beans) and *picadillo de ternera con arroz y plátano frito* (spicy veal with rice and fried banana), while top desserts include a delicious *pasta de guayaba con queso* (guava jelly with cheese). Zara's cocktails are legendary, especially the daiquiris, which many claim are the best in the capital.

Calle Infantas 5. ℂ **91-532-20-74.** Main courses 10€–14€ ($13–$18). Set menus 20€–27.50€ ($25–$34). AE, DC, MC, V. Mon–Fri 1–4pm and 8pm–midnight. Closed Aug. Metro: Chueca or Gran Vía.

INEXPENSIVE

Carmencita *(Finds* SPANISH/BASQUE   Carmencita, founded in 1840 and exquisitely restored, is a street-corner enclave of old Spanish charm filled with 19th-century detailing and tile work. It was a favorite hangout for the poet Federico García Lorca, as well as a meeting place for intelligentsia in the pre–civil war days. Meals might include entrecôte with green pepper sauce, escalope of veal, braised mollusks with port, filet of pork, cod with garlic, and Bilbao-style hake. Every Thursday the special of the day is a complicated version of Madrid's famous *cocido,* which patrons wax lyrical over.

Libertad 16. ℂ **91-531-66-12.** Reservations recommended. Main courses 7.50€–18€ ($9.30–$23); fixed-price menu 12€ ($15) available only at lunch. AE, DC, MC, V. Mon–Fri 1–4pm; Mon–Sat 9pm–midnight. Metro: Chueca or Banco de España.

El Bierzo CASTILIAN   Good, honest fare from the northerly Castilian region of El Bierzo is the order of the day at this down-to-earth eating spot. One of Chueca's most popular and established home-cooking establishments, it boasts excellent-value set lunch and dinner menus. *Costillas* (beef ribs) and *lentejas con arroz* (lentils with rice) are among the favorite dishes. There's also a good range of tapas and *raciones* if you fancy something lighter.

Calle Barbieri 16. ℂ **91-531-91-10.** Main courses 9€–18.50€ ($11–$23); set menu (lunch and dinner) 9.50€ ($12). AE, DC, MC, V. Mon–Sat 1–4pm and 8–11:30pm. Metro: Chueca.

Nabucco ITALIAN   In a neighborhood of Spanish restaurants, the Italian trattoria format here comes as a welcome change. The decor resembles a postmodern update of an Italian ruin, complete with trompe l'oeil walls painted to look like marble. Roman portrait busts and a prominent bar lend a dignified air. Menu choices include cannelloni, a good selection of veal dishes, and such main courses as osso buco. You might begin your meal with a selection of antipasti.

Calle Hortaleza 108. ℂ **91-310-06-11.** Reservations recommended. Pizza 5.50€–7€ ($6.90–$8.75); main courses 7€–12€ ($8.75–$15). AE, DC, MC, V. Daily 1:30–4pm; Sun–Thurs 8:45pm–midnight; Fri–Sat 8:45pm–1am. Metro: Alonso Martínez. Bus: 7 or 36.

Ribeiro do Miño *(Finds* GALICIAN   Set on a quiet street between the busier thoroughfares of Horteleza and Fuencarral, this spacious multiroomed restaurant is probably the liveliest seafood eating spot in Madrid. It's nearly always packed—and the prices tell you why. Service is an admirable combination of the easygoing and the professional. No bookings are taken, so if you want to snag a table, get here early and avoid weekends; otherwise be prepared to wait. Shellfish is exceptional; the mainstay of the piscatorial menu is the shared platter of *gambas* (shrimp), *cangrejo* (crab), and *almejas* (clams). *Pulpo gallego* (Galician-style octopus) is a regular feature, and *percebes* (goose barnacles) occasionally show up (though this will thwart any plans for a budget meal). Salads are generous, and the low-priced house *vino blanco* is the perfect liquid accompaniment. You also get a glass of yellow green *orujo* (strong digestive spirit) on the house after your dessert.

Calle Santa Brigida 1. (🕿) 91-521-98-54. Main courses 10€–20€ ($13–$25); special shellfish platter (minimum 2) 25€ ($31). No credit cards. Tues–Sun 1–4pm and 8–11:30pm. Closed Aug. Metro: Tribunal.

Tienda de Vinos SPANISH   Officially this restaurant is known as Tienda de Vinos (the Wine Store), but ever since the 1930s Madrileños have called it "El Comunista" (The Communist). Its now-deceased owner was a fervent Communist, and many locals who shared his political beliefs patronized the establishment. This rickety old wine shop with a few tables in the back is quite fashionable with actors and journalists looking for Spanish fare without frills. There is a menu, but no one ever looks at it—just ask what's available. Nor do you get a bill; you're just told how much to pay. Guests sit at simple wooden tables with wooden chairs and benches; walls are decorated with old posters, calendars, pennants, and clocks. Start with garlic or vegetable soup or lentils, followed by lamb chops, tripe in a spicy sauce, or meatballs and soft-set eggs with asparagus.

Augusto Figueroa 35. (🕿) 91-521-70-12. Main courses 2.50€–7.50€ ($3–$9.40). No credit cards. Mon–Sat 1–4pm and 9pm–midnight. Metro: Chueca.

26 de Libertad INTERNATIONAL   Brainchild of owner Miguel Caro, this flamboyant and friendly '90s restaurant set in the heart of Chueca aims to blend hearty, good-value lunches with that little extra something special in the evenings. The lunch menu includes reliables such as *rabo de buey* (oxtail) or *lenguado* (sole), while in the evening you'll find items like *ensalada de boletus* (wild mushroom salad), *solomillo a la cebollo* (filet mignon with onions), and mandarin sorbet on the more exotic *menú de degustación*. Service is very attentive.

Calle Libertad 26. (🕿) 91-522-25-22. Main courses 12€–18€ ($15–$23); set lunch 10€ ($13); evening *menú de degustación* 25€ ($31). MC, V. Sept–June Mon–Thurs 1–4pm and 8pm–midnight, Fri–Sat 1–4pm and 8pm–1am, Sun 1–4pm; July–Aug Mon–Thurs 1–4pm and 8pm–midnight, Fri–Sat 1–4pm and 8pm–1am. Metro: Chueca.

(Kids) Family-Friendly Restaurants

Children visiting Spain will delight in patronizing any of the restaurants at the Parque de Atracciones in the **Casa de Campo** (see "Especially for Kids," in chapter 7). Another good idea is to go on a picnic (see "Picnic, Anyone?" later in this chapter). Or try taking the family to a local *tasca,* where children are bound to find something they like from the wide selection of tapas.

For a taste of the States, there are always the American-bred fast-food chains: McDonald's, Burger King, and Kentucky Fried Chicken are everywhere. Remember, however, that the burgers and chicken will have a slightly different taste from those served back home. A place with juicy hamburgers, plus lots of fare familiar to American kids, is **Foster's Hollywood** (p. 165).

WokCafe JAPANESE   This is a distinctly "pop" version of a Japanese eating spot, at least as far as dyed-in-the-wool aficionados are concerned, but that doesn't mean the food's not great or that it's not exceptional value. Permanently crowded and bustling, it lies in a narrow Chueca lane parallel to the Gran Vía and surrounded by other bars and restaurants. Decor is clean and elegant, service erratic, and the dishes cover traditional stalwarts like tempura, noodles, and sushi, as well as Wokburgers and Wok pizzas should your taste veer toward McDonalds. Brash, honest good value and a good place to put you in a party mood.

Calle Infantas 44. (✆ **91-522-90-69.** Main courses 7€–14€ ($8.75–$18); set lunch 12€ ($15). AE, MC, V. Mon–Sat 1–4pm and 9pm–2am. Metro: Gran Vía.

12 Retiro/Salamanca

VERY EXPENSIVE

Santceloni ★★★ MEDITERRANEAN   Santi Santamaría is ranked among the top three chefs of Spain, along with his chief rivals, Juan Mark Arzak and Ferrán Adriá. Santamaría gets my vote as the leader of the "troika," as these chefs are often called by food critics. He made his fame in his restaurant outside Barcelona. As his acclaim grew, he decided to open this branch of his fabled restaurant in Madrid. It's been hailed as an immediate success. Few chefs know how to present such an enticing and imaginative cuisine of the Mediterranean.

Santamaría's cuisine is called *de mercado,* meaning that it's based on the freshest ingredients available that day in the marketplace. The same painstaking and fine care that goes into the selections of ingredients is also demonstrated when the produce hits those skillets, pots, and pans. The taste of most dishes is sublime. Backed by an impressive, even daring, wine list, the menu includes such starters as a terrine of tuna and foie gras, an unusual combination that is both appealing, startling, and a taste sensation. Large and well-flavored red prawns appear with sweet-tasting and lightly sautéed onions. The Atlantic fish John Dory is appetizingly wed with fennel. One of the best examples of Santamaría's marriage of ingredients is cream of pumpkin with crisp sweetbreads and black olives, a tasty "troika" unto itself. And, of course, his caviar with pork jowl and creamy potatoes is better than your mother made, as are his frogs' legs with garlic paste and a parsley emulsion.

In the Hotel Hesperia, Paseo de la Castellana 57. (✆ **91-210-88-40.** Reservations required. Main courses 27€–36€ ($34–$45). AE, DC, MC, V. Mon–Fri 2–4pm; Mon–Sat 9–11pm. Closed Aug. Metro: Gregorio Marañón.

Zalacaín ★★★ INTERNATIONAL   Outstanding in both food and decor, Zalacaín is credited with bringing nouvelle cuisine to Spain when it opened its doors back in 1973. It is reached by an illuminated walk from Paseo de la Castellana and housed at the garden end of a modern apartment complex. It's within an easy walk of such deluxe hotels as the Castellana and the Miguel Angel. The name of the restaurant comes from the intrepid hero of Basque author Pío Baroja's 1909 novel, *Zalacaín El Aventurero.* Zalacaín is small, exclusive, and expensive. It has the atmosphere of an elegant old mansion: The walls are covered with textiles, and some are decorated with Audubon-type paintings. Men should wear jackets and ties.

The menu features many Basque and French specialties, often with nouvelle cuisine touches. It might offer a superb sole in a green sauce, but it also knows the glory of grilled pigs' feet. Among the best dishes are oysters with caviar and sherry jelly; crepes stuffed with smoked fish; ravioli stuffed with mushrooms, foie gras, and truffles;

bouillabaisse; and veal escalopes in orange sauce. For dessert, I'd suggest one of the custards, perhaps raspberry or chocolate.

Alvarez de Baena 4. ✆ **91-561-48-40.** Reservations required. Main courses 25€–40€ ($31–$50); fixed-price menu 82€ ($103). AE, DC, MC, V. Mon–Fri 1:15–4pm; Mon–Sat 9pm–midnight. Closed week before Easter and Aug. Metro: Gregorio Marañón.

EXPENSIVE

Alkalde ⌖ BASQUE   For decades Alkalde has been known for serving top-quality Spanish food in an old tavern setting, and it continues to do so exceedingly well. Decorated like a Basque inn, it has beamed ceilings with hams hanging from the rafters. Upstairs is a large *típico* tavern; downstairs is a maze of stone-sided cellars that are pleasantly cool in summer (although the whole place is air-conditioned).

Basque cookery is the best in Spain, and Alkalde honors that noble tradition. Begin with the cream of crabmeat soup, followed by *gambas a la plancha* (grilled shrimp) or *cigalas* (crayfish). Other recommended dishes include *mero salsa verde* (brill in green sauce), trout Alkalde, stuffed peppers, and chicken steak. The dessert specialty is *copa Cardinal* (ice cream topped with fruit).

Jorge Juan 10. ✆ **91-576-33-59.** Reservations required. Main courses 27€–39€ ($34–$49); fixed-price menu from 36€ ($45). AE, DC, MC, V. Daily 1:15pm–midnight. Closed Sat–Sun in July–Aug. Metro: Retiro or Serrano. Bus: 8, 20, 21, or 53.

El Amparo ⌖⌖ BASQUE   Behind the cascading vines on El Amparo's facade is one of Madrid's most elegant gastronomic enclaves. Inside this converted carriage house, three tiers of rough-hewn wooden beams surround tables set with pink linens and glistening silver. A sloping skylight floods the interior with sun by day; at night, pinpoints of light from the high-tech hanging lanterns create intimate shadows. Polite, uniformed waiters serve well-prepared nouvelle cuisine versions of cold marinated salmon with a tomato sorbet, cold cream of vegetable and shrimp soup, bisque of shellfish with Armagnac, ravioli with crayfish dressed with balsamic vinegar and vanilla-scented oil, roast lamb chops with garlic purée, breast of duck, ragout of sole, roulades of lobster with soy sauce, and steamed hake with pepper sauce.

Callejón de Puigcerdà 8 (at corner of Jorge Juan). ✆ **91-431-64-56.** Reservations required. Main courses 15€–30€ ($19–$38). AE, MC, V. Mon–Fri 1:30–3:30pm; Mon–Sat 9–11:30pm. Closed week before Easter. Metro: Serrano. Bus: 21 or 53.

El Bodegón INTERNATIONAL/BASQUE/SPANISH   El Bodegón is imbued with the atmosphere of a gentleman's club for hunting enthusiasts. The restaurant is near such deluxe hotels as the Castellana and the Miguel Angel, and attracts a number of international globetrotters, especially in the evening. King Juan Carlos and Queen Sofía have dined here.

Waiters in black and white, with gold braid and buttons, bring dignity to the food service. Even bottled water is served champagne-style, chilled in a silver floor stand. There are two main dining rooms, both conservative and oak-beamed in the country-inn style. I recommend starting with cream of crayfish bisque or velvety vichyssoise. Main-course selections include grilled filet mignon with classic béarnaise sauce and venison bourguignon. Other choices include shellfish au gratin Escoffier, quails Fernand Point, tartare of raw fish marinated in parsley-enriched vinaigrette, and smoked salmon.

Pinar 15. ✆ **91-562-88-44.** Reservations required. Main courses 20€–30€ ($25–$38). AE, DC, MC, V. Mon–Fri 1:30–4pm; Mon–Sat 9pm–midnight. Closed holidays and Aug. Metro: Rubén Darío or Gregorio Marañón.

El Pescador ☞ SEAFOOD   El Pescador is a popular spot, packing in crowds with more than 30 kinds of fish served, all prominently displayed in a glass case. Many of them are unknown in North America, and some are found off the coast of Galicia. The management airfreights the fish in and prefers to serve them *a la plancha* (grilled). You might start off with spicy fish soup and accompany it with one of the many good wines from northeastern Spain. If you're not sure what to order, try one of the several varieties and sizes of shrimp. They go under the names *langostinos, cigalas, santiaguinos,* and *carabineros.* Many are expensive and priced by weight, so take care when you order.

Calle José Ortega y Gasset 75. ✆ **91-402-12-90.** Reservations required. Main courses 18€–36€ ($23–$45). MC, V. Mon–Sat noon–4pm and 8pm–midnight. Closed Aug. Metro: Lista or Diego de León.

Horcher ☞ GERMAN/INTERNATIONAL   Horcher originated in Berlin in 1904. In 1943, prompted by a tip from a high-ranking German officer that Germany was losing the war, Herr Horcher moved his restaurant to Madrid. For years it was known as the best dining room in the city, but fierce competition of late has stolen that crown. Nevertheless, the restaurant is still going strong, continuing its grand European traditions, including excellent service.

You might try the skate or shrimp tartare or the distinctive warm hake salad. Both the venison stew with green pepper and orange peel and the crayfish with parsley and cucumber are typical of the elegant fare served with style. Spanish aristocrats often come here in autumn to sample game dishes, including venison, wild boar, and roast wild duck. Other main courses include veal scaloppine in tarragon and sea bass with saffron. For dessert, the house specialty is crepes Sir Holden, prepared at your table with fresh raspberries, cream, and nuts.

Alfonso XII 6. ✆ **91-532-35-96.** Reservations required. Jackets and ties for men. Main courses 36€–60€ ($45–$75). AE, DC, MC, V. Mon–Fri 1:30–4pm; Mon–Sat 8:30pm–midnight. Metro: Retiro.

La Gamella ☞☞ CALIFORNIAN/CASTILIAN   La Gamella established its gastronomic reputation shortly after it opened several years ago in another part of town. In 1988, its Illinois-born owner Dick Stephens moved his restaurant into the 19th-century building where the Spanish philosopher Ortega y Gasset was born. The prestigious Horcher, one of the capital's legendary restaurants (see above), is just across the street, but the food at La Gamella is better. The russet-colored, high-ceilinged design invites customers to relax. Mr. Stephens has prepared his delicate and light-textured specialties for the king and queen of Spain, as well as for Madrid's most talked-about artists and merchants, many of whom he knows and greets personally between sessions in his kitchen.

Typical menu items include a ceviche of Mediterranean fish, sliced duck liver in truffle sauce, a dollop of goat cheese served over caramelized endive, duck breast with peppers, and an array of well-prepared desserts, including an all-American cheesecake. Traditional Spanish dishes such as chicken with garlic have been added to the menu, plus what has been called "the only edible hamburger in Madrid."

Alfonso XII 4. ✆ **91-532-45-09.** Reservations required. Main courses 30€–45€ ($38–$56). AE, DC, MC, V. Daily 1:30–4pm and 9pm–midnight. Closed 4 days around Easter. Metro: Retiro. Bus: 19.

La Paloma ☞ BASQUE/FRENCH   In the exclusive Barrio Salamanca, this small but comfortable restaurant is the showcase for the culinary talents of chef-owner Segundo Alonso, who made a stellar reputation at the more exclusive El Amparo. Many of his fans followed him here and have since become regulars. His restaurant is in a nostalgic old restored house with high ceilings and wooden beams. His French and Basque dishes are some of the finest of their kind in Madrid. His food is robust; he's known for what is called "variety meats," especially pigs' trotters. Even if you have never sampled this dish before, dare to here—you may be glad you did. You could settle instead for his equally celebrated wood pigeon stuffed with foie gras. He also does an excellent lasagna with crabmeat, spinach, and leeks, and a fine *rabo de toro* (bull's tail) stewed in red-wine sauce. The best fish dish is grilled turbot with tomato paste and thyme or sea urchin gratinéed and served with quail eggs. For dessert, try fresh dates with Chantilly cream or a velvety almond mousse with cinnamon ice cream.

Jorge Juan 39. ℂ **91-576-86-92**. Reservations recommended. Main courses 17€–26€ ($21–$33); *menú completo* 51€ ($64). AE, DC, MC, V. Mon–Sat 1:30–4pm and 9pm–midnight. Metro: Vergara or Velázquez.

La Trainera ⚓ SEAFOOD   This restaurant is more expensive, and more chic, than its sprawling, paneled interior might imply. Capable of seating up to 300 diners at a time, it occupies a quartet of dining rooms within a turn-of-the-20th-century building in the glamorous shopping neighborhood of Serrano. Look for vaguely Basque-inspired platters of very fresh seafood, which arrive steaming hot and drizzled with subtle combinations of herbs, wines, and olive oils. No meat of any kind is served here. Instead, you'll find spicy and garlic-enriched versions of fish soup, filet of sole prepared in any of several different versions, Cantabrian crayfish, and well-conceived versions of a *salpicón de mariscos* (a platter of shellfish). Other fish include red mullet, swordfish with capers, monkfish, and virtually anything else that swims. Any of them can be preceded with a heaping platter of shellfish set atop a bed of artfully arranged seaweed. Succulent shellfish, including lobster, shrimp, crab, and mussels, plus an array of other items, is market-priced by weight.

Calle Lagasca 60. ℂ **91-576-80-35**. Reservations recommended. Main courses 18€–40€ ($23–$50). AE, DC, MC, V. Mon–Sat 1–4pm and 8pm–midnight. Metro: Serrano.

Pedro Larumbe ⚓ BASQUE/FRENCH   You dine in style here in an opulent section of La Castellana close to the Plaza de Colón. This century-old building was once the headquarters of the famous newspaper *ABC*. Today, it is the elegant restaurant of National Gastronomic Award winner Pedro Larumbe. There are three dining areas, each as elegant as the others: the classic Salón Pompeyano, the Art Deco Salón Fundador, and the beautifully tiled Patio Andalús. This Navarrese chef not only likes a *fin-de-siècle* decor, he prefers turn-of-the-20th-century cookery as well. His specialties are often from the tried-and-true recipes of yesterday, as evoked by his *solomillo a la mostaza,* or steak with mustard sauce. He also specializes in hake in green sauce with mussels, a favorite dish of the Basque country. One of his specialties is *ensalada de bocavante con salsa de almendras* (lobster salad with almond dressing), a true delight. The service is impeccable, the wine list well chosen, and the desserts something to write home about: tiramisu with a sweet wine and caramel sauce or "tear drops" of chocolate—dark and rich tear-shaped chocolate pieces.

Serrano 61. ℂ **91-575-11-12**. Reservations required. Main course 17€–30€ ($21–$38); *menú completo* 45€ ($56). AE, DC, MC, V. Mon–Fri 1:30–4pm and 9pm–midnight; Sat 9pm–midnight. Closed Aug 15–30 and Easter week. Metro: Rubén Darío or Núñez de Balboa.

Suntory ⚓ JAPANESE   This is Madrid's leading Japanese restaurant. Already acclaimed for its chain restaurants around the world, Suntory has invaded an attractive section of La Castellana and is winning converts to its impeccably prepared cuisine. Decorated in a minimalist style evocative of other Japanese restaurants around the world, this is the domain of Ken Sato, acclaimed as the finest Japanese chef in Spain. There are three dining areas, including the Teppan Yaki, the Shabu-Shabu, and a sushi bar. The finest and freshest of fish and shellfish is served here, and visiting Japanese praise the quality of fish found in Spanish waters. Try some of the exquisite sushi or the Mediterranean prawn tempura. The red tuna sashimi is my favorite. Finish these delicacies with a tempura helado or cake with vanilla icing.

Paseo Castellana 36. 🕾 **91-577-37-34.** Reservations recommended. *Menú completo* 39€–72€ ($49–$90). AE, DC, MC, V. Mon–Sat 1:30–3:30pm and 8:30–11:30pm. Metro: Rubén Darío.

Thai Gardens THAI   Part of a high-class chain whose branches extend from Casablanca to Sao Paolo, this "in" Thai restaurant is a favorite with celebrities and visitors looking for something special. Traditional delights such as *khum phom pha* prawns and *kai satee* kebabs, using monosodium-glutamate-free ingredients mainly flown in from Thailand, are served in a garden-like setting of lush vegetation and trickling fountains. The attentive and friendly staff wear colorful Thai costumes.

Jorge Juan 5, 28001. 🕾 **91-577-88-84.** www.thaigardensgroup.com. Main courses 18€–30€ ($23–$38). AE, DC, MC, V. Daily lunch and dinner; call for hours. Metro Serrano

Viridiana 🕿🕿 INTERNATIONAL   Viridiana—named after the 1961 Luis Buñuel film classic—is widely regarded as one of the finest restaurants of Madrid, renowned for the creative imagination of its chef and part-owner, Abraham García, who has lined the walls with stills from Buñuel films. (He's not just a self-taught chef; he's also a film historian.) Menu specialties are contemporary adaptations of traditional recipes, and they change frequently according to availability. Examples of the individualistic cooking include a salad of exotic lettuces served with smoked salmon, a chicken *pastilla* (pie) laced with cinnamon, baby squid with curry served on a bed of lentils, roasted lamb served in puff pastry with fresh basil, and the choicest langostinos from Cádiz. The food is sublime, and the inviting ambience makes you relax as you sit back to enjoy dishes that dazzle the eye, notably venison and rabbit arranged on a plate with fresh greens to evoke an autumnal scene in a forest.

Juan de Mena 14. 🕾 **91-531-52-22.** Reservations recommended. Main courses 28€–48€ ($35–$60). V. Mon–Sat 1:30–4pm and 9pm–midnight. Closed 1 week at Easter. Metro: Banco de España.

MODERATE

El Buey SPANISH   This *casera* (homely) eating spot, with its cozy ambience and colorful bullfighting decor, lies in residential Salamanca close to Goya and Alcalá street. Twin of a more boisterous branch near Opera, it's a meat-eater's haven, specializing in quality steaks and joints cooked to individual needs. After an initial *picoteo* (selection of tidbits such as olives, stuffed anchovies, or *jamón Serrano*), go for the main favorite *lomo de buey* (ox loin or beef filet). Nonmeat specialties on the menu may include *pimientos rellenos de mariscos* (peppers stuffed with shellfish). Homemade desserts such as *crepes rellenos de chocolate* (chocolate-filled crepes) are good follow-ups.

General Pardiñas 10. 🕾 **91-431-44-92.** Main courses 12€–20€ ($15–$25). AE, DC, MC, V. Mon–Sat 1–4pm and 9pm–midnight. Metro: Goya.

La Galette VEGETARIAN/INTERNATIONAL   La Galette was one of Madrid's first vegetarian restaurants, and it remains one of the best. Small and charming, it lies in a residential and shopping area in the exclusive Salamanca district, near Plaza de la Independencia and the northern edge of Retiro Park. It has a limited selection of meat dishes, but the true allure lies in this establishment's imaginative preparation of vegetables. Examples include baked stuffed peppers, omelets, eggplant croquettes, and even vegetarian hamburgers. Some of the dishes are macrobiotic. The place is also noted for its mouth-watering pastries. The same owners also operate La Galette II, in the same complex.

Conde de Aranda 11. (✆ 91-576-06-41. Reservations recommended. Main courses 6€–18€ ($7.50–$23); fixed-price lunch 7€ ($8.75). AE, DC, MC, V. Mon–Sat 2–4pm and 9pm–midnight. Metro: Retiro.

Taberna de la Daniela ✶ *Finds* MADRILEÑO   Just up the road from El Buey, this much-loved *castizo* taberna, with its traditional zinc-top bar and wall tiles, is among the very best Madrileño eating spots for enjoying *cocido*. They even include a junior version *(cocido pequeño)* on their *menú infantil*. Another great specialty here is *besugo la madrileña—besugo* (or bream) being the most highly esteemed fish in the capital, more for its exquisite flavor than for its price. Other homemade dishes include *sopa de fideos* (noodle soup) and *huesos de tuétano* (marrow bone). The dining area, set back beside pillars from the tapas bar, is quiet and relaxing and the service friendly.

General Pardiñas 21. (✆ 91-575-23-29. Reservations recommended. Main courses 12€–18€ ($15–$23). MC, V. Daily 1–4pm and 8–11:30pm (weekends till 1am). Metro: Goya.

Teatriz ✶ ITALIAN   Decorated by the famed French architect and designer Philippe Starck, this old theater is now transformed into a top-notch Italian restaurant. Theater seats have long given way to dining tables, but Starck kept many of the elements of the old theater. As you head for the restrooms, you encounter a stunning fountain of marble, silver, and gold, everything bathed in a bluish light, making you think you're in a nightclub. The kitchen closes at midnight, but the bar remains open until 3am. The dishes are genuine and cleverly crafted. Launch yourself with fresh mozzarella with tomatoes in virgin olive oil or raw salmon and turbot flavored with fresh dill. One of the best pastas is a tortellini filled with Parmesan-flavored ground meat. The desserts are worth saving room for, including cannelloni stuffed with dark chocolate or a fresh cheese mousse with mango ice cream. There is also a velvety-smooth tiramisu.

Calle Hermosilla 15. (✆ 91-577-53-79. Reservations recommended. Main courses 11€–17€ ($14–$21); *menú completo* 20€ ($25). AE, DC, MC, V. Daily 1:30–4pm and 8:30pm–12:30am. Closed Aug. Metro: Serrano.

INEXPENSIVE

Iroco ✶ INTERNATIONAL   This well-run and popular Salamanca restaurant, known for its *nueva cocina* (nouvelle cuisine), attracts businessmen and -women for its lunch and a trend-setting and younger crowd in the evening. Yes, that was Felipe, the crown prince of Spain, I spotted entering the restaurant with an entourage. Some of the more daring dishes, such as mixing apples with asparagus, may not be to your tastes, but you may find other dishes enticing, including my recently sampled tuna steak in a marinade (then grilled to perfection). The eggplant lasagna served here is also a delight, with fresh mushrooms and lots of creamy mozzarella. Whitefish salad in a delightful sherry vinaigrette is a good luncheon choice on a hot day. Inspired by Asian fusion cuisine, the prawn rolls make a delightful beginning. Another good dish is *merluza* (hake) from the north coast, served in an asparagus sauce. Desserts are always tempting and made fresh daily.

Calle Velázquez 18. (✆ 91-431-73-81. Reservations required. Main courses 13€–17€ ($16–$21). AE, DC, MC, V. Daily 1:30–4pm and 8:30pm–midnight. Metro: Goya.

13 Chamberí

VERY EXPENSIVE

Jockey ✦✦✦ INTERNATIONAL   This is a deluxe culinary citadel. For decades, it was the premier restaurant of Spain. A favorite of international celebrities, diplomats, and heads of state, it was once known as the Jockey Club, although "Club" was eventually dropped because it suggested exclusivity. The restaurant, with tables on two levels, isn't large. Wood-paneled walls and colored linen provide a cozy ambience. Against the paneling are a dozen prints of jockeys mounted on horses—hence the name.

Since Jockey's establishment shortly after World War II, each chef who has come along has prided himself on coming up with new and creative dishes. You can still order Beluga caviar from Iran but might settle happily for the goose-liver terrine or slices of Jabugo ham. Cold melon soup with shrimp is soothing on a hot day, especially when followed by grill-roasted young pigeon from Talavera or sole filets with figs in chardonnay. Stuffed small chicken Jockey-style is a specialty, as is *tripa madrileña,* a local dish. Desserts are sumptuous.

Amador de los Ríos 6. © 91-319-24-35. Reservations required. Main courses 21€–35€ ($26–$44). AE, DC, MC, V. Daily 1–4pm and 9pm–midnight. Closed Aug. Metro: Colón.

EXPENSIVE

Belagua BASQUE   This glamorous restaurant was originally built in 1894 as a small palace in the French neoclassical style. In 1991 Catalan designer Josep Joanpere helped transform the building into a carefully detailed hotel (the Santo Mauro), which I've recommended separately (p. 110). On the hotel premises is this highly appealing postmodern restaurant, today one of the capital's finest.

Assisted by the well-mannered staff, you'll select from a menu whose inspiration and ingredients change with the seasons. Examples include watermelon-and-prawn salad, light cream of cold ginger soup, haddock baked in a crust of potatoes tinted with squid ink, filet of monkfish with prawn-and-zucchini sauce, and duck with honey and black cherries. Depending on the selection that day, dessert might include miniature portions of flan with strawberry sauce and an array of the day's pastries. The restaurant's name, incidentally, derives from a village in Navarre known for its natural beauty.

In the Santo Mauro Hotel, Calle Zurbano 36. © 91-319-69-00. Reservations recommended. Main courses 15€–25€ ($19–$31). AE, DC, MC, V. Daily 1:30–3:30pm and 8:30–11:30pm. Metro: Rubén Darío or Alonso Martínez.

La Broche ✦✦ CATALAN   The Catalan chef, Sergi Arola, is generating culinary excitement in Madrid, a Castilian city that in the past never paid a lot of respect to the cuisine of Barcelona. Arola trained under Catalonia's greatest chef, El Ferran Adrià of El Bulli. Arola learned from the master, but in Madrid he is creating his own magic with imaginative dishes. Forget the dull lobby of the Hotel Miguel Angel, a holdover from the 1970s, and enter this elegant dining enclave. Deluxe ingredients, personally selected by the chef and changed to take advantage of the best in any season, are fashioned into some of the capital's most flavor-filled dishes. Launch yourself into your repast with raw seafood and seawater gelée and then proceed across the heavenly menu, perhaps selecting a salmon risotto or a carpaccio of wild mushrooms. Even the bread placed on your table is freshly made and a delight, as are the creative desserts.

Calle Miguel Angel 29. © 91-399-34-37. Reservations required. Main courses 24€–26€ ($30–$33). AE, DC, MC, V. Mon–Fri 2–3:15pm and 9–11:30pm. Closed Aug. Metro: Rubén Darío or Gregorio Marañón.

Las Cuatro Estaciones 😊😊😊 MEDITERRANEAN   Las Cuatro Estaciones is placed by gastronomes and horticulturists alike among their favorite Madrid dining spots, and is neck and neck with the prestigious Jockey. In addition to superb food, the establishment prides itself on decorating with mass arrangements of flowers that change with the season. Depending on the time of year, the mirrors surrounding the multilevel bar near the entrance reflect thousands of hydrangeas, chrysanthemums, or poinsettias. Each person involved in food preparation spends a prolonged apprenticeship at restaurants in France before returning home to try their talents on the taste buds of aristocratic Madrid.

Representative specialties include crab bisque; a petite marmite of fish and shellfish; and a nouvelle cuisine version of blanquette of monkfish so tender it melts in your mouth. The desserts include daily specials brought temptingly to your table.

General Ibáñez Ibero 5. 🕐 **91-553-63-05.** Reservations required. Main courses 42€–54€ ($53–$68); fixed-price dinner 45€ ($56). AE, DC, MC, V. Mon–Fri 1:30–4pm; Mon–Sat 9pm–midnight. Closed Easter and Aug. Metro: Guzmán el Bueno.

MODERATE

Annapurna INDIAN   Regarded by many as the best Indian restaurant in Madrid, this refined locale stands in a relaxing Chamberí backwater just west of the Castellana. Immaculate and helpful service and a stylish dining room with charming views of an interior garden enhance the superlative cuisine. You might start with a delicious meat and vegetable *samosa* and then go on to a main course choice of Jeenga Annapurna (shrimp in tamarind sauce) or one of the Annapurna's incomparable oven tandoori roasts. Among the array of tempting desserts, Gajar Halva (a carrot-and-almond-based tartlet) is a must.

Calle Zurbano 5. 🕐 **91-319-87-16.** Reservations recommended. Main courses 15€–25€ ($19–$31). *Menú de degustación* 25€ ($31). AE, DC, MC, V. Mon–Fri 1:45–4pm and 9–11:45pm; Sat 1:45–4pm. Closed public holidays. Metro: Alonso Martínez.

Balear PAELLA/SEAFOOD   Only a handful of other restaurants in Madrid focus as aggressively as this one on the national dish of Spain, paella, which here comes in 14 different versions with permutations that might surprise even the most jaded aficionado. Once seated in the yellow-and-white dining room loaded with potted plants, you can order any of several paellas, including versions with shellfish, with chicken and shellfish, with pork, with crabs, with lobster, and an all-black version that's tinted with squid ink for extra flavor. There's even a vegetarian version if you absolutely, positively hate fish. Lots of journalists, writers, poets, and artists seem to have adopted this place.

Calle Sagunto 18. 🕐 **91-447-91-15.** Reservations recommended. Main courses 10€–14€ ($13–$18). AE, MC, V. Daily 1:30–4pm; Tues–Sat 8:30–11:30pm. Metro: Iglesia.

Casa Mundi MADRILEÑO   A traditional no-frills Madrileño restaurant that is very popular with local Chamberí residents. Its flavorsome dishes range from hearty leg of lamb and *cocido* (stew) to baked *besugo* (sea bream). The service is down-to-earth efficient. There's a fairly limited wine list, so best to go for a reliable Rioja.

Calle Donoso Cortes 14. 🕐 **91-446-60-06.** Main courses 15€–20€ ($19–$25) AE, DC, MC, V. Mon–Sat lunch and dinner; call for hours. Metro: Quevedo.

Ciao Madrid ITALIAN   Members of the extended Laguna family run two of these successful Italian eating spots in Madrid. The first was established 15 years ago on Calle Apodaca and the second (Calle Argensola; 🕐 **91-308-25-19**) followed shortly after. Both feature minimalist Milanese decor, dark furnishings, and a tasty menu highlighted by risottos and homemade pastas—here it's quite okay to have pasta as a main dish. Tagliatelle with mushrooms is a recommended favorite. For a more substantial repast, you might also consider osso buco or veal parmigiana or choose from the interesting fish selection. (See also Chueca branch, p. 148.)

Calle Apodaca 20. ✆ **91-447-00-36.** Pasta 10€–12€ ($13–$15); main courses 12€–24€ ($15–$30) AE, DC, MC, V. Mon–Fri 1:30–3:45 pm and Mon–Sat 9:30pm–12:30am. Apodaca branch closes in Sept and the Argensola branch closes in Aug. Metro: Tribunal.

La Cava Real 🏵🏵 FRENCH/BASQUE   If your wine is as important to you as the meal itself, this is the Madrid restaurant of choice for connoisseurs of *vino*. When the tavern opened in 1983, it was the first real wine bar Madrid had ever seen. Since then, there have been many others, but La Cava Real remains the best. It's linked to Spain's largest wine club. Just don't mention the word *beer* here and you should do fine. There are more than 350 wines in the cellar, and you can order a staggering 50 of them by the glass, which allows you to sample more than one wine at the same meal if you so desire.

Turn to the skilled maitre d', Chema Gómez, for advice on wine. The chef, Javier Collar, hardly neglects the cuisine in favor of the wine, turning out a smooth and well-executed cuisine that weds two great kitchens, that of France and that of the Basque country. I was enchanted with his pimientos stuffed with cod and his grilled and sweet-tasting *merluza* (hake) caught along the Basque coast. He also does wine, and in the autumn wild game such as partridge appears on the menu. The cheese selection deserves an award, and the chef also makes marvelous, really sumptuous, desserts fresh daily; it's worth saving room for one.

Espronceda 34, Chamberí. ✆ **91-442-54-32.** Reservations required. Main courses 14€–21€ ($18–$26); *menú de degustación* 46€ ($58). AE, DC, MC, V. Mon–Sat 1:30–4pm and 9pm–midnight. Closed Aug. Metro: Río Rojas.

Kikuyu 🏵 MEDITERRANEAN   No African dishes from the heart of Kenya are provided here, in spite of the name. Instead the light, healthy, rice-and-fish-dominated menu conjures up the Mediterranean shores of Levante. It's also very strong on vegetarian *platos* such as *setas* (mushroom) carpaccio, and it has a good wine list. The atmosphere is cool with metal-gray decor offset by a plant-filled inner courtyard that's illuminated at night.

Barbara de Braganza 4. ✆ **91-319-66-11.** Main courses 12.50€–22.50€ ($16–$28). MC, V. Mon–Sat 2–4pm and 9pm–midnight. Closed first 2 weeks in Aug. Metro: Colon or Alonso Martínez.

Mosaiq 🏵 MOROCCAN   Vividly decorated in exotic turquoise, orange, and cream-hued silks, Mosaiq is a visual treat even before you get started on the delicious food. One of Madrid's most stimulating non-Spanish-eating spots (with the added bonus of discreetly attentive service), it specializes in North African dishes of the highest order: *montabal* (eggplant dip), prawn brochettes, chicken tagine, and lamb *klefta,* among its gourmet highlights. The three dining areas all have traditional low-level tables with cushions and hassocks. After dinner, choose from an excellent selection of teas.

Calle Caracas 21. ✆ **91-308-44-46.** Set menu for two: 25€–30€ ($31–$38). AE, DC, MC, V. Metro: Alonso Martínez.

14 Chamartín

VERY EXPENSIVE

El Chaflán 🏵 SPANISH   One of Madrid's hot new chefs, Juan Pablo Felipe Pablado, is a master in the kitchen. He can take almost any dish, including the classics, and give it a new flavor and texture. For example, he virtually deconstructs the most famous soup of Spain, gazpacho, and reassembles it into *glaces* and mousses. There's a firm hand in control here, and the chef personally selects the best produce, fish, and local meats to concoct his dishes. A recent mushroom risotto was perfectly prepared and full of flavor, as was the main course, a roast suckling pig that would rival any in Segovia, where they say this dish is prepared better than anywhere else in the world.

Av. Pío XII 34. *C* **91-350-61-93.** Reservations required. Main courses 22€–30€ ($28–$38); fixed-price menus 45€–89€ ($56–$111). AE, DC, MC, V. Mon–Fri 1:30–4pm; Mon–Sat 9–11:30pm. Metro: Pío XII.

EXPENSIVE

Cabo Mayor 🔍🔍 SEAFOOD   Near Chamartín train station, this is one of the best, most popular, and most stylish restaurants in Madrid, attracting on occasion the king and queen of Spain. An open-air staircase leading to the entranceway descends from a manicured garden on a quiet side street where a battalion of uniformed doormen stands ready to greet arriving taxis. The restaurant's decor is nautically inspired, with hardwood panels, brass trim, pulleys and ropes, a tile floor custom-painted with sea-green and blue replicas of waves, and hand-carved models of fishing boats. Some dozen bronze statues honoring anglers and their craft are displayed in brass portholes in illuminated positions of honor.

Menu choices include paprika-laden peppers stuffed with fish, a salad composed of Jabugo ham and foie gras of duckling, Cantabrian fish soup, stewed sea bream with thyme, asparagus mousse, salmon in sherry sauce, and loin of veal in cassis sauce. Desserts include a rice mousse with pine-nut sauce.

Juan Ramón Jiménez 37. *C* **91-350-87-76.** Reservations recommended. Main courses 15€–31€ ($19–$39). AE, DC, MC, V. Mon–Sat 1:30–4pm and 8:45–11:45pm. Closed 1 week at Easter. Metro: Cuzco.

El Olivo Restaurant 🔍🔍 MEDITERRANEAN   Locals praise the success of a non-Spaniard (in this case, French-born Jean Pierre Vandelle) in recognizing the international appeal of two of Spain's most valuable culinary resources: olive oil and sherry. Designed in tones of green and amber, this is the only restaurant in Spain that wheels a cart stocked with 40 regional olive oils from table to table. From the cart, diners select a variety to soak up with chunks of rough-textured bread seasoned with a dash of salt.

Menu specialties prepared by Chef Gonzalo Omiste include grilled filet of monkfish marinated in herbs and olive oil, then served with black-olive sauce over compote of fresh tomatoes, and four preparations of cod arranged on a single platter and served with a *pil-pil* sauce (cod gelatin and herbs whipped into a mayonnaise-like consistency with olive oil). Among the other delicious olive-based dishes are *ensalada de bogavante a las finas hierbas* (lobster salad with fine herbs), *salmón y mero* (oil-marinated salmon and grouper), and *Pedro Ximénez foie gras con frutas rojas.* Dessert might be one of several different chocolate pastries.

Note: Many clients deliberately arrive early as an excuse to linger in El Olivo's one-of-a-kind sherry bar. Although other drinks are offered, the bar features more than 100 brands of *vino de Jerez,* more than practically any other establishment in Madrid. Priced at 1.50€ to 4.50€ ($1.70–$5.15) per glass, they make the perfect aperitif. Also note that most main courses fall at the lower end of the price listing below.

General Gallegos 1. *C* **91-359-15-35.** Reservations recommended. Main courses 19€–27€ ($24–$34); fixed-price meals 42€ ($53). AE, DC, MC, V. Tues–Sat 1–4pm and 9pm–midnight. Closed Aug 15–31 and 4 days around Easter. Metro: Plaza de Castilla.

Moments **Picnic, Anyone?**

On a hot day, do as the Madrileños do: Secure the makings of a picnic lunch and head for Casa de Campo (Metro: El Batón), those once-royal hunting grounds in the west of Madrid across the Manzanares River. Children delight in this adventure, as they can also visit a boating lake, the Parque de Atracciones, and the Madrid zoo.

Your best choice for picnic fare is **Rodilla**, Preciados 25 (© **91-522-54-67**; Metro: Callao), where you can find sandwiches, pastries, and takeout tapas. Sandwiches, including vegetarian, meat, and fish, begin at .75€ (94¢). It's open Monday and Tuesday from 8:30am to 10:30pm; Wednesday, Thursday, and Sunday from 9am to 11pm; Friday and Saturday from 9am to 11:30pm.

Príncipe de Viana _☞_ BASQUE   This place has gotten rave reviews. Fish is of course the most important staple of Basque cuisine, and here you have a wide selection from which to choose. You might go the traditional route, with _bacalao ajoarriera_ (cod with red peppers and tomatoes) or _merluza en salsa verde_ (hake in parsley, garlic, and olive oil sauce). More adventurous modern concoctions include a salad with _chipirones_ (baby squid) and _mollejas_ (sweet meats) in a soy vinaigrette. Those with a sweet tooth will be more than satisfied with the dessert of cream cheese and mango sorbet. From the many Spanish and occasional foreign wines to choose from, the Albariño from Galicia is particularly recommended.

Calle Manuel de Falla 5. © **91-457-15-49**. Reservations required. Main courses 12€–18€ ($15–$23). AE, DC, MC, V. Mon–Fri 1–4pm and 9–11:30pm; Sat 9–11:30pm. Closed Aug. Metro: Lima or Cuzco.

MODERATE

Goizeko Kabi _☞_ BASQUE   This restaurant serves some of the best Basque dishes in Madrid in an intimate, understated interior. Particularly delicious is the starter of _boquerones,_ almost sweet anchovies marinated in garlic and olive oil. I loved the _bacalao pil-pil vizcaina_ (cod in a Basque garlic sauce) and the wonderfully juicy king prawns. Dessert lovers will revel in the orange mousse with a coating of bitter chocolate or the more experimental black bread ice cream with coffee sauce.

Comandante Zorita 37. © **91-533-01-85**. Reservations recommended. Main courses 11€–30€ ($14–$38). AE, DC, MC, V. Mon–Sat 1–4pm and 8:30pm–midnight. Metro: Alvarado.

INEXPENSIVE

Alfredo's Barbacoa AMERICAN   Alfredo's is a popular rendezvous for Americans longing for home-style food. Al himself arrives at his bar/restaurant wearing boots, blue jeans, and a 10-gallon hat; his friendly welcome has made the place a center for both his friends and newcomers to Madrid. You _can_ have hamburgers here, but they are of the barbecued variety, and you might prefer the barbecued spareribs or chicken. The salad bar is an attraction. And it's a rare treat to be able to have corn on the cob in Spain.

The original **Alfredo's Barbacoa,** Lagasca 5 (© **91-576-62-71;** Metro: Retiro), is still in business, and also under Al's auspices.

Juan Hurtado de Mendoza 11. © **91-345-16-39**. Reservations recommended. Main courses 6.75€–15€ ($8.40–$19). AE, DC, MC, V. Mon–Sat 1–4:30pm and 8:30pm–midnight (Fri–Sat until 1am). Metro: Cuzco.

15 In the Arturo Soria District

MODERATE

Nicómedes (Finds) EXTREMADURAN   This is a real discovery. This colonial-style building has been completely refurbished by the charming Suárez sisters into a modern-looking chateau of five floors with beautiful, tall bay windows covering the full height of this impressive edifice. The immensity of the windows allows copious amounts of natural light to flood into the dining areas. The pervading atmosphere is one of openness combined with friendly hospitality. Customers often dine out in fine weather on a summer terrace. The modernity of the building is reflected in the style of the cuisine as well. The dishes from the western province of Extremadura are given a Madrid showcase here. Goat cheese with glazed onions is a tasty opener, as are *bolsitas rellenas de gamba y queso fresco* (crispy pasta balls stuffed with shrimp and freshly made cheese). *Rapa al horno con habitas y ajetes* (baked monkfish with beans and tender garlic) is a savory offering, although *solomillo de buey* (fondue of ox steak) is more typical of the region. For dessert, try the homemade cake of the day or a special sweet "biscuit" made with prunes and served with a caramel sauce.

Moscatelar 18. (©) **91-388-78-28.** Reservations recommended. Main courses 12€–16€ ($15–$20). AE, DC, V. Tues–Sat 1:30–3:30pm and 9:30pm–midnight; Sun 1:30–3:30pm. Closed Aug. Metro: Esperanza or Arturo Soria.

16 Near Plaza República Argentina

EXPENSIVE

Casa Benigna MEDITERRANEAN/SCANDINAVIAN   This small bistro lies in the northern sector of Madrid and has been run by the family of Jorge García for more than a decade. It is decorated in typically inviting Mediterranean style with blue walls and with murals of rural landscapes, even a library of books. The restaurant is the only one in Madrid that blends the cuisine of the far north of Europe with that of the sunny Mediterranean countries. The family has a close relative in Norway who contributes to their Scandinavian recipes. The dishes are exquisitely prepared and based on the finest ingredients. Here, you can order everything from Norwegian herring in delectable marinades to *arroz abanda,* a variation of traditional paella using different varieties of seafood. One especially good dish is the roast ribs of tender baby lamb. Many vegetarians appreciate their *parrillada de verduras,* or grilled fresh vegetables. For dessert, opt for the Norwegian cookies with wild berries or freshly made crepes with applesauce.

Benigno Soto 9. (©) **91-413-33-56.** Reservations required. Main courses 42€–48€ ($53–$60). AE, DC, MC, V. Mon–Sat 1:30–3:30pm and 9–11pm; Sun 1:30–4pm. Metro: Concha Espina.

MODERATE

Nodo (Finds) SPANISH/JAPANESE   Ironically named after the old Franco-era news agency (Noticias Documentales), which used to be housed across the road, this trendy eating spot offers a polar-opposite atmosphere of cool minimalism and ultrachic decor that tends to attract a high number of celebrity customers. There's nothing commonplace about the food, either. The restaurant's owner, Alberto Chicote, has successfully fused East and West gourmet tastes with dishes like *tataki de atún con ajo blanco malagueño* (Asian tuna with Málaga white garlic sauce) and sushi tempura. Other individual delights include *chipirones en su tinta* (baby squid cooked in its own ink), sushi, *guachalomo,* and "parcels" of leaf-enclosed fish. Japanese sake is also served. Simple but exotically named desserts like white chocolate bombe and *napoleón de fresas* finish off the meal. Service is extremely attentive, and prices are not as high as you might expect.

Calle Velázquez 150, 28002. ✆ **91-564-40-44.** Main courses 12€–24€ ($15–$22.50). AE, DC, MC, V. Mon–Thurs 1:30–4pm and 9pm–midnight; Fri–Sun 1:30–4pm and 9pm–1am. Metro: República Argentina.

Príncipe y Serrano ✰ CASTILIAN   In an exclusive area of the Serrano district, this classic restaurant exudes distinction. Its sophisticated dining areas on both floors offer a warm and cozy atmosphere, and the outside lawns and flowered patios (one of them resembling a miniature golf course with small swimming pools) make you forget you are in the center of a big city. There is the big *salón central,* two small dining areas for more private dinners, plus a bar downstairs. The cooking is simple, yet cosmopolitan, and always done to perfection. One especially good dish is roast potatoes with mussels. Based on the sea's bounty, try the *manitas de ibérico rellenas de morcilla* (pork filled with chorizo). I delight in the freshly made apple tart with prune sauce or the crepes filled with mango and served in a fancy caramel cream sauce.

Serrano 240. ✆ **91-458-62-31.** Reservations recommended. Main courses 12€–22€ ($15–$28). AE, DC, MC, V. Daily 1:30–4pm; Mon–Sat 9pm–midnight. Closed Aug. Metro: Colombia or Concha Espina.

INEXPENSIVE

Casa Mingo ASTURIAN/SPANISH   Casa Mingo has been known for decades for its cider, both still and bubbly. The perfect accompanying tidbit is a piece of the local Asturian *cabrales* (goat cheese), but the roast chicken is the specialty of the house, with a large number of helpings served daily. There's no formality here; customers share big tables under the vaulted ceiling in the dining room. In summer, the staff sets up tables and wooden chairs out on the sidewalk. This is not so much a restaurant as a *bodega/taberna* that serves food.

Paseo de la Florida 34. ✆ **91-547-79-18.** Main courses 3.30€–7€ ($4.10–$8.75). No credit cards. Daily 11am–midnight. Metro: Príncipe Pío, and then 15-min. walk.

Cervecería Alemana TAPAS   This place earned its name because of its long-ago German clients. Opening directly onto one of the liveliest little plazas in Madrid, it clings to its turn-of-the-20th-century traditions. Young Madrileños are fond of stopping in for a mug of draft beer. You can sit at one of the tables leisurely sipping beer or wine since the waiters make no attempt to hurry you along. To accompany your beverage, try the fried sardines or a Spanish omelet. Many of the *tascas* on this popular square are crowded and noisy—often with blaring loud music—but this one is quiet and a good place to have a conversation.

Plaza de Santa Ana 6. ✆ **91-429-70-33.** Beer 1.50€–2.50€ ($1.90–$3.10); tapas 1.80€–12€ ($2.25–$15). No credit cards. Sun–Thurs 11am–12:30am; Fri–Sat 11am–2am. Metro: Tirso de Molina.

Cervecería Santa Bárbara TAPAS   Unique in Madrid, Cervecería Santa Bárbara is an outlet for a beer factory, and the management has done a lot to make it modern and inviting. Hanging globe lights and spinning ceiling fans create an attractive ambience, as does the black-and-white checkerboard marble floor. You go here for beer, of course: *cerveza negra* (black beer) or *cerveza dorada* (golden beer). The local brew is best accompanied by homemade potato chips or by fresh shrimp, lobster, crabmeat, or barnacles. You can either stand at the counter or go directly to one of the wooden tables for waiter service.

Plaza de Santa Bárbara 8. ✆ **91-319-04-49.** Beer 1.50€–2.50€ ($1.90–$3.10); tapas 2.10€–24€ ($2.60–$30). MC, V. Daily 11:30am–midnight. Metro: Alonso Martínez. Bus: 3, 7, or 21.

The Best of the *Tascas*

Don't starve waiting around for Madrid's fashionable 9:30 or 10pm dinner hour. Throughout the city you'll find *tascas,* bars that serve wine and platters of tempting hot and cold hors d'oeuvres known as tapas: mushrooms, salads, baby eels, shrimp, lobster, mussels, sausage, ham, and, in one establishment, bull testicles. Keep in mind that you can often save euros by ordering at the bar rather than occupying a table. Here are two of my favorites:

La Atalaya *Value* CANTABRIAN   The owner of this pleasant restaurant, Gena Sánchez, hails from Santander in northern Spain and, in the typical style of her hometown, has decorated the yellow walls of her establishment with a plethora of modern paintings. The food is also typical of Spain's green northern coast, with an emphasis on fresh fish. Every Thursday and Saturday the chefs prepare the most typical dish of Santander, a hearty cabbage soup. Called *cocido montanés,* it is also made with sausage, green beans, and black pudding. *Caracoles marucas,* or clams Santander style, prepared in a spicy sauce, is another good offering, as is *sopa de pescado,* or fish soup, one of the finest of its kind in Madrid. You might opt for a *torta de queso caliente,* a warm cheese soufflé. For dessert, traditional regional puddings are served.

Joaquín Costa 31. (℮) **91-562-87-45.** Reservations recommended. Main courses 10€–16€ ($13–$20); fixed-price menu 12€ ($15). AE, DC, MC, V. Tues–Sat 1:30–4pm and 9pm–midnight. Metro: República de Argentina.

La Taberna de Antonio Sánchez ℱ TAPAS   Named in 1850 after the founder's son, who was killed in the bullring, this *taberna* is full of bullfighting memorabilia, including the stuffed head of the animal that gored young Sánchez. Also featured on the dark paneled walls are three works by the Spanish artist Zuloaga, who had his last public exhibition in this restaurant near Plaza Tirso de Molina. A limited array of tapas, including garlic soup, is served with Valdepeñas wine drawn from a barrel—though many guests ignore the edibles in favor of smoking cigarettes and arguing the merits of this or that bullfighter. A restaurant in the back serves Spanish food with a vaguely French influence.

Mesón de Parades 13. (℮) **91-539-78-26.** Tapas (in the bar) 1.50€–2.10€ ($1.90–$2.60); main courses 7€–11€ ($8.75–$14); fixed-price lunch (Mon–Fri) 6.60€ ($8.25). MC, V. Daily 1–4pm; Mon–Sat 8pm–midnight. Metro: Tirso de Molina.

Foster's Hollywood *Kids* AMERICAN   When your addiction to Stateside food becomes overwhelming, head here. When Foster's opened its doors in 1971, it was not only the first American-style restaurant in Spain, but one of the first in Europe. Since those early days, it has grown to 15 restaurants in Madrid and has even opened branches in Florida. A popular hangout for both locals and visiting Yanks, it offers a choice of dining rooms, ranging from classical club to a faux film studio with props. The varied menu includes Tex-Mex selections, ribs, steaks, sandwiches, freshly made salads, and, as its signature product, hamburgers grilled over natural charcoal. The *New York Times* once claimed that it had "probably the best onion rings in the world."

Paseo de la Castellana 116–118. ✆ **91-564-63-08.** Main courses 6€–17€ ($7.50–$21). AE, DC, MC, V. Sun–Thurs 1pm–midnight; Fri–Sat 1pm–2am. Metro: Nuevos Ministerios.

17 Cuatro Caminos

EXPENSIVE

O'Pazo ✷ GALICIAN This deluxe Galician restaurant is viewed by local cognoscenti as one of the top seafood places in the country. The fish is flown in daily from Galicia and mostly priced by weight at market rates. In front is a cocktail lounge and bar, all polished brass, with low sofas and paintings. Carpeted floors, cushioned Castilian furniture, soft lighting, and colored-glass windows complete the picture.

The fish and shellfish soup is delectable, although others gravitate to the seaman's broth as a beginning course. Natural clams are succulent, as are *cigalas* (a kind of crayfish), spider crabs, and Jabugo ham. Main dishes range from baby eels to sea snails, from Galician-style scallops to *zarzuela* (a seafood casserole).

Calle Reina Mercedes 20. ✆ **91-553-23-33.** Reservations required. Main courses 13€–25€ ($16–$31). MC, V. Mon–Sat 1–4pm and 8:30pm–midnight. Closed Aug. Metro: Nuevos Ministerios or Alvarado. Bus: 3 or 5.

San Mamés ✷ BASQUE/SPANISH/MADRILEÑO Situated in the north of the city in a historic building, this restaurant has been in the hands of the García family more than 50 years. The *tasca* (tavern) is decorated with colorful ceramic tiles and photographs of the celebrities who have dined here over the years. It is considered something of a secret address. With only two rooms, it has a homelike atmosphere of intimacy and good cheer. The cuisine offered is some of the best from both the Madrid and Basque kitchens. The owners shop carefully for the ingredients to prepare a repertoire of very tasty and well-flavored dishes. Their most typical dish is *callos a la madrileña,* a tripe stew with meat and chickpeas, beloved by their habitués. Otherwise, you might opt for *bacalao ajoarriero* (salt cod prepared with green peppers, tomatoes, and onions). Another dish favored in the Basque country is *cocochas de merluza,* which are the cheeks of the hake fish served with a bread sauce. For dessert, the owners recommend their *requesón con pasas* (cheesecake with raisins) or a hearty pudding called *tocino de cielo.*

Bravo Murillo 88. ✆ **91-534-50-65.** Reservations recommended. Main courses 17€–22€ ($21–$28); fixed-price menus 30€–36€ ($38–$45). AE, DC, MC, V. Mon–Fri 1:30–4pm and 8:30–11:30pm; Sat 1:30–4pm. Closed Aug. Metro: Cuatro Caminos.

INEXPENSIVE

Ceres VEGETARIAN Opened over a decade ago in the northwestern corner of the city, this is one of the longest-running green restaurants in Madrid, with a dedicated and faithful band of regulars so best to book a table before calling in. The eclectic range of dishes is based on fresh market ingredients; there is even a small on-site shop selling local products. Smoking, surprisingly for a vegetarian restaurant, is not frowned upon, so be warned.

Topete 32. ✆ **91-553-77-28.** Reservations recommended. Main courses 10€–15€ ($13–$19); midday menu 9€ ($11). Mon–Sat 1:30–4pm; Fri–Sat 8:30–11pm. Metro: Alvarado.

Las Batuecas *(Value)* SPANISH This restaurant unpretentiously calls itself a *casa de comidas,* or "meal house." Since 1954, the little restaurant of José Pascual and his family has been located near the *ciudad universitaria*. Many of their customers originally came here as students, and over the years have become devotees of the homemade Spanish food, which is wholesome and good without being pretentious. The decoration is plain, with old paintings and newspaper articles intermixed with cartoons and reviews by travel and food magazines in different languages. It has two floors with tables, all in the rustic style. But no one comes here for decor; the food is the attraction. Come here with a big appetite and launch yourself into a fine meal with such dishes as *tortilla de callos* (omelet with tripe), or perhaps squid cooked in its ink. You can try the fresh artichokes cooked with white wine and ham or *berenjenas rebosadas* (sliced eggplant batter-fried). One of the tastiest main dishes is shoulder flank of lamb roast, perfectly done. Desserts include almond, vanilla, or chocolate cakes, or a fine selection of puddings. Note that dinner is served only 2 nights a week.

Av. Reina Victoria 17. ℃ **91-554-04-52**. Reservations required. Main courses 16€–24€ ($20–$30); *menú completo* 18€ ($23). No credit cards. Mon–Sat 1–4pm; Thurs–Fri 9–11pm. Closed Aug. Metro: Guzmán El Bueno or Cuatro Caminos.

18 Fuencarral

Casa Pedro *(Finds* CASTILIAN   Largely unknown to outside visitors, this culinary oasis in the earthy northernly suburb of Fuencarral (a town in its own right 2 centuries ago) is the second-oldest restaurant in Madrid—after Sobrino de Botin. Founded in 1825 as a modest eating house for passing travelers, it was first known as La Casa de la Silvestra and then La Casa de la Pascuala in honor of the consecutive chunky Amazons who supervised its ever-busy kitchen. In the 1940s it acquired a new patron who upgraded its menu and standard of fare, and today it's entering its fifth generation of family ownership. The restaurant is divided into several different sections (separate rooms of the original house), where from its array of Castilian *asados* (roasts) you can savor a mouth-watering *conejo* (rabbit) dish that's considered by many to be the best in Madrid.

Nuestra Señora de Valvarde 119, Fuencarral. ℃ **91-734-02-01**. Main courses 12€–24€ ($15–$30). Major credit cards accepted. Mon–Sat 2–4:30pm and 9pm–midnight; Sun 2–4:30pm.

What to See & Do

Gone are the days when cynics would say there was nothing worth visiting in Madrid except the Prado (always a glibly patronizing statement anyway). Today, you're spoiled for choice with cultural amenities running the whole gamut from grandiose palaces and churches to information-crammed museums and art galleries, and possibly hedonistic attractions ranging from theater, concert halls, and international cinemas to a nonstop array of restaurants and round-the-clock nightspots. Not forgetting the upward of 18,000 bars and cafes liberally sprinkled throughout the city for whenever you need a breathing space and a *copa* (stemmed glass) of wine.

Greenbelts abound, with some of the finest parks you'll find anywhere (p. 187), and leisure and sports facilities exist in abundance—whether you want to participate or simply sit on the side as a spectator. Families with children are particularly fond of these grassy expanses. It's easy to get around with the inexpensive and well-run combination of bus, Metro, and *cercanías* (suburban-line train) transport. Taxis, too, are still good value. So dive in and enjoy the fun.

As in all European cities whose centers were originally designed for the horse and carriage, traffic is a problem, especially at rush-hour times. Best to avoid driving downtown yourself, especially during the heaviest traffic times.

1 The Major Museums: The "Golden Triangle" of Art

A cheap way to see many of the Spanish capital's cultural attractions is to purchase the **Madrid Card,** which combines a transportation pass (including Madrid Vision bus tours) with free entry to various museums and art centers. The cost is 28€ ($35) for a day, 42€ ($53) for 2 days, and 55€ ($69) for 3 days. Buy it at the at the main Plaza Mayor tourist office, on Madrid Vision buses, at newspaper *kioskos,* or online at **www.madridcard.com.**

Museo del Prado ★★★   With more than 7,000 paintings, the Prado is one of the most important repositories of art in the world. It began as a royal collection and was enlarged by the Habsburgs, especially Charles V, and later the Bourbons. In paintings of the Spanish school the Prado has no equal; on your first visit, concentrate on the Spanish masters (Velázquez, Goya, El Greco, and Murillo).

Major Italian works are exhibited on the ground floor. You'll see art by Italian masters—Raphael, Botticelli, Mantegna, Andrea del Sarto, Fra Angelico, and Correggio. The most celebrated Italian painting here is Titian's voluptuous Venus being watched by a musician who can't keep his eyes on his work.

The Prado is a trove of the work of El Greco (ca. 1541–1614), the Crete-born artist who lived much of his life in Toledo. You can see a parade of "The Greek's" saints, Madonnas, and Holy Families—even a ghostly John the Baptist.

Goya or No Goya, *The Milkmaid* & *The Colossus* Are Still Great Art

Spain's most fabled museum, the Prado, shocked the art world—and visitors, too—when it recently announced that two of its most famous paintings, *The Milkmaid of Bordeaux* and *The Colossus,* attributed to Francisco de Goya, are not in fact the work of this Spanish master. Goya specialists agree. The paintings still hang in the Prado, although their attribution has been changed to "attributed" to Goya instead of "by" Goya. Want to see some real Goyas? The Prado has some 150 actual paintings by the artist. At least I think that they do. Some Goya experts are questioning the authorship of some other "supposed" Goyas, especially several portraits. There was such a market for Goyas at the turn of the 19th century that many art dealers—surprise—kept turning up with "long-lost" Goyas.

You'll find a splendid array of works by the incomparable Diego Velázquez (1599–1660). The museum's most famous painting, in fact, is his *Las Meninas,* a triumph in the use of light effects. The faces of the queen and king are reflected in the mirror in the painting itself. The artist in the foreground is Velázquez, of course.

The Flemish painter Peter Paul Rubens (1577–1640), who met Velázquez while in Spain, is represented by the peacock-blue *Garden of Love* and by the *Three Graces.* Also noteworthy is the work of José Ribera (1591–1652), a Valencia-born artist and contemporary of Velázquez whose best painting is the *Martyrdom of St. Philip.* The Seville-born Bartolomé Murillo (1617–82)—often referred to as the "painter of Madonnas"—has three *Immaculate Conceptions* on display.

The Prado has an outstanding collection of the work of Hieronymus Bosch (1450?–1516), the Flemish genius. *The Garden of Earthly Delights,* the best-known work of "El Bosco," is here. You'll also see his *Seven Deadly Sins* and his triptych *The Hay Wagon.* See also *The Triumph of Death,* by another Flemish painter, Pieter Breughel the Elder (ca. 1525–69), who carried on Bosch's ghoulish vision.

Francisco de Goya (1746–1828) ranks along with Velázquez and El Greco in the trio of great Spanish artists. Hanging here are his unflattering portraits of his patron, Charles IV, and his family, as well as the *Clothed Maja* and the *Naked Maja.* You can also see the much-reproduced *Third of May* (1808), plus a series of Goya sketches (some of which, depicting the decay of 18th-c. Spain, brought the Inquisition down on the artist) and his expressionistic "black paintings."

Paseo del Prado. ☎ **91-330-28-00.** http://museoprado.mcu.es. Admission 6€ ($7.50) adults, 1.50€ ($1.90) students and seniors. Audio guides 3€. ($3.75) Tues–Sat 9am–7pm; free on Sun and holidays 9am–2pm. Closed Jan 1, Good Friday, May 1, and Dec 25. Metro: Banco de España or Atocha. Bus: 10, 14, 27, 34, 37, or 45.

Thyssen-Bornemisza Museum ★★★   Until around 1985, the contents of this museum virtually overflowed the premises of a legendary villa near Lugano, Switzerland. One of the most frequently visited sites of Switzerland, the collection had been laboriously amassed over a period of about 60 years by the Thyssen-Bornemisza family, scions of a century-old shipping, banking, mining, and chemical fortune with roots in Holland, Germany, and Hungary. Experts had proclaimed it as one of the world's most extensive and valuable privately owned collections of paintings, rivaled only by the legendary holdings of Queen Elizabeth II.

What to See & Do in Central Madrid

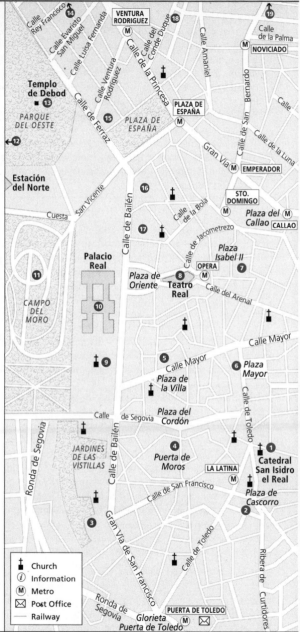

† Church
ⓘ Information
Ⓜ Metro
✉ Post Office
— Railway

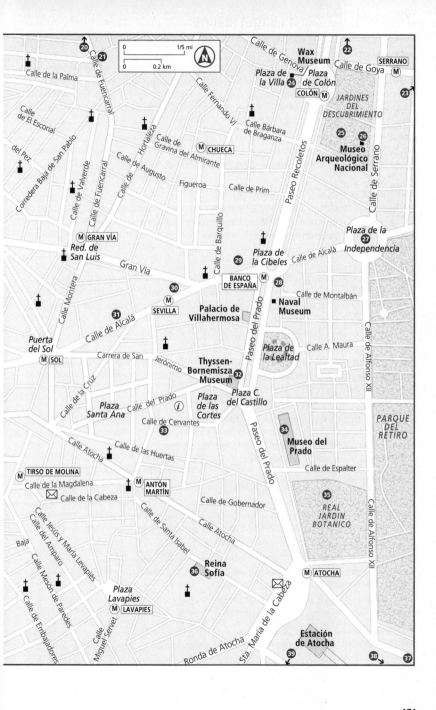

Calle de la Palma
Calle de la Palma
Calle de Fuencarral
Calle de Genova
Calle de Goya
Wax Museum
Plaza de la Villa
Plaza de Colón
SERRANO
COLÓN
JARDINES DEL DESCUBRIMIENTO
Calle de El Escorial
del Pez
Corredera Baja de San Pablo
Calle Fernando VI
Calle Bárbara de Braganza
Calle de Gravina del Almirante
Calle de Hortaleza
CHUECA
Calle de Valverde
Calle de Fuencarral
Calle de Augusto
Figueroa
Calle de Prim
Paseo Recoletos
Museo Arqueológico Nacional
Calle de Serrano
GRAN VÍA
Red. de San Luis
Gran Vía
Calle de Barquillo
Plaza de la Cibeles
Calle de Alcalá
Plaza de la Independencia
Calle Montera
BANCO DE ESPAÑA
Calle de Montalbán
SEVILLA
Palacio de Villahermosa
Naval Museum
Puerta del Sol
SOL
Calle de Alcalá
Carrera de San Jerónimo
Paseo del Prado
Plaza de la Lealtad
Calle A. Maura
Calle de Alfonso XII
Thyssen-Bornemisza Museum
Calle de la Cruz
Plaza Santa Ana
Calle del Prado
Plaza de las Cortes
Plaza C. del Castillo
Calle de Cervantes
PARQUE DEL RETIRO
Calle Atocha
Calle de las Huertas
Museo del Prado
TIRSO DE MOLINA
Calle de la Magdalena
Calle de la Cabeza
ANTÓN MARTÍN
Calle de Gobernador
Calle de Espalter
Calle Jesús y María
Calle del Amparo
Baja
Calle Mesón de Paredes
Calle de Santa Isabel
Calle Atocha
REAL JARDÍN BOTÁNICO
Calle de Alfonso XII
Reina Sofía
ATOCHA
Calle de Embajadores
Plaza Lavapiés
LAVAPIÉS
Calle Miguel Servet
Sta. María de la Cabeza
Estación de Atocha
Ronda de Atocha

1/5 mi
0.2 km

N

For tax and insurance reasons, and because the collection had outgrown the boundaries of the lakeside villa that contained it, the works were discreetly marketed in the early 1980s to the world's major museums. Amid endless intrigue, a litany of glamorous supplicants from eight different nations came calling. Among them were Margaret Thatcher and Prince Charles; trustees of the Getty Museum in Malibu, California; the president of West Germany; the duke of Badajoz, brother-in-law of King Carlos II; even emissaries from Walt Disney World in Orlando, Florida—all hoping to acquire the collection for their respective countries or entities.

Eventually, thanks partly to the lobbying by Baron Hans Heinrich Thyssen-Bornemisza's fourth wife, a Spanish-born beauty (and former Miss Spain) named Carmen Tita Cervera, the collection was awarded to Spain for $350 million. Controversies over the public cost of the acquisition raged for months. Despite the brouhaha, various estimates have placed the value of this collection between $1 billion and $3 billion.

To house the collection, an 18th-century building adjacent to the Prado, the Villahermosa Palace, was retrofitted with the appropriate lighting and security devices, and renovated at a cost of $45 million. Rooms are arranged numerically so that by following the order of the various rooms (nos. 1–48, spread out over three floors), a logical sequence of European painting can be traced from the 13th through the 20th centuries. The nucleus of the collection consists of 700 world-class paintings. They include works by, among others, El Greco, Velázquez, Dürer, Rembrandt, Watteau, Canaletto, Caravaggio, Hals, Memling, and Goya.

Unusual among the world's great art collections because of its eclecticism, the Thyssen group also contains goodly numbers of 19th- and 20th-century paintings by many of the notable French Impressionists, as well as works by Picasso, Sargent, Kirchner, Nolde, and Kandinsky—artists whose previous absence in Spanish museums had become increasingly obvious.

In addition to European paintings, major American works can also be viewed here, including paintings by Thomas Cole, Winslow Homer, Jackson Pollock, Mark Rothko, Edward Hopper, Robert Rauschenberg, Stuart Davis, and Roy Lichtenstein. There is also an agreeable and moderately priced cafeteria and restaurant on-site.

In 2004 an additional new exhibition opened in an extension occupying the site of two mansions (one the former Palace of Goyeneche) on adjoining Marqués de Cubas street. Known as the **Carmen Thyssen-Bornemisza Collection,** it occupies two floors, with Salas A to H on the second floor and Salas I to P on the first. The latter includes sculptures by Rodin, Fauvism, North American and German Impressionism, Post Impressionism, and Early Avant-Gardes of the 20th century. Among the standouts are works by Braque *(Marina a l'Estaque)* and Picasso *(Los Segadores)*. The second floor display contains 17th- to 19th-century paintings by Italian, Dutch, and Flemish artists. Realism and Early Impressionism are the main themes. Salas E and F feature some magnificent North American landscapes.

Palacio de Villahermosa, Paseo del Prado 8. ✆ **91-369-01-51** or 91-420-39-44. www.museothyssen.org. Admission 6€ ($7.50) adults, 4€ ($5) students and seniors, free for children 11 and under. Additional special exhibits: 4€ ($5) adults. Tues–Sun 10am–7pm. Metro: Banco de España. Bus: 1, 2, 5, 9, 10, 14, 15, 20, 27, 34, 45, 51, 52, 53, 74, 146, or 150.

Museo Nacional Centro de Arte Reina Sofía ★★★   Filling for the world of modern art the role that the Prado has filled for traditional art, the "MoMA" of Madrid (its nickname) is the greatest repository of 20th-century art in Spain. Set within the echoing, futuristically renovated walls of the former General Hospital, originally built between 1776 and 1781, the museum is a sprawling, high-ceilinged showplace named

after the Greek-born wife of Spain's present king. Once designated "the ugliest building" in Spain" by Catalan architect Oriol Bohigas, the Reina Sofía has a design that hangs in limbo somewhere between the 18th and the 21st centuries. It incorporates a 50,000-volume art library and database, a cafe, a theater, a bookstore, Plexiglas-sided elevators, and systems that calibrate security, temperature, humidity, and the quality of light surrounding the exhibits.

Special emphasis is paid to the great artists of 20th-century Spain: Juan Gris, Salvador Dalí, Joan Miró, and Pablo Picasso (the museum has been able to acquire a handful of his works). The work many critics feel is Picasso's masterpiece, *Guernica,* now rests at this museum after a long and troubling history of traveling. Banned in Spain during Franco's era (Picasso refused to have it displayed here anyway), it hung until 1980 at New York's Museum of Modern Art. The fiercely antiwar painting immortalizes the shameful blanket bombing of the town by the German Luftwaffe, fighting for Franco during the Spanish Civil War. Guernica was the cradle of the Basque nation, and Picasso's canvas made it a household name around the world.

Santa Isabel 52. © **91-467-50-62.** http://museoreinasofia.mcu.es. Admission 3€ ($3.75) adults, 1.50€ ($1.90) students, free after 2:30pm on Sat and all day Sun. Mon and Wed–Sat 10am–9pm; Sun 10am–2:30pm. Free guided tours Mon and Wed at 5pm, Sat at 11am. Metro: Atocha. Bus: 34, 41, or 55.

2 Near the Plaza Mayor & Puerta del Sol

Museo de la Real Academia de Bellas Artes de San Fernando (Fine Arts Museum) ☺☺   An easy stroll from Puerta del Sol, the Fine Arts Museum is located in the restored and remodeled 17th-century baroque palace of Juan de Goyeneche. The collection—more than 1,500 paintings and 570 sculptures, ranging from the 16th century to the present—was started in 1752 during the reign of Fernando VI (1746–59). It emphasizes works by Spanish, Flemish, and Italian artists. You can see masterpieces by El Greco, Rubens, Velázquez, Zurbarán, Ribera, Cano, Coello, Murillo, Goya, and Sorolla.

The same building also accommodates the **Museo de Calcografía Nacional** (© **91-524-08-83;** Mon–Sat 10am–2pm and 5–8pm; Sun 10am–2pm; free admission), which contains original plates used by Goya and other painters for engraving on copper or brass (an art known as chalcography). It's possible to buy limited edition prints here.

Alcalá 13. © **91-524-08-64.** Tues–Sat admission 3€ ($3.75) adults, 1.50€ ($1.90) students, free for children under 18. Tues–Fri 9am–7pm; Sat–Mon 9am–2pm. In July and Aug, open till 8:30pm Thurs. Free Wed. Metro: Puerta del Sol or Sevilla. Bus: 3, 15, 20, 51, 52, 53, or 150.

Palacio Real (Royal Palace) ☺☺   No longer occupied by royalty, but still used for state occasions, the Royal Palace stands on a ridge above the Manzanares River and Campo del Moro park. It was begun in 1738 on the site of the Madrid Alcázar, which burned to the ground in 1734. Some of its 2,000 rooms—which that "enlightened despot" Charles III called home—are open to the public; others are still used for state business. The palace was last used as a royal residence in 1931, before King Alfonso XIII and his wife, Victoria Eugénie, fled Spain.

Highlights of a visit include the Reception Room, the State Apartments, the Armory, and the Royal Pharmacy. To get an English-speaking guide, say *"inglés"* to the person who takes your ticket.

The Reception Room and State Apartments should get priority here if you're rushed. They include a rococo room with a diamond clock; a porcelain salon; the Royal

Value Hop on a Bus

It's always fun to explore a city by public transport. In Madrid you can do it for next to nothing, traveling as far as you like on the urban **red line buses** for 1.35€ ($1.70) a trip. Even more economical is the 10-pack metrobus ticket (5.35€/$6.70), valid for both buses and the Metro, which works out to only .55€ (70¢) a trip. You can buy the tickets at any Metro station or newspaper kiosk. To orient yourself, pick up a *Consorcio Transportes de Madrid* from one of the kiosks in the Puerta del Sol (1.50€/$1.90). This city bus route map marks all bus routes clearly. Here I've chosen half a dozen of the best red line bus trips around the city. Hope you enjoy them.

33: Príncipe Pío to Casa de Campo   This short run starts at the Príncipe Pío bus, Metro, and train junction at the end of Paseo de la Florida, just northwest of the Royal Palace. First follow the tree-lined avenue to the west of the Campo del Moro; then turn right across the Manzanares River at Puente de Toledo (Toledo bridge) before passing through the built-up zone of Puerta del Angel. From here cross the busy Paseo de Extremadura to enter the parklands of the Casa de Campo, stopping at the Parque de Atracciones (a fun park for teenagers), Batán (where bulls are penned prior to participating in *corridas* at the Ventas bullring), and the zoo. It's a great trip for families with children. Service runs every 15 minutes from 10am to 10pm.

54: Atocha to Vallecas   This route starts at Atocha and heads southeast along the Ciudad de Barcelona and Albufera avenues, via the lively junction of Puente Vallecas and across the M-40 highway to the Villa de Vallecas—a self-contained town which retains its earthy individuality (it still has its own football team) in spite of now being part of the Madrid community. "Gentrification" in the form of duplex flats, pedestrian *paseos,* and tree-lined avenues has transformed the center, but it remains at heart a traditional character-filled place, whose huge, 18th-century church of San Pedro Ad Vincula is a cultural monument. On your way back to Madrid, jump off at the Calle Pío Felipe stop just above the Buenos Aires Metro station and stroll onto the high grassy knolls of Cerro del Tío Pío park. From here you can enjoy panoramic views of Madrid, and on very clear days you can see the Gredos mountains of Avila province 100km (62 miles) to the west. Service runs every 5 minutes from 6am to 10pm.

75: Callao to Colonia Manzanares   This route takes you up the Gran Vía to Plaza España, where you turn left down the Cuesta de San Vicente to the Príncipe Pío junction, and then west along Avenida de la Florida to turn left again opposite the Casa Mingo restaurant and the Ermita de San Antonio de la Florida (an ornate chapel that contains some important Goya frescoes). Crossing the bridge over the River Manzanares, you enter the uniquely laid-back world of Colonia de Manzanares, which is nestled between the river and Casa del Campo. Its center is a small conglomeration of shops and cafes bordered by avenues of mature residential villas with gardens; on its riverside promenade you may see people fishing. The unexpected aura of peace and relaxation of this charming backwater seems light years—rather than just a 20-minute bus ride—away from the bustling Gran Vía. Service runs every 10 to 15 minutes from 6:15am to 11:30pm.

106: Manuel Becerra to Vicálvaro   This route starts at the Plaza de Manuel Becerra on the eastern edge of Salamanca district, follows Calle Alcalá past the imposing Ventas bullring, and heads over the M-30 highway before turning right down the quieter Avenida Daroca. Continuing past the cypress-filled Nuestra Señora de la Almudena cemetery (the largest in Spain) and the newly built flats and the parklands of San Blas and Las Rosas, you cross the M-40 and M-45 highways to reach Vicálvaro on the eastern fringe of Madrid. Like Vallecas, this historic little town is now officially part of the Spanish capital but remains a self-contained urban entity with a central 16th-century church, a local university, a modern Metro link, and a neighboring rail station with connections to Guadalajara and Atocha. Services run every 5 minutes from 7am to 10pm.

146: Callao to Barrio de la Concepción   Here is your chance to check out the city's changing architectural styles and moods as you progress along the length of Madrid's great east-west artery, Calle Alcalá. Starting at the center of the Gran Vía, you first pass the emblematic Cibeles fountain-statue and flamboyant turn-of-the-20th-century Palacio de Comunicaciones (Post Office) before continuing uphill to the neoclassical Puerta de Alcalá archway, opposite the main entrance to Retiro Park. From here the avenue extends farther east with the Retiro and neo-Mudéjar Antiguas Escuelas Aguirre building on your right, plus the shop-filled Velázquez and Príncipe Vergara streets of the elegant 19th-century Salamanca district on your left. Passing through Goya and Manuel Becerra squares to the Ventas bullring, you finally cross the M-30 bridge and turn left into the newer (ca. 1940s), homelier district of Barrio de la Concepción, which runs parallel to Alcalá. Step off at the tiny Calero park and stroll among the flowers, trees, and playgrounds, where hordes of toddlers play on swings next to a pine-shrouded open-air summer cinema—one of only two in Madrid. Then relax at an outdoor terrace table in the adjoining promenade-like Calle Virgen de Nuria and enjoy a Mahou beer and tapas in the sun. Service runs every 5 to 10 minutes from 7am to 11:30pm.

148: Callao to Méndez Alvaro (Parque Tierno Galván)   Route 148 heads north up the Gran Vía to Plaza España, and then turns sharp left into Calle Bailén, passing the Royal Palace, Almudena cathedral, and San Francisco el Grande Church. From here it sweeps down via the Ronda de Toledo and southerly districts of Embajadores and Legazpi to Méndez Alvaro, whose main-line bus station covers national and international destinations as far off as Romania. The route now leads west into a spacious park, named after Ernesto Tierno Galván, Madrid's most progressive mayor in the past 2 decades. Exit here and explore the surrounding greenery concealing a small amphitheater, IMAX theater, planetarium, and museum dedicated to Spain's top motorcyclist, Angel Nieto. Fine views north across the city abound from a small pergola. Service runs from 7:25am to 11:30pm every 10 to 15 minutes.

Chapel; the Banquet Room, where receptions for heads of state are still held; and the Throne Room. The empty thrones of King Juan Carlos and Queen Sofía are among the highlights of the tour.

The rooms are literally stuffed with art treasures and antiques—salon after salon of monumental grandeur, with no apologies for the damask, mosaics, stucco, Tiepolo ceilings, gilt and bronze, chandeliers, and paintings.

If your visit falls on the first Wednesday of the month, look for the changing of the guard ceremony, which occurs at noon and is free to the public.

In the Armory, you'll see the finest collection of weaponry in Spain. Many of the items—powder flasks, shields, lances, helmets, and saddles—are from the collection of Carlos V (Charles of Spain). From here, the comprehensive tour takes you into the Pharmacy.

Right in front of the Palacio Real is the **Plaza de Oriente,** a semicircular area of gardens and regal statues centered around an imposing re-creation of Felipe IV on horseback. The brainchild of Joseph Bonaparte and finished during the reign of Isabel II, it has an elegant European aura.

Plaza de Oriente, Calle de Bailén 2. (℃) **91-454-87-00.** Admission 9€ ($11; guided tour) adults, 8€ ($10; unguided tour) 3€ ($3.75) students and children. Mon–Sat 9am–6pm; Sun 9am–3pm. Metro: Opera or Plaza de España. Bus: 3, 39 or 148.

Almudena Cathedral   This highly controversial building—built on the site of Santa María de la Almudena, which in turn occupied the site of Madrid's first Muslim mosque—must be one of the longest delayed projects in modern times (110 years from inception to conception, in fact). Work began on the cathedral in 1883 following a neo-Gothic plan by the Marqués de Cubas. The first thing to be completed was the crypt, which today retains the 16th-century image of Madrid's patroness the Virgen de la Almudena. After that, progress was halted until 1944, when a new architect Fernando Chueca took over, introducing a neoclassical style. It was eventually finished in 1993 and graced with a visit from the pope. The bright interior reflects an uncertain blend of hybrid styles and its stained-glass windows are of the "pop art" variety; the windows were recently revealed to have been copied. (In defense, their creator claims they were "a vision from God.") The building was given a much-needed shot in the arm with the sumptuous wedding of Prince Felipe and Doña Letizia (a former newscaster) in May 2004, the first such royal event in nearly a century.

Calle Bailén 8–10. (℃) **91-542-22-00.** Free admission. Daily 9am–8:30pm. Metro: Opera. Bus: 3, 39, or 148.

Basílica de San Isidro   This huge twin-towered baroque church—also known as La Colegiata from its early days as part of a Jesuit college—acted as a substitute cathedral from 1885 until the completion of the Almudena. Designed by Pedro Sánchez in the style of the Gesu in Rome, and built by Francisco Bautista in the 17th century, it shelters the remains of Madrid's patron saint San Isidro and his wife, Santa María de la Cabeza. On the Thursday of Easter week, their two images are taken out and paraded around the streets of Madrid.

Calle Toledo 37. (℃) **91-369-20-37.** Free admission. Sept–July Mon–Sat 7:30am–1pm and 6:30–8:30pm; Aug Mon–Sat 7:30am–8:30pm, Sun 7:15–8:30pm. Metro: La Latina or Tirso de Molina. Bus: 17, 18, 23, 35, or 60.

Real Basílica de San Francisco el Grande   Prior to the inauguration of the Almudena, this imposing 18th-century church shared honors with San Isidro as the most important religious building in Madrid. Its dome is larger than that of St. Paul's in London and its interior is filled with a number of ecclesiastical works, notably a

Goya painting of St. Bernardinus of Siena. A guide will show you through.

Plaza de San Francisco el Grande, San Buenaventura 1. © **91-365-38-00**. Admission .70€ (80¢). Tues–Sat 11am–1pm and 4–6:30pm. Metro: La Latina or Puerta del Toledo. Bus: 3, 60, C, 148, or M4.

San Nicolás de los Servitas Church
Officially confirmed as the oldest church in the city, San Nicolás retains a—slightly renovated—12th-century Mudéjar bell tower built by Muslims under Christian rule, though the rest of the church was reconstructed 3 centuries later. The tiny interior contains paintings by Pedro de Mena and sculptures by Nicolás Busi.

Plaza San Nicolás. © **91-559-40-64**. Free admission. Mon 8:30am–1pm; Tues–Sat 9–9:30am and 6:30–8:30pm; Sun 10am–2pm and 6:30–8:30pm. Metro: Opera. Bus: 3.

San Pedro el Leal
Also known as San Pedro el Viejo, and roughly the same size as San Nicolás, this is Madrid's second oldest church and boasts the city's other remaining Mudéjar tower, said to be in its exact original form. Built in the 14th century, the tower has a slight inclination and has been jokingly called Madrid's answer to the leaning Tower of Pisa. (For a more modern comparison with the famed Italian structure, see the listing for KIO Towers, later in this chapter.)

Costanilla de San Pedro. © **91-365-12-84**. Free admission. Daily 6–8pm. Metro: La Latina. Bus: 50 or 55.

Museo de San Isidro
Situated in San Andrés square in the heart of the Austrias, this more recent addition to Madrid's historical museums contains interesting perspectives on the city's progress through the ages, via Paleolithic, Roman, and Muslim eras to the present day, using plans, sketches, models, paintings, and archaeological finds transferred from the Municipal Museum. The museum stands on the site where San Isidro, Madrid's patron saint, is said to have rescued his son from a well, into which the latter had fallen, by making the water rise. The well, purportedly the original, is located in the middle of the building.

Plaza de San Andrés 2. © **91-366-74-15**. Free admission. Mon–Fri 9:30am–8pm, Sat–Sun 1am–2pm; Aug Mon–Sat 9:30am–2:30pm. Metro: La Latina. Bus: 60.

3 Along or near the Paseo del Prado

Note: The **Museo del Ejército (Army Museum)** is closed until 2008 when it will reopen in Toledo.

Museo Nacional de Artes Decorativas
In 62 rooms spread over several floors, this museum, near the Plaza de la Cibeles, displays a rich collection of furniture, ceramics, and decorative pieces. Emphasizing the 16th and 17th centuries, the eclectic collection includes Gothic carvings, alabaster figurines, festival crosses, elaborate dollhouses, elegant baroque four-poster beds, a chapel covered with leather tapestries, and even kitchens from the 18th century. Two newer floors focusing on the 18th and 19th centuries have been added.

Calle de Montalbán 12. © **91-532-64-99**. Admission 2.40€ ($3) adults; 1.20€ ($1.50) students, children, and seniors. Tues–Fri 9:30am–3pm; Sat–Sun 10am–2pm. Metro: Banco de España. Bus: 14, 27, 34, 37, or 45.

Museo Naval
The history of nautical science and the Spanish navy, from the time of Isabella and Ferdinand until today, comes alive at the Museo Naval. The most fascinating exhibit is the map made by the first mate of the *Santa María* to show the Spanish monarchs the new discoveries. There are also souvenirs of the Battle of Trafalgar.

Paseo del Prado 5. © **91-379-52-99**. Free admission. Tues–Sun 10am–2pm. Closed Aug. Metro: Banco de España. Bus: 2, 14, 27, 40, 51, 52, or M6.

Fun Fact **Do You Know . . .**

Why the bear and the *madroño* tree are the symbols of Madrid?

You see them everywhere—from the small bronze statue in the Puerta del Sol to the insignia on the side of city taxis: A squat bear on its hind legs attempting to eat the berries on a equally squat *madroño,* or so-called strawberry tree. They are the official symbol of Madrid. But why? Opinions vary. The practical theory is that the bear standing on its hind legs with its front paws on the tree trunk represent possession and ownership of wood necessary for constructing buildings. The sentimental theory is based on the fact that bears love sweet things and constantly try to extract honey from beehives. According to legend, because they suffer from sore eyes, they get stung and bleed from their wounds to such an extent that it relieves them of some of the pain. Next, they grope around desperately for a *madroño* tree and start gobbling the fruit, whose bitterness belies its rich red exterior (it only *looks* like a strawberry) and shocks the palate into further reducing the pain by virtue of sheer distraction. So, masochistically, they rid themselves of their discomfort. The first theory makes sense as a metaphor for how Madrid has grown. The second is rather cute but doesn't seem to have any particular relevance. Take your pick.

Why Madrileños are known as "gatos" (cats)?

Most people believe this stems from the fact that Madrileños like to stay up late, especially on the weekend, when many of them barely sleep at all. Out on the tiles with a vengeance! (*Note:* This expression literally means to stay up all night like cats, which are often out all night and on rooftops.) However, the official explanation is historical. During a siege at the time of the Arabic invaders, when the city went by the name of Magerit, a particularly adept soldier managed to climb the outer walls with the agility of a cat by inserting his dagger between gaps in the outer walls to gain footholds. The story passed into legend, and the soldier and his family assumed the name of Gato. They eventually had a street—the Callejón del Gato—named after one of their descendants, a court poet at the time of Juan II named Juan Alvarez Gato.

Why the Manzanares River has had such bad press?

The insults and quips came thick and fast in the old days when it was a malodorous trickle that dried up in summer. "An apprentice river," the Golden Age poet Quevedo called it, "in which the water barely comes up to the sole of my foot." Another writer claimed that "the elms that decorate its banks die of thirst and the river itself begs for an umbrella if it rains," adding that

Bolsa de Comercio de Madrid (Stock Exchange)   For a fascinating look into the workings of the Spanish stock market, visit this impressive building designed by 19th-century architect Enrique María Rapulles. Located in the same small square as the Ritz hotel and just a short walk from the Prado, its neoclassical facade attracts almost as much attention as that of its illustrious neighbors. Visits are made at noon on weekdays, but you must make a prior call to arrange an appointment. You can view "the Manzanares barely dampens the ground as if a finger moistened with saliva was stroking the soil." King Fernando VII, passing one day in summer, is said to have requested his consorts to water it so that the dust wouldn't rise so much. Visiting French writer Alexander Dumas once pleaded with a friend not to throw away the glass of water he'd half finished but to throw it into the parched and needy Manzanares. And so on.

Today, if not quite comparable with the Seine, Thames, or Potomac, the Manzanares looks more like a real river thanks to tidied-up banks and diverted water channels that have helped replenish it, although that coyly secluded location in the dip between the Royal Palace and the Casa de Campo still prevents many visitors from realizing it's even there. As part of Mayor Gallardón's visionary plans for a "greener" Madrid, the current proliferation of cranes and excavations along the river herald an ambitious move to turn the whole area into a traffic-free parkland (with the road running underneath), which will link up with the adjoining Casa de Campo to form one big *zona verde*.

Why they bury sardines at Lent?

In the weeks before Lent, food, fun, fireworks, and general frolicking take place during a period known as Carnaval. The highlight of Carnaval is Shrove Tuesday (or Martes de Carnaval). The mood becomes more somber on the following day, Ash Wednesday. If you're anywhere down near Paseo de la Florida by the river, you can see men in top hats and black suits carrying a cardboard effigy of a sardine in a mock coffin to a riverside spot, where the sardine is ceremonially buried.

The origin of this eccentric event, known as the Entierro de la Sardina, can be traced back to the 18th century, when a cargo of sardines destined for the Lent festivities arrived in such a putrid state that the reigning monarch Charles III ordered them all to be buried. Sardines symbolize the end of Carnaval and its hedonism, and the advent of Lent fasting (fish being the recommended diet for this period). So in memory of their tragic premature demise 2 centuries ago—which caused the Madrid populace to be deprived of its abstinence diet for the next 40 days—the city decided that sardines should be mourned in style. Hence, the Entierro ceremony.

Side note: The ceremony was banned under General Franco's dictatorship, partly because of its irreverent nature and partly because it allowed folks to wander freely about in disguise—something that absolutely could not be tolerated during those rigid times.

the stock exchange floor through a glass partition above and see a small exhibition on the history of the market.

Plaza de la Lealtad 1. ℂ **91-589-22-64.** Free admission. Reservations essential. Mon–Fri at noon. Metro: Banco de España. Bus: 10, 14, 27, 34, 37, or 45.

Moments Taking the Bull by the Horns

Madrid draws the finest matadors in Spain. If a matador hasn't proven his worth in the **Plaza de Toros Monumental de las Ventas,** Alcalá 237 (*©* **91-356-22-00;** www.las-ventas.com; Metro: Ventas), he hasn't been recognized as a top-flight artist. The major season begins during the Fiestas de San Isidro, patron saint of Madrid, on May 15. This is the occasion for a series of fights, during which talent scouts are in the audience. Matadors who distinguish themselves in the ring are signed up for Majorca, Málaga, and other places. The bullfight season ends during the last two weekends in October (Feria del Otoño).

The best way to get tickets to the bullfights is to go to the stadium box office (Fri–Sun 10am–2pm and 5–8pm). Concierges for virtually every upper-bracket hotel can also acquire tickets. Alternatively, you can contact one of Madrid's best ticket agents, **Localidades Galicia,** Plaza del Carmen 1 (*©* **91-531-27-32;** Metro: Puerto del Sol), open Tuesday to Saturday 9:30am to 1:30pm and 4:30 to 7pm, Sunday 9:30am to 1:30pm. Tickets to bullfights are 12€ to 126€ ($15–$158), depending on the event and the position of your seat. Front-row seats are *barreras. Delanteras*—third-row seats—are available in both the *alta* (high) and the *baja* (low) sections. The cheapest seats, *filas,* afford the worst view and are in the sun *(sol)* the whole time. The best and most expensive seats are in the shade *(sombra).* Bullfights are held on Sunday and holidays throughout most of the year, and every day during certain festivals, which tend to last around 3 weeks, usually in the late spring. Starting times are adjusted according to the anticipated hour of sundown on the day of a performance, usually 7pm from March to October and 5pm during late autumn and early spring. Late-night fights by neophyte matadors are sometimes staged under spotlights on Saturday around 11pm. During the winter months of November to February, bullfights are replaced by a short circus season (see the "Especially for Kids" section, later).

Casa Museo de Lope de Vega   Just uphill from the Paseo, this atmospheric town house, former home of Spain's foremost "Golden Age" playwright, is paradoxically situated on a street named after the country's greatest novelist. A 17th-century gem with delightful gardens at the back, it's well worth the visit.

Cervantes 11. *©* **91-429-92-16.** Tues–Fri 9:30am–2pm; Sat 10am–2pm. Admission 2€ ($2.50); free Sat (check before to ensure it's not already booked). Metro Anton Martín. Bus: 34, 38, or 45.

4 Near Malasaña

Museo Municipal   Famed for its outstanding baroque facade, this 18th-century building has a collection of documents, models, paintings, drawings, and sketches that amply covers the history of the Spanish capital. Formerly an orphanage, it's located on the eastern edge of the Malasaña district a short walk up from the Gran Vía. It re-opened in 2005 after 2 years of renovation work.

Calle Fuencarral 78. *©* **91-588-86-72.** Admission free. Tues–Fri 9:30am–8pm, Sat and Sun 10am–2pm; mid-July–mid-Sept Tues–Fri 9:30am–2:30pm, Sat–Sun 10am–2pm. Metro: Tribunal.

5 Near the Plaza de España

Monasterio de las Descalzas Reales ✿✿   In the mid–16th century, aristocratic women—either disappointed in love or "wanting to be the bride of Christ"—stole away to this convent to take the veil. Each brought a dowry, making this Habsburg gem, which was founded by Joan of Austria in the 16th century, one of the richest convents in the land. By the mid–20th century it sheltered mostly poor women. True, it still contained a priceless collection of art treasures, but the sisters were forbidden to auction anything; in fact, they were literally starving. The state intervened, and the pope granted special dispensation to open the convent as a museum in 1960. A quarter of a century later, the European Council rated it "Museum of the Year," and today the public can look behind the walls of what had been a mysterious presence on one of the most beautiful squares in Old Madrid.

In the reliquary are the noblewomen's dowries, one of which is said to contain bits of wood from Christ's Cross; another, some of the bones of St. Sebastian. The most valuable painting is Titian's *Caesar's Money.* The Flemish Hall shelters other fine works, including paintings by Hans de Beken and Breughel the Elder. All of the tapestries were based on Rubens' cartoons, displaying his chubby matrons. Tours are in Spanish.

Plaza de las Descalzas Reales s/n. ✆ **91-454-88-00.** Admission 5€ ($6.25) adults, 2.60€ ($3.25) children. Sat and Tues–Thurs 10:30am–12:30pm and 3–5:45pm; Fri 10:30am–12:30pm; Sun 11am–1:15pm. Bus: 1, 2, 5, 20, 46, 52, 53, 74, M1, M2, M3, or M5. From Plaza del Callao, off the Gran Vía, walk down Postigo de San Martín to Plaza de las Descalzas Reales; the convent is on the left.

Monasterio de la Encarnación ✿   Central Madrid's other royally endowed Habsburg monastery nestles quietly in a charming little square between the Royal Palace and Plaza España. Though paling slightly in comparison with the incomparable Descalzas Reales, it still remains by any other standards a must-see. Founded by Margaret of Austria and Philip III in 1611 and rebuilt after a disastrous fire by Ventura Rodriguez in 1767, it's inhabited by Augustine Recoletos nuns who remain out of sight in their cloisters during visiting hours. The facade is a fine example of post-Herreran style, and inside there's an impressive selection of polychrome sculptures and paintings, highlighted by Ribera's superb portrait of John the Baptist. The most extraordinary of its many salons is the *reliquario* (relics room), where the solidified blood of Saint Pantaleon, permanently kept in a glass orb, supposedly liquefies for 24 hours every year beginning at midnight on July 27 (the eve of his saint's day). According to legend, if it does not liquefy disaster will follow. On display all around it are the bone fragments and bronze, copper, and gold reliquaries of other saints and martyrs. The main cloister and church are also well worth a look. As in the Descalzas Reales, tours are conducted in Spanish.

Plaza de la Encarnación 1. ✆ **91-547-05-10.** Admission: 3.50€ ($4.35). Tues–Thurs and Sat 10:30am–12:45pm and 4–5:45pm; Sun 10:30–1:45pm. Metro: Opera or Santo Domingo. Bus: 25, 39, or 148.

Templo de Debod   This Egyptian temple near Plaza de España once stood in the Valley of the Nile, 31km (19 miles) from Aswan. When the new dam threatened the temple, the Egyptian government dismantled and presented it to Spain. Taken down stone by stone in 1969 and 1970, it was shipped to Valencia and delivered by rail to Madrid, where it was reconstructed and opened to the public in 1971. Photos upstairs depict the temple's long history. The museum is located in the open garden area adjoining Pintor Rosales Avenue close to the Parque del Oeste and with panoramic views westwards of the Casa del Campo.

Paseo Pintor de Rosales 2. ℭ **91-366-74-15.** www.munimadrid.es/templodebod. Admission free. Apr 1–Sept 30 Tues–Fri 9:45am–1:45pm and 6.15–8:15pm; Oct 1–Mar 31 Tues–Fri 9:45am–1:45pm and 4.15–6:15pm; Sat–Sun 9:45am–1:45pm year-round. Metro: Plaza de España or Ventura Rodríguez. Bus: 25, 39, 46, 74, or 138.

Museo Cerralbo   This very personal museum close to the Debod temple was once owned by the 17th Marquis of Cerralbo, Enrique de Aguilera y Gamboa. Housed in an Italian-style 19th-century mansion, it provides a unique visiting experience, as its contents are laid out in exactly the same order as when he was living there. The Marquis was a great traveler as well as an erudite man of letters, and the museum is filled with collections (bequeathed to the state on his death in 1922) gathered during his colorful life. Forty years later it was declared a national monument. Among its multitude of artistic treasures and eclectic knick-knacks (estimated at around 50,000) are paintings by Titian, Tintoretto, Zurbarán, and El Greco (including his classic *Ecstasy of St. Francis of Assisi*), sculptures, 18th-century English watches, Venetian lamps, Saxon porcelain, and European and Japanese armor. The garden, planned in a classical-romantic style, has a small central pond and surrounding busts of Roman emperors.

Ventura Rodríguez 17. ℭ **91-547-36-46.** Admission 2.40€ ($3) adults, 1.20€ ($1.50) students, Sept–June free for those under 18 or over 65. Free for everyone Wed and Sun. Tues–Sat 9:30am–3pm, Sun 10am–3pm; July–Aug Tues–Sat 9:30am–2pm, Sun 10am–2pm. Metro: Ventura Rodríguez. Bus: 25, 39, 46, 74, or 138.

Conde Duque   A remarkable conversion from 18th-century barracks to one of Madrid's most evocative cultural centers, the Conde Duque is peacefully situated a short walk away from the Plaza España. Two galleries give permanent exhibitions, one located in a basement, the other in the main building, and two vast patios are used for open-air sculpture exhibitions. This is also home of the Museo Municipal de Arte Contemporáneo, which reopened in 2004 after 3 years of substantial renovation work. Bosch and Goya paintings feature among the collection, which was donated by financial magnate José Lazaro Galdiano. Other attractions include a video library and concert venue.

Conde Duque 11. ℭ **91-588-58-34.** Admission free. Tues–Sat 10am–2pm and 5:30–9pm. Closed Sun–Mon. Metro: Noviciado or Ventura Rodríguez. Bus: 1, 2, 44, 74, 133, or C.

6 Near Atocha

Real Fábrica de Tapices (Royal Tapestry Factory)   At this factory, located a short walk southeast of the Atocha railway station, the age-old process of making exquisite (and very expensive) tapestries is still carried on with consummate skill. Nearly every tapestry is based on a cartoon by Goya, who was the factory's most famous employee. Many of these patterns, such as *The Pottery Salesman,* are still in production today. (Goya's original drawings are in the Prado.) Many of the other designs are based on cartoons by Francisco Bayeu, Goya's brother-in-law.

Fuenterrabía 2. ℭ **91-434-05-50.** www.realfatapices.com. Admission 3€ ($3.50). Mon–Fri 10am–2pm. Closed Aug and holidays. Metro: Menéndez Pelayo. Bus: 10, 14, 26, 32, 37, C, or M9.

7 Salamanca

Museo Arqueológico Nacional   This stately mansion is a storehouse of artifacts from the prehistoric to the baroque. One of the prime exhibits here is the Iberian statue *The Lady of Elche* 👁👁👁, a piece of primitive carving (from the 4th c. B.C.) discovered on the southeastern coast of Spain. Finds from Ibiza, Paestum, and Rome are on display, including statues of Tiberius and his mother, Livia. The Islamic collection

Private Galleries

Madrid has about 150 private art galleries, where you can view and buy the work of modern artists of all styles. Some of the best galleries are located on Claudio Coello (Metro: Retiro or Serrano; bus no. 21 or 53) in the Salamanca district. These include **Guillermo de Osma,** Claudio Coello 4–1° izda. (© 91-435-59-36; Mon–Fri 10am–2pm and 4:30–8:30pm, Sat noon–2pm); **Urbino,** Claudio Coello 17 (© 91-576-51-98; Mon–Fri 10am–2pm and 5–8pm, Sat 11am–2pm); **Paz Feliz,** Claudio Coello 17 (© 91-575-86-86; Mon–Fri 10am–2pm and 5–8pm, Sat 11am–2pm); **Oliva Arauna,** Claudio Coello 19 (© 91-435-18-08; Mon–Fri 10am–2pm and 5–8pm, Sat 11am–2pm; p. 215); and **Jorge Alcolea,** Claudio Coello 28 (© 91-431-65-92; 10:30am–2:30pm and 5:30–9:30pm). If you're keen on sculptures, visit **Capa Esculturas,** Claudio Coello 19 (© 91-431-05-93; Mon–Fri 10am–2pm and 5–8pm, Sat 11am–2pm).

from Spain is outstanding. There are also collections of Spanish Renaissance lusterware, Talavera pottery, Retiro porcelain, and some rare 16th- and 17th-century Andalusian glassware. Many of the exhibits are treasures that were removed from churches and monasteries. A much-photographed choir stall from the palace of Palencia dates from the 14th century. Also worth a look are the reproductions of the Altamira cave paintings (chiefly of bison, horses, and boars), discovered near Santander in northern Spain in 1868.

Serrano 13. © **91-577-79-12.** Admission 3€ ($3.75), free for children and adults over 65. Free for everyone all day Sat and Sun. Tues–Sat 9:30am–8pm; Sun 9:30am–2:30pm. Metro: Serrano or Retiro. Bus: 1, 9, 19, 51, or 74.

Museo Lázaro Galdiano 👀   Imagine 37 rooms in a well-preserved 19th-century mansion bulging with artworks—including many by the most famous Old Masters of Europe. Visitors usually take the elevator to the top floor and work down, lingering over such artifacts as 15th-century hand-woven vestments, swords and daggers, royal seals, 16th-century crystal from Limoges, Byzantine jewelry, Italian bronzes from ancient times to the Renaissance, and medieval armor.

One painting by Bosch evokes his own peculiar brand of horror, the canvas peopled with creepy fiends devouring human flesh. The Spanish masters are the best represented—among them El Greco, Velázquez, Zurbarán, Ribera, Murillo, and Valdés-Leal.

One section is devoted to works by the English portrait and landscape artists Reynolds, Gainsborough, and Constable. Italian artists exhibited include Tiepolo and Guardi. Salon 30—for many, the most interesting—is devoted to Goya and includes paintings from his "black period."

This off-the-beaten-track museum, closed for a year and reopened after tasteful renovations in 2003, is a gem and usually enjoyably underpopulated, a nice contrast to the overcrowded Prado, Thyssen, and Reina Sofía museums.

Serrano 122. © **91-561-60-84.** Admission 3€ ($3.75). Tues–Sun 10am–2pm. Closed holidays and Aug. Metro: Rubén Darío or Núñez de Balboa. Bus: 9, 16, 19, 27, 45, 51, 61, 89, or 114.

Museo de Escultura al Aire Libre   As its name implies, this small "museum" is really an open-air collection of mainly bronze abstract sculptures by the likes of Chillida and Miró dating from the 1920s and situated next to busy Castellana Avenue. At

its center is a sparkling cascade designed by sculptor Eusebio Sempere, brainchild of this tiny gem.

Paseo de la Castellana 41. ℂ **91-588-86-72.** www.munimadrid.es/museoairelibre. Free. Open daily; call for hours. Metro: Ruben Darío.

8 Chamberí

Museo Sorolla　From 1912, painter Joaquín Sorolla and his family occupied this elegant Madrileño town house off Paseo de la Castellana. His widow turned it over to the government, and it is now maintained as a memorial. Much of the house remains as Sorolla left it, right down to his stained paintbrushes and pipes. The museum wing displays a representative collection of his works.

Although Sorolla painted portraits of Spanish aristocrats, he was essentially interested in the common people, often depicting them in their native dress. On view are the artist's self-portrait and the paintings of his wife and their son. Sorolla was especially fond of painting beach scenes of the Costa Blanca.

General Martínez Campos 37. ℂ **91-310-15-84.** www.museosorolla.mcu.es. Admission 2.40€ ($3). Tues–Sat 9:30am–3pm; Sun 10am–3pm. Metro: Iglesia or Rubén Darío. Bus: 5, 16, 61, 40, or M3.

9 Moncloa

Museo del Traje　Opened in March 2004 in Ciudad Universitaria, a 20-minute subway ride from the center, this museum displays more than 500 costumes, even frocks from the 1700s, along with bullfighters' "suits of light." Spanish folk dress is highlighted as well, along with Chanel designs and a 1967 metal dress made by designer Paco Rabanne. Movie scenes show fashions, including Bogie's *Casablanca* and Audrey Hepburn in Givenchy as she appeared in *Funny Face.* Attracting the most attention is Marilyn Monroe in a subway-blown William Travilla dress in *The Seven Year Itch.* Some exhibits are hands-on—you can try on a corset or the frame of a hoop skirt, say, or even check out your derrière in a bustle. On-site is an excellent Basque restaurant, **Bokado.** Ever had gazpacho made with watermelon and lobster?

Av. Jean de Herrera 2. ℂ **91-549-71-50.** http://museodeltraje.mcu.es. Admission 3€ ($3.75). Daily 10am–5pm. Metro: Moncloa or Ciudad Universitaria.

Museo de América (Museum of the Americas)　This museum near the university campus houses an outstanding collection of pre-Columbian, Spanish-American, and Native American art and artifacts. Various exhibits chronicle the progress of the inhabitants of the New World, from the Paleolithic period to the present day. One exhibit, "Groups, Tribes, Chiefdoms, and States," focuses on the social structure of the various peoples of the Americas. Another display outlines the various religions and deities associated with them. Also included is an entire exhibit dedicated to communication, highlighting written as well as nonverbal expressions of art.

Av. de los Reyes Católicos 6. ℂ **91-549-26-41.** Admission 3.01€ ($3.75) adults, 1.50€ ($1.70) students, free for children 18 and under and seniors over 65. Tues–Sat 10am–3pm; Sun 10am–2:30pm. Metro: Moncloa.

10 Cuatro Caminos

Museo Tiflológico　This museum is designed for sightless and sight-impaired visitors. Maintained by Spain's National Organization for the Blind, it's one of the few museums in the world that emphasizes tactile appeal. All the exhibits are meant to be

Frommer's Favorite Madrid Experiences

Tasca **Hopping.** This is the quintessential Madrid experience and the fastest way for a visitor to tap into the local scene. *Tascas* are Spanish pubs serving tapas, those tantalizing appetizers. You can go from one to the other, sampling each tavern's special dishes and wines.

Eating around Spain. The variety of gastronomic experiences is staggering: You can literally restaurant-hop from province to province without ever leaving Madrid.

Viewing the Works of Your Favorite Artist. Spend an afternoon at the Prado, savoring the works of your favorite Spanish artist.

Bargain Hunting at El Rastro. Madrid has one of the greatest flea markets in Europe, if not the world. Wander through to discover that hidden treasure you've been searching for.

Enjoying a Night of Flamenco. Flamenco folk songs *(cante)* and dances *(baile)* are an integral part of the Spanish experience. Spend at least 1 night in a flamenco tavern listening to the heart-rending laments of gypsy sorrows and dreams.

Outdoor-Cafe Sitting. This is a famous experience for the summertime, when Madrileños come alive again on their *terrazas*. The drinking and good times can go on until dawn. From glamorous hangouts to lowly street corners, the cafe scene takes place mainly along the axis formed by the Paseo de la Castellana, Paseo del Prado, and Paseo de Recoletos (all of which make up one continuous street). Other ideal open-air spots lined with terrace cafes are the park-side promenade of Pintor Rosales on the western edge of Argüelles near the *teleférico*, and Calle Argumosa in the southern part of Lavapiés.

touched and felt; to that end, the museum provides audiotapes, in English and Spanish, to guide visitors as they move their hands over the object on display. It also offers pamphlets in large type and Braille.

One section of the museum features small-scale replicas of such architectural wonders as the Mayan and Aztec pyramids of Central America, the Eiffel Tower, and the Statue of Liberty. Another section contains paintings and sculptures created by blind artists, such as Miguel Detrel and José Antonio Braña. A third section outlines the status of blind people throughout history, with a focus on the sociology and technology that led to the development of Braille during the 19th century.

La Coruña 18. (C) **91-589-42-00.** Free admission. Tues–Fri 10am–2pm and 5–8pm; Sat 10am–2pm. Metro: Estrecho. Bus: 3, 42, 43, 64, or 124.

11 Príncipe Pío

Ermita San Antonio de la Florida and the Panteón de Goya (Goya's Tomb) ⊛

Nestled in an avenue close to the River Manzanares and just beyond the Príncipe Pío Station are two beautiful domed hermitages, built between 1792 and 1798. The one on the right contains Goya's tomb and one of his most unusual masterpieces—an elaborately beautiful fresco depicting the miracles of St. Anthony on the dome and cupola. This has been called Goya's Sistine Chapel. Already deaf when he began the painting, Goya labored dawn to dusk for 16 weeks, painting with sponges rather than brushes. By depicting common street life—stonemasons, prostitutes, and beggars—Goya raised the ire of the nobility who held judgment until the patron, Carlos IV, viewed it. When the monarch approved, the formerly outrageous painting was deemed acceptable. Discreetly placed mirrors will help you see the ceiling better.

Glorieta de San Antonio de la Florida s/n. (C) **91-542-07-22.** Free admission. Tues–Fri 9am–8pm; Sat–Sun 10am–2pm (in summer daily 10am–2pm only). Metro: Príncipe Pío. Bus: 41, 46, 75, or C.

12 Ventas

Museo Taurino (Bullfighting Museum)   This museum might serve as a good introduction to bullfighting for those who want to see the real event. Here you'll see the death costume of Manolete, the *traje de luces* (suit of lights) he wore when he was gored to death at age 30 in Linares's bullring. Other memorabilia evoke the heyday of Juan Belmonte, the Andalusian who revolutionized bullfighting in 1914 by performing close to the horns. Other exhibits include a Goya painting of a matador, as well as photographs and relics that trace the history of bullfighting in Spain from its ancient origins to the present day.

Plaza de Toros de las Ventas, Alcalá 237. (C) **91-725-18-57.** Free admission. Mar–Oct Tues–Fri and Sun 9:30am–2:30pm; Nov–Feb Mon–Fri 9:30am–2:30pm. Metro: Ventas. Bus: 12, 21, 38, 53, 146, M1, or M8.

13 Outside the City Center

Museo del Aire/Museo Aeronautico   Named **Cuatro Vientos** (Four Winds) after an airplane that crashed in the Mexican jungles of Campeche during a long-distance flight via Cuba in the 1930s, this time-warp paradise for vintage-plane observers is 8km (5 miles) west of Madrid close to the satellite town of Alcorcón. A wide range of military and civil airplanes dating from 1911 to the 1970s is on display both out in the open and in various large hangars. One of the most evocative is the English-piloted *Dragon Rapide,* in which General Franco flew to the mainland from Africa and the Canaries in 1936 to launch his coup attempt and initiate the civil war, which ended democratic rule of the country for nearly 40 years. A small cafeteria is on-site.

Carretera Extremadura Km 10.5. (C) **91-509-16-90.** www.museodelaire.com. Admission .60€ (75¢); Wed free. Tues–Sun 10am–2pm. Closed Mon. Bus: Green line 512, 513, 514, and 516 from Principe Pío.

Cerro de los Angeles (Hill of the Angels)   Located 10km (6.2 miles) south of Madrid on the outskirts of Getafe, this 670m (2,299-foot) rise surrounded by pines rivals the town of Pinto as official geographical center of Spain. It offers marvelous views of the fertile plains and less picturesque industrial estates of southern Madrid. The hill's baroque **Ermita de Nuestra Señora de los Angeles** and **Convento de las Carmelitas Descalzas** date from the 17th century. The towering white-stoned **Monumento de Sagrado Corazón,** with its statue of Jesus, was built from public subscriptions after the original monument (inaugurated by King Alfonso XIII in 1919) was dynamited by Republican forces in 1936 at the beginning of the civil war. Amid the pines you'll find picnic areas and kiddie play zones and a small cafeteria up near the statue. A colorful pilgrimage wends its way here from Getafe every May.

Carretera de Andalucía Km 13. www.diocesisgetafe.es. Bus: 446 from Legazpi Square (easier access by car).

shifting alliances favored adjacent Castile. The historical linkage between León and Old Castile is now recognized in the formal name of the region, Castilla y León.

Lleida *(Lérida)*

Map **14**D9. *Lleida. 156km (87 miles) w of Barcelona; 144km (90 miles) e of Zaragoza. Population: 120,000* **i** *Arc del Pont s/n* ☎*(973) 248 120.*

The military history of this now industrialized provincial capital is long and painful, and inevitably as a result there is little of ancient origin or artistic accomplishment to see. It was fought over by the Romans, Moors, Catalan rebels and, not least in destructiveness, the French. The center of the city lies on the w bank of the river Segre, rising sharply to the fortified hilltop whose remaining ramparts is the **Seu Vella** (old cathedral). The Gothic structure, built between the 12th and 14thC, was a target of constant bombardment and was desecrated by its use as an army barracks from the 1707 War of Succession to 1948.

☛ By the main Lleida exit on the A2 *autopista* is the comfortable **Lleida** (☎(973) 116 023 ⬛⬛ *to* ⬛⬛⬛⬛); in the closer suburbs, try the functional **Condes de Urgel II** (*Av. Barcelona 17* ☎(973) 202 300 ⬛⬛).

🍴 **Forn del Nastasi** (*Salmerón 10* ☎(973) 234 510 ⬛⬛) has an ambitious and creative kitchen that justifies a detour: consider lobster with spinach, eggplant mousse or sea bass in champagne sauce. **Sheyton Pub** (*Av. Prat de la Riba 39* ☎(973) 240 033 ⬛⬛ *to* ⬛⬛⬛) imitates an English club in decor and menu.

Logroño

Map **13**C7. *Logroño. 128km (80 miles) e of Burgos; 92km (57 miles) s of Vitoria. Population: 116,000* **i** *Miguel Villanueva 10* ☎*(941) 251 500.*

The capital and major distribution center of the agricultural province of **La Rioja**, Logroño lacks the charm that might be expected of the major wine-producing region of Spain. Textile and other manufacturing firms have brought prosperity but little visual appeal. The superb wines of Rioja are among the best in the world yet relatively unappreciated. Vines have been cultivated here since prehistoric times. Asparagus, olives and other vegetables are also grown in abundance in the fields that stretch to the horizon.
Events In Sept, celebrations of the Rioja grape harvest.

Sights and places of interest

The Baroque exterior ornamentation of the **Catedral de Santa María de la Redonda** (*Plaza del Mercado s/n*) masks the plain 15thC Catalan Gothic interior. There is a striking Churrigueresque doorway and 18thC chapel immediately inside. The **Iglesia de Santa María de Palacio** (*Marqués de San Nicolás*) is a 12thC church that was once part of a royal palace; despite renovation, it retains its Gothic aspect. The 17thC Baroque **Palacio del Espartero** (*Plaza de San Agustín s/n* 🔲 *open 10am-2pm, 4-7pm, closed Mon*) has now been converted into the **provincial museum.**

☛ **Carlton Rioja** (*Rey Juan Carlos 1* ☎(941) 240 033 ⬛⬛⬛ *to* ⬛⬛⬛⬛) and **Los Bracos** (*Bretón de los Herreros 29* ☎(941) 246 608 ⬛⬛⬛ *to* ⬛⬛⬛⬛) are modern and unremarkable, but located in the town center.

🍴 **Mesón de la Merced** (*Mayor 109* ☎(941) 221 166 ⬛⬛), a small palace luxuriously renewed, is the sybaritic setting for Castilian dishes executed with unusual delicacy and dash, complemented by an extensive selection of Rioja wines; the service is admirably professional. Otherwise, try **San Remo** (*Av. España 2* ☎(941) 230 838 ⬛⬛) for regional meat and fish recipes.

Lugo

Map 10B3. Lugo. 85km (59 miles) SE of La Coruña; 96km (60 miles) N of Orense. Population: 74,000 i Plaza Soledad 15 ☎(982) 211 361.

A Celtiberian settlement and later a Roman, then Arab agricultural center, Lugo retains impressive walls built by these and subsequent occupiers. Modern buildings of the new town outside the unbroken 2km (1¼ mile) perimeter conceal them from the approach roads. Inside nearly 9m (30ft) ramparts is a pleasant old quarter with 16th-18thC mansions, including a floridly Baroque **Ayuntamiento**, an 18thC **Palacio Episcopal**, a **provincial museum** containing Roman antiquities, a 12thC cathedral, and several good restaurants. There is little of interest beyond the walls.

☞ **Lugo Husa** (*Av. Ramón Ferreiro s/n ☎(982) 224 152* ▐▐▐) offers competent service and functional facilities; **Méndez Núñez** (*Reina 1 ☎(982) 230 711* ▐▐) is an alternative if Lugo Husa is full.

≕ There are locals who claim that the **bus station restaurant** (*Plaza Angel López Pérez ☎(982) 223 968* ▐ *above the bus station*) is the best in town, unlikely as that might seem; **Mesón de Alberto** (*Cruz 4 ☎(982) 228 310* ▐▐) is its match, however, providing vast platters of grilled mixed seafood and other Galician specialties; a few steps away is **Verruga** (*Cruz 12 ☎(982) 229 855* ▐▐), with a *tapas* bar and no-nonsense regional dishes.

Madrid

Map 2-3, 12E6. Madrid. 626km (386 miles) W of Barcelona; 346km/115 miles) NW of Valencia. Population: 3,350,000 i Plaza Mayor 3 ☎(91) 266 4874.

By European standards, Madrid is a young capital. Although settlements existed here from prehistoric times and most of Iberia's successive conquerors occupied it for various periods, it remained a backwater while the seat of government was moved from Toledo to Sevilla to Valladolid at the whims of monarchs currently in power. Only when Philip II chose it as capital in 1561 did it begin to receive the royal largesse that was to make it Spain's largest city and repository of most of its greatest works of art. Only rarely thereafter has it lost its status.

In selecting Madrid for his capital Philip II had political considerations in mind, as well as the clear, dry climate. A capital at the geographical center of Spain might have helped to keep the volatile outlying regions in check. As it happened, centrifugal forces have often been as powerful.

Growth has been especially apparent in Madrid since the Civil War, through almost the whole of which it was held in siege by the Nationalists. Much of it was destroyed or damaged during those two and a half years, through constant shelling and bombardment. Parks became bivouacs, churches were desecrated, palaces and museums plundered. Most have been restored or replaced, and the great monuments of the 16th-18thC survive. Although there is no proper cathedral in Madrid, there are sweeping avenues, fountains, elegant Neoclassical buildings and over 40 museums, which compensate. This cosmopolitan city, with its vast number of hotels and restaurants, has expanded primarily to the N and S, where new districts have been created by blocks of flats and office buildings. The NE precinct is now a grid of banks, glass and steel skyscrapers and corporate headquarters, most of which did not exist 30yrs ago. Madrid is a logical base from which to explore a ring of smaller, older cities (see *Places nearby*). There is also skiing in the Gredos mountains, and a plenitude of summer country palaces to visit. Madrileños leave the city to visitors in August, when many stores and restaurants close.

Event In May, Fiesta de San Isidro, with bullfights and other celebrations.

Sights and places of interest

Casa del Campo
This substantial area of heath and woodland was once a royal park and hunting ground for Philip II, laid out in 1562 and extended and improved by subsequent monarchs. Its 1,747 hectares (4,370 acres) lie w of the canalized Manzanares river, which forms the western edge of the central city, and contain an **amusement park** (🏯 *open Apr-Oct Mon-Fri 11am-4pm, Sat-Sun 11am-1pm; Nov-Mar Sat-Sun 11am-8pm, closed Mon-Fri*) and a **zoo** (🏯 *open Apr-Sept 10am-9pm, Oct-Mar 10am to sunset*), which is Spain's best and is famous for its panda couple, among over 2,000 other creatures.

Casón del Buen Retiro ☆
Map 3D5. Felipe IV 13 🏯 *Open Tues-Sun 10am-2pm in summer, 10am-5pm in winter. Closed Mon. Metro Antón Martin.*
This ugly Neoclassical building faces El Retiro park, four streets E of the main Prado museum. Its principal attraction is the famous Picasso painting *Guernica*. A savage condemnation of the terror bombing of that Basque city during the Civil War, the anguished study in grays and blacks was held at the Museum of Modern Art in New York for 40yrs. It was only brought back to Spain, according to the artist's wishes, when democracy returned after Franco's death. The rest of the collection is concerned with 19thC Spanish painting.

Convento de las Descalzas Reales
Map 2D3. Plaza de las Descalzas Reales 3 🕿 *(91) 222 0687* 🏯 *𝄍 compulsory. Open Mon-Thurs 10.30am-12.45pm, 4-5.15pm, Fri-Sun 10.30am-12.45pm. Metro Sol.*
This 16thC convent is noted for its rich collection of tapestries, paintings and sculptures, its sumptuous Baroque staircase and its landings crowded with polychrome decorative carvings and lined with rare marble veneers.
Aristocratic benefactors who sought spiritual retreat here clearly saw no need to condemn themselves to the unrelenting sobriety normally associated with such establishments.

Ermita de San Antonio
Glorieta de San Antonio de la Florida 🕿 *(91) 247 7921* 🏯 *Open Mon-Tues, Thurs-Sat 11am-1pm, 3-6pm, Sun and holidays 11am-1.30pm. Closed Wed. Metro Norte.*
Built in 1797, this most recent of three hermitages now functions as a shrine to the artist Goya who is buried here. An unusual dome fresco, the *Miracle of St Anthony of Padua*, which he completed in 1789, is preserved, together with related scenes, in the cross vault.

Estudio y Museo Sorolla
Martínez Campos 37 🕿 *(91) 410 1584* 🏯 *Open 10am-2pm. Closed Mon. Metro Rubén Darío.*
The home of the Valencian artist Joaquín Sorolla y Bastida is preserved essentially as it was during his creative lifetime, which ended in 1923. His large landscapes and figurative paintings are well displayed in the rooms in which he lived and worked.

Museo de la Academia de Bellas Artes de San Fernando
Map 3D4. Alcalá 13 🕿 *(91) 276 2564* 🏯 *Open Tues-Sat 9am-5pm, Sun, Mon 9am-2pm. Metro Sevilla.*
Powerful Goya canvases of his expressionistic later years dominate these galleries, which represent centuries of Spanish painting. Murillo, El Greco, Vicente López, Ribera and Sorolla are on display, as well as the work of artists such as Rubens and Bellini.

Museo de América ☆
Reyes Católicos 6 🕿 *(91) 243 9537* 🏯 *Open 10am-7pm. Closed Mon and some holidays. Metro Moncloa.*
Spanish America produced the bulk of this collection although the name is sufficiently elastic to include arts and crafts from the Philippines. Mayan Palenque is represented by steles and by a calendar more accurate than the European version, Peru by funerary relics, Colombia by boisterous clay figurines, and all the colonies by folk art that preceded and followed the arrival of the conquistadors.

Madrid

Museo Arqueológico Nacional ☆
Map 3B5. Serrano 13 ☎(91) 403 6607 ▧ Open Tues-Sun 9.15am-1.45pm. Closed Mon, holidays. Metro Colón.

To the left of the street entrance and down stairs into an artificial cave is a reproduction of the paintings at Altamira (see *Sight nearby* in *Santillana del Mar*). It is not an especially compelling display, but is worth a visit, as the original requires special permission to visit.

Inside the museum itself, galleries to the right are concerned primarily with Iberian and Roman artifacts. The pride of the collection is the **Dama de Elche**, a bust of a woman of rare sophistication, with an unusual disc headdress and serpent-head necklace; it dates back to the 4thCBC. The galleries that follow have sculpture, mosaics, jewelry, pottery and minor arts of the Roman epoch. Proceeding counter clockwise, next encountered is the revamped Visigothic section, with striking installations of clothing, jewelry, glasswork and architectural fragments.

Iberian prehistory is illustrated in the basement, with reconstructed human and animal skeletons and models. Particularly intriguing are exhibits dealing with ancient ceremonial and domestic structures still on view in the Balearic Islands. Other rooms contain substantial displays of Greek pottery and Egyptian funerary objects.

On the first floor, the museum's definition is stretched to include decorative arts — tapestries, furnishings, bronzes — of the Middle Ages and the Renaissance.

Museo Cerralbo
Map 2B2. Ventura Rodríguez 17 ☎(91) 247 3646 ▧ Open Tues-Sat 10am-2pm, 4-7pm, Sun 10am-2pm. Closed Mon and Aug.

The Marqués de Cerralbo was a voracious collector, and this mansion is filled with artworks that he left to the country after his death in 1922. His catholic tastes drew him to Celtiberian weaponry, Greek ceramics, Flemish tapestries, jewelry, clocks, paintings by Zurbarán, Van Dyck and El Greco, and drawings by Goya and Tintoretto. Although it is lacking in scholarly discipline, it is a stunning collection.

Museo del Ejército ☆
Map 3D5. Méndez Núñez 1 ☎(91) 222 0628 ▧ Open Tues-Sun 10am-2pm. Closed Mon. Metro Banco.

Thousands of weapons and related implements are well displayed in the 17thC Buen Retiro palace. Although most of the exhibits are of interest primarily to military buffs and scholars, there are displays of Moorish ivory and silver daggers, firearms and the reputed sword of El Cid, who apparently had a very dainty hand for an epic hero.

Museo Español de Arte Contemporáneo
Av. Juan de Herrera 2 ☎(91) 449 7150 ▧ Open Tues-Sat 10am-6pm, Sun and holidays 10am-3pm. Closed Mon. Metro Moncloa.

"Contemporary" is defined here as the mid-19thC late Romantics onward, including the 1960s Spanish abstractionists such as Antonio Tapies. Works by Eduardo Vicente, Picasso, Juan de Echevarría, Solana and Rosales represent every major modern art movement in Spain.

Museo Lázaro Galdiano ☆
Serrano 122 ☎(91) 261 6084 ▧ Open 10am-2pm. Closed Mon. Metro Rubén Darío.

This impressive 19thC mansion, given to the city by the well-known author-financier, is celebrated for its comprehensive display of enamels and silverwork, which span the Middle Ages in three continents. The museum also exhibits paintings by Gainsborough, Bosch, Murillo, Rembrandt, Velázquez, Constable and Turner.

Museo Municipal
Map 3B4. Fuencarral 78 ☎(91) 221 6656 ▣ Open Tues-Sat 10am-2pm; 5-9pm, Sun 10am-3pm. Closed Mon. Metro Tribunal.

The former 18thC hospice of San Fernando has now been converted into the municipal museum. The wildly Baroque portal is in fierce contrast with the plain brick facade. Exhibitions concentrate on the history of the city, and the most interesting show maps and models of Madrid in earlier centuries.

Museo Nacional de Artes Decorativas ☆
Map 3D5. Montalbán 12 ☎(91) 221 3440 ▧ Open Tues-Fri 10am-5pm, Sat, Sun 10am-2pm. Closed July, Aug, Sept and Mon. Metro Banco.

Domestic arts and crafts of the last four centuries are captivatingly presented in period rooms reflecting Gothic, Baroque, Mudejar, Levantine and folk persuasions. Included in the displays are ceramics, china, leatherwork, furniture, clothing, crystal, lace and jewelry. The sumptuously furnished rooms re-created on the first floor and second floors deserve particular attention.

Museo del Prado ★

Map 3D5. Paseo del Prado s/n ☎(91) 230 3439 ▦ but ⬚ on Sat ✗ ▦ Open Apr-Sept Tues-Sat 10am-6pm, Sun 10am-2pm; Oct-Mar Tues-Sat 10am-5pm, Sun 10am-2pm. Closed Mon. Metro Antón Martín.

Whatever their many deficiencies as rulers, such monarchs as Philip II and IV and Charles I and V and their aides had true collectors' eyes for the artistic achievements of their times. The Prado contains the cream of the royal collections. Although the Spanish masters, Velázquez, Goya, Murillo, El Greco and Zurbarán, are abundantly represented, there are also numerous favorites of the various foreign courts. Particularly evident are the Flemish Baroque painter Rubens, the Italians Titian, Bellini, Tintoretto, Botticelli and Fra Angelico, the Dutch Van der Weyden, Van Dyck and Rembrandt, the Germans Dürer and Holbein.

An extensive, multi-million-peseta renovation is in its final stages, its principal objective being the installation of air conditioning for canvases in danger of deterioration from the extreme temperature changes of the capital. Artworks are therefore moved frequently and as a result only a sketchy guide to the galleries is possible at present. Entrance to the undistinguished late 18thC Neoclassical building is made at street level. This and the floor above is where the principal galleries are located, with an additional smaller space below.

Turn right (s) into a wing dominated by the vast 17thC allegorical and religious canvases of Rubens. In the far right-hand corner is his powerful *Death of Seneca* and beyond, a circular salon of Greek sculptures. Return to the main hall, and turn right (E) into a series of galleries, which also highlight Rubens but phase into Dutch still-lifes and landscapes. Return to the main vestibule, then continue into the N hall and a glorious profusion of early Gothic panels surrounded by astonishing gilt frames. Walk in a clockwise direction, taking the exit on the left (E) up the stairs past a sign with an arrow pointing to "Goya."

The first small room that you come to includes one of Rembrandt's luminous self-portraits. In the next chamber hangs Goya's famous portrayal of a massacre of peasants by a Napoleonic firing squad, and in an opposite corner a portrait of *Fernando VII* — a subject the artist clearly held in contempt. The so-called "black" paintings are in the next gallery; huddled, despairing figures are expressively grouped in unknown terror. Most of these were lifted from the walls of Goya's country home. Less well-known than his earlier paintings, they are his most profoundly moving works.

The gallery beyond has the side-by-side nude and clothed portraits of the Maja, possibly Goya's mistress. Continuing counter clockwise, you come to his scathing group portrait of the family of Carlos IV. Carry on in the same direction, back through the Rembrandt room and into the Gothic hall.

The first-floor vaulted central hall is devoted to Velázquez, with equestrian portraits of royalty, mythological and court scenes. Velázquez did not tweak the sensibilities of his patrons, instead concentrating on painterly techniques and a masterly use of light that is reminiscent of Rembrandt. A portal in the E wall leads to a gallery of El Greco's work, although none of his most famous pictures are here, for he was not in favor until relatively recently and many of his canvases were taken abroad; those displayed are representative of his expressive style.

This account serves merely as an introduction, highlighting some of the most memorable works. The Prado repays repeated visits, however, to explore on different occasions such varied delights as Romanesque murals, fine inlaid Florentine furniture, the florid works of Watteau and other artists of the 18th-19thC Romantic period, the splendid collections of Titian and the Venetian school, and the mysterious paintings of Bosch. The best advice is to be organized: decide before you set out what you want to see.

Seven hundred of the choicest works from the Thyssen Collection, one of the finest private art collections in the world, have recently been given on long loan to the Prado. The collection is to be housed at the Villa Hermosa Palace.

Palacio Real ★

Map 2C2. Plaza de Oriente ☎(91) 248 7404 ▦ four separate tickets are required for official apartments, painting galleries, library and armory ✗ compulsory ✿ Open May-Sept Mon-Sat 10am-12.45pm,

4-5.45pm, Sun and holidays 10am-1.30pm; Oct-Apr Mon-Sat 10am-12.45pm, 3.30-5.15pm, Sun and holidays 10am-2pm. Metro Opera.

This huge Renaissance Neoclassical building lies to the N of a great courtyard formed by colonnaded halls and ancillary structures. It was completed in 1764, the same year that Carlos III took up residence here. The palace has 2,000 rooms, although visitors can see only fifty.

The main facade is comparatively restrained; the ground floor of plain granite blocks is surmounted by Corinthian columns and pilasters and a balustraded balcony. The interior, however, shows all the extravagance of the final stage of the Baroque era, the last flamboyant burst of Rococo. The double marble staircase ascends to the first floor beneath a florid ceiling painting by the 18thC Italian Conrado Giaquinto. Circular windows and arches pierce the domed ceiling, encrusted with medallions, stucco cherubim, and white and gold carved garlands.

The **Salón de Alabarderos** is next, named after the royal guards whose quarters were once here; Spanish tapestries of the 18thC illustrate episodes from the lives of Solomon, Joseph and David. The following rooms include the **Salón de Columnas** and the apartments that constituted the principal residence of Charles III and his family. The **Saleta de Gasparni**, named after the designer, is in lavish Rococo style, with fine chandeliers, gilt-framed mirrors, and a circular sofa with an extravagant candelabra, a gift of the French monarchs. An antechamber contains portraits of *Charles IV* and *Queen María Luisa* by Goya. The **Salón de Gasparini** has an astonishing profusion of entwined tendrils and garlands in high painted relief leaping up the walls and across the arched ceiling.

Nearly as astonishing is the **Sala de Porcelana**, in which 400 panels of exquisitely modeled and handpainted scenes in porcelain are joined to cover the entire walls and ceiling, but even these are surpassed in grandeur by the **state dining room**, its single long table set for 145 guests, the gold-edged china glinting beneath 15 ornate chandeliers. The present king uses the hall for ceremonial dinners.

After rooms devoted to collections of fans, clocks and silverware, the tour leads to the **Capilla Real** (Royal Chapel) completed in 1757. Beneath the dome are columns of veined black marble with gilded capitals, statues of saints, paintings by Giaquinto and an image of the 10yr-old St Félix. Finally, the **Throne Room**, used occasionally by the present monarchs, contains chairs bearing their carved profiles. There are two curiosities in the **painting galleries**: a portrait with the face and hands by El Greco but completed by his son, and a rearing horse by Velázquez that was to be an equestrian portrait. The artist died before he could paint in his royal subject.

The tour ends in the waiting room. As you leave through the W door, bear right (N) toward the **Biblioteca Real** (Royal Library), which is interesting for its maps, engravings, Renaissance musical instruments and 300,000 books. Turning left (S) from the waiting room, walk across the courtyard to the **Armería Real** (Royal Armory). A superb display of over 100 suits of armor, many mounted on horseback, with plumed helmets, is supplemented by crossbows, lances, shields, swords, wheel-lock pistols and rifles.

Other museums

Casa-Museo de Lope de Vega (*Cervantes 11* ☎(91) 429 9216 ☎ open *Tues-Sun 11am-2pm, closed Mon, July 15-Sept 15* ☎) is a painstaking reproduction of the famous playwright's 17thC home. **Centro de Arte Reina Sofía** (*Santa Isabel 52* ☎(91) 467 5062 ☎ open *Wed-Mon 10am-9pm*) is a new museum housed in a former hospital and named for the present queen. At the moment, it is a major exhibition venue for names such as Jasper Johns and Diego Rivera, but a permanent collection is being assembled. Ornate horsedrawn carriages, harnesses and related implements of the age of royalty are the concern of the small **Museo de Carrozas** (*Bailén s/n* ☎(91) 276 2564 ☎ open *Mon-Sat 10am-1.30pm, 3.30-5.15pm, Sun and holidays 10am-1.30pm*). At **Museo de Cera** (*Paseo de Recoletos 41* ☎(91) 419 2282 ■ ✳ open *10.30am-1.30pm, 4-8.30pm*) over 300 figures in wax represent famous personalities from Spanish and world history. The exhibits in **Museo de Ciencias Naturales** (*José Gutiérrez Abascal 2* ☎(91) 261 8607 ☎ open *Mon-Sat 9am-2pm, 3-6pm, Sun and holidays 10am-2pm*) are concerned with geology, entomology, paleontology and zoology, and include stuffed animals.

Museo Naval (*Montalbán 2* ☎(91) 221 0419 ☎ open *10.30am-1.30pm; closed Aug and Mon*) displays delightful models of ships and a chart of the New World made by Juan de la Cosa in 1500. A mid-19thC *palacio*, **Museo**

Romántico (*San Mateo 13* ☎(91) 448 1045 🖼 *open Tues-Sat 10am-6pm, Sun and holidays 10am-2pm; closed Aug to mid-Sept, and Mon*) is aptly filled with paintings, objects and furnishings of the latter part of the Romantic era. An annex of the Las Ventas bullring, **Museo Taurino** (*Alcalá 237* ☎(91) 255 1857 🖼 *open Tues-Sun 9am-3pm, closed Mon*) chronicles the history of the *corrida* in carefully organized pictorial exhibits showing the careers of the great matadors.

Other sights

Parque del Oeste (Park of the West) has the loveliest plants of any of Madrid's parks, and contains the reconstructed Egyptian **Templo de Debod** (🖼 *open 10am-1pm, holidays 10am-3pm*), which dates from the 4thCBC and was moved here to save it from the rising waters created by the Aswan Dam. Another park, **El Retiro**, was once the grounds of a palace that belonged to Philip IV but no longer exists. There are flower gardens, tree-shaded walks, an artificial lake, fountains, an extravagant pavilion and a glass-domed conservatory.

Plaza de la Cibeles boasts the most handsome of the capital's many fountains. It celebrates the Greek goddess Cybele, who commands a chariot and team of horses. On the SE side of the plaza is the **Palacio de Comunicaciones**, a Neo-Baroque extravaganza that houses the main post office. The **Plaza Mayor**, an enclosed pedestrian square, is the focus of old Madrid. The equestrian statue in the center is of *Philip III*, during whose reign the surrounding structures were built. As it has always been, the square is still the setting for carnivals, music festivals, plays and other events.

Hotels

Barajas 🏨
Av. de Logroño 205, Madrid 22
☎(91) 747 7700 ☏ 22255 ▥ 230
rms ▭ 230 ▦ ▰ ⇌ AE ⊙ ⊙
VISA

Location: Near the airport, 14km (8 miles) from the city center. Were it in town, this hotel would rank among the more desirable. It possesses most reasonable amenities, including a pool, gymnasium and convenient golf course. As it is, only those with chauffeured limousines, unlimited expense accounts for taxis or very early flights from the nearby airport are likely to want to spend more than one night.

⌂ ‡ ᵫ □ ◪ ✿ ≋ ✔ ☵ ☂

Eurobuilding
Padre Damián 23, Madrid 16
☎(91) 457 3100 ☏ 22548 ▥ 412
rms ▭ 412 ▦ ▰ ⇌ ⇌ AE CB
⊙ ⊙ VISA *Metro Tetuán.*

Location: In the northern district. Expect neither warmth nor charm in this modern high-rise, but once you are ensconced there is little reason to leave. There are two swimming pools, a gym, saunas, stores, a hairdresser, four bars and four restaurants.

‡ □ ◪ ✿ ≋ ☵ ☂ ⊙

Liabeny
Map 2C3. Salud 3, Madrid 13
☎(91) 232 5306 ☏ 49024 ▥ 158
rms ▭ 158 ▦ ▰ ⇌ AE *Metro Sol.*

Location: Near the Puerta del Sol.

Heavy but comfortable furnishings in the rooms carry out the promise of the spacious lobby. There is an animated "American" bar as well as a restaurant and snack bar. The *plaza mayor* and lively *tapas* districts are close at hand.

‡ □ ◪ ✿ ≋ ☵ ☂

Meliá Madrid
Map 2B2. Princesa 27, Madrid 8
☎(91) 241 8200 ☏ 22537 ▥ 250
rms ▭ 250 ▦ ▰ ▰ ⇌ AE ⊙
⊙ VISA *Metro Ventura Rodríguez.*

Location: Near the Plaza de España. Although both architecture and staff are rather chilly, the Meliá Madrid strives to overcome these deficiencies. In addition to the expected amenities, there is a projection room, hairdresser, barber, gymnasium, sauna, and substantial conference space with the latest types of audio-visual devices.

‡ □ ◪ ✿ ≋ ☵ ☂ ⊙

Miguel Angel 🏨
Miguel Angel 31, Madrid 10
☎(91) 442 0022 ☏ 44235 ▥ 307
rms ▭ 307 ▦ ▰ ⇌ ⇌ AE CB
⊙ ⊙ VISA *Metro Rubén Darío.*

Location: N of the city center, off the important Paseo de la Castellana. No reasonable facility or amenity is denied guests of this five-star luxury hotel, including an indoor pool, a sauna and stores. Staff attend quickly to client needs. Bedrooms are decorated in mellow, darker hues and the furniture is carefully chosen.

Television sets have movies in
English. Reserve well ahead.
✪ ▭ ◻ ◪ ◪ ⚓ ⚓ ⌿ ☂ ▨ ◉

Palace ♨
*Map 3D4. Plaza de las Cortes 7,
Madrid 14 ☎(91) 429 7551*
◎22272 ▥ 520 rms ▭ 520 ▤
▰ ◥ ▭ ◪ AE VISA *Metro Sevilla.*
Location: Three streets from the Prado.
Second only to the **Ritz** among the
capital's *grande dame* hotels, glamor,
intrigue, diplomacy and statecraft are
associated with the Palace's
commodious halls and bedchambers.
Regular guests include star
bullfighters, rock musicians,
politicians, artists and executives.
Perhaps because it is three times the
size of its principal competitor,
service can be offhand. An
impressive glass dome shelters the
busy main reception room.
Renovations underway will include a
new health club.
◪ ✪ ▭ ◻ ◪ ⚓ ☂ ▨

Ritz ♨
*Map 3D5. Plaza de la Lealtad 5,
Madrid 14 ☎(91) 221 2857*
◎43986 ▥ 156 rms ▭ 156 ▤
▰ ◥ ▭ ◪ AE VISA *Metro Banco.*
Location: Two streets N of the Prado.
From 1910, the Ritz has cosseted
the cultured and wealthy elite with
exquisitely precise service and lavish
Edwardian-style appointments. With
a maximum of 306 guests, the staff of
230 is rarely unable to attend to
needs with quicksilver grace. They
make it a practice to learn clients'
names upon registration, which per-
mits the doorman to hand over the
correct room key and the elevator
operator to press the appropriate
floor button without a word. The
bedcovers will be turned back, a
butler will quickly bring a nightcap.
There aren't ten hotels in the whole
of Spain that can match the experience of staying at the Ritz.
✪ ▭ ◻ ◪ ⚓ ▨

Villa Magna ♨
*Map 3A6. Paseo de la Castellana
22, Madrid 1 ☎(91) 261 4900*
◎22914 ▥ to ▥ 194 rms ▭ 194
▤ ▰ ◥ AE *Metro Colón.*
*Location: Halfway between the
northern district and the city center.*
This hotel strives to be a
contemporary manifestation of the
aristocratic **Ritz**, and succeeds.
Scrupulously tended gardens set off
the gleaming glass and steel tower.
Public rooms are 18thC in theme,
bedrooms are large and dining rooms
are opulent.
✪ ▭ ◻ ◪ ◪ ⚓ ☂ ▨

Wellington
Velázquez 8 ☎(91) 275 4400
▥ 258 rms ▭ 258 ▤ ▰ ✪ ▭
◻ ◪ ⚓ ◥ ▭ ☂ ▨ AE ◉ ◎ VISA
Location: Near El Retiro Park. Given
a soupçon more polish here, a dash of
creativity there, this stately middle
sized entry would be among Madrid's highest tier of hotels. Lacking
those smidgens of extra care, it remains among the more desirable,
especially with participants and fol-
lowers of the art/sport of bullfighting.

🕭Other recommendations include:
Aitana (*Paseo de la Castellana 152,
Madrid 16* ☎(91) 250 7107 ▥);
Alcalá (*Alcalá 66, Madrid 9* ☎(91)
435 1060 ▥ to ▥); **(Arosa** (*Salud
21, Madrid 13* ☎(91) 232 1600 ▥);
Carlos V (*Maestro Vitoria 5, Madrid
13* ☎(91) 231 4100 ▥); **Charmatín**
(*Estación de Chamartín 378, Madrid
16* ☎(91) 450 9050 ▥); **Emperatriz**
(*Lopez de Hoyos 4* ☎(91) 413 6511
▥); **Luz Palacio** (*Castellana 57*
☎(91) 442 5100 ▥); **Mercator**
(*Atocha 123, Madrid 12* ☎(91) 239
2600 ▥ to ▥); **Sanvy** (*Goya 3,
Madrid 1* ☎(91) 276 0800 ▥ to ▥);
Sideral (*Casado del Alisal 14, Madrid
14* ☎(91) 467 1200 ▥); **Suecia**
(*Marqués de Casa Riera 4, Madrid 14*
☎(91) 231 6900 ▥).

Restaurants

El Amparo △
*Callejón de Piugcerdá 8 ☎(91)
431 6456 ▥ ▭ ▤ ▰ ☂ AE VISA*
*Last orders 11.30pm. Closed Aug,
Holy Week, Sat lunch, Sun. Metro
Wellington.*
El Amparo hides its considerable
light down a mews off Calle Jorge
Juan (E of the intersection with Calle
de Claudio Coello). Carriage lights, a
vine-covered wall and a brass plate
announce its presence. You usually
have to knock to be let in. But it is

worth the effort, for this is among the
elite of Madrid's culinary temples.
French Basque dishes include *terrina
de hígado*, *lubina* and *hojaldre de
cigalas* (crayfish in puff pastry) and
are distributed by staff whose
professionalism is a joy to witness.
Make sure that you have plenty of
cash with you as prices are stiff.

El Bodegon
*Pinar 15 ☎(91) 262 8844 ▥ △
▭ ▤ ▰ ◥ ▤ AE ◉ ◎ VISA*

Last orders 11.30pm. Closed Sun, holidays, Aug.

A gracious welcome awaits patrons in this converted townhouse in a tranquil neighborhood near fashionable Calle Serrano. The understated decor draws the eye to the effulgent garden behind. Tables are large, chairs upholstered. Well-schooled waiters guide diners through the elaborate selections and ceremoniously whisk away the silver bells that cover each course. The *menu degustacíon* (changed frequently) might include baby lima beans and tiny string beans in pastry with a just a wisp of sauce, *lenguado* with slivers of assorted mushrooms, tasty *filets de buey* drizzled with paprika sauce and twin mounds of sorbet. Reserve for Fri and Sat evenings.

Botín

*Map **2D3**. Cuchilleros 17 ☎(91) 266 4217* ▥ ▭ ▆ ▦ ▣ ⊕ ▥ ▥ *Last orders 11pm. Metro Tirso de Molina.*

Successive managements since 1725 have packed these three floors as well as a subterranean *bodega* with enough picturesque detail for a dozen restaurants. Hemingway was a habitué, and every foreigner arriving in Madrid since has made it a visit as obligatory as the Prado. Roast meat and fowl are the specialties, the tastiest of which are chicken and kid.

Cabo Mayor

Juan Hurtado de Mendoza 11 (at the rear) ☎(91) 250 8776 ▥ ▭ ▆ ▦ ▣ ⊕ ▥ *Last orders 11.30pm. Closed Sun, last two weeks of Aug, first two weeks of Jan. Metro Cuzco.*

Nautical trappings of boat hulls and squared portholes belie the marked sophistication of the inspired kitchen. Disciplined young cooks under the direction of the celebrated Pedro Larumbe observe the essentials of the Basque tradition, but eschew thickened sauces and play with new combinations. One example is the tender medallions of anglerfish (monkfish) showered with baby eels and bracketed with tiny clams and afloat in an aromatic saffron sauce. Others are *lomo de merluza* and *cigalas y langostinos con verduras al jerez sibarita*. Desserts are well above the Spanish norm.

Jockey ⌂

*Map **3B5**. Amador de los Rios 6 ☎(91) 419 2435* ▥ ▭ ▆ ▭ ▣ ⊕ ▥ *Last orders 11pm. Closed Aug, Sun and holidays. Metro Colón.*

For years this restaurant was called the "Jockey Club," but now the second word has been dropped to eliminate the suggestion of exclusiveness. Certainly one of the top places in Madrid, it is not, however, as has been claimed, one of the "great restaurants of the world." An unbroken banquette covered in emerald velvet runs from the curtained entrance past the far service bar. Horse prints of the 19thC hang on polished wood paneling, and curb and snaffle bits and Toby mugs enhance the ambience. Tables are snugly spaced, as it is a small room. The host will be suavely anxious about your well-being, for he is intent upon maintaining the restaurant's reputation. Everything on the menu is likely to please, most of it Spanish in origin but with a light French touch. *Perdiz Española, lomo de lubina* and *mousse de anguila* are among the most delicious specialties.

Lhardy

*Map **3D4**. Carrera de San Jerónimo 8 ☎(91) 221 3385* ▥ ▭ ▆ ▦ ▣ *Closed Sun dinner and most holidays. Metro Sevilla.*

Lhardy is a delightful throwback to gentler times. Downstairs there is a delicatessen-pastry shop combined with a confectioner-tea room. Customers patiently wait for thin crustless sandwiches accompanied by thimbles of sherry or cups of consommé. Queen Isabella II was on the throne when the business started in 1839, and the upstairs dining room reflects these origins. Apart from the *cocido*, the cooking is routine, with specialties such as *crema de mariscos* and roast beef. Its atmosphere is Lhardy's appeal, and it is worth the expensive prices to soak it in.

Mesón Txistl

Plaza Angel Carbajo 6 ☎(91) 270 9651 ▥ ▭ ▆ ▦ ▣ ▣ ⊕ ▥ ▥ *Last orders 11.30pm. Metro Valdeacederas.*

Noisy, hectic and decked out with rows of hanging hams, this Basque restaurant provides heaps of atmosphere as well as sturdy examples of what many people argue is Spain's superior regional cuisine. It might lack subtlety, but certainly not taste. Try one of the house specialties: *pâté de perdiz, merluza romana, cazuela Txistl* and *chuletón Vasco.*

O'Pazo ⌂
Reina Mercedes 20 ☎ *(91) 253 2333* ⅢⅢ ▭ 🍽 ⏛ *Last orders 11.30pm. Closed Aug and Sun. Metro Alvarado.*
This busy, homey Galician restaurant is usually full for both lunch and dinner. The menu is strictly seafood, which is of the highest quality. You will be presented with a plate of unbidden cold snails to accompany the aperitif. Everything that follows, including *mero*, *besugo* and *cigalas a la plancha*, is good to excellent.

Peñas Arriba
Francisco Gervás 15 ☎ *(91) 279 2966* ⅢⅢ ▤ ⏛ ▭ *Closed Sun.*
Apart from some forgivable infelicities in service, owing perhaps to the youth of the staff, Peñas Arriba nearly deserves the fevered praise it has received since its opening. Chef Javier Otaduy sends forth pretty plates that celebrate the fruits of the sea over those of the land, as with roasted peppers stuffed with *merluza* and a terrine of salmon and spinach. Located in the northerly commercial district, the clientele is overwhelmingly male and suited, especially at lunch. Wait a bit before ordering a *digestif*, because they will probably offer you an icy fruit liqueur, an increasingly common lagniappe in the city's restaurants.

Sixto Gran Mesón
Map 3D4. Cervantes 28 ☎ *(91) 429 2255* ⅢⅢ ▭ 🍽 ▤ AE CB ⊙ ⊙ VISA *Last orders 11.30pm. Closed Sun dinner. Metro Palacio.*
Beams, white plaster and terra cotta accurately reflect the thoroughly Castilian bias of this restaurant, in both surroundings and menu. The ground floor has a *taberna* atmosphere; the long room upstairs is more sedate. Waiters speedily bring well-prepared classic dishes, such as *paella*, *chuletas de cordero* and

pollo asado. Try if possible to sit by the fireplace.

Zalacaín ⌂
Alvarez de Baena 4 ☎ *(91) 261 4840* ⅢⅢ ▭ ➤ ▤ 🍽 ⏛ ⅋ *Last orders 11.30pm. Closed Aug, Holy Week, Sat lunch, Sun.*
Mercedes and Lancias growl in the street outside as preliminary testimony to the reputation of a grand luxury restaurant. Zalacaín gathers awards in profusion. By any legitimate gauge, the creation of Jesús María Oyarbide has few peers in Spain or in Europe. He has left little to chance. Patrons are received graciously. Tables shimmer with gleaming glasses, polished silverware and arrangements of fresh flowers, fruit or even dried vegetables. Ingredients are top quality and purchased daily. Any selection of specialties is hopelessly inadequate, for no dish will disappoint. The only reservations are the closeness of the tables and the size of the bill, which by Spanish standards tends to be stunning. Vintage wines are very expensive, but the house versions are more than adequate.

⏛ Among the other restaurants worth trying are: **Asador Donostiarra** (*Pedro Villar 14* ☎ *(91) 279 7340* ⅢⅢ); **Cafe de Oriente** (*Plaza Oriente 2* ☎ *(91) 247 1564* ⅢⅢ); **Club 31** ⌂ (*Alcalá 58* ☎ *(91) 231 0092* ⅢⅢ); **La Dorada** (*Orense 64* ☎ *(91) 270 2004* ⅢⅢ); **La Fonda** (*Príncipe de Vergara 211* ☎ *(91) 250 6147* ⅢⅢ); **La Gran Tasca** (*Ballesta 1* ☎ *(91) 231 0044* ⅢⅢ); **Luis XIII** (*Carrera de San Jerónimo 29* ☎ *(91) 429 8104* ⅢⅢ); **Mesón del Corregidor** (*Plaza Mayor 8* ☎ *(91) 266 5056* ⅢⅢ); **Pazo de Monterrey** (*Alcalá 4* ☎ *(91) 232 8280* ⅢⅢ); **El Pescador** (*José Ortega y Gasset 75* ☎ *(91) 402 1290* ⅢⅢ); **Príncipe de Viana** (*Manuel de Falla 5* ☎ *(91) 259 1448* ⅢⅢ); **Señorío de Bertiz** (*Comandante Zorita 4* ☎ *(91) 233 2757* ⅢⅢ); **Trabuco** (*Mesonero Romanos 19* ☎ *(91) 221 8489* ⅢⅢ).

Nightlife
As in all cities and towns, many **discos** in the capital flare and fade like fireflies, but a surprising number survive for years. Young Madrileños throng to the numerous nightclubs along the Calle de Orense, their older cousins choosing parallel Capitán Haya for its plusher bistros and music clubs. The choices are inexhaustible. More ambitious discos, with elaborate fixtures and superior sound systems, are dotted about the city. Standard practice is to charge an admission fee at the door, which usually include the first drink. Many discos have "afternoon" sessions, from about 7-9.30pm, closing for dinner and reopening at 11pm or later. At the chic spots, business rarely picks up until 1am, and most close at 4 or 4.30am

14 Parks & Gardens

Madrid is now officially one of the greenest cities in the world, thanks to energetic programs for planting a multitude of trees, flowers, and grasslands organized in the last decade by the Comunidad de Madrid. Some parks—such as Casa del Campo and the Retiro—have been around for centuries, but new green zones are springing up annually. Overall, the change from just a few decades ago is remarkable.

Casa de Campo ☆ (Metro: Lago or Batán) is the former royal hunting grounds—miles of parkland lying south of the Royal Palace across the Manzanares River. Until 1931 it was exclusively a hunting ground and leisure area for royalty. You can see the gate through which the kings rode out of the palace grounds, either on horseback or in carriages, on their way to the tree-lined park. A lake in the park is usually filled with rowers. You can have drinks and light refreshments around the water or go swimming in a municipally operated pool. Children will love both the zoo and the Parque de Atracciones (p. 189). The Casa de Campo can be visited daily from 8am to 9pm.

Parque de Retiro ☆ (Metro: Retiro), originally a playground for the Spanish monarchs and their guests, extends over 140 hectares (350 acres). The huge palaces that once stood here were destroyed in the early 19th century; only the former dance hall, the Casón del Buen Retiro (housing the modern works of the Prado), and the building containing the Army Museum remain. The park boasts numerous fountains and statues, plus a large pristine and carp-filled rowing lake, whose borders were modernized and waters drained and replenished and between 2002 and 2003. There are also two exposition centers, the Velázquez and Crystal palaces (built to honor the Philippines in 1887—see "Architectural Standouts," later), and a lakeside monument, erected in 1922 in honor of King Alfonso XII. In summer, the rose gardens are worth a visit, and you'll find several places for inexpensive snacks and drinks. The park is open daily 24 hours, but it is safest from 7am to about 8:30pm.

El Real Jardín Botánico (Botanical Garden) ☆
This garden is a short walk west of the Retiro, and adjacent to the Museo del Prado. Founded in the 18th century by Fernando VI at the Huerto de Migas Calientes and subsequently moved to its present location by Carlos III, the garden celebrated its 250th anniversary in 2005. Today it contains more than 104 species of trees and 30,000 types of plants. Also on the premises are an exhibition hall and a library specializing in botany.

Plaza de Murillo 2. ℭ **91-420-30-17.** www.rjb.csic.es. Admission 2€ ($2.50). Daily from 10am; closing hours vary from 6–9pm according to the month. Closed Aug. Metro: Atocha. Bus: 10, 14, 19, 32, or 45.

Campo del Moro ☆
These extremely beautiful gardens slope down westward from the Royal Palace toward the River Manzanares. Named after a medieval Arab chieftain who attempted a siege of the fortress that occupied the spot where the palace now stands, the park boasts a well-tended profusion of lawns, trees, and flowers. There are also two magnificent fountains: the 17th-century Triton originally located in the Aranjuez Palace gardens and the other, Las Conchas, built by Ventura Rodríguez a century later. The still-advertised Museo de Carruajes (Carriage Museum), tucked away in a corner of the grounds, has, alas, been closed for many years. You can only enter the park from the lower side beside the Paseo de la Virgen del Puerto (which involves a longish roundabout walk via Cuesta de la Vega if you are visiting the Royal Palace first).

Paseo de la Virgen del Puerto. ℭ **91-454-88-00.** Free admission. Oct–Mar Mon–Sat 9am–6pm, Sun 9am–6pm; Apr–Sept 10am–8pm, Sun 9am–8pm. Metro: Príncipe Pío. Bus: 26, 33, 39, 41, 138, or 500.

Parque de Oeste   Beautifully laid out by landscape gardener Cecilio Rodríguez at the beginning of the 20th century, this peaceful and relaxing park slopes from the northwestern edge of Argüelles down toward the River Manzanares and Casa del Campo. Meandering paths follow a well-marked "nature route" past birch, cedar, cypress, and pine trees and every May a rose festival is held in the 17,000-sq.-m (182,986-sq.-ft.) Rosaleda close to the *teleférico* and the terrace cafe–lined Pintor Rosales Promenade. Main entrance is at Moncloa where Paseo de Moret meets the Avenida Arco de la Victoria.

Metro: Moncloa. Bus: 16, 44, 61, or 133.

Parque Tierno Galván   This is one of Madrid's newer parks, built in honor of the city's popular 1980s mayor Enrique Tierno Galván. Located in the southwest of the city close to the Méndez Alvaro bus station (also known as Estación Sur), it's a sunny open park with lawns, cypresses, panoramic city views, and a Greek-style outdoor amphitheater where occasional concerts are held. It's also the site of three major attractions for families: the IMAX cinema, the Planetarium, and the Angel Nieto motorcycle museum (named after Spain's former world-champion motorcyclist).

Metro: Méndez Alvaro. Bus: 102 or 148.

Fuente del Berro *(Finds)*   An oasis of unexpected peace beside the busy M30 at the western end of Salamanca district, this mature gem of a park dates from the 17th century and within its small confines boasts a wide selection of trees from all over the world. An information section was opened inside the grounds in 2003. Around the park is the tiny district known as Quinta del Berro, where a number of stylish detached 1920s villas stand sedately in quiet tree-lined lanes.

Metro: O'Donnell. Bus: 15 or 28.

Parque Juan Carlos   This new park sprawls beside a golf course at the far western end of the city between Barajas airport and the Feria de Madrid buildings. A vast conglomeration of waterways, gardens, and cycling and walking paths, with views north to the distant Guadarrama mountains, it's still finding its way as a leisure area, and in summer the present lack of full-size trees means there is little shade. The abundant olive groves were there long before the park was conceived, but the newly planted pines, oaks, and eucalyptus will need many years of growth before the park can achieve a much-needed sense of completeness.

Metro: Canillejas (south entrance) or Campo de las Naciones (north entrance). Bus: 122.

El Capricho de Alameda de Osuna *(Finds)*   Just below the southern end of Juan Carlos park, in complete contrast, is this fully mature, French-style park, designed by J. B. Mulot (Marie Antoinette's gardener) for the duchess of Osuna at the end of the 18th century. It's cool, green, and tranquil, with every conceivable kind of European tree, plus gazebos, lodges, an artificial lake with islands in the middle, and a labyrinthine hedge-bordered maze (alas, the latter is not open to the public). After years of abandonment and decay (it was used as a military barracks during the civil war), it was restored to its full glory in the mid-1970s with later work carried out in the 1990s.

Paseo de la Alameda de Osuna. 010 for Madrid Information Service. Free admission. Weekends and fiesta days only. Oct–Mar 9am–6:30pm; Apr–Sept 9am–9pm. Metro: Canillejas. Metro station to open beside park in 2007. Extension of no. 5 line from Canillejas. Bus: 101 or 105.

15 Especially for Kids

Plaza de Toros Monumental de las Ventas   It's not all bulls and blood (see "Taking the Bull by the Horns," earlier in this chapter) in this, well, monumental venue. For periods of several weeks between November to March, when the air is distinctly cooler and the skies—for Madrid, that is—are grayer, a whole new mood takes over when the circus comes to town and, under a giant cover, elephants, clowns, and trapeze artists perform for kids of all ages in the bullfighting arena.

Calle Alcalá 237. ℰ 91-726-35-70. www.las-ventas.com. Tickets at bullring. Nov–Mar. Metro: Ventas. Bus: 53 or 146.

Museo de Cera de Madrid (Wax Museum)   The kids will enjoy seeing a lifelike wax Columbus calling on Ferdinand and Isabella, as well as Marlene Dietrich checking out Bill and Hillary Clinton. The 450 wax figures also include heroes and villains of World War II. Two galleries display Romans and Arabs from the ancient days of the Iberian Peninsula; a show in multivision gives a 30-minute recap of Spanish history from the Phoenicians to the present.

Paseo de Recoletos 41. ℰ 91-319-26-49. Admission 12€ ($15) adults, 8€ ($10) children, children 3 and under free. Daily 10am–2pm and 4–8pm. Metro: Colón. Bus: 27, 45, or 53.

Parque de Atracciones   The park was created in 1969 to amuse the young at heart with an array of rides and concessions. The former include a toboggan slide, a carousel, pony rides, an adventure into outer space, a walk through a transparent maze, a visit to a jungle, a motor-propelled series of cars disguised as a tail-wagging dachshund puppy, and a gyrating whirligig clutched in the tentacles of an octopus named El Pulpo. The most popular rides are a pair of roller coasters named "7 Picos" and "Jet Star." The park also has diversions for adults (see chapter 10 for details).

Casa de Campo. ℰ 91-463-29-00. http://parquedeatracciones.es. Admission to all amusements 24.40€ ($31) adults, 13.90€ ($17) children under 7. Apr–May Tues–Fri noon–8pm, Sat–Sun noon–10pm; June–Aug Tues–Fri 6pm–1am, Sat 6pm–2am, Sun noon–1am; Sept Tues–Sun (variable hours; call to check before going); Oct–Mar Sat noon–8pm (sometimes 9pm), Sun 11am–8pm (sometimes 9pm). Take the Teleférico cable car (below); at the end of this ride, microbuses take you the rest of the way. Alternatively, take the suburban train from Plaza de España and stop near the entrance to the park (Entrada de Batán).

Teleférico   Strung high above several of Madrid's verdant parks, this cable car was originally built in 1969 as part of a public fairgrounds (Parque de Atracciones) modeled vaguely along the lines of Disneyland. Today, even for visitors not interested in visiting the park, the *teleférico* retains an allure of its own as a high-altitude method of admiring the cityscape of Madrid. The cable car departs from Paseo Pintor Rosales at the eastern edge of Parque del Oeste (at the corner of Calle Marqués de Urquijo) and carries you high above two parks, railway tracks, and over the Manzanares River to a spot near a picnic ground and restaurant in Casa de Campo. Weather permitting, there are good views of the Royal Palace along the way. The ride takes 11 minutes. At the Pintor Rosales entrance to the *teleférico* is the famed Bruin Ice Cream Parlour, which has been around for decades and offers a wide choice of *helados* (ice creams) and *granizados* (iced drinks).

Paseo del Pintor Rosales s/n. ℰ 91-541-11-18. Fare 3.50€ ($4.35) one-way, 4.80€ ($6) round-trip. Apr–Sept daily noon–8 or 9pm (depending on month); Oct–Mar Sat–Sun noon–7pm. Metro: Plaza de España or Argüelles. Bus: 21.

Faro de Madrid   Topped by what looks like a control tower and boasting a marvelous panorama of both city and countryside, this thin 90m-high (300 ft.) tower (known as the "Lighthouse of Madrid") rises on the western outskirts of University

City, just above Moncloa and right opposite the Museo de America. With the aid of telescopes (.50€/.60¢ for 5 min.), you can check out the Plaza Mayor's rooftops or (on a clear day) the rugged peaks of the Guadarramas 97km (60 miles) away. An elevator takes you up to the viewing area—which is glassed in for safety—and floor diagrams point out the main city highlights. A major advantage is that relatively few people know about it, so you rarely have to wait in line (thankfully, since elevator space is limited). *Note:* The Faro was closed at press time but due to be opened by late 2006; call ahead to make sure it's open before you go.

Av. de los Reyes Católicos. ⓒ **91-544-81-04.** Admission 1€ ($1.25). Tues–Sun 10am–1:45pm and 5–8:45pm. Metro: Moncloa. Bus: 12, 44, or 133.

Zoo Aquarium de la Casa de Campo   This modern, well-organized facility allows you to see about 3,000 animals from five continents. Most are in simulated natural habitats, with moats separating them from the public. There's a petting zoo for the kids and a show presented by the Chu-Lin band. The zoo/aquarium complex includes a 520,000-gallon tropical marine aquarium, a dolphinarium, and a parrot club. You can also take a camel, pony, or mini-train ride, and live your own *Jaws* experience in the walk-through shark tank.

Casa de Campo. ⓒ **91-512-37-70.** www.zoomadrid.com. Admission 14.90€ ($19) adults, 12.20€ ($15) seniors and children 3–8, free for children 2 and under. Daily 10:30am–sunset. Metro: Batán. Bus: 33.

Faunia   Initially set up in 2001 under the name *Parque Biológico de Madrid,* Faunia (as it is now called) aims at educating children (and adults) about the natural world by using state of the art technology. Within its 140,000-sq.-m (1.5-million-sq.-ft.) grounds, a variety of ecosystems from tropical rainforests to deserts and polar regions have been ingeniously created. In addition to a wide variety of vegetation, there are hundreds of species of animals on view. Facilities include dining areas, nursery, an animal hospital, and a lake. Though it's out in the eastern suburbs of the city, it can be easily reached by Metro or bus.

Av. de las Comunidades 28. ⓒ **91-301-62-10.** www.faunia-es.com. Admission 21€ ($26) adults, 15€ ($19) children 3–9 and seniors over 65. Mon–Fri 10:30am–8pm; Sat–Sun 10:30am–9pm. Metro: Valdebernardo. Bus: 71.

IMAX Madrid   Incredibly realistic 3-D and Omnimax presentations of science, travel, and wildlife movies make this very special movie house a must for the kids, even though the shows only last an hour and are in Spanish. It's located inside Tierno Galván park in the southwest of Madrid, a short walk from the Metro.

Parque Tierno Galván. ⓒ **91-467-48-00.** Admission 7€ ($8.75) adults. Reduced rates Mon 5.90€ ($7.35) adults and seniors over 65; 10€ ($13) for 2 shows. Mon–Thurs, Sun noon–1pm and 5–10pm; Fri–Sat noon–1pm and 5–11pm. Metro: Méndez Alvaro. Bus: 102 or 148.

⌒*Tips* **An Area You May Want to Avoid**

The zone by the *teleférico* in the Casa de Campo has a very good self-service restaurant with a terrace section enjoying fine views of the park—an excellent place to enjoy a relaxing lunch before walking down a wood-fringed park to Lago. But some 500m (1,640 ft.) to the west it's different story. There the road that runs just inside the park is a pickup zone for prostitutes with cars stopping and negotiating deals. It's also a drug zone, so you may want to avoid that particular section of the park entirely.

El Planetario de Madrid   Also in Tierno Galván park is Madrid's impressive Planetarium, with regular 45-minute shows taking you on virtual-reality trips across the solar system—and you never leave your seat. It's Spanish-speaking narration only but sensational enough to keep kiddies of all ages watching.

Parque Tierno Galván. ℂ **91-467-38-98**. Admission 3€ ($3.75) adults, 1.20€ ($1.50) children 2–14 and seniors, 2.25€ ($2.80) groups. Mid-Sept–mid-June Tues–Fri 9:30am–1:45pm and 5–7:45pm, Sat–Sun 11:45am–1:45pm and 5–8:45pm; mid-June to mid-Sept Tues–Sun 11am–1:45pm and 5–7:45pm. Metro: Méndez Alvaro. Bus: 102 or 148.

Museo del Ferrocarril (Railway Museum)   Located just south of Atocha in the barrio of Delicias, this ironwork trainspotter's delight was built in 1880 by Gustave Eiffel. Once trains ran from here as far as Portugal, but all services stopped in 1968. Today, in a locomotive timewarp, it's the only station in Madrid that still looks like it belongs to the 19th century. Climb aboard the trains (check out the 1950s Talgo that looks like the one Spencer Tracy took in the movie *Bad Day at Black Rock*), watch early locomotive movie footage, attend short "theater shows," and see the "clock room" whose array of timers includes the one that clocked the very first train trip in Spain, a trip from Barcelona to Mataró. A buy-and-sell model-train market is sometimes on-site.

Paseo de las Delicias 61. ℂ **91-506-83-33**. www.museodelferrocarril.org. Admission: 4€ ($5) adults, 2.50€ ($3.10) children 4–12. Free Sat. Tues–Sun 10am–3 pm. Theater shows Tues–Fri 10:30–11:45am. Metro: Delicias.

OUT OF TOWN

Museo de la Ciencia Cosmo Caixa   Huge fun for kids of all ages is guaranteed at this interactive science museum on the outskirts of the northerly suburb of Alcobendas, just a short bus trip from Plaza Castilla. Here activity rooms show how nature's laws work and how matter evolves from atomic structure into the most complex forms of life. There's also a Bubble Planetarium and two year-round exhibitions that are worth a couple of hours of anyone's time. In between visiting the different attractions you can recharge with a snack and drink at the cafeteria.

Pintor Velázquez s/n, Alcobendas, 16km (10 miles) from Madrid. ℂ **91-484-52-00**. Admission: 3€ ($3.50) permanent exhibitions; 1.50€ ($1.85) per activity room. Tues–Sun 10am–8pm. Ten-min train ride from Atocha station or 15-min bus ride from Plaza Castilla.

Warner Brothers Movie World   Newest addition to Madrid's great child attractions, this long-awaited movie theme park—Spain's answer to Disneyworld—opened in April 2002. It's not cheap (and you're not allowed to take your own food and drink), but it's proved a smash for the family and could be worth stretching the budget for a day. Its five themed areas cover Old West Territory, Hollywood, DC Super Heroes, Cartoon Village, and Warner Bros. Studios. Note that the park closes for 6 months in winter and 6 weeks in summer (see below).

San Martín de la Vega. ℂ **91-821-12-34**. www.warnerbrospark.com. Admission 32€ ($40) adults, 24€ ($30) children 5–11. Apr–June, Sept Mon–Thurs 10am–8pm, Fri–Sun 10am–midnight. Closed mid-Oct to Mar and Aug to mid-Sept. Metro: Atocha RENFE. By train C-3 from Atocha railway station. By car N-IV to Km 22 then M-506 to San Martín de la Vega.

Safari Park   This animal-lover's paradise is located near the village of Aldea del Fresno just west of Navalcarnero, and is close to a lake and the beach-bordered Alberche River, where you can rent a *pedalo* and swim in summer. A colorful range of nearly 500 animals, from tigers and monkeys to giraffes and elephants, roam wild on the extensive grounds—you can view them in safety from a car. An exciting highlight is the daily lion taming show. Birds of prey are among the many species that fill the aviary, and for fans of slithery things, the reptile house boasts snakes galore.

Aldea del Fresno, Carretera de Extremadura N-V Km 32. (✆ **91-862-23-14**. Admission 11€ ($14) adults, 7€ ($8.75) children 3–10. Daily 10:30am–sunset. Car essential. Take N-V to Navalcarnero, and then M-507 to Aldea del Fresno.

Tren de la Fresa   Known as "The Strawberry Train" because *fresas* (strawberries) are handed out on it to travelers by hostesses dressed in period costumes, this trip from Atocha station to the town of Aranjuez takes place on a old steam train. This not only offers a relaxing and atmospheric way of travel, evoking an era of bygone days, but also gives you a full day out to visit Aranjuez palace and gardens and enjoy a lunch beside the Tagus River. It's particularly popular in spring.

Estación de Atocha. (✆ **902-22-88-22**. Fare 24€ ($30) adults, 16€ ($20) children 2–12. Departs 10am and returns from Aranjuez at 6:30pm. Closed mid-Oct to Mar and Aug to mid-Sept. Metro: Atocha RENFE, and then *cercanías* train to Aranjuez.

Aquasur   Also in Aranjuez, this superb open-air pool with its five giant slides is an ideal fun location for the kids if you're visiting Madrid in the full heat of summer. Catch the regular *cercanías* train from Atocha for the 40-minute trip. Free buses run from Aranjuez town center (Calle Príncipe) to the pool. Better value on weekdays.

Estación de Atocha. (✆ **91-891-60-34**. Admission Mon–Fri 5€ ($6.25) adults, 3€ ($3.75) children 3–9; Sun 10€ ($12) adults, 7€ ($8.75) children 3–9. June–Sept 11am–8pm. Metro: Atocha RENFE, and then *cercanías* train to Aranjuez.

Aquópolis-Villanueva   One of two Aquópolis water parks in Madrid province (the other is in San Fernando de Henares), this well-equipped summer favorite is among the biggest pool leisure centers in all Europe. Among its main attractions are its wave pools and huge water slides.

Av. de la Dehesa, Villanueva de la Cañada. (✆ **91-815-69-11**. Admission Mon–Fri 13€ ($16) adults, 9€ ($11) children 3–9, 9.25€ ($12) seniors; Sat–Sun 16.50€ ($21) adults. Mid-June to mid-Sept noon–9pm. Metro: Moncloa. Bus: 627 from Moncloa bus station. Free bus service from Cuesta de San Vicente.

16 Special-Interest Sightseeing

ARCHITECTURAL STANDOUTS

Plaza Mayor 🞱🞱   In the heart of Madrid, this famous square was known as the Plaza de Arrabal during medieval times, when it stood outside the city wall. The original architect of Plaza Mayor itself was Juan Gómez de Mora, who worked during the reign of Philip III. Under the Habsburgs, the square rose in importance as the site of public spectacles, including the abominable *autos de fé*, in which heretics were burned. Bullfights, knightly tournaments, and festivals were also staged here.

Three times the buildings on the square burned—in 1631, 1672, and 1790—but each time the plaza bounced back. After the last big fire, it was completely redesigned by Juan de Villanueva.

Nowadays a Christmas fair is held around the equestrian statue of Philip III (dating from 1616) in the center of the square. On summer nights the Plaza Mayor becomes the virtual living room of Madrid, as tourists sip sangria at the numerous cafes and listen to the music performances, many of which are spontaneous. The walls of the former **Casa de la Panadería** on the square's northern side feature murals that some have compared unflatteringly to comic strips.

Metro: Puerta del Sol.

Sociedad General de Autores de España   This extraordinary building, former home of the banker Javier González Longoria (and also known as Palacio Longoria), is the only example of Catalan Art Nouveau architecture in Madrid. Gaudí and other exponents of this distinctive style never really got a look in, probably because of the fierce rivalry between the Spanish capital and Barcelona. Designed at the beginning of the century by José Grases Riera in a style that also shows French influence, the building bears more than a passing resemblance to an exotic fairy-tale sand castle. Today it's home of the Association of Spanish Writers and artists, and though it's not open to the public the unique exterior alone is well worth a look.

Calle Fernando VI 6. ✆ **91-349-95-14.** Metro: Alonso Martínez. Bus: 3, 40, or 149.

La Casa de las Siete Chimeneas (House of the Seven Chimneys)   Located in the historic Plaza del Rey on the western edge of Chueca, this remarkable little Habsburg building was the late-16th-century creation of El Escorial architect Juan de Herrera. Celebrated visitors over the years have included Charles I of England and the Marquis of Esquilache, who caused a minor mutiny when he tried to abolish the wearing of capes and broad-brimmed hats in the 18th century.

Plaza del Rey. Metro: Banco de España. Bus: 1, 9, 74, 146, or 150.

Palacio de Comunicaciones   This is the grandiose name for Madrid's imposing Correos (Post Office) building, which was completed at the end of the First World War by Antonio Palacios and Joaquín Otamendi. An extravagant wedding cake lookalike that gleams cream-ochre above the Plaza de Cibeles, it's one of the most emblematic images of 20th-century Madrid. An ambitious blend of Spanish and Viennese Art Nouveau, the building is anything but functional in style, and contrasts strongly with the stark modernity of many buildings lining the nearby Castellana avenue. Inside it's just as dramatic, with high ceilings, soaring pillars, marble floors, and a palatial staircase. You won't find a more impressive place to buy stamps for your postcards.

Plaza de Cibeles. ✆ **91-521-65-00.** Mon–Fri 8:30am–9:30pm; Sat 9:30am–9:30pm; Sun 8:30am–2pm. Metro: Banco de España. Bus: 5, 14, 27, 37, 45, 53, or 146.

Banco de España   On the other side of Cibeles Square from the *Correos* building, Spain's most prestigious bank is housed in an equally impressive 19th-century French Second Empire–influenced landmark designed by Eduardo Adaro and Severiano Sanz de Lastra. Standouts inside include a Carrara marble stairway, glass-domed central patio, and variety of stained-glass windows. Guided tours can be arranged, and the bank's collection of Goyas viewed by appointment.

Plaza de Cibeles or Paseo del Prado 2. ✆ **91-338-53-65.** Guided tours by arrangement Mon and Wed–Thurs 9:30 and 11:30am. Write at least 1 week in advance to the Protocol Service, Banco de España, Alcalá 50, Madrid 28014. Metro: Banco de España. Bus: 1, 9, 74, 146, or 150.

Edificio Metrópolis   Another familiar Madrid landmark that stands out as prominently as the bow of ship is this French-built 1911 structure designed by the brothers Jules and Raymond Février for the Union and Fenix Insurance Company. Topped by the bust of a phoenix symbolizing winged victory, its ornate dome of dark slate and interwoven gilt decor towers above the junction of Alcalá and the beginnings of the Gran Vía. Colonnaded floors have statues representing Trade, Agriculture, Industry, and Mining. Now owned by the Metropolis insurance company, it has remained largely unchanged in appearance since the beginning of the century (though the phoenix was replaced by a newer one in the 1970s). Unfortunately the building is not open to the public, so its charms can only be viewed from outside.

Calle de Alcalá 39. Metro: Sevilla. Bus: 1, 5, 9, 15, 20, 51, 52, 74,146, or 150.

Puerta de Alcalá   Designed by the prominent Italian architect Francesco Sabatini for Carlos III, this granite neoclassical gateway, comprising five arches topped by angels, marked the eastern edge of the city up to the mid-1800s. Today it stands in the middle of the Plaza de Independencia roundabout surrounded by a small flower-garden area, just opposite the entrance to the Retiro and next to the beginning of stylish Calle Serrano.

Plaza de la Independencia. Metro: Retiro. Bus: 1, 9, 19, 20, 28, 51, 52, or 146.

Palacio de Cristal (Crystal Palace)   Modeled on London's Crystal Palace of the 1850s, Madrid's greatest wrought-iron and glass-domed Industrial Revolution structure was launched just 30 years later to stage an exhibition of Philippine tropical plants. It stands in the heart of the Retiro Park, reflecting charismatically in a small lake inhabited by ducks, grey lag geese, and black swans, and forms one of Madrid's most enduring bucolic images. Exhibitions of modern art are regularly held inside the building; these range from surrealistic metal sculptures to aviary shows.

Parque del Retiro. ℂ 91-574-66-14. Free admission. Oct–May Mon and Wed–Sat 10am–6pm; June–Sept Mon and Wed–Sat 11am–8pm. Metro: Retiro.

KIO Towers   Madrid's very own ultramodern twin version of the leaning tower of Pisa, this pair of highly controversial gravity-defying *torres* were built at the beginning of the booming '80s to symbolize a new economic dawn. The towers were financed by the Kuwaiti Investment Office (hence the name), and their completion was delayed well over a decade due to a financial scandal. Evocative icons of smoked glass and concrete, they now loom at the northern end of the Castellana Avenue on either side of Plaza Castilla like jet-age exit gates to the city.

Plaza Castilla. Metro: Plaza Castilla. Bus: 5, 27, 66, 70, 124, or 147.

17 Organized Tours

A large number of agencies in Madrid book organized tours and excursions to sights and attractions both in and outside the city limits. Although your mobility and freedom might be somewhat hampered with an organized tour, many visitors appreciate the ease and convenience of being able to visit so many sights in a single efficiently organized day.

IN THE CITY

BUS TOURS   Many of the city's hotel concierges, and all of the city's travel agents, will book anyone who asks for a guided tour of Madrid or its environs with one of Spain's largest tour operators, **Pullmantours,** Plaza de Oriente 8 (ℂ 91-541-18-07). Regardless of their destination and duration, virtually every tour departs from the Pullmantours terminal, at that address. Half-day tours of Madrid include an artistic tour priced at 34€ ($43) per person, which includes entrance to a selection of the city's museums, and a panoramic half-day tour for 19€ ($24).

The hop-off, hop-on **Madrid Vision Bus** lets you set your own pace and itinerary. A scheduled panoramic tour lasts a half-hour, provided that you don't get off the bus. Otherwise, you can opt for an unlimited number of stops, exploring at your leisure. The Madrid Vision makes four complete tours daily, two in the morning and two in the afternoon; on Sunday and Monday buses depart only in the morning. Check with **Trapsa Tours** (ℂ 91-767-17-43) for the latest departure times, which vary. The full-day tour, with unlimited stops, costs 11€ ($14). You can board the bus at the Madrid tourist office.

ORGANIZED WALKING TOURS   If you're interested in organized walking tours of the city, the **Patronato Municipal de Turismo** (Tourist Office; Plaza Mayor 3; ℂ **91-588-16-36;** www.munimadrid.es/turismo) provides English-speaking guides and routes that cover the history, monuments, and leading figures of Madrid. You can get details and buy tickets at the tourist office in Plaza Mayor. Local travel agencies also sell tickets for various sightseeing tours in and around Madrid.

For something a little more out of the ordinary, check out the program arranged by **Stephen Drake-Jones,** an English ex-lecturer who's lived in the city more than 30 years. His half-dozen erudite and slightly eccentric walks around old Madrid are pleasantly broken up by refreshments—liquid and otherwise—at local taverns (ℂ **60-914-32-03;** www.wellsoc.org).

Another organized program of interesting guided walks is provided by **Olé Spain Tours** (Paseo Infanta Isabel 21; ℂ **91-551-52-94;** www.olespaintours.com).

If you'd like to combine a walking tour with an eating tour, contact **Adventurous Appetites,** a tapa-bar tour run by two enterprising young resident Englishmen. James Fraser and Will Leonard (ℂ **63-933-10-73;** www.adventurousappetites.com; tours@adventurousappetites.com). Their trips depart from the statue of the bear and *madroño* tree in the Puerta del Sol at 8pm Monday through Saturday and cost 40€ ($50) a head. Maximum size of tour group is six.

OUTSIDE THE CITY

Pullmantours (see information above) also offers guided tours to destinations outside Madrid. **Toledo** is the most popular full-day excursion **outside the city limits.** Trips cost from 60€ ($75). These tours (including lunch) depart daily at 9:45am from the Pullmantours terminal at Plaza de Oriente 8, last all day, and include ample opportunities for wandering at will through the city's narrow streets. You can, if you wish, take an abbreviated morning tour of Toledo, without stopping for lunch, for 40€ ($50).

Another popular tour stops briefly in Toledo and continues on to visit both the monastery at **El Escorial** and the **Valle de los Caídos** (Valley of the Fallen) before returning the same day to Madrid. With lunch included, this all-day excursion costs 90€ ($113).

The third major destination of bus tours from Madrid's center to the city's surrounding attractions is Pullmantours' full-day guided excursion to **Avila** and **Segovia,** which takes in a heady dose of medieval and ancient Roman monuments. With lunch included, the price per person is 70€ ($88).

18 Sports

ACTIVE SPORTS

GOLF   Golf is not cheap in Madrid, where it still has the faint aura of an elitist activity. (Weekends are particularly expensive so avoid them if you can.) Among the few venues around the capital, the best is the **Club de Campo Villa de Madrid** (**Madrid Country Club;** Carretera de Castilla Km 2; ℂ **91-550-08-40;** http://club-demadrid.com), which has a challenging par-71 course. This is a full-fledged sports center with tennis, squash, horseback-riding, pigeon shooting, and a swimming pool among its other facilities.

Another topnotch venue, located on the eastern outskirts of Madrid between the Juan Carlos Exhibition Halls and Barajas airport, is the **Club de Golf Olivar de la Hinojosa** (Avenida de Dublin s/n, Campo de la Naciones; ✆ **91-721-18-89;** http:// golfolivar.com), which has one 9-hole course and one 18-hole course. You'll need a handicap card to play there.

TENNIS You'll find reasonably priced courts for hire (around 4€/$5 per hour) at large *polideportivos* (multifacility sports centers) run by the Madrid municipality. **Casa del Campo** (✆ **91-464-91-67**), **Barrio del Pilar, Barrio de la Concepción,** and **La Elipa** are among the main locales. Private courts with high membership fees and court fees are also available at the **Club de Tenis de Chamartín** (✆ **91-345-25-00;** www. ctchamartin.es).

SWIMMING There's a good choice of municipal pools run by the **Instituto Municipal de Deportes** (✆ **010** for info on areas and rates; www.imd.es). Their best **indoor** pool is the Olympic-size one at Chamartín (✆ **91-350-12-23**), which closes in August but is open the rest of the year. Smaller is the centrally located indoor **La Latina pool** (✆ **91-365-80-31**). During the summer months from June to August the municipality has a wider variety of good-size **open-air** pools. Among the best are those at **La Elipa** and **Lago.** The **Comunidad de Madrid** also runs a popular summer pool at **Canal de Isabel II** (✆ **91-533-96-42**) in Chamberí.

KEEPING FIT If you want to stay trim in order to do justice to the sights, many hotels either have their own fitness facilities or have agreements with private clubs for clients to use their facilities. One of the best-run of these is the **Bodhidharma** in the southerly suburb of Embajadores (✆ **91-517-28-16**).

WALKING The Guadarrama mountains are nearer than you think. Just 1 hour and 20 minutes by suburban train from Chamartín takes you to the town of Cercedilla (see chapter 11), which has an information center and six graded trails in them thar hills. Another fine walking spot—reached by bus from Plaza de Castilla—is **Manzanares el Real,** with its beautiful and dramatic La Pedriza park, where many scenes from the Charlton Heston '60s epic *El Cid* were filmed (p. 252).

HORSEBACK RIDING The closest place for taking to the saddle is the **Club de Campo Villa de Madrid** sports complex on the edge of the leafy Casa del Campo park (see "Golf," above, for details). At the nearby upmarket suburb of Pozuelo, you can also hire horses by the hour or day at the **Escuela de Equitación Pozuelo.** Further countryside riding facilities are available at outlying towns such as Cercedilla and **Manzanares el Real** (p. 252).

SKIING The most popular resort near Madrid for this strictly midwinter activity (Nov–Feb) is **Puerto de Navacerrada,** with its 15 ski slopes and chairlift up to the 2,100m (7,000-ft.) Bola del Mundo. **Valdesqui** near Cotos has 24 slopes and usually the best snow, while **Valcotos** has the most attractive setting. For up-to-date details on skiing accommodations, locations, and snow conditions around Madrid in general, contact **ATUDEM** (✆ **91-350-20-20**). They only speak Spanish, so you may want to get someone (your concierge, for example) to help translate. Skiing conditions are generally limited; for many the main pleasure in such outings is seeing the beautiful surrounding countryside covered in a white blanket of snow.

SPECTATOR SPORTS

SOCCER   If you're a fan of English-style football, then the place to go is **Santiago Bernabeu** (Estadio Santiago Bernabeu, Paseo de la Castellana 144; ℭ **91-229-17-09;** www.realmadrid.es), Madrid's largest stadium: total capacity 75,000 spectators. This is the home of Spain's most successful team Real Madrid, regarded by diehard fanatics as even more important than the Prado or Palacio Real. And whose host of charismatic international stars ranges from Brazil's Ronaldinho to Britain's Beckham. Tickets are 15€ to 80€ ($19–$100).

BASKETBALL   Basketball is almost as popular as soccer all over Spain, and there are several locales in the city where you watch the sport. Best is the 15,000-capacity **Palacio Alegre stadium** (Calle Utebo 1; ℭ **91-422-07-81;** www.palaceiovistaalegre. com), situated in the southwestern suburbs and rebuilt in 2000 over the old Plaza de Toros. It's also a venue for bullfights as well as rock and opera concerts.

ATHLETICS   Madrid's largest (20,000 capacity) athletic stadium, ambitiously aimed at expanding fourfold to host the 2012 Olympics (if its bid is successful), is the **Estadio de la Comunidad de Madrid** (Av. de Arcantales s/n; ℭ **91-720-24-00**). Located on the rapidly expanding eastern edge of the city, it features a variety of athletic events as well as periodic music shows.

8

Strolling Around Madrid

Start:	Southeastern corner of the Palacio Real.
Finish:	Calle del Arenal.
Time:	3 hours.
Best Times:	Saturday or Sunday, when you can also visit the flea market of El Rastro.
Worst Times:	Monday to Saturday from 7:30 to 9:30am and 5 to 7:30pm—because of heavy traffic.

This tour encompasses 16th- and 17th-century Madrid, including the grand plazas and traffic arteries that the Habsburg families built to transform a quiet town into a world-class capital.

The tour begins at the:

❶ Palacio Real (Royal Palace)
This palace is at the corner of Calle de Bailén and Calle Mayor. The latter was built by Philip II in the 1560s to provide easy access from the palace to his preferred church, San Jerónimo el Real.

Walk east to:

❷ Calle Mayor
Walk on the south side of the street. Within a block, you'll reach a black bronze statue of a kneeling angel, erected in 1906 to commemorate the aborted assassination of King Alfonso XIII (grandfather of the present king, Juan Carlos).

Across the street from the kneeling angel is the:

❸ Palacio de Abrantes
Today, this palace, at Calle Mayor 86, is occupied by the Italian Institute of Culture.

On the same side of the street as the kneeling angel, to the statue's left, is the:

❹ Palacio de Uceda
This palace, at Calle Mayor 79, is now the headquarters of the Spanish military

(their version of the Pentagon). Both of these palaces are among the best examples of 17th-century civil architecture in Madrid.

Walk half a block east, crossing to the north side of Calle Mayor and detouring about 18m (60 ft.) to the left, down narrow Calle de San Nicolás. You'll come to the somber facade of the oldest church in Madrid, the 12th-century:

❺ Church of St. Nicolás
Only a brick tower remains from the original building at the Plaza de San Nicolás. It is one of the few examples of the Mudéjar style in the capital. The reredos at the high altar is the work of Juan de Herrera, also the architect of El Escorial.

Retrace your steps to Calle Mayor. Turn left and continue to walk east. You'll pass Plaza de la Villa on your right, and, 1 block later:

❻ Plaza de San Miguel
This is an iron-canopied meat-and-vegetable market (Mon–Fri 9am–2pm and 5–8pm, Sat 9am–2pm). You might stock up on ingredients for a picnic here.

Walking Tour 1: Habsburg Madrid (The Austrias)

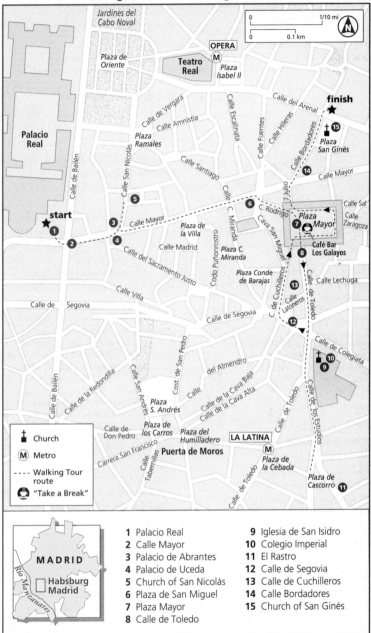

Jardines del Cabo Noval

Plaza de Oriente

Teatro Real

OPERA Ⓜ

Plaza Isabel II

Calle del Arenal

finish ★

Plaza San Ginés

Calle de Vergara

Calle Amnistia

Plaza Ramales

Calle Escalinata

Calle Fuentes

Calle Hileras

Calle Bordadores

Palacio Real

Calle San Nicolás

Calle Santiago

Calle Mayor

Calle Sal

Calle Zaragoza

Calle de Bailén

start ★
1

2

3

5

Calle Mayor

Plaza de la Villa

Calle Madrid

Calle C. Miranda

6

C. Rodrigo

Cava San Miguel

Plaza Mayor

7

Café Bar Los Galayos

8

4

Calle del Sacramento Justo

Codo Puñonrostro

Plaza C. Miranda

Plaza Conde de Barajas

C. de Cuchilleros

Calle Latoneros

Calle Lechuga

13

Calle Villa

Calle de Segovia

Calle de Toledo

Calle de Segovia

12

Calle de Colegiata

10

9

Calle de Bailén

Calle de la Redondilla

Calle San Andrés

Cost. de San Pedro

del Almendro

Calle

Calle de la Cava Baja

Calle de la Cava Alta

Calle de Toledo

Calle de los Estudios

Plaza S. Andrés

Calle de Don Pedro

Plaza de los Carros

Plaza del Humilladero

LA LATINA Ⓜ

Carrera San Francisco

Calle Tabernillas

Puerta de Moros

Plaza de la Cebada

Plaza de Cascorro

11

✝ Church

Ⓜ Metro

---- Walking Tour route

"Take a Break"

MADRID

Río Manzanares

Habsburg Madrid

1 Palacio Real
2 Calle Mayor
3 Palacio de Abrantes
4 Palacio de Uceda
5 Church of San Nicolás
6 Plaza de San Miguel
7 Plaza Mayor
8 Calle de Toledo

9 Iglesia de San Isidro
10 Colegio Imperial
11 El Rastro
12 Calle de Segovia
13 Calle de Cuchilleros
14 Calle Bordadores
15 Church of San Ginés

Leave Plaza de San Miguel by Ciudad Rodrigo (there might not be a sign), which leads under a soaring granite archway and up a sloping street to the northwestern corner of:

❼ Plaza Mayor

This landmark square is at the heart of Old Madrid.

☕ **TAKE A BREAK**
Café Bar Los Galayos, Plaza Mayor 1 (✆ 91-366-30-28), has long been one of the best places for tapas along this square. If you're taking the walking tour during the day, you may want to return to this cafe/bar at night, when it is most lively. In summer you can select one of the outdoor tables for your drinks and tapas. The cafe is open daily from noon to 1am.

Stroll through Plaza Mayor, crossing it diagonally and exiting at the closer of its two southern exits. A steep, dingy flight of stone stairs leads down to the beginning of the:

❽ Calle de Toledo

Note in the distance the twin domes of the yellow-stucco and granite:

❾ Iglesia de San Isidro

This is the legendary burial place of Madrid's patron saint and his wife, Santa María de la Cabeza. The church lost its status as a cathedral in 1992, when the honor went to the larger Church of La Almudena.

Adjacent to San Isidro is the baroque facade of the:

❿ Colegio Imperial

Lope de Vega, Calderón, and many other famous men studied at this institute, which was also run by the Jesuits.

If your tour takes place on a Saturday or Sunday before 3pm, visit:

⓫ El Rastro

This is Madrid's world-famous flea market. Continue along Calle de Toledo, then fork left onto Calle Estudios, and proceed to Plaza de Cascorro, named after a hero of the Cuban wars. El Rastro begins here.

If your tour takes place Monday to Friday, skip the Rastro neighborhood. Instead, turn right onto:

⓬ Calle de Segovia

This street intersects Calle de Toledo just before it passes in front of the Catedral de San Isidro.

Walk 1 block and turn right onto the first street:

⓭ Calle de Cuchilleros

Follow this street north past 16th- and 17th-century stone-fronted houses. Within a block, a flight of granite steps forks to the right. Climb the steps (a sign identifies the new street as Calle Arco de Cuchilleros) and you'll pass one of the most famous *mesones* (typical Castilian restaurants) of Madrid, the Cueva de Luis Candelas.

Once again you will have entered Plaza Mayor, this time on the southwestern corner. Walk beneath the southernmost arcade and promenade counterclockwise beneath the arcades, walking north underneath the square's eastern arcade. Then walk west beneath its northern arcade. At the northwest corner, exit through the archway onto Calle 7 de Julio. Fifteen meters (50 ft.) later, cross Calle Mayor and take the right-hand narrow street before you. This is:

⓮ Calle Bordadores

During the 17th century, this street housed Madrid's embroidery workshops, staffed exclusively by men.

As you proceed, notice the 17th-century brick walls and towers of the:

⓯ Church of San Ginés

This church at Arenal 15 is one of Madrid's oldest parishes. It owes its present look to the architects who reconstructed it after a devastating fire in 1872.

At the end of this tour, you'll find yourself on traffic-congested Calle del Arenal, at the doorstep of many interesting old streets.

WALKING TOUR 2	**THE CASTIZO QUARTER (LA LATINA & LAVAPIÉS)**

Start: Plaza General Vara del Rey.
Finish: Calle Mesón de Paredes.
Time: 2 hours (slow pace).
Best Times: Any day.
Worst Times: No particularly bad time as rush tour traffic doesn't affect too much of this route.

This short, leisurely tour takes you across one of Madrid's oldest quarters: a warren-like network of narrow lanes and medieval buildings that still represents the *castizo* (traditional) heart of Madrid. In recent years it's attracted a genuine ethnic mix, with new resident nationalities ranging from Chinese and North African to Indian and Turkish.

The tour begins at the:

❶ Plaza General Vara del Rey

We start our walk just west of El Rastro at this small, intimate square named after a Spanish commander who died during the 1898 war with Cuba. The adjoining Museo de Artes Populares has examples of local arts and crafts.

Continue west to Calle Toledo and then south to the:

❷ Puerta de Toledo

Originally planned to celebrate France's victory over Spain in 1808, the prominent archway at the end of Calle Toledo took 6 years to build and eventually served to commemorate the reverse: the expulsion of the French from Spain.

Turn east now though the Plaza Campillo Mundo Nuevo past the Ministerio de la Economía building and along the Ronda de Toledo to:

❸ Glorieta de Embajadores

Together with Puerta de Toledo, this great roundabout forms the southern fringe of the Embajadores district where many ambassadors moved in the 15th century when a plague was spreading through Madrid. Close by is the 18th-century Fábrica de Tabaco (Tobacco Factory).

Continue west along Calle Embajadores and then turn left into Calle Mira al Sol arriving at:

❹ La Corrala

Here—in a well-preserved example of the area's once widespread typical 16th-century architecture—is a building of windowless adjoining apartments, known as *corralas,* whose long continuous balconies overlook an open communal courtyard or well. This is one of the few such buildings that remain in Madrid.

Westward along narrow Calle Sombrete we come now to:

❺ Plaza de Lavapiés

Named after a fountain that once adorned it, Lavapiés square is the focal point of this colorful barrio, medieval in character and multi-ethnic in atmosphere today. Arabic, Indian, Chinese, and Turkish shops and eating spots abound. Narrow lanes radiate upwards and outwards from it as they've done for centuries, but there's no trace of the fountain that once gave it its name. (*Lavapiés* means literally "wash feet.")

From the square take a southeasterly turn into:

❻ Calle Argumosa

Known locally as the "promenade of Lavapiés," this wide, lively street leading east to the Ronda de Atocha is virtually one long row of cafes and bars with outdoor terraces in summer.

TAKE A BREAK
La Heladería, Argumosa 7 (© **91-528-80-09**), is a great summer place not only for ice cream and *horchata,* but also for coffee or something a bit stronger. Sit on the pavement *terraza* in the sun or under the stars and watch the world go by. The owners are very welcoming. Open April to October only; Monday to Thursday and Sunday 10am to midnight, Friday and Saturday 10am to 1am. No credit cards are accepted. Metro: Lavapiés.

Return to Lavapiés square, turn north into Calle Ave María, and then right (east) at Calle Esperanza into:

❼ Calle Torrecilla del Leal

Turn left and climb up this typically narrow and atmospheric street, which unobtrusively shelters two of the best wine and tapas bars in Madrid: Aloque (20) and El Sur (12). Both are ideal spots to pop into if you're taking an evening stroll (they don't open till 8pm).

Continue to the top and turn right at Plaza Anton Martin to reach the:

❽ Filmoteca Cine Doré

Located next to Anton Martín square and its adjoining well-stocked two-story food market, this mecca for movie buffs offers by far the best value in Madrid (seats are only 2.50€/$3.10!). Despite threats a couple of decades back to raze it and build a block of modern offices in its place, this small, ornate '50s monument to art managed to survive thanks to the mass protest of artists, musicians, and writers. Programs cover the most adventurous and eclectic range of original-language movies in Madrid. There are outdoor projections with a rooftop bar in summer and a small downstairs movie bookshop.

Return to Plaza Anton Martín and walk west along Calle de la Magdalena till you arrive at:

❾ Plaza Tirso de Molina

Named after the prolific Golden Age playwright Tirso de Molina (the pseudonym

of Fray [Brother] Gabriel Téllez, who died in 1648), this once historic but now blandly modernized square on the northern edge of Lavapiés is dominated by a statue in honor of him. Tirso was the first of many dramatists to write about the legendary romantic figure Don Juan.

On Sundays, the mainly pedestrianized plaza is crowded with overflows from the Rastro market. It usually has colorfully unsalubrious—albeit harmless—bunches of marginal semi-residents. Close to it are the Nuevo Apolo theater, with its Art Deco–cum–neo-Mudéjar facade and regular big musical productions, and superb Asador Frontón Basque restaurant, whose steaks are second to none.

At the western end of the square turn left (south) into:

❿ Calle Mesón de Paredes

This long, narrow thoroughfare is one of the oldest streets in Lavapiés, leading right down to La Corrala and then continuing on to the Ronda de Valencia on the outskirts of the Old City. It's named after Simón Miguel Paredes, who ran one of the largest medieval *mesónes* in Madrid. Though the *mesón* no longer exists, we have in its place one of the city's most distinctive *tabernas:* the cavernlike, bullfight-oriented Antonio Sánchez.

TAKE A BREAK
Taberna de Antonio Sánchez, Mesón de Paredes 13 (© **91-539-78-26**), is a snug 19th-century tavern, the oldest in central Madrid, whose atmospheric features include bullfight decor, dark wood paneling, paintings by artist Ignacio Zuloaga, and a traditional zinc bar top. Here you can enjoy a glass or two of modestly priced wine together with a tasty tapa. Larger *raciones* are also available. Open daily from 1 to 4pm and Monday to Saturday from 8pm to midnight. Metro: Tirso de Molina.

Walking Tour 2: The Castizo Quarter (La Latina & Lavapiés)

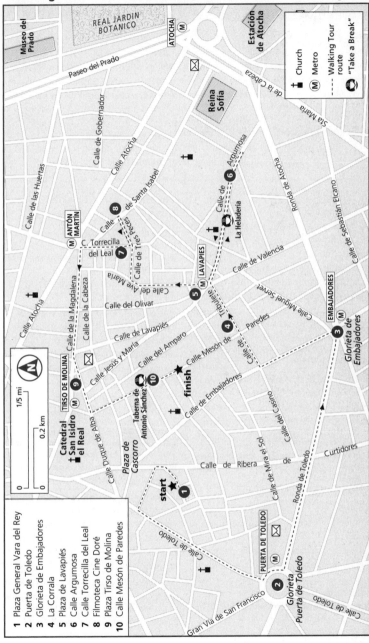

REAL JARDIN BOTANICO

Museo del Prado

ATOCHA Ⓜ

Estación de Atocha

Church
Metro Ⓜ
Walking Tour route ----
"Take a Break"

Paseo del Prado

Reina Sofía

Calle de Gobernador

Calle Atocha

Calle de las Huertas

Calle de Santa Isabel

Calle de Tres Peces

ANTÓN MARTÍN Ⓜ

C. Torrecilla del Leal

Calle del Ave María

Calle del Olivar

Calle de la Magdalena

Calle de la Cabeza

LAVAPIÉS Ⓜ

Calle de Valencia

Calle de Argumosa

La Heladería

Calle de Miguel Servet

EMBAJADORES Ⓜ

Glorieta de Embajadores

Calle de Sebastián Elcano

Ronda de Atocha

Sta María

Calle de la Cabeza

Calle de Lavapiés

Calle de Paredes

Calle Mesón de

Taberna de Antonio Sánchez

Calle Jesús y María

TIRSO DE MOLINA Ⓜ

Catedral San Isidro el Real

Calle Duque de Alba

Plaza de Cascorro

Calle del Amparo

Calle de Embajadores

Calle del Casino

Calle de Mira el Sol

Ronda de Toledo

Curtidores

Calle de Ribera de

finish ★

1/5 mi

0.2 km

N

start ★ ❶

Calle de Toledo

PUERTA DE TOLEDO Ⓜ

Glorieta Puerta de Toledo

Gran Vía de San Francisco

Calle de Toledo

1 Plaza General Vara del Rey
2 Puerta de Toledo
3 Glorieta de Embajadores
4 La Corrala
5 Plaza de Lavapiés
6 Calle Argumosa
7 Calle Torrecilla del Leal
8 Filmoteca Cine Doré
9 Plaza Tirso de Molina
10 Calle Mesón de Paredes

WALKING TOUR 3   PUERTA DEL SOL, ALCALA & HUERTAS

Start:	Puerta del Sol.
Finish:	Plaza Canalejas.
Time:	2 hours (excluding a visit to the Convento de las Descalzas Reales).
Best Times:	Any day.
Worst Times:	Avoid rush hours on weekdays 7:30 to 9:30am and 5 to 7:30pm because of heavy traffic.

A circular tour extending east from the Puerta de Sol to a fan-shaped area bordered by Calle Alcalá in the north and Calle Huertas in the south, taking in a wide, compact range of historical, cultural, and fun sights en route.

The tour begins at:

❶ Puerta del Sol

This half-moon-shaped square is not only the acknowledged central point of the capital but also kilometer zero for the entire country (all distances in Spain are measured from outside the Casa de Correos on the south side of the square). Prior to assuming its present central position in the 19th century, this "Gateway of the Sun" marked the eastern entry point to the city. Traditionally symbolic of Madrid, and a favorite rendezvous point, is the bronze statue of the *Oso y el Madroño* (Bear and the Strawberry Tree), which stands on the northern edge of the square at the entrance to the pedestrianized Calle del Carmen.

From here head west up Calle Arenal and then take the second right turn into Calle San Martín to arrive at the:

❷ Convento de las Descalzas Reales

Founded by Carlos V's daughter Juana of Austria in 1557, this haven of tranquillity, with its chapels, baroque art masterpieces, grandiose stairway, and (hidden) inner gardens, is still home to an enclosed order of nuns. Visitors are allowed in 20 at a time, which at times makes for large queues—so be prepared for a possible wait.

Return to the Puerta del Sol and then head east along Calle Alcalá past the impressive Ministerio de Economia y Hacienda building to the adjoining:

❸ Real Academia de Bellas Artes de San Fernando

Started in 1744 by Felipe V and bought by Carlos III 30 years later, this art museum—located at number 13 Calle Alcalá—is the oldest in Madrid. It boasts a rich collection of works by El Greco, Zurbarán, and Velázquez as well as masterpieces by Van Dyck and Rubens. An entire room is devoted to Goya.

Cross the road and continue down the southern side of Alcalá past the Sevilla Metro station until you reach Calle Marqués de Casa Riera. Turn right for the entrance to the:

❹ Círculo de Bellas Artes

A multipurpose 1920s-style cultural center refurbished in the 1990s and complete with four exhibition rooms where continuous displays are held. It also boasts a superb cafe with high ceilings, where you can enjoy a drink and watch the city life outside swirl by. There is a top-floor library and adjoining bookshop, theater, and cinema showing international movies in their original language.

Walking Tour 3: Puerta del Sol, Alcalá & Huertas

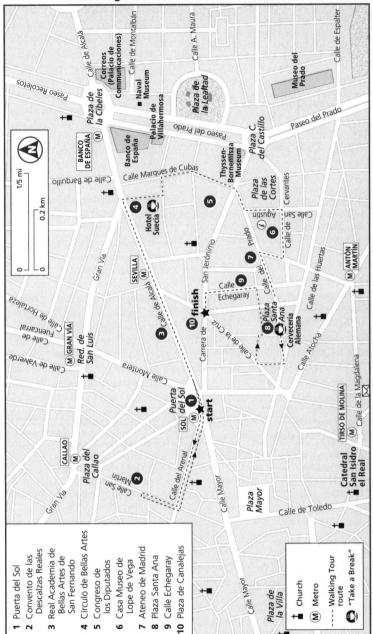

1 Puerta del Sol
2 Convento de las Descalzas Reales
3 Real Academia de Bellas Artes de San Fernando
4 Círculo de Bellas Artes
5 Congreso de los Diputados
6 Casa Museo de Lope de Vega
7 Ateneo de Madrid
8 Plaza Santa Ana
9 Calle Echegaray
10 Plaza de Canalejas

✝■ Church
Ⓜ Metro
- - - - Walking Tour route
🔴 "Take a Break"

TAKE A BREAK
If you're not tempted by the Círculo de Bellas Artes' cafe, then try the **Hotel Suecia** just 50m (164 ft.) farther down Calle Marqués de Casa Riera at no. 4 (✆ **91-531-69-00**). The ground-floor cafe lounge is an ideal spot to sink into a sofa, relax, and enjoy a coffee and pastry. Staff members are very friendly and welcoming, and the decor and setting are bright and modern—all very civilized. (This is said to have been one of Hemingway's haunts.)

Continue along Calle Marqués de Casa Riera, then turn left into Calle de los Madrazo, and almost immediately right into Calle Marqués de Cubas. This leads you eventually to Carrera de San Jerónimo where on your immediate right you'll see the:

❺ Congreso de los Diputados

This mid-19th-century building, also known as the Palacio de las Cortes, houses the lower house of the Spanish parliament. Its classical portico and twin bronze lions facing the Plaza del Cortes create an impressive front entrance, and visitors can enjoy guided tours of the interior on Saturday mornings.

Cross the plaza, head south down Calle San Agustín, and turn right (south) at Calle Cervantes to the:

❻ Casa Museo de Lope de Vega

The prolific Golden Age playwright Lope de Vega Carpio wrote some of his 2,000-plus works in this small 16th-century house at number 18, uniquely preserved and opened as a museum in 1935. Due to its size, only 10 people can visit it at one time. Farther along is the Convento de las Trinitarias, where rival pensmith Miguel de Cervantes' ashes were kept in an urn, which subsequently got mislaid. (The author of *Don Quixote,* incidentally, lived not on this street but on adjoining Calle León, though his abode was pulled down centuries ago. Only a commemorative plaque remains.)

Continue along Calle Cervantes to Calle León. Here turn right to Calle de Prado where almost opposite—at number 21—you'll see the:

❼ Ateneo de Madrid

Founded in 1820, this is one of the capital's great literary institutions and home of Spain's second largest library. You have to pay a yearly subscription to be a member, but visitors are allowed to climb up the marble stairs, wander around, eye the array of portraits of key Spanish essayists, novelists, and poets, and soak up the untrammeled/slightly run-down 19th-century atmosphere. It also has a small, unpretentious cafe if you feel like a refreshing taste of something.

Turn left along Calle del Prado to arrive at:

❽ Plaza Santa Ana

A legacy of the brief French rule under Joseph Bonaparte, this sunny square is one of the most popular in Madrid, lined with tree-shaded pavement cafes and boasting a small statue to García Lorca. On its eastern side in Calle Príncipe is the stylish Teatro Español, which dates from the 18th century and reopened after lengthy refurbishment work in 2002. A theater has existed on this spot since 1583 when the Corral del Príncipe would put on shows to a raucously demanding audience.

TAKE A BREAK
Hemingway time again. Try one of his all-time favorites, the 80-year-old **Cervecería Alemana** at Plaza Santa Ana 6 (✆ **91-429-70-33**) for coffee or delicious cold beer. Sit at a table in the traditional wood-paneled interior in winter or outside under the trees in summer.

Leave Plaza Santa Ana via Calle Príncipe to the north and turn right into the tiny Manuel González y Fernández alleyway passing, or pausing in, the Trucha tapas bar and the tile-and-wood-furnished Viva Madrid cafe to arrive in:

❾ Calle Echegaray

This long, narrow street, so quiet and unassuming by day, comes to life at night when its multinational array of watering holes and eating spots makes progressing from one end to the other a very slow ramble. Among its highlights are Los Gabrieles, a former bordello whose series of salons boast the best ornamental wall tiles in Madrid, and La Venencia, an uncompromising cellar bar dating from the 1920s that sells nothing but sherry by the glass (covering the full gamut from dry *manzanillas* to heavy *olorosos*).

At the northern end of Calle Echegaray, turn left into Carrera de San Jerónimo and continue to the:

⑩ Plaza de Canalejas

Placed at the closely knit junction of four roads, this attractive but busy little square was once aptly named the Plaza de los Cuatro Calles. It owes its present name to the 19th-century politician José Canalejas, who was assassinated while peering in the window of a bookshop in the Puerta del Sol (just a couple of hundred meters away). Nearby look out for the inimitable Lhardy's French restaurant with its downstairs deluxe snack bar.

WALKING TOUR 4   GRAN VIA, MALASAÑA & CHUECA

Start:	Edificio Metropolis at junction of Gran Vía and Calle Alcalá.
Finish:	Casa de las Siete Chimeneas in Chueca.
Time:	2 to 3 hours.
Best Times:	Weekends or midmornings.
Worst Times:	Rush-hour times 8 to 10am or 5 to 7pm (especially on the Gran Vía).

This comprehensive walk takes you from east to west along the city's great central artery and returns via the intricate, narrow-laned districts of Malasaña and Chueca with their traditional squares and architecture.

---

❶ Edificio Metrópolis

The French-styled Metropolis building, built in 1911 for the Union and Fenix Español insurance company, stands at the beginning of the Gran Vía on the corner of the junction with Alcalá. An essential part of the central Madrid skyline, it looks back toward the equally symbolic Cibeles fountain and Correos building. On the pavement in front of it is a small statue in honor of La Violetera, or violet seller, representing all the young ladies who used to sell flowers, "Pygmalion" style, to theatergoers. (International movie buffs may wish to note that it was the theme of an early flick starring Sara Montiel, Spain's answer to Elizabeth Taylor.)

Start walking up the Gran Vía and then make an immediate deviation to the left into Calle Caballero de Gracia to the:

❷ Oratorio del Caballero de Gracia

One of the city's least-known ecclesiastical gems, this late-18th-century church is considered one of the finest examples of neoclassical work in Madrid. The Gran Vía was actually rerouted during its construction so that it could be preserved.

Return to the Gran Vía at the junction of Calle Montera and the San Luis roundabout. Passing the imposing 1924 Edificio Telefónica on your right, in its time Madrid's highest building, continue up the Gran Vía to the:

❸ Plaza de Callao

Named after a naval battle fought between Spain and allied South American forces off Peru in 1866, this busy square stands just over halfway along the Gran Vía. Running off it toward the Puerta del Sol are the central pedestrian-only streets of Preciados and del Carmen with their big shopping stores, and on either side of it are some of Madrid's longest-established cinemas and theaters (Spanish-language showings only).

Continue on down to the end of the Gran Vía where you reach the:

❹ Plaza de España

Separating the Gran Vía from Calle Princesa, this large, perennially busy square is famed as much for its Don Quixote and Sancho Panza statue (on horseback in front of a taller one of Cervantes) as for the two concrete Francoist structures that tower beside it: Edificio España, built between 1947 and 1953, has 23 stories, while Torre Madrid (nicknamed "the Giraffe"), completed in 1953 with 10 more stories, was at its time the largest concrete building in the world.

Cross the square at its northwesterly corner and walk up Calle Ferraz to Calle de Ventura Rodriguez. Turn right into it and on your right is the:

❺ Museo Cerralbo

This highly personal 19th-century mansion-museum provides an intimate contrast with the grandeur of the Paseo del Prado's "Big Three." It contains the lifetime personal collection of former owner Enrique de Aguilera y Gamboa, the 17th Marquis of Cerralbo, who died in 1922. All is as he left it, from his Japanese armor collection to his Goya and Zurbarán masterpieces.

Leaving the museum, turn left along Ventura Rodriguez and cross Calle Ferraz to look at the:

❻ Templo de Debod

Situated at the far end of the Parque del Oeste on the western edge of the city (beside the tiny Ferraz gardens), this remarkable 4th-century temple built by the Pharaoh Zakheramon was transferred stone by stone from Egypt, in thanks for help given by Spain in building the Aswan dam. There are spectacular views west from the edge of the park of the Casa del Campo and distant Guadarrama mountains.

Return across Calle Ferraz and along Calle Ventura Rodríguez to reach Calle Princesa. Cross here to the:

❼ Palacio de Liria

This marvelous neoclassical 18th-century palace can only be visited if you book in a group beforehand. The tours take place each Friday at 10:45am, 11:30am, and 12:15pm and are free. From outside, the gardens and imposing facade convey all the grandeur of an elegant bygone era. Formerly the private residence of the Duchess of Alba, the palace has an art collection with paintings by Rembrandt, Rubens, and Goya (Princesa 20; ✆ **91-547-53-02;** or send a letter by fax 91-541 03-77).

Next take the lane to the right of the palace to join the Calle de Conde Duque, which leads to the:

❽ Centro Cultural Conde Duque

Converted from a huge 18th-century barracks built for Felipe V's guards, complete with two spacious courtyards, this ambitious arts center provides around a dozen different exhibitions a year as well as concert performances and conferences. There's also a well-stocked video library.

Continue to the end of Calle Conde Duque and turn left (east) into Calle Alberto Aguilera, following the northern border of the Malasaña district. Cross the Glorieta (roundabout) de Ruíz Giménez and continue to the Glorieta de Bilbao.

TAKE A BREAK
Here's a chance to step back in time and sample what literary cafe life was like at the turn of the last century. The **Café Comercial,** Glorieta de Bilbao 7 (✆ **91-521-56-55**), has dauntlessly clung to its age-old mood of unadorned—almost spartan—charm where other establishments have yielded to crass developers. Its roomy interior, spare marble-topped tables, and painted iron pillars create a stimulatingly low-keyed aura. Coffee drinkers can spend hours uninterrupted here over their books, notepads, or thoughts or exchange profound ideas on life with their companions. Along with the mellow—and let's face it, snootier—Gijon in Recoletos, it's a survivor from another age. (The only concession to modernity is the Internet cafe upstairs.)

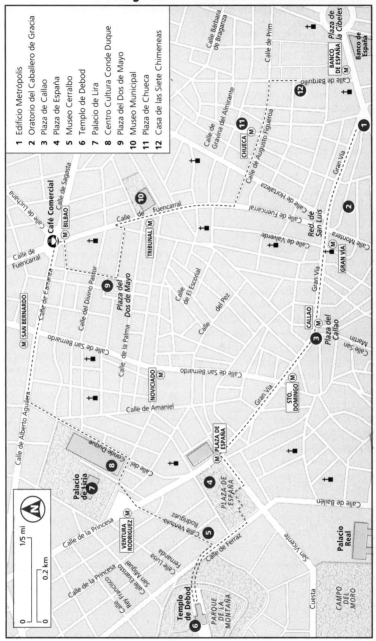

1 Edificio Metrópolis
2 Oratorio del Caballero de Gracia
3 Plaza de Callao
4 Plaza de España
5 Museo Cerralbo
6 Templo de Debod
7 Palacio de Lira
8 Centro Cultura Conde Duque
9 Plaza del Dos de Mayo
10 Museo Municipal
11 Plaza de Chueca
12 Casa de las Siete Chimeneas

Return into the Malasaña district by crossing Calle Fuencarral, which runs south, into the narrow Calle Mañuela Malasaña, named after the young woman who, so one story goes, was executed for carrying a dangerous weapon (namely scissors) by the occupying French forces during the Peninsula War. Turn left into Calle Andrés to reach another potent symbol of rebellion, the:

9 Plaza del Dos de Mayo

This small square, less impressive aesthetically than in its historical associations, celebrates the uprising of the populace against the French army on May 2, 1808. Formerly, it was the site of the Monteléon barracks where captains Daoiz and Velarde launched their famed counterattack. Today a statue in their memory stands in the plaza, and the streets to west and east of the square are named after them. An archway representing the main barracks gate stands next to the statue. The liveliest time here is during the San Isidro festivities in May when concerts and outdoor parties are held. (Less salubrious was the trash-strewn aftermath of youngsters' impromptu weekend *botellón* soirées, which lasted till dawn, though these have now theoretically been cleaned up by urban authorities.)

Head east from the square along Calle Velarde and then turn right (south) into Calle Fuencarral. On your left after Calle Barceló is the:

10 Museo Municipal

Originally built as a 17th-century orphanage, this museum bears an ornate facade by Pedro de Ribera featuring San Fernando, patron saint of orphans. Inside is a vast array of maps, drawings, and photos of Madrid up to 1840. A major attraction is the superb large model of the whole city as laid out in 1833. It was reopened to the public after renovation work in 2005.

Continue south down Calle Fuencarral and take the sixth street on your left, Calle August Figueroa. Continue along this road across Calle Hortaleza. Two streets later you'll see Calle Barbieri on your right. Opposite this on your left is:

11 Plaza de Chueca

Dedicated to the *zarzuela* composer Federico Chueca, who died in 1908, this tiny square with its surrounding 19th-century buildings has evolved into the bustling epicenter of gay Madrid. In summer the square is packed with as many cafe tables and raucous crowds as is humanly possible. Around the square, the Chueca district's intricate network of narrow lanes shelter what is probably the highest concentration of cafes, restaurants, bars, and clubs—some straight, most of them not—in the city. On weekends the area barely sleeps. (Not surprisingly, inhabitants of the apartments overlooking the square feel compelled to hang signs from their balconies pleading for a reduction in noise.)

From here return to Augusto Figueroa and turn left (east) till you reach Calle Barquillo. Turn right (south) and continue till you see on your right the:

12 Casa de las Siete Chimeneas

Built in 1585, The "House of the Seven Chimneys" achieved fame as the place where Charles I of England stayed in 1624 during a marriage-seeking visit to Madrid (in the end, his plan to wed the Infanta María was unsuccessful). Designed by Juan de Herrera, the Escorial architect, this superb Habsburg building is a surviving gem of Felipe II's regal Madrid, quietly set beside a charming plaza and topped by—of course—seven tall chimneys. Just a few minutes yet a world away from Plaza de Chueca.

Shopping in Madrid

Seventeenth-century playwright Tirso de Molina called Madrid "a shop stocked with every kind of merchandise," and it's true—an estimated 50,000 stores sell everything from high-fashion clothing to flamenco guitars to art and ceramics.

Madrid still boasts many personal specialist shops, especially around the Plaza Mayor and Sol areas, but if your time is limited, go to one of the big department stores (later in this chapter), which carry a bit of everything.

1 The Shopping Scene

SHOPPING AREAS **The Center** The sheer diversity of shops in Madrid's center is staggering. Their densest concentration lies immediately north of the Puerta del Sol, radiating out from Calle del Carmen, Calle Montera, and Calle Preciados.

Calle Mayor & Calle del Arenal Unlike their more stylish neighbors to the north of Puerta del Sol, shops in this district to the west tend toward the small, slightly dusty enclaves of coin and stamp dealers, family-owned souvenir shops, clock makers, sellers of military paraphernalia, and an abundance of stores selling musical scores.

Gran Vía Conceived, designed, and built in the 1910s and 1920s as a showcase for the city's best shops, hotels, and restaurants, the Gran Vía has since been eclipsed by other shopping districts. Its Art Nouveau–Art Deco glamour still survives in the hearts of most Madrileños, however. The bookstores here are among the best in the city, as are outlets for fashion, shoes, jewelry, furs, and handcrafted accessories from all regions of Spain.

El Rastro It's the biggest and most frenetic flea market in Spain, and its makeshift stalls draw collectors, dealers, buyers, and hopefuls from throughout Madrid and its suburbs every Sunday morning. For more information, refer to the "Flea Markets" section under "Shopping A to Z," below.

Plaza Mayor Under the arcades of the square itself are exhibitions of lithographs and oil paintings, and every weekend there's a loosely organized market for stamp and coin collectors. Within 3 or 4 blocks in every direction you'll find more than the average number of souvenir shops.

On Calle Marqués Viudo de Pontejos, which runs east from Plaza Mayor, is one of the city's headquarters for the sale of cloth, thread, and buttons. Also running east, on Calle de Zaragoza, are silversmiths and jewelers. On Calle Postas you'll find housewares, underwear, soap powders, and other household items.

Near the Carrera de San Jerónimo Several blocks east of Puerta del Sol is Madrid's densest concentration of gift shops, crafts shops, and antiques dealers—a decorator's delight. Its most interesting streets include Calle del Prado, Calle de las Huertas, and Plaza de las Cortés. The neighborhood is pricey, so don't expect bargains here.

Northwest Madrid   A few blocks east of Parque del Oeste is an upscale neighborhood that's well stocked with luxury goods and household staples. Calle de la Princesa, its main thoroughfare, has shops selling shoes, handbags, fashion, gifts, and children's clothing. Thanks to the presence of the university nearby, there's also a dense concentration of bookstores, especially on Calle Isaac Peral and Calle Fernando el Católico, several blocks north and northwest, respectively, from the subway stop of Argüelles.

Salamanca District   It's known throughout Spain as the quintessential upper-bourgeois neighborhood, uniformly prosperous, and its shops are correspondingly exclusive. They include outlets run by interior decorators, furniture shops, fur and jewelry shops, several department stores, and design headquarters whose output ranges from the solidly conservative to the high-tech. The main streets of this district are Calle de Serrano and Calle de Velázquez. The district lies northeast of the center of Madrid, a few blocks north of Retiro Park. Its most central Metro stops are Serrano and Velázquez.

HOURS   Major stores are open (in most cases) Monday to Saturday from 9:30am to 8pm. Many small stores take a siesta between 1:30 and 4:30pm. Of course, there is never any set formula, and hours can vary greatly from store to store, depending on the idiosyncrasies and schedules of the owner.

SHIPPING   Many art and antiques dealers will crate and ship bulky objects for an additional fee. Whereas it usually pays to have heavy objects shipped by sea, in some cases it's almost the same price to ship crated goods by airplane. Of course, it depends on the distance your crate will have to travel overland to the nearest international port, which, in many cases for the purposes of relatively small-scale shipments by individual clients, is Barcelona. Consequently, it might pay to call two branches of **Emery Worldwide** from within Spain to explain your particular situation, and receive comparable rates. For information about sea transit for your valuables, call **Emery Worldwide Ocean Services** at their only Spanish branch, in Barcelona (© **93-479-30-50**). For information about **Emery Worldwide Air Freight,** call the main Spanish office in Madrid (© **91-747-56-66**) for advice on any of the dozen air-freight pickup stations the company maintains throughout Spain. These include, among many others, Barcelona, Alicante, Málaga, Bilbao, and Valencia. For more advice on this, and the formalities that you'll go through in clearing U.S. Customs after the arrival of your shipment in the United States, call **Emery Worldwide** in the United States at © **800/ 488-9451.**

For most small- and medium-size shipments, air freight isn't much more expensive than ocean shipping. **Iberia's Air Cargo Division** (© **800/221-6002** in the U.S.) offers air-freight service from Spain to New York, Chicago, Miami, or Los Angeles. What will you pay for this transport of your treasured art objects or freight? Here's a rule of thumb: For a shipment under 100 kilograms (220 lb.), from either Barcelona or Madrid to New York, the cost is approximately 4.40€ ($5.05) per pound. The per-pound price goes down as the weight of the shipment increases, declining to, for example, 1.50€ ($1.70) per pound for shipments of more than 1,000 kilograms (2,200 lb.). Regardless of what you ship, there's a minimum charge enforced.

For an additional fee, Iberia or one of its representatives will also pick up your package. For a truly precious cargo, ask the seller to build a crate for it. For information within Spain about air-cargo shipments, call Iberia's cargo division at Madrid's Barajas Airport (© **91-587-33-07**) or at Barcelona's airport (© **93-401-34-26**).

> ## *Tips* When the Weather & the Sales Are Hot!
>
> The best sales are usually in summer. Called *rebajas,* they start in July and go through August. As a general rule, merchandise is marked down even more in August to make way for the new fall wares in most stores.

Remember that your air-cargo shipment will need to clear Customs after it's brought into the United States. This involves some additional paperwork, costly delays, and in some cases a trip to the airport where the shipment first entered the United States. It's usually easier (and in some cases, much easier) to hire a commercial customs broker to do the work for you. **Emery Worldwide,** a division of CF Freightways, can clear most shipments of goods for around $138, which you'll pay in addition to any applicable duty you owe your home government. For information, you can call ✆ **800/443-6379** within the United States.

TAX & HOW TO RECOVER IT   If you are not a European Union resident and you make purchases in Spain worth more than 90€ ($104), you can get a tax refund. (The internal tax, known as VAT in most of Europe, is called **IVA** in Spain.) Depending on the goods, the rate usually ranges from 7% to 16% of the total worth of your merchandise. Luxury items are taxed at 33%.

To get this refund, you must complete three copies of a form that the store gives you, detailing the nature of your purchase and its value. Citizens of non–E.U. countries show the purchase and the form to the Spanish Customs Office. The shop is supposed to refund the amount due you. Inquire at the time of purchase how they will do so and discuss in what currency your refund will arrive.

DUTY-FREE—WORTH IT OR NOT?   Before you leave home, check the regular retail price of items that you're most likely to buy. Duty-free prices vary from one country to another and from item to item. Sometimes you're better off purchasing an item in a discount store at home. If you don't know the prices back home, you can't tell when you're getting a good deal.

BARGAINING   The days of bargaining are, for the most part, long gone. Most stores have what is called *precio de venta al público* (PVP), a firm retail price not subject to negotiation. With street vendors and flea markets, it's a different story, because haggling *a la española* is expected. However, you'll have to be very skilled to get a considerable reduction in cost—most of these street-smart vendors know exactly what their merchandise is worth and are old hands at getting that price.

2 Shopping A to Z

Spain has always been known for its craftspeople, many still working in the time-honored and labor-intensive traditions of their grandparents. It's hard to go wrong if you stick to the beautiful handcrafted Spanish objects—hand-painted tiles, ceramics, and porcelain; hand-woven rugs; handmade sweaters; and intricate embroideries. And, of course, Spain produces some of the world's finest leather. Jewelry, especially gold set with Majorca pearls, represents good value and unquestioned luxury.

Some of Madrid's art galleries are known throughout Europe for discovering and encouraging new talent. Antiques are sold in highly sophisticated retail outlets. Better suited to the budgets of many travelers are the weekly flea markets.

Spain continues to make inroads into the fashion world. Its young designers are regularly featured in the fashion magazines of Europe. Excellent shoes are available, some highly fashionable. But be advised that prices for shoes and quality clothing are generally higher in Madrid than in the United States.

ANTIQUES

A large concentration of antiques shops is found in Ribera de Curtidores, where the Sunday flea market is located (see "El Rastro," later); while you're there, you can browse the flea market for vintage goods. You'll find a more widespread choice in the prestigious Salamanca district, especially on Lagasca and Jorge Juan streets.

Centro de Anticuarios Lagasca   You'll find about a dozen antiques shops here, clustered into one covered arcade. They operate as individual businesses, although by browsing through each you'll find an impressive assemblage of antique furniture, porcelain, and whatnots. Open Monday to Saturday from 10am to 1:30pm and 5 to 8pm. Lagasca 36. ℂ 91-577-37-52. Metro: Serrano or Velázquez.

Galería de Arte del Lubre   Housed in a mid-19th-century building are several unusual antiques dealers (and a large carpet emporium as well), many of whom specialize in antique, sometimes monumental paintings. Each establishment maintains its own schedule, although the center itself has overall hours. Open Monday to Saturday from 10am to 2pm and 5 to 8:15pm. Serrano 5. ℂ 91-576-96-82. Metro: Retiro: Bus: 9 or 15.

Galerías Piquer   This huge arcade of new shops selling old things is set on the same street as the Rastro and has an equally varied choice of antiques and knick-knacks. It's all a bit neater and tidier and for some lacks the full-blooded exhilaration of the gritty street market itself. It's certainly worth a look, however, as the locales total up to 70 and you're bound to find something you like. Gallery opens Monday to Friday 10:30am to 2pm and 5 to 8pm; Saturday and Sunday 10:30am to 2pm. Times vary from shop to shop, so check www.dai.es/piquer. Ribera de Curtidores 29. No phone. Metro: Puerta de Toledo or La Latina. Bus: 17, 18, 23, 35, or 60.

Mercado Puerta de Toledo   Another deluxe conglomeration of locales (14 in all) selling antiques, located at the Puerta de Toledo, a short stroll from Ribera de Curtidores. Great places to look for quality vintage brass and ceramic goods. Open Tuesday to Saturday 10:30am to 9pm; Sunday 10:30am to 2:30pm. Puerta de Toledo 1. ℂ 91-366-72-09. Metro: Puerta de Toledo.

ART GALLERIES

The greatest concentration of galleries is in Salamanca, in particular **Claudio Coello, Chueca (Calle Almirante),** and **Chamberí** (especially on **Calle Orfila**). You'll also find a few near the Reina Sofía modern-art museum.

Galería Kreisler   One successful entrepreneur on Madrid's art scene is Ohio-born Edward Kreisler, whose gallery, now run by his son Juan, specializes in figurative and contemporary paintings, sculptures, and graphics. The gallery prides itself on occasionally displaying and selling the works of artists who are critically acclaimed and displayed in museums in Spain. Open Monday to Saturday 10:30am to 2pm and 5 to 9pm. Closed in August and on Saturday afternoons from July 15 to September 15. Hermosilla 8. ℂ 91-431-42-64. Metro: Serrano. Bus: 27, 45, or 150.

Guillermo de Osma   For lovers of early-20th-century avant-garde art from Kandinsky to Klee, this discreet little gallery, tucked away on the first floor of an elegant Salamanca building, is a good place to look. At least three interesting shows are held each year.

Open Monday to Friday 10am to 2pm and 4:30 to 8:30pm; Saturday noon to 2pm. Claudio Coello 4–1° izda. ℂ 91-435-59-36. Metro: Retiro. Bus: 2, 19, 20, 21, 28, 53, or 146.

Marlborough   Set on a stylish Chamberí street, this deceptively spacious gallery was designed by Stateside architect Richard Gluckman. International artists from David Hockney to Luis Gordillo are regularly represented and the gallery has branches in New York, London, and Monte Carlo. Orfila 5. ℂ 91-319-14-14. Metro: Alonso Martínez. Bus: 7, 40, or 147.

Oliva Arauna   The main focus of this gallery is sculpture with a strong interest in photography and video. Samples of these three art forms are regularly represented in Arco and PhotoEspaña exhibitions. Open Monday to Saturday 10:30am to 2pm and 4:30 to 8:30pm (closed in Aug and afternoons in summer). Claudio Coello 19. ℂ 91-435-18-08. Metro: Retiro or Serrano. Bus: 2, 19, 20, 21, 28, 53, or 146.

Estiarte   This 30-odd-year-old gallery is the place to go if you want to see some first-rate graphic art. Max Ernst and Picasso are some of the luminaries who've been represented here. Open Monday to Friday 10:30am to 2pm and 4:30 to 8:30pm; Saturday 10am to 2pm. Almagro 44. ℂ 91-308-15-69. Metro: Rubén Darío.

Juana de Aizpuru   This renowned Chueca gallery exhibits mainly vanguardist and avant-garde art and sculptures by local and international artists such as Alex García Rodero and William Wegman. Open Monday 4:30 to 8:30pm; Tuesday to Saturday 10:30am to 2pm and 4:30 to 8:30pm. Closed in August. Barquillo 44. ℂ 91-310-55-61. www.galeriajuanadeaizpuru.com. Metro: Chueca.

Galería Soledad Lorenzo   This bright, spacious Chamberí gallery features works by topnotch contemporary Spanish painters such as Tàpies and Miguel Barceló. Open Monday 4:30 to 8:30pm; Tuesday to Saturday 11am to 2pm and 4:30 to 8:30pm (closed evenings mid-June to mid-Sept). Orfila 5. ℂ 91-308-28-87. www.soledadlorenzo.com. Metro: Alonso Martínez. Bus: 7, 40, or 147.

BOOKS

Booksellers   The only bookshop in town specializing solely in English-language books, from the latest U.K. and U.S. novels to travel, history, and teaching material. Plenty of children's literature and English-language video, too. It also has a wide selection of children's literature and English-language videos and DVDs. Open Monday to Friday 9:30am to 2pm, 5 to 8:30pm; Saturday 10:30am to 2:30pm; closed Sunday. Calle Hernández de la Hoz 40. ℂ 91-442-79-59. Metro: Gregorio Marañón. Bus: 7, 40, or 147.

Casa del Libro   By far the most comprehensive bookshop in Madrid, the three-story Casa del Libro is conveniently positioned right in the center of the Gran Vía. The basement offers a great selection of dictionaries and grammar books, while a ground floor alcove has an up-to-date selection of English-language literature (alongside current French, German, Italian, and Portuguese tomes). The first floor houses a well-stocked international travel section with plenty of books on Madrid. Open Monday to Saturday 9:30am to 9:30pm; Sunday 11am to 9pm. Gran Vía 29. ℂ 91-521-21-13. Metro: Gran Vía. Bus: 1, 2, 46, 74, 146, or 149.

Cuesta de Moyano   A sort of smaller literary Rastro, this collection of wooden bookstalls and *kioskos* climbs the slope from the Atocha end of the Paseo del Prado—alongside the railings of the Botanical Gardens—right up to the southwestern corner of the Retiro Park. Practically all the books are secondhand and in Spanish, but whether you read Castilian or not it's great fun to wander, browse, and simply absorb the scene, unchanged over many decades and one of the great traditional sights of outdoor Madrid. Most stalls are open daily from 10am to 7pm; Sunday mornings are the liveliest time. No phone. Metro: Atocha. Bus: 6, 10, 14, 26, 27, 32, 34, 37, or 45.

Hartley's Good Bookshop   Opened in 2005 and the most recent of Madrid's new crop of English-language bookshops, modern Hartley's is located in the Goya area of the Salamanca district. New books are upstairs and a quality collection of secondhand classics and others are downstairs. Talks and presentations are regularly given by locally based English-speaking writers. There's also a small selection of English-language videos. Calle Padilla 74 (corner of Alcántara). ℂ 91-401-90-77. Metro: Diego de León or Lista.

J & J   This friendly English-language *librería,* opened at the beginning of 2004 in the Malasaña district, J & J's—like Petra's (see below)—is one of the best places to find secondhand book bargains. It's named after husband-and-wife team Jamie and Javi, who wanted to create a meeting place for English-speaking residents and visitors as well as a comprehensive bookshop. A genial cafe sits on the ground floor, while the basement contains over 15,000 books ranging from horror stories to the classics. There is also a small selection of English language videos. The second Wednesday of every month is the *hora del libro* (book hour) when participants discuss a specific book; other social events include quiz night and story time for kids. Open Monday to Thursday noon to 8pm; Friday and Saturday noon to 10pm; and Sunday 2 to 8pm. Espíritu Santo 47. ℂ 91-521-87-76. Metro: Noviciado. Bus: 147.

Pasajes   First-rate bookshop on two levels with international choice that include English-language fiction, nonfiction, children's books, and videos, as well as a wide variety of books in French, German, Italian, Portuguese, and Russian. Open Monday to Friday 10am to 2pm and 5 to 8pm; Saturday 10am to 2pm. Génova 3. ℂ 91-310-12-45. Metro: Alonso Martínez. Bus: 3, 7, 21, 40, or 147.

Petra's Bookshop   A small but cavernous shop that extends back from a narrow street centrally located between Opera and the Gran Vía. It's run by an American (who is the owner of a well-fed cat called Petra—hence the name) and has a wide choice of both new and secondhand English-language books. Here you can trade as well as buy. There's also a notice board and a regular coming and going of international visitors. Open Monday to Friday 11am to 2:30pm and 4:30 to 7:30pm; Saturday 10am to 2pm. Campomanes 13. ℂ 91-541-72-91. Metro: Opera or Santo Domingo. Bus: 44, 133, or 147.

La Tienda Verde   Not one but two highly individual shops in the same Cuatro Caminos street offering a compact but comprehensive selection of travel, ecology, and nature books and maps, especially on Spain. An invaluable source of information for hikers, walkers, and mountaineers, its stock is almost entirely in Spanish. Open Monday to Friday 9:30am to 2pm and 5 to 8:30pm; Saturday 9:30am to 2pm and 5 to 8pm. Maudes 23 (books) and 38 (maps). ℂ 91-535-38-10. www.tiendaverde.org. Metro: Cuatro Caminos. Bus: C.

CAPES

Capas Seseña   Founded shortly after the turn of the 20th century, this shop manufactures and sells wool capes for both women and men. The wool comes from the mountain town of Béjar, near Salamanca. Celebrities who have been spotted donning Seseña capes include Picasso, Hemingway, and, more recently, Hillary Rodham Clinton and daughter, Chelsea. Open Monday to Friday 10am to 2pm and 4:30 to 8pm; Saturday 10am to 2pm. Cruz 23. ℂ 91-531-68-40. Metro: Sevilla or Sol. Bus: 5, 39, 51, or 52.

CARPETS

Ispahan   In this 19th-century building, behind bronze handmade doors, are three floors devoted to carpets from around the world, notably Afghanistan, India, Nepal, Iran, Turkey, and the Caucasus. One section features silk carpets. It's open Monday through Saturday 10am to 2pm and 4:30 to 8:30pm (till 8pm on Sat). Serrano 5. (✆ 91-575-20-12. Metro: Retiro. Bus: 1, 2, 9, 15, or 19.

CERAMICS

Adamá   This attractive shop in the heart of Salamanca district is one of the best places to find top contemporary Spanish ceramics. Leading figures such as Claudi Casanovas display their inventively creative wares here—at high prices, however! Open Monday to Saturday 10am to 2pm and 4:30 to 8:30pm. Av. Felipe II 24. (✆ **91-435-99-88.** Metro: Goya. Bus: 15, 21, 29, 43, 53, or 146.

Antigua Casa Talavera   "The first house of Spanish ceramics" has wares that include a sampling of regional styles from every major area of Spain, including Talavera, Toledo, Manises, Valencia, Puente del Arzobispo, Alcora, Granada, and Seville. Sangria pitchers, dinnerware, tea sets, plates, and vases are all handmade. Inside one of the showrooms is an interesting selection of tiles, painted with reproductions of scenes from bullfights, dances, and folklore. There's also a series of tiles depicting famous paintings in the Prado. At its present location since 1904, the shop is only a short walk from Plaza de Santo Domingo. Open Monday to Friday 10am to 1:30pm and 5 to 8pm; Saturday 10am to 1:30pm. Isabel la Católica 2. (✆ **91-547-34-17.** Metro: Santo Domingo. Bus: 1, 2, 46, 70, 75, or 148.

CRAFTS

El Arco de los Cuchilleros Artesanía de Hoy   Set within one of the 17th-century vaulted cellars of Plaza Mayor, this shop is entirely devoted to unusual craft items from throughout Spain. The merchandise is one of a kind and in most cases contemporary; it includes a changing array of pottery, leather, textiles, woodcarvings, glassware, wickerwork, papier-mâché, and silver jewelry. The hardworking owners deal directly with the artisans who produce each item, ensuring a wide inventory of handicrafts. The staff is familiar with the rituals of applying for tax-free status of purchases here, and speaks several different languages. Open January to September Monday to Saturday 11am to 8pm; October to December Monday to Saturday 11am to 9pm. Plaza Mayor 9 (basement level). (✆ **91-365-26-80.** Metro: Sol or Opera. Bus: 3 or 50.

La Tierra   This gem of a shop, located in a stylish Chueca street, offers a wide selection of Spanish *artesanía,* covering just about everything from terra-cotta ceramics and Sevillan tiles to wrought-iron grills and antique wooden chests. The array of traditional kitchenware includes decorative plates and *botijos* (jars for storing water). Open Monday to Friday 9:30am to 1:30pm and 5 to 8pm; Saturday 9:30am to 1:30pm. Almirante 28. (✆ **91-521-21-34.** Metro: Chueca. Bus: 5, 14, 27, 37, 45, 53, or 150.

DEPARTMENT STORES

El Corte Inglés   This flagship of the largest department-store chain in Madrid sells hundreds of souvenirs and Spanish handicrafts, such as damascene steelwork from Toledo, flamenco dolls, and embroidered shawls. Some astute buyers report that it also sells glamorous fashion articles, such as Pierre Balmain designs, for about a third less than equivalent items in most European capitals. Services include interpreters, currency-exchange windows, and parcel delivery either to a local hotel or overseas. Open

Monday to Saturday 10am to 10pm; some stores also open Sunday noon to 8pm. Preciados 3. ⓒ **91-379-80-00.** Metro: Sol. Bus: 5, 15, 20, 39, 51, 52, or 53.

FNAC   Located in the bustling pedestrian zone between Sol and the Gran Vía, this multistory French store provides a wealth of media fare from a multilingual book section with everything from current bestsellers to travel and history to a huge stock of DVDs and CDs (the second floor has a section where you can sit and listen before you buy). On the ground floor are a travel agency, a cafeteria, and newsagents with a choice of international periodicals. Open Monday to Saturday 10am to 9:30pm; Sunday noon to 9:30pm. Preciados 28. ⓒ **91-595-61-00.** www.fnac.es. Metro: Callao. Bus: 44, 46, 75, 143, 146, 147, 148, or 149.

EMBROIDERIES

Casa Bonet   The intricately detailed embroideries produced in Spain's Balearic Islands (especially Majorca) are avidly sought for bridal chests and elegant dinner settings. A few examples of the store's extensive inventory are displayed on the walls. Open Monday to Friday 10:45am to 2pm and 5 to 8pm; Saturday 10:15am to 2pm. Núñez de Balboa 76. ⓒ **91-575-09-12.** Metro: Núñez de Balboa. Bus: 1 or 74.

ESPADRILLES

Casa Hernanz   A brisk walk south of Plaza Mayor delivers you to this store, in business since the 1840s. In addition to espadrilles, it sells shoes in other styles, as well as hats. Open Monday to Friday 9am to 1:30pm and 4:30 to 8pm; Saturday 10am to 2pm. Toledo 18. ⓒ **91-366-54-50.** Metro: Sol, Opera, or La Latina. Bus: 17, 18, 23, 35, or 60.

FANS & UMBRELLAS

Casa de Diego   Here you'll find a wide inventory of fans, ranging from plain to fancy, from plastic to exotic hardwood, from cost-conscious to lavish. Some fans tend to be a bit overpriced; you may have to shop around to find a real bargain. Now open year-round, Monday to Saturday 9:45am to 8pm. Puerta del Sol 12. ⓒ **91-522-66-43.** Metro: Sol. Bus: 5, 15, 20, 51, 52, 53, or 150.

FASHIONS FOR MEN

For the man on a budget who wants to dress reasonably well, the best outlet for off-the-rack men's clothing is one of the branches of the Corte Inglés department-store chain (see above). Most men's boutiques in Madrid are very expensive and may not be worth the investment.

FASHIONS FOR WOMEN

Adolfo Domínguez   This controversial Gallego designer from Orense has developed a cool laid-back style of clothing that caters to both sexes. Its fans appreciate the no-frills (verging on austere) style and impressive cost-to-value ratio. Snazzier shoes and a sports range aimed at younger buyers are also available. Open Monday to Saturday 10:15am to 2pm and 5 to 8:30pm. Ortega y Gasset 4. ⓒ **91-576-00-84.** Metro: Núñez de Balboa. Bus: 1 or 74.

Agatha Ruiz de la Prada   A former leading light of the dynamic *movida* period of the late '80s, Agatha Ruiz de la Prada faded in popularity and then made a resurgence a decade ago in the ground floor of this Chamberí locale built by her grandfather. Here you'll find the full gamut of her latest bright, accessible, easy-to-wear style of clothing. Another store has recently opened in stylish Serrano and children's and men's clothes are also made to order. Open Monday to Friday 10am to 2pm and 5 to 8pm.

During the month of August, it also opens Saturdays from 10am to 2pm and 5 to 8pm. Marqués de Riscal 8. ✆ **91-319-05-01**. Metro: Rubén Darío. Bus: 7, 40, or 147.

Herrero   The sheer size and buying power of this popular retail outlet for women's clothing make it a reasonably priced emporium for all kinds of feminine garb as well as various articles for gentlemen. An additional outlet lies on the same street at no. 16 (✆ **91-521-15-24**). Both are open Monday to Saturday 10:30am to 8pm; some Sundays from noon to 8pm. Preciados 7. ✆ **91-521-29-90**. Metro: Sol. Bus: 5, 15, 20, 51, 52, or 53.

Modas Gonzalo   This boutique's baroque, gilded atmosphere evokes the 1940s, but its fashions are strictly up-to-date, well made, and intended for stylish adult women. Open Monday to Saturday 10am to 1:30pm and 4:30 to 8pm. Gran Vía 43. ✆ **91-547-12-39**. Metro: Callao or Santo Domingo. Bus: 46, 74, 75, 133, 146, 147, or 150.

Sybilla   The *fashionistas* of Madrid are buzzing with excitement over the clothes displayed in this tiny atelier. Fashion critics have hailed Sybilla's clothing as "wearable, whimsical, and inevitably original." Everything is stylish. The outlet also sells articles for the home like sheets, towels, and dishes. Open Monday through Friday 10am to 2pm and 4 to 8:30pm; Saturday 11am to 3pm and 5 to 8:30pm. Gran Vía 43. ✆ **91-547-12-39**. Metro: Callao. Bus: 46, 74, 75, 133, 146, 147, or 150.

Zara   One of Spain's top fashion shops, the Galician-run Zara offers stylish outfits at very reasonable prices. Apart from state-of-the-art clothes, Zara also sells quality suits and conventional office wear. Very popular, especially on Saturdays. Open Monday to Saturday 10am to 8:30pm. Princesa 45. ✆ **91-541-09-02**. Metro: Argüelles. Bus: 1, 2, 44, 74, 133, or C.

FLEA MARKETS

El Rastro   Foremost among markets is the Sunday morning El Rastro (translated as either "flea market" or "thieves' market"), occupying a roughly triangular district of streets and plazas a few minutes' walk south of Plaza Mayor. Its center is Plaza Cascorro and Ribera de Curtidores. This market will delight anyone attracted to a mishmash of fascinating junk interspersed with bric-a-brac and paintings. *Note:* Thieves are rampant here (hustling more than just antiques), so secure your wallet carefully, stay alert, and proceed with caution. Insofar as scheduling your visit to El Rastro, bear in mind that this is a flea market involving hundreds of merchants who basically pull up their display tables and depart whenever their goods are sold or they get fed up with the crowds. Sunday only; opens from dawn but gets busy by 9am. Metro La Latina Bus: 17, 18, 23, 35, or 60.

FOOD & WINE

Al Dente   Products from Tuscany, Umbria, and Puglia dominate this little corner of Italy in Chueca, owned by Alicia Carulla, who's also on hand to give advice on recipes and dispense general culinary tips. Pasta rules in a rich variety of forms: *toconi, cavatelli, orecchiette,* and *tagliolini* among them. Rich sauces and a fine selection of Italian wines and grappas are also available, and the stylish shelves are lined with housewares with famous names like Fiordalisi, Fattorie, and Umbre. Fernando Vi 2. ✆ **91-650-39-43**. Metro: Alonso Martínez. Bus: 3, 7, 21, 40, or 147.

Chiacchere   Owner Patrizia Bonfiglio comes from Milan and has projected much of that city's style into this chic, friendly locale, whose name means chitchat or gossip, but whose atmosphere is both cosmopolitan and essentially Italian. You can select from a wide range of native produce, including pastas from Bari and rich tomato sauces flavored with basil and Gorgonzola. If the sight of all these goodies makes you hungry, sample the delicious 10€ ($12) menu in the small dining area. A typical combination would be carpaccio di Bresaola, penne al pesto, and tiramisu, all made from produce sold in the shop. Libertad 9. ℭ **91-521-26-90.** Metro: Chueca. Bus: 3, 40, or 149.

Deli Deluxe   Another American-inspired creation is this stylish multipurpose deli-cum-restaurant run by brother-and-sister team Astrid and Randy Romero. While deciding which of the international food products on display you want to buy, relax over a coffee or—depending on the time of day—one of the Romeros' marvelous cocktails. The restaurant section offers colorful salads and Cuban sandwiches as well as a 9€ ($10) menu. A catering service is also available. Open 11am to 11pm. San Marcos 33. ℭ **91-522-42-04.** Metro: Chueca. Bus: 3, 40, or 149.

González *(Finds)*   Quietly concealed on a character-filled Huertas street, this charming deli-cum-wine bar sells top-rate cheeses and hams at the counter by the entrance and vintage wines by the glass or bottle at the bar or in the cozily unpretentious inner salon, where the discreet movie posters and stills bedeck the walls. Open Tuesday to Saturday 10:30am to 3pm and 7pm to midnight. León 12. ℭ **91-429-56-18.** Metro: Antón Martín. Bus: 6, 26, or 32.

Hespen & Suárez   Kay Hespen and her husband, José Suárez, launched this bright compact international deli in 2003 and if it feels a bit like a real New York deli, maybe that's because both Kay and her husband lived many years in the Big Apple, where Kay was a marketing expert and José was head chef at Placido Domingo's restaurant. Products on its shelves range from Lebanese coffee and tandoori pasta to Japanese noodles. Their own products include bagels and takeout minestrone, and if you want to eat on the spot you can sample their modest menu (up to 7€/$8.05) or just enjoy a coffee and cake at the bar. Barceló 15. ℭ **91-445-39-03.** Metro: Chueca. Bus: 3, 40, or 149.

Lavinia   If you can't find the wine you want here, you won't find it anywhere. Lavinia claims to be not only the largest wine shop in Madrid but also in the whole of Europe. It's big, alright: Its two floors of racked *vinos* run the full range from Tokai to Tío Pepe. Smart, bright, and ultramodern, it's light-years away from the traditional concept of musty-barrel-lined bodegas, and the switched-on, multilingual staff complements it perfectly. Open Monday to Saturday 10am to 9pm. Ortega y Gasset 16. ℭ **91-426-06-04.** www.lavinia.es. Metro: Núñez de Balboa. Bus: 1 or 74.

Mallorca   Madrid's best-established gourmet shop opened in 1931 as an outlet selling a pastry called *ensaimada,* and this is still one of the store's most famous products. Tempting arrays of cheeses, canapés, roasted and marinated meats, sausages, and about a dozen kinds of pâté accompany a spread of tiny pastries, tarts, and chocolates. Don't overlook the displays of Spanish wines and brandies. A stand-up tapas bar is always clogged with clients three deep, busy sampling the wares before they buy larger portions to take home. Tapas cost from .90€ to 2.40€ ($1.05–$2.75) per *ración* (portion). Open daily from 9:30am to 9:30pm. Velázquez 59. ℭ **91-431-99-09.** Metro: Velázquez. Bus: 1, 9, 19, 51, 74, or 89.

Taste of America   Yanks feeling homesick might want to head here for a taste of the States. Set in the leafy residential north of the city at the end of Calle Serrano, it offers a wealth of specialties including pretzels, fudge brownies, candy, and Newman's Own sauces. Homesick Brits can stock up on marmite, Colman's mustard, and cheddar cheese. Opens Monday to Saturday 10am to 2pm and 4 to 8pm. Serrano 149. ℭ **91-562-02-78.** Metro: República Argentina. Bus: 16, 19, or 51.

FOOD MARKETS

On the booming outskirts of the city and in nearby satellite towns like Las Rozas and Madahonda, American-style malls and other modern commercial centers are sprouting up at an alarming rate and superseding the traditional image of the covered market. Luckily, the latter still reigns supreme in the heart of the city. Vibrantly alive and brimming with rich atmosphere, with its goodies and kaleidoscope of colors (and, let's face it, smells), it still survives as an indelible reminder of old Spain. As such it's well worth taking a stroll around one whether you buy anything or not—if only to reassure yourself that some things never change. Here are five prime examples.

Anton Martín   One of the homeliest and friendliest—and surprisingly least known—of the traditional Madrileño markets, with two floors serving every conceivable kind of produce from Spain and farther afield. Adjoining street stalls sell a tantalizing variety of fish and smoked products. Calle Santa Isabel (near Cine Doré) Metro: Antón Martín.

El Mercado de Chamartín   A close rival to La Paz in the chic market stakes is residential Chamartín's traditional two-story food emporium. Noted for its small but immaculate fresh fish selection and marvelous range of olive oils and sauces, it also boasts an impressive range of quality meats, fruits, and vegetables. Bolivia 9. *C* **91-457-53-50.** Metro: Colombia. Bus: 7, 16, 29, or 51.

La Cebada   In spite of its ugly functional outward appearance, this La Latina landmark right on the edge of the historic Plaza de la Cebada is a bustling old-style market with a attractive variety of produce spread over two spacious levels. Plaza de la Cebada. *C* **91-365-91-76.** Metro: La Latina. Bus: 60.

La Paz   The neatest and most stylish market in Madrid, possibly in all Spain, La Paz is located on the western edge of fashionable Salamanca district. Pride of place goes to its charcuterie counters, but everything is top quality, hyper-clean, and served with attentive professionalism. Classic cheese stall **La Boulette** boasts over 200 international cheeses. Ayala 28. *C* **91-435-07-43.** Metro: Serrano. Bus: 1, 74, or 89.

Maravillas   Situated between the northwesterly districts of Cuatro Caminos and Tetuan, this is the biggest of the Madrid's old-style markets: noisier, grittier, and more Rabelaisian than the previous two. Its choice of fish is the largest and most varied in the capital. At the bargain-priced bar counters, you can buy as fine a coffee as you'll taste in the Ritz. Bravo Murillo 122. *C* **91-534-84-29.** Metro: Alvarado. Bus: 3, 64, 66, 124, or 127.

San Miguel   This 19th-century Industrial Revolution–style market set right in the heart of the Austrias district is a real work of art. Inside its eye-catching exterior of ironwork and glass are rows of stalls selling a wide range of fresh fruit, vegetables, meat, and fish. There's also a lively little cafe if you feel like a pick-me-up. Plaza de San Miguel. *C* **91-548-12-14.** Metro: Sol. Bus: 3.

GUITARS

José Ramírez   A true Hispanic original, this long-established shop located just a stone's throw from the Puerta del Sol sells nothing but guitars. Not any old guitar, though. These handmade gems are purchased worldwide, and all shipping orders must be placed in the shop itself. You can also visit the workshop to see these instruments being made on weekdays. Open Monday to Friday 10am to 2 pm and 4:30 to 8pm; Saturday 10:30am to 2 pm. Calle de la Paz 8. *C* **91-531-42-29.** www.guitarrasramirez.com. Metro Sol.

HERBALISTS

Although vegetarian restaurants are a relatively recent phenomenon (p. 125), Spain has been a health-conscious country for some time and herbalist shops *(herbolarios)* are traditional institutions. Here are two of the longest established.

Herbolario la Fuente *(Finds* Founded in 1856, this family run business began with a love of and fascination with plants and their curative powers and continued ever since, making few concessions to modern fads or trends. All plants and herbs sold are freshly collected on a regular basis from the countryside and preserved either in large glass jars made at La Granja or in 19th-century drawers that slide into niches. Apart from relishing the guaranteed quality of their products, you'll be taking a stimulating trip back into the past. Open Monday to Friday, 10am to 1:30pm and 5 to 8pm; Saturday 10am to 1:30pm. Pelayo 70. ℂ **91-308-13-98.** Metro: Alonso Martínez. Bus: 3, 40, or 149.

Viuda de Patricio Morando In business since 1916, this veteran shop contains a large store of medicinal herbs, though in recent years market pressures have also drawn it into the spheres of garden produce, diet foods, spices, and natural cosmetics. Though it still retains the original drawers used for storing its products, today these are purely decorative. Open Monday to Friday 9:30am to 1:30pm and 4:45 to 8pm; Saturday 9:45am to 1:30pm; Sunday 10:30am to 2:30pm. Duque de Alba 15. ℂ **91-369-08-26.** Metro: La Latina. Bus: 17, 18, 23, 35, or 60.

LEATHER

Excrupulus Net Highly innovative shoe, jacket, and briefcase designs from Cataluña and Valencia—all of the highest-quality leather—are sold in this prestigious Chueca shop. The notable Muxart range includes stylish windcheaters. Open Monday to Saturday 11am to 2pm and 5:30 to 8:30pm. Almirante 7. ℂ **91-521-72-44.** Metro: Chueca. Bus: 5, 14, 27, 37, 45, 53, or 150 (all to Recoletos).

Farrutx One of the most well-known names in the world of footwear, Farrutx originates from the Balearic island of Mallorca (its *zapaterías,* or shoe shops, are renowned for producing elegant quality goods). Belts and handbags feature highly among other leather products on sale here. Open Monday to Saturday 10am to 2pm and 5 to 8:30pm (July 10am–2pm and 5:30–8:30pm). Serrano 7. ℂ **91-577-09-24.** Metro: Serrano. Bus: 1, 74, or 89.

Loewe ⊕ Since 1846, this has been the most elegant leather store in Spain. Its gold medal–winning designers have always kept abreast of changing tastes and styles, but the inventory retains a timeless chic. The store sells luggage, handbags, and jackets for men and women (in leather or suede). Open Monday to Saturday 9:30am to 8:30pm. There's another branch with the same hours, and much of the same merchandise, at Serrano 26 (ℂ **91-577-60-56**). Gran Vía 8. ℂ **91-522-68-15.** Metro: Banco de España or Gran Vía. Bus: 1, 2, 74, or 146.

PERFUMES

Alvarez Gómez This is a marvelously old-fashioned *perfumería.* It's been around so long it's newly fashionable again. The shop markets its own fragrances, many based on almost long-forgotten formulas. Even if you're not specifically looking for perfume, you'll find an array of unusual merchandise here, including tortoiseshell accessories, custom jewelry, and even women's handbags and belts. Open Monday through Friday day 10am to 8pm; Saturday 10am to 2pm. Castellana 111. ℂ **91-555-59-61.** Metro: Cuzco. Bus: 5, 27, 147, or 150.

Oriental Perfumeries   Located at the western edge of the Puerta del Sol, this shop carries one of the most complete stocks of perfume in Madrid—both national and international brands. It also sells gifts, souvenirs, and costume jewelry. Open Monday through Friday from 10am to 9pm, Saturday from 10am to 12:30pm and 5 to 9pm. Calle Mayor 1. ✆ **91-521-59-05**. Metro: Sol. Bus: 3.

PORCELAIN

Lasarte   This imposing outlet is devoted almost exclusively to Lladró porcelain; the staff can usually tell you about new designs and releases the Lladró company is planning for the near future. Open Monday to Friday from 9:30am to 8pm, Saturday from 10am to 8pm. Gran Vía 44. ✆ **91-521-49-22**. Metro: Callao. Bus: 46, 74, 75, 133, 146, or 150.

SHOPPING MALLS

ABC Serrano   Set within what used to be the working premises of a well-known Madrileño newspaper *(ABC)*, this is a complex of about 85 upscale boutiques that emphasize fashion, housewares, cosmetics, and art objects. Although each of the outfitters inside are independently owned and managed, most maintain hours of Monday to Saturday from 10am to midnight. On the premises, you'll find cafes and restaurants to keep you fed between bouts of shopping, lots of potted and flowering shrubbery, and acres and acres of Spanish marble and tile. Serrano 61 or Castellana 34. ✆ **91-577-50-31**. Metro: Serrano. Bus: 1, 74, or 89 (Serrano); 7, 14, or 27 (Castellana).

La Vaguada   This megamall has pretty much everything. Among its countless shops, cafes, and restaurants you'll find an El Corte Inglés department store and a multi-screen cinema (Spanish movies only). Open Monday to Saturday and first Sunday of every month 10am to 10pm (most shops, except for the department stores, close at 8:30pm; on Sun many shops open for shorter hours). Monforte de Lemos 36. ✆ **91-730-10-00**. Metro Barrio del Pilar. Bus: 124, 134.

Moda Shopping   Located just off the Castellana in Salamanca district, this stylish mall has over 50 locales from pricey boutique and fashion stores to hairdressers and an art showroom. Open Monday to Saturday 8am to 10pm; first Sunday of every month 11am to 10pm (some shops open at noon on Sun). Ave. General Peron 40 (at the corner of Paseo de la Castellana), ✆ **91-581-15-25**. www.modashopping.com. Metro: Santiago Bernabeu.

Plenilunio   Claiming to be the largest mall in all Spain, with over 200 premises including multiscreen cinemas, this is also the newest commercial center to sprout up in the Madrid area. It was launched in May 2006 and lies on the northerly outskirts of the city close to the Eisenhower junction section of the Barcelona highway.

Xanadu   This huge out-of-town complex boasts over 200 shops, including an El Corte Ingles and HiperCor. Other facilities include cafes, bars, and a 15-screen cinema. Don't miss the Parque de Nieve, an indoor artificial ski slope. Stores open every day from 10am to 10pm. Leisure zones open Sunday to Thursday 10am to 2am; Friday and Saturday 10am to 4am. Carretera de Extremadura (N-5), Km 23.5 (13 mi/22 km southwest of Madrid), Arroyomolinos. www.madridxanadu.com.

10

Madrid After Dark

Madrid abounds in dance halls, *tascas,* cafes, theaters, movie houses, music halls, and nightclubs. Proceed carefully through this maze of offerings—you'll discover that many are strictly for residents or Spanish-speakers.

Because dinner is served late in Spain, nightlife doesn't really get under way until after 11pm, and it generally lasts until around 3am—Madrileños are so fond of prowling about at night that they're known around Spain as *gatos* (cats). In fact, if you arrive at 9:30pm at a club, you'll have the place all to yourself, if it's even open.

In most clubs a one-drink minimum is the rule: Feel free to nurse one drink through the entire evening's entertainment.

In summer, Madrid sponsors a series of plays, concerts, and films, making the city a virtual free festival. Pick up a copy of the *Guía del Ocio* (available at most newsstands) for listings of these events. This guide also provides information about occasional discounts for commercial events, such as the concerts that are given in Madrid's parks. Also check the program of *Fundación Juan March,* Calle Castelló 77 (© **91-435-42-40;** Metro: Núñez de Balboa). Tapping into funds that were bequeathed to it by a generous financier (Sr. Juan March), it stages free concerts of Spanish and international classical music within a concert hall at its headquarters at Calle Castelló 77. In most cases, these are 90-minute events that are presented every Monday and Saturday at noon, and every Wednesday at 7:30pm.

Like flamenco clubs, discos tend to be expensive, but they often open for what is erroneously called afternoon sessions (7–10pm). Although discos charge entry fees, at an afternoon session the cost might be as low as 3€ ($3.75), rising to 15€ ($19) and beyond for a night session—that is, beginning at 11:30pm and lasting until the early morning hours. Therefore, go early, dance until 10pm, and then proceed to dinner (you'll be eating at the fashionable hour).

Nightlife is so plentiful in Madrid that the city can be roughly divided into the following "night zones."

Plaza Mayor/Puerta del Sol   The most popular areas from the standpoint of both tradition and tourist interest, they can also be dangerous, so explore them with caution, especially late at night. They are filled with tapas bars and *cuevas* (drinking caves). Here it is customary to begin a *tasca* crawl, going to tavern after tavern, sampling the wine in each, along with a selection of tapas. The major streets for such a crawl are Cava de San Miguel, Cava Alta, and Cava Baja. You can order *pinchos y raciones* (tasty snacks and tidbits).

Gran Vía   This area contains mainly cinemas and theaters. Most of the after-dark action takes place on little streets branching off the Gran Vía.

Plaza de Isabel II/Plaza de Oriente Another area much frequented by tourists. Many restaurants and cafes flourish here, including the famous Café de Oriente.

> ⟨ *Tips* **Champagne Entertainment on a Beer Budget**
>
> Flamenco in Madrid is geared mainly to prosperous tourists with fat wallets, and nightclubs are expensive. But since Madrid is preeminently a city of song and dance, you can often be entertained at very little cost—in fact, for the price of a glass of wine or beer, if you sit at a bar with live entertainment.

Chueca Along such streets as Hortaleza, Infantas, Barquillo, and San Lucas, this is the gay nightlife district, with dozens of clubs. Cheap restaurants, along with a few female striptease joints, are also found here. This area can also be dangerous in the early hours of the morning, though the customary presence of weekend revelers who throng the streets till around 3am often manages to deter potential pickpockets and muggers. The reasonably active police presence at night also helps.

Argüelles/Moncloa For university students, this part of town sees most of the action. Many dance clubs are found here, along with ale houses and fast-food joints. The area is bounded by Pintor Rosales, Cea Bermúdez, Bravo Murillo, San Bernardo, and Conde Duque.

1 The Performing Arts

Madrid has a number of theaters, opera companies, and dance companies. To discover where and when specific cultural events are being performed, pick up a copy of *Guía del Ocio* at any city newsstand. The sheer volume of cultural offerings can be staggering; for a concise summary of the highlights, see below.

Tickets to dramatic and musical events usually range in price from 4.20€ to 40€ ($5.25–$50), with discounts of up to 50% granted on certain days of the week (usually Wed and matinees on Sun).

The concierges at most major hotels can usually get you tickets to specific concerts, if you are clear about your wishes and needs. They charge a considerable markup, part of which is passed along to whichever agency originally booked the tickets. You'll save money if you go directly to the box office to buy tickets. In the event your choice is sold out, you may be able to get tickets (with a reasonable markup) at **Localidades Galicia** at Plaza del Carmen 1 (✆ **91-531-27-32;** Metro: Puerta del Sol). This agency also markets tickets to bullfights and sporting events. It is open Tuesday to Saturday from 9:30am to 1:30pm and 4:30 to 7:30pm, Sunday from 9:30am to 1:30pm.

Here follows a grab bag of nighttime diversions that might amuse and entertain you. First, the cultural offerings:

MAJOR PERFORMING-ARTS COMPANIES

For those who speak Spanish, the **Compañía Nacional de Nuevas Tendencias Escénicas** is an avant-garde troupe that performs new and often controversial works by undiscovered writers. On the other hand, the **Compañía Nacional de Teatro Clásico,** as its name suggests, is devoted to the Spanish classics, including works by the ever-popular Lope de Vega and Tirso de Molina.

Among dance companies, the national ballet of Spain—devoted exclusively to Spanish dance—is the **Ballet Nacional de España.** Their performances are always well attended. The national lyrical ballet company is the **Ballet Lírico Nacional.**

World-renowned flamenco sensation Antonio Canales and his troupe, **Ballet Flamenco Antonio Canales,** offer spirited high-energy performances. Productions are centered on Canales's impassioned *Torero,* his interpretation of a bullfighter and the physical and emotional struggles within the man. For tickets and information, you can call Madrid's most comprehensive ticket agency, the previously recommended **Localidades Galicia,** Plaza del Carmen 1 (℃ **91-531-27-32**), for tickets to cultural events and virtually any other event in Castile. Other agencies include **Casa de Cataluña** (℃ **91-538-33-00**) and **Corte Inglés** (℃ **91-432-93-00**). Both Casa de Cataluña and Corte Inglés have satellite offices located throughout Madrid.

Madrid's opera company is the **Teatro de la Opera,** and its symphony orchestra is the outstanding **Orquesta Sinfónica de Madrid.** The national orchestra of Spain—widely acclaimed on the continent—is the **Orquesta Nacional de España,** which pays particular homage to Spanish composers.

CLASSICAL MUSIC

Auditorio del Parque de Atracciones   The schedule of this 3,500-seat facility might include everything from punk-rock musical groups to the more high-brow warm-weather performances of visiting symphony orchestras. Check with Localidades Galicia (℃ **91-531-27-32**) to see what's on at the time of your visit. Metro: Casa del Campo, Batán, or Lago.

Auditorio Nacional de Música   Sheathed in slabs of Spanish granite, marble, and limestone and capped with Iberian tiles, this hall is the ultramodern home of both the National Orchestra of Spain and the National Chorus of Spain. Standing just north of Madrid's Salamanca district, it ranks as a major addition to the competitive circles of classical music in Europe. Inaugurated in 1988, it is devoted exclusively to the performances of symphonic, choral, and chamber music. In addition to the Auditorio Principal (Hall A), whose capacity is almost 2,300, there's a hall for chamber music (Hall B), as well as a small auditorium (seating 250) for intimate concerts. Príncipe de Vergara 146. ℃ **91-337-01-39**. Tickets 4.20€–40€ ($5.25–$50). Metro: Cruz de Rayo.

Centro Cultural de la Villa   Spanish-style ballet along with *zarzuelas* (musical reviews or operettas), orchestral works, and theater pieces, are presented at this cultural center. Tickets go on sale 5 days before the event of your choice, and performances are usually presented at two evening shows (8 and 10:30pm). Plaza de Colón. ℃ **91-575-60-80**. Tickets, depending on event, 12€–27€ ($15–$34). Metro: Serrano or Colón.

Fundación Juan March   This foundation sometimes holds free concerts at lunchtime. The advance schedule is difficult to predict, so call for information. Castelló 77. ℃ **91-435-42-40**. Metro: Núñez de Balboa.

La Fidula   Serving as a bastion of civility in a sea of rock-and-roll and disco chaos, this club was converted from an 1800s grocer. Over the past 2 decades, it has been presenting chamber music concerts nightly at 11:30pm in cooperation with the Royal Music Conservatory with an additional show at 1am on weekends. The club offers the prospect of a tranquil, cultural evening on the town, at a moderate price. They take performances here seriously—late arrivals may not be seated for concerts. It's open Monday to Thursday and Sunday 7pm to 3am; Friday and Saturday 7pm to 4am. Calle Huerta 57. ℃ **91-429-29-47**. Cover 2.15€ ($2.70). Metro: Antón Martín.

Teatro de la Zarzuela   Modeled on La Scala in Milan, this 150-year-old theater is the best place in Madrid to see the unfashionably nostalgic though still enjoyable

Spanish operetta, or *zarzuela*. A resident company gives spirited performances year-round, but the main season is October to July. Plays, ballets, and the occasional opera and family show also feature on the agenda, as does an annual program devoted to the 19th-century German *Lied.* Box office is open noon to 8pm. Shows usually start at 8pm. Jovellanos 4 ℭ **91-524-54-00.** Tickets 8€–60€ ($10–$75). http://teatrodelazarzuela.mcu.es. Metro: Banco de Espana.

Teatro Real   Reopened in 1997 after a massive $157-million renovation, this theater is one of the world's finest stage and acoustic settings for opera. Its extensive state-of-the-art equipment affords elaborate stage designs and special effects. Today, the building is the home of the Compañía del Teatro Real, a company specializing in opera and the occasional ballet, and often working with leading Spanish lyric talents, including Plácido Domingo. The theater is also a major venue for classical music. On November 19, 1850, under the reign of Queen Isabel II, the Royal Opera House opened its doors with Donizetti's *La Favorita.* Plaza Isabel II, 7 ℭ **91-547-45-77** and 90-233 22 11. Tickets 30€–192€ ($38–$240). Metro: Opera.

MAINSTREAM THEATER

Madrid offers many different theater performances, useful to you only if you are very fluent in Spanish. If you aren't, check the *Guía del Ocio* for performances by English-speaking companies on tour from Britain, or select a concert or subtitled movie instead.

In addition to the major ones listed below, there are at least 30 other theaters, including one devoted almost entirely to children's plays, the **Sala la Bicicleta,** in the Ciudad de los Niños at Casa de Campo. Nonprofessional groups stage dozens of other plays in such places as churches.

Teatro Calderón   This is the largest theater in Madrid, with a seating capacity of 2,000. Although in the past this venue included everything from dramatic theater to flamenco, in recent years it has moved to a more serious approach that focuses mostly on opera, with performances beginning most evenings at 8pm. A long-running favorite is Bizet's *Carmen,* whose Spanish setting partly justified its enduring popularity among Madrileños. Atocha 18. ℭ **91-429-58-90.** Tickets 27€–50€ ($34–$63). Metro: Tirso de Molina.

Teatro de Bellas Artes   Adjoining the Círculo de Bellas Artes cultural center, this long-established theater offers around three or four works a year ranging from Golden Age to modern plays. In its early days, audiences enjoyed a more prolific program organized by the colorful 19th-century novelist and playwright Ramón de Valle-Inclán. Box office is open from 11:30am to 1:30pm, and 5pm till the commencement of the performance. Open Tuesday to Sunday. Marqués de Casa Riera 2. ℭ **91-532-44-37.** Tickets 18€–24€ ($23–$30) Metro: Banco de España

Teatro de la Comedia   This is the home of the Compañía Nacional de Teatro Clásico. Here, more than anywhere else in Madrid, you're likely to see performances from the classic repertoire of such great Spanish dramatists as Lope de Vega and Calderón de la Barca. There are no performances on Wednesday, and the theater is closed during July and August. The box office is open daily from 11:30am to 1:30pm and 5 to 6pm, and for about an hour before the performances. Príncipe 14. ℭ **91-521-49-31.** Tickets 8€–16€ ($10–$20), 50% discount Thurs. Metro: Sevilla. Bus: 15, 20, or 150.

Teatro Español   This company is funded by Madrid's municipal government, its repertoire a time-tested assortment of great and/or favorite Spanish plays. The box office is open daily from 11:30am to 1:30pm and 5 to 6pm. Príncipe 25. © **91-429-62-97**. Tickets 3€–20€ ($3.75–$25), 50% discount Wed. Metro: Sevilla.

Teatro Lara   Reopened in the mid-1990s after years of disuse, the Teatro Lara stands on a steep narrow lane in Malasaña. It's a marvelous example of a 19th-century theater, and its evocatively traditional architecture has remained largely unchanged since refurbishment. Family plays and musicals such as *Annie* and *Blood Brothers* are generally shown here. The box office is open Tuesday to Sunday from 11:30am to 1pm and 5pm till the start of the show. Corredera Baja de San Pablo 15. © **91-521-05-52**. Tickets 12€–16€ ($15–$20). Metro: Callao.

Teatro Nuevo Apolo   Nuevo Apolo is the permanent home of the renowned Antología de la Zarzuela company. It is on the restored site of the old Teatro Apolo, where these musical variety shows have been performed since the 1930s. Prices and times depend on the show. The box office is open daily from 11:30am to 1:30pm and 5 to 6pm. Plaza de Tirso de Molina 1. © **91-369-06-37**. Tickets 20€–45€ ($25–$56). Metro: Tirso de Molina.

Nuevo Teatro Alcalá   Specializing in Spanish versions of big Broadway hits such as *Cats* and *Cabaret,* this renovated and recently reopened theater lies just off Alcalá in the Salamanca district. Calle Jorge Juan 62 © **91-426-47-79**. Advanced bookings for tickets: © **90-288-87-88**. Tickets from 12€–65€ ($15–$81). Metro: Príncipe de Vergara.

ALTERNATIVE THEATER

Madrid offers a modest but fascinating choice of imaginative and original "alternative" shows—ranging from sharp satires to esoteric sketches but—unlike the more accessible mainstream theater where you can usually get by without a full command of Spanish—a knowledge of the language and thought processes is essential if you decide on a visit to one of these venues.

Alfil   Although it's officially a mainstream theater, the Alfil repertoire dips so frequently into the avant-garde (recent performances have included *The Vagina Monologues*) that it's fair to include it in this section. A popular venue for stand-up comics—having in the past hosted the Internacional Teatro de Humor—it also provides a regular program of satirical and humorous plays. The box office opens 1 hour before each performance. Check with theater for exact shows and times. Open daily. Calle Pez 10. © **91-521-58-27** and **90-248-84-88**. Tickets 12€–20€ ($15–$25). Metro: Callao or Noviciado.

Cuarta Pared   The "Fourth Wall" is another key fringe rendezvous. It boasts its own company as well as an enthusiastic training section and innovative contributors whose plays deal frankly and uncompromisingly with contemporary Spanish social themes. Another highly praised feature is its lively children's theater. The box office opens 1 hour before performances. Open September to July; closed August. Ercilla 17. © **91-517-23-17**. Tickets 10€ ($13). Metro: Embajadores.

El Canto de la Cabra   Not many theaters go by the name of "The Goat's Bleat," so that alone makes this one different. Its experimental productions, performed by up to a score of Spanish companies throughout the year, are very popular. Indoor seating is limited to 70 persons, but in summer there are outdoor patio shows. Box office opens 1 hour before performances. Open September to June Thursday to Sunday at 9pm, and July and August Wednesday to Sunday at 10pm. San Gregorio 8. © **91-310-42-22**. Tickets 10€ ($13). Metro: Chueca.

Sala Triángulo   For alternative theater aficionados, this is the best of Madrid's alternative theaters, offering some of the most adventurously original satires and surrealistic sketches in town. Some programs may start at midnight. The box office opens 30 minutes before each show. Check with the theater for exact performance times. Open Thursdays to Sundays. Calle Zurita 20. ℭ **91-530-68-91.** Tickets 10€–12€ ($13–$15). Metro Antón Martín or Lavapiés.

ENGLISH-LANGUAGE THEATER

The **Madrid Players,** with their combined troupe of American, English, and Spanish artistes, put on spirited performances throughout the year in a range of venues. A standout is the Christmas Pantomime for children of all ages, but they also do plays and musical shows, occasionally in alternative theaters such as the Triángulo, above. For details of performances and venues, call ℭ **91-445-36-00** or 91-530-68-91. Also check **www.madridplayers.org**.

MOVIES

There are 13 single-screen and multiplex cinemas with a combined total of over 50 *salas* (theaters) showing original-language movies in Madrid.

MAINSTREAM

Alphaville Golem   The first of Madrid's four-screen art houses, the Alphaville opened in 1977 and has been committed to showing an adventurously contrasting blend of popular and nonmainstream movies ever since. The comfortable basement restaurant was the original movie house. Programs start at 4:30pm. Late-night shows are on Friday and Saturday at 12:30am. Martín de los Heros 14. ℭ **91-559-38-36.** Tickets 4€–6€ ($5–$7.50) Tues–Sun, 4.50€–6.50€ ($5.30–$7.50) Mon (except for holidays). Metro: Ventura Rodríguez or Plaza España.

Ideal Yelmo Cineplex   A favorite with locals and foreigners alike, this established eight-screen movie palace offers a full mix of commercial and independent productions. Programs start at 4pm. Late-night shows on Friday and Saturday start around midnight. Dr. Cortezo 6. ℭ **90-222-09-22.** Tickets 6.10€ ($7.60). Metro: Tirso de Molina.

Princesa   This larger, nine-screen multiplex is located in a small modern plaza adjoining Calle Princesa. It shows a wide selection of current international and national movies. Programs start 4:05pm. Late-night shows on Friday and Saturday start at 12:30 or 12:45am. Princesa 3. ℭ **91-541-41-00** or 90-222-91-22. Tickets 6€–6.20€ ($7.50–$7.75). Metro: Plaza de España or Ventura Rodríguez.

Renoir   There are four branches of these comfortable, well-run cinemas in the city, all equipped with high-quality sound and vision. Each has compact-size *salas* showing an up-to-date blend of international movies. Programs start around 4pm. Late-night shows on Friday and Saturday start at 12:30am. Tickets (6€–6.20€/$7.50–$7.75) for any Renoir theater can be booked by calling ℭ **90-222-91-22.**

Renoir Cuatro Caminos   Four screens. On the avenue close to northerly Cuatro Caminos's large central roundabout. Has a small bar. Raimundo Fernández Villaverde 10. ℭ **91-541-41-00.** Metro: Cuatro Caminos.

Renoir Plaza de España   Five theaters. Right next to the Alphaville and sharing the same street number. Opened in 1896. Martín de los Heros 14. ℭ **91-541-41-00.** Metro: Plaza de España or Ventura Rodríguez.

Renoir Princesa   Two screens. In the covered arcade running between Martín de los Heros and Calle Princesa. Princesa 5. © **91-541-41-00.** Metro: Plaza de España or Ventura Rodríguez.

Renoir Retiro   Four screens. In stylish Salamanca avenue 2 blocks east of the Retiro Park. Narváez 42. © **90-288-89-02.** Metro: Goya.

Verdi   Immaculately refurbished and reopened as a *versión original* cinema in 2002, the Chamberí-based, five-screen Verdi offers an enticing choice of mainstream and lesser-known international movies. There's also a small bar where you can enjoy a pre-movie coffee or *copa de vino.* Programs start 4pm. Last performances start at 10:30pm. Bravo Murillo 28. © **91-447-39-30.** Tickets 5.80€ ($7.25) Tues–Sun, 4€ ($5) Mon and 1st show Tues–Fri. Metro: Canal or Quevedo.

INDEPENDENT OR ART HOUSE

In addition to the theaters listed below, French, German, Italian, and Brazilian **cultural centers** have regular V. O. *(versión original)* performances of their country's movies. The **Casa de América,** Paseo de Recoletos 2, often features offbeat Latin American films in Spanish or Portuguese.

Cine Doré (Filmoteca) (*Finds*)   Founded in 1953 and a miraculous survivor of the philistine attempts in the '80s to turn it into a block of offices (thanks largely to a mass protest by journalists and artists), the Doré, or Filmoteca, is both a movie buff's delight and a marvelous example of Art Deco architecture. Madrid's richest and most eclectic variety of original-version movies—from '20s classics to offbeat or commercial international productions—can be found here. It also offers bargain ticket prices, a cozy cafe, and a small but well-stocked movie bookshop. There are two indoor theaters plus an open-air one upstairs in summer. Situated right next to the Antón Martín covered food market on the northern edge of Lavapiés, it's open Tuesday to Sunday 4pm to midnight. In April 2006 the Filmoteca raised its prices for the first time in 15 years (from 1.35€/$1.70 to 2.50€/$3.10), but it remains a bargain compared with mainstream cinema entry charges of around 5.80€ ($7.25). Programs usually start at 5:30pm. Last performance 10pm. Santa Isabel 3. © **91-369-21-18.** Tickets 2.50€ ($3.10), block of 10 tickets (each useable for any show) 20€ ($25) Metro: Antón Martín.

Cine Estudio Círculo de Bellas Artes   This stylishly renovated art cinema, just a few steps up the road from the Círculo de Bellas Artes cultural center, is noted for its varied alternative movie program. Pleasantly free of the crush that plagues some of the other movie houses, it's a relaxing backwater of comfort and taste. Programs start at 5:30pm. Last performance 10pm. Marqués de Casa Riera 2. © **91-522-50-92.** Tickets: 4€ ($5). Metro: Banco de España.

La Enana Marrón   As experimental a movie center as you'll find in Madrid, the tiny *Enana Marrón* (Brown Dwarf) nestles unobtrusively in a quiet lane between Chueca and Malasaña. A cineaste's cinema with a repertoire ranging from avant-garde retrospectives to new independent releases, it's little given to advertising, so you'll need to ring or pass by to check current programs and timetables. Travesía de San Mateo 8. © **91-308-14-97.** Tickets 4€ ($5) Metro: Tribunal.

Pequeño Cine Estudio   If you're a fan of '40s Hollywood film noir, British '50s comedies, or international classics in general you're likely to find what you're looking for here in this modest shrine to celluloid nostalgia, tucked away in an offbeat corner of Chamberí. Three or four different films are shown every day from 4pm to midnight. Last program 10pm. Magallanes 1. ☏ **91-447-29-20.** Tickets 6€ ($7.50) Thurs–Tues, 1st session 4.50€ ($5.60; except public holidays). Metro: Quevedo.

2 The Club & Music Scene

CABARET

Madrid's nightlife is no longer steeped in prudishness, as it was (at least officially) during the Franco era. You can now see glossy cabaret acts and shows with lots of nudity.

Café del Foro   This old-time favorite in the Malasaña district has suddenly in the 1990s become one of the most fashionable places in Madrid to hang out after dark. Patronizing the club are members of the literati along with a large student clientele. You never know exactly what the show for the evening will be, although live music of some sort generally starts at 11:30pm. Cabaret is often featured, along with live merengue, bolero, and salsa. There's a faux starry sky above the stage area, plus Roman colonnades that justify the name Café del Foro. Open daily from 7pm to 3am. Calle San Andrés 38. ☏ **91-445-37-52.** Cover may be imposed for specially booked act. Metro: Bilbao. Bus: 40, 147, 149, or N-19.

Scala Meliá Castilla   Madrid's most famous dinner show is a major Las Vegas–style spectacle, with music, water, light, and color. The program is varied, including international or Spanish ballet, magic acts, ice skaters, whatever. Most definitely a live orchestra will entertain you. It's open Tuesday to Saturday from 8:30pm to 3am. Dinner is served beginning at 9pm; the show is presented at 10:45pm. The show with dinner costs 70€ ($88), and if you partake you don't have to pay the cover charge; it's included in the show/dinner price. Reservations are essential. Calle Capitán Haya 43 (entrance at Rosario Pino 7). ☏ **91-571-44-11.** Cover 36€ ($45) including 1st drink. Metro: Cuzco.

FLAMENCO

Café de Chinitas   One of the best flamenco clubs in town, Café de Chinitas is set one floor above street level in a 19th-century building midway between the Opera and the Gran Vía. It features an array of (usually) gypsy-born flamenco artists from Madrid, Barcelona, and Andalusia, with acts and performers changing about once a month. You can arrange for dinner before the show, although many Madrileños opt for dinner somewhere else and then arrive just for drinks and the flamenco. Open Monday to Saturday, with dinner served from 9 to 11pm and the show lasting from 10:30pm to 2am. Reservations are recommended. Torrija 7. ☏ **91-559-51-35.** Dinner and show 66€ ($83), show without dinner (but includes 1 drink) 30€ ($38) Metro: Santo Domingo. Bus: 1 or 2.

Candela   Though this popular Lavapiés bar has no live music, the atmosphere is pure flamenco as gypsies and Andaluz artistes performers regularly drop in and do their stuff. The "jam sessions" at the rear are deservedly famous, though it may be hard to get access. Open Monday to Thursday and Sunday 11pm to 5:30am; Friday and Saturday 11pm to 6am. Olmo 2. ☏ **91-467-33-82.** Metro: Tirso de Molina.

Casa Patas   This club is now one of the best places to see "true" flamenco as opposed to the more tourist-oriented version presented at Corral de la Morería (see below). It is also a bar and restaurant, with space reserved in the rear for flamenco. Shows are presented midnight on Thursday, Friday, and Saturday and during Madrid's major fiesta month of May. The best flamenco in Madrid is presented here: Proof of the pudding is that flamenco singers and dancers often hang out here after hours. Tapas are priced at 2.70€ to 15€ ($3.40–$19) and are available at the bar. The club

The Sultry Sound of Flamenco

The lights dim and the flamenco stars clatter rhythmically across the dance floor. Their lean bodies and hips shake and sway to the music. Accompanied by stylized guitar music, castanets, and the fervent clapping of the crowd, the dancers are filled with tension and emotion.

Flamenco dancing, with its flash, color, and ritual, is evocative of Spanish culture. The word *flamenco* has various translations, meaning everything from "gypsified Andalusian" to "knife," and from "blowhard" to "tough guy." Experts disagree as to where it came from, but most claim Andalusia as its seat of origin. Although its influences were both Jewish and Islamic, it was the gypsy artist who perfected both the song and the dance. Gypsies took to flamenco like "rice to paella," in the words of the historian Fernando Quiñones.

The deep song of flamenco represents a fatalistic attitude toward life. Marxists used to say it was a deeply felt protest of the lower classes against their oppressors, but this seems unfounded. Protest or not, over the centuries, rich patrons, often brash young men, liked the sound of flamenco and booked artists to stage *juergas* or fiestas where dancer-prostitutes became the erotic extras. By the early 17th century, flamenco was linked with pimping, prostitution, and lots and lots of drinking, by both the audience and the artists.

By the mid–19th century, flamenco had gone legitimate and was heard in theaters and *café cantantes.* By the 1920s, even the pre-Franco Spanish dictator, Primo de Rivera, was singing the flamenco tunes of his native Cádiz. The poet Federico García Lorca and the composer Manuel de Falla preferred a purer form, attacking what they viewed as the degenerate and "ridiculous" burlesque of *flamenquismo,* the jazzed-up, audience-pleasing form of flamenco. The two artists launched a Flamenco Festival in Grenada in 1922. Of course, in the decades since, their voices have been drowned out, and flamenco is more *flamenquismo* than ever.

In his 1995 book *Flamenco Deep Song,* Thomas Mitchell draws a parallel to flamenco's "lowlife roots" and the "orgiastic origins" of jazz. He notes that early jazz, like flamenco, was "associated with despised ethnic groups, gangsters, brothels, free-spending bluebloods, and whoopee hedonism." By disguising their origins, Mitchell notes, both jazz and flamenco have entered the musical mainstream.

is open daily from 8pm to 2:30am. Calle Cañizares 10. ℂ **91-369-04-96.** Admission 20€ ($25). Metro: Tirso de Molina.

Corral de la Morería   Right on the western edge of the Austrias quarter near the remains of the old Arabic walls, the Morería (meaning "where the Moors reside") sizzles with flamenco. Colorfully costumed strolling performers warm up the audience around 11pm; a flamenco show follows, with at least 10 dancers. It's much cheaper to eat somewhere else first, and then pay only the one-drink minimum. Open daily from

9pm to 3am. Morería 17. ℭ **91-365-84-46.** Dinner and show 70€ ($88), show without dinner (includes 1 drink) 29€ ($36). Metro: La Latina or Sol.

Corral de la Pacheca   Located in the pricey Cuzco district close to Castellana Avenue, this fashionable locale features flamenco performers who both sing and dance. Open daily from 9pm to 3am. This show usually starts around 10pm. Juan Ramon Jimenez 26 station). ℭ **91-359-2660.** One drink and show 32€ ($40); dinner and show 70€–90€ ($88–$113). Metro: Cuzco.

Las Carboneras   A fairly new competitor in the flamenco stakes, Las Carboneras is a stylish venue combining dinners and floor shows. Though decidedly commercial and priced accordingly, it offers top-value dance entertainment and regular invited quality acts. Open Monday to Saturday at 8:30pm and closed in the early hours. Shows are at 10:30pm Monday to Wednesday and 11pm Friday and Saturday. Plaza del Conde de Miranda 1. ℭ **91-542-86-77.** Admission 35€–45€ ($44–$56) for 3-course meal with drinks included, 20€ ($25) without a meal and including 1 drink. Metro: La Latina or Opera.

La Soleá   This small late-night locale, set in the heart of a narrow bar-filled street, is a lively impromptu spot with a resident guitarist accompanying whomever chooses to try his or her hand (or rather vocal chords) at singing flamenco. Not as karaoke as it sounds, since many visitors are proficient in the genre and some inspired results often arise. The atmosphere is friendly and very good natured. Open from 11pm to 6am Monday to Saturday. Cava Baja 27. ℭ **91-366-05-34.** Metro: La Latina.

Las Tapas ☆ *(Finds*   Fed up with *faux* flamenco on the tourist circuit and all those frilly costumes, dancers Antonia Moya and Marisol Navarro opened their own little place. In a minimalist room, they perform some of the most authentic flamenco in Madrid. Sometimes the owners themselves star in a show. This place is for flamenco devotees. The cover charge of 14€ ($18) includes your first drink. Shows are held nightly at 10:30pm, and reservations are needed on weekends. Plaza de España 9. ℭ **91-542-05-20.** Metro: Plaza de España.

Torres Bermejas   Located in the very center of the city, on a narrow road leading off the Gran Vía, this colorful dinner and flamenco venue features regular live shows. Open 8:30pm. Calle de Mesonero Romanos 11. ℭ **91-532-33-22.** Metro: Gran Vía.

DANCE CLUBS

The Spanish dance club takes its inspiration from those of other Western capitals. In Madrid most clubs are open from around 6 to 9pm, later reopening around 11pm. They generally start rocking at midnight or thereabouts.

Alquimia   This stylishly individual disco has the unexpectedly relaxing atmosphere of an elegant old house. The eclectic, sometimes bizarre, music repertoire is intended to accommodate all tastes. Open from 9pm. Villanueva 2. ℭ **91-577-27-85.** Cover 10€ ($13) including one drink. Metro: Colon or Retiro.

Ananda   Located close to the Atocha train station complex, this huge (2000 sq. m/21,528 sq. ft.) nightclub boasts 10 bars and two dance floors, one inside and one outdoors. Things don't really liven up till around 2am, when a lavish dance show performed by drag queens begins. The Terrace is open nightly May to October 11pm to sunrise. The Covered Zone is open October to May Thursday, Friday, and Saturday 11pm to sunrise. Calle Ciudad de Barcelona 2. ℭ **91-781-95-40.** Cover 15€ ($19). Metro: Atocha.

Cool   It's cool all right, among the coolest clubs in the capital. No club in Madrid seems to blend a gay and straight (or else bi) crowd as successfully as this major production set on two levels. Sometimes the most stunning drag queens in Madrid appear here (often billed as "more beautiful than actual girls"). Video projections are always enticing, and the crowd of patrons in their 20s and early 30s are a medley of Madrileños and international folk, especially Brits and Yanks. One special feature of the club is the heavily attended Shangay Tea Dance taking place on Sunday from 9pm to 2am. If you're a "circuit queen" seeking out the hottest gay males in the Spanish capital, you're likely to encounter these "Urban Cowboys" here at this time. Open Friday and Saturday, from midnight to 6am and Sunday from 9pm to 2am. Isabel la Católica 6. ✆ **91-548-20-22.** Cover 8€–12€ ($10–$15). Metro: Callao.

Joy Eslava   Near the Puerta del Sol, this place has survived the passing fashions of Madrileño nightlife with more style than many of its (now-defunct) competitors. Virtually everyone in Madrid is likely to show up here, ranging from traveling sales reps in town from Düsseldorf to the youthful members of the Madrileño *movida*. Open nightly 10pm to 6:30am. Drinks are 9€ ($11) each. Arenal 11. ✆ **91-366-37-33.** Cover 15€ ($19) including 1st drink. Metro: Sol.

Kapital   This is the most sprawling, labyrinthine, and multicultural disco in Madrid at the moment. Set within what was originally a theater, it has seven different levels, each sporting at least one bar and an ambience that's often radically different from the one on the previous floor. Voyeurs of any age can take heart—there's a lot to see at the Kapital, with a mixed crowd that pursues whatever form of sexuality seems appropriate at the moment. Open Thursday to Sunday from 11:30pm to 5:30am. Second drinks cost from 10€ ($13) each. Atocha 125. ✆ **91-420-29-06.** Admission 12€–15€ ($15–$19) including 1st drink. Metro: Atocha.

Kathmandu   This is Madrid's club of the moment, where cutting-edge music echoes through the night—reggae, jungle, hip-hop, jazzy funk. At this alternative disco, be prepared for a dizzy psychedelic experience. The club would feel right at home among the scores in New York's West Chelsea. Decidedly androgynous, it's an Oriental-inspired, ultramodern scoff at normalcy. The bar on the top floor is a curious retreat, with Tibetan textiles draped from the ceiling. Nepalese art decorates part of the downstairs. At times the floor becomes so overcrowded you think the club will sink, but it carries on with wild abandon. Open Thursday from 11am to 5am and Friday and Saturday from 10am until 6am. Señores de Luzón 3. No phone. Cover 10€ ($13) including 1st drink. Metro: Sol.

Magik Room   Small and friendly psychedelic-style disco co-owned by Oscar nominee Javier Bardem of Hispanic-acting-family fame. Said to be the narrowest—and for many the coziest—locale in town. It opens Tuesday to Thursday midnight to 5am and Friday and Saturday midnight to 5:30am, and doesn't really get going till the early hours. Colón 12. ✆ **91-531-34-91.** Metro: Tribunal.

Ohm/Bash Line   This ultralively disco is also known as **Bash Line** during the week and on Sundays. But on peak Friday and Saturday nights, it comes into its own as **Ohm,** a must both with regular devotees to hedonism and newcomers in search of something alternative. Top DJs keep the action going, and organized theme parties are regular features. Open Wednesday to Sunday midnight to 6am. Plaza de Callao 4. ✆ **91-531-01-32.** Cover 8€–10€ ($10–$13), Sat 10€–12€ ($13–$15). Metro: Callao.

Pachá   The carefully contrived setting is pseudo-opulent and the drinks sometimes hard to get because of the milling crowds. Despite that, Pachá thrives as one of the late-night staples in Madrid for the mid-20s to late-40s clientele (a crowd that often segregates itself by age into distinctly different areas of the place). More than other nightclubs in Madrid, this has been the subject of complaints from neighbors about late-night noise. Open Tuesday to Sunday from 11pm to 5am. Barceló 11. ℂ **91-446-01-37**. Cover 12€–15€ ($15–$19) including 1st drink. Metro: Tribunal.

Palacio Gaviria   Its construction in 1847 was heralded as the architectural triumph of one of the era's most flamboyant aristocrats, the Marqués de Gaviria. Famous as one of the paramours of Queen Isabella II, he outfitted his palace with the ornate jumble of neoclassical and baroque styles that later became known as *Isabelino*. In 1993, after extensive renovations, the building was opened to the public as a concert hall for the occasional presentation of classical music and as a late-night cocktail bar. Ten high-ceilinged rooms now function as richly decorated, multipurpose areas for guests to wander in, drinks in hand, reacting to whatever, or whomever, happens to be there at the time. (One room is discreetly referred to as having been the bedroom-away-from-home of the queen herself.) No food is served, but the libations include a stylish list of cocktails and wines. The often-dull music doesn't match the elegance of the decor. Dance nights are usually Thursday through Saturday, everything from the tango to the waltz. Cabaret is usually featured on most other nights. Open Monday to Friday from 9pm to 3am; Saturday and Sunday from 9pm to 5am. Arenal 9. ℂ **91-526-60-69**. www.palaciogaviria.com. Cover 8€–15€ ($10–$19), including 1st drink. Metro: Sol or Opera.

Pasapoga   This club personifies the Madrid of today, drawing the most sophisticated crowd of beautiful people in their 20s and 30s of almost any club in the capital. On many nights the clientele is about 90% gay. The interior is also sleek and beautiful, with a grand staircase with ivory banisters. Under a mammoth and glittering chandelier, the princes and princesses of Madrid dance into the wee hours to recorded music featuring house, pop, and techno. The club is open Monday through Thursday from 6 to 10:30pm and Friday and Saturday from midnight to 6:30am. Gran Vía 37. ℂ **91-547-57-11**. Cover 8€–12€ ($10–$15). Metro: Callao.

The Room at Stella's   This weekend-only mecca, with its '70s decor and glistening mosaic ceiling, is one of the most stylish all-night spots around, featuring house techno music, a smooth DJ, and a tiny dance floor packed with seasoned revelers of the chic variety. Open Friday and Saturday 1 to 7am. Arlabán 7. No phone. Cover 12€ ($15) including 1 drink. Metro: Sevilla.

Sweet   Glamorously refurbished in 2002, this club lives up to its name. It doesn't even open its doors until 1 o'clock in the morning. Even so, the place doesn't get rocking until 2 hours later. Once it does, it's the hottest scene in Madrid. Steel doors with steel vines open up to reveal a wildly campy scene that attracts a 90% gay clientele most nights. Look for suspended cages and a "disco ball" dance floor packed with some of the prettiest girls and handsomest men in Madrid. Wear your most daring apparel. Open only Friday and Saturday from 1am to daybreak. Dr. Cortezo 1. ℂ **91-869-40-38**. Cover 8€–12€ ($10–$15) including 1st drink. Metro: Tirso de Molina.

Torero   If you're not one of the *gente guapa* (beautiful people), head elsewhere. The tough bouncer at the door only admits those young men and women he judges to be beautiful; otherwise, it's away with you. If you can pass such a tough door policy, you'll find yourself in one of the city's most glamorous after-dark rendezvous. The club is on two levels, with the top floor more attractive and Iberian with its leather chairs. The downstairs is more functional and less desirable. Some entertainment is provided on most nights, with drag shows a feature on Thursday. The latest Spanish recordings are played here, especially "pop Español." Hours are Friday and Saturday from 11pm to 6am; Sunday to Thursday from 11pm to 5am. Cruz 26. © **91-523-11-29.** Cover 12€ ($15). Metro: Sol or Tirso de Molina.

JAZZ

Café Central   Off the Plaza de Santa Ana, beside the famed Gran Hotel Victoria, the Café Central has a vaguely turn-of-the-20th-century Art Deco interior, with an unusual series of stained-glass windows. Many of the customers read newspapers and talk at the marble-top tables during the day, but the ambience is far more animated during the nightly jazz sessions, which are ranked among the best in Spain and often draw top artists. Open Sunday to Thursday from 1:30pm to 2:30am and Friday and Saturday from 1:30pm to 3:30am; live jazz is offered daily from 10pm to midnight. Beer costs 2.75€ ($3.40). Plaza del Angel 10. © **91-369-41-43.** Cover 8€–10€ ($10–$13); prices can vary according to the show. Metro: Antón Martín.

Café Populart   This club is known for its exciting jazz groups, which encourage the audience to dance. It specializes in Brazilian, Afro-bass, reggae, and new wave African music. When the music starts, usually around 11pm, the price of drinks nearly doubles. Open daily from 6pm to 2 or 3am. After the music begins, beer costs 4€ ($5); whiskey with soda 7.50€ ($9.35). Huertas 22. © **91-429-84-07.** Metro: Antón Martín or Sevilla.

Clamores   With dozens of small tables and a huge bar in its dark and smoky interior, Clamores, which means "noises" in Spanish, is the largest and one of the most popular jazz clubs in Madrid. Established in the early 1980s, it has thrived because of the diverse roster of American and Spanish jazz bands that have appeared here. The place is open daily from 6pm to around 3am, but jazz is presented only Tuesday to Saturday. Tuesday to Thursday, performances are at 11pm and again at 1am; Saturday, performances begin at 11:30pm, with an additional show at 1:30am. There are no live performances on Sunday or Monday nights, when the format is recorded disco music. Regardless of the night of the week you consume them, drinks begin at around 4.20€ ($5.25) each. Albuquerque 14. © **91-445-79-38.** Cover Tues–Sat usually 5€–24€ ($6.25–$30), but varies with act. Metro: Bilbao.

Segundo Jazz   It's over 3 decades since it first opened this spacious locale in Madrid's gritty Tetuan district, and Segundo Jazz is now officially the city's oldest jazz club. The eclectic range of artistes performing varies from completely new faces to the most famous of Spanish jazz performers. *Cantautores* (singer-composers) and traditional bands both make regular appearances. The club opens from 7pm to 4am daily. Comandante Zorita 8. © **91-554-94-37.** Cover 4€–8€ ($5–$10). Metro Cuatro Caminos.

POP & ROCK

El Perro (de la Parte Atras del Coche)   The bar's name ("the dog in the back of the car," referring to the wobble-headed toy dog you still sometimes see in car rear windows) gives you a hint of the zany retro mood. Corny kitsch decor, an eclectic mix of straight and bohemian clientele, and a background of soul, funk, and rock-'n'-roll sounds. Live acts include heavy metal groups. Open from 9pm to 3:30 am. Calle de la Puebla 15. © **91-521-03-25.** Cover 8€ ($10) Metro: Gran Vía.

Honky Tonk   This lively locale in the Chamberí district combines live pop music and stylish dining out with art and photography exhibitions. Open nightly 9pm to 5am. Covarrubias 24. © **91-445-68-86.** Entrance free, but after 3am a cover charge of 8€ ($10). Metro: Alonso Martinez.

La Via Lactea   Still a favorite with young fun ravers, this pioneer bar dates from the late '70s, when the famed post-Franco *movida* movement began. The place specializes in rock and hip-hop, and its walls are lined with posters of pop stars of the past 2 or more decades, including the Beatles, the Who, and the Rolling Stones. Open nightly from 9pm. Velarde 18 ℭ **91-446-75-81.** Cover around 6€ ($7.50). Metro: Tribunal.

Siroco   Highly popular rock locale with live shows by Spanish and international pop groups till around 2am followed by a lively blend of DJ-inspired soul and funk till the early hours. Open Thursday to Saturday from 9:30 or 10pm. San Dimas 3. ℭ **91-593-30-70.** www.siroco.es. Cover around 6€–10€ ($7.50–$13). Metro: San Bernardo.

CUBAN SALSA/BRAZILIAN

Café La Palma   Live Cuban groups playing salsa dominate the agenda here. As in Paris, anything Cuban is suddenly chic in Madrid. This is a convivial club and one of the most happening clubs in the capital. It's open daily from 4pm to 3am, but go after 10pm for the most action. A group made up of people mainly in their 20s and 30s is attracted here by the live music. La Palma 62. ℭ **91-522-50-31.** Cover 5€–6€ ($6.25–$7.50). Metro: Noviciado.

Galileo Galilei   Under the same ownership as the popular Clamores (see above), this spacious venue hosts a wide selection of performers of all types and persuasions from flamenco and jazz to Eastern dance—though salsa is its specialty. The place used to be a cinema and today retains much of its original kitschy imitation Greek decor. It opens daily from 6pm to 3am. Galileo 100. ℭ **91-534-75-57.** Cover 6€–13€ ($7.50–$16). Metro: Quevedo or Islas Filipinas.

El Son   This Cuban-run establishment has live salsa shows. You can also take dancing lessons given by wholesome native instructors. It's open from 7pm till early hours. Calle de la Victoria 6. ℭ **91-532-32-83.** Cover 8€ ($10). Metro: Sol.

Negro Tomasa   This is a Cuban music bar, drawing big crowds on the weekends. A Caribbean setting is evoked by fishermen and palm fronds. Pictures of Cuba on the walls also evoke the ambience. Cuban music and salsa attract a crowd in their 20s and 30s, and the place is very fashionable. The drinks served here—*mojitos,* daiquiris, and piña coladas—are familiar to barflies the world over. But have you ever had a Cubanito? It's tomato juice and lime with rum. Hours are daily from midnight to 3:30am. Calles Espoz y Mina and Cádiz. ℭ **91-523-58-30.** Fri–Sat cover 6€ ($7.50). Metro: Sol. Bus: 3, 15, 20, or 51.

Oba-Oba   A little slice of Rio in Madrid, this established Brazilian club is now in its third decade of entertaining grateful customers with its sambas and caipirinha cocktails. Regular live performances with Brazilian artistes. Open daily from 11pm to 6am. Jacometrezo 4. No phone. Cover usually 8€ ($10). Metro: Callao.

3 The Bar & Pub Scene

Aloque   Come to this cozy little bar with an even cozier little alcove at the back to sample the incomparable choice of wines, either by the glass or bottle. The latest "in" tipples are chalked on a blackboard, but you'll have over 200 national and international varieties to choose from—enough to satisfy the most demanding oenophile. Particularly interesting are the selections from burgeoning new Spanish wine-producing areas such as Somontano near Huesca. Excellent tapas ranging from *cecina de Astorga* (smoked beef) to *carpaccio de buey con queso parmesano* (ox carpaccio with

Parmesan cheese) match the quality of the vino. Open daily 7:30pm to 1am. Closed in August. Torrecilla del Leal 20. ☎ **91-528-36-62.** Metro: Antón Martín.

Balmoral   Its exposed wood and comfortable chairs evoke a cross between a London club and a Scottish hunting lodge. The clientele tends toward journalists, politicians, army brass, owners of large estates, bankers, diplomats, and the occasional literary star. *Newsweek* magazine dubbed it one of the "best bars in the world." No food other than tapas is served. Open Monday to Saturday noon to midnight or 1am. Beer is 3€ ($3.75); drinks are from 6€ ($7.50). Hermosilla 10. ☎ **91-431-41-33.** Metro: Serrano.

Balneario   Clients enjoy potent drinks in a setting with fresh flowers, white marble, and a stone bathtub that might have been used by Josephine Bonaparte. Near Chamartín Station on the northern edge of Madrid, Balneario is one of the most stylish and upscale bars in the city. It is adjacent to and managed by one of Madrid's most elegant and prestigious restaurants, El Cabo Mayor, and often attracts that dining room's clients for aperitifs or after-dinner drinks. Tapas include endive with smoked salmon, asparagus mousse, and anchovies with avocado. Open Monday to Saturday from noon to 2:30am. Drinks are 4€ to 8€ ($5–$10); tapas cost 3€ to 12€ ($3.75–$15). Juan Ramón Jiménez 37. ☎ **91-350-87-76.** Metro: Cuzco.

Bar Cock   This bar on two floors attracts some of the most visible artists, actors, models, and filmmakers in Madrid. The name comes from the word *cocktail,* or so they say. The decor is elaborate and unique, in contrast to the hip clientele; the martinis are Madrid's best. Open daily from 7pm to 3am; closed December 24 to 31. Drinks are 8€ ($10). Reina 16. ☎ **91-532-28-26.** Metro: Gran Vía.

Bar Taurino   This bar remains the top gathering spot for bullfight aficionados. A multitiered place, it is still a shrine to the greatest matador of the 1950s, Manolete, who was praised by Hemingway. This is no rough-and-tumble bar, but a cultured space often attracting Madrid society. It reaches the peak of its excitement during the San Isidro bullfighting festival, when Spain's top bullfighters often make appearances here in their full death-in-the-afternoon suits of light. Hours are daily 11am to midnight. In the Hotel Reina Victoria. Plaza Santa Ana. ☎ **91-531-45-00.** Metro: Antón Martín.

Chicote   This is Madrid's most famous cocktail bar. It's classic retro chic, with the same 1930s interior design it had when the foreign press came to sit out the Spanish Civil War, although the sound of artillery shells along the Gran Vía could be heard at the time. Long a favorite of artists and writers, the bar became a haven for prostitutes in the late Franco era. No more. It's back in the limelight again, a sophisticated and much-frequented rendezvous. Open daily from 8am to 3am. Drink prices can be high—from 6€ ($7.50)—but the waiters serve them with such grace you don't mind. Gran Vía 12. ☎ **91-532-67-37.** Metro: Gran Vía.

Del Diego   The latest "in" place to appear (well, late 1980s) in competition with Chicote and the Cock as a civilized place to enjoy a good cocktail. Try the daiquiris and you'll have to agree they're the best in town. The margaritas and dry martinis are also excellent, and the service is effortlessly attentive. Cool decor, low-key atmosphere, and smooth service add to the charm of this discreet locale, tucked away in a quiet street just below the Gran Vía. Open daily Monday to Thursday 7pm to 3am and Friday and Saturday 7pm to 3:30am; closed the month of August. Cocktails start around 5€ ($6.25). Reina 12. ☎ **91-523-31-06.** Metro: Gran Vía.

Hispano Bar/Buffet   This establishment does a respectable lunch trade every day for members of the local business community, who crowd in to enjoy the amply portioned *platos del día.* These might include a platter of roast duck with figs or orange sauce, or a supreme of hake. After around 5pm, however, the ambience becomes that of a busy after-office bar, patronized by stylishly dressed women and many local entrepreneurs. The hubbub continues on into the night. Open daily from 1:30pm to 1:30am. Full meals at lunchtime cost from around 33€ to 36€ ($41–$45), while beer costs from 1.80€ ($2.25). Paseo de la Castellana 78. ⓒ **91-411-48-76.** Metro: Nuevos Ministerios.

James Joyce Bar   This spacious and atmospheric bar, situated between Cibeles and the Puerta de Alcalá, is another Irish favorite, with a penchant for name changes. Known until early 2006 as Kitty O'Shea's, it was called Café Lion in the 1940s when it was the key meeting spot for the literati. Today, local rugby club members gather for weekly get-togethers and fuel themselves on draught Guinness and no-nonsense pub food. No rowdy locale this, though. The atmosphere is always good-natured and easygoing, and in summer you can sit at tables and chairs outside. In winter there are regular live music shows. Open Monday to Thursday from 11am to 2am; Friday and Saturday from 11am to 4am. A pint of beer costs 4€ ($5). Alcalá 59. ⓒ **91-575-49-01.** Metro: Banco de España.

La Venencia   On one of the traditional *tasca* streets in Old Madrid, this tavern has a distinct personality. It is dedicated to the art of serving Spain's finest sherry—and that's it. Don't come here asking for an extra dry martini. My favorite remains *manzanilla,* a delicate fino with just a little chill on it. If Luis Buñuel were to need extras in a film, surely the patrons here would be ideal. To go with all that sherry, the waiters (a little rough around the edges) will serve tapas, especially those garlicky marinated olives, *majoama* (cured tuna), and blue-cheese canapés. Barrels form the decor, along with antique posters long turned tobacco-gold from the cigarette smoke. Open daily from 7pm to 1:30am. Echegaray 7. ⓒ **91-429-62-61.** Metro: Sevilla.

Moore's   If not the oldest Irish pub in Madrid, at least Moore's is in the oldest building. Set just off the Plaza Mayor, this former medieval house has a basement that was once an "interrogation room" for the Inquisition. Now it features Eminem and pool tables. The main salon is relaxing and comfortable with dark wood-paneled walls and cozy alcoves. Guinness is the tipple par excellence and Wednesdays are curry evenings. Open daily noon to 1am. Pint of beer costs 4€ ($5). Felipe III 4. ⓒ **91-365-58-02.** Metro: Sol.

Teatriz   Part of its function is as a restaurant where soft lighting and a decor by world-class decorator Philippe Starck create one of the most stylish environments in Madrid. A meal averages around 20€ ($25) at lunch and 24€ ($30) in the evening, but if it's just a drink you're looking for, consider an extended session at any of the site's three bars. Here, within a setting not quite like a disco, but with a sound system almost as good, you'll find a music bar environment where stylish folk of all persuasions enjoy drinks and the gossip that often seems to originate at places like this. The restaurant is open daily from 1:30 to 4pm and 9pm to 1am. The bars are best appreciated every night from 9pm to 3am. Hermosilla 15. ⓒ **91-577-53-79.** Metro: Serrano.

Viva Madrid   A congenial and sudsy mix of students, artists, and foreign tourists cram into the turn-of-the-20th-century interior here, where antique tile murals and blatant Belle Epoque nostalgia contribute to an undeniable charm. In the good old days (the 1950s, that is), the fabled beautiful people showed up here, notably Ava Gardner with the bullfighter Manolete when they couldn't take their hands off each other. But Orson Welles and even Louis Armstrong used to pop in as well. Crowded and noisy, it's a place where lots of beer is swilled and spilled. It's set in a neighborhood of antique houses and narrow streets near the Plaza de Santa Ana. Open Friday from noon to 1am; Saturday from noon to 2am. Beer costs 3.50€ ($4.40); whiskey begins at 6€ ($7.50). Manuel Fernández y González 7. ℭ **91-429-36-40.** Metro: Sol.

CAVE CRAWLING

To capture a peculiar Madrid joie de vivre of the 18th century, visit some *mesones* and *cuevas,* many found in the *barrios bajos,* the area south of Plaza Mayor. From Plaza Mayor, walk down the Arco de Cuchilleros until you find a gypsylike cave that fits your fancy. Young people love to meet in the taverns and caves of Old Madrid for communal drinking and songfests. The sangria flows freely, the atmosphere is charged, and the room is usually packed; the sounds of guitars waft into the night air. Sometimes you'll see a strolling band of singing students going from bar to bar, colorfully attired, with ribbons fluttering from their outfits.

Mesón de la Guitarra   My favorite *cueva* in the area, Mesón de la Guitarra is loud and exciting on any night of the week, and it's as warmly earthy as anything you'll find in Madrid. The decor combines terra-cotta floors, antique brick walls, hundreds of sangria pitchers clustered above the bar, murals of gluttons, old rifles, and faded bullfighting posters. Like most things in Madrid, the place doesn't get rolling until around 10:30pm, although you can stop in for a drink and tapas earlier. Don't be afraid to start singing an American song if it has a fast rhythm—60 people will join in, even if they don't know the words. Open daily from 7pm to 1:30am. Beer is 2€ ($2.50); wine is from 1€ ($1.25); tapas are 6€–10€ ($7.50–$13). Cava de San Miguel 13. ℭ **91-559-95-31.** Metro: Sol.

Mesón del Champiñón   In English the name of this place means "mushroom," and that is exactly what you'll see depicted in various sizes along sections of the vaulted ceilings. The bartenders keep a brimming bucket of sangria behind the long stand-up bar as a thirst quencher for the crowd. A more appetizing way to experience a *champiñón* is to order a *ración* of grilled, stuffed, and salted mushrooms, served with toothpicks. Two tiny, slightly dark rooms in the back are where Spanish families go to hear organ music performed. Unless you want to be exiled to the very back, don't expect to get a seat. Practically everybody prefers to stand. Open daily from 6pm to 2am. Cava de San Miguel 17. No phone. Metro: Sol.

Sesamo   In a class by itself, this *cueva,* dating from the early 1950s, draws a clientele of young painters and writers with its bohemian ambience. Hemingway was one of those early visitors (a plaque commemorates him). At first you'll think you're walking into a tiny snack bar—and you are. But proceed down the flight of steps to the cellar. Here, the walls are covered with contemporary paintings and quotations. At squatty stools and tables, an international assortment of young people listens to piano music and sometimes guitar playing. Open daily from 6:30pm to 2am. A pitcher of sangria (for four) is 10€ ($13); beer costs 2.50€ ($3.10). Príncipe 7. ℭ **91-429-65-24.** Metro: Sevilla or Sol.

GAY & LESBIAN BARS

Black and White   This is the major gay bar of Madrid, in the center of the Chueca district. A guard will open the door to a large room—painted, as you might expect, black and white. There's a disco in the basement, but the street-level bar is the premier gathering spot, featuring drag shows beginning at 3am Thursday to Sunday, male

---

Moments **Summer *Terrazas***

At the first blush of spring weather, Madrileños rush outdoors to drink, talk, and sit at a string of open-air cafes, called *terrazas,* throughout the city. The best and most expensive ones are along Paseo de la Castellana between the Plaza de la Cibeles and the Plaza Emilio Castelar, but there are dozens more throughout the city.

You can wander up and down the boulevard, selecting one that appeals to you; if you get bored, you can go on later to another one. Sometimes these *terrazas* are called *chirinquitos.* You'll find them along other paseos, the Recoletos and the Prado, both fashionable areas but not as hip as the Castellana. For old traditional atmosphere, the terraces at the Plaza Mayor win out. The Plaza Santa Ana has several atmospheric choices within the old city. Friday and Saturday are the most popular nights for drinking; many locals sit here all night.

---

striptease, and videos. Old movies are shown against one wall. Open Monday to Friday from 8pm to 5am; Saturday and Sunday from 8pm to 6am. Beer is 4€ ($5); whiskey costs 6€ ($7.50). Gravina (at the corner of Libertad). © 91-531-11-41. Metro: Chueca.

Café Figueroa   This turn-of-the-20th-century cafe attracts a diverse clientele, including a large number of gay men and lesbians. It's one of the city's most popular gathering spots for drinks and conversation. Open Sunday through Thursday from 4pm to midnight; Friday and Saturday from 4pm to 2:30am. Beer is from 2.50€ ($3.10); whiskey costs from 5€ ($6.25). Augusto Figueroa 17 (at corner of Hortaleza). © 91-521-16-73. Metro: Chueca.

Cruising   One of the predominant gay bars of Madrid, a center for gay consciousness-raising and gay cruising (though they say the name refers to automobile driving), this place has probably been visited at least once by every gay male in Castile. There are practically no women inside, but many a hustler looking for a tourist john. It doesn't get crowded or lively until late at night. Open Monday to Friday from 8pm to 3:30am; Saturday and Sunday from 8pm to 4:30am. Beer costs 2.75€ to 3.50€ ($3.40–$4.35). Pérez Galdós 5. © 91-521-51-43. Metro: Chueca.

Leather Bar   This is another of the premier bars for gay men in Madrid, but despite its supposed emphasis on leather and uniforms, only about 25% of the men who show up actually wear them. You'll find two bars on the establishment's street level and a disco in the basement where same-sex couples can dance. Beer costs 3.50€ ($4.35). It's open Sunday through Thursday from 7pm to 3am; Friday and Saturday from 8pm to 3:30am. Pelayo 42. © 91-308-14-62. Admission 4€ ($5). Metro: Chueca.

Rick's   Rick's takes its name from "Everybody Comes to Rick's," the original title of the Bogie classic *Casablanca.* Many gay bars in the Chueca barrio are sleazy, but this is a classy joint—just like the fictional Rick's in Morocco. It's decorated with Bogie paraphernalia, including marble floors and gilt columns. The only thing missing is a piano player singing "As Time Goes By"—and Bergman, of course. Gay men patronize the place, with the occasional woman showing up, too. Incongruously, it has a foosball table in the bar but lavender walls. Open daily from 11:30pm "until some-time in the early morning." Clavel 8. ℂ **91-531-91-86**. Cover 8€ ($10). Metro: Chueca.

4 A Casino

Casino Gran Madrid is at Km 29 along the Carretera La Coruña (the A-6 highway running between Madrid and La Coruña), Apartado 62 (ℂ **91-856-11-00**). The largest place for gambling in Madrid, it appeals to nongamblers to boot with a well-choreographed roster of dining and entertainment facilities, including two restaurants, four bars, and a nightclub. And if you happen to enjoy gambling, there are facilities for French and American roulette, blackjack, *punto y banco,* baccarat, and chemin de fer. Presentation of a passport at the door is essential—without it, you won't be admitted. Entrance costs 4€ ($5), although that fee is often waived for residents of some of Madrid's larger hotels who arrive with a ticket that's sometimes provided gratis by the hotel management. The casino and all of its facilities are open daily from 4pm to 5am.

An a la carte restaurant in the French Gaming Room offers international cuisine, with dinners costing from 40€ to 55€ ($50–$69). A buffet in the American Gaming Room will cost around 25€ ($31). The restaurants are open 9:15pm to 2am.

The casino is about 29km (18 miles) northwest of Madrid. If you don't feel like driving, the casino has buses that depart from Plaza de España 6 every afternoon and evening at 4:30, 6, 7:30, 11pm, and 1am. Note that between October and June, men must wear jackets and ties; T-shirts and tennis shoes are forbidden in any season.

Side Trips from Madrid

Madrid makes an ideal base for excursions. Most of the day trips listed below range from 14 to 100km (9–62 miles) outside Madrid, allowing you to leave in the morning and be back by nightfall. Quickest to reach now is Toledo (just half an hour by high speed train from Atocha), which makes the most manageable day out. Others are an hour or more by bus or train.

Should you choose to stay overnight I've also included a selection of hotels in each town.

The trips are divided into two parts: villages and towns inside Madrid province, and three cities in provinces bordering it to the west.

Madrid province—also known as the "Comunidad de Madrid"—is a geographical kaleidoscope of plains, valleys, rivers, and mountains that belie the clichéd image of a beleaguered capital surrounded by arid badlands. The trips I recommend take you to a variety of places ranging from the known to the unknown, from the wondrous palace of **Aranjuez** and monastery of **El Escorial** to the picturesque hill village of **Patones de Arriba** and the castle town of **Manzanares el Real.**

In the provinces radiating around the "Comunidad de Madrid" you can explore the world-famous cities of **Toledo,** with its El Greco masterpieces; **Segovia,** whose fairy-tale castle seems to float in the clouds; and **Avila,** the most complete walled city in Europe.

1 Alcalá de Henares

29km (18 miles) E of Madrid

Despite its outwardly modern appearance, Alcalá de Henares is a historic city with a glorious past. Its discreetly hidden medieval center still abounds with colleges, monasteries, and palaces, and its Calle Mayor (main street) is among the oldest in Madrid province. When a university was founded here in the 15th century, Alcalá became a cultural and intellectual center. Europe's first polyglot Bible (supposedly with footnotes in the original Greek and Hebrew) was published here in 1517, but the town declined during the 1800s when the university moved to Madrid. Today, Alcalá is one of the main centers of North American academics in Spain, cooperating with the Fulbright Commission, Michigan State University, and Madrid's Washington Irving Center. Overall, the city has taken on new life. Commuters have turned it into a virtual suburb, dubbing it "the bedroom of Madrid." (Prominent among its non-commuting inhabitants is the perennial community of highly urbanized storks that nonchalantly squat in their roof- and spire-top nests or, wide winged, wheel effortlessly overhead.)

EXPLORING ALCALA DE HENARES

Colegio Mayor de San Ildefonso   Adjacent to the main square, Plaza de Cervantes, is the Colegio Mayor de San Ildefonso, where Lope de Vega and other famous Spaniards studied. You can see some of their names engraved on plaques in the examination room. The old university's Plateresque **facade** ⚜ dates from 1543. From here you can walk across the Patio of Saint Thomas (from 1662) and the Patio of the Philosophers to reach the Patio of the Three Languages (from 1557), where Greek, Latin, and Hebrew were once taught. Here is the *Paraninfo* (great hall or old examination room), now used for special events. The hall has a Mudéjar carved-panel ceiling. The Paraninfo is entered through a restaurant, **Hostería del Estudiante** (see "Where to Dine," below).

Plaza San Diego. ℂ **91-885-41-22.** Admission 3€ ($3.75). Tours (mandatory) Mon–Fri 11:30am, 12:30, 1:30, 5, and 6pm; Sat–Sun 11 and 11:45am, 12:30, 1:15, 2, 4:30, 5:15, 6, 6:45, and 7:30pm.

Museo Casa Natal de Cervantes   Visitors come to see the birthplace of Spain's literary giant Miguel de Cervantes, the creator of *Don Quixote,* who may have been born here in 1547. This 16th-century Castilian house was reconstructed in 1956 around a beautiful little courtyard, which has a wooden gallery supported by pillars with Renaissance-style capitals, plus an old well. The house contains many Cervantes manuscripts and, of course, copies of *Don Quixote,* one of the world's most widely published books (available here in many languages).

Calle Mayor 50. ℂ **91-889-96-54.** Free admission. Tues–Sun 10:15am–1:30pm and 4:15–6:30pm.

ESSENTIALS

GETTING THERE   **Trains** travel between Madrid's Atocha or Chamartín station and Alcalá de Henares every day and evening. Service is every 15 minutes (trip time: 30 min.) and round-trip fare from Madrid costs 3.35€ ($4.15). The train station (ℂ **90-224-02-02**) in Alcalá is at Paseo Estación.

   Buses from Madrid depart from Av. América 18 (Metro: América), every 15 minutes. A one-way fare is 1.90€ ($2.35). Bus service is provided by Continental-Auto, and the Alcalá bus station is on Av. Guadalajara 36 (ℂ **91-888-16-22**), 2 blocks past Calle Libreros.

   Alcalá lies adjacent to the main national highway (N-11), connecting Madrid with eastern Spain. As you leave central Madrid, follow signs for Barajas Airport and Barcelona.

VISITOR INFORMATION   The **tourist information office,** Callejón de Santa María 1 (ℂ **91-889-26-94;** www.alcaladehenares-turismo.com), provides a map showing all the local attractions. It is open daily from 10am to 2pm and 4 to 6:30pm (until 7:30pm July–Sept).

WHERE TO DINE

Hostería del Estudiante ⚜ CASTILIAN   Located within the university complex, this remarkable 1510 building is an attraction in its own right. It opened as a restaurant in 1929, and its typically Castilian recipes haven't been altered since. In the cooler months, if you arrive early you can lounge in front of a 4.5m (15-ft.) open fireplace. Oil lamps hang from the ceiling, pigskins are filled with local wine, and rope-covered chairs and high-backed carved settees capture the spirit of the past. Run by the Spanish parador system, the restaurant offers a tasty (and huge) three-course set-price lunch or dinner featuring such regional specialties as roast suckling lamb, *huevos comigos*

Madrid Environs

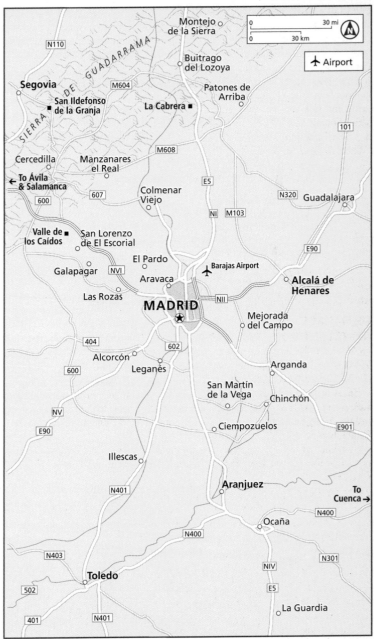

Montejo de la Sierra

Buitrago del Lozoya

N110

SIERRA DE GUADARRAMA

M604

Segovia

San Ildefonso de la Granja

La Cabrera ■

Patones de Arriba

101

✈ Airport

0   30 mi
0   30 km

Cercedilla

Manzanares el Real

M608

E5

N320

Guadalajara

← To Ávila & Salamanca

600

607

Colmenar Viejo

NI   M103

Valle de los Caídos ■

San Lorenzo de El Escorial

El Pardo

Galapagar

NVI

Aravaca

E90

Barajas Airport ✈

Alcalá de Henares

Las Rozas

MADRID ★

NII

Mejorada del Campo

404

602

Alcorcón

600

Leganés

Arganda

San Martín de la Vega

Chinchón

NV

E90

Ciempozuelos

E901

Illescas

N401

Aranjuez

To Cuenca →

N400

Ocaña

N400

N301

N403

NIV

Toledo

502

E5

401

N401

La Guardia

245

(three eggs fried with mushrooms), and trout Navarre style. For dessert, try the cheese of La Mancha.

Calle Colegios 3. © **91-888-03-30**. Reservations recommended. Main courses 21€–35€ ($26–$45); fixed-price menus 25€ ($31). AE, DC, MC, V. Daily 1–4pm; Mon–Sat 9–11:30pm; Sun 9–10:30pm. Closed Aug.

2 Aranjuez

47km (29 miles) S of Madrid, 48km (30 miles) NE of Toledo

This Castilian town, at a confluence of the Tagus and Jarama rivers, was once home to Bourbon kings in the spring and fall. With its manicured shrubbery, stately elms, fountains, and statues of the Palacio Real and surrounding compounds, Aranjuez remains a regal garden oasis in what is otherwise an unimpressive agricultural flatland known primarily for its strawberries and asparagus.

ESSENTIALS

GETTING THERE   **By Train**   Trains depart about every 20 minutes from Madrid's Atocha Railway Station to make the 50-minute trip to Aranjuez, a one-way fare costing 3€ ($3.75). Twice a day you can take an express train from Madrid to Toledo, which makes a brief stopover at Aranjuez. This trip takes only 30 minutes. Trains run less often along the east-west route to and from Toledo (a 40-min. ride). The spring highlight is the **Tren de la Fresa (Strawberry Express)** trip, taking 3 hours (the train is wooden and steam-powered). Travel on this and you get to sample local strawberries handed out by hostesses in traditional costumes. The Aranjuez station lies about 1.6km (1 mile) outside town. For information and schedules, call © **90-224-02-02**. You can walk it in about 15 minutes, but taxis and buses line up on Calle Stuart (two blocks from the city tourist office). The bus that makes the run from the center of Aranjuez to the railway station is marked N-Z.

By Bus   Buses for Aranjuez depart every 30 minutes from 7:30am to 10pm from Madrid's Estación Sur de Autobuses, Calle Méndez Alvaro. In Madrid, call © **91-530-46-05** for information. Buses arrive in Aranjuez at the City Bus Terminal, Calle Infantas 8 (© **91-891-01-83**).

By Car   Driving is easy; it takes about 30 minutes once you reach the southern city limits of Madrid. To reach Aranjuez, follow the signs to Aranjuez and Granada, taking highway N-IV.

VISITOR INFORMATION   The **tourist information office** is at Plaza de San Antonio 9 (© **91-891-04-27**), open Monday to Friday from 10am to 2pm and 4 to 6pm.

SEEING THE SIGHTS

Casa del Labrador   "The House of the Worker," modeled after the Petit Trianon at Versailles, was built in 1803 by Charles IV, who later abdicated in Aranjuez. The queen came here with her youthful lover, Godoy (whom she had elevated to the position of prime minister), and the feeble-minded Charles didn't seem to mind a bit. Surrounded by beautiful gardens, the "bedless" palace is lavishly furnished in the grand style of the 18th and 19th centuries. The marble floors represent some of the finest workmanship of that day; the brocaded walls emphasize the luxurious lifestyle; and the royal toilet is a sight to behold (in those days, royalty preferred an audience). The clock here is one of the treasures of the house. The casita lies .8km (½ mile) east of the

Royal Palace; those with a car can drive directly to it through the tranquil Jardín del Príncipe.

Calle Reina, Jardín del Príncipe. (©) **91-891-03-05**. Admission 3€ ($3.75) adults, 1.50€ ($1.85) students and children. Apr–Sept Tues–Sun 10am–6:30pm; Oct–Mar Tues–Sun 10am–5:30pm.

Jardín de la Isla ✨ After the tour of the Royal Palace, wander through the Garden of the Island. Spanish impressionist Santiago Rusiñol captured its evasive quality on canvas, and one Spanish writer said that you walk here "as if softly lulled by a sweet 18th-century sonata." A number of fountains are remarkable: the "Ne Plus Ultra" fountain, the black-jasper fountain of Bacchus, the fountain of Apollo, and the ones honoring Neptune (god of the sea) and Cybele (goddess of agriculture).

You may also stroll through the Jardín del Parterre, located in front of the palace. It's much better kept than the Garden of the Island, but not as romantic.

Directly northwest of the Palacio Real. No phone. Free admission. Apr–Sept daily 8am–8:30pm; Oct–Mar daily 8am–6:30pm.

Palacio Real ✨✨ Since the beginning of a united Spain, the climate and natural beauty of Aranjuez have attracted Spanish monarchs: Ferdinand and Isabella; Philip II, when he managed to tear himself away from El Escorial; Philip V; and Charles III.

The structure you see today dates from 1778 (the previous buildings were destroyed by fire). The palace is lavishly and elegantly decorated: Salons show the opulence of a bygone era, with room after room of royal extravagance. Especially notable are the dancing salon, the throne room, the ceremonial dining hall, the bedrooms of the king and queen, and a remarkable Salón de Porcelana (Porcelain Room). Paintings include works by Lucas Jordan and José Ribera. A guide conducts you through the huge complex (a tip is expected).

Plaza Palacio. (©) **91-891-13-44**. Admission 5€ ($6) adults, 2.40€ ($3) students and children. Tues–Sun 10am–6:15pm. Bus: Routes from the rail station converge at the square and gardens at the westernmost edge of the palace.

WHERE TO STAY
Hostal Castilla *Value* On one of the town's main streets north of the Royal Palace and gardens, the Castilla consists of the ground floor and part of the first floor of a well-preserved early-18th-century house. Most of the accommodations overlook a courtyard with a fountain and flowers. All units contain well-kept bathrooms. Owner Martín Soria, who speaks English fluently, suggests that reservations be made at least a month in advance. There are excellent restaurants nearby, and the *hostal* has an arrangement with a neighboring bar to provide guests with an inexpensive lunch. This is a good location from which to explore either Madrid or Toledo on a day trip.

Carretera Andalucía 98, 28300 Aranjuez. (©) **91-891-26-27**. 22 units. 54€ ($68) double. AE, DC, MC, V. Free parking on street. Rates include breakfast. **Amenities:** Lounge; laundry/dry cleaning. *In room:* A/C, TV.

WHERE TO DINE
Casa José ✨✨ SPANISH/INTERNATIONAL Set near Town Hall and the Church of Antonio, this well-managed restaurant occupies two ground-floor rooms of a 300-year-old house in the heart of town; it's the premier restaurant of the entire area, and local gastronomes drive for miles around to dine here. The regionally based repertoire of food is prepared with an intelligent association of flavors. Any of the daily offerings is well worth ordering. Menu items focus on fresh ingredients that the staff buys every morning at the town markets. Look for a menu that changes at least four times a year, with an emphasis on pork, veal, fish, chicken, and shellfish. Of special

note are braised lamb chops in a fresh tomato and cilantro sauce, Jabugo ham with broad beans, shrimp in garlic sauce, hake with green sauce, and thick juicy steaks.

Calle Abastos 32. ℭ **91-891-14-88**. Reservations recommended. Main courses 18€–24€ ($23–$30). AE, DC, MC, V. Tues–Sun 1–4pm and Tues–Sat 9pm–midnight.

La Rana Verde ☆ SPANISH   "The Green Frog," just east of the Royal Palace and next to a small bridge spanning the Tagus, is still the traditional choice for many. Opened in 1905 by Tomás Díaz Heredero, it is owned and run by a third-generation member of his family, who has decorated it in a 1920s style. The restaurant looks like a summerhouse, with its high-beamed ceiling and soft ferns drooping from hanging baskets. The preferred tables are in the nooks overlooking the river. As in all the restaurants of Aranjuez, asparagus is a special feature. Game, particularly partridge, quail, and pigeon, can be recommended in season; fish, too, including fried hake and fried sole, makes a good choice. Strawberries are served with sugar, orange juice, or ice cream.

Reina 1. ℭ **91-891-32-38**. Reservations recommended. Main courses 8€–25€ ($10–$31); fixed-price menu 15€–24€ ($19–$30). MC, V. Daily 9pm–midnight.

3 Buitrago del Lozoya

75km (47 miles) N of Madrid

The only township inside Madrid province to have retained its original Arabic walls, charming Buitrago is the last stop before the high Somosierra pass at the eastern end of the province's northerly mountain range. Poised like the prow of a ship on the curve of the Lozoya River, this small town of just over a thousand inhabitants boasts a picturesque medieval center and a unique little Picasso museum. To the east lies the slate and shrub-dotted Sierra Negra (Black Mountains), replete with hidden streams, reservoirs, and villages, one of which, Montejo de la Sierra, shelters the most southerly beech tree forest in Europe.

ESSENTIALS
GETTING THERE   By Bus   Continental Auto buses (Línea Sierra Norte) depart from the Plaza Castilla Intercambiador station hourly and the journey time is about 90 minutes. They operate between 6:15am and 11pm on weekdays and between 8am and 10:30pm on Saturday and Sunday. Last bus back to Madrid is at 8pm (ℭ **91-314-57-55**).

By Car   Take the northerly N-1 highway which leads straight through Buitrago del Lozoya on its way to Burgos. Once clear of the city you should get there easily in an hour.

VISITOR INFORMATION   The **town hall** in Buitrago (ℭ **91-868-00-56**) gives useful local information. Also go to **www.buitrago.org**.

SEEING THE SIGHTS
IN TOWN
Alcázar   This ruined medieval castle in the town center was declared a national monument in 1931. The well-preserved ramparts enclose the former courtyard where—amazingly—summer bullfights are now held. Early in the new year, notwithstanding the mountain cold, locals reenact biblical scenes in living tableaux known as the *Belén Viviente* here.

Buitrago del Lozoya

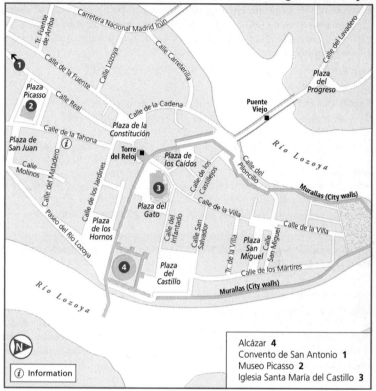

Alcázar **4**
Convento de San Antonio **1**
Museo Picasso **2**
Iglesia Santa María del Castillo **3**

Iglesia Santa María del Castillo   Within in the castle grounds this Gothic church is reached via a vaulted arch and is noted for its 17th-century sepulchers and Mudéjar tower. Unusually, the interior also features Bulgarian icons created by an artist living close by.

La Murallas   The outer walls that surround the city, still intact from the times of the Arabic occupation, date from the 11th century. The tiny **Paseo de la Concha (Shell Promenade)** running alongside their eastern edge beside the river is a particularly peaceful and attractive spot.

Museo Picasso   Located in the same building as the town hall, this unique little museum contain relics and souvenirs given to Picasso's barber, a Buitrago native called Eugenio Arias, when the two Spaniards shared a post–civil war exile in southern France. Among the small but priceless exhibits are a wooden "Barber's Box" with pyrographed bullfight scenes and various ink sketches.

OUT OF TOWN

Convento de San Antonio *(finds*   Founded in the 11th century, this little-known gem is the oldest convent in Madrid province. Noted for its exceptionally well-preserved tower, it nestles idyllically on the richly wooded slopes of La Cabrera mountain just 15km (9.4 miles) south of Buitrago and some 60km (37 miles) from the capital. The most practical way to get here is by rental car, though it's possible to catch the Buitrago bus from Madrid to the village of La Cabrera, at the base of the mountain, and take the steep 45-minute walk up. The trip's well worth the effort whichever way you make it—the views from the monastery are superb.

℡ 91-868-85-61. Open to public Tues, Thurs, Sat, and Sun 11:30am–1pm and 5–6:30pm.

WHERE TO STAY
Hostal Madrid-París A modest but comfortable converted stone house on the outskirts of town, just on your right as you arrive. The *hostal* offers excellent-value rooms and a neat traditional dining room.

Av. de Madrid 23. ℡ 91-868-11-26. 25 units. 30€ ($38) double. V. **Amenities:** Restaurant. *In room:* A/C, TV.

WHERE TO DINE
Mesón Serrano Attractive old-fashioned hostelry specializing in Castilian roast dishes. Try the outstanding lamb, which is cooked in a traditional oven.

Real 30. (facing the town hall). ℡ 91-868-01-13. Main courses 15€–20€ ($19–$25). V. Daily 1:30–5pm.

4 Cercedilla

57km (35 miles) NW of Madrid

By the time you reach this laid-back little town you're already in the foothills of the Guadarrama mountains and the hassle of the big city is far, far behind you. If you come by train, the center—with its cafes, small square, and alpine-style chalets and modern apartments—is hidden over to your right. The main attraction of Cercedilla, though, is that it's a walker's paradise with a variety of sylvan trails leading off from the pine-wooded Fuenfría Valley that rises just ahead of you, blending into enticing ridges and peaks above the town.

ESSENTIALS
GETTING THERE   By Train By far the most convenient way to get to Cercedilla is by *cercanías* (suburban line C-8b) train from Chamartín. They run at least once an hour and the journey time is an hour and 20 minutes. Once at the town you can take an additional single-gauge train trip via Puerto de Navacerrada and spectacular pine forest scenery up to the 1,700m-high (5,577-ft.) Cotos—a ski center in winter and mountain walker's base in summer. This runs every 2 hours and the trip last 40 minutes. The last train back to Madrid leaves Cercedilla at 10:35pm.

By Bus The Larrea bus company provides an hourly service (no. 684) from Moncloa bus station.

By Car Take the N-VI highway to Guadarrama town and then bear left on the M-995 which brings you to Cercedilla.

VISITOR INFORMATION   An information office is located in the town center near the town hall (℡ 91-852-02-00). A kilometer inland from the railway station is the **Fuenfría Valley Information Center,** which gives details of six differently graded walks in the area along routes where tree trunks are marked in different colors according to each individual route so you don't lose your way. It's open all year-round from 9am to 6pm except for the following Christmas and New Year fiesta days: December 25 and 31 and January 1 and 6.

SEEING THE SIGHTS   Although the surrounding scenery provides the major attractions, the town's main church, the **Iglesia Parroquial de San Sebastián**— originally medieval Romanesque and rebuilt after the civil war—is well worth a look. It also enjoys spectacular views of the Guadarrama Valley.

Inland up the Fuenfría Valley, the **Calzada Romana (Roman Road)** is the real thing, with original stones and remains of four Roman bridges along its route. It's a tiny section of a road that once connected the township of Titulcia south of Madrid with Segovia on the other side of the mountains.

WHERE TO STAY

Hostal El Aribel ⚐   This is the best and most atmospheric place to bed down. Vaguely alpine in style, it was once a hostelry for miners. Today it's noted for its warm timber decor, neat well-appointed rooms, and friendly service. (A sister hotel, **Los Longinos,** with similar standards and amenities, adjoins it.)

Emilio Serrano 71. ✆ **91-852-15-11.** 50 units. 45€ ($56) double. V. **Amenities:** Lounge; bar. *In room:* TV, central heating.

WHERE TO DINE

Casa Gómez   This highly regarded traditional eating spot is on the first floor of a building right opposite the railway station. Dishes like *sopa de hongos y castañas* (mushroom and chestnut soup) and *merluza con almejas y gambas* (hake with clams and prawns) are among the menu's main attractions.

Emilio Serrano 40. ✆ **91-852-01-46.** Dinner main courses 10€–15€ ($13–$19); lunch 10€ ($13). V. Fri–Sat 1–5pm and 9pm–midnight.

---

5 Chinchón

52km (32 miles) SE of Madrid, 26km (16 miles) NE of Aranjuez

Many visitors to Chinchón are attracted by the *cuevas* **(caves),** where Anís de Chinchón, a strong digestive aniseed spirit, is manufactured, and you can buy bottles of Chinchón *dulce, seco,* or *extra seco* at shops in the center of town. But it's the **Plaza Mayor** ⚐⚐, or main square, that's the real architectural highlight of Chinchón and the image that will linger on in the memory long after you've returned home. Dominated by its church, this photogenic arcaded plaza—which captivated artist Goya in the 18th century—is surrounded by three-story frame houses with wooden balconies, and in summer its central lamppost is removed, cars that usually park there are told to park elsewhere, and—shazam!—you have a colorful *plaza de toros* where half a dozen top bullfights take place between June and September.

Wander along the town's steep and narrow streets, past houses with large bays and spacious carriageways. Although closed to the public, the 15th-century **Chinchón Castle,** seat of the Condes of Chinchón, can be viewed from outside. The most interesting church, **Nuestra Señora de la Asunción,** dating from the 16th and 17th centuries, contains a painting by Goya.

GETTING THERE   Chinchón is most often visited from Aranjuez (see earlier in this chapter), which is only a 15-minute ride away. **Buses** run twice a day from Aranjuez but only Monday through Friday, leaving from Calle Almíbar next to the Plaza de Toros in Aranjuez. Schedules tend to be erratic, so call for information (✆ **91-891-01-83**). A one-way fare is 1.55€ ($1.90).

You can drive from Alcalá to Toledo, bypassing Madrid by taking the C-300 in a southwesterly arc around the capital. About halfway there, follow signs to CUEVAS DE CHINCHON. Another option is to take the E-901 southeast of Madrid toward Valencia, turning southwest at the turnoff for Chinchón.

WHERE TO STAY

Parador de Chinchón 🎔🎔🎔   Set near the town center, this hotel lies within the carefully restored 17th-century walls of what was originally an Augustinian convent. After a stint as both a civic jail and a courthouse, it was transformed in 1972 into a government-run parador and is the best place to stay in town. A team of architects and designers converted it handsomely, with glass-walled hallways opening onto a stone-sided courtyard. The hotel has two bars and two dining halls. Severely dignified rooms still manage to convey their ecclesiastical origins. Rooms range from small to medium, each with a quality mattress and fine linens along with well-maintained tiled bathrooms with showers.

Av. Generalísimo 1, 28370 Chinchón. ✆ **91-894-08-36.** Fax 91-894-09-08. www.paradores.es. 38 units 130€ ($162) double; 175€ ($219) suite. AE, DC, MC, V. Parking 9€ ($11). **Amenities:** Restaurant; bar; outdoor pool (June–Sept only); room service; babysitting; laundry service; dry cleaning. *In room:* A/C, TV, minibar, hair dryer, safe.

WHERE TO DINE

Mesón Cuevas del Vino 🎔 SPANISH   This establishment is known for its wine cellars, and you can sample the stock at lunch or dinner. Hanging from the rafters are hams cured by the owners, along with flavorful homemade spiced sausages. Chunks of ham and sausage cooked in oil, plus olives and crunchy bread, are served. Your meal might begin with sliced *chorizo* (Spanish sausage); blood pudding; slices of La Mancha cheese; *sopa castellana* made with garlic, ham, and eggs; and thin-sliced cured ham. Main courses place heavy emphasis on roast suckling lamb and pig that emerge crackling from a wood-burning oven. Desserts include flan, biscuits coated in cinnamon and sugar, and liquefied and sweetened almonds presented in a soupy mixture in a bowl.

Benito Horteliano 13. ✆ **91-894-02-85.** Reservations recommended on holidays. Main courses 6€–20€ ($7.50–$25). No credit cards. Wed–Mon 1:30–4pm and 8–11pm. Closed Aug 1–20.

6 Manzanares el Real

48km (30 miles) N to NW of Madrid

Located near the source of the River Manzanares, this charming little town is well worth the trip for two very good reasons. First and foremost, to see its famous medieval castle, best preserved in the entire province of Madrid. Second, to explore the Cuenca Alta del Manzanares national park, whose astonishing Pedriza rock formations provide a fairy-tale backdrop to both town and castle and are an ideal location for walking and picnicking.

ESSENTIALS
GETTING THERE

By Bus   The Hnos. De Colmenarejo SL 724 bus runs regularly from the Plaza Castilla Intercambiador station. The journey lasts about an hour.

By Car   Take the M-607 to Cerceda and then swing right on to the M-608 which brings you straight to Manzanares.

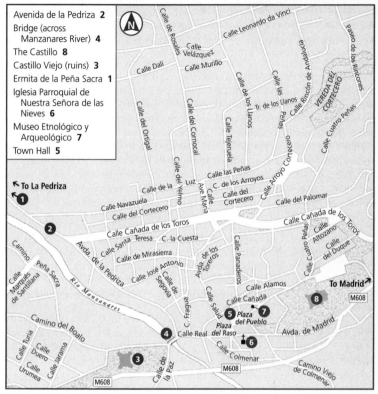

Avenida de la Pedriza **2**

Bridge (across
Manzanares River) **4**

The Castillo **8**

Castillo Viejo (ruins) **3**

Ermita de la Peña Sacra **1**

Iglesia Parroquial de
Nuestra Señora de las
Nieves **6**

Museo Etnológico y
Arqueológico **7**

Town Hall **5**

VISITOR INFORMATION

Staff at the **Town Hall,** Plaza del Pueblo 1 (© **91-853-00-09**), will give you full information on the town and its castle. There is also a small information kiosk at the
entrance to the castle.

SEEING THE SIGHTS

The **castillo** (© **91-853-00-08**) stands beside the Santillana reservoir, its high turrets
reflecting in the clear still waters. Built in 1475 by the powerful Mendoza family, it
was eventually converted into a palace. The original Mudéjar and Gothic walls
remain, and the tastefully renovated interior hosts a library, observatory, exhibition
room (named after the Marqués de Santillana), and tapestry-lined vestibule. From
here, climb to the parapets with their octagonal keep and trio of cylindrical towers and
enjoy the superb mountain and reservoir views. It's open Tuesday to Sunday June to
September 10am to 1:15pm and 4 to 7:15pm, October to May 10am to 5:15pm.
Admission is 1.80€ ($2.25), concessionary charges .80€ ($1).

The **Iglesia Parroquial de Nuestra Señora de la Nieves** also dates from the 15th
century and has a fine Renaissance portal. It's home to a permanent colony of storks
who have made nests on its roof.

Museo Etnológico y Arqueológico Tiny museum dedicated to ethnology and archaeology with background prehistoric information on the surrounding area.

In the Casa de Cultura in the town center. ✆ 91-853-03-40. Free admission. Daily 5–9pm.

La Pedriza As spectacular a natural phenomenon as you'll find in the whole province, the surrealistically shaped granite formations of La Pedriza rise 2km (1¼ miles) north of the town, just off the road to Real de Cerceda. The surrounding paths and gullies of the Cuenca Alta de Manzanares national park are best avoided on weekends—especially in summer—when they tend to get packed with picnickers and hikers. Don't miss the marvelous views from the mirador at the Quebrantaherraduras Pass.

Near the entrance to the park, 3km (1¾ miles) above the town on Carretera de la Pedriza, you can visit the **Centro de Interpretación** (✆ **91-853-99-78**). This information center provides interesting facts on La Pedriza (geography, history, legends, and so on) and is open daily from 10am to 6pm. Short audiovisual shows about the park are given at 10 and 11:30am, and 1, 1:30, and 4:45pm. Admission is free.

Ermita de la Peña Sacra This tiny 16th-century hermitage, set high up in the national park's wild Peña Sacra (Holy Peak) area, also enjoys spectacular vistas. To get to it, follow Avenida de Pedriza up from the town. Unfortunately, the interior is now closed to the public (due to earlier instances of vandalism). You can, however, see the interior shrine through the window and take photographs of the simple but charming exterior. From its high vantage point, the Ermita enjoys spectacular views of the surrounding countryside.

WHERE TO STAY

El Tranco This modest hostelry offers neat comfortable rooms and a homely atmosphere at very reasonable prices. It's popular and tends to get fully booked on weekends, so best to reserve in advance or go midweek.

Tranco 4. ✆ 91-853-00-63. 9 units. 30€ ($38) double with bathroom in hallway; 45€ ($56) double with private bathroom. V. **Amenities:** Restaurant. *In room:* TV.

WHERE TO DINE

Casa Goyo One of the town's favorite eating spots, the Goya provides a wide variety of delicious but uncompromisingly traditional dishes ranging from *cabrito asado* (roast kid) to *chipirones en su tinta* (cuttlefish cooked in its own ink). It prides itself on using fresh market produce in all its dishes, and these are priced accordingly.

Plaza del Sagrado Corazón 2. ✆ **91-853-94-84**. Main courses 15€–20€ ($19–$25). V. Mon–Tues, Thurs–Sun 1:30–4pm and 9pm–midnight.

7 Patones de Arriba

60km (37 miles) NW of Madrid

A highly atmospheric village of black slate houses, Patones de Arriba (Upper Patones) clings to the rugged slopes of the Sierra Negra in the mountainous northwest corner of Madrid province, enjoying fine views of the Jarama valley and distant cliff-top township of Uceda just inside the Guadalajara border. Its claims to fame are that it once had its own peasant king (who thought himself the equal of Felipe II) and it was one of the few spots unconquered by the French in the Peninsula War. After decades of abandon it has reemerged in recent years as a favorite getaway spot for Madrileños, dotted with fine restaurants and tastefully converted houses, and surrounded by off-the-beaten-track walking trails. Its modern counterpart Patones de Abajo (Lower Patones), 2km (1¼ miles) below, is in contrast a functional town with a single main street bordered by modern low-level houses.

ESSENTIALS

GETTING THERE **By Bus** The Continental Auto SA 197 bus runs several times a day from the Plaza Castilla Intercambiador through Torrelaguna to Patones de Abajo. From here you can either catch a taxi or follow the steep path up a gorge to the village, depending on how energetic you're feeling.

By Car Drive up the N-1 Burgos highway to Venturada, then take the N-320 to Torrelaguna, and finally take the M-102, which brings you right to Patones de Arriba's tiny main square.

VISITOR INFORMATION Situated right on the square is the village's surprisingly well-equipped **Centro Initiativas Turisticas Educativas Culturales y de Ocio (CITECO),** occupying a stone house with the grandiose name of Palacio de los Reyes de Patones. Here you can follow Patones' history from ancient times right up to the present via a series of plans, sketches, and scaled models. You can also watch a half-hour video. It's on Plaza de Llano (✆ **91-843-20-26** weekdays, or 91-843-29-06 weekends). It's open Saturday, Sunday, and fiestas from noon to 6pm.

SEEING THE SIGHTS The whole village is a scenic delight where you can wander along higgledy-piggledy lanes, look at slate houses whose wild gardens overflow with luminous oleander bushes and outsize fig trees, and get enjoyably lost.

Torrelaguna This larger town just 7km (4⅓ miles) away is worth a visit on its own to see its monasteries, ancient walls, and magnificent 16th-century main square and church of Santa María Magdalena.

Presa de Atazar One of the walks to the north leads you to this dam bordering a reservoir fringed by pine woods. In summer it's a great spot for picnicking or enjoying watersports.

Cueva del Reguerillo Hidden away near the Atazar dam is this small but impressive cave whose stalactites and prehistoric sketches earned it a rating as an artistic-historic monument in 1931.

WHERE TO STAY

El Tiempo Perdido 🏵🏵 Outwardly resembling just another village house, this is in fact one of the most original and prestigious little hotels in the whole of Madrid province. Its individually furnished rooms have all been in furnished in superb taste by its French owner with fine paintings, antiques, and quality linens. There's also a choice of classic videos if you're a movie buff. Booking ahead is essential.

Travesía del Ayuntamiento 7. ✆ **91-843-21-52.** Reservations: 650-381-730. 7 units. Double 180€–260€ ($225–$325). MC, V. Fri–Sun and certain fiestas only. Closed Aug. **Amenities:** Lounge.

WHERE TO DINE

El Poleo Regarded by many as Patones' top eating spot, this beautifully converted village house exudes atmosphere and style. The cuisine is mainly French Basque influenced, and specialties include *cordero en miel de Patones* (roast lamb cooked in Patones honey). (Opposite is a twin eating spot, **El Jardín del Poleo,** with a large outdoor terrace ideal for summer dining.)

Travesía de Arroyo 1. ℂ **91-843-21-01.** Main courses 16€–25€ ($20–$31). No credit cards. Fri–Sun and fiesta days 2–5pm and 9:30pm–midnight.

8 San Lorenzo de El Escorial ✟★

48km (30 miles) W of Madrid, 52km (32 miles) SE of Segovia

Without a doubt one of the most unforgettable excursions from Madrid is to the austere royal monastery of San Lorenzo de El Escorial. Philip II ordered the construction of this granite-and-slate behemoth in 1563, 2 years after he moved his capital to Madrid. Once the haunt of aristocratic Spaniards, El Escorial is now a resort where hotels and restaurants flourish in summer, as hundreds come to escape the heat of the capital. Aside from the appeal of its climate, the town of San Lorenzo itself is not very noteworthy. But because of the monastery's size, you might decide to spend a night or two at San Lorenzo—or more if you have the time.

ESSENTIALS
GETTING THERE   By Train   More than two dozen trains depart daily from Madrid's Atocha, Nuevos Ministerios, and Chamartín train stations. Trip time is little more than an hour. During the summer extra coaches are added. For schedules and information, call ℂ **90-224-02-02.** A one-way fare costs 2.80€ ($3.50).

The railway station for San Lorenzo de El Escorial is located about 1.6km (1 mile) outside of town along Carretera Estación (ℂ **91-890-07-14**). The Herranz bus company meets all arriving trains with a shuttle bus that ferries arriving passengers to and from the Plaza Virgen de Gracia, about a block east of the entrance to the monastery.

By Bus   The Office of Empresa Herranz, Calle Reina Victoria 3, in El Escorial (ℂ **91-890-41-22** or 91-890-41-25), runs some 40 buses per day back and forth between Madrid and El Escorial. On Sunday, service is curtailed to 10 buses. Trip time is an hour, and a round-trip fare costs 5.50€ ($6.90). The same company also runs one bus a day to El Valle de los Caídos. It leaves El Escorial at 3:15pm with a return at 5:30pm. The ride takes only 15 minutes, and a round-trip fare is 8€ ($10), El Valle only.

By Car   Follow the N-VI highway (marked on some maps as A-6) from the northwest perimeter of Madrid toward Lugo, La Coruña, and San Lorenzo de El Escorial. After about a half-hour, fork left onto the C-505 toward San Lorenzo de El Escorial. Driving time from Madrid is about an hour.

VISITOR INFORMATION   The **tourist information office** is at Calle Grimaldi 2 (ℂ **91-890-53-13**). It is open Monday to Thursday from 11am to 6pm, Friday to Sunday from 10am to 7pm.

⸨Tips⸩ A More Convenient Base than Madrid

San Lorenzo makes a good base for visiting nearby Segovia, the royal palace at La Granja, and the Valley of the Fallen.

SEEING THE SIGHTS

Casa de Príncipe (Prince's Cottage) ⧉   This small but elaborately decorated 18th-century palace near the railway station was originally a hunting lodge built for Charles III by Juan de Villanueva. Most visitors stay in El Escorial for lunch, visiting the cottage in the afternoon.

Calle Reina s/n. ℂ **91-890-59-03.** Admission included in comprehensive ticket to Real Monasterio de San Lorenzo de El Escorial (see below). Sat–Sun and holidays 10am–6:45pm.

El Valle de los Caídos (Valley of the Fallen) ⧉   This is Franco's El Escorial, an architectural marvel that took 2 decades to complete, dedicated to those who died in the Spanish Civil War. Its detractors say that it represents the worst of neofascist design; its admirers say they have found renewed inspiration by coming here.

A gargantuan cross nearly 150m high (492 ft.) dominates the Rock of Nava, a peak of the Guadarrama Mountains. Directly under the cross is a basilica with a vault in mosaic, completed in 1959. Here José Antonio Primo de Rivera, the founder of the Falange party, is buried. When this Nationalist hero was buried at El Escorial, many, especially influential monarchists, protested that he was not a royal. Infuriated, Franco decided to erect another monument. Originally it was slated to honor the dead on the Nationalist side only, but the intervention of several parties led to a decision to include all the *caídos* (fallen). In time the mausoleum claimed Franco as well; his body was interred behind the high altar.

A funicular extends from near the entrance to the basilica to the base of the gigantic cross erected on the mountaintop above (where there's a superb view). The fare is 2.50 € ($3.10) round trip, and the funicular runs daily from 10:30am to 1:15pm and 4 to 6pm.

On the other side of the mountain is a Benedictine monastery that has sometimes been dubbed "the Hilton of monasteries" because of its seeming luxury.

ℂ **91-890-56-11.** Admission 5€ ($6.25) adults, 2.90€ ($3.60) students and children. Apr–Sept Tues–Sun 9:30am–6pm; Oct–Mar Tues–Sun 10am–7pm. Bus: Tour buses from Madrid usually include an excursion to the Valley of the Fallen on their 1-day trips to El Escorial (see "By Bus," above). By Car: Drive to the valley entrance, about 8km (5 miles) north of El Escorial in the heart of the Guadarrama Mountains. Once here, drive 6km (3½ miles) west along a wooded road to the underground basilica.

Real Monasterio de San Lorenzo de El Escorial ⧉⧉⧉   This huge granite fortress houses a wealth of paintings and tapestries and also serves as a burial place for Spanish kings. Foreboding both inside and out because of its sheer size and institutional look, El Escorial took 21 years to complete, a remarkably short time considering the bulk of the building and the primitive construction methods of the day. After his death, the original architect, Juan Bautista de Toledo, was replaced by Juan de Herrera, the greatest architect of Renaissance Spain, who completed the structure.

Philip II, who collected many of the paintings exhibited here in the New Museums, did not appreciate El Greco and favored Titian instead. But you'll still find El Greco's *The Martyrdom of St. Maurice,* rescued from storage, and his *St. Peter.* Other superb works include Titian's *Last Supper* and Velázquez's *The Tunic of Joseph.*

The **Royal Library** houses a priceless collection of 60,000 volumes—one of the most significant in the world. The displays range from the handwriting of St. Teresa to medieval instructions on playing chess. See, in particular, the Muslim codices and a Gothic *Cantigas* from the 13th-century reign of Alfonso X ("The Wise").

You can also visit the **Philip II Apartments;** these are strictly monastic, and Philip called them the "cell for my humble self" in this "palace for God." Philip became a religious fanatic and requested that his bedroom be erected overlooking the altar of the 90m-high (295-ft.) basilica, which has four organs and whose dome is based on Michelangelo's drawings for St. Peter's. The choir contains a crucifix by Cellini. By comparison, the Throne Room is simple. On the walls are many ancient maps. The Apartments of the Bourbon Kings are lavishly decorated, in contrast to Philip's preference for the ascetic.

Under the altar of the church you'll find one of the most regal mausoleums in the world, the **Royal Pantheon,** where most of Spain's monarchs—from Charles I to Alfonso XII, including Philip II—are buried. In 1993 Don Juan de Borbón, the count of Barcelona and the father of King Juan Carlos (Franco passed over the count and never allowed him to ascend to the throne), was interred nearby. On a lower floor is the "Wedding Cake" tomb for children.

Allow at least 3 hours for a visit. The guided tour doesn't take you to all the sites, but you are free to explore on your own afterward.

Calle Juan de Borbón s/n. (C) **91-890-59-03**. Comprehensive ticket 8€ ($10) adults, 4€ ($5) children, guided tour 9€ ($11). Free on Wednesdays. Apr–Sept Tues–Sun 10am–7pm; Oct–Mar Tues–Sun 10am–6pm.

WHERE TO STAY
MODERATE
Hotel Botánico ✿✿ True to its name, the hotel stands in a lovely manicured garden consisting of both indigenous and exotic shrubbery. Although the building is traditionally Castilian, the decor seems vaguely alpine, with wood paneling and beams in the reception rooms. The clean, well-lit rooms are large and comfortable, with well-kept bathrooms. There is a restaurant inside the hotel.

Calle Timoteo Padros 16, 28200 San Lorenzo de El Escorial. (C) **91-890-78-79**. Fax 91-890-81-58. 20 units. 115€– 150€ ($144–$188) double; 215€ ($269) suite. Breakfast included. AE, V. Free parking. **Amenities:** Restaurant; bar; room service; babysitting; laundry/dry cleaning. *In room:* A/C, TV, minibar, hair dryer.

Hotel Victoria Palace ✿✿ The Victoria Palace, with its view of El Escorial, is the finest hotel in town, a traditional establishment that has been modernized without losing its special aura of style and comfort. The rooms (some with private terraces) are well furnished and maintained. All units contain neatly kept bathrooms. The rates are reasonable enough, and a bargain for a government-rated four-star hotel. The dining room serves some of the best food in town.

Calle Juan de Toledo 4, 28200 San Lorenzo de El Escorial. (C) **91-896-98-90**. Fax 91-896-98-96. www.hotelvictoria palace.com. 87 units. 120€–145€ ($150–$181) double. AE, MC, V. Parking 11€ ($13). **Amenities:** Restaurant; bar; room service; outdoor pool (June–Sept); babysitting; laundry service; dry cleaning. *In room:* TV, hair dryer, safe.

INEXPENSIVE
Hostal Cristina ✿ 🅥𝐚𝐥𝐮𝐞 An excellent budget choice, this hotel is run by the Delgado family, which opened it in the mid-1980s. It doesn't pretend to compete with the comfort and amenities of the Victoria Palace (see above), but it has its devotees nonetheless. About 45m (148 ft.) from the monastery, it stands in the center of town, offering clean and comfortable but simply furnished rooms. Every room has a well-kept bathroom. The helpful staff will direct you to the small garden. The food served in the restaurant is both good and plentiful, making this a popular booking among Spanish visitors for a summer holiday. Parking is available along the street.

Juan de Toledo 6, 28200 San Lorenzo de El Escorial. (C) 91-890-19-61. Fax 91-890-12-04. 16 units. 45€–50€ ($56–$63) double. MC, V. **Amenities:** Lounge. *In room:* TV.

WHERE TO DINE
MODERATE
Charolés ✰ SPANISH/INTERNATIONAL   The thick and solid walls of this establishment date, according to its managers, "from the monastic age"—and probably predate the town's larger and better-known monastery of El Escorial. The restaurant contained within was established around 1980, and has been known ever since as the best dining room in town. It has a flower-ringed outdoor terrace for use during clement weather. The cuisine doesn't quite rate a star, but chances are you'll be satisfied. The wide choice of menu items based entirely on fresh fish and meats includes such dishes as grilled hake with green or hollandaise sauce, shellfish soup, pepper steak, a *pastel* (pie) of fresh vegetables with crayfish, and herb-flavored baby lamb chops. Strawberry or kiwi tart is a good dessert choice.

Calle Floridablanca 24. (C) 91-890-59-75. Reservations required. Main courses 18€–28€ ($23–$35). AE, DC, MC, V. Daily 1–4pm and 9pm–midnight.

NEAR THE VALLEY OF THE FALLEN
Hostelería Valle de los Caídos SPANISH   There aren't a lot of dining options around the Valley of the Fallen, and of the few that exist, this is about as good a bet as you'll get. Built in 1956, it's set amid a dry but dramatic landscape halfway along the inclined access road leading to Franco's monuments, reachable only by car or bus. It's a mammoth modern structure with wide terraces and floor-to-ceiling windows. The *menú del día* usually includes such dishes as cannelloni Rossini, pork chops with potatoes, a dessert choice of flan or fruit, and wine. The typical fare of roast chicken, roast lamb, shellfish, and paella is somewhat cafeteria-style in nature.

Valle de los Caídos. (C) 91-890-55-11. Reservations not accepted. Fixed-price menu 10€ ($13). No credit cards. Tues–Sun 9–10am, 2–3:30pm, and 9–10pm. Closed Dec 15–Jan 15.

EL ESCORIAL AFTER DARK
No longer the dead place it was during the long Franco era, the town comes alive at night, fueled mainly by the throngs of young people who pack into the bars and taverns, especially those along Calle Rey and Calle Floridablanca. Some of my favorite bars, offering vats of wine or kegs of beer, include the **Piano Bar Regina,** Floridablanca ((C) 91-890-68-43); **Gurriato,** Leindro Rubio 3 ((C) 91-890-47-10); and **Don Felipe II,** Floridablanca ((C) 91-896-07-65). The hottest disco is **Move it,** Plaza de Santiago 11 ((C) 91-890-54-91), which rarely imposes a cover unless some special group is featured.

9 Toledo ✰✰

68km (42 miles) SW of Madrid, 137km (85 miles) SE of Avila

Don't miss a trip to Toledo—a place made special by its Arab, Jewish, Christian, and even Roman and Visigothic elements. A national landmark, the city that so inspired El Greco in the 16th century has remained relatively unchanged. You can still stroll through streets barely wide enough for a man and his donkey—much less for an automobile.

Surrounded on three sides by a bend in the Tagus River, Toledo stands atop a hill overlooking the arid plains of New Castile—a natural fortress in the center of the Iberian Peninsula. It was a logical choice for the capital of Spain, though it lost its political

Toledo

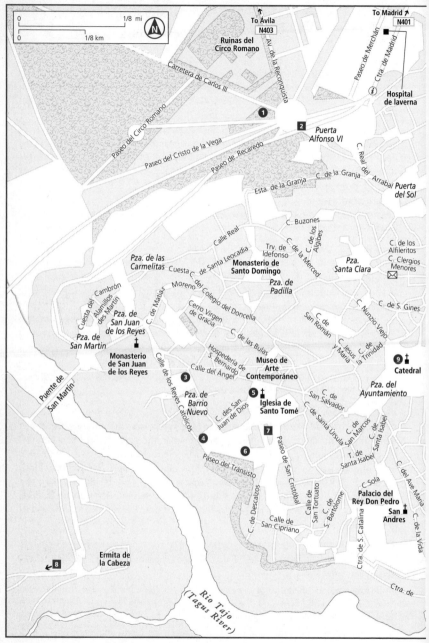

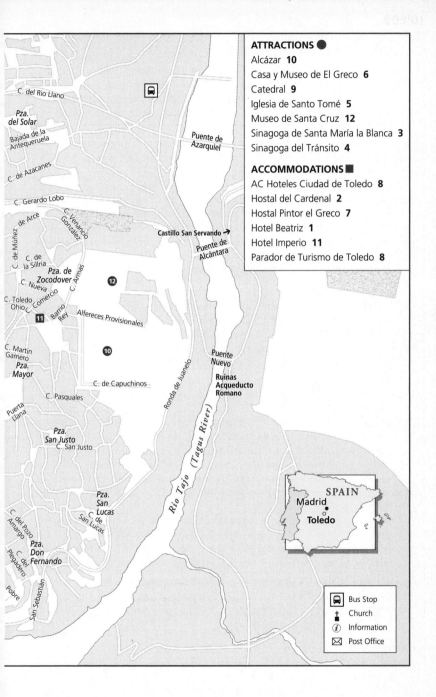

ATTRACTIONS ●
Alcázar **10**
Casa y Museo de El Greco **6**
Catedral **9**
Iglesia de Santo Tomé **5**
Museo de Santa Cruz **12**
Sinagoga de Santa María la Blanca **3**
Sinagoga del Tránsito **4**

ACCOMMODATIONS ■
AC Hoteles Ciudad de Toledo **8**
Hostal del Cardenal **2**
Hostal Pintor el Greco **7**
Hotel Beatriz **1**
Hotel Imperio **11**
Parador de Turismo de Toledo **8**

C. del Rio Llano
Pza. del Solar
Bajada de la Antequeruela
C. de Azacanes
C. Gerardo Lobo
de Arce
C. de Muñez
C. Venancio González
C. de la Sillria
Pza. de Zocodover
C. Nueva
C. Armas
C. Comercio
C. Toledo Ohio
Barrio Rey
Alfereces Provisionales
C. Martin Gamero
Pza. Mayor
C. de Capuchinos
C. Pasquales
Puerta Llana
Pza. San Justo
C. San Justo
Pza. San Lucas
C. de San Lucas
C. del Pozo Amargo
Pza. Don Fernando
C. de Piegadero
Pobre
San Sebastián

Puente de Azarquiel
Castillo San Servando →
Puente de Alcántara
Puente Nuevo
Ruinas Acqueducto Romano
Ronda de Juanelo
Rio Tajo (Tagus River)

12
11
10

SPAIN
Madrid ●
Toledo ○

🚌 Bus Stop
✝ Church
ⓘ Information
✉ Post Office

Moments A Great Scenic Drive

Another Toledan highlight is the **Carretera de Circunvalación,** the route that threads through the city and runs along the Tagus. Clinging to the hillsides are rustic dwellings, the *cigarrales* of the Imperial City, immortalized by 17th-century dramatist Tirso de Molina, who named his trilogy *Los Cigarrales de Toledo.*

status to Madrid in the 1500s. Toledo has remained the country's religious center, as the seat of the Primate of Spain.

If you're driving, the much-painted skyline of Toledo will come into view about 6km (3½ miles) from the city. When you cross the Tagus River on the 14th-century Puente San Martín, the scene is reminiscent of El Greco's moody, storm-threatened *View of Toledo,* which hangs in New York's Metropolitan Museum of Art. The artist reputedly painted that view from a hillside that is now the site of **Parador Nacional de Conde Orgaz.** If you arrive at the right time, you can enjoy an aperitif on the parador's terrace and watch one of the famous violet sunsets of Toledo.

ESSENTIALS

GETTING THERE   By Train   RENFE trains run here frequently every day. Those departing Madrid's Atocha Railway Station for Toledo run daily from 7am to 9:50pm; those leaving Toledo for Madrid run daily from 7am to 9pm. Traveling time by direct high-speed train (12 services a day) is now just 30 minutes! One-way fare 8.30€ ($10). For detailed information, call ✆ **90-224-02-02;** in Toledo call ✆ **92-522-30-99.**

By Bus   Bus transit between Madrid and Toledo is faster and more convenient than travel by train. Buses are maintained by several companies, the largest of which include Continental or Galiano. They depart from Madrid's Estación Sur de Autobuses (South Bus Station), Calle Méndez Alvaro (✆ **91-468-42-00** for information), every day between 6:30am and 10pm at 30-minute intervals. The fastest leave Monday to Friday on the hour. Those that depart weekdays on the half-hour, and those that run on weekends, take a bit longer. Travel time, depending on whether the bus stops at villages en route, is between 1 hour and 1 hour 20 minutes. One-way transit costs 3.60€ ($4.50).

Once you reach Toledo, you'll be deposited at the Estación de Autobuses, which lies beside the river, about 1.2km (¾ mile) from the historic center. Although many visitors opt to walk, be advised that the ascent is steep. Bus nos. 5 and 6 run from the station uphill to the center, charging .80€ ($1) for the brief ride. Pay the driver directly.

By Car   Exit Madrid via Cibeles (Paseo del Prado) and take the N-401 south.

VISITOR INFORMATION   The **tourist information office** is at Puerta de Bisagra (✆ **92-522-08-43**). It's open Monday to Friday from 9am to 6pm, Saturday from 9am to 7pm, and Sunday from 9am to 3pm.

EXPLORING THE TOWN

Alcázar   The Alcázar, located at the eastern edge of the old city, dominates the Toledo skyline. It became world famous at the beginning of the Spanish Civil War, when it underwent a 70-day siege that almost destroyed it. Today it has been rebuilt and turned into an army museum, housing such exhibits as a plastic model of what the fortress looked like after the civil war, electronic equipment used during the siege, and photographs taken during the height of the battle. A walking tour gives a realistic simulation of the siege. Allow an hour for a visit.

Calle General Moscardó 4, near the Plaza de Zocodover. ☏ **92-522-16-73**. Admission 3€ ($3.75) adults, free for children under 10. Tues–Sun 9:30am–2pm. Bus: 5 or 6.

Casa y Museo de El Greco ✦   Located in Toledo's *antiguo barrio judío* (the old Jewish quarter, a labyrinth of narrow streets on the old town's southwestern edge), the House of El Greco honors the great master painter, although he didn't actually live here. In 1585 the artist moved into one of the run-down palace apartments belonging to the Marquís of Villena. Although he was to live at other Toledan addresses, he returned to the Villena palace in 1604 and remained there until his death. Only a small part of the original residence was saved from decay. In time, this and a neighboring house became the El Greco museum; today it's furnished with authentic period pieces.

You can visit El Greco's so-called studio, where one of his paintings hangs. The museum contains several more works, including a copy of *A View of Toledo* and three portraits, plus many pictures by various 16th- and 17th-century Spanish artists. The garden and especially the kitchen also merit attention, as does a sitting room decorated in the Moorish style.

Calle Samuel Leví 3. ☏ **92-522-40-46**. Admission 2.40€ ($3) adults, free for children under 10. Tues–Sat 10am–2pm and 4–6pm; Sun 10am–2pm. Bus: 5 or 6.

Catedral ✦✦✦   Ranked among the greatest Gothic structures, the cathedral actually reflects several styles, since more than 2½ centuries elapsed during its construction (1226–1493). Many historic events transpired here, including the proclamation of Joanna the Mad and her husband, Philip the Handsome, as heirs to the throne of Spain.

Among its art treasures, the *transparente* stands out—a wall of marble and florid baroque alabaster sculpture overlooked for years because the cathedral was too poorly lit. Sculptor Narcisco Tomé cut a hole in the ceiling, much to the consternation of Toledans, and now light touches the high-rising angels, a *Last Supper* in alabaster, and a Virgin in ascension.

The 16th-century Capilla Mozárabe, containing works by Juan de Borgona, is another curiosity of the cathedral. Mass is still held here using Mozarabic liturgy.

The Treasure Room has a 500-pound 15th-century gilded monstrance—allegedly made with gold brought back from the New World by Columbus—that is still carried through the streets of Toledo during the feast of Corpus Christi.

Other highlights of the cathedral include El Greco's *Twelve Apostles* and *Spoliation of Christ* and Goya's *Arrest of Christ on the Mount of Olives*. The cathedral shop, where you buy tickets to enter, is well organized and stocks a variety of quality souvenirs, including ceramics and damascene (see "Shopping," below).

Cardenal Cisneros 1. ☏ **92-522-22-41**. Free admission to cathedral; Treasure Room 5€ ($6). Mon–Sat 10:30am–6:30pm; Sun 2–6:30pm.

Iglesia de Santo Tomé   This modest little 14th-century chapel, situated on a narrow street in the old Jewish quarter, might have been overlooked had it not possessed El Greco's masterpiece ***The Burial of the Count of Orgaz*** ✦✦✦, created in 1586. To avoid the hordes, go when the chapel first opens.

Plaza del Conde 4, Vía Santo Tomé. ☏ **92-525-60-98**. Admission 1.75€ ($2.20). Daily 10am–6:45pm (closes at 5:45pm in winter). Closed Dec 25 and Jan 1.

Museo de Santa Cruz ⭐⭐   Today a museum of art and sculpture, this was originally a 16th-century Spanish Renaissance hospice, founded by Cardinal Mendoza— "the third king of Spain"—who helped Ferdinand and Isabella gain the throne. The facade is almost more spectacular than any of the exhibits inside. It's a stunning architectural achievement in the classical Plateresque style. The major artistic treasure inside is El Greco's *The Assumption of the Virgin,* his last known work. Paintings by Goya and Ribera are also on display along with gold items, opulent antique furnishings, Flemish tapestries, and even Visigoth artifacts. In the patio of the museum, you'll stumble across various fragments of carved stone and sarcophagi lids. One of the major exhibits is of a large Astrolablio tapestry of the zodiac from the 1400s. In the basement, you can see artifacts, including elephant tusks, from various archaeological digs throughout the province.

Calle Miguel de Cervantes 3. ℂ **92-522-10-36.** Free admission. Mon–Sat 10am–6pm; Sun 10am–2pm. Bus: 5 or 6. Pass beneath the granite archway on the eastern edge of the Plaza de Zocodover and walk about 1 block.

Sinagoga de Santa María La Blanca ⭐   In the late 12th century, the Jews of Toledo erected an important synagogue in the *almohada* style, which employs graceful horseshoe arches and ornamental horizontal moldings. Although by the early 15th century it had been converted into a Christian church, much of the original remains, including the five naves and elaborate Mudéjar decorations, mosquelike in their effect. The synagogue lies on the western edge of the city, midway between the El Greco museum and San Juan de los Reyes.

Calle Reyes Católicos 2. ℂ **92-522-72-57.** Admission 1.90€ ($2.40) Apr–Sept daily 10am–2pm and 3:30–7pm; Oct–Mar daily 10am–2pm and 3:30–6pm. Bus: 2.

Sinagoga del Tránsito ⭐   One block west of the El Greco home and museum stands this once-important house of worship for Toledo's large Jewish population. A 14th-century building, it is noted for its superb stucco Hebrew inscriptions, including psalms inscribed along the top of the walls and a poetic description of the Temple on the east wall. The synagogue is the most important part of the **Museo Sefardí (Sephardic Museum),** which opened in 1971 and contains art objects as well as tombstones with Hebrew epigraphy, some of which are dated before 1492.

Calle Samuel Leví. ℂ **92-522-36-65.** Admission 2.40€ ($3). Tues–Sat 10am–1:45pm and 4–5:45pm; Sun 10am–1:45pm. Closed Jan 1, May 1, Dec 24–25, and Dec 31. Bus: 2.

SHOPPING

In swashbuckling days, the swordsmiths of Toledo were world renowned. They're still here and still turning out **swords** today. Toledo is equally renowned for its *damasquinado,* or damascene work, the Moorish art of inlaying gold, even copper or silver threads, against a matte black steel backdrop. Today Toledo is filled with souvenir shops hawking damascene. The price depends on whether the item is handcrafted or machine made. Sometimes machine-made damascene is passed off as the more expensive handcrafted item, so you have to shop carefully. Bargaining is perfectly acceptable in Toledo, but if you get the price down, you can't pay with a credit card—only cash.

   Marzipan (called *mazapán* locally) is often prepared by nuns and is a local specialty. Many shops in town specialize in this treat made of sweet almond paste.

   The province of Toledo is also renowned for its **pottery,** which is sold in so many shops at competitive prices that it's almost unnecessary to recommend specific branches hawking these wares. However, over the years I've found that the prices at the large roadside emporiums on the outskirts of town on the main road to Madrid often have better bargains than the shops within the city walls, where rents are higher.

Casa Bermejo   Established in 1910, this factory and store employs almost 50 artisans, whom you observe at work as part of a visit to its premises. The outlet carries a wide array of damascene objects fashioned into Toledo's traditional Mudéjar designs. These include swords, platters, pitchers, and other gift items. Don't think, however, that everything this place manufactures follows the inspiration of the medieval Arabs. The outfit engraves many of the ornamental swords that are awarded to graduates of West Point in the United States, as well as the decorative, full-dress military accessories used by the armies of various countries of Europe, including France. Open Monday to Friday from 9am to 1pm and 3 to 6pm, Saturday from 8am to 1pm. Closing times are later in July and August, determined solely by business traffic. Calle Airosas 5. ℂ **92-528-53-67.**

Casa Telesforo   Many long-time residents of Toledo remember this place as the supplier of the marzipan consumed at their childhood birthday parties and celebrations. A specialist in the almond-and-sugar confection whose origins go back to the year 1806, it sells the best marzipan in town, cunningly made into such whimsical shapes as hearts, diamonds, flowers, and fish. Open daily from 9am to 10pm, later in summer, depending on the crowds. Plaza de Zocodover 13. ℂ **92-522-23-79.**

Santiago Sánchez Martín   This is one of the most prestigious manufacturers of damascene work in Toledo. It specializes in the elaborately detailed arabesques whose techniques are as old as the Arab conquest of Iberia. Look for everything from decorative tableware (platters, pitchers) to mirror frames, jewelry, letter openers, and ornamental swords. Open Monday to Friday from 9am to 2pm and 5 to 7pm. Río Llano 15. ℂ **92-522-77-57.**

WHERE TO STAY
EXPENSIVE

AC Hoteles Ciudad de Toledo 🏵🏵   Opened in 1998, this is the first hotel in years that has emerged as a superior choice to the government-run parador. If El Greco were painting his *A View of Toledo* today, he would surely have come to this site instead of the parador location. On a beltway south of the city—follow the directions to the Parador Nacional de Conde Orgaz—this deluxe property is a member of a chain that also includes the swanky **Santo Mauro** in Madrid. The epitome of luxury living and contemporary lines, this hotel across the river from Toledo is entered at the third floor. You move down through the spiraling architectural design to reach the rest of the hotel. Bedrooms are spacious and luxuriously furnished, all in contemporary styling, each with tiled bathrooms. The suites have oversize bathtubs and hydromassage.

Carretera de Circunvalación 15, 41005 Toledo. ℂ **92-528-51-25.** Fax 92-528-47-00. www.ac-hoteles.com. 49 units. 120€–130€ ($150–$163) double; 180€–210€ ($225–$263) suite. AE, MC, V. Free parking. Bus: 5. **Amenities:** Restaurant; bar; room service; babysitting; laundry service; dry cleaning. *In room:* A/C, TV, minibar, hair dryer.

Hotel Beatriz 🏵🏵 *(Kids)*   This is the first really *luxe* hotel ever constructed in the city. It is also the city's largest hotel, although it gives its guests personal attention. The building dates from the early 1990s but was completely refurbished during the post-millennium, making it your best bet for up-to-date technology. Even though it lacks the atmosphere of the Parador, that government-run hostelry is often fully booked, so you'll have a far better chance of getting in here.

All the modern amenities have been installed, ranging from special make-up mirrors to hydromassages in the more expensive rooms. Junior suites are also blessed with private Jacuzzi. The furnishings are tasteful and comfortable, and the location is only a 5-minute drive from the Old Town. The activities here are the best of any hotel, including the bamboo-constructed **Kiosk Bar** with its great cocktails. Children's games and activities are also the best in town. The piano bar features live music plus an on-site dance club. The hotel restaurant, **Alacena** (p. 267), is among Toledo's most luxurious.

Carretera de Avila, 45005 Toledo. ℂ **92-526-91-00.** Fax 92-521-58-65. www.hotelbeatriztoledo.com. 295 units. 95€–145€ ($119–$181) double; 175€ ($219) junior suite; 275€ ($344) suite. AE, DC, MC, V. Parking 9€ ($12). **Amenities:** 2 restaurants; bar; outdoor pool; gym; sauna; business center; room service (7:30am–midnight); babysitting; laundry service; rooms for those w/limited mobility. *In room:* A/C, TV, minibar, beverage maker (in some), hair dryer, safe.

Parador de Turismo de Toledo 👁👁👁 You'll have to make reservations well in advance to stay at this parador, which is built on the ridge of a rugged hill where El Greco is said to have painted his *View of Toledo.* That view is still here, and it is without a doubt one of the grandest in the world. The main living room/lounge has fine furniture—old chests, brown leather chairs, and heavy tables—and leads to a sunny terrace overlooking the city. On chilly nights, you can sit by the public fireplace. The guest rooms are the most luxurious in all of Toledo, far superior to those at María Cristina. Spacious and beautifully furnished, they contain reproductions of regional antique pieces.

Cerro del Emperador, 45002 Toledo. ℂ **92-522-18-50.** Fax 92-522-51-66. www.paradores.es. 76 units. 130€ double ($163); 175€ ($219) suite. AE, DC, MC, V. Free parking. Drive across Puente San Martín and head south for 4km (2½ miles). **Amenities:** Restaurant; bar; room service; outdoor pool (June–Sept only); babysitting; laundry service; dry cleaning. *In room:* A/C, TV, minibar, hair dryer, safe.

MODERATE

Hostal del Cardenal 👁👁 Although it has long been acclaimed as the best restaurant in Toledo (p. 268), the fact that this establishment has rooms available is still a well-kept secret. They're not as grand as those at the Parador, but they are choice nevertheless, sought by those wanting to capture an old Toledan atmosphere. The entrance to this unusual hotel is set into the stone fortifications of the ancient city walls, a few steps from the Bisagra Gate. To enter the hotel, you must climb a series of terraces to the top of the crenellated walls of the ancient fortress. Here, grandly symmetrical and very imposing, is the *hostal* (hostel), the former residence of the 18th-century cardinal of Toledo, Señor Lorenzana. Just beyond the entrance, still atop the city wall, you'll find flagstone walkways, Moorish fountains, rose gardens, and cascading vines. The establishment has tiled walls; long, narrow salons; dignified Spanish furniture; and a smattering of antiques. Each room has a private bathroom equipped with a tub/shower combination. A member of the hotel staff will call you a taxi if you don't want to walk the steep ascent (on narrow to nonexistent sidewalks) into the historic district.

Paseo de Recaredo 24, 45003 Toledo. ℂ **92-522-49-00.** Fax 92-522-29-91. www.hostaldelcardenal.com. 27 units. 90€–110€ ($113–$138) double; 115€–150€ ($144–$188) suite. AE, DC, MC, V. Parking nearby 13€ ($16). Bus: 2 from rail station. **Amenities:** Restaurant; bar; babysitting; laundry service; dry cleaning. *In room:* A/C, TV, hair dryer.

Hotel Pintor El Greco 👁 In the old Jewish quarter, one of the most traditional and historic districts of Toledo, this hotel was converted from a typical *casa toledana* (house in Toledo) that had once been used as a bakery. With careful restoration, especially of its ancient facade, it was transformed into one of Toledo's best and most atmospheric small hotels—the only one to match the antique charm of Hostal del Cardenal (see above), although, it too, seems relatively unknown. Decoration in both the public rooms and bedrooms is in a traditional Castilian style. Bedrooms come in a variety of shapes and sizes, as befits a building of this age, but all are equipped with small bathrooms with tub/shower combinations and adequate shelf space. At the doorstep of the hotel are such landmarks as the Monasterio de San Juan de los Reyes, Sinagoga de Santa María la Blanca, Sinagoga del Tránsito, Casa y Museo de El Greco, and Iglesia de Santo Tomé.

Alamillos del Tránsito 13, 45002 Toledo. ℭ 92-528-51-91. Fax 92-521-58-19. www.hotel-pintorelgreco.com. 33 units. 95€–120€ ($119–$150) double. AE, DC, MC, V. Parking 5€ ($6). **Amenities:** Lounge; babysitting; laundry service; dry cleaning. *In room:* A/C, TV, minibar, hair dryer, safe.

INEXPENSIVE
Hotel Imperio *Value* Long a budget favorite, this modest hotel is a few yards from the Alcázar and the cathedral. Built in the '80s, the hotel was recently renovated (and just in time), adding more comfort to the small rooms. The furnishings are in a rather severe style, but the beds are comfortable—and for the price, this is one of the city's best choices. Rooms on the second floor have balconies overlooking the street. A snack bar is on-site, but some fine restaurants lie just outside the door.

Cadena 5, 45001 Toledo. ℭ 92-522-76-50. Fax 92-525-3183. www.hotelimperio.com.ar. 21 units. 45€ ($56) double. AE, DC, MC, V. Parking nearby 14€ ($18). **Amenities:** Bar; lounge; babysitting; laundry service. *In room:* A/C, TV.

WHERE TO DINE
MODERATE
Alacena *⊙* TOLEDAN/SPANISH Located in the previously recommended Hotel Beatriz, this is the most elegant and comfortable restaurant in Toledo, although Hostel del Cardenal maintains a slight edge in cuisine. Using some of the area's best products and the finest produce shipped from the international markets in Madrid, La Alacena hires the finest chefs in the region as well, who are dedicated to flavor, taste, and texture. The chefs also celebrate the dying art of hunting, as evoked by such specialties as stewed partridge or sirloin of deer in a sauce of fresh mushrooms. Filet of hare is yet another specialty. Sometimes the chefs feature a specialty month, such as November, when they celebrate the cuisine of Galicia province in the northwest, shipping in turbot, hake, bullock, and goose barnacles caught off the coast of Spain. Savory Mediterranean rice dishes are another specialty. Starters may include a cream of lobster soup studded with shrimp, or a succulent salad of Iberian cured ham with duck liver.

In the Hotel Beatriz, Carretera de Avila. ℭ 92-526-91-00. Reservations recommended. Main courses 12€–22€ ($15–$28). Fixed-price menu 36€–38€ ($45–$58). AE, DC, MC, V. Mon–Sat 1:30–4pm; daily 8–11:30pm.

Asador Adolfo *⊙* SPANISH Less than a minute's walk north of the cathedral, at the corner of Calle Hombre de Palo behind an understated sign, Asador Adolfo is one of the finest restaurants in town (though I prefer the Hostal del Cardenal). Sections of the building were first constructed during the 1400s, but the thoroughly modern kitchen has recently been renovated. Massive beams support the dining room ceilings, and here and there the rooms contain faded frescoes dating from the original building.

Game dishes are a house specialty; such choices as partridge with white beans and venison consistently rate among the best anywhere. Other offerings include hake flavored with local saffron as well as a wide array of beef, veal, or lamb dishes. To start, try the *pimientos rellenos* (red peppers stuffed with pulverized shellfish). The house dessert is marzipan, prepared in a wood-fired oven and noted for its lightness.

La Granada 6. 🕐 **92-522-73-21.** Reservations recommended. Main courses 18€–28 € ($23–$35). AE, DC, MC, V. Daily 1–4pm; Mon–Sat 8pm–midnight. Bus: 5 or 6.

Casón de los López 🏵🏵 CASTILIAN A short walk from the heartbeat Plaza de Zocodover, this charmer of a restaurant serves the lightest and most sophisticated cuisine in Toledo. Its setting alone would make it an enticing choice. In an antique building, it's a virtual museum, furnished with antiques, some from as far back as the 16th century. Castilian iron bars, Mudéjar-style wooden ceilings, Arab stucco decorations, a patio ringed with marble statues, a splashing fountain, and caged birds create this mellow atmosphere. And get this: Much of the furniture is for sale. Hopefully, some other diner won't buy the table out from under you when your main course is being served.

In such a mellow ambience, you can plunge into a cuisine that sees me returning again and again to sample the bounty of the countryside, especially such game as hare, rabbit, partridge, and pigeon. A recent specialty I enjoyed, loin of venison with fresh, garlic-flecked spinach in a velvety smooth mushroom cream sauce, was irresistibly juicy and a combination of blissful contrasts. Launch yourself with the garlic-ravioli soup, a first for many diners, and top the meal with an extravagant cheese and fresh plum mousse.

Sillería 3. 🕐 **92-525-47-74.** Reservations required. Main courses 15€–24€ ($19–$30). Set-price menus 35€–48€ ($44–$60). AE, DC, MC, V. Daily 1:30–4pm; Mon–Sat 9–11pm.

Hostal del Cardenal 🏵🏵 SPANISH Treat yourself to Toledo's best-known restaurant, owned by the same people who run Madrid's Sobrino de Botín (see chapter 6). The chef prepares regional dishes with flair and originality. Choosing from a menu very similar to that of the fabled Madrid eatery, begin with "quarter of an hour" (fish) soup or white asparagus, and then move on to curried prawns, baked hake, filet mignon, or smoked salmon. Roast suckling pig is a specialty, as is partridge in casserole. Arrive early to enjoy a sherry in the bar or in the courtyard.

Paseo de Recaredo 24. 🕐 **92-522-08-62.** Reservations required. Main courses 10€–20€ ($13–$25); fixed-price menu 20€ ($25). AE, DC, MC, V. Daily 1–4pm and 8:30–11:30pm. Bus: 2 from rail station.

INEXPENSIVE

La Perdiz 🏵 *Finds* CASTILIAN La Perdiz is named from the favorite dish of Toledans—partridge. That bird is best showcased here in a dish called *perdiz estofada a la toledana,* partridge stew with white wine, bay leaf, and onions. Another excellent choice is venison in a mushroom sauce. The menu also has some imaginative offerings such as a fresh fried cheese tossed in an orange dressing.

The best dessert is that local favorite, marzipan, here served as a tart with almond biscuits. On occasion a roast suckling pig is featured. The location is in the center of the old Jewish ghetto, about midpoint between two synagogues, Santa María la Blanca and Tránsito. The restaurant has two floors with views of the historic district, and walls are of wood and brick. Locals, and with good reason, cite the place for its good quality cuisine at affordable prices. The same people who run La Perdiz also operate Asador Adolfo, Toledo's premier restaurant (see above). But prices at La Perdiz are far more reasonable.

Calle Reyes Católicos 7. ℭ **92-521-46-58.** Reservations recommended. Main courses 12€–18€ ($15–$23); set menu 20€ ($25). AE, MC, V. Tues–Sat noon–11pm; Sun noon–4pm.

TOLEDO AFTER DARK

Begin your nighttime crawl through Toledo with a stop at **Bar Ludeña,** Plaza de la Magdalena 13, Corral de Don Diego 10 (ℭ **92-522-33-84**), where a loyal clientele comes for glasses of wine and *tapas* of *calamares,* olives, or ham that are as generous as the bar is small. Drop in next to **Trébol,** Calle Santa Fe 1 (ℭ **92-521-37-02**), to sample their wine, their excellent tapas, and their *bombas* (stuffed potato bombs). Another wine bar hangout is **Enebro,** on the postage stamp–size Plaza Santiago Balleros, off Calle Cervantes (ℭ **92-522-21-11**).

Toledo is quiet at night, with fewer dance clubs than you'd expect from a town of its size. If you want to hear some recorded music, head for **Bar La Abadía,** Plaza San Nicolás 3 (ℭ **92-525-11-40**), where crowds of local residents, many of them involved in the tourism industry, crowd elbow to elbow for pints of beer, glasses of wine, and access to the music of New York, Los Angeles, or wherever. Other spots to hit include **O'Brien's Irish Pub,** Calle Armas 12 (ℭ **92-521-26-65**), which seems more appropriate for the streets of Dublin than old Toledo. A crowd in their 20s flocks here, and there's live music every Thursday at 10:30pm.

10 Segovia ✶✶✶

91km (57 miles) NW of Madrid, 68km (42 miles) NE of Avila

Less commercial (!) than Toledo, Segovia, more than anywhere else, typifies the glory of Old Castile. Wherever you look, you'll see reminders of a golden era—whether it's the most spectacular Alcázar on the Iberian Peninsula or the well-preserved, still-functioning Roman aqueduct.

Segovia lies on the slope of the Guadarrama Mountains, where the Eresma and Clamores rivers converge. This ancient city stands in the center of the most castle-rich part of Castile. Isabella herself was proclaimed queen of Castile here in 1474.

The narrow, winding streets of this hill city must be covered on foot to fully view the Romanesque churches and 15th-century palaces along the way.

ESSENTIALS

GETTING THERE   By Train   Fifteen trains leave Madrid's Chamartín Railway Station every day and arrive 2 hours later in Segovia, where you can board bus no. 3, which departs every quarter-hour for the Plaza Mayor. The trains that leave from Chamartín first travel through Atocha Station, making it closer to some travelers' hotels. The station at Segovia lies on the Paseo Obispo Quesada s/n (ℭ **921-42-07-74**), a 20-minute walk southeast of the town center.

By Bus   Buses arrive and depart from the Estacionamiento Municipal de Autobuses, Paseo de Ezequiel González 10 (ℭ **92-142-77-07**), near the corner of the Avenida Fernández Ladreda and the steeply sloping Paseo Conde de Sepúlveda. There are 10 to 15 buses a day to and from Madrid (which depart from Paseo de la Florida 11; Metro: Norte), and about four a day traveling between Avila, Segovia, and Valladolid. One-way tickets from Madrid cost around 5.35€ ($6.70).

By Car   Take the N-VI (on some maps it's known as the A-6) or the Autopista del Nordeste northwest from Madrid, toward León and Lugo. At the junction with Route 110 (signposted SEGOVIA), turn northeast.

VISITOR INFORMATION   The **tourist information office** is at Plaza Mayor 10 (© **92-146-03-34**). It is open daily from 9am to 3pm and 5 to 7pm.

SEEING THE SIGHTS

El Alcázar 🏰🏰   If you've ever dreamed of castles in the air, then all the fairy-tale romance of childhood will return when you view the Alcázar. Many have waxed poetic about it, comparing it to a giant boat sailing through the clouds. View the Alcázar first from below, at the junction of the Clamores and Eresma rivers. It's on the west side of Segovia, and you may not spot it when you first enter the city—but that's part of the surprise.

The castle dates from the 12th century, but a large segment, which contained its Moorish ceilings, was destroyed by fire in 1862. Restoration has continued over the years.

Royal romance is associated with the Alcázar. Isabella first met Ferdinand here, and today you can see a facsimile of her dank bedroom. Once married, she wasn't foolish enough to surrender her royal rights, as replicas of the thrones attest—both are equally proportioned. Philip II married his fourth wife, Anne of Austria, here as well.

Walk the battlements of this once-impregnable castle, from which its occupants hurled boiling oil onto the enemy below. Or ascend the hazardous stairs of the tower, originally built by Isabella's father as a prison, for a panoramic view of Segovia.

Plaza de La Reina Victoria Eugenia. © **92-146-07-59**. Admission 3.50€ ($4.35) adults, 2.50€ ($3.10) children 8–14, free for children 7 and under. Apr–Sept daily 10am–7pm; Oct–Mar daily 10am–6pm. Bus: 3. Take either Calle Vallejo, Calle de Velarde, Calle de Daoiz, or Paseo de Ronda.

Cabildo Catedral de Segovia 🏰   Constructed between 1515 and 1558, this is the last Gothic cathedral built in Spain. Fronting the historic Plaza Mayor, it stands on the spot where Isabella I was proclaimed queen of Castile. Affectionately called *la dama de las catedrales,* it contains numerous treasures, such as the Blessed Sacrament Chapel (created by the flamboyant Churriguera), stained-glass windows, elaborately carved choir stalls, and 16th- and 17th-century paintings, including a reredos portraying the deposition of Christ from the cross by Juan de Juni. The cloisters are older than the cathedral, dating from an earlier church that was destroyed in the so-called War of the Comuneros. Inside the cathedral museum you'll find jewelry, paintings, and a collection of rare antique manuscripts.

Plaza Catedral, Marqués del Arco. © **92-146-22-05**. Free admission to cathedral; cloisters, museum, and chapel room 2€ ($2.50) adults, children 11 and under are free. Spring and summer daily 9am–7pm; off-season daily 9:30am–6pm.

Iglesia de la Vera Cruz 🏰   Built in either the 11th or the 12th century by the Knights Templar, this is the most fascinating Romanesque church in Segovia. It stands in isolation outside the walls of the old town, overlooking the Alcázar. Its unusual 12-sided design is believed to have been copied from the Church of the Holy Sepulchre in Jerusalem. Inside you'll find an inner temple, rising two floors, where the knights conducted nightlong vigils as part of their initiation rites.

Carretera de Zamarramala. © **92-143-14-75**. Admission 2€ ($2.50). Apr–Sept Tues–Sun 10:30am–1:30pm and 3:30–7pm; Oct–Mar Tues–Sun 10:30am–1:30pm and 3:30–6pm.

Monasterio del Parral 🏰 *(Finds*   The restored "Monastery of the Grape" was established for the Hieronymites by Henry IV (1425–74), a Castilian king known as "The Impotent." The monastery lies across the Eresma River about .8km (½ mile) north of the city. The church is a medley of styles and decoration—mainly Gothic, Renaissance, and Plateresque. The facade was never completed, and the monastery itself was abandoned when religious orders were suppressed in 1835. Today it's been restored and is once again the domain of the *jerónimos,* Hieronymus priests and brothers. Inside, a robed monk will show you the various treasures of the order, including a polychrome altarpiece and the alabaster tombs of the Marquis of Villena and his wife—all the work of Juan Rodríguez.

Subida del Parral 2 (across the Eresma River). (© 92-143-12-98. Free admission. Mon–Sat 10am–2:30pm and 4–6:30pm; Sun 10–11:30am and 4–6:30pm. Take Ronda de Sant Lucía and cross the Eresma River.

Roman Aqueduct (Acueducto Romano) ✸✸✸   This architectural marvel was built by the Romans nearly 2,000 years ago. Constructed of mortarless granite, it consists of 118 arches, and in one two-tiered section it soars 29m (95 ft.) to its highest point. The Spanish call it El Puente. It spans the Plaza del Azoguejo, the old market square, stretching nearly 720m (2,362 ft.). When the Moors took Segovia in 1072, they destroyed 36 arches, which were later rebuilt under Ferdinand and Isabella in 1484.

Plaza del Azoguejo.

WHERE TO STAY
EXPENSIVE
Parador de Segovia ✸✸✸   This 20th-century tile-roofed parador sits on a hill 3km (2 miles) northeast of Segovia (take the N-601). It stands on an estate called El Terminillo, which used to be famous for its vines and almond trees, a few of which still survive. If you have a car and can get a reservation, book here; the comfort level dwarfs that found at Los Arcos (see below). The guest rooms are deluxe; furnishings are tasteful (often in blond pieces), and large windows open onto panoramic views of the countryside. Some of the older rooms are a bit dated, however, with a lackluster decor. The in-house restaurant is one of the best places to enjoy a meal in Segovia.

Carretera Valladolid s/n (N-601), 40003 Segovia. (© 92-144-37-37. Fax 92-143-73-62. www.parador.es. 113 units. 130€ ($163) double; from 210€ ($263) suite. AE, DC, MC, V. Covered parking 7€ ($8.75), free outside. **Amenities:** Restaurant; bar; room service; outdoor pool (June–Sept); indoor heated pool (Oct–May); 2 tennis courts (1 floodlit); fitness center; sauna; babysitting; laundry service; dry cleaning. *In room:* A/C, TV, minibar, hair dryer, safe.

MODERATE
Hotel Infanta Isabel ✸   Named after Queen Isabel, the great-grandmother of the present-day king, the hotel stands overlooking the charming central square and is within a stone's throw of the majestic cathedral. This is where she would stay when on her way to the nearby summer palace of La Granja. The present owners have modernized the interior considerably, but a good deal of the building's 19th-century grandeur, such as the staircase, remains. Each room is decorated in its own style, and each is furnished with an eye to comfort. Despite its old-fashioned style, the hotel has every convenience.

Plaza Mayor, 40001 Segovia. (© 92-146-13-00. Fax 92-146-22-17. 37 units. 80€–100€ ($100–$125) double. AC, DC, MC, V. Parking 9€ ($11). **Amenities:** Bar; lounge; room service; babysitting; laundry service; dry cleaning. *In room:* A/C, TV, minibar, hair dryer, safe.

Hotel Los Arcos   This concrete-and-glass five-story structure opened in 1987 and is generally cited as the best lodging in town. Well run and modern, it attracts the business traveler, although tourists frequent the place in droves as well. Rooms are generally spacious but furnished in a standard international bland way, except for the beautiful rug-dotted parquet floors. Built-in furnishings and tiny bathrooms are part of the offering. Rooms are well kept, although some furnishings look worn.

Even if you don't stay here, consider dining at the hotel's **La Cocina de Segovia,** the only hotel dining room that competes successfully with Mesón de Cándido (see below). As at the nearby competitors, roast suckling pig and roast Segovia lamb—perfectly cooked in specially made ovens—are the specialties. There's also a tavernlike cafe and bar. In all, it's a smart, efficiently run, and pleasant choice, if not a terribly exciting one.

Paseo de Ezequiel González 26, 40002 Segovia. ✆ **92-143-74-62.** Fax 92-142-81-61. 59 units. 110€–125 € ($138-$156) double. AE, DC, MC, V. Parking 10€ ($13). **Amenities:** Restaurant; bar; lounge; health club; room service; babysitting; laundry service; dry cleaning. In room: A/C, TV, minibar, hair dryer, safe.

INEXPENSIVE
Las Sirenas   Standing on the most charming old plaza in Segovia, opposite the Church of St. Martín, this hotel was built around 1950 and has been renovated several times. However, it has long since lost its Franco-era supremacy to Los Arcos (see above). It is modest and well maintained, and decorated in a conservative style. Each bedroom is filled with functional, simple furniture and well-kept bathrooms. Breakfast is the only meal served, but the staff at the reception desk can direct clients to cafes and *tascas* nearby.

Juan Bravo 30, 40001 Segovia. ✆ **92-146-26-63.** Fax 92-146-26-57. 39 units. 60€–70€ ($75–$88) double. AE, DC, MC, V. **Amenities:** Breakfast salon. In room: A/C, TV.

WHERE TO DINE
Mesón de Cándido ✦✦ CASTILIAN   For years this beautiful old Spanish inn, standing on the eastern edge of the old town, has maintained a monopoly on the tourist trade. Apart from the hotel restaurants—specifically La Cocina de Segovia at the Los Arcos—it is the town's finest dining choice. The Cándido family took it over in 1905, and fourth- and fifth-generation family members still run the place, having fed, over the years, everybody from Hemingway to Nixon. The oldest part of the restaurant dates from 1822, and the place has gradually been enlarged since then. The proprietor of the House of Cándido is known as *mesonero mayor de Castilla* (the major innkeeper of Castile). He's been decorated with more medals and honors than paella has grains of rice. The restaurant's popularity can be judged by the crowds of hungry diners who fill every seat in the six dining rooms. The a la carte menu includes those two regional staples: *cordero asado* (roast baby lamb) and *cochinillo asado* (roast suckling pig). Some of the seating areas are cramped and confining. Opt for a table on the second floor, facing the Aqueduct, or else one of the outdoor cafe tables in front.

Plaza del Azoguejo 5. ✆ **92-142-59-11.** Reservations recommended. Main courses 12€–20€ ($15–$25). AE, DC, MC, V. Daily 12:30–4:30pm and 8pm–midnight.

Restaurante Duque ✦ CASTILIAN   Set on the street that links Segovia's ancient Roman aqueduct with the city's medieval core, this restaurant was established in 1895, and has fed many successive generations of local residents ever since. The severely dignified interior looks almost unchanged since it was built. The decor includes heavy ceiling beams, exposed stone, rough-textured plaster, and battered 19th-century artifacts from long-ago farms. Come here for the kind of cuisine that was in vogue when the restaurant was built, with very few concessions to modern cuisine. There's an excellent version of cream of crabmeat soup; roast suckling pig slow-cooked on a spit; savory roasted lamb with aromatic rosemary, thyme, and garlic; and different preparations of grilled chicken, veal, beef, and pork. An excellent accompaniment for any of these might include kidney beans cooked with chunks of salted cod, fresh spinach, and mounds of mashed potatoes or rice.

Calle Cervantes 12. ℂ **92-146-24-87**. Reservations recommended. Main courses 12€–24€ ($15–$30). AE, DC, MC, V. Daily 12:30–5pm and 8–11:30pm.

AN EASY EXCURSION TO LA GRANJA

To reach La Granja, 11km (7 miles) southeast of Segovia, you can take a 20-minute bus ride from the center of the city. Six to 10 buses a day leave from Paseo Conde de Sepulveda at Avenida Fernández Ladreda. A one-way fare costs 9€ ($11). For information, call ℂ **92-142-77-07**.

Palacio Real de La Granja   San Ildefonso de la Granja was the summer palace of the Bourbon kings of Spain, who replicated the grandeur of Versailles in the province of Segovia. Set against the snowcapped Sierra de Guadarrama, the slate-roofed palace dominates the village that grew up around it (which, these days, is a summer resort).

The founder of La Granja was Philip V, grandson of Louis XIV and the first Bourbon king of Spain (his body, along with that of his second queen, Isabel de Fernesio, is interred in a mausoleum in the Collegiate Church). Philip V was born at Versailles on December 19, 1683, which may explain why he wanted to re-create that atmosphere at Segovia.

Before the palace was built in the early 18th century, a farm stood here—hence the totally incongruous name *la granja,* meaning "the farm" in Spanish. Inside you'll find valuable antiques (many in the Empire style), paintings, and a remarkable collection of tapestries based on Goya cartoons from the Royal Factory in Madrid.

Most visitors, however, seem to find a stroll through the gardens more pleasing, so allow adequate time for that. The fountain statuary is a riot of cavorting gods and nymphs, hiding indiscretions behind jets of water. The gardens are studded with chestnuts and elms. A spectacular display takes place when the water jets are turned on.

Plaza de España 17, San Ildefonso (Segovia). ℂ **92-147-00-19**. Admission 5€ ($6.25) adults, 2.50€ ($3.10) children 5–14, free for children 4 and under. Apr–Sept Tues–Sun 10am–6pm; Oct–Mar Tues–Sat 10am–1:30pm and 3–5pm; Sun 10am–2pm.

SEGOVIA AFTER DARK

Some of the most spontaneous good times can be created around the Plaza Mayor, Plaza Azagejo, and the busy Calle del Carmen that runs into the Plaza Azagejo. Each of those sites contains a scattering of simple bars and cafes that grow more crowded at night as the days grow hotter. If you want to go dancing, two of the most popular discos are **Mansión,** Calle de Juan Bravo (no phone), which is open nightly from 11pm till dawn for dancing, drinking, and flirting with the 20- to 30-year-old crowd; and its somewhat more stylish competitor, **Bar Ginasio,** Paseo del Salon (no phone), which is open nightly from 8pm till dawn, a bit more atmospheric and frequented by persons from ages 25 to around 50.

11 Avila ★★

109km (68 miles) NW of Madrid, 67km (42 miles) SW of Segovia

The ancient city of Avila is completely encircled by well-preserved 11th-century walls, which are among the most important medieval relics in Europe. The city has been declared a national landmark, and there is little wonder why. The walls aren't the only attraction, however. Avila has several Romanesque churches, Gothic palaces, and a fortified cathedral. It is among some 80 cities designated by UNESCO as World Heritage Sites (six of these are in Spain; the other five are Santiago de Compostela, Segovia, Toledo, Cáceres, and Salamanca).

Avila's spirit and legend are most linked to St. Teresa, born here in 1515. This Carmelite nun, who helped defeat the Reformation and founded a number of convents, experienced visions of the devil and angels piercing her heart with burning-hot lances. She was eventually imprisoned in Toledo. Many legends sprang up after her death, including the belief that a hand severed from her body could perform miracles. Finally, in 1622, she was declared a saint.

Note: Bring warm clothes if you're visiting in the early spring.

ESSENTIALS

GETTING THERE   There are more than two dozen **trains** leaving daily from Madrid for Avila, about a 1½- to 2-hour trip each way. Depending on the schedule, trains depart from Chamartín, Atocha, and Príncipe (Norte) railway stations. The 8am train from Atocha, arriving in Avila a t 9:26am, is a good choice, considering all there is to see. Tickets cost 5.75€ to 15€ ($7.20–$19). The Avila station is at Avenida José Antonio (© **90-224-02-02**), about a mile east of the Old City. You'll find taxis lined up in front of Avila's railway station and at the more central Plaza Santa Teresa. For taxi information, call © **92-025-09-00.**

Buses leave Madrid daily from Paseo Florida 11 (Metro: Norte), in front of the Norte railway station. In Avila the bus terminal (© **92-025-65-05**) is at the corner of Avenida Madrid and Avenida Portugal, northeast of the center of town. A one-way ticket from Madrid costs around 6.80€ ($8.50).

To drive there, exit Madrid from its northwest perimeter and head northwest on highway N-VI (A-6), toward La Coruña, eventually forking southwest to Avila. Driving time is around 1½ hours.

VISITOR INFORMATION   The **tourist information office,** Plaza Catedral 4 (© **92-021-13-87**), is open Monday through Friday from 9am to 2pm and 5 to 7pm, Saturday and Sunday from 10am to 2pm and 5 to 8pm.

EXPLORING THE TOWN

Begun on orders of Alfonso VI as part of the general re-conquest of Spain from the Moors, the 11th-century **Walls of Avila** 🎔🎔, built over Roman fortifications, took 9 years to complete. They average 10m (33 ft.) in height and have 88 semicircular towers and more than 2,300 battlements. Of the nine gateways, the two most famous are the St. Vincent and the Alcázar, both on the eastern side. In many respects the walls are best viewed from the west. Whatever your preferred point of view, you can drive along their entire length: 2km (1½ miles).

Basílica de San Vicente 🎔🎔   Outside the city walls at the northeast corner of the medieval ramparts, this Romanesque-Gothic church in faded sandstone encompasses styles from the 12th to the 14th century. It consists of a huge nave and a trio of apses. The eternal struggle between good and evil is depicted on a cornice on the southern portal. The **western portal** 🎔🎔, dating from the 13th century, contains Romanesque carvings. Inside is the tomb of St. Vincent, martyred on this site in the 4th century. The tomb's medieval carvings, which depict his torture and subsequent martyrdom, are fascinating.

Plaza de San Vicente. © **92-025-52-30**. Admission 1.40€ ($1.75). Daily 10am–2pm and 4–6:30pm.

Catedral de Avila ⭐⭐   Built into the old ramparts of Avila, this cold, austere cathedral and fortress (begun in 1099) bridges the gap between the Romanesque and the Gothic, and, as such, enjoys a certain distinction in Spanish architecture. One local writer compared it to a granite mountain. The interior is unusual, built with a mottled red-and-white stone.

Like most European cathedrals, Avila lost its purity of design through the years as new chapels and wings—one completely in the Renaissance mode—were added. A Dutch artist, Cornelius, designed the seats of the choir stalls, also in Renaissance style, and the principal chapel holds a reredos showing the life of Christ by Pedro Berruguete, Juan de Borgoña, and Santa Cruz. Behind the chapel the tomb of Bishop Alonso de Madrigal—nicknamed El Tostado (The Parched One) because of its brownish color—is Vasco de Zarza's masterpiece. The Cathedral Museum contains a laminated gold ceiling, a 15th-century triptych, a copy of an El Greco painting, as well as vestments and 15th-century songbooks.

Plaza Catedral. ☎ **92-021-16-41.** Admission 4€ ($5) adults, free for children under 10. May–Sept daily 9:30am–1:30pm and 3:30–8pm; Oct–Apr daily 10am–1:30pm and 3:30–6pm.

Convento de Santa Teresa   This 17th-century convent and baroque church, two blocks southwest of the Plaza de la Victoria, is at the site of St. Teresa's birth. To the right of the convent is the tiny Sala de Reliquias exhibiting some of her relics, including a finger from her right hand, the sole of one of her sandals, and a cord she used to flagellate herself.

Plaza de la Santa 2. ☎ **92-021-10-30.** Admission 2€ ($2.50). Convent May–Sept daily 9:30am–1:30pm and 3:30–9pm; Oct–Apr daily 9:30am–1:30pm and 3:30–8:30pm. Sala de Reliquias daily 9:30am–1:30pm and 3:30–7:30pm. Bus: 1, 3, or 4.

Monasterio de Santo Tomás ⭐   This 15th-century Gothic monastery was once the headquarters of the Inquisition in Avila. For 3 centuries it housed the tomb of Torquemada, the first general inquisitor, whose zeal in organizing the Inquisition made him a notorious figure in Spanish history. Legend has it that after the friars were expelled from the monastery in 1836, a mob of Torquemada-haters ransacked the tomb and burned the remains somewhere outside the city walls. His final burial site is unknown.

Prince John, the only son of Ferdinand and Isabella, was also buried here, in a sumptuous sepulcher in the church transept. The tomb was desecrated during a French invasion; now, only an empty crypt remains.

Visit the Royal Cloisters, in some respects the most interesting architectural feature of the place. In the upper part of the third cloister, you'll find the Museum of Far Eastern Art, which exhibits Vietnamese, Chinese, and Japanese art and handicrafts.

Plaza Granada 1. ☎ **92-035-22-37.** Admission to museum 2€ ($2.50); cloisters 1€ ($1.25). Museum Tues–Sun 11am–12:45pm and 4–6pm; cloisters Mon–Sun 10am–1pm and 4–8pm. Bus: 1, 2, or 3.

WHERE TO STAY

Avila is a summer resort—a refuge from Castilian heat—but the hotels are few in number, and the Spanish book nearly all the hotel space in July and August. Make sure to have a reservation in advance. Las Cancelas (see "Where to Dine," below) also rents rooms.

MODERATE
Gran Hotel Palacio de Valderrábanos   Set immediately adjacent to the front entrance of the cathedral behind an entryway that is a marvel of medieval stonework,

this is one of the most elegant and historic hotels of Castile. Originally built in the 1300s as a private home by an early bishop of Avila (and a member of the Valderrábanos family), it contains a once-fortified lookout tower (whose circumference encloses one of the suites), high-beamed ceilings, and intricately chiseled stonework. The public rooms have a somber elegance, with slightly faded baronial furniture that adds to the old-fashioned feeling. If possible, ask for a bedroom overlooking the cathedral. Rooms come in a variety of shapes, but each is usually medium in size, well furnished with comfortable beds and firm mattresses.

Plaza Catedral 9, 05001 Avila. ℂ **92-021-10-23.** Fax 92-025-16-91. www.palaciovalderrabanoshotel.com. 73 units. 115€ ($144) double; 160€ ($200) suite. AE, DC, MC, V. Parking 9€ ($11) per day. Bus: 1, 2, or 3. **Amenities:** Restaurant; bar; room service; babysitting; laundry service; dry cleaning. *In room:* A/C, TV, minibar, hair dryer, safe.

Hostería Ayala Berganza ★★ *Finds*   This 15th-century building was once the abode of one of Spain's most famous painters, Ignacio Zuloaga (1870–1945). It has been turned into one of the most atmospheric little inns in Castile. Part of the hotel is the original Castilian palace, dating from the 15th century and declared a historic monument, plus a modern structure completed in 1998. The location is next to the Romanesque church of San Millán, only a few minutes' walk from the Aqueduct. The hotel lies just outside the ramparts of the center of Segovia, a 5-minute walk to the heart of town and the cathedral. Care and attention went into the design of the modernized bedrooms and two suites, each individually decorated and containing a private bathroom. In a stone-columned central patio, an excellent Castilian cuisine based on seasonal dishes and roasted meats from a wood-fired oven is served.

Calle Carretas 5, 40001 Segovia. ℂ **92-146-04-48.** Fax 92-146-23-77. www.innsofspain.com. 18 units. 110€–135€ ($138–$169) double; 165€–200€ ($206–$250) suite. Rates include breakfast. AE, MC, V. **Amenities:** Restaurant; coffee shop; bar; business center; babysitting; laundry service; garden. *In room:* A/C, TV, minibar, hair dryer, safe.

Hotel Reina Isabel ★   Cited for its elegant decoration, this hotel stands behind a severe facade but warms considerably once you're inside. Rated four stars by the government, it lies about a 6-minute walk outside the walls of the old city. The interior is classically designed, with separate areas depicting various epochs in Spanish history, complete with furnishings and objets d'art from the 14th to the 18th century, including a magnificent altarpiece from the 15th century. The spacious bedrooms are similarly decorated and furnished with classical motifs, with marble floors and comfortable beds. All have state-of-the-art bathrooms; each unit contains a tub/shower combo, and each suite has a whirlpool tub. The hotel also operates an excellent restaurant nearby, **Copacabana,** San Millán 9 (ℂ **92-021-11-10**).

Paseo de la Estación 17, 05001 Avila. ℂ **92-025-10-22.** Fax 92-025-11-73. www.reinaisabel.com. 60 units. 85€–120€ ($106–$150) double; 165€ ($206) suite. AE, DC, MC, V. Parking 8€ ($10). **Amenities:** Restaurant; bar; room service; laundry service; dry cleaning. *In room:* A/C, TV, minibar, hair dryer, safe.

Palacio de Los Velada ★★★   When the Spanish chain Meliá opened this splendid gem to guests in 1995, it quickly became the most sought-after accommodation in the province, surpassing even the government-run *paradores*. Four centuries ago, this palace sheltered the likes of Charles V and Philip II. Arrayed around a central courtyard, today's hotel offers a luxury that was unimaginable when those kings spent the night.

The styling in the public rooms and the luxuriously furnished guest rooms make even the *paradores* look like they need a face-lift. Enjoying the best location in town—right in the center near the cathedral—the hotel receives guests in the setting of a medieval palace, with massive stones and antiques throughout. All the modern conveniences, including wide, comfortable beds have been installed, along with state-of-the-art plumbing. A shopping arcade is nearby.

Plaza de la Catedral 10, 05001 Avila. © **92-025-51-00.** Fax 92-025-49-00. www.veladahoteles.com. 145 units. 135€ ($169) double; 280€ ($350) suite. AE, MC, V. Parking 13€ ($16)]. **Amenities:** Restaurant; bar; room service; laundry service; dry cleaning. *In room:* A/C, TV, minibar, hair dryer, safe.

Parador de Avila ⌖   Two blocks northwest of Plaza de la Victoria, this parador stands on a ridge overlooking the banks of the Adaja River. Once it was known as the Palace of Benavides, from the 15th century; its facade forms part of the square. The palace has a dignified entranceway, with most of its public lounges opening onto a central courtyard with an inner gallery of columns. The refurbished rooms contain tasteful furnishings: stone fireplaces, highly polished tile floors, old chests, leather armchairs, paintings, and sculptures. The rooms, generally medium-size, come with all the modern comforts, including good mattresses and tiled bathrooms.

Marqués de Camales de Chozas 2, 05001 Avila. © **92-021-13-40.** Fax 92-022-61-66. www.parador.es. 61 units. 100€–120€ ($125–$150) double; 275€ ($344) suite. AE, DC, MC, V. Free outside parking; garage 12€ ($15). **Amenities:** Restaurant; bar; room service; laundry service; dry cleaning. *In room:* A/C, TV, minibar, hair dryer, safe.

INEXPENSIVE

El Rastro *(Value)*   Situated near the junction of Calle Caballeros and Calle Cepadas, this is the best choice for the bargain hunter. Few visitors know that they can spend the night at this old Castilian inn built into the city walls. The small guest rooms are basic and clean, containing private bathrooms with tubs.

Plaza del Rastro 1, 05001 Avila. © **92-021-12-18.** Fax 92-025-16-26. 10 units. 35€–42€ ($44–$53) double. AE, MC, DC, V. **Amenities:** Restaurant; bar; lounge. *In room:* TV, no phone.

Hostería de Bracamonte ⌖⌖ *(Finds)*   The most tranquil spot in town is this little gem decorated in a classic Castilian style. It lies 1 block north of Plaza de Victoria, the main square within the city walls. A restful and quiet oasis, it has a number of charming features, including a lovely patio and a dark-wood Castilian motif throughout. Converted to a small inn in 1989, the *hostería* retains some of its aristocratic origins as the town house of Gov. Don Juan Teherán y Monjaraz. Rooms are spacious and have whitewashed walls; some have fireplaces and four-poster beds. All contain neatly kept bathrooms with tubs. There is also an excellent restaurant.

Bracamonte 6, 05001 Avila. © **92-025-12-80.** 22 units. 60€–75€ ($75–$94) double. MC, V. Parking nearby 10€ ($13). **Amenities:** Restaurant; bar; lounge. *In room:* TV, minibar.

WHERE TO DINE
MODERATE
El Molino de la Lasa ⌖ *(Finds)* SEGOVIAN   A mill dating from the 1400s and standing near the Adaja River has been turned into one of the best restaurants in Segovia. Instead of disguising the building's former functions, the owners decided to preserve and display the machinery. Try to arrive before your reservations to enjoy a drink in the animated and charming bar, filled with a mix of locals and visitors. The chef uses top-quality ingredients that he fashions into a savory cuisine with both fish and meat dishes. Try his garlic-studded roast pork or his *merluza* (hake) in a zesty marinara sauce. Some excellent, tender, and well-flavored lamb dishes are also served along with tasty veal chops. The trout served is caught in the Adaja River. Try for a side dish of *judías de El Barco,* from the nearby village of El Barco, whose farmers are

said to produce the tastiest beans in Old Castile. In the garden is a little playground for the kids.

Bajada de la Losa 12. ✆ **92-021-11-01.** Reservations required. Main courses 19€–25€ ($24–$31). AE, DC, MC, V. Tues–Sun 1:30–4:30pm and 9–11:30pm.

INEXPENSIVE

El Rastro CASTILIAN   An old inn built into the 11th-century town walls, El Rastro serves typical Castilian dishes, with more attention given to freshness and preparation than to culinary flamboyance. Specialties include roast baby lamb and tender white veal, raised in the region and known for its succulence. It is prepared at least four different ways. Dessert recipes have been passed down from Avila's nuns. Try, if you dare, the highly touted *yemas de Santa Teresa* (St. Teresa's candied egg yolk). Travel expert Arthur Frommer found it a particularly horrible dessert—and I agree. Yet Avila residents keep praising it as a specialty. To my taste, there are far better selections on the menu. They also maintain a small hotel with 10 comfortable rooms (see "Where to Stay," above).

Plaza del Rastro 1. ✆ **92-021-12-19.** Reservations required on weekends only. Main courses 12€–16€ ($15–$20); fixed-price menu 15€ ($19). AE, DC, MC, V. Daily 1–4pm and 9–11pm.

Las Cancelas ✦ *Value* CASTILIAN   A recent discovery for me, Las Cancelas is where the locals go, whereas tourists crowd into several restaurants nearby. You get good food, regional specialties, a time-mellowed Castilian ambience, and affordable prices, a rather unbeatable combination. I begin my evenings in Avila at the restaurant's tapas bar up front. Tasty tidbits, almost mystical conversations, and good wine flow freely. Later you can head back to the dining room where simple paper covers the old wooden tables. A carafe of regional wine arrives at your table as you tear off hunks of the freshly baked bread. The restaurant itself is in a stone-columned patio where seasonal dishes emerge from the kitchen. Meats are roasted in a wood-fired oven and are the house specialties. I can never resist the *chuletón de Avila,* a mammoth T-bone steak and the chef's specialty. Platters of roast chicken, baked lamb, and other delights will also tempt you.

The Castilian inn is also one of the bargain places to stay in Avila, offering 14 small but modernized and comfortable bedrooms, each with a private shower, costing only 57€ ($71) a night for a double. Each has a TV and phone and in some cases air-conditioning as well.

Cruz Viejo 6. ✆ **92-021-22-49.** Reservations recommended. Main courses 12€–20€ ($15–$25). AE, DC, MC, V. Daily 1:30–4pm and 8:30–10:30pm.

Appendix A:
Madrid in Depth

Madrid was conceived, planned, and built when Spain was at the peak of its confidence and power in the 16th century during the reign of Phillip II, and the city became the solid and dignified seat of a great empire stretching around the world. Madrid glitters almost as much as Paris, Rome, or London and parties more than any other city. Although it lacks the spectacular Romanesque and Gothic monuments of older Spanish cities, Madrid never fails to convey its own sense of grandeur.

Madrid has the highest altitude (600m/1,969 ft.) of any European capital, and although it gets quite cold in winter, the city can be blisteringly hot in summer. Traffic roars down wide boulevards that stretch for miles—from the narrow streets of the city's historic 17th-century core to the ugly concrete suburbs that have built up in recent years.

Don't come to Madrid expecting a city that looks classically Iberian. True, many of the older buildings in the historic core look as Spanish as those you might have encountered in rural towns across the plains of La Mancha. But a great number of the monuments and palaces mirror the architecture of France—an oddity that reflects the genetic link between the royal families of Spain and France.

Most striking is how the city has blossomed since the demise of the 20th-century Spanish dictator Franco. Madrid was the epicenter of *la movida* (the movement), a renaissance of the arts after years of dictatorial creative repression. Today, despite stiff competition from such smaller cities as Barcelona and Seville, Madrid still reigns as the country's artistic and creative centerpiece.

More world-class art is on view in the central neighborhood around the stellar Prado museum than in virtually any other concentrated area in the world: the Caravaggios and Rembrandts at the Thyssen-Bornemisza; the El Grecos and Velázquezes at the Prado itself; and the Dalís and Mirós—not to mention Picasso's wrenching *Guernica*—at the Reina Sofía. Ironically, much of the city's art was collected by 18th-century Spanish monarchs whose artistic sensibility was frequently more astute than their political savvy.

Regrettably, within the city limits you'll also find sprawling expanses of concrete towers, sometimes paralyzing traffic, a growing incidence in street crime, and entire districts that, as in every other metropolis, bear no historic or cultural interest for the tourist. Many long-time visitors find that the city's quintessential Spanish feel has subsided somewhat in the face of a Brussels-like "Europeanization" that has occurred since Spain's 1986 induction into the European Union. The city's gems remain the opulence of the **Palacio Real,** the bustle of **El Rastro**'s flea market, and the sultry fever of late-night flamenco. When urban commotion starts to overwhelm, seek respite in the **Parque del Retiro,** a vast, verdant oasis in the heart of the city a stone's throw from the Prado.

1 A Look at the Past

BARBARIAN INVASIONS, THE MOORISH KINGDOM & THE RECONQUEST Around 200 B.C. the Romans vanquished the Carthaginians and laid the foundations of the present Latin culture. Traces of Roman civilization can still be seen today. By the time of Julius Caesar, Spain (Hispania) was under Roman law and had begun a long period of peace and prosperity.

When Rome fell in the 5th century, Spain was overrun, first by the Vandals and then by the Visigoths from eastern Europe. The chaotic rule of the Visigothic kings lasted about 300 years, but the barbarian invaders did adopt the language of their new country and tolerated Christianity as well.

In A.D. 711, Moorish warriors led by Tarik crossed over into Spain and conquered the disunited country. By 714, they controlled most of it, except for a few mountain regions around Asturias. For 8 centuries the Moors occupied their new land, which they called *al-Andalús*, or Andalusia, with Córdoba as the capital. A great intellectual center, Córdoba became the scientific capital of Europe; notable advances were made in agriculture, industry, literature, philosophy, and medicine. The Jews were welcomed by the Moors, often serving as administrators, ambassadors, and financial officers. But the Moors quarreled with one another, and soon the few Christian strongholds in the north began to advance south.

In A.D. 852, under Emir Mohamed I Córdoban, Moors constructed the wooden *Alcázar* (fortress) in Mayrit—subsequently named Magerit and later Madrid—on the site of the present *Palacio Real* (Royal Palace). Its strategic position deterred 11th-century Castilian invaders who mistook what was then little more than a rural village for the bigger city of Toledo.

The Reconquest, the name given to the Christian efforts to rid the peninsula of the Moors, slowly reduced the size of the Muslim holdings, with Catholic monarchies forming in northern areas. The three powerful kingdoms of Aragón, Castile, and León were joined in 1469, when Ferdinand of Aragón married Isabella of Castile. Catholic kings, as they were called, launched the final attack on the Moors and completed the Reconquest in 1492 by capturing Granada.

That same year Columbus, the Genoese sailor, landed in the West Indies, laying the foundations for a far-flung empire that brought wealth and power to Spain during the 16th and 17th centuries.

The Spanish Inquisition, begun under Ferdinand and Isabella, sought to eradicate

Dateline

- **11th century B.C.** Phoenicians settle Spain's coasts.
- **650 B.C.** Greeks colonize the east.
- **600 B.C.** Celts cross the Pyrenees and settle in Spain.
- **6th–3rd century B.C.** Carthaginians make Cartagena their colonial capital, driving out the Greeks.
- **218–201 B.C.** Second Punic War: Rome defeats Carthage.
- **2nd century B.C.–2nd century A.D.** Rome controls most of Iberia. Christianity spreads.
- **5th century** Vandals, then Visigoths, invade Spain.
- **8th–9th century** Moors conquer most of Spain, and found Mayrit on original site of Madrid.
- **10th century** Madrid occupied by Christian king Ramiro II.
- **1202** Madrid officially given town status.
- **1214** More than half of Iberia is regained by Catholics.
- **1339** First parliament (Cortés) held in Madrid by Alfonso XI.

all heresy and secure the primacy of Catholicism. Non-Catholics, Jews, and Moors were mercilessly persecuted, and many were driven out of the country.

Around this time, Madrid was chiefly of interest as a great hunting area, much favored by the monarchs of Castile, and today the El Prado Park north of the city still contains a host of protected wildlife.

THE GOLDEN AGE & LATER DECLINE Columbus's voyage to America and the conquistadors' subsequent exploration of that land ushered Spain into its golden age.

In the first half of the 16th century, Balboa discovered the Pacific Ocean, Cortés seized Mexico for Spain, Pizarro took Peru, and a Spanish ship (initially commanded by the Portuguese Magellan, who was killed during the voyage) circumnavigated the globe. The conquistadors took Catholicism to the New World and shipped cargoes of gold back to Spain. The Spanish Empire extended all the way to the Philippines. Charles V, grandson of Ferdinand and Isabella, was the most powerful prince in Europe—king of Spain and Naples, Holy Roman Emperor and lord of Germany, duke of Burgundy and the Netherlands, and ruler of the New World territories.

But much of Spain's wealth and human resources were wasted in religious and secular conflicts. First Jews, then Muslims, and finally Catholicized Moors were driven out—and with them much of the country's prosperity. When Philip II ascended the throne in 1556, Spain could indeed boast vast possessions: the New World colonies; Naples, Milan, Genoa, Sicily, and other portions of Italy; the Spanish Netherlands (modern Belgium and the Netherlands); and portions of Austria and Germany. But the seeds of decline had already been planted.

Philip II, a bureaucrat of the first order, made Madrid his capital in 1561 for the simple reason that it was the geographical center of the country, and apart from a temporary 6-year transfer to Valladolid in 1600, the city has occupied that position ever since. As a result of Phillip's decision, the population suddenly expanded fourfold to over 80,000 in barely 40 years, and some of the city's finest sights, from the Plaza Mayor to the Monastery of the Descalzas Reales, emerged in their full glory.

Also a fanatic Catholic, Phillip devoted his energies to subduing the Protestant revolt in the Netherlands and to becoming the standard-bearer for the Counter-Reformation. He tried to return England to Catholicism, first by marrying Mary I ("Bloody Mary") and later by wooing her half-sister, Elizabeth I, who rebuffed him. When, in 1588, he resorted to sending the Armada, it was ignominiously defeated;

- **1469** Ferdinand of Aragón marries Isabella of Castile.
- **1492** Catholic monarchs seize Granada, the last Moorish stronghold. Columbus lands in the New World.
- **1519** Cortés conquers Mexico. Charles I is crowned Holy Roman Emperor, as Charles V.
- **1556** Philip II inherits throne and launches the Counter-Reformation.

- **1561** Phillip II establishes Madrid as Spain's capital.
- **1588** England defeats Spanish Armada.
- **1600** Capital moved from Madrid to Valladolid by Phillip II, but returned to Madrid 6 years later.
- **1700** Philip V becomes king. War of Spanish Succession follows.

- **1713** Treaty of Utrecht ends war. Spain's colonies reduced.
- **1734** Madrid's Moorish Alcázar fortress burned down. Royal Palace completed on same site 30 years later.
- **1759** Charles III ascends throne.
- **1808** Napoleon places brother Joseph on the Spanish throne. Resistance and rebellion in Madrid.

(continues)

and that defeat symbolized the decline of Spanish power.

In 1700, a Bourbon prince, Philip V, raised at Versailles, became king, and the country fell under the influence of France. Many of the changes in Madrid around this time, such as the rebuilding of the Palacio Real and construction of La Granja near Segovia, demonstrate this "Europeanizing" effect. Philip V's right to the throne was challenged by the Archduke Charles of Austria, thus giving rise to the War of the Spanish Succession. When it ended, Spain had lost Flanders, its Italian possessions, and Gibraltar (still held by the British today).

During the 18th century, Spain's direction changed with each sovereign. The "enlightened" Charles III (1759–88) developed the country economically, culturally, and aesthetically. He cleaned up the by then "dark foul smelling" capital by building sewers, introducing street lights, constructing monuments, and creating the wide tree-lined Prado Avenue and incomparable Botanical Gardens. But his successor, Charles IV, became embroiled in wars with France, and the weakness of the Spanish monarchy allowed Napoleon to place his brother Joseph Bonaparte on the throne in 1808. The *Madrileños* put up a spirited but hopeless resistance against these superior odds and it was 4 more years before an allied force under the duke of Wellington was able to drive out the French and restore Madrid and Spain to the Spaniards.

THE 19TH & 20TH CENTURIES

Although Britain and France had joined forces to restore the Spanish monarchy, the European conflicts encouraged Spanish colonists to rebel. Ultimately, this led the United States to free the Philippines, Puerto Rico, and Cuba from Spain in 1898.

In 1876, Spain became a constitutional monarchy. But labor unrest, disputes with the Catholic Church, and war in Morocco combined to create political chaos. Conditions eventually became so bad that the Cortés, or parliament, was dissolved in 1923, and Gen. Miguel Primo de Rivera formed a military directorate. Early in 1930, Primo de Rivera resigned, but unrest continued.

On April 14, 1931, a revolution occurred, a republic was proclaimed, and King Alfonso XIII and his family were forced to flee. Initially, the liberal constitutionalists ruled, but soon they were pushed aside by the socialists and anarchists. These adopted a constitution separating church and state, secularizing education, and containing several other radical provisions (for example, agrarian reform and the expulsion of the Jesuits).

- **1813** Wellington drives French out of Spain; the monarchy is restored.
- **1876** Spain becomes a constitutional monarchy.
- **1898** Spanish-American War leads to Spain's loss of Puerto Rico, Cuba, and the Philippines.
- **1906** Grand opening of Madrid's Ritz hotel.
- **1908** Construction work on Gran Vía begins.

- **1921** Launching of Madrid Metro.
- **1923** Primo de Rivera forms military directorate.
- **1930** Right-wing dictatorship ends; Primo de Rivera exiled.
- **1931** King Alfonso XIII abdicates; Second Republic is born.
- **1933–35** Falange party formed.

- **1936–39** Civil war between the governing Popular Front and the Nationalists led by Gen. Francisco Franco. Ends when Franco enters Madrid victoriously after a 3-year siege.
- **1939** Franco establishes dictatorship, which will last 36 years.
- **1941** Spain technically stays neutral in World War II, but Franco favors Germany.

The extreme nature of these reforms fostered the growth of the conservative Falange party (*Falange española,* or Spanish Phalanx), modeled after Italy and Germany's fascist parties. By the 1936 elections, the country was divided equally between left and right, and political violence was common. On July 18, 1936, the army, supported by Mussolini and Hitler, tried to seize power, igniting the Spanish Civil War. Gen. Francisco Franco, coming from Morocco to Spain, led the Nationalist (rightist) forces in fighting that ravaged the country.

The popular front opposing Franco was forced to rely mainly on untrained volunteers, including a few heroic Americans called the "Lincoln brigade." For those who want an insight into the era, Ernest Hemingway's novel *For Whom the Bell Tolls* is a good read. It took time to turn untrained militias into an army fit to battle Franco's forces, and time was something the popular front didn't have.

It was a war that would attract the attention of the world. By the summer of 1936, the USSR was sending rubles to aid the revolution by the republicans. Even Mexico sent war materiel to the popular front. Most—but not all—the volunteers were communists. Italy and Germany contributed war materiel to Franco's forces.

Madrid, controlled by the popular front, held out through a brutal siege that lasted for 28 months. Eventually, the government of the popular front moved to Valencia for greater safety in 1936.

But in the winter of 1936–37, Franco's forces slowly began to establish power, capturing the Basque capital of Bilbao and eventually Santander. The war shocked the world with its ruthlessness (World War II hadn't happened yet). Churches were burned, and mass executions occurred, especially memorable in the Basque town of Guernica, which became the subject of one of Picasso's most fabled paintings.

By October 1, 1936, Franco was clearly in charge of the leadership of nationalist Spain, abolishing popular suffrage and regional autonomy—in effect, launching a totalitarian rule for Spain.

The republicans were split by internal differences, and spy trials were commonplace. At the end of the first year of war, Franco held 35 of Spain's provincial capitals. In 1937, the republican forces were cut in two, and Madrid was left to fend for itself.

The last great offensive of the war began on December 28, 1938, with an attack by Franco's forces on Barcelona, which fell on January 26 after a campaign of 34 days. Republican forces fled toward France, as a succession of presidents occurred. On March 28 some 200,000 nationalist troops marched into Madrid,

- **1955** Spain joins the United Nations.
- **1969** Franco names Juan Carlos as his successor.
- **1975** Juan Carlos becomes king. Franco dies.
- **1976** *El País,* Spain's first world-class democratic newspaper, launched in Madrid.
- **1978** New democratic constitution initiates reforms.
- **1981** Coup attempt by right-wing officers in Madrid's parliament building fails.

- **1982** Socialists gain power after 43 years of right-wing rule.
- **1986** Spain joins the European Community (now the European Union).
- **1992** Barcelona hosts the Summer Olympics; Seville hosts EXPO '92.
- **1996** A conservative party defeats Socialist party, ending 13-year rule. José María Aznar chosen prime minister.

- **1998** Two cultural milestones for Spain: the inauguration of the controversial Guggenheim Museum at Bilbao and the reopening of Madrid's opera house, Teatro Real. Real Madrid soccer team wins European Cup for a record seventh time.
- **1999** Spain falls under the euro umbrella.

(continues)

meeting no resistance. The war was over the next day when the rest of republican Spain surrendered. The war lasted 2 years and 254 days, costing some one million lives.

To get a sense of the Spanish Civil War, visitors can travel to El Valle de los Caídos (the Valley of the Fallen) outside El Escorial (see chapter 11).

Although Franco adopted a neutral position during World War II, his sympathies obviously lay with Germany and Italy. Spain, although a nonbelligerent, assisted the Axis powers. This action intensified the diplomatic isolation into which the country was forced after the war's end—in fact, it was excluded from the United Nations until 1955.

Before his death, General Franco selected as his successor Juan Carlos de Borbón y Borbón, son of the pretender to the Spanish throne. After the 1977 elections, a new constitution was approved by the electorate and the king; it guaranteed human and civil rights, as well as free enterprise, and canceled the status of the Roman Catholic Church as the church of Spain. It also granted limited autonomy to several regions, including Catalonia and the Basque provinces, both of which, however, are still clamoring for complete autonomy.

In 1981 the fledgling democracy overcame its first test. A group of right-wing military officers seized the Cortés (parliament building) in Madrid and called upon Juan Carlos to establish a Francoist state. The king, however, refused, and the conspirators were arrested. The government's second major accomplishment—under the Socialist administration of Prime Minister Felipe González, the country's first leftist government since 1939—was to gain Spain's entry into the European Community (now Union) in 1986.

The '80s was a progressive decade for Madrid, with a highly innovative and imaginative Socialist mayor Enrique Tierno Galván at the helm, still revered and honored with a park in his name today. This was the effervescent and optimistic period of the *movida,* when the creative arts, long repressed, exploded with an inventive energy that was unprecedented. (It was alas subsequently dampened by his pallid and reactionary '90s Partido Popular successor Alvarez de Manzano, who—unlamented—ceded his role in 2004 to the potentially more promising but as yet unproven Alberto Ruiz-Gallardón.)

The most shocking news for 2000 was not political, or artistic, but social. Spain came under increasing pressure to conform to short lunch breaks like those in the other E.U. countries. What? No 3-hour siesta? It was heresy. Pro-siesta forces

---

- **2000** Economy goes on an upswing. Complete euro unity looms.
- **2001** Spain moves forward as an economic powerhouse in Latin America.
- **2002** Spain gives up its historic currency, the peseta, and adopts the euro as its national currency.
- **2004** Al Qaeda–linked terrorists bomb three suburban Madrid trains, killing almost

200 people; PSOE (Spanish Socialist party) candidate Zapatero is elected as prime minister, ending 8 years of rule by Aznar's Populist party.
- **2006** Basque terrorist organization ETA declares a "permanent" truce. PSOE and PP differ in opinion regarding negotiations.

in Spain cited the American custom of "power naps" as reason to retain their beloved afternoon break. In spite of the opposition, large companies began to cut lunch to 2 hours.

So the siesta appears to be under serious attack, perhaps as a consequence of the Spanish economy's upswing, which created more new jobs than in any other country in the E.U. More and more families are moving to the suburbs, and more women are joining the workforce. A survey has revealed that only 25% of Spaniards still take the siesta.

On other fronts, Spain moved ahead as an economic powerhouse in Latin America, where only 20 years ago it was a minor economic presence. Today, the long-held monopoly of the U.S. in the region is being challenged for the first time since the Spanish-American War of 1898. In the last tally, Spaniards in 1 year poured $20 billion worth of investment value into Latin America.

Spain officially abandoned its time-honored peseta and went under the euro umbrella in March 2002. During the transition period, as Spaniards struggled to adjust to the new currency, counterfeiters had a field day.

The tragedy of March 11, 2004, when Al Qaeda–linked terrorists blew up three suburban trains in and near the main station of Atocha, causing nearly 200 deaths, revealed the subsequent unity, resilience, and individuality of spirit of the Madrileños. "We were all on that train" became a popular slogan. Three days later—after 8 years in the wilderness—the PSOE (Spanish Socialist Party) was reelected to power in an overt rejection of former President Aznar's policy in general and his contribution to the Iraq incursion in particular. The country's populace held him and his party responsible for these terrible consequences. Only time will tell how Aznar's successor, the idealistic, youthful, and yet untried President Zapatero, succeeds in guiding the new democracy.

In 2005 Madrid lost out to London in its bid to host the 2012 Olympics, but is still surging ahead with city development plans originally aimed to coincide with that event. It's even advanced some projects so that they'll be ready in time for the municipal elections in 2007.

After 4 decades of violence aimed indiscriminately at the military and civil population alike, the Basque terrorist organization ETA announced a "permanent" ceasefire in 2006. As they had already announced a ceasefire several years back only to renege on it 18 months later, the first reaction to this statement was one of extreme caution. However, general revulsion at the 2004 atrocity was such that terrorist groups in Spain have lost most of their remaining supporters, and the likelihood is that this truce will hold. In all events the PSOE is anxious to go ahead with negotiations, with or without the help of the PP, who refuse under any circumstances to deal with ETA.

2 A Taste of Madrid

Meals are an extremely important social activity in the Spanish capital, whether that means eating out late at night or hosting large family gatherings for lunch. Although the city is faster paced than it once was, few Madrileños race through a meal on the way to an appointment.

The food choices in the capital are extremely varied, and culinary traditions from all over the country are well represented. Portions are immense, but prices, by North American standards, can be high. Whenever possible, try the traditional Castilian specialties. Most restaurants close 1 day a week, so be sure to check ahead. Hotel dining rooms are generally open all week long. Generally, reservations are not necessary, except at

The Spectacle of Death

For obvious reasons, many people consider bullfighting cruel and shocking, but as Ernest Hemingway pointed out in *Death in the Afternoon:* "The bull-fight is not a sport in the Anglo-Saxon sense of the word; that is, it is not an equal contest or an attempt at an equal contest between a bull and a man. Rather it is a tragedy: the death of the bull, which is played, more or less well, by the bull and the man involved and in which there is danger for the man but certain death for the bull."

When the symbolic drama of the bullfight is acted out, some believe it reaches a higher plane, the realm of art. Some people argue that it is not a public exhibition of cruelty at all, but rather a highly skilled art form that requires the will to survive, courage, showmanship, and gallantry. Regardless of how you view it, the spectacle is an authentic Spanish experience and reveals much about the character of the land and its people.

The *corrida* (bullfight) season lasts from early spring until around mid-October. Fights are held in a *plaza de toros* (bullring), and the big-time Ventas bullring in Madrid is the largest in all Spain. Sunday is *corrida* day *par excellence,* though Madrid also regularly has fights on Saturdays and fiestas, and during the San Isidro festivities there are 4 continuous weeks of daily bullfights. At the back of the Plaza de Toros in the Patio de Caballos (Courtyard of the Horses) is the atmospheric little **Museo Taurino (Bullfight Museum;** ✆ **91-725-18-57)**, where, among less ghoulish *corrida* souvenirs, you can see the *traje de luces* (luminous suit)—complete with faded bloodstains—that the legendary Spanish bullfighter Manolete wore during his last fateful bullfight in Linares in 1947.

Tickets fall into three classifications, and prices are based on your exposure to the famed Spanish sun: *sol* (sun), the cheapest; *sombra* (shade), the most expensive; and *sol y sombra* (a mixture of sun and shade), the medium-price range.

the most popular or highly acclaimed restaurants.

MEALS

BREAKFAST The day starts with a continental breakfast of coffee, hot chocolate, or tea, with assorted rolls, butter, and jam. Spanish breakfast might also consist of *churros* (fried fingerlike doughnuts) or *porras* (basically larger *churros* that Madrileños habitually down in threes; note, however, that you should be wary of eating more than a couple yourself—they're *very* filling). Either version can be accompanied by hot chocolate that is very sweet and thick, but most Spaniards simply have coffee, usually strong, served with hot milk: either a *café con leche* (half coffee, half milk) or *cortado* (a shot of espresso "cut" with a dash of milk). If you find it too strong and bitter for your taste, you might ask for a more diluted *café americano.*

LUNCH The most important meal of the day in Spain, lunch is comparable to the farm-style midday "dinner" in the United States. It usually includes three or

The *corrida* begins with a parade. For many viewers, this may be the high point of the afternoon's festivities, as all the bullfighters are clad in their *trajes de luces.*

Bullfights are divided into thirds. The first is the *tercio de capa* (cape), during which the matador tests the bull with various passes and gets acquainted with him. The second portion, the *tercio de varas* (sticks), begins with the lance-carrying *picadores* on horseback, who weaken, or "punish," the bull by jabbing him in the shoulder area. The horses are sometimes gored, even though they wear protective padding, or the horse and rider might be tossed into the air by the now-infuriated bull. The *picadores* are followed by the *banderilleros,* whose job it is to puncture the bull with pairs of boldly colored darts.

In the final *tercio de muleta,* the action narrows down to the lone fighter and the bull. Gone are the fancy capes. Instead, the matador uses a small red cloth known as a *muleta,* which, to be effective, requires a bull with lowered head. (The *picadores* and *banderilleros* have worked to achieve this.) Using the *muleta* as a lure, the matador wraps the bull around himself in various passes, the most dangerous of which is the *natural;* here, the matador holds the *muleta* in his left hand, the sword in his right. Right-hand passes pose less of a threat, since the sword can be used to spread out the *muleta,* making a larger target for the bull. After a number of passes, the time comes for the kill, the moment of truth.

After the bull dies, the highest official at the ring may award the matador an ear from the dead bull, or perhaps both ears, or ears and tail. For a truly extraordinary performance, the hoof is sometimes added. Spectators cheer a superlative performance by waving white handkerchiefs, imploring the judge to award a prize. The bullfighter may be carried away as a hero, or if he has displeased the crowd, he may be jeered and chased out of the ring by an angry mob. At a major fight, usually six bulls are killed by three matadors in one afternoon.

four courses, beginning with a choice of soup or several dishes of hors d'oeuvres called *entremeses.* Often a fish or egg dish is served after this, and then a meat course with vegetables. Wine is always part of the meal. Dessert is usually pastry, custard, or assorted fruit—followed by coffee. Lunch is served from 1 to 4pm, with "rush hour" at 2pm.

TAPAS After the early evening stroll, many Spaniards head for their favorite *tascas,* bars where they drink wine and sample assorted tapas, or snacks, such as bits of fish, eggs in mayonnaise, or olives.

Because many Spaniards eat dinner very late, they often have an extremely light breakfast, certainly coffee, and perhaps a pastry. However, by 11am they are often hungry and lunch might not be until 2pm or later, so many Spaniards have a late-morning snack, often at a cafeteria. Favorite items to order are an *empanada* (slice of meat or fish pie from Galicia) or *tortilla* (Spanish omelet with potatoes) accompanied by a *copa* of wine or a *caña* (small glass) of beer. (If you want a larger beer ask for a *doble*.) Many request a large tapa, such as *calamares* (squid) or *callos* (tripe) also served with bread and wine (or beer).

DINNER   Dinner in Madrid is another extravaganza. A typical meal starts with a bowl of soup, followed by a second course, often a fish dish, and by another main course, usually veal, beef, or pork, accompanied by vegetables. Again, desserts tend to be fruit, custard, or pastries.

Naturally, if you had a heavy and late lunch and stopped off at a tapas bar or two before dinner, supper might be much lighter, perhaps some cold cuts, sausage, a bowl of soup, or even a Spanish omelet made with potatoes. Wine is always part of the meal. Afterward, you might have a demitasse and a fiery Spanish brandy, *orujo* (equivalent of the gritty French *marc* or Italian *grappa*) or *anís* (anise-flavored liquor, a specialty of nearby Chinchón). The normal dining hour is 10 or 10:30pm.

THE CUISINE

SOUPS & APPETIZERS   Soups are usually served in big bowls. Cream soups, such as asparagus and potato, can be fine; too often, however, they are made from powdered envelope soups such as Knorr and Liebig. Served year-round, chilled gazpacho is tasty and particularly refreshing during the hot months. The combination is pleasant: olive oil, garlic, ground cucumbers, and raw tomatoes with a sprinkling of croutons. Spain also offers several varieties of fish soup—*sopa de pescado*—and many of these are superb.

In the *paradores* (government-run hostelries) and top restaurants, as many as 15 tempting hors d'oeuvres are served. In lesser-known places, avoid these *entremeses,* which often consist of last year's sardines and shards of sausage left over from the Moorish conquest.

EGGS   These are served in countless ways. A Spanish omelet, a *tortilla española,* is made with potatoes and usually onions. A simple omelet is called a *tortilla francesa.* A *tortilla portuguesa* is similar to the American Spanish omelet.

FISH   Spain's fish dishes tend to be outstanding and vary from province to province. One of the most common varieties is *merluza* (sweet white hake). *Langosta,* a variety of lobster, is seen everywhere—it's a treat but terribly expensive. (Gourmets relish the seawater taste; others find them tasteless.) *Rape* (pronounced "*rah-*peh") is the Spanish name for monkfish, a sweet, wide-boned ocean fish with a scalloplike texture. Also try a few dozen half-inch baby eels. They rely heavily on olive oil and garlic for their flavor, but they taste great. Squid cooked in its own ink is suggested only to those who want to go native. Charcoal-broiled sardines, however, are a culinary delight—a particular treat in the Basque provinces. Trout Navarre is one of the most popular fish dishes, usually stuffed with bacon or ham. Among the superb shellfish brought in daily from Spain's Atlantic coasts, *gambas* (prawns) and *mejillones* (mussels) are widely available. *Gambas al ajillo* (prawns cooked in garlic in a small earthenware dish) and *mejillones al vapor* (steamed mussels) are two popular variations.

PAELLA   You can't go to Spain without trying the country's celebrated paella. Flavored with saffron, paella is an aromatic rice dish usually topped with shellfish, chicken, sausage, peppers, and local spices. Served authentically, it comes steaming hot from the kitchen in a metal pan called a *paellería.* (Incidentally, what is known in the U.S. as Spanish rice isn't Spanish at all. If you ask an English-speaking waiter for Spanish rice, you'll be served paella.)

MEATS Don't expect Kansas City steak, but do try the spit-roasted suckling pig, so sweet and tender it can often be cut with a fork. The veal is also good, and the Spanish *lomo de cerdo,* loin of pork, is unmatched anywhere. Tender chicken is most often served in the major cities and towns today, and the Spanish are adept at spit-roasting it until it turns a delectable golden brown. However, in more remote spots of Spain, "free-range" chicken is often stringy and tough.

VEGETABLES & SALADS Through more sophisticated agricultural methods, Spain now grows more of its own vegetables, which are available year-round, unlike days of yore, when canned vegetables were used all too frequently. Both potatoes and rice are a staple of the Spanish diet, the latter a prime ingredient, of course, in the famous paella originating in Valencia. Salads don't usually get the attention they do in California, here often made simply with just lettuce, onions, and tomatoes.

DESSERTS The Spanish do not emphasize dessert, often opting for fresh fruit. Flan, a home-cooked egg custard, appears on all menus—sometimes with a burnt-caramel sauce in a version known as *crema catalana.* Ice cream appears on nearly all menus as well. Your best bet is to ask for a basket of fruit, which you can wash at your table. Homemade pastries are usually moist and not too sweet. As a dining oddity—although it's not at all odd to Spaniards—many restaurants serve fresh orange juice for dessert.

OLIVE OIL & GARLIC Olive oil is used lavishly in Spain, the largest olive grower on the planet. If you prefer your fish grilled in butter, the word is *mantequilla.* (In some instances, you'll be charged extra for the butter.) Garlic is also an integral part of the Spanish diet, and even if you love it, you may find Spaniards love it more than you do and use it in even the oddest combinations.

WHAT TO DRINK

WATER It is generally safe to drink water in Madrid. If you're traveling in remote areas, play it safe and drink bottled water. Among the most popular noncarbonated bottled drinks in Spain are Font Vella from Cataluña, Solan de Cabras from Cuenca, Lanjarón from Granada, and Solares, which is from Andalusia. Nearly all restaurants and hotels have it. Bubbly water is *agua mineral con gas* (Vichy Catalan is a good one to try here); noncarbonated, *agua mineral sin gas.* Note that bottled water in some areas may cost as much as the regional wine.

SOFT DRINKS In general, avoid the carbonated citrus drinks on sale everywhere. Most of them never saw an orange, much less a lemon. If you want a citrus drink, order old, reliable Schweppes. An excellent noncarbonated drink for the summer is called Tri-Naranjus, which comes in lemon and orange flavors. Your cheapest bet is a liter bottle of *gaseosa,* which comes in various flavors. In summer you should also try an *horchata.* Not to be confused with the Mexican beverage of the same name, the Spanish horchata is a sweet, milklike beverage made of tubers called *chufas.* In hot weather *granizados* (crushed-ice drinks) of lemon, orange or even coffee are very popular but watch the price if you're having one in an outdoor cafe in the Castellana avenue or Retiro park.

COFFEE Even if you are a dedicated coffee drinker, you may find the *café con leche* (coffee with milk) a little too strong. I suggest *leche manchada,* a little bit of strong, freshly brewed coffee in a glass that's filled with lots of frothy hot milk. If you're really desperate for American-style coffee, you can now try Starbucks, which has opened several Madrid branches in the past couple of years.

MILK In the largest cities you get bottled milk, but it loses a great deal of its flavor in the process of pasteurization. In all cases, avoid untreated milk and milk products. The best brand of fresh milk is Lauki.

BEER Beer *(cerveza)* is now drunk everywhere and is rapidly superseding wine as the most popular tipple. Domestic brands include San Miguel, Aguila, Cruz Blanca, Cruzcampo, and, last but not least, Mahou (which is made in Madrid). Bottled or draft versions of the latter are widely available, usually in the form of a *caña,* a small glass drawn from the *barril* or cask.

Note: There is an old Madrid ruling that alcoholic drinks—beer, wine, *vermut*—must be accompanied by a nourishing tidbit in order to "lessen their noxious influence," so you usually get a small free tapa thrown in with your tipple, especially in the cheaper, more traditional bars.

WINE Sherry *(vino de Jerez)* has been called "the wine with a hundred souls." Drink it before dinner (try the topaz-colored *finos,* a dry and very pale sherry) or whenever you drop into some old inn or bodega for refreshment; many of them have rows of kegs with spigots. *Manzanilla,* a golden-colored medium-dry sherry, is extremely popular. The sweet cream sherries (Harvey's Bristol Cream, for example) are favorite after-dinner wines (called *olorosos*). While the French may be disdainful of Spanish table wines, they can be truly noble, especially two leading varieties, Rioja and Navarra. Wines from westerly Extremadura are also beginning to make an impact, and several Extremeño wine bars have recently opened in the capital. If you're not too exacting in your tastes, you can always ask for the *vino de la casa* (house wine) wherever you dine. (This is likely to be a quaffable drop from Toledo or La Mancha.) The Priorat of Catalonia, meanwhile, is heavy, though its rival Penedès comes across as a more subtle vino. From Andalusia comes the fruity sherry-like Montilla. Spain has some good local sparkling wines *(cavas),* such as Freixenet and Codorníu, especially the Non Plus Ultra variety. One brand, Benjamín, comes in individual-size bottles.

Beginning in the 1990s, based partly on subsidies and incentives from the European Union, Spanish vintners have scrapped most of the country's obsolete winemaking equipment, hired new talent, and poured time and money into the improvement and promotion of wines from even high-altitude or arid regions not previously suitable for wine production. Thanks to irrigation, improved grape varieties, technological developments, and the expenditure of billions of pesetas, bodegas and vineyards are sprouting up throughout the country, opening their doors to visitors interested in how the stuff is grown, fermented, and bottled. These wines are now earning awards at wine competitions around the world for their quality and bouquet. Even Madrid province wines, ignored for years and still straining at the leash to prove themselves, have improved out of all recognition. The Jesús Díaz *bodega* from Colmenar de Oreja, south of the capital near Chinchón, has already won several prizes for its fragrant reds.

Interested in impressing a newfound Spanish friend over a wine list? Consider bypassing the usual array of Riojas, sherries, and sparkling Catalonian *cavas* in favor of, say, a Galician white Albariño from Rías Baixas, which some connoisseurs consider the perfect accompaniment for seafood. Among reds, make a beeline for vintages from the fastest-developing wine region of Europe, the arid, high-altitude district of Ribera del Duero, near Burgos, whose alkaline soil, cold nights, and sunny days have earned unexpected praise from winemakers (and encouraged massive investments) in the past 5 years.

For more information about these or any other of the 10 wine-producing regions of Spain (and the 39 officially recognized wine-producing *Denominaciones de Orígen* scattered across those regions), contact **Wines from Spain,** c/o the Commercial Office of Spain, 405 Lexington Ave., 44th Floor, New York, NY 10174-0331 (© **212/661-4959**).

SANGRIA   The all-time favorite refreshing drink in Spain, sangria is a red-wine punch that combines wine with oranges, lemons, *gaseosa* (seltzer), and sugar. Be careful, however; many joints that do a big tourist trade produce a sickly-sweet Kool-Aid version of sangria for unsuspecting visitors. Other places may also add an unwelcome amount of cheap *coñac* or *anís* to the drink.

WHISKEY & BRANDY   Imported whiskeys are available at most Spanish bars but at a high price. If you're a drinker, switch to brandies and cognacs, where the Spanish reign supreme (though Spanish *coñacs* tend to be sweeter and darker than their French counterparts). Try Fundador, made by the Pedro Domecq family in Jerez de la Frontera. If you find this a bit raw and want a slightly smoother coñac, ask for the "103" white label, while for something yet more mellow—and pricey—Magno or Carlos III are an appreciable step up. If money is no object, splash out on a Lepanto or Gran Duque de Alba, both of which are served from decanters and guaranteed to send you floating in a mellow haze up the Gran Vía.

In appendix B you'll find a short glossary of Spanish words connected with food, drink, and restaurants.

Appendix B:
Useful Terms & Phrases

1 Basic Vocabulary

Most Spaniards are very patient with foreigners who try to speak their language. Although you might encounter several regional languages and dialects in Spain, Castilian (*Castellano,* or simply *Español*) is understood everywhere. In Catalonia, they speak *Catalán* (the most widely spoken non-national language in Europe with roots in French, Italian, and Latin); in the Basque country, they speak *Euskera* (a complex "non–Indo European" language whose real origins remain a mystery); in Galicia, you'll hear *Gallego* (a Romance language closely linked to Portuguese). Still, a few words in Castilian will usually get your message across with no problem.

When traveling, it helps a lot to know a few basic phrases, so we've included a list of certain simple phrases in Castilian Spanish for expressing basic needs. Two pronunciation points to note: In Spain, the "ll" sound is a combination of "l" and "y" rather than just "y," which is South American pronunciation, and the "rr" is pronounced with an exaggerated guttural Scottish or Germanic intonation.

ENGLISH & CASTILIAN SPANISH PHRASES

English	Spanish	Pronunciation
Good day	**Buenos días**	*bweh*-nohs *dee*-ahs
How are you?	**¿Cómo está?**	*koh*-moh es-*tah*
Very well	**Muy bien**	mwee byehn
Thank you	**Gracias**	*grah*-syahs
You're welcome	**De nada**	deh *nah*-dah
Goodbye	**Adiós**	ah-*dyohs*
Please	**Por favor**	pohr fah-*vohr*
Yes	**Sí**	see
No	**No**	noh
Excuse me	**Perdóneme**	pehr-*doh*-neh-meh
	Discúlpeme	dees-*kul*-peh-meh
Give me	**Déme**	*deh*-meh
Where is . . . ?	**¿Dónde está . . . ?**	*dohn*-deh es-*tah*
the station	**la estación**	lah es-tah-*syohn*
a hotel	**un hotel**	oon oh-*tel*

English	Spanish	Pronunciation
a gas station	una gasolinera	*oo*-nah gah-so-lee-*neh*-rah
a restaurant	un restaurante	oon res-tow-*rahn*-teh
the toilet	el baño	el *bah*-nyoh
a good doctor	un buen médico	oon bwehn *meh*-dee-coh
the road to . . .	el camino a/ hacia . . .	el cah-*mee*-noh ah/ *ah*-syah
To the right	A la derecha	ah lah deh-*reh*-chah
To the left	A la izquierda	ah lah ees-*kyehr*-dah
Straight ahead	Derecho	deh-*reh*-choh
I would like	Quisiera	kee-*syeh*-rah
I want	Quiero	*kyeh*-roh
to eat.	comer	ko-*mehr*
a room.	una habitación	*oo*-nah ah-bee-tah-*syohn*
Do you have?	¿Tiene usted?	tyeh-neh oo-*sted*
a book	un libro	oon *lee*-broh
a dictionary	un diccionario	oon deek-syoh-*na*-ryo
How much is it?	¿Cuánto cuesta?	*kwahn*-toh *kwehs*-tah
When?	¿Cuándo?	*kwahn*-doh
What?	¿Qué?	keh
There is (Is there . . . ?)	(¿)Hay (. . . ?)	aye
What is there?	¿Qué hay?	keh aye
Yesterday	Ayer	ah-*yehr*
Today	Hoy	oy
Tomorrow	Mañana	mah-*nyah*-nah
Good	Bueno	*bweh*-noh
Bad	Malo	*mah*-loh
Better (Best)	(Lo) Mejor	(loh) meh-*hor*
More	Más	mahs
Less	Menos	*meh*-nohs
No smoking	Se prohibe fumar	seh proh-*ee*-beh foo-*mahr*
Postcard	Tarjeta postal	tar-*heh*-tah pohs-*tahl*
Insect repellent	Repelente contra insectos	reh-peh-*lehn*-teh *cohn*-trah een-*sehk*-tohs

NUMBERS

1	**uno** (*oo*-noh)	17	**diecisiete** (dyeh-see-*syeh*-teh)
2	**dos** (dohs)	18	**dieciocho** (dyeh-see-*oh*-choh)
3	**tres** (trehs)	19	**diecinueve** (dyeh-see-*nweh*-beh)
4	**cuatro** (*kwah*-troh)	20	**veinte** (*bayn*-teh)
6	**seis** (says)	30	**treinta** (*trayn*-tah)
7	**siete** (*syeh*-teh)	40	**cuarenta** (kwah-*rehn*-tah)
8	**ocho** (*oh*-choh)	50	**cincuenta** (seen-*kwehn*-tah)
9	**nueve** (*nweh*-beh)	60	**sesenta** (seh-*sehn*-tah)
10	**diez** (dyehs)	70	**setenta** (seh-*tehn*-tah)
11	**once** (*ohn*-seh)	80	**ochenta** (oh-*chehn*-tah)
12	**doce** (*doh*-seh)	90	**noventa** (noh-*behn*-tah)
13	**trece** (*treh*-seh)	100	**cien** (*syehn*)
14	**catorce** (kah-*tohr*-seh)	200	**doscientos** (doh-*syehn*-tohs)
15	**quince** (*keen*-seh)	500	**quinientos** (kee-*nyehn*-tos)
16	**dieciséis** (dyeh-see-*says*)	1,000	**mil** (meel)

2 Eating in Spain

Look for the fixed menu (comprising three courses, usually with wine), which is much better value than the the a la carte choice. See "A Taste of Madrid" in appendix A for more vocabulary on restaurants, food, and drink.

THE BASICS
MEALS & COURSES

English	Spanish	Pronunciation
Breakfast	**Desayuno**	deh-sah-*yoo*-noh
Lunch	**Almuerzo**	al-*mwehr*-thoh
Dinner	**Cena**	*theh*-nah
Meal	**Comida**	ko-*mee*-thah
Appetizers	**Entremeses**	en-treh-*meh*-sehs
Main course	**Primer plato**	*pree*-mehr *plah*-toh
Dessert	**Postre**	*pohs*-treh

TABLE SETTING

English	Spanish	Pronunciation
Glass	**Vaso**	*bah*-soh
	or **Copa**	*koh*-pah
Napkin	**Servilleta**	sehr-vi-*lye*-tah
Fork	**Tenedor**	teh-neh-*dor*
Knife	**Cuchillo**	koo-*chee*-lyoh
Spoon	**Cuchara**	koo-*chah*-rah
Bottle	**Botella**	boh-*teh*-lyah
Cup	**Taza**	*tah*-thah

DECODING THE MENU

English	Spanish	Pronunciation
Baked	Al horno	ahl ohr-noh
Boiled	Hervido	ehr-*vee*-thoh
Charcoal grilled	A la brasa	ah lah *brah*-sah
Fried	Frito	*free*-toh
Grilled	A la plancha	ah lah *plan*-chah
Rare	Poco hecho	*poh*-koh *eh*-choh
Medium	Medio hecho	*meh*-dyo *eh*-choh
Well done	Muy hecho	mwee *eh*-choh
Roasted	Asado	ah-*sah*-thoh
Sauce	Salsa	*sahl*-sah
Spicy	Picante	pee-*kahn*-teh
Stew	Estofado	ess-toh-*fah*-doh

DINING OUT

English	Spanish	Pronunciation
Check/bill	Cuenta	*kwen*-tah
Waiter	Camarero *(masc.)*	kah-mah-*reh*-roh
	Camarera *(fem.)*	kah-mah-*reh*-rah

ASSORTED FOODS
BEVERAGES

English	Spanish	Pronunciation
Beer	Cerveza	thehr-*veh*-thah
Coffee	Café	kah-*feh*
Milk	Leche	*leh*-cheh
Pitcher	Jarra	*hah*-rah
Tea	Té	teh
Water	Agua	*ah*-gwah
Wine	Vino	*bee*-noh
Red	Tinto	*teen*-toh
Rosé	Rosado	roh-*sah*-thoh
White	Blanco	blahn-*koh*
Wine list	Carta de vinos	*kahr*-tah deh *bee*-nohs

MEAT, SAUSAGES & COLD CUTS

English	Spanish	Pronunciation
Beef	Buey	*bway*
Duck	Pato	*pah*-toh
Meat	Carne	*kahr*-neh
Chicken	Pollo	*po*-lyoh

English	Spanish	Pronunciation
Cold meat	Fiambre	*fyam*-breh
Cutlet	Chuleta	choo-*leh*-tah
Ham	Jamón	hah-*mohn*
Cooked ham	Jamón York	hah-*mohn* york
Cured ham	Jamón Serrano	hah-*mohn* seh-*rah*-noh
Lamb	Cordero	kohr-*deh*-roh
Kidneys	Riñones	ree-*nyoh*-nehs
Liver	Hígado	ee-gah-thoh
Partridge	Perdiz	*pehr*-deeth
Pheasant	Faisán	fahy-*thahn*
Pork	Cerdo	*thehr*-doh
Rabbit	Conejo	koh-*neh*-hoh
Ribs	Costilla	kos-*tee*-lyah
Sausage	Salchicha	sahl-*chee*-chah
Spicy sausage	Chorizo	choh-*ree*-thoh
Steak	Bistec	*bee*-stehk
Sirloin	Solomillo	so-loh-*mee*-lyoh
Tripe	Callos	*kah*-lyohs
Turkey	Pavo	*pah*-voh
Veal	Ternera	tehr-*neh*-rah

SEAFOOD & SHELLFISH

English	Spanish	Pronunciation
Anchovy		
salt	Anchoa	ahn-*choh*-ah
fresh	Boquerón	boh-*keh*-rohn
Bass	Lubina	loo-*bee*-nah
Bream (porgy)	Besugo	beh-*soo*-goh
Cod	Bacalao	bah-kah-*lah*-oh
Crab	Cangrejo	kan-*greh*-hoh
Crayfish	Cigala	see-*gah*-lah
Cuttlefish	Jibia	*hih*-byah
Fish	Pescado	pess-*kah*-thoh
Flounder	Platija	plah-*tee*-hah
Hake	Merluza	mehr-*loo*-thah
Grouper	Mero	*meh*-roh
Lobster	Langosta	lahn-*goss*-tah
Mackerel	Caballa	cah-*ba*-lyah
Monkfish	Rape	*rah*-peh
Mussel	Mejillón	meh-hee-*lyohn*

English	Spanish	Pronunciation
Octopus	**Pulpo**	*pool*-poh
Oyster	**Ostra**	*ohs*-trah
Prawn	**Gamba**	*gahm*-bah
Red mullet	**Salmonete**	sal-moh-*neh*-teh
Salmon	**Salmón**	sal-*mohn*
Sardine	**Sardina**	sahr-*dee*-nah
Scallop	**Peregrina**	peh-reh-*gree*-nah
Shellfish	**Mariscos**	mah-*reess*-kohs
Sole	**Lenguado**	len-*gwah*-tho
Shrimp	**Camarón**	ka-mah-*rohn*
Squid	**Calamar**	kah-lah-*mahr*
Swordfish	**Pez espada**	*peth* ess-*pah*-thah
Trout	**Trucha**	*troo*-chah
Tuna	**Atún**	ah-*toon*
Turbot	**Rodaballo**	roh-dah-*ba*-lyoh

VEGETABLES & LEGUMES

English	Spanish	Pronunciation
Carrot	**Zanahoria**	thah-nah-*oh*-ryah
Cabbage	**Col**	kohl
Red cabbage	**Lombarda**	lom-*bahr*-dah
Celery	**Apio**	*ah*-pyoh
Chickpea	**Garbanzo**	gahr-*bahn*-thoh
Corn	**Maíz**	mah-*eeth*
Eggplant	**Berengena**	beh-rehn-*jeh*-nah
Fava (broad) beans	**Habas**	*ah*-bahs
Green beans	**Judías**	hoo-*dee*-yahs
Lentil	**Lenteja**	lehn-*teh*-hah
Leek	**Puerro**	*pweh*-roh
Lettuce	**Lechuga**	leh-*choo*-gah
Mushroom	**Seta**	*seh*-tah
Potato	**Patata**	pah-*tah*-tah
Pumpkin	**Calabacín**	kah-lah-bah-*theen*
Salad	**Ensalada**	enn-sah-*lah*-dah
Spinach	**Espinaca**	ess-pee-*nah*-kah
Onion	**Cebolla**	theh-*bo*-lyah
Tomato	**Tomate**	toh-*mah*-teh
Vegetables	**Verduras**	vehr-*doo*-rahs

Index

See also Accommodations and Restaurant indexes, below.

RESTAURANTS

FROMMER'S® COMPLETE TRAVEL GUIDES

Alaska
Amalfi Coast
American Southwest
Amsterdam
Argentina & Chile
Arizona
Atlanta
Australia
Austria
Bahamas
Barcelona
Beijing
Belgium, Holland & Luxembourg
Belize
Bermuda
Boston
Brazil
British Columbia & the Canadian
 Rockies
Brussels & Bruges
Budapest & the Best of Hungary
Buenos Aires
Calgary
California
Canada
Cancún, Cozumel & the Yucatán
Cape Cod, Nantucket & Martha's
 Vineyard
Caribbean
Caribbean Ports of Call
Carolinas & Georgia
Chicago
China
Colorado
Costa Rica
Croatia
Cuba
Denmark
Denver, Boulder & Colorado Springs
Edinburgh & Glasgow
England
Europe
Europe by Rail
Florence, Tuscany & Umbria

Florida
France
Germany
Greece
Greek Islands
Hawaii
Hong Kong
Honolulu, Waikiki & Oahu
India
Ireland
Israel
Italy
Jamaica
Japan
Kauai
Las Vegas
London
Los Angeles
Los Cabos & Baja
Madrid
Maine Coast
Maryland & Delaware
Maui
Mexico
Montana & Wyoming
Montréal & Québec City
Moscow & St. Petersburg
Munich & the Bavarian Alps
Nashville & Memphis
New England
Newfoundland & Labrador
New Mexico
New Orleans
New York City
New York State
New Zealand
Northern Italy
Norway
Nova Scotia, New Brunswick &
 Prince Edward Island
Oregon
Paris
Peru
Philadelphia & the Amish Country

Portugal
Prague & the Best of the Czech
 Republic
Provence & the Riviera
Puerto Rico
Rome
San Antonio & Austin
San Diego
San Francisco
Santa Fe, Taos & Albuquerque
Scandinavia
Scotland
Seattle
Seville, Granada & the Best of
 Andalusia
Shanghai
Sicily
Singapore & Malaysia
South Africa
South America
South Florida
South Pacific
Southeast Asia
Spain
Sweden
Switzerland
Tahiti & French Polynesia
Texas
Thailand
Tokyo
Toronto
Turkey
USA
Utah
Vancouver & Victoria
Vermont, New Hampshire & Maine
Vienna & the Danube Valley
Vietnam
Virgin Islands
Virginia
Walt Disney World® & Orlando
Washington, D.C.
Washington State

FROMMER'S® DAY BY DAY GUIDES

Amsterdam
Chicago
Florence & Tuscany

London
New York City
Paris

Rome
San Francisco
Venice

PAULINE FROMMER'S GUIDES! SEE MORE. SPEND LESS.

Hawaii

Italy

New York City

FROMMER'S® PORTABLE GUIDES

Acapulco, Ixtapa & Zihuatanejo
Amsterdam
Aruba
Australia's Great Barrier Reef
Bahamas
Big Island of Hawaii
Boston
California Wine Country
Cancún
Cayman Islands
Charleston
Chicago
Dominican Republic

Dublin
Florence
Las Vegas
Las Vegas for Non-Gamblers
London
Maui
Nantucket & Martha's Vineyard
New Orleans
New York City
Paris
Portland
Puerto Rico
Puerto Vallarta, Manzanillo &
 Guadalajara

Rio de Janeiro
San Diego
San Francisco
Savannah
St. Martin, Sint Maarten, Anguila &
 St. Bart's
Turks & Caicos
Vancouver
Venice
Virgin Islands
Washington, D.C.
Whistler

FROMMER'S® CRUISE GUIDES

Alaska Cruises & Ports of Call

Cruises & Ports of Call

European Cruises & Ports of Call

FROMMER'S® NATIONAL PARK GUIDES

Algonquin Provincial Park
Banff & Jasper
Grand Canyon

National Parks of the American West
Rocky Mountain
Yellowstone & Grand Teton

Yosemite and Sequoia & Kings
Canyon
Zion & Bryce Canyon

FROMMER'S® MEMORABLE WALKS

London
New York

Paris
Rome

San Francisco

FROMMER'S® WITH KIDS GUIDES

Chicago
Hawaii
Las Vegas
London

National Parks
New York City
San Francisco

Toronto
Walt Disney World® & Orlando
Washington, D.C.

SUZY GERSHMAN'S BORN TO SHOP GUIDES

France
Hong Kong, Shanghai & Beijing
Italy

London
New York

Paris
San Francisco

FROMMER'S® IRREVERENT GUIDES

Amsterdam
Boston
Chicago
Las Vegas

London
Los Angeles
Manhattan
Paris

Rome
San Francisco
Walt Disney World®
Washington, D.C.

FROMMER'S® BEST-LOVED DRIVING TOURS

Austria
Britain
California
France

Germany
Ireland
Italy
New England

Northern Italy
Scotland
Spain
Tuscany & Umbria

THE UNOFFICIAL GUIDES®

Adventure Travel in Alaska
Beyond Disney
California with Kids
Central Italy
Chicago
Cruises
Disneyland®
England
Florida
Florida with Kids

Hawaii
Ireland
Las Vegas
London
Maui
Mexico's Best Beach Resorts
Mini Mickey
New Orleans
New York City

Paris
San Francisco
South Florida including Miami &
the Keys
Walt Disney World®
Walt Disney World® for
Grown-ups
Walt Disney World® with Kids
Washington, D.C.

SPECIAL-INTEREST TITLES

Athens Past & Present
Best Places to Raise Your Family
Cities Ranked & Rated
500 Places to Take Your Kids Before They Grow Up
Frommer's Best Day Trips from London
Frommer's Best RV & Tent Campgrounds
in the U.S.A.

Frommer's Exploring America by RV
Frommer's NYC Free & Dirt Cheap
Frommer's Road Atlas Europe
Frommer's Road Atlas Ireland
Great Escapes From NYC Without Wheels
Retirement Places Rated

FROMMER'S® PHRASEFINDER DICTIONARY GUIDES

French

Italian

Spanish

THE NEW TRAVELOCITY GUARANTEE

EVERYTHING YOU BOOK WILL BE RIGHT, OR WE'LL WORK WITH OUR TRAVEL PARTNERS TO MAKE IT RIGHT, RIGHT AWAY.

To drive home the point, we're going to use the word "right" in every single sentence.

Let's get right to it. Right to the meat! Only Travelocity guarantees everything about your booking will be right, or we'll work with our travel partners to make it right, right away. Right on!

Here's a picture taken smack dab right in the middle of Antigua, where the guarantee also covers you.

The guarantee covers all but one of the items pictured to the right.

For example, what if the ocean view you booked actually looks out at a downright ugly parking lot? You'd be right to call – we're there for you. And no one in their right mind would be pleased to learn the rental car place has closed and left them stranded. Call Travelocity and we'll help get you back on the right track.

Now, you may be thinking, "Yeah, right, I'm so sure." That's OK; you have the right to remain skeptical. That is until we mention help is always right around the corner. Call us right off the bat, knowing that our customer service reps are there for you 24/7. Righting wrongs. Left and right.

Now if you're guessing there are some things we can't control, like the weather, well you're right. But we can help you with most things – to get all the details in righting,* visit **travelocity.com/guarantee**.

*Sorry, spelling things right is one of the few things not covered under the guarantee.

I'd give my right arm for a guarantee like this, although I'm glad I don't have to.

IF YOU BOOK IT, IT SHOULD BE THERE.

Only Travelocity guarantees it will be, or we'll work with our travel partners to make it right, right away. So if you're missing a balcony or anything else you booked, just call us 24/7. **1-888-TRAVELOCITY.**

travelocity
You'll never roam alone.